WASHBURN, KEMP & WAGENSEIL
ONE EMBARCADERO CENTER, SUITE 2407
SAN FRANCISCO, CALIFORNIA 94111

Legal Secretary's Encyclopedic Dictionary

SECOND EDITION

Legal Secretary's
Encyclopedic Dictionary

SECOND EDITION

By The Prentice-Hall Editorial Staff

Revised by
BETTY KENNEDY THOMAE

PRENTICE-HALL, INC.   Englewood Cliffs, New Jersey

Prentice-Hall International, Inc., *London*
Prentice-Hall of Australia, Pty. Ltd., *Sydney*
Prentice-Hall of Canada, Ltd., *Toronto*
Prentice-Hall of India Private Ltd., *New Delhi*
Prentice-Hall of Japan, Inc., *Tokyo*
Prentice-Hall of Southeast Asia Pte. Ltd., *Singapore*
Whitehall Books, Ltd., *Wellington, New Zealand*

Library of Congress Cataloging in Publication Data

Main entry under title:

Legal secretary's encyclopedic dictionary.

   1. Legal secretaries--United States--Handbooks,
manuals, etc. I. Thomae, Betty Kennedy.
II. Prentice-Hall, inc.
KF319.L36 1977   340'.03   76-50563
ISBN 0-13-528943-2

Printed in the United States of America

**To
all legal secretaries everywhere**

ACKNOWLEDGMENTS

I wish to thank Mr. James L. Young, Director of the Ohio Legal Center Institute, for permission to reprint the material on no-fault divorce.

A special thanks to Kenneth P. Bessey, Esquire, and Joseph F. Frasch, Jr., Esquire, for helping me with certain definitions.

A special thanks also to West Publishing Company for permission to reprint many of the legal definitions from *Black's Law Dictionary*.

Betty Kennedy Thomae

Announcing the new, revised and updated . . .

LEGAL SECRETARY'S ENCYCLOPEDIC DICTIONARY

This Second Edition of the Prentice-Hall *Legal Secretary's Encyclopedic Dictionary* offers a broad range of new material which substantially increases its practical value.

For example, suppose you need specific data on incorporation for lawyers in a law firm. Just turn the pages to Lawyers' Incorporated, and you'll find the procedures described. The Internal Revenue Service now recognizes professional corporations, which offer tax advantages to individuals in the corporation, and many states now allow lawyers to incorporate. You'll also learn what the initials LPA after a firm of lawyers means.

Or, suppose you want information on Paralegals or legal assistants. Just turn to Paralegals by referring to the convenient, alphabetized listing of subject areas. Perhaps you need additional information on the PLS rating. Just refer to The National Association of Legal Secretaries (NALS) and find out all about this exclusive rating for legal secretaries—what the examination covers and where to write for more information. An increasing number of states have adopted the "No-Fault" Divorce procedure. This recent development is now covered, as well as secretarial procedures when paying an abstracter and how to set up a filing system for abstract continuations when they are typed in the law office.

A new section has also been added on accounting methods used in the law office—how to credit the attorney who originated the fee—how to manage trust funds—how to separate different types of income on the lawyer's books, *i.e.*, probate income, real estate income, etc.

Whenever you need information on legal ethics and the specific relationships between lawyers and their clients, you will now be able to refer directly to the canons of the American Bar Association. Does your lawyer need a print-out of an amortization schedule for a buyer of a new home? You can quickly find out where and how to get one under Amortization Schedules. This new edition also includes a section on Guardians and Guardianships. Find out how you, the Secretary, can handle Guardianships for your lawyer by depositing income, taking care of expenditures and even preparing the accounting for the Probate Court for him.

When you are concerned about whether or not you may be doing something that might amount to the practice of law (and most legal secretaries are confronted by this dilemma)—just review the new section on Unauthorized Practice of Law—to make certain you do not infringe in this area.

These are just a few examples that show how this new publication has been thoroughly updated. Many new Latin terms have been added, many new legal definitions are included and a large variety of new cross-references have been inserted.

This latest edition is a complete guide to the skills, crafts and essential reference data needed by the professional legal secretary. Experienced secretaries, legal assistants, beginners—*anyone* who needs information that is essential to the legal secretary *in any of the 50 states of the country*—will find flick-of-the-finger answers to *all* the secretarial know-how needed for *every* kind of law office.

In quick, easy-to-find style, the book combines the best features of an alphabetical dictionary with the illustrative power and thoroughness of an encyclopedia. It gives the secretary a full understanding of law office duties and includes step-by-step instructions for every phase of her work. Ways to save your lawyer time and money are explored—not only in the general law office field, but also in these special practices: *Real Estate—Criminal Law—Domestic Relations—Negligence Cases—Corporate Practice—Commercial Collections—Labor Relations—Patents—Probate and Estate Administration—Tax Practice—Trial Law—Admiralty Practice—Administration of Trusts—Constitutional Law.*

Here, between the covers of one book, the legal secretary has easy access to the essential information she needs to help her succeed in the law office. The legal secretary or assistant can speedily refresh, "up-date" her knowledge, or find the precise requirements and procedures in the special field of law that interests her. A broad range of specimen legal forms, filled-in law blanks, sample letters, court papers, diary pages and drawings are included. They illustrate every procedure and situation the legal secretary is likely to encounter. Moreover, the book shows you—*how to set up court papers correctly . . . how to type legal documents . . . the meaning of Latin terms and phrases . . . legal terminology in simple language . . . special follow-up methods . . . how to use the law library . . . the secretary's responsibilities in court procedures . . . how to keep the lawyer's suit register . . . how to process a new case report . . . correct methods of filing for the law office . . . how to address court officials . . . where to write for Government publications . . . how to order redemption tables for Series E bonds . . . and much, much more.*

You need no special instructions in order to use this book. The alphabetical entries make for rapid reference. Simply turn to the word or phrase you want explained. You may find a word capitalized within the text of a definition; it means that the capitalized word is defined elsewhere. Cross-reference to it may not be necessary for an understanding of the term you are consulting, but you can refer to it if you wish.

Betty Kennedy Thomae

A

AFL-CIO. A united labor federation in the United States, formed by the merger of the AMERICAN FEDERATION OF LABOR and the CONGRESS OF INDUSTRIAL ORGANIZATIONS in December, 1955. George Meany was elected the first president of the AFL-CIO. See also LABOR UNION.

Abandonment. See DESERTION.

Abandonment of Leased Premises. Leaving of premises by the lessee (tenant) before TERMINATION OF LEASE, without the lessor's (landlord's) consent. Abandonment does not relieve the lessee of liability for rent. Leases generally provide specifically that if the lessee abandons the premises before expiration of the LEASE, he continues to be liable for rent.

Abduction. The offense of taking away a wife or child by FRAUD or open violence. The most frequent type of abduction is the carrying away of a female to force her to marry or, with her consent, for the purpose of marriage even though she cannot legally marry without the consent of her parents. The crime also includes such conduct as enticing children away from their parents and enticing females for the purpose of sexual intercourse or prostitution. See KIDNAPPING.

Abeyance. A condition in which the ownership of REAL PROPERTY or PERSONAL PROPERTY is undetermined.

Abortion. The destruction, or the bringing forth prematurely of the human foetus before the natural time of birth.

Abrogation. The annulment or repeal of a law or obligation by an authoritative act. For example, the COMMON LAW is abrogated by statute.

Abstract Company. A business enterprise whose main function is to search land records and to make a summary of the material parts of every recorded instrument affecting the title to a particular tract of land. The summary is called an ABSTRACT OF TITLE. See also LAND DESCRIPTION.

Abstract of Title. Evidence of TITLE to REAL PROPERTY. An abstract is a history of the title to a particular tract of land. It consists of a summary of the material parts of every recorded instrument affecting the title. It begins with a description of the land covered by the abstract, and then shows the original government grant and all subsequent deeds, mortgages, releases, wills, judgments, mechanics' liens, FORECLOSURE proceedings, tax sales, and other matters affecting title.

Of course, only a summary of these items is shown. For example, a deed is summarized as shown below.

FREDERICK SCOTT AND ETHEL SCOTT, HIS WIFE to JAMES LAKE	WARRANTY DEED Dated June 16, 1912 Ack. June 19, 1912 Rec. June 21, 1912 Transfer Tax Consideration Witnesses Bk. 35, page 38
Conveys a large plot of land including the premises under examination.	

The abstract concludes with the abstracter's certificate. This discloses what records the abstracter has examined, and what records he has not examined. For example, if the abstracter certifies that he has made no search of Federal court proceedings affecting the property, it will be necessary to write to the Clerk of the District Court, who will supply the search for a small charge.

Abstract companies, lawyers, and public officials prepare abstracts. (See ABSTRACT COMPANY.) Abstract companies do by far the greatest portion of the abstracting, except in a few states where there are no abstract companies.

What the secretary does. The secretary should always keep in her desk directory the name, address, and telephone number of the abstract company or other abstracter used by her firm. The secretary to the lawyer for the purchaser or the *mortgagee* (see MORTGAGE) in communities where abstracts are acceptable evidence of title will frequently have to order abstracts. When the abstract is ordered, the secretary should make a follow-up entry in her DIARY or an extra copy of the letter for the follow-up file. (See FOLLOW-UP FILING SYSTEM.) It is important to get the abstract as soon as possible because the deal cannot be closed until the purchaser's attorney has examined the abstract of title. When the abstract is received, the cost is charged to the client; the lawyer will pay the abstracter.

A CONTRACT OF SALE frequently provides that the seller shall furnish an abstract of title. This usually means that he will give the purchaser an abstract of title to the date that the seller obtained the property. The seller will have it brought up to date. The secretary will then be asked to order a *continuation* or an extension. The original abstract is sent to the abstract company and the company *recertifies* its accuracy and brings it down to date.

Letter asking for a continuation:

The enclosed abstract of title covers the west three rods of Lots 26 and 27, Leonard Berg's Addition to Kingston, Ulster County, New York, according to the recorded plat thereof.

Please continue this to date for the land owned by Jennifer Green and return it to us as soon as possible.

Paying the Abstracter

When abstract continuations are typed in the law office, the secretary should keep a close record of the continuations so that the abstracter may be paid. An arrangement should be made with the abstracter as to how often he is to be paid, i. e. once a week or the first of the month. A simple method is to use a 3 x 5 card with columns for debit, credit and balance. These may be ordered from the stationer. At the top of the card the secretary should write the abstracter's name and rate of pay per section. When a continuation is completed, enter the date, the surname of the person who owns the real estate, and the number of sections. On the first day of the month (or other pay period) the secretary should multiply the number of sections in each entry by the rate per section and enter the resultant figure in the debit column. She should then add up all debits and draw a check to the abstracter for the total amount. She should make an entry in the credit column of the amount of the check, along with the date the check is issued.

Numbering and Filing Continuations

When continuations are typed in the law office a numbering system should be used to facilitate filing the continuations and retrieving them. At the bottom of each tail sheet (last page of continuation containing abstracter's or attorney's signature) the secretary should type at the bottom the abstracter's initials and her initials and the number assigned to that continuation. The number should be entered in a small notebook alphabetically by owner's name. To keep track of numbers used the secretary should keep a running list of numbers in numerical order with the owner's name after each number. This list can also be kept in the small notebook. Then numbers should be

placed on the caption sheet of the file copy and the continuations can be filed in file folders in numerical order (usually 25 to a folder). The folders can be marked "Abstract Continuations 1 through 25," and filed in a special cabinet.

Acceleration Clause. An essential statement contained in a CONTRACT evidencing debt (as in MORTGAGE or INSTALLMENT CONTRACT), which provides that if the interest or installment is not paid when due, the entire debt becomes payable immediately. Without this clause, the mortgagee or seller would have to sue for the amount of each payment as it becomes due, or wait until the entire debt matures. For example, the *acceleration clause* in a MORTGAGE contract might read: *That the whole of said principal sum shall become due after default in the payment of any installment of principal or of interest for . . . .days, or after default in the payment of any tax, water rate or assessment for . . .days, after notice and demand.*

Acceptance. See CONTRACTS.

Accessory. One who, after the commission of a FELONY, helps the felon to avoid or escape arrest, prosecution, or punishment with knowledge of the offender's wrongful act or liability for such act. The one who aids is known as an *accessory after the fact,* and the felon who is aided is known as the principal. See also ACCOMPLICE; AIDING AND ABETTING.

Accomplice. One who has taken part with the one accused in perpetration of, or in preparation for, a crime, with intent to assist in the crime. Whether or not a person is classified as an accomplice is important, since many states have statutes forbidding conviction where the only incriminating evidence is that given by an accomplice. See ACCESSORY; AIDING AND ABETTING.

Accounting Records for the Lawyer (business). It is essential to the law office that books of account be kept regularly and accurately. A law office should be run on a business-like basis and only well-kept books of account can determine how it is run. In a smaller office the lead secretary may also be the bookkeeper. A basic bookkeeping course such as is given in high school would be most helpful to the legal secretary.

Some bookkeeping procedures are peculiar and incidental to the law office. For example:

Cash Receipts

If the lawyers like to know the source of their fees a columnar journal should be used for cash receipts. The columns other than cash itself could be labeled with classifications such as Probate income, Real Estate income, Personal Injury income, Income Tax income, Trial income, Bankruptcy income, etc., and a column for Miscellaneous income. The columns should be footed at the bottom of each page and at the end of the month. At the end of the month they should be balanced across the page. The debit cash column should equal the sum of all the credit balances (cash basis system).

Recovering Costs Advanced

Recovering costs advanced is a very important step in a law office, and

there are many systems for recording such costs. A simple one is to use Time-Cost record sheets put out by Day-Timers, Inc. These are 8 ½ x 11 sheets punched for a 3-ring notebook. (Day-Timers, Inc. furnishes a notebook.) An alphabetical index may also be obtained from Day-Timer, and the sheets can be arranged alphabetically for quick locating. As costs are expended they should be posted on the sheet for each client, and when billing time comes around, a check with the Day-Timer book will indicate just what costs have been advanced. You can write to Day-Timers at:

Day-Timers, Inc.
P.O. Box 2368
Allentown, Pennsylvania 18001

A column should also be set aside for Costs Advanced in your Cash Disbursed Journal and Cash Receipts Journal. When the costs are advanced and the money comes in as payment, payment should be broken down and credit given for, say, $25 to the Costs Advanced and $100 in the appropriate fee column. Only the $100 should be entered and credited to the attorney who originated it. (See below.)

Crediting the Attorney Who Originates the Fee

If the attorney wishes to know how many fees are brought in by each attorney in his office, a column should be set aside in the Cash Receipts Journal for each attorney, and each time a fee is recorded it should be credited to the appropriate attorney column. These are information columns only and are not to be taken into consideration when balancing debits and credits. To double-check the accuracy of the posting, however, the sum of the attorney columns, plus the total of the Costs Advanced column, plus any unearned income should equal the Cash Receipts column.

Setting Up a Trust Account for Clients' Funds

Since clients often pay funds to the attorney to be forwarded to others, i.e. Clerk of Courts for court costs, alimony payments to a spouse and attorney; or monies to be held for a few months such as small estate funds, a separate account for these funds must be set up. It is unethical for an attorney to co-mingle this type of fund with his own funds. The secretary who handles trust monies should be extremely careful with records and disburse the funds only at the direction of the attorney responsible, and for the purpose intended, lest the attorney be accused of mishandling funds. Funds should be disbursed from this account up to the amount deposited in the individual's name.

A simple, effective method of recording trust funds is to use a small card file for 3 x 5 cards for each client depositing funds. The card should be an account card with columns for debits, credits, and balances. Each card should be marked "Trust Account" in case it should become mixed with other cards. The client's last name should come first. The name or initials of the attorney who is responsible for the funds should also be placed on the card.

As funds come into the account, an entry should be made immediately. As funds are disbursed, the entry should be made on the card immediately. Part of the essence of the system is its "instant" reference. At any moment the secretary should be able to determine how much is in a client's trust fund.

When the funds are disbursed, the card should be removed from the file and placed in another file for storage. It can be pulled if the same client again brings in funds.

Once a month the trust account checkbook balance should be reconciled with the bank statement. Also once a month the balance on all cards should be totaled and should equal the current balance in the checking account. This is a double check on the accuracy of record keeping.

Accounting Records for the Lawyer (personal). Although the size of the lawyer's estate might not justify a formal set of books, every lawyer must keep a record of income and expenditures for tax purposes, if for no other reason. Frequently, the secretary maintains these records. Three broad classes of records are usually kept:

1. Records of what the lawyer owns, such as stocks, bonds, and real estate.

2. Records that must be kept for income and other tax purposes.

3. Records of living expenses that are not deductible under the income tax law, in addition to records for other purposes.

A columnar book, or journal, supported by detailed records of income-producing property, is adequate. Columnar books are available in single or double pages with from two to thirty-six money columns, and columns for date, number and amount of checks, and for an explanation of the item being entered in the journal.

Separate columns should be allotted to income and to expenditures. There should be a separate column for each source of recurring income and a miscellaneous column for nonrecurring items. Because of the special tax treatment accorded stock dividends, it is important that dividends be kept separate from other income.

A separate column should be allotted to each class of deductible expenses that recur frequently. Deductible items that occur only occasionally may be entered in an *Other Deductions* column and analyzed at the end of the year for the lawyer's Federal income tax return. Nondeductible expenditures may be kept in a *Nondeductible Expenses* column unless the lawyer wants to know what a particular class of expenses has cost him. In that case, a separate column is allotted to each class of expenses in which he is interested. He may want a record of one or more of the following expenses:

1. House expenses, if he owns the home he lives in. This includes expenditures for repairs, replacements, decoration, outside painting, grounds, and the like. Taxes and mortgage interest are deductible expenses.

2. Wages paid to servants. These records must be kept for SOCIAL SECURITY TAX purposes and for filing an information return required by the Government. Also in some localities an employer of one or more domestic servants must pay state unemployment and disability insurance taxes on their wages.

3. Life insurance and other premiums. The cost can be determined from the INSURANCE RECORDS.

4. Education of children.

5. Clothes.

6. Recreation, including expenses incurred at country clubs and other social clubs.

7. Money spent in support of a dependent.

8. Travel, other than in connection with business. A record of business travel expenditures must be kept for income tax purposes. (See EXPENSE ACCOUNT.)

9. Automobile expenses, other than in connection with business. A record of business automobile expenses must be kept for income tax purposes.

10. Membership dues, other than those that are deductible.

11. Hobbies, such as expenditures on greenhouses, raising chickens, keeping stables, and the like.

12. Gifts.

Account Stated. An account balance, as determined by the creditor, which has been accepted as correct by the debtor. In law, the *account stated* operates as an admission of liability by the debtor. He is barred from disputing the accuracy of the computation, the bar being raised either by the debtor's explicit approval of the account or by his failure within a reasonable time to indicate any exception to it.

Acknowledgment. In law, the act by which a person who has signed an instrument goes before an authorized officer, such as a NOTARY PUBLIC, and vows that he executed the instrument. The notary public signs what is called *the certificate of acknowledgment*. The function of the certificate of acknowledgment is twofold: It entitles the instrument to be recorded or filed and it authorizes the instrument to be given in evidence without further proof of its execution.

Laws governing acknowledgments. Most states, under the Uniform Acknowledgment Act, require the acknowledgment of an instrument before it can be recorded or filed. In those states that have adopted the Uniform Acknowledgment Act the laws governing the use of acknowledgments and their form are similar. Otherwise the law varies with the state, and each state's statutes must be

New York will follow the New York laws governing the certificate of acknowledgment, although it will show that the acknowledgment was made in Florida.

The lawyer usually dictates, or makes available to the secretary, a form of the acknowledgment he wants

```
STATE OF WISCONSIN)
                   : ss.
COUNTY OF CHIPPEWA)


        On this the      day of       , 19—, before me,
                the undersigned officer, personally ap-
peared ALBERT JONES, known to me to be the person whose.
name is subscribed to the within instrument and acknowledged
that he executed the same for the purpose therein contained.
        IN WITNESS WHEREOF, I have hereunto set my hand
and official seal.



                            _____
                                    Notary Public
My commission expires
```

Acknowledgment: Figure 1. *Certificate of acknowledgment of individual.*

adhered to strictly. A basic principle of law governing acknowledgments is that *the law of the state where the instrument is recorded governs.* For example, an instrument prepared in a New York office which is to be recorded in Florida will use the form and wording that follow the Florida statutes, even though the certificate will show that the acknowledgment was made in New York. An instrument sent to Florida to be signed and returned for recording in

used. Pages 15 to 18 show how various acknowledgments may be typed. The illustrations (Figures 1 to 4) are not meant to be copied word for word, but serve merely as examples of acknowledgments.

Essentials of an Acknowledgment. Although acknowledgments vary with the state, they all have certain basic essentials. These are:

1. *Venue.* An acknowledgment always begins with a recital of the

venue, that is, the name of the state and county in which the acknowledgment is made. In Kentucky, Massachusetts, Pennsylvania, and Virginia, the venue recites the name of the *commonwealth* instead of the *state;* in Lousiana, the *parish* instead of the *county*. Type the statement of the venue in solid caps, bracket it, and follow with *ss.*, the ab-

breviation for *scilicet*. The abbreviation may be caps or small letters. Like all abbreviations, it is followed by a period. Technically, a colon should also follow because scilicet means "to wit," but few law offices observe this technicality.

2. *Date of acknowledgment*. An acknowledgment always recites the

STATE OF GEORGIA)
: ss.
COUNTY OF BAKER)

I, ELAINE BAKER, a notary public in and for the said state and county, duly commissioned and sworn, hereby certify that HENRY R. DAVIS and NANCY R. DAVIS, his wife, who are to me personally known, this day appeared before me personally, and severally acknowledged that they signed, sealed, and delivered the foregoing deed for the purposes therein stated. The said NANCY R. DAVIS, wife of said HENRY R. DAVIS, being duly examined by me, separate and apart from her said husband, did declare that she signed, sealed, and delivered the said deed freely and voluntarily, and without compulsion by her said husband, with intention to renounce and convey all dower or other right, title, and interest in the property thereby conveyed, for the uses and purposes therein stated.

IN WITNESS WHEREOF, I have hereunto set my hand and official seal this 30th day of April, 19—.

_____
Notary Public

Acknowledgment: Figure 2. *Certificate of acknowledgment by husband and wife—separate examination.*

date on which the acknowledgment is made. When you type the certificate of acknowledgment, leave blank spaces for the day of the month, and also for the name of the month if you are preparing the instrument near the end of the month. Although a client is supposed to sign and acknowledge an instrument on the 30th of April, he might not get into the office until the 1st day of May. The date of the acknowledgment does not necessarily coincide with the date of the instrument, but the date of an acknowledgment must *never* precede the date the instrument was signed.

3. *Designation of person making acknowledgment.* The name of the person making the acknowledgment always appears in the certificate. Type it in solid caps. If the person making the acknowledgment is making it in a capacity other than that of an individual, that capacity is also stated,

---

STATE OF FLORIDA)
: SS.:
COUNTY OF DUVAL)

        I hereby certify that on this day before me, an officer duly authorized in the state aforesaid and in the county aforesaid to take acknowledgments, personally appeared ALFRED JONES and LESTER S. SMITH, to me known and known to be the persons described in and who executed the foregoing instrument as president and secretary, respectively, of National Company, Inc., a corporation named therein, and severally acknowledged before me that they executed the same as such officers, in the name of and for and on behalf of the said corporation.

        IN WITNESS WHEREOF, I have hereunto set my hand and affixed my official seal this   day of September, 19—.

                                        _____
                                             Notary Public

My commission expires

Acknowledgment: Figure 3. Certificate of acknowledgment
by corporation—two officers.

```
STATE OF CALIFORNIA)
                    : ss.
COUNTY OF EL DORADO)


        On this      day of          , 19—, before me,
Nancy Jones, notary public in and for said county and state,
personally appeared FRED C. BELL, known to me to be one of
the partners of the partnership that executed the within
instrument, and acknowledged to me that such partnership
executed the same.



                              _____
                              Notary Public in and for said
                                    County and State
```

Acknowledgment: Figure 4. Certificate of acknowledgment by partnership.

but not in solid caps. For example, when a person makes an acknowledgment as secretary of a corporation, the designation is written, ". . . EDWARD WILLIAMS, secretary of Royal Matches, Inc., . . ." The person who makes the acknowledgment does not sign the certificate.

Signature and designation of officer taking acknowledgment. The officer who takes an acknowledgment signs the certificate. In typing the certificate, type a blank line for his signature four spaces beneath the body of the certificate. Type his title underneath the line. (In Indiana and Ohio, the name of the notary must also be typed, or printed.) In many states the certificate also recites the name and full title of the officer taking the acknowledgment. If you do not know who is to take the acknowledgment, leave a blank space long enough for the average name to be inserted in handwriting.

Date of expiration of commission. Many states require ·hat an acknowledgment taken by a notary public show the date of the expiration of his commission. On acknowledgments to be used in those states, type "My commission expires. . . . . . . , 19 . . ." two spaces below the signature. Notaries usually have a rubber stamp showing the expiration date of their commission, and the typed line is not necessary except as a reminder that the date of expiration must appear on the certificate.

4. *Notary's seal.* In almost all cases the certificate of acknowledgment must also bear the notary's seal, especially if the instrument is acknowledged outside the state where it is to be recorded. See NOTARY'S SEAL.

Acknowledgment of Claim. See COLLECTIONS.

Acquittal. CONTRACTS. A release, absolution, or discharge from an obligation, liability, or engagement.

CRIMES. The legal and formal certification of the innocence of a person who has been charged with crime; a deliverance or setting free of a person from a charge of guilt.

Action Number. See CLERK'S INDEX SYSTEM.

Additur. The power of a judge to increase the amount of an inadequate award of money in a jury verdict. The DAMAGES are increased, with the consent of the defendant, as condition for the denial of plaintiff's motion for a new trial on the grounds that the damages awarded are inadequate. Additur is usually proposed in informal, off-the-record discussion between the judge and counsel for both sides.

Additur, as well as REMITTER, is an effective means of giving a just award without the expense and trouble of a new trial.

Add-ons. Additional purchases made on installment accounts before payments on the previous contract are completed. A new CONTRACT is drawn, combining the terms of the old and new contracts. For example, suppose a customer owes a balance of $25 on furniture on which she has already paid $200. She makes an additional purchase of $150 and enters into a new contract. This arrangement, after the down payment, brings her balance payable up to $168.10. Assume that after paying $100 of the $168.10, she defaults on her contract. In most of the states, the items that were purchased under the first contract are subject to repossession until the entire new balance is paid. Several states, however, have enacted laws to protect retail customers against the apparent

injustice of this practice. These laws provide that items originally purchased are security for the debt only until the *original balance is paid.* They also provide how the payments under the new contract shall be prorated to the old and new purchases. These laws apply to *consumer installment credit,* not to *productive installment credit.* (See INSTALLMENT CREDIT.)

Address on Letters. The INSIDE ADDRESS and the address on the envelope are written in exactly the same form. The points on which questions arise in the law office, to which the secretary should know the answers, appear below:

The addressee's name. A man's name is dear to him. If it begins with *Mac,* he wants it written that way, not *Mc.* The same is true of firms and companies. Some law firms omit the comma between names of the members of the firm (for example, *Case White Jones Engel*); others insert the ampersand between each name (*Case & White & Jones & Engel*). Some companies include *Company, Co., The, Inc.,* or & as part of the official name. It is the secretary's duty to write a name the way the owner writes it. She should never take a chance and write it the way she thinks it should be written—it should be verified from incoming correspondence, the file, or some other reference source.

Titles. Generally, the following forms apply to titles in an address:

1. Always precede a name by a title, unless initials indicating degrees or *Esquire* follow the name. The use of a business title or position or of *Sr.* or *Jr.* after a name does not take the place of a title.

Right
Mr. Ralph P. Edwards, President

Wrong
Ralph P. Edwards, President

2. *Esquire,* or *Esq.,* never precedes a name and is never used with any other title, not even with *Mr.* In business correspondence *Esquire* or *Esq.* is used only to address high-ranking professional men who have no other title, but the practice is different in law offices. Many law offices always address a lawyer as *Esquire.* Some firms also address their clients as *Esquire.* You, of course, must be guided by the instructions of the dictator. Clerks of courts and justices of the peace are properly addressed as *Esquire.* There is no feminine of *Esquire.*

Right
Dr. Richard W. Nelson
William S. Richey, Esquire
Robert Wilson, Jr., Esq.

Wrong
Dr. Richard W. Nelson, Esq.
Mr. William S. Richey, Esquire
Mr. Robert Wilson, Jr., Esq.

The title *Esq.* is commonly used in England. There it is the proper title to use in addressing the heads of business firms, banking executives, doctors, and the like.

Correct in England
Robert E. Meade, Esq., President
Laurence D. Goode, Esq., M.D.

3. It is preferable not to use the title *Esquires* after a firm name composed of two or more lawyers' surnames. Such firm names become entities in themselves and are not regarded from the standpoint of the lawyers as individuals. Of course, if the letter is addressed to a *particular* lawyer in that firm (whether or not his name appears as part of the firm name) his name, and the title, *Esquire,* is written as the first line of the address, followed by the firm name on the second line of the address.

Right
William S. Trask, Esquire
Trask, Whiting & Case

John L. Mewes, Esquire
Trask, Whiting & Case

Wrong
William S. Trask
Trask, Whiting & Case, Esquires

John L. Mewes, Esquire
Trask, Whiting & Case, Esquires

4. *Messrs.* is used for addressing a firm of attorneys, as *Messrs. Jackson, Bell & Hunt.* It may be used in addressing a business firm of men, or men and women, when the names denote individuals, but not in addressing corporations or other business organizations that bear impersonal names.

Right
Messrs. Marvin Tobin Smart
  Attorneys at Law
James Marshall & Sons

Wrong
Messrs. James Marshall & Sons

5. Initials or abbreviations indicating degrees and other honors are sometimes placed after the name of the person addressed. Use only the initials of the highest degree; more than one degree may be used, however, if the degrees are in different fields. A scholastic title is not used in combination with the abbreviation indicating that degree, but another title may be used in combination with abbreviations indicating degrees.

Right

Robert E. Saunders, Ph.D.

Dr. Ralph Jones *(preferred)* or

Ralph Jones, M.D.

The Reverend Perry E. Moore,
D.D., LL.D.

To a professor

Professor Robert E. Saunders

Wrong

Robert E. Saunders, A.B., A.M.,
Ph.D.

Business titles or position 1. The designation of a business position follows the name. It does not take the place of a title.

Right

Mr. Ralph E. Edwards, President

Wrong

Ralph E. Edwards, President

President Ralph E. Edwards

2. Do not abbreviate business titles or positions such as President, Secretary, and Sales Manager. *Mr.* (or *Mrs.* or *Miss*) precedes the individual's name, even when the business title is used. If a person's business title is short, place it on the first line; if it is long, place it on the second line.

Mr. James E. Lambert, President
Lambert & Woolf Company
1005 Tower Street
Cleveland, Ohio   44103

Mr. George F. Moore
Advertising Manager
Price & Patterson
234 Seventh Avenue
New York, New York   10005

The modern trend is to omit the business title, particularly if it makes the address run over four lines.

3. Do not hyphenate a title unless it represents two or more offices.

Right

Secretary-Treasurer

Vice President

Wrong

Secretary Treasurer

Vice-President

4. If a letter is addressed to a particular department in a company, place the name of the company on the first line and the name of the department on the second line.

5. In addressing an individual in a firm, corporation, or group, place the individual's name on the first line, and the company's name on the second line.

Forms for addressing women

1. *Firm composed of women.* In addressing a firm composed of women, either married or unmarried, use *Mesdames* or *Mmes.*

2. *Unmarried woman.* Use *Miss* or *Ms.* when addressing an unmarried woman or when the dictator does not know whether she is married or unmarried.

3. *Married woman.* Socially a married woman is addressed by her husband's full name preceded by *Mrs.* In business, she may be addressed either by her husband's name or by her given name and her married name, preceded by *Mrs.* Use the form she prefers if known.

4. *Widow.* Socially a widow is addressed by her husband's full name preceded by *Mrs.* In business either her husband's full name or her given name and her married name, preceded by *Mrs.*, is correct. Use the form that she prefers if known.

5. *Divorcee.* If a divorcee retains her married name, the title *Mrs.* is

21

preferable to *Miss.* If she uses her maiden name, she may use either *Miss, Mrs.,* or *Ms.* In business she may be addressed by her given name combined with her married name or by both her maiden and married names. Follow the form she prefers if known. Socially she is addressed by her maiden name combined with her married name.

6. *Wife of a titled man.* Do not address a married woman by her husband's title. Address her as *Mrs. Robert E. Adams* or *Mrs. R. E. Adams.* If she is addressed jointly with her husband, the correct form is *Dr. and Mrs. Robert E. Adams, Judge and Mrs. Irving Levy.*

7. *Professional women.* Address a woman with a professional title by her title, followed by her given and last names. A married woman sometimes uses her maiden name and, if so, should be addressed by it. In social correspondence her title is sometimes dropped in addressing her and her husband.

When you do not know whether an addressee is a man or a woman, use the form of address appropriate for a man. *Women in official or honorary positions are addressed just as men in similar positions, except that Madam, Mrs., Ms., or Miss replaces Sir or Mr.* See ADDRESSING OFFICIALS.

How to type the street address. The inside address and the address on the envelope are the same. The following instructions for writing it are standard, although various authorities give different rules for writing addresses.

1. Do not precede the street number with a word or a sign.

Right
70 Fifth Avenue
Wrong
No. 70 Fifth Avenue
#70 Fifth Avenue

2. Spell out the numerical names of streets and avenues if they are numbers of 12 or under. When figures are used, do not follow with *d, st,* or *th.* Use figures for all house numbers except *One.* Separate the house number from a numerical name of a thoroughfare with a space, a hyphen, and a space.

23 East Twelfth Street
23 East 13 Street
One Fifth Avenue
2 Fifth Avenue
234 - 72 Street

3. If a room, suite, or apartment number is part of the address, it should follow the street address. This position facilitates mail delivery. If the address is an office building instead of a street, the suite number may precede the name of the building.

Right
700 Baylor Drive, Room 289
1010 First National Bank Building
Wrong
Room 289, 700 Baylor Drive

4. Never abbreviate the name of a city. States, territories, and possessions may be abbreviated. See ENVELOPES.

5. The Zip Code follows the state.

6. If there is no street address, put the city and state with Zip Code on separate lines.

7. Use post-office box number if you have it instead of street address.

For the correct form of addressing persons in official or honorary positions, see ADDRESSING OFFICIALS.

Addressing Officials. A secretary in a law office is frequently asked to write a letter to a person who holds an official or honorary position.

See the charts that follow:

UNITED STATES GOVERNMENT OFFICIALS

Personage	Envelope and Inside Address	Formal Salutation	Informal Salutation	Formal Close	Informal Close	1. Spoken Address 2. Informal Introduction or Reference[1]
The President	The President The White House Washington, D.C. 20500[2]	Mr. President	My dear Mr. President:	Respectfully yours,	Faithfully yours, (official) Very respectfully yours, (private individual)	1. Mr. President 2. NOT INTRODUCED (The President)
Vice President	The Vice President United States Senate Washington, D. C. *or* The Honorable John R. Blank Vice President of the United States Washington, D. C.	Sir:	My dear Mr. Vice President:	Very truly yours,	Sincerely yours,	1. Mr. Vice President *or* Mr. Blank 2. The Vice President
Chief Justice of the United States	The Chief Justice The Supreme Court Washington, D. C.	Sir:	My dear Mr. Chief Justice:	Very truly yours,	Sincerely yours,	1. Mr. Chief Justice 2. The Chief Justice
Associate Justice of the United States Supreme Court	Mr. Justice Blank The Supreme Court Washington, D. C.	Sir:	My dear Mr. Justice:	Very truly yours,	Sincerely yours,	1. Mr. Justice *or* Mr. Justice Blank 2. Mr. Justice Blank
Speaker of the House of Representatives	The Honorable John R. Blank Speaker of the House of Representatives Washington, D. C.	Sir:	My dear Mr. Speaker:	Very truly yours,	Sincerely yours,	1. Mr. Speaker *or* Mr. Blank 2. The Speaker, Mr. Blank (The Speaker or Mr. Blank)
Cabinet Officer (man)	*Formal* The Honorable the Secretary of State Washington, D. C. *Informal* The Honorable John R. Blank Secretary of State Washington, D. C. *If written from abroad* The Honorable John R. Blank Secretary of State of the United States of America Washington, D. C.	Sir:	My dear Mr. Secretary:	Very truly yours,	Sincerely yours,	1. Mr. Secretary *or* Mr. Blank 2. The Secretary of State, Mr. Blank (The Secretary or Mr. Blank)

[1] The form of introduction and the form of reference to a person are usually similar. When they differ, the form of reference is shown here in parentheses.
[2] On the inside address it is permissible to omit "Washington 25, D. C."

23

UNITED STATES GOVERNMENT OFFICIALS (Continued)

Personage	Envelope and Inside Address	Formal Salutation	Informal Salutation	Formal Close	Informal Close	1. Spoken Address 2. Informal Introduction or Reference[1]
Cabinet Officer (woman)	Formal The Honorable the Secretary of Labor Washington, D. C.	Madam:	My dear Madam Secretary:	Very truly yours,	Sincerely yours,	1. Madam Secretary or Mrs. (Miss) Blank 2. The Secretary of Labor, Mrs. (Miss) Blank (The Secretary or Mrs. (Miss) Blank)
Under Secretary of a Department	The Honorable John R. Blank Under Secretary of the Treasury Washington, D. C.	My dear Mr. Blank:	My dear Mr. Blank:	Very truly yours,	Sincerely yours,	1, 2. Mr. Blank
Assistant Secretary of a Department	The Honorable John R. Blank Assistant Secretary of Agriculture Washington, D. C.	My dear Mr. Blank:	My dear Mr. Blank:	Very truly yours,	Sincerely yours,	1, 2. Mr. Blank
Director of an Office, Chief of a Division or Bureau	John R. Blank, Esquire Chief, Bureau of Labor Statistics Department of Labor Washington, D. C.	My dear Mr. Blank:	My dear Mr. Blank:	Very truly yours,	Sincerely yours,	1, 2. Mr. Blank
United States Senator (man)	The Honorable John R. Blank United States Senate Washington, D. C.	Sir:	My dear Senator Blank:	Very truly yours,	Sincerely yours,	1. Senator Blank or Senator 2. Senator Blank
United States Senator (woman)	The Honorable Mary Blank United States Senate Washington, D. C.	Madam:	My dear Senator Blank: or My dear Mrs. (Miss) Blank:	Very truly yours,	Sincerely yours,	1. Senator Blank or Mrs. (Miss) Blank 2. Senator Blank
United States Representative (man)	The Honorable John R. Blank House of Representatives Washington, D. C.	Sir:	My dear Mr. Blank:	Very truly yours,	Sincerely yours,	1. Mr. Blank 2. Mr. Blank or Representative Blank
United States Representative (woman)	The Honorable Mary Blank House of Representatives Washington, D. C.	Madam:	My dear Mrs. (Miss) Blank:	Very truly yours,	Sincerely yours,	1, 2. Mrs. (Miss) Blank

	Address				
Territorial Delegate	The Honorable John R. Blank / Delegate of Alaska / House of Representatives / Washington, D. C.	Sir:	My dear Mr. Blank:	Very truly yours,	Sincerely yours,	1, 2. Mr. Blank
Resident Commissioner	The Honorable John R. Blank / Resident Commissioner of / Puerto Rico / Washington, D. C.	Sir:	My dear Mr. Blank:	Very truly yours,	Sincerely yours,	1, 2. Mr. Blank
Secretary to the President	The Honorable John R. Blank / Secretary to the President / The White House / Washington, D.C. 20500	Sir:	My dear Mr. Blank:	Very truly yours,	Sincerely yours,	1, 2. Mr. Blank
Secretary to the President with military rank	Major General John R. Blank / Secretary to the President / The White House / Washington, D.C. 20500	Sir:	My dear General Blank:	Very truly yours,	Sincerely yours,	1, 2. General Blank
Assistant Secretary to the President	The Honorable John R. Blank / Assistant Secretary to the / President / The White House / Washington, D.C. 20500	Sir:	My dear Mr. Blank:	Very truly yours,	Sincerely yours,	1, 2. Mr. Blank
High Officials of the United States, in general: Comptroller General, Director of Bureau of the Budget, Librarian of Congress	*Formal* / The Comptroller General of / the United States / Washington, D. C. // *Informal* / The Honorable John R. Blank / Comptroller General of the / United States / Washington, D. C.	Sir:	My dear Mr. Blank:	Very truly yours,	Sincerely yours,	1, 2. Mr. Blank
Heads of Independent Federal Agencies, Boards, Commissions, Establishments, Organizations, etc.	*Formal* / The Chairman of the Board of / Governors of the Federal / Reserve System / Washington, D. C. // *Informal* / The Honorable John R. Blank / Director, Mutual Security / Agency / Washington, D. C.	Sir:	My dear Mr. Chairman (or Mr. Director): / or / My dear Mr. Blank:	Very truly yours,	Sincerely yours,	1, 2. Mr. Blank

STATE AND LOCAL GOVERNMENT OFFICIALS

Personage	Envelope and Inside Address	Formal Salutation	Informal Salutation	Formal Close	Informal Close	Spoken Address / Informal Introduction or Reference[1]
Governor of States[3]	The Honorable John R. Blank Governor of Iowa Des Moines	Sir:	My dear Governor Blank:	Respectfully yours,	Sincerely yours,	1. Governor Blank *or* Governor 2. Governor Blank *or* The Governor (Outside his own state: The Governor of Iowa)
Lieutenant Governor	The Honorable John R. Blank Lieutenant Governor of Iowa Des Moines, Iowa	Sir:	My dear Mr. Blank:	Respectfully yours, *or* Very truly yours,	Sincerely yours,	1. Mr. Blank 2. The Lieutenant Governor of Iowa, Governor Blank (The Lieutenant Governor *or* Mr. Blank)
Secretary of State	The Honorable John R. Blank Secretary of State of Iowa Des Moines	Sir:	My dear Mr. Secretary:	Very truly yours,	Sincerely yours,	1, 2. Mr. Blank
Attorney General	The Honorable John R. Blank Attorney General of New York Albany, New York	Sir:	My dear Mr. Attorney General	Very truly yours,	Sincerely yours,	1, 2. Mr. Blank
State Representative or Assemblyman	The Honorable John R. Blank House of Representatives Nashville, Tennessee	Sir:	My dear Mr. Blank:	Very truly yours,	Sincerely yours,	1. Mr. Blank 2. Mr. Blank *or* Representative Blank
Mayor of a city	The Honorable John R. Blank Mayor of Memphis Tennessee	Sir:	My dear Mayor Blank:	Very truly yours,	Sincerely yours,	1. Mayor Blank *or* Mr. Mayor 2. Mayor Blank

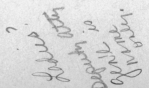

Commissioners of a city	*Formal* The Commissioners of the City of Buffalo New York	Sirs:	Sirs:	Very truly yours,	Very truly yours,	1. Gentlemen 2. The Commissioners
President of Board of Commissioners	*Formal or Informal* The Honorable John R. Blank President, Board of Commissioners of the City of Buffalo New York	Sir:	My dear Mr. Blank:	Very truly yours,	Sincerely yours,	1, 2. Mr. Blank
District Attorney	The Honorable John R. Blank District Attorney, Sunflower County County Courthouse Indianola, Mississippi	Dear Sir:	Dear Mr. Blank:	Very truly yours,	Sincerely yours,	1, 2. Mr. Blank
City Attorney City Counsel Corporation Counsel	The Honorable John R. Blank City Attorney (City Counsel, Corporation Counsel) Aliceville, Alabama	Dear Sir:	Dear Mr. Blank:	Very truly yours,	Sincerely yours,	1, 2. Mr. Blank
Aldermen	Alderman John R. Blank City Hall Aliceville, Alabama	Dear Sir:	Dear Mr. Blank:	Very truly yours,	Sincerely yours,	1, 2. Mr. Blank

[3] The form of addressing Governors varies in the different states. The form given here is the one used in most states. In Massachusetts by law and in some other states by courtesy, the form is *His Excellency, the Governor of Massachusetts.*

27

COURT OFFICIALS

Personage	Envelope and Inside Address	Formal Salutation	Informal Salutation	Formal Close	Informal Close	1. Spoken Address 2. Informal Introduction or Reference[1]
Chief Justice of a State Supreme Court	The Honorable John R. Blank Chief Justice[4] of the Supreme Court of Minnesota Minneapolis, Minnesota	Sir:	My dear Mr.[5] Chief Justice: *or* My dear Judge Blank:	Very truly yours,	Sincerely yours,	1. Mr. Chief Justice *or* Judge Blank 2. Mr. Chief Justice Blank *or* Judge Blank
Associate Justice Presiding Justice	The Honorable John R. Blank Associate (Presiding) Justice, Appellate Division Supreme Court, New York, New York	Sir:	My dear Mr. Justice:	Very truly yours,	Sincerely yours,	1, 2. Mr. Justice (*or* Judge) Blank
Judge of a Court[6]	The Honorable John R. Blank Judge of the United States District Court for the Southern District of California Los Angeles, California	Sir:	My dear Judge Blank:	Very truly yours,	Sincerely yours,	1, 2. Judge Blank
Clerk of a Court	John R. Blank, Esquire Clerk of the Superior Court Boston, Massachusetts	Sir:	My dear Mr. Blank:	Very truly yours,	Sincerely yours,	1, 2. Mr. Blank

[4] If his official title is *Chief Judge*, substitute *Chief Judge for Chief Justice*.
[5] Never use *Mr.* with *Chief Judge* or *Judge*.
[6] This does not apply to a Justice of the United States Supreme Court. See page 18.

Ademption. The failure of a *specific legacy* (see LEGACY) because the subject matter no longer belongs to the testator's estate at his death. See also ADVANCEMENT.

Adjective Law. See SUBSTANTIVE LAW.

Adjustment of Charges and Income. (Real estate) Upon a sale of REAL PROPERTY, an equitable apportionment between seller and purchaser of the charges against the property to be conveyed and of any income produced by the property.

Date of adjustment. The date as of which charges and income are apportioned between purchaser and seller varies with the locality. In many instances, adjustments are made as of the day immediately preceding the day on which TITLE is closed; that is, the purchaser bears the charges and receives the income beginning with and including the day on which title passes to him. The CONTRACT OF SALE may, however, fix some earlier date of adjustment. If the date for CLOSING TITLE is postponed, the consent to adjournment may indicate a new date of adjustment.

Items adjusted. The following are generally apportioned between purchaser and seller:

1. Taxes: These include county, town, city, village, and school taxes. The basis for adjustment depends upon local custom and the agreement of the parties. As to taxes paid for the year for which they are levied and in which title is closed, seller is generally entitled to an amount representing the unexpired portion of that year.

2. Water charges: These include both municipal and private water charges.

3. Insurancce premiums: These include fire, plate glass, rent, boiler, and other similar insurance. Liability and compensation insurance premiums are generally not apportioned; the purchaser obtains such insurance on his own account immediately upon taking title.

4. Interest on mortgages: Interest is adjusted from the date of the last payment.

5. Rents: In the case of rents collected by the seller for the month in which title is closed, the purchaser is entitled to that portion representing the unexpired part of the month. If rents that have become due have not been paid at the date of closing, the purchaser may give to the seller written assurance, in the form of a letter, that upon receipt of the rent he will turn over to the seller the portion to which the seller is entitled.

The contract of sale may enumerate the items to be adjusted. Other items not mentioned, for example fuel on hand, prepayments on service contracts, and the like, may also be prorated according to local practice. If payment due on the closing is to be made by certified check, the purchaser should bring to the closing a check for the approximate amount and suffcient *cash* to cover adjustments.

Method of calculating adjustments. The method of computing adjustments varies with the locality. For the purpose of simplification, many local real estate boards recommend the practice of computing by a 360-day method, rather than a 365-day method. Each month represents 1/12 of the annual charge, and each day 1/30 of the monthly charge. Where the period for which computation is made is more than one month, the time is computed by full months and by the actual number of days in excess of such full months. For example, the period between March 15 and June 3 is 2 months (April and May) and 20 days (17 days in March and 3 days in June).

Examples of calculation of adjustments. Following are some examples of calculations of adjustments. For the purpose of the examples, assume that title closes June 8, 19___.

Tax adjustment: Taxes in the locality are payable semi-annually, April 1 and October 1. The seller paid taxes on April 1 for the preceding 6-month period. During the current 6-month period, the seller is responsible for taxes from April 1 to, but not including, June 8, the closing date. He would have to allow the buyer the amount of the taxes for that period—2 months (April and May) and 7 days. Assuming that the taxes for the 6-month period amount to $1,500, the taxes for one month are $250 ($1,500 ÷ 6), for one day, $8.33⅓ ($250 ÷ 30). An adjustment of $558.33 is made in favor of the purchaser [2 x $250 + (7 x $8.33⅓)].

Interest adjustment: Suppose there is a mortgage of $20,000 on the property, with interest at 6 percent payable quarterly on 15th of December, March, June, and September. When title closed on June 8, interest had been paid to but not including March 15. The purchaser is entitled to an allowance for interest from and including March 15 through June 7, or for a period of 2 months (April and May) and 24 days (17 days in March, 7 days in June). The interest on $20,000 at 6 percent annum is $100

per month, $3.33⅓ per day ($100 ÷ 30). The interest for 2 months, 24 days is $200 (2 x $100) + $80 (24 x $3.33⅓). An adjustment of $280 is made in favor of the purchaser.

Insurance adjustment: Suppose there is a fire policy on the property which had been paid up for three years. The expiration date of the policy is August 1, 1977. The seller is therefore entitled to an adjustment of insurance for 13 months and 23 days (June 8, 1976, the date of the closing, to August 1, 1977). The premium is $10 per month [$360 ÷ (12 x 3)], or 33⅓¢ per day ($10 ÷ 30). An adjustment of $137.67 (13 x $10) + (23 x 33⅓¢) is made in favor of the seller.

Rent adjustment: The seller had collected the rents in advance for the month of June. They amounted to $5,000. The purchaser is entitled to an adjustment for the period from and including June 8 through June 30, or 23 days. Since June has only 30 days, the rent per day is $5,000 ÷ 30, or $166.66⅔ per day. The purchaser is entitled to an adjustment of $3,833.33 (23 × $166.66⅔). If there is more than one tenant, the rent for each must be prorated separately, unless the rents had all been collected for the same period.

Administrative Law. The rules and regulations framed by an administrative body created by a state legislature or by Congress to carry out a specific statute. For example, the Federal income tax law is administered by the Internal Revenue Service, which issues regulations and rules that have the weight of law as long as they keep within the scope of the income tax statute. Frequently such regulations interpret in a specific way the legislature's general intent when it enacted the statute. Thus, administrative bodies, which are primarily executive in nature, may also have powers that resemble legislative or judicial authority.

Administrator. See LETTERS OF ADMINISTRATION.

Admiralty. A court empowered to enforce maritime law and exercise JURISDICTION over a maritime CONTRACT, TORT, and certain maritime crimes. Admiralty jurisdiction is placed by the Constitution within the Federal judicial system, although state and Federal common law courts can and do enforce most maritime rights. Only a Federal court can enforce a MARITIME LIEN, however. There is no requirement of diversity of citizenship or of a minimum amount of monies involved as there is in Federal civil cases. Federal admiralty courts may hear all such cases involving waters that are navigable in foreign or INTERSTATE COMMERCE. Whether a particular water is navigable is a question of fact of which the courts may take JUDICIAL NOTICE, but should the point be in doubt, evidence may be introduced and considered.

Admiralty has devloped its own procedure and terminology, and attorneys in this field (see PROCTOR) generally insist that its peculiar customs be followed. The secretary who works for a lawyer specializing in admiralty, therefore, must be aware of terms that are unique in admiralty. See CITATION (ADMIRALTY PROCEEDING); LIBEL (IN ADMIRALTY PRACTICE); RESPONDENT; CLAIMANT; PETITION. An example of a verified libel and answer (corresponding to the complaint and answer in a common law proceeding) demonstrating the correct form and terminology to be used follows. The cause of action involves the alleged damage of goods aboard ship.

LIBEL

TO THE HONORABLE THE JUDGES OF THE UNITED STATES DISTRICT COURT FOR THE SOUTHERN DISTRICT OF NEW YORK

The libel and complaint of JONES IMPORTING COMPANY against the Steamship DAUNTLESS, her engines, boilers, etc., and SMITH SHIPPING COMPANY, in a cause of contract, civil and maritime, alleges upon information and belief, and respectfully shows to this Honorable Court, as follows:

FIRST: At all times hereinafter mentioned, libelant was, and now is, a corporation organized and existing under and by virtue of the laws of the State of New York, with an office and place of business at 500 Fifth Avenue, in the City and State of New York.

SECOND: At all times hereinafter mentioned, the Steamship DAUNTLESS was, and now is, a general merchant ship engaged in the common carriage of goods by water for hire and is now or will be during the pendency of this action within this District and subject to and within the jurisdiction of the Honorable Court.

THIRD: At all times hereinafter mentioned, SMITH SHIPPING COMPANY was, and now is, a corporation organized and existing under and by virtue of the laws of the Republic of Liberia, with an office and place of business at 50 Water Street, City and State of New York.

FOURTH: On or about June 15, 19__, at London, England, John Doe, Inc., as shipper, delivered to the respondent and to the Steamship DAUNTLESS a shipment consisting of 50 cartons of linen in good order and condition, and the respondents then and there accepted the said merchandise so delivered to them and in consideration of the payment of certain freight charges, paid or agreed to be paid, agreed to transport said merchandise as a common carrier to the Port of New York, and there deliver the same in like good order and condition as when shipped to shipper's order, notify Jones Importing Company, in accordance with the valid terms and conditions of its bill of lading No. 42 dated June 15, 19__, at London issued that date by the duly authorized agent of the respondent and the Steamship DAUNTLESS.

FIFTH: Thereafter the respondent loaded the said merchandise on board the Steamship DAUNTLESS, and the said vessel having the said merchandise on board, sailed from the Port of London and subsequently arrived at the Port of New York where the DAUNTLESS and the repondent failed to deliver the merchandise in the same like order and condition as when received by the respondent, but on the contrary, delivered it crushed and damaged and contaminated by water and other substances unknown to libelant.

SIXTH: At all said times, libelant was the ultimate consignee of the merchandise and brings this action not only on its own behalf but on behalf of and for the benefit of all parties who may become interested, as their respective interests may ultimately appear.

SEVENTH: Libelant and said other parties have duly complied with all valid obligations and conditions of the aforesaid contract of carriage on their respective parts to be performed.

EIGHTH: By reason of the premises, libelant and said other parties have sustained damages in the amount of $5,000, as nearly as the same can now be estimated, no part of which has been paid although duly demanded.

NINTH: All and singular the premises are true and within the admiralty and maritime jurisdiction of the United States and of this Honorable Court.

WHEREFORE, libelants pray:

1. That process in due form of law, according to the course and practice of this Honorable Court in causes of Admiralty and Maritime jurisidiction, may issue against the respondent, SMITH SHIPPING COMPANY, and that the said respondent be cited to appear and answer, all and singular, the matters aforesaid.

2. That process in due form of law, according to the course and practice of this Honorable Court in causes of Admiralty and Maritime juridiction, may issue against the Steamship DAUNTLESS, her engines, etc., and that all persons claiming any interest in the said vessel be cited to appear and answer, all and singular, the matters aforesaid.

3. That this Honorable Court may adjudge and decree that the said resondent pay to libelant its damages as aforesaid, together with interest and costs and that the Steamship DAUNTLESS be condemned and sold to pay the same.

4. Libelant may have such other and further relief in the premises as in law and justice it may be entitled to receive.

BLACKSTONE & BLACKSTONE
Proctors for Libelant
Office & P.O. Address
11 John Street
New York, New York 10001

VERIFICATION

STATE OF NEW YORK
COUNTY OF NEW YORK } ss.:

JOHN W. JONES, being duly sworn, deposes and says:

That he is the Vice President of JONES IMPORTING COMPANY, the libelant herein.

That he has read the foregoing libel and knows the contents thereof and the same is true of his own knowledge except as to matters therein stated to be alleged upon information and belief, and as to those matters he believes them to be true.

That the reason why this verification is made by deponent and not by libelant is that libelant is a corporation and deponent is an officer thereof.

That the sources of deponent's information and the grounds of his belief are reports made to him by employees, and libelant's records.

. . . .

Sworn to before me this
    day of August, 19. . .

ANSWER

TO THE HONORABLE THE JUDGES OF THE UNITED STATES DISTRICT COURT FOR THE SOUTHERN DISTRICT OF NEW YORK

The answer of respondent SMITH SHIP-PING COMPANY to the libel of JONES IM-PORTING COMPANY, in an alleged cause of contract, civil and maritime, alleges upon infor-mation and belief, as follows:

FIRST: It denies knowledge or information sufficient to form a belief as to the allega-tions of article First of the libel.

SECOND: It admits that the Steamship DAUNTLESS was and is a general merchant ship engaged in the common carriage of good by water for hire, denies that it is now within this district and subject to and within the jurisdiction of this Honorable Court and denies knowledge or information sufficient to form a belief as to its future whereabouts.

THIRD: It admits the allegations of article Third of the libel.

FOURTH: It admits that at London, England on or about June 15, 19— it received from John Doe, Inc., a shipment consisting of 50 cartons, contents and condition of contents un-known to it, for transportation to the Port of New York for an agreed freight, and delivery there as ordered by the shipper, in accordance with and subject to the terms, conditions and exceptions of its bill of lading No. 42 dated June 15, 1977, issued to and accepted by the said shipper at London by respondent's duly authorized agent. Except as above admitted, respond-ent denies the allegations of article Fourth of the libel.

FIFTH: It admits that the shipment referred to in article Fourth herein was loaded on board the DAUNTLESS and carried by it from London to New York where it was delivered in accordance with the terms of the aforementioned bill of lading, which constituted the con-tract of carriage. Except as herein admitted, it denies the allegations of article Fifth of the libel.

SIXTH: It denies knowledge or information sufficient to form a belief as to the allega-tions of article Sixth of the libel.

SEVENTH: It denies the allegations of article Seventh of the libel.

EIGHTH: It admits demand and non-payment and denies the remaining allegations of article Eighth of the libel.

NINTH: It admits the admiralty and maritime jurisdiction of the United States and of this Honorable Court and denies the remaining allegations of article Ninth of the complaint.

TENTH: Further answering, respondent alleges that the 50 cartons referred to in the libel were received at London and transported subject to the terms, conditions and exceptions of bill of lading referred to in article Fourth of the libel, conditions and exceptions of bill of lading referred to in article Fourth of the libel, which constituted the contract of carriage, and in accordance with the Carriage of Goods by Sea Act.

The following exception was noted on the face of the said bill of lading:

"CARTONS WATER-STAINED BUT
APPARENTLY DRY"

The said Carriage of Goods by Sea Act provided in part as follows:

"Sec. 3 (6) ***." In any event the carrier and the ship shall be discharged from all liability in respect of loss or damage unless suit is brought within one year after delivery of the goods or the date when the goods should have been delivered.***."

"Sec.4 (2). Neither the carrier nor the ship shall be responsible for loss or damage arising or reulting from—

(i) Act or omission of the shipper or owner of the goods, his agent or representative;

* * *

(n) Insufficiency of packing;

* * *

(q) Any other cause arising without the actual fault and privity of the carrier and without the fault or neglect of the agents or servants of the carrier***."

Any damage sustained by the shipment occurred before it was delivered to the respondent, and respondent is not liable.

Suit was not brought against respondent within one year after delivery of the goods, and repondent is not liable.

Any loss or damage to the shipment which occurred while it was in respondent's custody was the result of one or more causes excepted in the Carriage of Goods by Sea Act, and respondent is not liable.

All and singular the premises are true.

WHEREFORE, respondent prays that the libel herein be dismissed with costs.

WHITESTONE AND WHITESTONE
Proctors for Respondent
26 Broadway
New York, N.Y. 10001

VERIFICATION

SOUTHERN DISTRICT OF NEW YORK ⎫
COUNTY OF NEW YORK   ⎬ ss.:
⎭

GEORGE W. WHITESTONE, being duly sworn, says:

I am one of the proctors for the respondent herein. I have the foregoing answer and know the contents thereof, and the same is true to the best of my knowledge, information and belief. The sources of my knowledge or information are communications received from the respondent and an examination of the papers relating to the matter in suit. The reason why this verification is not made by respondent is that the said respondent is a foreign corporation.

. . . .

Sworn to before me this
     day of August, 19___

- -

See also MARITIME LIEN; CHARTER-PARTY; GENERAL AVERAGE LOSS; SALVAGE.

Admission to the Bar. The status that allows a person to practice law within a state. Each state has its own requirements for admission to the bar. In every state, the requirements include these four factors: academic training, legal training, moral character, and belief in and loyalty to the form of the United States Government.

In almost all states the applicant for admission to the bar must take an examination, even though he is a graduate of law school. Admission to practice in one state does not license the attorney to practice in another state. He must comply with the rules that state has for admission of an "attorney applicant." However, almost all of the states will admit an attorney from another state without examination after he has practiced a specified length of time, provided he meets other requirements. A few states require the attorney applicant to take an examination.

License to practice in one or more states does not admit the lawyer to practice in Federal Courts. To be admitted to the United States Supreme Court, an attorney must have practiced three years in the highest court in his state or territory. A member of the bar moves the attorney's admission in open court. Requirements for admission to the Federal courts of appeals and district courts vary with the circuit and the district.

An attorney may obtain special permission to argue a particular case before a court in which he is not licensed to practice. This often happens in criminal cases when the accused wants a nationally famous criminal lawyer to represent him in the state in which he is to be tried.

Adoption. The taking and receiving as one's own that to which he bore no prior relation, colorable or otherwise. The act of one who takes another's child into his own family, treating him as his own, and giving him all the rights and duties of his own child. Adoptions are made legal by making application to the Probate Court for the right to adopt. Adoptions are usually very secret and in the case of infants, the adoptive parents do not usually know the original surname of the infant they are adopting. The secretary should be very careful never to divulge information to the adoptive parents. See sample Petition and Judgment Entry following.

IN THE COURT OF COMMON PLEAS, FRANKLIN COUNTY, OHIO
PROBATE DIVISION

IN THE MATTER OF THE ADOPTION OF
JOHN EDWARD JONES   Case No._____

PETITION FOR ADOPTION

The undersigned, Thomas Lee Jones and Josephine Ellen Jones represent to the Court that they are husband and wife and they respectfully petition the Court for permission to adopt as their own child, John Edward Smith, and to have the name of said child changed to John Edward Jones.

Your petitioners represent to the Court that the following is a correct statement concerning the petitioner, the child and the child's custody:

PETITIONERS

NAME:	Thomas Lee Jones
ADDRESS:	3013 Hardesty Place West, Columbus, Ohio 43204
DATE & PLACE OF BIRTH:	November 18, 1943 Cleveland, Ohio
NAME:	Josephine Ellen Jones
ADDRESS:	3013 Hardesty Place West, Columbus, Ohio 43204
DATE & PLACE OF BIRTH:	October 9, 1945 Columbus, Ohio
DATE & PLACE OF MARRIAGE:	April 1, 1966 Columbus, Ohio
RELATIONSHIP TO CHILD:	None

CHILD

NAME:	John Edward Smith
ADDRESS:	3013 Hardesty Place West, Columbus, Ohio 43204
DATE & PLACE OF BIRTH:	March 7, 1965 Columbus, Franklin County, Ohio
PROPERTY:	None

The following information is given to determine the persons or person whose consent to said adoption is required to be obtained pursuant to R. C. 3107.06; are required to be notified of the filing to the Petition for Adoption pursuant to R. C. 3107.08.

The child is in the permanent custody of the Franklin County Children Services Board, a certified organization.

The said child is living in the home of the petitioners herein and was placed in said home on the 1st day of November, 1974, for purposes of adoption by the Franklin County Children Services Board.

A certified copy of the child's birth certificate is attached herewith.

Your petitioners represent that they are possessed of sufficient means and ability to properly maintain and educate the said child.

Your petitioners hereby waive notice of any hearing on the petition filed in this cause pursuant to the provisions of Sec. 2101.28 of the Ohio Revised Code. Your petitioners further waive notice of any investigation made or report submitted, or availability for examination of the contents of any reports hereafter submitted, by the next friend of said child appointed by the Court in this case.

WHEREFORE, your petitioners pray that upon the final hearing in this cause, they may be permitted by order of Court to adopt John Edward Smith and that the name of said child be changed to John Edward Jones, all in accordance with Chapter 3107 of the Ohio Revised Code, pertaining to adoptions.

_____

Thomas Lee Jones

_____

Josephine Ellen Jones

STATE OF OHIO, COUNTY OF FRANKLIN, SS:

The undersigned, the petitioners in the foregoing petition for adoption, being first duly sworn, say that the statements contained in the foregoing petition are true, as they verily believe.

_____

Thomas Lee Jones

_____

Josephine Ellen Jones

Sworn to before me and subscribed in my presence this 15th day of May, 19__.

_____

Notary Public

IN THE COURT OF COMMON PLEAS, FRANKLIN COUNTY, OHIO
PROBATE DIVISION

IN THE MATTER OF THE ADOPTION OF:
JOHN EDWARD JONES   Case No._____

FINAL DECREE OF ADOPTION

This day this cause came on to be heard on the petition for adoption and change of name of John Edward Jones and the evidence. The Court, being fully advised according to law, is of the opinion that the facts stated in the petition are true; that the petitioners, Thomas Lee Jones and Josephine Ellen Jones, husband and wife, residing at 3013 Hardesty Place West, Columbus, Ohio 43204, are of good moral character and of reputable standing in the community, and have ability and means properly to care for, rear, and educate said child by them sought to be adopted, according to law in this proceeding; and that the best interests of said child would be promoted by such adoption.

Further, the Court finds that such child is suitable for adoption, and is satisfied that all the statutory provisions relative to adoption have been complied with; that the child is in the permanent custody of the Franklin County Children Services Board, a certified agency, which has answered and consented to the adoption and change of name, and the same is on file herein.

Further, the Court finds that the said child has resided with the petitioners for more than six (6) months; and the Court, having examined Thomas Lee Jones and Josephine Ellen Jones, each separate and apart from the other, is satisfied that each desires such adoption of his own free will and accord.

THEREFORE, IT IS ORDERED, ADJUDGED AND DECREED that said adoption be and hereby is made, that the name of said child be and hereby is changed to John Edward Jones; that said child shall hereafter be known by said name, and that from this day henceforth said child shall for all purposes in the adoption statutes of this state provided, be the child of Thomas Lee Jones and Josephine Ellen Jones.

_____
Probate Judge

Approved:

_____
Attorney

Adultery. The conscious act of sexual intercourse between a married person and a person other than his legal spouse. Adultery is grounds for DIVORCE in every state in this country.

Ad Valorem Tax. A tax or duty based on the value of property. In contrast, a _specific_ tax is levied as a fixed sum on each article of class, without regard to its value. (See DUTIES.)

Advancement. (Inheritance) A payment given to an HEIR by a person who does not intend to leave a WILL (see INTESTATE). He makes the payment with the intention that it substitute for the share of his estate that such heir would ordinarily receive under the laws of intestacy.

Advancement does not apply where there is a will, unless the will expressly so provides. The maker of a will may refer to advancements made by him to his donees (see DONEE) during his lifetime, and direct that such advancements be deducted from the donee's LEGACY. See also ADEMPTION.

Advance Sheets. See NATIONAL REPORTER SYSTEM.

Affiant. A person making an affidavit. He may also be known as the _deponent._ See AFFIDAVIT.

Affidavit. A written statement of facts sworn to by the person making the statement in the presence of an officer authorized to administer the oath. The purpose of the affidavit is to help establish or prove a fact. For example, an affidavit may be used to prove a person's identity, age, marital status, and possession of property. It may also be used as an essential part of a court case or action. The person making the affidavit is the _affiant_ or _deponent._ An affidavit is always a complete instrument within itself, whereas an ACKNOWLEDGMENT is always part of, or rather an appendage to, another instrument. An affidavit is sworn to but an acknowledgment is not. Both the person making the affidavit and the officer administering the oath sign an affidavit; only the officer taking an acknowledgment signs it. An affidavit has a JURAT but an acknowledgment does not.

Essentials of an affidavit. Some affidavits are written in the first person and some in the third person, but they all have the following basic essentials.

1. *Venue.* When an affidavit is used in a court case, it is always preceded by the caption of the case. The affidavit itself begins with a recital of the venue.

2. *Name of affiant.* The name of the person making the affidavit is written in solid caps.

3. *Averment of oath.* The introduction to the affidavit avers that the affiant was sworn, or made the statement under oath.

4. *Statement of facts.* The body of the affidavit is a narrative of the facts that the affiant wishes to state.

5. *Signature of affiant.* The affiant always signs the affidavit, even those that are written in the third person.

6. *Jurat.* A jurat is a clause in an official certificate attesting that the affidavit or deposition was sworn to at a stated time before an authorized officer. It is often referred to as the "sworn to" clause. The form of jurat varies slightly in the different states. In a few states, the jurat recites the title of the officer and the state, or state and county, in which he is authorized to act. In a few other states, the name of the affiant is repeated in the jurat. The most common form of jurat is:

Subscribed and sworn to before me this
. . . . . . .day of. . . . .,
19. . . .   .
Notary Public

7. *Signature of notary.* The notary signs immediately beneath the jurat. He also affixes his seal and the expiration date of his commission. In some states the expiration date precedes the signature.

STATE OF SOUTH CAROLINA)
                         ; ss.
COUNTY OF FLORENCE   )

ROBERT T. SMITH, being duly sworn, deposes and says:

He is the Secretary of National Corporation, and that no stockholder of said Corporation has filed with the Secretary thereof a written request (other than such written request or requests as may have heretofore expired or been withdrawn) that notices intended for him shall be mailed to some address other than his address as it appears on the stock book of the said Corporation.

_____
Secretary

Sworn to before me this
day of   , 19—

_____
Notary Public

Affidavit: Figure 1.

Affidavit of Title. An AFFIDAVIT executed by the seller upon sale of REAL PROPERTY to assure the purchaser that there are no defects in the seller's TITLE to the property. The affidavit of title supplements a title examination; it covers matters which may not be revealed by a TITLE SEARCH. It furnishes additional protection to the purchaser, for a false affidavit of title may subject the seller to criminal prosecution. The affidavit of title also serves as a means of identifying the person executing the papers to be delivered on CLOSING TITLE to the satisfaction of the title company that insures the title. (See TITLE INSURANCE.)

FORM OF AFFIDAVIT OF TITLE

STATE OF NEW YORK } ss.:
COUNTY OF

Title No. . . . .
. . . ., being duly sworn, says:
I reside at No. . . . . Street,
. . . . . . City, State of . . . .
I am the *. . . . .
owner in fee simple of premises . . . . . .
and . . . . . . the grantee described in a certain deed of said premises recorded in the Register's Office of . . . . County in Liber . . . . of Conveyances, page . . . .

Said premises have been in my/its possession since 19 . . . . . .; that my/its possession thereof has been peaceable and undisturbed, and the title thereto has never been disputed, questioned or rejected, nor insurance thereof refused, as far as I know. I know of no facts by reason of which said possession or title might be called in question, or by reason of which any claim to any part of said premises of any interest therein adverse to me/its might be set up. There are no judgments against me/its unpaid or unsatisfied of record entered in any court of this state, or of the United States, and said premises are, as far as I know, free from all leases, mortgages, taxes, assessments, water

cnarges and other liens and encumbrances, except . . . .

Said premises are now occupied by . . . .

No proceedings in bankruptcy have ever been instituted by or against me/it in any court or before any officer of any state, or of the United States, nor have I/has it at any time made an assignment for the benefit of creditors, nor an assignment, now in effect, of the rents of said premises or any part thereof.

† I am a citizen of the United States, and am more than 21 years old. I am by occupation . . . . I am married to . . . . who is over the age of 21 years and is competent to convey or mortgage real estate. I was married to her on the . . . . day of . . . . . 19 . . . . . I have never been married to any other person now living. I have not been known by any other name during the past ten years.

‡ That the charter of said corporation is in full force and effect and no proceeding is pending for its dissolution or annulment. That all license and franchise taxes due and payable by said corporation have been paid in full.

There are no actions pending affecting said premises. That no repairs, alterations or improvements have been made to said premises which have not been completed more than four months prior to the date hereof. There are no facts known to me relating to the title to said premises which have not been set forth in this affidavit.

This affidavit is made to induce . . . . to accept a . . . . of/on said premises, and to induce . . . . Title Company to issue its policy of title insurance numbered above covering said premises knowing that they will rely on the statements herein made.

Sworn to before me this . . . .
day of . . . ., 19 . . . .

---

*If owner is a corporation, fill in office held by deponent and name of corporation.

†This paragraph to be omitted if owner is a corporation.

‡This paragraph to be omitted if owner is not a corporation.

Affirmance. See RATIFICATION.

Affreightment Contract. A contract by a carrier to transport goods. See BILL OF LADING; CHARTER-PARTY.

Agency. The relationship that exists when one person authorizes another to act for him. The one granting the authority is the *principal;* the one authorized to act is the *agent.* For an agent to act, a *third party*, with whom he contracts, is necessary. An agency relationship is created when a person gives a POWER OF ATTORNEY or a PROXY, and in other situations. An agency may be *general*—the agent has broad powers to represent the principal; or the agency may be special.

Agreement. See CONTRACT.

Aiding and Abetting. Words, acts, or presence by one person to assist another person, the principal, to do the physical acts in the commission of a crime. If one aids and abets, he is liable for the same punishment as the principal doing the act. The principal must actually commit the crime if the aider and abetter is to be liable. See ACCOMPLICE; ACCESSORY; CONSPIRACY.

Airplane Reservation. A plane reservation may be made by telephoning *Reservations* at the desired airline or through a TRAVEL AGENCY. Information necessary to make a reservation includes (1) point of departure and destination, (2) date desired, (3) time of departure, (4) airline and flight number. The secretary to a lawyer does not ordinarily leave the selection of flight, route, and the like to the airline representative or travel agent but might ask for suggestions if it is not possible to get the desired reservation. The airline representative making the reservation at the point of departure will follow through on reservations, for the entire trip. See RESERVATIONS, LETTERS MAKING, for form of letter to be used in writing for reservations. (See AIRPLANE TRANSPORTATION.)

Cancellation of reservation. Frequently a plane reservation is not available at the time the request is entered. The airline will then enter the request and notify the customer if the space later becomes available. In a situation of this kind, it is customary to enter a request for space with other lines or with a railroad. As soon as the secretary is notified of space being available on one line, she should cancel requests entered with other lines. Good will of the transportation companies is kept by the prompt cancellation of any space that is not going to be used. As the reservation is usually made locally, it may be canceled by phone. A reservation for a return flight for stages of an interrupted flight is not held if the traveler does not confirm the reservation within a certain number of hours before his flight is to be resumed.

Airplane Transportation. (See also AIRPLANE RESERVATION.) When planning a business trip by plane the traveler is interested in (1) airlines that can be used for the trip, (2) time schedules, (3) whether meals are served on flight, (4) cost, and (5) baggage facilities.

If the legal secretary is asked to make

41

plane reservations and get accurate travel information (either for domestic or foreign travel) for the lawyer for whom she works, she should know that one of the easiest and most efficient ways to obtain service is through a qualified travel agency. If the lawyer for whom she works has never used a travel agency, the knowledgeable secretary can suggest it to her employer as a great convenience and time-saver to both herself and him. There is no charge for obtaining airline or hotel reservations through an agency, because the agency receives its commission from the airline or hotel.

The secretary need only tell the agency her employer's name, his business and home phone numbers, detailed information on proposed dates, times of arrival and departure at each city, type of plane transportation preferred. The agency makes the desired reservations. The usual procedure is for the agency to bill the employer when delivering the tickets, unless he has a credit TRAVEL CARD. It is, however, a wise precaution for the secretary to follow up with the agency a reasonable time after the call has been placed, to be sure the reservations have been made and that the tickets will arrive at the office in plenty of time. On arrival of the tickets, the secretary should check carefully the date, time, destination, and the like before giving them to the lawyer.

If the secretary prefers to work directly with the airline, she may choose one or more likely airlines by consulting the classified section in her local directory. Then she can ask them for necessary information and, at the same time, get the timetables of those lines. When she decides on the airline to use and selects the flight best suited to her employer's needs she should, of course, check very carefully at the time the reservation is actually placed, for flights listed in the timetables are subject to change.

Alias Summons. A SUMMONS that is issued when the original one is not effective because of defective form or improper manner of service. It is prepared like the original summons, except that *alias* precedes *summons*. If the alias summons is not served, and it is necessary to issue a following summons, the third one is designated as a *pluries summons*.

Alibi. An inference that one could not have committed a crime because he was elsewhere at the time of its commission.

Alien Corporation. A CORPORATION organized outside the United States. See also FOREIGN CORPORATION; DOMESTIC CORPORATION; STATE OF INCORPORATION.

Alignment of Paper. The "lining up" of a large pack of paper and carbons for insertion in the typewriter in such a way that a uniformity of all the sheets is attained. Many legal secretaries make a special *feeding device* to assure perfect alignment. Figure 1 shows how to make such a device; Figure 2 shows it after completion, with paper inserted.

1. Fold a 5 by 8½ inch strip of flimsy Manila tag (a cheap file folder will do) across the center, lengthwise.

2. Cut three U-shaped slots across the upper half of the folded strip, about one-half inch from the crease.

3. Lift up and bend backward the tongues formed by the slots.

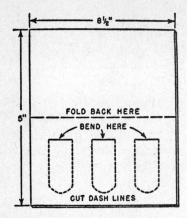

Alignment of paper: Figure 1.
Device for feeding paper
to typewriter—process of making device.

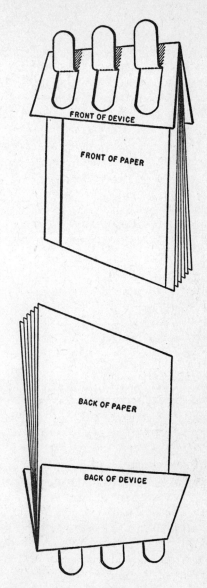

Alignment of Paper: Figure 2.
Device for feeding paper
into typewriter with papers inserted.

4. Insert the assembled sheets of paper in the folded strip.

5. Feed the tongues from the U-slots into the typewriter. The platen grasps them more readily than it does a thick pack of paper.

6. Remove the folded strip before beginning to type.

Several sheets of paper and carbon may be inserted easily in the typewriter by placing them beneath the flap of an envelope. The platen, however, does not grasp a large pack as readily, and the alignment is not as perfect, as when the device described here is used.

Alimony. Allowances that a court orders a husband to pay his wife for maintenance while they are separated or after they are divorced. The amount of alimony to be awarded is discretionary with the court. In determining the amount to be paid, the court considers the husband's income and his ability to provide for himself and his family.

Temporary alimony is an allowance made pending a suit for DIVORCE or SEPARATION. It includes a reasonable allowance for expenses in preparing the suit as well as for support. In determining the amount of temporary alimony, the court looks into the chances of the wife's success in the action.

For the purpose of Federal income

taxes, periodic alimony payments are included in the gross income of the wife and are deductible by the husband in the year of payment. Generally, alimony payable in a lump sum or in a fixed number of installments is not deductible by the husband.

Allegation. A statement made by a party who claims it can be proved as a fact. See also COMPLAINT.

All-time Bottom. An expression used to denote the time of the lowest period of business activity throughout the United States.

All-time High. An expression used to denote the time of the highest peak of business activity throughout the United States.

Allonge. (French) A piece of paper attached to a bill of exchange or a promissory note, on which to write endorsements when there is no room on the instrument itself.

Alphabetical Filing, Law Office. (For client's files) The methodical system of laying away certain law office papers in an arrangement based on the order of the alphabet. In this system, clients' folders are filed alphabetically according to name or subject. A cross-index (see NUMERICAL FILING SYSTEM) is not necessary with this system of filing but is sometimes desirable.

How to use the alphabetical system. Each client has a general folder and each of his matters has a separate folder. All matters of a specific client are filed under his name. The order of arrangement of the various folders is similar to that of the index cards in a numerical system: the general folder comes first and is followed by the non-suit files arranged alphabetically according to subject. These are followed by the litigation files arranged alphabetically according to opposing party. The various matters of Client Desmond & Lake, Inc. might be labeled and filed as follows:

Desmond & Lake, Inc.—General
Desmond & Lake, Inc.—Arbitration— R. E. Brown
Desmond & Lake, Inc.—Arbitration— L. F. Jones
Desmond & Lake, Inc.—Profit-sharing Plan
Desmond & Lake, Inc. ads. Bates & Co.
Desmond & Lake, Inc. vs. Cordell Lighting Effects Co.

If the active files of a client are very numerous, they might be numbered and a card index made of that client's files.

Another method of using the alphabetical system in a law office is to file under the name of the plaintiff, whether the plaintiff is the client or not. Lawyers have a tendency to think of suits and claims in terms of plaintiff vs. defendant. Non-litigation matters are filed under the name of the client. When this method of filing is followed, cross-index cards are desirable. The secretary makes the index cards in the name of the client and others connected with the case, and shows on the card under which name the folder is filed.

How to transfer alphabetical files. When alphabetical files are closed or transferred to storage, cross-index cards *must* be made. The simplest method of transferring them is to assign the file a transfer number and make cross-index cards for each party connected with the matter. The files are then placed in the storage files in numerical order. This avoids shifting of files.

Some offices transfer alphabetically. The file drawers are then numbered and the drawer number in which the file is placed is indicated on the cross-index cards. Each year's transferred files may be filed together alphabetically. However, this entails shifting of files from drawer to drawer unless ample space under each letter is kept open for files to be stored under that letter in the future.

See also NUMERICAL FILING SYSTEM (APPLIED TO CLIENT'S FILES.); FILING (IN A LAW OFFICE).

Amendment of the Constitution. A method of changing the Constitution, as provided by Article V in the Constitution, itself. Amendments are proposed by two-thirds of each House of Congress. To become law, they must then be ratified by the legislatures or conventions in three-fourths of the states.

American Association of Law Libraries. An association of law libraries. They may be reached by writing:

American Association of Law Libraries
53 West Jackson Boulevard
Chicago, Illinois 60604

American Bar. (Publication) A biographical directory of the leading lawyers of the United States and Canada published by James C. Fifield Co., Minneapolis, Minnesota. This annual publication lists lawyers under the names of their firms, which in turn are arranged geographically by state and city. Brief biographical material is given on the lawyers listed. The firm's address is given with information on the nature of practice.

American Bar Association. A national association for lawyers, to which most lawyers belong. The American Bar Association has published a list of Canons which govern their members' ethics. They are as follows:

1. A lawyer should assist in maintaining the integrity and competence of the legal profession.
2. A lawyer should assist the legal profession in fulfilling its duty to make legal counsel available.
3. A lawyer should assist in preventing the unauthorized practice of law.
4. A lawyer should preserve the confidences and secrets of a client.
5. A lawyer should exercise independent professional judgment on behalf of a client.
6. A lawyer should represent a client competently.
7. A lawyer should represent a client zealously within the bounds of the law.
8. A lawyer should assist in improving the legal system.
9. A lawyer should avoid even the appearance of professional impropriety.

The American Bar Association may be reached at 1155 E. 60th Street, Chicago, Illinois 60637.

American Court System. The plan by which American courts are organized and conducted. The American court system consists of Federal courts plus the various systems of all the states. The courts of the District of Columbia and Puerto Rico are part of the Federal court system.

The Supreme Court of the United States is the highest tribunal in our land—it is the apex in the hierarchy of courts, both Federal and state. The power of this court demands respect from every member of the legal profession.

State courts. Each state system consists of the state's highest AP-PELLATE COURT and of courts of original jurisdiction, that is, courts where suits are instigated. States with a large volume of cases also have INTERMEDIARY APPELLATE COURTS to relieve the congestion of cases in the highest court. A case is brought and tried in a lower court and may be appealed to a higher court having appellate jurisdiction until it reaches the state's highest AP-PELLATE COURT, or, in some cases, the United States Supreme Court.

Under some of the state systems, the state is divided into circuits or districts with a court for each. Usually court is held in each county seat and the judges travel the "circuit" to the county seats to hold court. (For a list of the judicial circuits and the states within each circuit, see Table III below.) Other states have only one superior, or trial court, which is composed of geographical divisions. The distinction is reflected in the wording of the captions on court papers. For example, Mississippi is divided into 17 judicial circuits, with a separate court for each. The captions on the court papers read:

IN THE CIRCUIT COURT OF THE FIRST JUDICIAL DISTRICT OF HINDS COUNTY, MISSISSIPPI

On the other hand, there is only one superior court of Massachusetts, which is composed of divisions according to counties. The captions read:

COMMONWEALTH OF MASSACHUSETTS
ESSEX, ss   SUPERIOR COURT

In many jurisdictions the courts are also divided into Parts for the purpose of facilitating the court's work. There is no standard principle upon which the division is based. For example, the Chancery Court of Davidson County, Tennessee, is divided into Part One and Part Two, and members of the Nashville Bar can bring their suits in either part. The caption designates the part. In Kings County, New York, Part One of the Supreme Court is the part in which all cases are called when they appear on the ready day calendar. (See CALENDAR CALL). The judge presiding in Part One sends cases to the different trial parts. After a case is assigned to a certain part, that part is designated in the caption.

The courts in one state have no control over, or relation to, the courts in another state—the hierarchy in each state is complete. Nor do the Federal courts, with the exception of the Supreme Court of the United States, have any relation to the state courts.

Federal courts. When our country first adopted its Constitution, a rivalry and jealousy existed among the states that made up the Union, and between the Federal Government and the respective state governments. The citizens of one state were fearful that they would not receive a fair verdict from judge or jury in another state. The Federal Government feared that the state courts would not interpret and enforce the national laws to the best of their ability. To avoid any miscarriage of justice that might result from interstate antagonism, the Congress provided for a Federal system of courts for the trial of cases involving Federal laws and interstate commerce and, also, cases involving diversity of citizenship—cases brought by a citizen of one state against a citizen of another state.

The Federal system of courts consists of the Supreme Court of the United States, 11 courts of appeal, district courts, a court of claims, a customs court, an emergency court of appeals, and a tax court. (See Table I, below.) The United States is divided into 11 judicial circuits—ten are comprised of several states each, and there is in addition the District of Columbia Circuit. Table III gives a list of the states in each circuit; Table IV, page 55, lists the states alphabetically and shows the circuit each state is in.

Federal district courts. Each state has at least one district court. Twenty-six of the states are divided into two, three, or four districts with a court for each district. For example, in Alabama we have the United States District Court for the Northern District of Alabama; the United States District Court for the Middle District of Alabama; and the United States District Court for the Southern District of Alabama. The states that have only one Federal district court are indicated by an asterisk in Table IV, page 55.

Many of the district courts are divided into divisions. For example, we have the United States District Court for the Western District of Arkansas, El Dorado Division. It is important to know whether or not a district court is divided into divisions because the division must appear in the caption on papers filed in that court. In the following examples, the words in italics change according to the state, district, and division:

EXAMPLE 1.

IN THE UNITED STATES
DISTRICT COURT FOR THE
DISTRICT OF *IDAHO*
(*SOUTHERN* DIVISION)

EXAMPLE 2.

IN THE UNITED STATES
DISTRICT COURT FOR THE
SOUTHERN DISTRICT OF
MISSISSIPPI
(*JACKSON* DIVISION)

TABLE I

FEDERAL COURTS OF RECORD IN THE UNITED STATES AND THEIR MEMBERS

Court	Members
Supreme Court of the United States	Chief Justice Justices
United States Court of Appeals for the District of Columbia	Circuit Justice Chief Judge Circuit Judges

TABLE I (Continued)

United States Court of Appeals for the (First) Circuit	Circuit Justice Chief Judge Circuit Judges
United States District Court for the (Southern) District of (New York) *Or where the state is all in one district* United States District Court for the District of Maryland)	Chief Judge District Judges
United States Court of Claims	Chief Judges Judges
United States Court of Customs and Patent Appeals	Chief Judge Judges
United States Customs Court	Chief Judge Judges
United States Emergency Court of Appeals	Chief Judge Judges
The Tax Court of the United States	Chief Judge Judges

TABLE II

STATE COURTS OF RECORD IN THE UNITED STATES AND THEIR MEMBERS

(Asterisks indicate intermediate appellate courts.
Municipal courts are not included.)

State	Court	Members of Court
Alabama	Supreme Court	Chief Justice Associate Justices
	*Court of Appeals	Presiding Judge Associate Judges
	Circuit Courts	Judges
	Probate Courts	Judge
Alaska	Supreme Court	Chief Justice Associate Justices
	Superior Court	Judges
Arizona	Supreme Court	Chief Justice, Justices
	Superior Courts	Judges

TABLE II (Continued)

State	Court	Members of Court
Arkansas	Supreme Court	Chief Justice
		Associate Justices
	Circuit Courts	Judges
	Chancery Courts	Chancellors
	Probate Courts	Judges
California	Supreme Court	Chief Justice
		Associate Justices
	*District Courts of Appeal	Presiding Justice
		Justices
	Superior Courts	Judges
Colorado	Supreme Court	Chief Justice, Justices
	District Courts	Judges
	County Courts	Judges
Connecticut	Supreme Court of Errors	Chief Justice
		Associate Justices
	Superior Court	Judges
	Courts of Common Pleas	Judges
	Probate Courts	Judges
Delaware	Supreme Court	Chief Justice
		Associate Justices
	Court of Chancery	Chancellor
		Vice Chancellor
	Superior Court	President Judge
		Associate Judges
	Registers' Courts	Register of Wills
Florida	Supreme Court	Chief Justice, Justices
	District Courts of Appeal	Chief Judge, Judges
	Circuit Courts	Judges
	Civil Court of Record	Judges
	Probate Courts	Judges
Georgia	Supreme Court	Chief Justice
		Presiding Judge
		Associate Justices
	*Court of Appeals	Chief Judge
		Presiding Judge
		Judges
	Superior Courts	Judges
	Courts of Ordinary	Ordinaries
Hawaii	Supreme Court	Chief Justice
		Associate Justices

TABLE II (Continued)

State	Court	Members of Court
Idaho	Supreme Court	Chief Justice Justices
	District Courts	Judges
	Probate Courts	Judges
Illinois	Supreme Court	Chief Justice Justices
	*Appellate Courts	Judges
	Circuit Courts	Judges
	Court of Claims	Chief Justice Judges
	County Courts	Judges
	Probate Courts	Judges
Indiana	Supreme Court	Chief Justice Associate Judges
	*Appellate Court	Chief Judge Presiding Judge Associate Judges
	Circuit Court	Judges
	Superior Court	Judges
	Probate Courts	Judges
Iowa	Supreme Court	Chief Justice Justices
	District Courts	Judges
Kansas	Supreme Court	Chief Justice Justices
	District Courts	Judges
	Probate Courts	Judges
Kentucky	Court of Appeals	Chief Justice Associate Justices Commissioners of Appeals Special Commissioners
	Circuit Courts	Judges
	County Courts	Judges
Louisiana	Supreme Court	Chief Justice Associate Justices
	*Court of Appeal	Judges
	District Courts	Judges
Maine	Supreme Judicial Court	Chief Justice Associate Justices
	Superior Court	Justices
	Probate Courts	Judges, Registers

TABLE II (Continued)

State	Court	Members of Court
Maryland	Court of Appeals	Chief Judge
		Associate Judges
	Circuit Courts	Chief Judges, Judges
	Orphan's Courts	Judges
		Register of Wills
Massachusetts	Supreme Judicial Court	Chief Justice
		Associate Justices
	Superior Court	Chief Justice
		Associate Justices
	Probate Courts	Judges
	Land Court	Judge, Associate Judges
	District Courts	Justice, Special Justices
	*Appellate Divisions of District Courts	Presiding Justice Associate Justices
Michigan	Supreme Court	Chief Justice
		Associate Justices
	Circuit Courts	State Presiding Circuit Judge
		Judges
	Court of Claims	Judge
	Probate Courts	Judges
Minnesota	Supreme Court	Chief Justice
		Associate Justices
	District Courts	Judges
	Probate Courts	Judges
Mississippi	Supreme Court	Chief Justice, Associate Justices
	Circuit Courts	Judges
	Chancery Courts	Chancellors
	County Courts	Judges
Missouri	Supreme Court	Chief Justice
		Presiding Judge
		Associate Judges
	*Court of Appeals	Presiding Judge
		Associate Judges
	Circuit Courts	Judges
	Probate Courts	Judges
Montana	Supreme Court	Chief Justice
		Associate Justices
	District Courts	Judges
Nebraska	Supreme Court	Chief Justice
		Associate Justices
	District Court	Judges
	County Courts	Judges

TABLE II (Continued)

State	Court	Members of Court
Nevada	Supreme Court	Chief Justice
		Justices
	District Courts	Judges
New Hampshire	Supreme Court	Chief Justice
		Associate Justice
	Superior Court	Chief Justice
		Justices
	Probate Courts	Presiding Judges
		Registers
New Jersey	Supreme Court	Chief Justice
		Justices
	*Superior Court, Appellate Division	Senior Judge
		Judges
	Superior Court, Chancery Division	Judges
	Superior Court, Law Division	Judges
	County Courts	Judges
	Surrogate's Courts	Surrogates
New Mexico	Supreme Court	Chief Justice
		Justices
	District Courts	Presiding Judge
		Judges
	Probate Courts	Judges
New York	Court of Appeals	Chief Judge
		Associate Judges
	*Supreme Court, Appellate Division	Presiding Justice
		Justices
	Supreme Court	Justices
	County Courts	Judges
	Surrogates' Courts	Surrogates
North Carolina	Supreme Court	Chief Justice
		Associate Justices
	Superior Courts	Judges
	County Courts	Judges
North Dakota	Supreme Court	Chief Justice
		Judges
	District Courts	Judges
	County Courts	Judges
Ohio	Supreme Court	Chief Justice
		Judges
	*Courts of Appeals	Judges
	Courts of Common Pleas	Judges
	Probate Courts	Judges

TABLE II (Continued)

State	Court	Members of Court
Oklahoma	Supreme Court	Chief Justice
		Vice Chief Justice
		Justices
	Criminal Court of Appeals	Presiding Judge
		Judges
	District Courts	Judges
	Superior Courts	Judges
	County Courts	County Judges
Oregon	Supreme Court	Chief Justice
		Acting Chief Justice
		Associate Justices
	Circuit Courts	Judges
	County Courts	County Judges
Pennsylvania	Supreme Court	Chief Justice
		Justices
	Superior Court	Presiding Judge
		Judges
	Courts of Common Pleas	Judges
	Orphans' Courts	Judges
Rhode Island	Supreme Court	Chief Justice
		Associate Justices
	Superior Court	Presiding Justice
		Justices
	District Court	Judges
	Probate Courts	Judges
South Carolina	Supreme Court	Chief Justice
		Associate Justice
	Circuit Courts	Judges
	County Courts	Judges
	Probate Courts	Judges
South Dakota	Supreme Court	Presiding Judge
		Judges
	Circuit Courts	Judges
	County Courts	Judges
Tennessee	Supreme Court	Chief Justice
		Associate Justices
	*Court of Appeals	Presiding Judge
		Associate Judges
	Chancery Courts	Chancellors
	Circuit Courts	Judges
	County Courts	Justices of the Peace
	Probate Court of Shelby County	Judge

TABLE II (Continued)

State	Court	Members of Court
Texas	Supreme Court	Chief Justice
		Associate Justices
	*Court of Civil Appeals	Chief Justice
		Associate Justices
	*Court of Criminal Appeals	Presiding Judge
		Commissioners Judges
	District Courts	Judges
	County Courts	Judges
Utah	Supreme Court	Chief Justice
		Justices
	District Court	Judges
Vermont	Supreme Court	Chief Justice
		Associate Justices
	County Courts	Judges
	Chancery Court	Chancellors
	Probate Courts	Judges
Virginia	Supreme Court of Appeals	Chief Justice
		Justices
	Circuit Courts	Judges
Washington	Supreme Court	Chief Justice
		Associate Judges
	Superior Courts	Judges
West Virginia	Supreme Court	President
		Judges
	Circuit Courts	Judges
	County Courts	Commissioners
Wisconsin	Supreme Court	Chief Justice
		Associate Justices
	Circuit Courts	Judges
	County Courts	Judges
Wyoming	Supreme Court	Chief Justice
		Associate Justice
	District Courts	Judges

TABLE III

FEDERAL JUDICIAL CIRCUITS AND THE STATES IN EACH CIRCUIT

District of Columbia Circuit	District of Columbia

First Circuit—   Maine, New Hampshire, Massachusetts, Rhode Island, and Puerto Rico

Second Circuit—   New York, Connecticut, and Vermont

Third Circuit—   New Jersey, Pennsylvania, Delaware, and Virgin Islands

Fourth Circuit—   Maryland, Virginia, West Virginia, North Carolina, and South Carolina

Fifth Circuit—   Texas, Lousisana, Mississippi, Alabama, Georgia, Florida, and Canal Zone

Sixth Circuit—   Tennessee, Kentucky, Ohio, and Michigan

Seventh Circuit—   Indiana, Illinois, and Wisconsin

Eighth Circuit—   Arkansas, Iowa, Minnesota, Missouri, Nebraska, North Dakota, and South Dakota

Ninth Circuit—   California, Arizona, Nevada, Oregon, Washington, Idaho, Montana, Alaska, and Hawaii

Tenth Circuit—   Colorado, Kansas, New Mexico, Oklahoma, Utah, and Wyoming

TABLE IV
STATES AND JUDICIAL CIRCUIT IN WHICH EACH IS LOCATED

State	Circuit	State	Circuit
Alabama	Fifth Circuit	Nebraska*	Eighth Circuit
Alaska	Ninth Circuit	Nevada*	Ninth Circuit
Arizona*	Ninth Circuit	New Hampshire*	First Circuit
Arkansas	Eighth Circuit	New Jersey*	Third Circuit
California	Ninth Circuit	New Mexico*	Tenth Circuit
Colorado*	Tenth Circuit	New York	Second Circuit
Connecticut*	Second Circuit	North Carolina	Fourth Circuit
Delaware*	Third Circuit	North Dakota*	Eighth Circuit
Florida	Fifth Circuit	Ohio	Sixth Circuit
Georgia	Fifth Circuit	Oklahoma	Tenth Circuit
Hawaii	Ninth Circuit	Oregon*	Ninth Circuit
Idaho*	Ninth Circuit	Pennsylvania	Third Circuit
Illinois	Seventh Circuit	Puerto Rico	First Circuit
Indiana	Seventh Circuit	Rhode Island*	First Circuit
Iowa	Eighth Circuit	South Carolina	Fourth Circuit
Kansas*	Tenth Circuit	South Dakota*	Eighth Circuit
Kentucky	Sixth Circuit	Tennessee	Sixth Circuit
Louisiana	Fifth Circuit	Texas	Fifth Circuit
Maine*	First Circuit	Utah*	Tenth Circuit
Maryland*	Fourth Circuit	Vermont*	Second Circuit
Massachusetts*	First Circuit	Virginia	Fourth Circuit
Michigan	Sixth Circuit	Washington	Ninth Circuit
Minnesota*	Eighth Circuit	West Virginia	Fourth Circuit
Mississippi	Fifth Circuit	Wisconsin	Seventh Circuit
Missouri	Eighth Circuit	Wyoming*	Tenth Circuit
Montana*	Ninth Circuit		

*Only one district court.

American Digest System. The most comprehensive DIGEST series, covering all printed cases in all American jurisdictions from the year 1658.

Organization. The American Digest system is tied in with the NATIONAL REPORTER SYSTEM. It is broken down as follows:

Century Digest	1658-1896	50 Vols.
First Decennial Digest	1897-1906	19 Vols.
Second Decennial Digest	1907-1916	24 Vols.
Third Decennial Digest	1916-1926	29 Vols.
Fourth Decennial Digest	1926-1936	34 Vols.
Fifth Decennial Digest	1936-1946	49 Vols.
Sixth Decennial Digest	1946-1956	29 Vols.
Seventh Decennial Digest	1956-1966	38 Vols.
Eighth Decennial Digest	1966-1976	50 Vols.
General Digest Fifth Series	1976 to date	

The bound volumes of the General Digest, cumulated about every four months, are followed by monthly pamphlets and by the weekly advance sheets of the reporters. The Decennials, as their names imply, are cumulated every 10 years and supersede the General Digest for that period.

The digest covers approximately 500 main topics, arranged alphabetically. The Century and Decennials are broken down alphabetically, each volume containing certain main topics. Thus, Volume 19 of the Fourth Decennial Digest, "Judgment to Kidnapping," contains a reference to each case published from 1926 to 1936 on the topics of Judgment, Judicial Sales, Jury, Justice of the Peace, and Kidnapping. Each volume of the General Digest Series contains a reference to all the cases on every topic published during the period of time covered by that particular volume. Thus, each volume of the General Digest, Third Series, contains the topic *Judgment.*

A detailed fact index constitutes part of the American Digest System. The index is contained in several volumes, with a binding differing from that on the digests, entitled DESCRIPTIVE WORD INDEX. The descriptive words are listed in black type in alphabetical order. Different situations involving the fact element are listed in lighter type and refer to the place in the digest where cases in point may be found. The reference is by means of topic and key number.

An analysis precedes each main topic. The digests of cases are grouped according to the point of law involved, and each point is given a key number. The key numbers in the First Decennial are preceded by the section symbol (§) instead of the key symbol, but the numbers correspond. The Century section numbers do not correspond to the key numbers but may be translated into key numbers (see below).

How to use the digest system. Suppose that the lawyer or his secretary is interested in the priority over other claims of an allowance by the executor to a widow.

1. The first step in finding the authorities through the digest system is to get the key number. There are three methods of getting the key number:

(a) If at least one case in point is already known, from the key numbers in the headnotes in the reporters, which correspond to the key numbers in the digests
(b) From the Descriptive Word Index
(c) From the analysis that precedes each topic

2. The search may be started with any of the Decennials or with the General Digest, and, then worked forward and backward. All of the cases involving the suggested question will be found under the topic Executors and Administrators, Key 182. The backbones of the volume will indicate in which volumes of the Decennials the topic Executors and Administrators can be found.

3. The topic is in every volume of the General Digest, First, Second, and Third Series, but there probably is not a case in point in all volumes. To avoid unnecessary research, use the cumulative tables of key numbers, which are paper pamphlets published in conjuction with the General Digest. These pamphlets list the topics in alphabetical order and list the key numbers under each topic. On a line with each key number are the numbers of the volumes of the General Digest in which reference is made to cases having that key number. Thus, in the table of key numbers to General Digest, Third Series, Volume 1-10, under the topic Executors and Administrators, is the notation:

Key
182—3, 5, 6, 7, 9

Thus, volumes 3, 5, 6, 7, and 9 refer to cases in point. There is no need to look in the other volumes of the General Digest, Third Series.

4. Continue the search for the key number through the monthly digests that are in pamphlet form, and through the digests in the reporter advance sheets published subsequent to the latest monthly digest.

5. Then search in the Century for cases decided prior to 1897. The second Decennial refers to the volume, topic, and section number in the Century, if there is a case in point referred to in the Century. Thus, Key 182 under Executors and Administrators in the Second Decennial shows this reference: Cent. Dig. & Ad. §§651, 686-693. If there is no reference, there are no cases in point digested in Century.

6. Possibly the search was begun with a reference in Century. It was found that cases in point were digested at §686 of the topic Executors and Administrators. To get subsequent authorities, translate the section number to the key number of the digest. In the front of Volume 21 of the First Decennial, there is a parallel table on pink sheets. The table gives under each topic, the section number in the Century and the corresponding key number in the Decennial.

Table of cases. If the name of a case is known, find where it is reported from the tables of cases. The last five volumes of the First Decennial (Volumes 21-25) cover the cases digested in the Century and in the First Decennial. The last volumes of the Second, of the Third, and of the Fourth Decennials are tables of cases. The back of each volume of the General Digest contains a table of cases. Since each unit of the American Digest System covers a period of time, the search is narrowed if the decade in which the case was decided is known.

American Federation of Labor (AFL).

A voluntary association of national labor unions organized along craft lines. The AFL was formed in 1886 with Samuel Gompers its first president. In 1955 AFL merged with the CONGRESS OF INDUSTRIAL

ORGANIZATIONS to form the AFL-CIO. See also LABOR UNION.

American Jurisprudence. A legal encyclopedia that gives comprehensive textual statements of American case law. *Am. Jur.*, as American Jurisprudence is commonly called, makes no attempt to cite every case in point in support of its text. It relies heavily on cases printed in the annotated case series (See AMERICAN LAW REPORTS), including *all* United States Supreme Court cases. *Am. Jur.* also cites and quotes pertinent RESTATEMENTS OF THE LAW.

American Law Reports (A.L.R.). Annotated opinions of appellate courts (see APPELLATE COURT) in all jurisdictions. A.L.R. contains a minimum of U.S. Supreme Court cases; they are taken care of by the annotations in the *Lawyer's Edition.*

A.L.R. cases are selected on the basis of probable usefulness to lawyers. They are illustrative of established principles and are not necessarily "leading cases." Parallel official and unofficial (see NATIONAL REPORTER SYSTEM) citations are supplied. The decision is summarized at some length and the subject of the annotation is noted. Headnotes are written by the editors and classified according to the *Permanent A.L.R. Digest* classification. There are frequent cross references to the legal encyclopedia, AMERICAN JURISPRUDENCE.

A.L.R. puts out a *Blue Book* that brings each A.L.R. case up to date by later cases in point.

A.L.R. is indispensable to the lawyer who has official reports of cases decided in his own state, but is interested in cases on the same point decided in other jurisdictions.

Amortization Schedules. A printed-out breakdown of principal and interest after each monthly payment and showing balance due on a note and mortgage load. Two copies may be obtained for $1.25 (present rate) by writing to:

The Financial Publishing Co.
82 Brookline Avenue
Boston, Massachusetts 02115

Send amount of loan, amount of monthly payment, rate of interest and type of interest (monthly reduction, annual or semi-annual). It is not necessary to send the names of the mortgagor or mortgagee. The secretary should mark the name of the client on the letter ordering the schedules so that she will be able to identify the schedules when they are returned, as there are no names on the schedules. After the initial order the company will send a convenient order card for the next order, or, if desired, prepaid order cards may be ordered. The order card is always sent back with the order, so the secretary may indicate the client's name on the order card to identify it when it is returned.

Ancillary. Auxiliary; subordinate. The term *ancillary letters* is used to apply to letters testamentary or letters of administration that are taken out in a state other than that of the decedent's domicile, but in which he had assets or debts. These letters are subordinate or supplementary to the letters issued in the decedent's domicile. The term *ancillary* also applies to court proceedings that are auxiliary to the main action—for example, a bill of discovery is ancillary to the principal action.

Annexed paper. An additional piece of paper containing auxiliary material, which is attached to a *notice,* such as a Notice of Appearance in Equity Case, Notice of Filing and Entry, Notice of Settlement, and Notice of Motion. The addition is also referred to as an *attached* paper. Both the notice and the *annexed paper* are stapled together, with the notice on top, unless the other paper is to be signed by the judge. Whenever a group of papers are given to the judge for signature, any paper that he is supposed to sign is placed on top, so that he will not have to search for the appropriate paper.

In the endorsement on the back of the instrument, the name of the annexed paper is placed first because it is the more important paper. See LEGAL BACK.

Announcement Card. A printed or engraved notification that is sent to clients, colleagues or other persons whom the lawyer wishes to advise concerning the address at which he is prac-

ticing. An attorney sends these announcement cards when he joins a new firm, or moves his offices. Figure 1, below, shows an announcement when the lawyer first enters practice; Figure 2, (page 60), when he resumes practice; Figure 3, when he moves his offices.

These cards cannot be mailed out indiscriminately to people whom the lawyer does not know. The secretary can be very helpful in compiling and maintaining a permanent list of people to whom announcements may be sent. Keep the list on 3 by 5 inch index cards, and enter regularly any additions or changes that come to mind.

The cards may be mailed to the groups listed below.

1. *Friends and acquaintances.* The secretary will have to depend largely upon the lawyer to compile this list originally, but she can maintain it by adding the name of contacts he makes that she knows about, also by keeping the addresses on the list up to date.

2. *Members of the local bar.* The

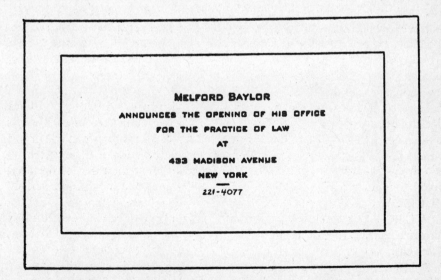

Announcement Cards: Figure 1. Announcement when entering practice.

Twenty Pine Street
New York , N.Y.

John R. Brown, having completed his
term as a Justice of the Supreme Court of the
State of New York, announces his return to the
practice of law with the firm of

Brown & Hartung

January 15, 19___   *222-4483*

Announcement Cards: Figure 2. Announcement when resuming practice.

BEGEL, BUDGE & MILLER

ANNOUNCE THE REMOVAL OF THEIR OFFICES TO

52 VANDERBILT AVENUE

NEW YORK , N.Y.

WHERE THEY WILL CONTINUE THE GENERAL PRACTICE

OF LAW UNDER THE FIRM NAME OF

BEGEL, BUDGE, MILLER & STEBLING

AUGUST 1, 19___   228-5800

Announcement Card: Figure 3. Announcement of removal of offices.

secretary can probably obtain this list from the classified telephone directory. Volumes I and II of MARTINDALE-HUBBELL LAW DIRECTORY contain a list of lawyers and their addresses in the United States and Canada. Every law library and almost every law office contain this directory; or it may be obtained from the local Bar Association for a fee.

3. *County Officials.* Each state publishes a "bluebook," directory, register, or roster, which contains the names of county officers, state officers,

judges, members of the senate and house, and names of departments and administrative offices. Probably a more accessible source for the names of county officials is the clerk's office in the county courthouse.

4. *Classmates.* The secretary can get the names and addresses of the lawyer's college classmates from the permanent secretary of his class. If there is no permanent class secretary, the Alumni Secretary will give the secretary the proper source for the information or send it direct.

5. *Other lawyers.* The names of lawyers in other localities with whom the secretary's employer is personally acquainted should be put on the announcement list.

6. *Clients.* The name of each client should be added to the announcement list.

Annulment of Marriage. A judicial decision that makes a marriage void and of no effect from its beginning. A basis for annulment would be a misrepresentation that amounts to FRAUD. For example, before marriage a spouse promises to have a family and during the marriage refuses to have sexual intercourse or uses some artificial means of birth control.

Married couples are increasingly resorting to annulment rather than DIVORCE for a judicial termination of their marriage.

Answer. The defendant's formal written statement of his defense, signed by his attorney. It denies some, or all, of the allegations of the COMPLAINT and sets forth the grounds of his defense. It may also set up claims that the defendant has against the plaintiff.

The answer consists of the following parts: (1) Caption; (2) Introduction; (3) Denials of allegations of the complaint; (4) Counterclaims, if any; (5) "Wherefore" clause; prayer, if answer contains a counterclaim; (6) Signature of attorney for defendant; (7) Verification if the complaint is verified.

How to prepare the answer. The lawyer will dictate the answer, but it is the secretary's responsibility to set it up in a workmanlike manner. Unless the lawyer indicates his preference, follow the style illustrated in Figure 1, pages 62 and 63.

1. Type on legal-size paper.

2. Make an original for the court, a copy to serve on each plaintiff's attorney, and a copy for thhe office file.

3. The caption is the same as that on the complaint, but if there are numerous parties the title of the case may be shortened by listing the first plaintiff or defendant only and adding *et al, et ux,* or *et vir.*

4. The index number must appear on the answer, at the right of the box.

5. The title of the document is "Answer."

6. Number the paragraphs consecutively throughout, except the last paragraph, which is the "wherefore" clause. Do not start new series of numbers for the paragraphs in each separate defense.

7. Type a line for signature of attorney.

8. The answer must be verified if the complaint is.

9. In some large cities, the attorney's name, address, and telephone number must appear after the verification, but usually this is not necessary. The attorney's address is on the legal back.

10. Endorse a legal back for each copy except your office copy. See

BMM:r 4/22/— 1-2-1

IN THE CIRCUIT COURT OF THE ELEVENTH
JUDICIAL CIRCUIT OF FLORIDA, IN AND
FOR DADE COUNTY. AT LAW.

———————————————————————————x
                                          :
AUGUSTUS N. ROBERTSON and ELIZABETH
R. ROBERTSON,   : Index No: 11660-19—

                    Plaintiffs, :

                 -against-   :   ANSWER

JOHNSTON-DOUGLAS MANAGEMENT CORPORA-   :
TION, a corporation, and FREDERICK
FASHIONS, INC., a corporation,

                                          :
                    Defendants.   :
———————————————————————————x

The defendant Johnston-Douglas Management Corporation, answering the amended complaint herein by his attorneys, Jones & Smith:

1. Admits_____

_____

_____.

2. Denies that he has knowledge or information
sufficient to form a belief as to the allegations contained
in the paragraph of the complaint designated "SECOND."

(*Continued on following page*)

Answer: Figure 1.

(Continued from preceding page)

```
            FOR A FIRST SEPARATE AND COMPLETE
            DEFENSE, DEFENDANT ALLEGES:


      3.    On information and belief_____
                  .#
      _____ .


            FOR A SECOND SEPARATE AND PARTIAL
            DEFENSE, DEFENDANT ALLEGES:



      4.    _____
      _____ .



            FOR A DISTINCT SEPARATE AND AFFIRM-
            ATIVE DEFENSE AND BY WAY OF A
            COUNTERCLAIM, DEFENSE ALLEGES:



      5.    _____
      _____ .



            WHEREFORE, defendant demands that the complaint be
      dismissed with costs and asks judgment in the amount _____
      _____ .




                                  _____
                                  Attorneys for Defendant
                                  Johnston-Douglas Manage-
                                  ment Corporation
```

Answer: Figure 1 (continued).

Figure 2, page 64. The endorsement differs from the endorsement on the complaint in that it shows the court's index number and the name of the attorney for the plaintiff, on whom a copy of the answer is served. When the complaint was prepared, the secretary for the plaintiff did not know the index number or who would represent the defendant.

11. Collate and staple in backs.

12. After signature and verification, conform exactly.

Methods of service of answer on plain-

```
┌─────────────────────────────────────┐
│  Index No.  11660-19 --             │
│                                     │
│  IN THE CIRCUIT COURT OF THE ELEV-  │
│  ENTH JUDICIAL CIRCUIT OF FLORIDA,  │
│  IN AND FOR DADE COUNTY.  AT LAW.   │
├─────────────────────────────────────┤
│  AUGUSTUS N. ROBERTSON, et ux.,     │
│                                     │
│              Plaintiffs,            │
│                                     │
│            -against-                │
│                                     │
│  JOHNSTON-DOUGLAS MANAGEMENT        │
│  CORPORATION, a corporation,        │
│  et al.,                            │
│                                     │
│              Defendants.            │
├─────────────────────────────────────┤
│                                     │
│              ANSWER                 │
│                                     │
├─────────────────────────────────────┤
│                                     │
│    Jones, Smith & Thompson          │
│        352 E.  Flagler St.          │
│        Miami, Florida               │
│                                     │
│  Attorneys for  Defendants          │
│  Johnston-Douglas Management        │
│  Corporation                        │
├─────────────────────────────────────┤
│  To Elwood & Adams, Esquires,       │
│     Attorneys for Plaintiffs.       │
│                                     │
│                                     │
└─────────────────────────────────────┘
```

Answer: **Figure 2.** Endorsed back of answer.

tiff's attorney. Although practice may vary with the jurisdiction, the answer is generally served on the plaintiff's attorney by (1) handing him a copy, or leaving it at his office with his clerk or other person in charge of the office; or (2) by mailing it to the attorney. No regular process server is necessary in the majority of jurisdictions. The secretary, or a clerk in the attorney's office, may serve the papers.

Proof of service. The attorney on whom the answer is served, or the secretary if she is authorized, writes on the back of the original a receipt similar to the following:

(date)

Copy received . . . .

(firm name)

. . . .

(name of client)

Attorneys for . . . .

Many offices have rubber stamps for this purpose.

Printed LEGAL BACKS have printed on them an admission of service, which usually contains the words "due and proper" service, "timely" service, or the like. When a secretary accepts service, she should strike out these words. Although she might be authorized to accept service, it is not her responsibility to admit that it was due, proper, or timely.

In some jurisdictions, the attorney whose office is serving the answer endorses on the back of the original:

I do hereby certify that copy hereof has been furnished to .... by mail (or delivery), this .... day of ...., 19 ...

Many jurisdictions require a formal affidavit when service is made by mail.

What the secretary does about the answer.

1. Prepares the answer, and verification if required.

2. Has answer signed, and verified, after approval by the attorney.

3. Notarizes verification.

4. Sees that the copy is served on plaintiff's attorney.

5. Makes certain that receipt of service is endorsed on back of original, or that affidavit of service is attached.

6. Conforms office copy.

7. Files original, with admission of service, in court, with fee if required.

8. Makes entry in SUIT REGISTER of service and filing.

9. The secretary to the attorney on whom the answer is served makes a notation on the back of the answer of the date and hour it was served; also makes entry in suit register.

10. *Enters in diary* date by which next action must be taken. See also PLEADING.

Answering the Calendar Call. See CALENDAR CALL.

Antenuptial Contract. A CONTRACT made before marriage. The property rights of the prospective husband or wife can be determined by contract. For example, there have been instances where a wife has given up all right to any portion of the estate of her husband by signing an antenuptial contract

Antitrust Laws. Legislation that forbids monopolistic trade practices and prohibits conspiracies and trusts that restrain INTERSTATE COMMERCE. Antitrust statutes are the Sherman Act; the Clayton Act; the Federal Trade Commission Act; the Robinson-Patman Act; the Miller-Tydings Act; the Wheeler-Lea Act. Antitrust laws do not apply to labor unions.

Appeal. The legal procedure by which decision of a lower court is brought to a higher court for review.

The procedure for taking a case to a higher court is governed by the rules of the highest state tribunal. These rules are based upon the civil practice acts or codes of civil procedure and are usually found in an appendix to the act or code. They may also be obtained in pamphlet form from the clerk of the APPELLATE COURT or from the state judicial council. The United States Supreme Court makes the rules for appeals to it and, also, for appeals from Federal district courts to Federal courts of appeal.

The secretary can easily find in these rules the information she should have in order to do her part of the appellate work in accordance with the court's requirements. The rules provide, among other things, for the following:

1. Methods for review
2. Content of the RECORD ON APPEAL

3. Form of testimony (question and answer, narrative, or abstract)
4. Preparation and format of record
5. Preparation and format of BRIEF
6. Time allowed for filing and service of papers
7. Method of service on opposing counsel
8. Costs

Methods for review by a higher court. The method for review by the higher tribunal is by appeal from the lower court to the higher court, in the majority of states. In a few states, the method is by a petition to the higher court for a WRIT OF ERROR. At one time chancery cases were reviewed by means of an appeal and law cases by means of a writ of error. This distinction in appellate procedure no longer exists except in a few states. Regardless of the method for review, the procedure is loosely referred to as *taking an appeal* or *appealing a case.* The use of the term appeal here embraces both appeals and writs of error.

A case may also be referred to a higher court, under special circumstances, by means of extraordinary writs, such as CERTIORARI, MANDAMUS, HABEAS CORPUS, PROHIBITION, QUO WARRANTO, and STAY writs. These writs eliminate the necessity of hearings and trials in the lower court.

In some states the appeal is to an intermediate appellate court and thence to the highest state court. In states that do not have intermediary appellate courts (and in certain cases even if they do), the appeal is direct from the trial court to the highest court. The procedure for taking an appeal to an intermediate appellate court is similar to, but not exactly the same as, taking an appeal to the highest state tribunal.

The main variations are in the details, such as the time allowed for the various steps taken, disbursements, to be paid, whether the papers are to be typewritten or printed, and the size and quality of paper that is to be used. The secretary should check the rules of the intermediate appellate court.

Appellant. The party making an APPEAL to a higher court for review of a decision rendered by a lower court. See PARTIES TO AN APPEAL; APPELLATE COURT.

Appellate Court. A tribunal empowered to hear arguments, pro and con, concerning the decision made by a lower court on a particular cause of action or trial. The appellate court has the power to affirm, reverse, or remand the original decision for retrial.

For example, a case tried in a lower court may be brought on APPEAL to a higher court having appellate jurisdiction until it reaches the state's highest appellate court or, in some cases, the United States Supreme Court. (See SUPREME APPELLATE COURT.) States with a large volume of cases have INTERMEDIARY APPELLATE COURTS to relieve the congestion of cases in the highest court. The party who loses a law suit, or who is dissatisfied with a JUDGMENT or court order or DECREE, may ask a higher court to review the decision of the lower court with the hope that the higher court will reverse or modify the lower court's decision. See also BRIEF; RECORD ON APPEAL; TIME TABLE ON APPEAL; CAPTION OF CASE ON APPEAL; PARTIES TO AN APPEAL.

Appointment, Reminders of. See REMINDERS TO THE LAWYER.

Arbitration. Submission of labor disputes to a third party for final and binding decision. Arbitration may be compulsory or voluntary. Compulsory arbitration takes place when a governmental agency compels the disputing parties to submit their differences to an outside body for settlement. Voluntary arbitration takes place by mutual and free consent of the parties. Most collective bargaining contracts provide for arbitration as the final step in grievance procedure. See MEDIATION; CONCILIATION.

Arms Length Sale. A transaction where the parties have equal bargaining power. One party does not exercise undue influence or superior knowledge over the other.

Arrest. See PROVISIONAL REMEDIES.

Arson. The crime of maliciously burning the house of another. In several states arson is divided into three degrees. First degree arson is the willful act of setting fire at night a dwelling house with a human being in it; second degree arson is the act of burning a dwelling house in the daytime with a human in it or the burning in the nighttime of an uninhabited building while endangering an adjoining building with human beings in it; arson in the third degree is setting a fire under circumstances not amounting to first or second degree arson or the burning of property with the intent to defraud the insurers.

Asportation. See LARCENY.

Assault and Battery. An assault is a threat made with the apparent intention of doing bodily harm to another. An essential element of assault is real or apparent ability on the part of the person making the threat to do bodily harm to another. Mere words do not constitute assault. A *battery* is the wrongful touching of another's person or clothing as a result of an assault. A battery always includes an assault, but an assault may be made without a battery. A person guilty of assault and battery is liable for damage to the injured party. Assault and battery may also be a crime punishable by the state.

Assessment. A tax levied upon property within a designated area to provide funds for local improvements, such as grading or widening streets, construction of sewers, erection of bridges. Assessments are generally payable in yearly installments. See also TAX LIEN.

Assignment. The transfer of one's rights to another. Assignments are made (a) by the act of the parties, as in the case of a tenant assigning his lease to another; or (b) by operation of law, as in the case of death or bankruptcy. The party transferring his right is the *assignor;* the party to whom the rights are transferred is the *assignee.*

An assignment need not be in any particular form. It may be oral or written, unless it involves a contract required by the STATUTE OF FRAUDS to be in writing. It may be a formal document or an endorsement on the contract signed by the assignor. An assignment does not require any consideration, but it must effect an immediate transfer to a specific assignee.

Assignment of Errors. See RECORD ON APPEAL.

Attachment. The method by which a debtor's property, real or personal, is placed in the custody of the law and held as security pending the outcome of a creditor's suit. Until the case is decided, the debtor cannot dispose of his property or place it beyond the reach of the creditor. The most usual grounds of attachment are the following: (1) the debtor is a nonresident or a foreign corporation; (2) the debtor has left the state or is in hiding; (3) the debtor is about to remove, conceal, or dispose of his property.

In many states the attaching creditor must put up a BOND; a debtor may then release the property by putting up a counterbond. See also LIEN.

Attempt. An act done with the intent to commit a crime and tending but failing to effect its commission. Four elements necessary to constitute the crime of attempt are intention, an overt act, failure, and closeness of success. See MERGER.

Attention Line. Designation of a specific person or department in letters addressed to a business firm. This practice marks the letter as a business rather than a personal letter and insures that it will be opened in the absence of the individual to whom it is directed.

Type the attention line two spaces below the address. The word *of* is not necessary. The attention line has no punctuation and is not underscored. When a letter addressed to a firm has an attention line, the salutation is *Gentlemen* because the salutation is to the firm, not the individual. It is permissible to direct the letter to the attention of an individual without including his given name or initials, if they are unknown.

Preferable
Attention Mr. Walter R. Richardson
Permissible
Attention Mr. Richardson

On the letter, the attention line is typed two spaces below the address. It is typed in the lower left-hand corner of the envelope.

Attestation. The act of signing a written instrument as witness to the signature of a party, at his request; for example, witnessing signatures to a CONTRACT or WILL. Because the witness signs the instrument he is called a *subscribing witness.* See also ATTESTATION CLAUSE.

Attestation Clause. The legend or clause that relates the circumstances surrounding the signing of an instrument. It usually precedes the signature of the attesting witnesses. For example, if Thomas I. Dean were testator, the attestation clause in his will might read: "Signed, sealed, published and declared by Thomas I. Dean, the above named testator, as and for his Last Will and Testament in our presence, and we, at his request, in his presence and in the presence of each other, have hereunto subscribed our names as witnesses this 5th day of September in the year of our Lord 19___." The wording of an attestation clause may be simply: "In the presence of." The clause is typed at the left of the signature. The legal secretary is often asked to attest documents that are signed in the attorney's office.

When the secretary of a corporation attests an instrument, he impresses the CORPORATE SEAL upon it. See also TESTIMONIUM CLAUSE.

Attorney at Law. A person licensed to practice law.

Attorney in Fact. One who is appointed by another, with the authority to act for him in matters specified in the terms of the appointment. (See also AGENCY.) An attorney at law may be an attorney in fact, but an attorney in fact is not necessarily an attorney at law. In a loose sense, the term is frequently used to mean all agents *except* attorneys at law.

Attractive Nuisance. A condition on private property that would be hazard-ous to children if they came in contact with it. The children, in states where the attractive nuisance doctrine applies, can be compensated for injury even though they are trespassers if it is foreseeable to the person who maintains the hazard that children might enter, be attracted to it, and become injured. New York, for example, has applied the doctrine in a case where children trespassed on personal property left on a public highway. The doctrine is an exception to the general rule that no duty of care is owed to a TRESPASSER.

B

Backing. See LEGAL BACK.

Bail. The security given the COURT in order to obtain the release of a prisoner and insure his later appearance at trial. The security as well as the persons who give it is known as *bail.* A *bail bond* is the document evidencing the monetary obligation to the court, signed by the defendant and those who put up the money for his release. The obligation is extinguished when the defendant appears at trial.

Bailment. A delivery of personal property for some particular purpose, upon a contract, express or implied, that the property will be returned to the person delivering it after the accomplishemnt of the purpose for which it was delivered. An essential of a bailment is that return of the property is contemplated.

The person delivering the property is a *bailor;* the person receiving it is a *bailee.* If under the terms of the contract the bailee is obligated to pay a sum of money instead of returning the goods, the obligation is a debt and not a bailment. Thus, a conditional sale is distinguished from a bailment, even though the contract calls the transaction a bailment. The parties to a consignment of goods expect that the goods will be sold for the account of the consignor or returned to him; a consignment is therefore considered a bailment. A bailee is liable for breach of his contract to keep the property in a particular manner in a particular place for a particular purpose.

The following transactions are bailments: lease of a car for hire; deposit of goods for storage or safekeeping; pledge of stocks as collateral. Title to the property remains in the bailor.

Bank Accounts. Law offices maintain two basic bank accounts: the *firm's* bank account and the *trust* bank account.

The *firm's* bank account reflects (1) *deposits* of all moneys belonging to the firm, that is, money that the lawyer or lawyers put into the bank when the law office is opened (the capital account); and all cash received from clients in payment for services rendered (accounts receivable); (2) cash *withdrawals* for operating expenses such as salaries, office supplies, taxes, and the like.

The *trust* bank account reflects all bank transactions relating to moneys belonging to the client, such as (1) *deposits* of advances made by clients for expenses, or deposits that represent any moneys collected on behalf of clients; (2) all *withdrawals*—checks drawn on the trust bank account for purposes of remitting to the client those collections that have been made for him, or any other moneys that may be due him. See ACCOUNTING, Trust Funds.

Bankruptcy. A state of IN-SOLVENCY in which the property of a debtor is taken over by a receiver or

70

trustee in bankruptcy for the benefit of the creditors. This action is performed under the jurisdiction of the courts as prescribed by the National Bankruptcy Act.

Voluntary bankruptcy. Voluntary bankruptcy is brought about by the filing of a petition in bankruptcy by the debtor. The form of the petition is prescribed by the act. By filing a voluntary petition, the debtor seeks, first, to have his assets equally distributed among all his creditors, and, second, to free himself of his debt. He is thus able to begin his business life anew, unencumbered.

Voluntary bankruptcy is open to all individuals, firms, and corporations, except banking, building and loan, insurance, railroad, and municipal corporations. No special amount of indebtedness is required; a person owing one dollar or several millions may file a petition in voluntary bankruptcy.

Involuntary bankruptcy. Involuntary bankruptcy is brought about by the filing of a petition by the creditors against an insolvent debtor. If there are fewer than twelve creditors, one creditor may file the petition; if there are more than twelve, three creditors must join in the filing. Before creditors can throw a debtor into bankruptcy, these conditions must exist:

1. The debtor must owe at least $1,000.

2. The creditor or creditors filing the petition must have provable claims aggregating $500.

3. The debtor must have committed an act of bankruptcy within four months preceding the filing of the petition.

Involuntary bankruptcy proceedings cannot be brought against a wage earner, a farmer, or a banking, building and loan, insurance, railroad, or municipal corporation.

Steps in bankruptcy proceedings. After a petition is filed in the Federal courts, in a form prescribed by the United States Supreme Court, the basic steps are: (1) application for receiver, (2) adjudication of the bankrupt, (3) referral to referee in bankruptcy, (4) filing of schedules by the bankrupt, (5) meetings of creditors, (6) election of trustee in bankruptcy, (7) proof and allowance of claims, and (8) discharge of the bankrupt.

Referee in bankruptcy. When the court signs a decree of adjudication it refers the case to a "referee" in bankruptcy. The referee, who is a lawyer, acts in place of the bankruptcy court, conducts all the usual proceedings, and grants the final discharge of the bankrupt from further liability for his debts. He presides over all creditors' meetings.

Filing of schedules by the bankrupt. Within five days after the debtor has been adjudged bankrupt he must file, in involuntary cases, a schedule of his assets and liabilities on a form prescribed by the United States Supreme Court. If the debtor files a voluntary petition, he must accompany the petition with similar schedules.

What the secretary does. Opens a file and processes a bankruptcy matter just as she does on any new matter. Makes diary entries and keeps a progress record sheet. The petition, application, schedules, and the like are prepared on forms prescribed by the United States Supreme Court. The secretary will have no difficulty filling them in.

Bar Associations. Professional organizations for lawyers. May be National, State, or Local. An attorney usually belongs to all three. See AMERICAN BAR ASSOCIATION.

Bastard. A child born of an illicit union and before the marriage of his parents. Nearly all the states have statutory provisions relating to the liability of the father criminally, as well as to the care and support of the child. If the parents marry subsequent to the birth of the child, many states consider the child to be legitimatized with all the rights of a legitimate child. The question as to whether a child is legitimate is important where a WILL is drawn up leaving money or property to the "children" of someone. The courts interpret "children" as meaning legitimate children.

Bequest. See LEGACY.

Best Evidence Rule. A regulation that requires a person who testifies in court seeking to prove the contents of a writing, to produce the original writing or to satisfactorily account for its absence. The rule prevents the fraudulent misrepresentation of the contents of a document. It also guards against errors arising from the inaccurate copying of the original writing, or from mistakes in reading it, or from faulty recollection of its contents. These dangers disappear when the writing itself is produced at trial.

Bigamy. A criminal offense whereby one marries when he has a living legal spouse, The law treats the second marriage as nonexistent and the innocent spouse is free to remarry.

Bill of Attainder. A law passed by Congress or a state legislature that inflicts punishment upon someone without the benefit of a judicial trial. The Constitution prohibits bills of attainder in order to prevent legislatures from usurping judicial functions.

Bill in Equity. See COMPLAINT.

Bill of Complaint. See COMPLAINT.

Bill of Lading. Written evidence of a contract between a shipper and carrier for the carriage and delivery of goods. A bill of lading is signed by the carrier or his agent. It describes the goods to be carried, states the name of the consignor (the shipper), the terms of the contract of transportation, the place where the goods are to be delivered, and the person to whom, or to whose order, the goods are to be delivered. A bill of lading serves three purposes: it is a receipt for the goods; it is a CONTRACT that defines the terms under which the carrier agrees to transport the goods; it is a document of title.

When the bill of lading states that the goods are to be delivered to the order of a particular person, it is an *order* or negotiable bill of lading and can be transferred by the original shipper to a third party. Bills of lading are often transferred or "negotiated" in connection with the sale of the goods by shippers to others. The buyer can claim the goods from the carrier by presenting the bill of lading.

Bill of Particulars. A written statement of information and details relating to a legal controversy furnished by one of the parties to the other. The information is produced either voluntarily in response to a DE-

MAND FOR A BILL OF PAR-
TICULARS, or in compliance with a
judge's order for that purpose.

Usually the lawyer dictates the bill of
particulars. The secretary should
follow Figure 1, page 74, for style unless otherwise instructed.

The bill of particulars is prepared
like the demand for bill of particulars,
except that in almost all jurisdictions it
must have a VERIFICATION. The
lawyer tells the secretary who is to
verify the bill.

Bill of Rights. The first ten amendments to the Constitution. They limit
the Federal Government by guaranteeing to the individual certain fundamental personal rights. Among the
guarantees are FREEDOM OF
SPEECH AND PRESS, RIGHT OF
ASSEMBLAGE AND PETITION,
and the RIGHT TO RELIGIOUS
LIBERTY.

Bill of Sale. A formal document issued by a seller to a buyer evidencing
the transfer of title to the particular
piece of personal property described in
the instrument. Some transactions require a bill of sale for purposes of
registration; for example, the sale of a
motor vehicle.

Billing Client. Instead of billing
clients once a month, the usual practice
in a law office is to bill them when a
case is completed, unless it is a long,
drawn-out matter. Then the client is
billed at intervals. The lawyer will
probably dictate the bill.

Law firms generally have printed
bill heads; otherwise, they use letterheads. The general practice is to
make an original and two copies—the
original for the client, a copy for the

case file, and a copy for the invoice file.
The bills are usually numbered and
filed in the invoice file according to
number. If they are not numbered, they
are filed according to date.

Charges made to clients. Fees for services and disbursements made in behalf
of a client are charged to his account.
The disbursements, which are itemized
in the bill, include:

Recording fees
Court costs
Fee paid process servers
Telephone charges
Office visits
Revenue or state documentary
stamps
Postage, when for heavy airmail or
registered documents; also when a
special job requires mailing a large
number of letters
Stenographic services when an out-
of-the-ordinary amount of clerical
work is required
Long-distance telephone calls
Telegrams
All fees paid for investigations, ac-
countings, abstracts, etc.
Photostats

*How the amount of the bill is
calculated.* When the lawyer is ready to
bill the client, he will want a report on
the time costs. The secretary will give
him a report of the total number of
hours spent on the case by each lawyer
from the time the case was opened, or
from the date of the last bill. Each
lawyer's time is listed separately,
because the cost per hour varies with
the lawyer. The lawyer knows the cost
per hour of each member of the firm
and of each associate lawyer (the
secretary might not), and calculates the
cost accordingly.

He will also want a record of the ad-

JMH:p 8/23/— 1-2-1

AUGUSTUS N. ROBERTSON and ELIZABETH R. ROBERTSON, Plaintiffs	*	IN THE
	*	CIRCUIT COURT
	*	OF BALTIMORE COUNTY
vs.	*	
	*	
JOHNSTON–DOUGLAS MANAGEMENT CORPORATION and FREDERICK FASHIONS, INC., Defendants	*	
	*	
	*	

*   *   *   *   *   *   *

<u>BILL OF PARTICULARS</u>

The following is a bill of the particulars of the plaintiffs' claim against the defendants, that is to say:

(a) The accident occurred on February 23, 19—, at approximately 9:30 o'clock A.M.

(b) The accident occurred in the aisle between the second and third counters from the entrance to defendants' store about midway between the ends of said counters and nearer to the third counter.

(c) The following amounts are claimed as special damages:

1.	Hospital bills	$ 1,758.03
2.	Physicians' services and medical supplies	1,023.50
3.	Nurses	1,160.00
4.	Household Assistance	904.60
5.	Transportation to hospital and doctor's office	43.10

(d) Plaintiffs reside at 162 Westchester Avenue, Baltimore, Maryland.

ELWOOD & ADAMS
Attorneys for Plaintiffs

Bill of Particulars: Figure 1.

74

vances made for the client, and the status of the account as a whole. He will get this from the client's account ledger sheet, or the secretary will give him a record of the disbursements. (See ACCOUNTING RECORD FOR THE LAWYER (business), *Recovering Costs Advanced*). Whenever a client is billed, the secretary should examine the current petty cash record to see if any expenditures have been made in his behalf; she also examines records of toll telephone costs. After a client is billed, the lawyer cannot very well send him a bill for 50 cents for a photostat that the secretary paid out of petty cash, but numerous small advances add up to sizeable sums.

Binder. 1. *Real Estate.* An agreement to cover a down payment for the purchase of REAL PROPERTY as evidence of good faith on the part of the purchaser. The payment itself is also called a binder.

2. *Insurance.* A temporary agreement given by an insurance company to pay the loss if damage from the peril insured against should occur before the policy is written. A binder need not be in writing.

Blacklist. An index of persons to be held under suspicion or censure. Employers' associations have occasionally kept a file of the names of men discharged for labor agitation, union affiliation, participation in a STRIKE, or other behavior distasteful to the employer. If the employers' association covers a wide area, it becomes practically impossible for a man on the blacklist to obtain work.

Blackmail. The use of any letter or writing threatening to injure another's person, property, or reputation for purposes of EXTORTION. The crime of blackmail is established merely by showing the act and the intent; it is not necessary for the writing actually to produce fear on the part of the victim.

Blanket Mortgage. One MORTGAGE on a number of parcels of REAL PROPERTY. Provision may be made for release of each parcel as certain payments are made in reduction of the loan. In the absence of such a provision for *partial release,* the mortgagee (lender) cannot be required to release any one parcel from his blanket mortgage upon payment of a pro rata share of the debt; he is entitled to hold all the prrroperties as security until the debt is paid in full.

Blind Copy Notation. See CARBON COPY DISTRIBUTION NOTATION.

Blue Book. See AMERICAN LAW REPORTS.

Blue-Sky Laws. Statutes that have been enacted by most states to protect the public from FRAUD in the offering of securities. The term probably derives from the fact that promoters, practicing fraud, were accused of selling stock that had as much worth as a piece of blue sky. These laws supplement interstate regulation of securities offerings, securities exchanges, and speculative practices, through the Securities and Exchange Commission. Actually, protection is achieved through (1) specific legislation—blue-sky laws; and (2) through enforcement of anti-fraud statutes.

Board of Directors. A group of individuals elected by stockholders, who *as a body* manage a CORPORATION.

Who is qualified to act as director. Any person who is legally competent to contract can be a director, unless the statute, CERTIFICATE OF INCORPORATION or BYLAWS provide otherwise.

Ownership of stock is generally, but not always, a statutory, charter or bylaw requirement. Some statutes require residence in the STATE OF INCORPORATION by one or more directors; a few require United States citizenship.

Number of directors. A minimum, usually three, is generally fixed by statute; maximum is also sometimes fixed by statute. Actually a number within statutory limits is fixed by charter or bylaws of the corporation. This number may be increased or decreased by amendment to the charter when the charter fixes the number; or by amendment to the bylaws when bylaws fix the number.

Election. The certificate of incorporation usually names the first board of directors; statutes give stockholders the right to elect directors annually thereafter. Election must take place once a year when the statute or certificate requires an annual election; no corporate bylaw or regulation can modify a statute directing the method of election. In the absence of an election, incumbent directors are retained in office.

Terms of office. Usually fixed by

	SECRETARY'S MEMORANDUM		
	MEETING OF BOARD OF DIRECTORS		
ORGANIZATION		Stated Annual Special	Reg. Notice Personal Waiver
DATE	19—	Hour	Standard
PRESENT CHAIRMAN SECRETARY MINUTES STATEMENTS RESOLUTIONS	No. present	Necessary for quorum	
#1	Proposed by Votes	Seconded by For Against	
#2	Proposed by Votes	Seconded by For Against	

(Continued on next page)

Board of Directors: Figure 1. Secretary's memorandum for entering notes of minutes of meeting.

```
RESOLUTIONS
CONTINUED

        #3   Proposed by          Seconded by
                                  For
             Votes                Against

        #4   Proposed by          Seconded by
                                  For
             Votes                Against

        #5   Proposed by          Seconded by
                                  For
             Votes                Against

        #6   Proposed by          Seconded by
                                  For
             Votes                Against

        #7   Proposed by          Seconded by
                                  For
             Votes                Against
NOTES

ADJOURNMENT

DISBURSEMENT  Fees    Per member present
              Expenses  "      "   present   Sundries  Total
                          (Signed).......................
                                        Secretary
```

Board of Directors: Figure 1 *(Continued)*.

bylaws. Directors continue to hold office and must discharge their duties until their successors are elected.

Resignation. A director may resign at any time unless prevented by the certificate of incorporation or bylaws or by statute of the state of incorporation. A director who has made a contract with a corporation to serve a definite period of time is liable for damages caused by his resignation before the expiration of that period. Written resignation is preferable, but an oral one is sufficient. Resignation should state when it is to become effective; otherwise, it is effective immediately

Powers. The directors have power to conduct the ordinary business activities of the corporation. They are free to exercise their independent judgment upon all matters before them, without interference by the stockholders except in matters requiring stockholders' consent. In many states the laws provide that matters affecting all the property of the company must be referred to the stockholders; for example, a sale of the assets, lease of all the assets, consolidation or merger, amendment of the charter to increase or decrease capital stock.

Liabilities. Directors must act in

good faith and with reasonable care and must handle the affairs of the corporation with the prudence that an ordinary man would use. The law presumes that they know everything concerning the corporation that they might have learned from the use of reasonable care and diligence. They are not personally liable for losses resulting from accident or mistakes of judgment. Their relation to the corporation is FIDUCIARY and they are accountable to it for any secret profits. They are not to use their positions of trust and confidence to further their private interests. They need not volunteer information affecting the value of stock when trading with the individual stockholder. Directors also incur liabilities under certain Federal and state statutes.

Meetings. Generally, directors can bind the corporation by their acts only when they are assembled in a meeting. Bylaws usually provide for the place of the meeting and the method of calling it. A majority of the members of the board is necessary to constitute a QUORUM. A director cannot vote by PROXY and he is forbidden to vote on any matter in which he is personally interested. It is advisable that he leave the meeting when the board is considering a matter of personal interest to him, because some courts hold that favorable action will not be binding if his vote is necessary to decide the question. (See DIRECTORS' MEETINGS.)

Compensation. Directors are not legally entitled to compensation for performing their duties as directors or for attending meetings in the absence of charter or bylaw provision. State corporation laws rarely regulate compensation of directors. Directors who perform duties beyond the scope of a director's duties are entitled to compensation for their services.

Boldface. (b.f.) A heavy-face type, used principally for side and center headings, emphasis, short quotations, display lines, and display headings. **This is boldface type.** A wavy line under the word or words indicates that it is to be set in boldface.

Bond and Mortgage. A legal instrument that is written evidence of an obligation under seal, the payment of which is secured by a MORTGAGE (the conditional conveyance) on the property of the issuer. In a *bond and mortgage* both the evidence of obligation and the terms and conditions of payment to be met are combined in the same document.

Bond. A written promissory agreement, under SEAL, by which one party, which may be a corporation, governmental unit or other body promises to pay a stated sum of money at some specified future time (known as the maturity date), and to pay interest at a stated rate at specified dates until the maturity date. The obligation or debt is evidenced by the written certificate for a stated amount and for a stated term. See also BOND AND MORTGAGE; BOND ISSUE: CORPORATE MORTGAGE BOND.

Bond Issue. A method of raising funds through issuance of a large number of similar bonds, all of which are covered by a trust indenture or DEED OF TRUST that sets forth the obligations of the borrower, the rights of the bondholders, and the duties of a bank or trust company designated as trustee for the bondholders. The borrower may be an individual, but generally bonds are issued by a CORPORATION (see CORPORATE MORTGAGE BOND). Each BOND represents the corporation's written promise, under SEAL to pay a specified sum of money at a fixed time in the future, usually more than ten years after the promise is made, with interest at a fixed rate payable at specified interest dates.

Bottomry Loan. A loan made to the owner or master of a ship, usually in a foreign port in cases of emergency, for which the ship itself is pledged as security. The development of modern means of communication enabling masters to get assistance from their owners in emergencies has rendered this device largely obsolete. The lender has a LIEN on the ship enforceable in ADMIRALTY upon its safe arrival at the port of destination. The lien becomes void, however, if the ship is lost before arrival. See also RESPONDENTIA: MARITIME LIEN.

Boycott. An effort of many persons to injure another by preventing anyone from doing business with him. Boycotts have been used as a coercive weapon by workers against management. An effective boycott could hurt the workers as well as management because wages and employment may be reduced for some time through the partial destruction of the market once boycotted.

A *secondary boycott* is an effort to injure another by putting economic pressure on a neutral party. A secondary boycott may take the form of union members refusing to handle nonunion goods. Secondary boycotts have been made illegal because they tend to injure to a greater extent parties not involved in a labor dispute than those directly concerned.

Breach of Contract. The failure or refusal by one of the parties to a CONTRACT to perform some act the contract calls for. A contract may also be breached by making performance impossible, as when a person contracts to sell a car and wrecks it before delivery; or by "anticipatory" breach, as the unqualified announcement by a seller, before delivery date, that he will not deliver the goods.

Breach of a contract by one party may discharge the other from performance. Or the injured party may sue for damages representing the loss directly incurred from the breach. Damages cannot be obtained for speculative or possible losses that cannot be shown to have resulted directly from the breach.

Breach of the Peace. Conduct by acts or words that disturbs the public tranquility and is likely to produce violence in others. An example of a breach of the peace is the conduct of a man who threatens another with violence, or who goes about in public with dangerous weapons in a threatening manner. One who commits a breach of the peace is also guilty of DISORDERLY CONDUCT.

Breach of Warranty. When a WARRANTY made by a vendor proves to be false, the warranty is said to be breached. For the breach, the buyer has a choice of four remedies: (1) Accept or keep the goods and set up the breach to reduce the purchase price. (2) Keep the goods and recover damages for the breach of warranty. (3) Refuse to accept the goods if title has not passed, and bring an action for damages for breach of warranty. (4) Rescind the CONTRACT, or if the goods have been delivered, return them, and recover any part of the purchase price that has been paid. The buyer can claim only *one* of these remedies.

Bribery. The act of offering, giving, receiving, or soliciting anything of value to a public officer in order to influence his action in the discharge of legal or public duty. The crime is committed whether or not the official does the act requested. Modern statutes punish the giving, receiving, asking, and offering of bribes.

Brief. (Litigation) A written document that an attorney prepares as the basis for his argument before an APPELLATE COURT.

The brief must contain a history of the case on APPEAL, a statement of the questions or points involved, and the argument. The history is a concise statement of the essential facts without argument. It states the purpose of the litigation, contains a chronological enumeration of the PLEADINGS, the issues, and the JUDGMENT of the trial court, giving references to applicable pages of the transcript. The questions or points should be stated as concisely as possible. Each one is numbered and set forth in a separate paragraph and is usually followed by a statement of whether it was answered in the negative or the affirmative by the trial court. The section of the brief entitled *Argument* contains a division for each of the questions involved, with discussion and citation of authorities.

Preliminaries to preparing the brief. Before the lawyer dictates the brief, he *briefs* cases to be used in support of his position. This means that he makes a summary, digest, or abstract of a case, quoting pertinent parts from the court's opinion. Although the lawyer will dictate notes of these abstracts to the secretary, the dictation will consist principally of instructions to TAKE-IN excerpts of the court's opinion. Each summary is typed on a separate sheet of paper. Put the name of the case and the CITATION at the top of the sheet, double space the lawyer's language and indent and single space the take-ins. No copy is necessary.

Check carefully the spelling of names and the volume and page number of citations. After typing the notes, have someone read back the take-ins, if possible. This is especially important if the book quoted from is a borrowed book that must be returned before the final brief is written.

Time element. The court rules provide that the appellant must file his brief within a specified number of days after the RECORD ON APPEAL is filed, and that the appellee has a specified number of days thereafter to file his brief. The appellant then has an additional time in which to file a reply brief. The timing is close. If the brief is to be printed, there is a deadline by which the MANUSCRIPT must reach the printer. Unfortunately, many lawyers are inclined to put off the preparation of a brief until the last minute, and there is nothing the secretary can do about it except remind the lawyer of the date the brief must be filed.

Preparation of the brief. A rough *draft* of the dictated brief is first typed. Occasionally the lawyer will dictate part of a brief and then, because of the

I

THE BROAD POWERS GIVEN UNDER THE WILL CLEARLY IN-
DICATE AN INTENTION TO PERMIT THE EXECUTORS AND
TRUSTEES TO MAKE THE PROPOSED TEN-YEAR LEASE AND
OTHER LONG-TERM LEASES

By the terms of Article EIGHT of the Last Will and

Testament of_____

_____

Article EIGHT reads in part as follows:

"I hereby give to my Executors or Executor and
to my Trustees or Trustee, as the case may be, and
to such of them and their successors or successor as
shall qualify or may be acting for the time being,
full power, authority and discretion to manage and
operate any property which I may leave; * * * and
in general to do and perform all acts which seem to
them wise and necessary for the proper management,
investment and reinvestment of my estate, it being
my intention and direction that they should have the
widest possible powers, authority and discretion in
relation thereto." (Italics ours.)

Among the powers expressly conferred upon the Trustees

by the testator_____

_____

In Corse v. Corse, 144 N. Y. 569, 572, power to grant

leases for a term not limited_____

_____

See cases in point.

Goddard v. Brown, 12 R. I. 31, 46, 47 (1821);
Holland v. Bogardus-Hill Drug Co., 314 Mo. 214;
      284 S. W. 121;
Lord v. Roberts, 84 N. H. 517; 153 Atl. Rep. 1, 3;
Matter of Jones, 122 F. 2d 853.

Brief: Figure 1. Page from typed brief.

press of other matters, be unable to complete the dictation for a day or two. In the meantime, the secretary should transcribe her notes and place a copy on his desk for reference when he is able to work again on the brief.

Number of copies. After the lawyer revises the draft, it is typed in final form unless the lawyer asks for a second draft. The number of copies depends upon the rules of the court where the brief is to be filed. If the brief is to be printed, an original and two copies are necessary—the original for the printer, a copy for the lawyer, and a copy for the secretary's file.

Format. Figure 1 (above) shows a page of a typed brief. It is important to note that the *questions* or *points* are typed in solid caps or printed in bold face. Also, when several cases are cited in support of the same proposition,

INDEX

Brief: **Figure 2.** Index to brief.

IN THE SUPREME COURT OF FLORIDA

MIAMI SHORES VILLAGE,
Appellant,
vs.
BESSEMER PROPERTIES, INCORPORATED,
Appellee.

BRIEF OF APPELLEE.

Connelly Karter Behnke Ott & Martin
627 Ingraham Building,
Miami, Florida,
Attorneys for Appellee.

Brief: Figure 3. Cover for brief on letter-size, or smaller, paper.

they are placed one under the other unless they are in a quotation.

Index and list of authorities cited. A brief of more than 12 pages (consult the rules) must be indexed and prefaced by an alphabetical list of the authorities cited. These pages are numbered with small roman numerals. The index is actually a table of contents. Figure 2,

page 82, shows an index. In the alphabetical list of authorities cited, the titles of the cases are not necessarily underscored or in italics. Underscoring of a long list of authorities takes considerable time.

It sometimes happens that a case is cited before the court's opinion is published in the reporter (see

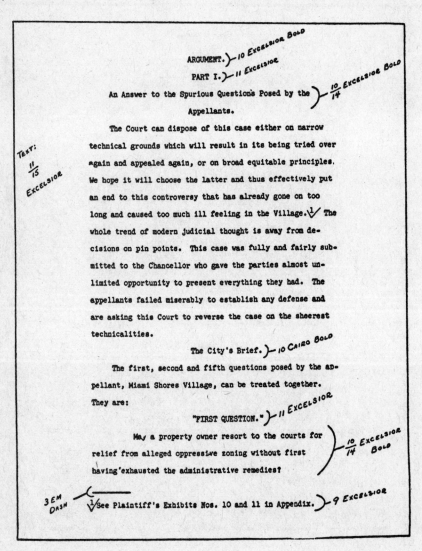

Brief: **Figure 4.** Page of manuscript from brief, marked for printer.

NATIONAL REPORTER SYSTEM), or even in the advanced sheets. The page and volume numbers are then left blank. Should the opinion be published before the brief is filed, the reference may be inserted.

Cover and binding. The cover of the brief contains the name of the court, the style of the case, identification of the brief (the party filing it), and the name and address of the attorneys representing the party filing the brief. When the brief is typed on legal size paper, a legal back, endorsed with these items, is used and stapled at the top. When the brief is typed on letter-size paper, double covers stapled at the side are used. Some rules specify different colors for the backs of the appellant's brief, the appellee's brief, and the appellant's reply brief. Figure 3 on page 83 illustrates a brief cover.

Filing and service. The rules specify the number of copies of the brief that must be filed with the clerk of the appellate court and the number of copies that must be served on opposing counsel. Service on opposing counsel may be by mail or in person. Proof of service must be made to the appellate court.

Procedure when having a brief printed. The secretary should follow all rules carefully when typing a brief and preparing it for the printer (see TYPING MANUSCRIPT; PROOFREADER'S MARKS; PROOFREADING: MARKED COPY.) Figure 4, page 84, is a page of typed manuscript from a brief, marked for the printer. Printers who specialize in court work are usually familiar with the requirements of the court rules.

Upon receipt of the galley proofs, the lawyer will read the brief again and make any changes he desires. The secretary has the following responsibilities:

1. Proofread for typographical errors.

2. Check the make-up, that is, to see that material that should be in boldface type is in boldface; quotations are indented, etc.

3. Compare the quotations with the source from which taken, or, if this is impractical, with the manuscript.

4. Check the citations, preferably by reference to the cited case in the reporter; otherwise, against the manuscript.

5. Check the record references against the record itself.

6. Return the corrected proof to the printer with instructions as to number of copies to be printed, stock and color of cover, and the like.

Bulk Sales Law. Legislation designed to protect the creditors of a seller who liquidates all or most of his assets to a single buyer at a single time. Sometimes a merchant desiring to go out of business will find someone to buy all of his assets at once. In order to protect the creditors of such a merchant from being defrauded, most states have enacted bulk sales legislation. Though the laws vary in detail from state to state, in general they provide that the purchaser of all or a major portion of a merchant's stock, other than in the regular course of business, should obtain from the seller, under oath, a list of all the seller's creditors, their addresses, and the amount owed to each of them. The buyer is then obliged to give each creditor notice of the pending sale, usually ten days before possession is transferred and payment is made. This procedure allows the creditors a brief period of time in which to press or secure their claims before the assets are beyond their reach.

The bulk sales laws do not apply to court conducted sales such as those resulting from proceedings in BANKRUPTCY or trusteeships. In some states the statutes apply only to retail merchants, in others to retailers and wholesalers, and in still other states to anyone disposing of most of his business assets to a single buyer.

A buyer failing to comply with the law may be liable to the seller's creditors on a pro rata basis up to the value of the goods received from the seller.

Burglary. A crime defined under the COMMON LAW as breaking and entering the house of another at night with the intent to commit a FELONY. Modern statutes have enlarged the scope of punishable burglary to include breaking and entering in the daytime into structures other than dwelling houses with the intent to commit a felony. Statutes have divided the crime into degrees, with burglary as defined under the common law bearing the severest punishment.

Business Law Articles, The. A looseleaf periodical used as a "secondary" source; useful in the law library.

Business Trust. See MASSACHUSETTS TRUST.

Bylaws. The rules adopted by a CORPORATION for its own government and that of its stockholders, directors, and officers. Bylaws are permanent and continuing, except for the changes that may be made by amendment.

The general corporation law of each state usually empowers the corporation to govern its internal affairs by bylaws and prescribes a method for their adoption and amendment. When either the corporation law or the CERTIFICATE OF INCORPORATION describes the manner in which bylaws should be adopted, they must be adopted in that prescribed way or they will not be valid.

Ordinarily the corporation may change its bylaws at will, provided the amended bylaw is (1) consistent with law, (2) consistent with the certificate of incorporation, (3) consistent with reason, (4) capable of being complied with, and (5) not violative of the rights of stockholders.

Preparation of bylaws. Like the certificate of incorporation, the bylaws usually follow a more or less routine pattern. The lawyer will dictate special clauses or paragraphs peculiar to the corporation being organized, and will dictate a memorandum that includes the following information:

1. Place of stockholders' meeting.
2. Day and hour of annual meeting of stockholders.
3. Time when notice of annual meeting of stockholders must be given (usually 10 days before meeting).
4. Who may call special meetings of stockholders (usually president, vice president, or upon request of two directors or holders of 25 percent of the outstanding stock).
5. Time when notice of special meeting of stockholders must be given (usually 10 days before meeting).
6. Percentage of stock that constitutes a QUORUM (usually a majority).

7. Place of directors' meetings.

8. When regular directors' meetings are to be held.

9. Time when notice of regular meetings of directors must be given (usually three or five days before the meeting).

10. Who may call special meetings of directors (usually president, vice president, or upon request of two directors).

11. Time when notice of special meetings of directors must be given (usually three or five days before the meeting).

12. Number of directors to constitute a quorum (usually a majority).

JOHNSON E. JONES, INC.

BY LAWS

ARTICLE I.

Office.

The principal office of the Corporation shall be located in the Borough of Manhattan, City of New York,

_____

_____

ARTICLE II.

Meetings of Stockholders.

Section 1. Annual Meeting. The annual meeting of the stockholders of the Corporation after the year 19___

_____

_____

Section 2. Inspectors of Election. The annual election of Directors shall be conducted by two inspectors

_____

_____

ARTICLE III.

Directors.

Section 1. Management. The property, business and affairs of the Corporation shall be managed by a

_____

_____

Bylaws: Figure 1. First page of bylaws.

13. Officers who are to sign and countersign checks.

14. Officers who are to sign and countersign stock certificates.

15. When the fiscal year of the company ends.

With the help of this memorandum and the certificate of incorporation the secretary will be able to follow a form and prepare the bylaws. Bylaws are too lengthy to be included here, but reference may be made to any book of incorporating forms. A printed copy of the bylaws of corporations that are listed on a stock exchange may also be obtained. Figure 1 shows how the bylaws should be set up. Letter-size paper is preferable.

C

COGSA (Carriage of Goods by Sea Act). A federal statute (46 U.S. Code Sec. 1300) passed in 1936 that is this country's adoption of the Hague Rules, which were drafed by representatives of the major maritime nations at an international convention. The statute defines the rights, liabilities and obligations of shippers and carriers of goods brought to or from the United States. Most of the leading maritime nations have adopted similar legislation See also ADMIRALTY; GENERAL AVERAGE LOSS; MARITIME LIEN.

Calendar. See DIARY.

Calendar Call. The list of cases to be called before a court. If the court hears cases every day the calendar call is referred to as the *daily call*. In courts that hear cases weekly, the calendar call is referred to as the *weekly call*.

The lists are published in the local law journal, so that the lawyers will know when their cases are to be called before the court. Both sides are supposed to be in court when the case is called. (See PARTIES TO AN ACTION). If the PLAINTIFF responds and the DEFENDANT does not appear, there will be a JUDGMENT or DECREE by default. If the defendant is ready and the plaintiff does not appear, the case will be dismissed for want of prosecution (DWP).

Answering the calendar call. Some lawyers have their secretaries answer the calendar call to save time for the lawyers. The cases are called by calendar number and by title. When the case is called, the secretary answers "Ready"; or, when the lawyer is trying a case in another court, "Ready subject to engagement." Then she explains to the court that the lawyer is trying a case in another court but will be available at a later hour. The lawyer will not send the secretary to answer the calendar call if he is not ready and must ask for an adjournment. If the case has been settled out of court, the secretary answers "Settled."

After all the cases on the list are called, they are called for trial, in turn. There is no need for the lawyer to sit through the trial of other cases. The secretary, or whoever is answering the call for him, waits in the courtroom until a reasonable time before his case is about to be reached for trial, and then telephones him to come to court to try the case.

Canvass. To scrutinize, discuss, solicit. Not to be confused with *canvas*.

Capital. 1. In the economic sense, one of the three "factors of production." The other two are "land" and "labor."

2. In the accounting sense, the net worth of a business as shown in the

capital account of a sole proprietor; the sum of the capital accounts of the partners in a PARTNERSHIP business; the sum of the CAPITAL STOCK and surplus in a CORPORATION.

3. In the legal sense, that portion of the consideration received by the corporation upon the issuance of stock that has been set up on its books as capital in accordance with the laws of the state in which the corporation is organized. It cannot be impaired through the payment of dividends or the acquisition of the corporation's own stock.

4. In a business sense, actual wealth or assets of a business in money, tangible property, such as plant and equipment, or intangible property, such as GOOD WILL, patents, trademarks and the like. Capital is used synonymously with total assets expressed in monetary forms.

Capital, Capitol. *Capital* is a city that is the seat of a government; *Capitol* is the building in which Congress meets, or a building in which a state legislature meets. State capitols may be spelled with either upper or lower case C, but the United States Capitol is spelled with an upper case C. CAPITAL has several other meanings but they do not cause confusion.

Capital Assets. Under the CAPITAL GAIN AND LOSS provisions of the Federal income tax law, a capital asset is any property held by the taxpayer, except

(a) Stock in trade or other property customarily includible in inventory if on hand at the close of the taxable year.

(b) Property held primarily for sale to customers in the ordinary course of the taxpayer's trade or business.

(c) Depreciable property used in trade or business.

(d) Real property used in trade or business.

(e) Copyrights; literary, musical or artistic compositions; and similar property; held by (1) a taxpayer whose personal efforts created such property, or (2) a taxpayer deriving a basis for such property, for the purpose of determining gain, from the person who created it; for example, a taxpayer who acquired a copyright from an author as a gift.

(f) Federal, state and municipal obligations issued on or after March 1, 1941, on a discount basis and payable without interest at a fixed maturity date not exceeding one year from the date of issue.

(g) Accounts or notes receivable acquired in the ordinary course of trade or business (1) for services rendered, or (2) from the sale of property held for sale to customers in the ordinary course of business.

The term "capital asset" includes such intangibles as shares of stocks and bonds unless they fall under one of the exceptions mentioned.

Capital Gain and Loss. The Federal INCOME TAX law and some of the state income tax laws have special provisions for the treatment of gains and losses on the sale or exchange of CAPITAL ASSETS by individuals and corporations. These are called the capital gain and loss provisions. The following explanation of the capital gain and loss provisions of the Federal income tax laws, as applied to security transactions by an individual, shows the principal factors of the provisions.

Gain or loss on security transaction. The disposition of securities for money (a sale) or for other property (an exchange) or for a combination of both, almost always results in a gain or loss. This is so because there is usually a difference between what was paid for the security given up and what was received for it. Before the taxable gain or loss, if any, on a security transaction can be determined, the taxpayer must know these principal factors:

1. The cost or other basis of the securities disposed of.

2. The amount realized upon the disposal of the security.

3. The period the investment was held before it was disposed of.

Basis for gain or loss on security-transactions. "Basis" is the term used in the tax law to indicate the amount to be compared with the sales proceeds in order to determine what the gain or loss is. The basis depends upon the manner in which the securities were acquired. It may be the actual cost, the fair market value, or a substituted basis.

The amount realized. The amount realized includes both money and fair market value of any property received on the sale or other disposition of the securities. Fair market value is a question of fact to be determined from evidence.

The period the investment was held. This factor is important because a deduction from gross income is allowed equal to 50 percent of the excess of the new long-term capital gain over the net short-term capital loss. Gains and losses from the sale or exchange of a security held for more than six months are long-term capital gains and losses, and gains and losses from the sale or exchange of a security held

for not more than six months are short-term capital gains and losses.

It is essential that the exact length of time the investment was held be determined. An error of one day might convert a short-term capital gain or loss into a long-term capital gain or loss, or vice versa. This could make a substantial difference in the tax. That is why a careful record must be kept of the exact date the investment was acquired and the exact date it was disposed of.

In computing the period held, the day on which the property was acquired is *excluded;* the day on which it was disposed of is *included.* For example, if property were purchased on April 10 of this year and sold on October 10 of this year, it would have been held for exactly six months (not more than six months) and it is therefore a short-term capital gain or loss.

In certain security transactions, particular rules must be followed for determining when the security was acquired. These rules give the *date basis.*

Illustration of computation of income and deduction (page 92). To illustrate how net capital gain and loss are figured and how the deduction is computed, assume these facts: gain from sale of securities held for more than six months, $1,500; loss from the sale of securities held for more than six months, $750; gain from the sale of securities held for six months or less, $800; loss from the sale of securities held for six months or less, $300.

A net capital gain is included in income. By reason of the so-called "alternative tax" (separate Schedule D, Form 1040) the tax on the gain will never be more than 25 per cent of the actual gain.

A net capital loss is deducted from

other income. But the taxpayer cannot deduct more than $1,000; any loss over $1,000 is carried over and deducted in the next five years against capital gains and up to $1,000 a year against other income. On a joint return, the losses of one spouse can be used to offset the gains of the other.

NET CAPITAL GAIN AND LOSS

1. Actual long-term
   capital gain $1,500
2. Actual long-term
   capital loss   750
                              _____
3. Net long-term capital
   gain . . . . $ 750
4. Short-term capital
   gain . . . . ,   800
5. Short-term capital
   loss   300
                              _____
6. Net short-term capital
   gain . . . . ,   500
                              _____
7. Net capital gain . . . , , , $1,250

DEDUCTION OF 50 PER CENT OF EXCESS OF NET LONG-TERM CAPITAL GAIN OVER NET SHORT-TERM CAPITAL LOSS

8. Net long-term capital
   gain (line 3) . . . . $ 750
9. Net short-term capi-
   tal loss   0
                              _____
10. Excess, if any, of line
    8 over line 9 (if
    line 9 exceeds line
    line 8 enter a zero) $ 750
11. Deduction (50% of
    line 10) . . . . $ 375
                              _____

Capital Loss. See CAPITAL GAIN AND LOSS.

Capital Stock. The aggregate proprietary interest of stockholders in a CORPORATION. This is not an interest in, or ownership of, any specific assets of the corporation; rather it is the collective ownership of the corporation itself. See also COMMON STOCK; PREFERRED STOCK; PAR VALUE STOCK; NO PAR STOCK; CERTIFICATE OF STOCK.

Caption. The heading that is written on a legal document or court paper. The caption consists of the following parts:

1. *Jurisdiction and venue.* Usually the jurisdiction, that is, the name of the court in which the case is brought, and the venue are recited together in phraseology similar to this:

IN THE DISTRICT COURT WITHIN AND FOR OKLAHOMA COUNTY, STATE OF OKLAHOMA
or
IN THE DISTRICT COURT OF SEDGWICK COUNTY, KANSAS

In a few states the venue is recited separately from the jurisdiction, thus:

STATE OF ILLINOIS }ss.:
COUNTY OF COOK

IN THE CIRCUIT COURT THEREOF

2. *The title of the case.* This gives the names and designation of the various parties to the action. The heading that appears on the summons and complaint is used throughout the action until it is appealed, unless (1) there should be a change of parties by amendment, or (2) there is more than one plaintiff or defendant. In the latter case, it is necessary to show only the first-named plaintiff and the first-named defendant, followed by appropriate words indicating that there are others, such as *et al., et ux., et vir.*

3. *The index number.* The index, docket, or action number is assigned by

the CLERK OF THE COURT. Although it is not known at the time the first paper is filed in court, it must be included on all future papers.

4. *Title of the pleading.* Each litigation paper has a designation or title, such as a COMPLAINT, or NOTICE OF TRIAL. The common practice is to include the title in the heading or just beneath it. All offices do not follow this practice.

How to type the caption. Court rules specify the information that goes into the caption, but only a few courts regulate the style in which the caption shall be typed. The secretary should ask the lawyer to designate the style he wants her to follow.

Caption of Case on Appeal. The part of a motion (see MOTIONS) or BRIEF that gives the name of the parties (see PARTIES TO AN APPEAL) and the name of the APPELLATE COURT where the APPEAL is being made. When the RECORD ON APPEAL is filed with the appellate court, the CAPTION has changed from what it was in the lower court. The new caption indicates the name of the appellate court, and the designation of the parties shows their appellate status. The lower court's INDEX NUMBER of the case is no longer indicated. For styles of designation of the parties on appeal and a table of the styles used in the 50 states see PARTIES TO AN APPEAL.

Carbon Copy Distribution Notation. The typed line that shows that a carbon copy is to be sent to another person. The notation is typed flush with the left-hand margin, below all other notations. If space permits, separate it from the other notations by two spaces.

SRE:NG
Enclosure
Copy to Mr. S. A. Williams

The abbreviation *c.c.* may be used instead of *Copy to.* In the simplified form of letter neither is used.

Blind copy notation. Type the carbon copy notation in the upper left hand portion of the letter *on the carbons only.* This indicates that the addressee of the letter does not know that a copy was sent to anyone.

Card Indexing. See NUMERICAL FILING SYSTEM (APPLIED TO CLIENTS' FILES), *Card indexing.*

Carry-Back and Carry-Over. A tax law provision that allows an individual or CORPORATION to use an operating or capital loss (see CAPITAL GAIN AND LOSS) in one year to reduce taxes for preceding (carry-back) or succeeding years (carry-over). See also INCOME TAX.

Case Law. The essential substance of law created by judicial decisions, as opposed to law stemming from statutory or other sources. See also SUBSTANTIVE LAW.

Censorship. The denial of the right of FREEDOM OF SPEECH AND PRESS and of all those rights and privileges which one expects under a free government. Totalitarian governments have generally censored on political grounds, but in democracies censorship has largely ceased, save on moral grounds or during wartime.

Center Heading. (Typing) To type a heading exactly in the center of a page, count the letters, spaces, and punctuation marks in the heading. Subtract one-half the number from the point on the typewriter scale that coincides with the center of the paper. (For example, if the paper extends from 0 to 102 on the scale, the center of the paper will be at 51 on the scale; if the paper extends from 5 to 95, the center will be at 45 on the scale.) The remainder will show the point on the typewriter at which the heading must begin. Thus, if the heading contains 26 characters, and the center point is 51, the starting point will be 38 [51 — (½ of 26)].

Or the starting point may be determined by beginning at the center point and back spacing once for each two characters in the heading while spelling out the heading. In spelling the heading, include spaces and punctuation marks as though they were letters. This will place the machine at the proper starting point.

If part of the left margin is to be used for binding, the center point will be moved toward the right one-half the number of spaces cut off for binding. For example, if 35 is the center point gauged by the entire width of the paper, and 10 spaces are to be allowed for binding purposes, the center point will be 40.

Centralized Filing. A system of keeping records whereby all correspondence and material are entrusted to one main filing center for safekeeping. Law offices generally maintain a *centralized* filing system. In a small office the secretary might be responsible for the centralized file. In addition, she maintains her lawyer's confidential or personal file quite apart from the regular centralized file. It usually contains papers that are pertinent to the lawyer's personal affairs. See also

PERSONAL FILE; FILING (IN A LAW OFFICE).

Certificate of Good Faith. A written statement by an attorney that he has filed a DEMURRER on behalf of his client in good faith and not for the purpose of delay.

Certificate of Incorporation. A written instrument that determines what the CORPORATION is authorized to do. It is sometimes referred to as *articles of incorporation, articles of association,* or *charter of the corporation.* The general corporation laws of each state provide what *must* and what *may* be included in the certificate. It is essential to valid incorporation that the provisions of the general corporation law prescribing the necessary contents of the articles be complied with.

Before the proposed certificate of incorporation is filed with the public official designated by law (usually the Secretary of State), it should be checked carefully to make certain that all provisions required by statutes are included. Failure to include a required provision may lead the designated public official to reject the proposed certificate, thus requiring redrafting and resubmission with attendant delay.

Generally, the certificate of incorporation must contain the following:

1. Name of corporation.

2. Purpose or objects of corporation or nature of its business.

3. Place of business.

4. Amount of CAPITAL STOCK and number of shares into which it is divided. If more than one class is created, a description of the different classes with terms on which respective classes are created.

5. Statement of maximum amount

of indebtedness which may be incurred and prohibition against exceeding that amount.

6. Duration of corporate existence.

7. Name and residence of incorporators.

8. Statement indicating what officers are to conduct corporate affairs.

9. Number of directors and names and addresses of directors selected for first year.

10. Statement showing compliance with requirements concerning subscription to, or payment for, capital stock, including amount required to be paid in before commencing business.

Preparation of certificate of incorporation. The law office will have, or the secretary will accumulate, a form file from certificates prepared for previous clients. These forms will serve as models in the preparation of the certificate for a corporation in the process of organization.

The secretary should observe these points:

1. Find out the number of copies that the law requires. *Make three extra copies*—one to be kept at the principal office of the corporation, one for the file, and one for the minute book. (In some states, including California, New Jersey, and Pennsylvania, an extra copy is required as an exhibit to the application for a permit to sell securities to the public. A copy of the charter must also be filed with the application to the Securities Exchange Commission.) Some states also require that a certified copy be filed in each county where the corporation owns real estate. The secretary will also have to make an extra copy for each state in which the proposed corporation expects to qualify. Two typings are necessary, the second being on minute paper.

2. Use either 8 ½ by 11 inches good quality bond paper, or legal cap. The trend is toward the use of the letter-size paper, except in those states where printed forms prepared by the state are used. When letter-size paper is used, the ribbon copy of the second typing is made on minute paper, thus saving the time required to copy the charter in the minute book.

3. If printed blank forms are used, as in Illinois, be sure they are of the same date of printing; otherwise, they might not be exact copies.

4. When typing the charter, always use PICA type and a very black ribbon, and double space it. These requirements are mandatory in nearly every state. Otherwise, there is no specific form in which the certificate of incorporation must be typed. Figures 1, 2, and 3 illustrate the first, second, and last pages of a charter and will serve as a model for style. The following details are customary, though not mandatory:

(a) The title of the document and name of the corporation are written in solid caps.

(b) The following words are written with initial caps whenever they refer to the corporation that is being organized: corporation, certificate of incorporation (or any other name by which the charter is known), BOARD OF DIRECTORS, BYLAWS.

(c) The left margin of indented material is indented five spaces from the principal left margin, and the first line of an indented paragraph is indented five additional spaces. The right margin is also indented.

(d) Subindentations are indented an additional five spaces.

(e) Numbered or lettered items are indented.

(f) Purpose clauses are indented.

CERTIFICATE OF INCORPORATION

OF

JOHNSON E. JONES, INC.

We, the undersigned, for the purpose of associating
to establish a corporation for the transaction of the business
and the promotion and conduct of the objects and purposes hereinafter stated, under the provisions and subject to the requirements of the laws of the State of Delaware (particularly Chapter 1,
Title 8 of the Delaware Code and the acts amendatory thereof and
supplemental thereto, and known, identified and referred to as
the "General Corporation Law of the State of Delaware"), do make
and file this Certificate of Incorporation in writing and do
hereby certify as follows, to wit:

FIRST, The name of the corporation (hereinafter
called the Corporation) is

JOHNSON E. JONES, INC.

SECOND: The respective names of the County and of the
City within the County in which the principal office of the
Corporation is to be located in the State of Delaware are the
County of Kent and the City of Dover. The name of the resident
agent of the Corporation is The Prentice-Hall Corporation System,
Inc. The street and number of said principal office and the ad-
dress by street and number of said resident agent is 229 South
State Street, Dover, Delaware.

Certificate of Incorporation: Figure 1. First page.

(g) Pages are numbered.

(h) Numbers are written out, followed by figures in parentheses.

5. Type a signature line for each signer.

6. In almost all states the charter is a sealed instrument. If the state of incorporation requires the seals of the signers, type (L.S.) or (SEAL) after each signature line.

7. If an acknowledgment is required, type the certificate of acknowledgment in the form required by the state of incorporation. The VENUE will recite the state and county where the incorporators sign, not the state of incorporation. The rules that govern the acknowledgment of any instrument govern the acknowledgment of a certificate. Some states require acknowl-

THIRD: The nature of the business and of the purposes to be conducted and promoted by the corporation, which shall be in addition to the authority of the corporation to conduct any lawful business, to promote any lawful purpose, and to engage in any lawful act or activity for which corporations may be organized under the General Corporation Law of the State of Delaware, is as follows:

To _____

_____

To _____

_____

FOURTH: The name and place of each of the incorporators are as follows:

NAME	PLACE OF RESIDENCE
E. G. Smith	Dover, Delaware
R. S. Lacey	Dover, Delaware
L. M. Stark	Dover, Delaware

FIFTH: The Corporation is to have perpetual existence.

SIXTH: The total number of shares of stock which the corporation shall have authority to issue is _____ with par value of $_____ each [or with no par value]. All such shares are of one class and are Common Stock. [Add additional clauses if there are to be different classes of stock, and if shares are to have preemptive rights].

SEVENTH: _____

_____

EIGHTH: The effective date of the certificate of incorporation of the Corporation, and the date upon which the existence of the corporation shall commence, shall be   , 19   [This clause is to be used if effective date of certificate of incorporation is to be a date after the date of filing and recording, but in no event later than 90 days after filing with the Secretary of State].

Certificate of Incorporation: **Figure 2.** Second page.

edgments taken outside the state to be authenticated. Therefore, if the acknowledgment is to be taken in a state other than the state of incorporation, consult the statutes of the state of incorporation to see if authentication is necessary. If all incorporators sign at the same time, one certificate of acknowledgment is sufficient, but if they sign at different times, there must be a separate acknowledgment for each. Some states do not require that all incorporators who sign shall acknowledge the instrument.

8. Prepare a cover for each copy except the one that is on minute paper. The only typing on the cover is, "Certificate of Incorporation (or articles, or charter, as the case may be) of (name of corporation)."

Execution of the certificate. In a few states all copies of the certificate of in-

```
        IN WITNESS WHEREOF, we, the undersigned, being all of the incorpo-
rators hereinabove named, do hereby further certify that the facts herein-
above stated are truly set forth and accordingly have hereunto set our
respective hands and seals.
Dated at Dover, Delaware
October 31, 19--

                              _____ (L.S.)

                              _____ (L.S.)

                              _____ (L.S.)


STATE OF DELAWARE)
                 ) SS.:
COUNTY OF KENT   )


        BE IT REMEMBERED that personally appeared before me, Robert R.
Steele, a Notary Public in and for the County and State aforesaid, E. G.
Smith, R. S. Lacey, and L. M. Stark, all the incorporators who signed the
foregoing Certificate of Incorporation, known to me personally to be such,
and I having made known to them and each of them the contents of said
Certificate of Incorporation, they did severally acknowledge the same to
be the act and deed of the signers, respectively, and that the facts there-
in stated are truly set forth.
        Given under my hand and seal of office this 31st day of October,
A. D. 19--.


                              _____
                                            Notary Public
        -10-
```

Certificate of Incorporation: Figure 3. Last page.

corporation required to be filed with the designated public official must be ribbon copies, carbons not being acceptable. In others, an original and duplicate originals or triplicate originals are acceptable. Some states will accept an original and conformed copies.

If the papers are to be executed in the office, notify the incorporators that the papers are ready for signature and arrange a time for them to come in to sign. (It is advisable to do this as soon as it is known when the papers will be ready, in order to avoid delay.) If some or all of the incorporators are to sign outside the office, forward the document with a covering letter

Each original, duplicate original, and triplicate original must be signed, but the copies that are to be conformed need not be signed. The signature must be the same on each copy, and must be written exactly as in the document. Thus, if an incorporator signs his name *R. P. Edwards,* his name should not be written *Richard P. Edwards* in the document.

When acknowledgments are required, take the acknowledgment of the incorporators, and notarize all signed copies of the charter. Conform the unsigned copies.

Filing the certificate and payment of fees. After the certificate of incorporation has been executed, send the required number of copies to the proper state official, with a letter of transmittal and a check in payment of the organization tax and fees. The letter of transmittal might read as follows:

The Honorable John R. Blank
Secretary of State of Delaware
Dover, Delaware

Dear Sir:

Re: Johnson E. Jones, Inc.
We are enclosing an original and two conformed copies of Certificate of Incorporation of Johnson E. Jones, Inc. Please record the original of the Certificate in your offices and certify and return to us the conformed copies.

We are also enclosing our check for $40, covering (1) the organization tax, $10; (2) filing and indexing fee, $5; (3) recording fee, $15; (4) certification of copy for recording, $6; and (5) certification of one extra copy, $4.

Very truly yours,
Brown & Wilson
Enclosures (4)

If the charter is acceptable, the public official will retain the original. He will mark the copy, or copies, to show that the charter has been filed with him and endorse his approval upon it, or attach a certificate of approval to it, and return it, together with receipt for tax and fees, to the office.

1. Conform the office copy, noting particularly the date of the official's filing marks. This date, rather than the date on which the charter was executed, is the date of incorporation.

2. Draw check for the local filing fee and file the certified copy of the charter in the appropriate local office if required.

3. Note on the office copy the date the certificate was filed locally.

4. Paste the tax receipt in the minute book.

Certificate of Stock. Written evidence of ownership of a certain number of shares in a CORPORATION. The certificate itself evidences the holder's right to a proportionate share in the declared dividends and in the assets of the corporation upon its dissolution. The certificate is an assignable CHOSE IN ACTION. See also CAPITAL STOCK.

Certificate of Title. An instrument, written and signed by a TITLE examiner, stating that in his opinion the seller has good title to property to be conveyed. A certificate of title may be issued by an attorney who examines the public records and states his opinion as to the validity of the title based on such examination. It offers no protection to the purchaser of property against any hidden defects in the title which an examination of the records could not reveal or against any unwarranted litigation attacking the title. The issuer of the certificate is liable only for DAMAGES due to negligence. A certificate of title is, in effect, TITLE IN-

SURANCE. See also ABSTRACT OF TITLE.

Certified Check. A CHECK that has been guaranteed by the bank both as to signature and amount. Either the maker of a check or the holder can present the check for certification at the bank on which the check is drawn. The bank examines the drawer's account, charges the account immediately for the amount of the check, and marks the check "accepted" or "certified."

The check then ceases to be an order on the bank and becomes an obligation of the bank. Hence, certification of a check makes it equivalent to cash. Certified checks are used principally in real estate and securities transaction in which cash payment is required. When the drawer has the check certified, he accepts the bank as his debtor and the drawer is not liable in case of insolvency of the bank before payment. The drawer of a certified check cannot stop payment on it. He should redeposit the check if it is still in his possession, and not destroy it. If a bank certifies a check by mistake, it may withdraw the certification if it acts promptly, provided the holder has lost no right.

Certified Mail. See POSTAL SERVICE.

Certiorari. (Latin) To be informed of; to be made certain in regard to. A writ issued by a superior court to an inferior court directing it to send to the former court the record of a particular case. A writ of certiorari is an extraordinary remedy resorted to in cases obviously entitled to redress where no direct appellate proceedings are provided by law. A writ of certiorari cannot be used as a substitute for an appeal or a writ of error. It is distinguished from an appeal in that it brings up the case on the record, whereas on appeal a case is brought up on the merits. A litigant is entitled to a writ of error as a matter of right, but a writ of certiorari lies within the court's discretion.

The dissatisfied party in the lower court petitions the appellate court for a writ of ceriiorari. If, on the face of the record, the appellate court determines that the lower court has not proceeded in accordance with the law, it will consent to issue the writ and hear the case. If the record itself does not indicate that the petitioner has been wronged by the proceeding, the court will deny the petition for a writ of certiorari. The denial is, in effect, an affirmance of the lower court's decision on the point of law before the appellate court, but the issuance of the writ does not mean that the appellate court will decide in favor of the petitioner. The court may then order the certiorari dismissed; or return it to the lower court with instructions; or render a final judgment which must finally govern the case.

See also HABEAS CORPUS; STAY; PROHIBITION; QUO WARRANTO; MANDAMUS; WRIT OF ERROR.

Chancery Court. A court or tribunal that has jurisdiction over EQUITY or chancery matters. Law actions usually have for their object the assessment of damages, but a court of equity or chancery goes further. It attempts to prevent the wrong itself or give the complainant what he bargained for.

A few states still have chancery courts (see Table II, AMERICAN COURT SYSTEM). Others do not separate cases in equity from cases at law, but apply equity principles when appropriate. In the majority of states, equity and law are organized under a single court, which has two dockets—one in equity and one in law.

Among the more common equity actions are injunction suits, partition suits, specific performance, rescission of contract, reformation of a contract, and all matters relating to trusts and trustees.

Charge to the Jury. Instructions given by the JUDGE to the jury on the principles of law which the jury is required to apply to the facts of the case in order to return a verdict. Many judges invite active participation by the lawyers in the preparation of a tentative charge. Each lawyer at a trial has an opportunity to object to the charge as finally given by the court.

How to prepare an instruction to the jury. Many offices keep printed forms of stock instructions, but the lawyer will dictate others.

1. Make an original for the judge, a copy for opposing counsel, and an office copy.

2. Type each instruction on a separate sheet of legal paper.

3. Number each instruction for identification purposes.

4. Identify the party submitting the instructions, thus, "Plaintiff's Instruction No......." (This may be placed at the top or bottom of the charge; numbers are inserted later in the order in which the charge is given.)

5. There is no CAPTION.

6. Instructions are not stapled in a legal back and are not enclosed.

Charter-Party. A CONTRACT by which a ship or a portion of it is leased to another for a specified time or use. There are three main types of charter-parties:

1. *Voyage charter.* A ship is engaged to carry cargo on a single voyage. The vessel is manned and navigated by the owner. The voyage charter is the form of charter-party most frequently encountered.

2. *Time charter.* The ship is engaged by the charterer for a fixed period of time for the carriage of goods anywhere in the world on as many voyages as approximately fit into the charter period. As in the voyage charter, the owner's people continue to navigate and manage the vessel. The crew is under the charterer's orders as to the ports touched, cargo loaded, and other business matters.

3. *Demise charter.* The charterer takes over the ship and mans her with his own people. In practice, virtually all demise charters are for a period of time. See also ADMIRALTY; MARITIME LIEN.

Chattel. An article of tangible personal property, as distinguished from real property (land and improvements) and intangibles (stocks, bonds, and the like). The term chattel derives from the word *cattle,* an early symbol of property.

Chattel Mortgage. A MORTGAGE on tangible PERSONAL PROPERTY (chattels). A chattel mortgage is distinguished from other instruments of conveyance by the condition contained in it that if the debt is paid by a day specified, the conveyance is void, and if payment is not made, the transfer is absolute. In some jurisdictions, a chattel mortgage, like a real estate mortgage, is not a conveyance transferring TITLE but merely a LIEN given as security for the debt. If the debt is not paid when due, or if some other condition of the mortgage has not been complied with, the mortgagee enforces his lien by a FORECLOSURE sale.

In some states, the foreclosure of a chattel mortgage, like the foreclosure of a real estate mortgage, can be effected only through court procedure. In many states the chattel mortgage must be recorded. The chattel mortgage does not in itself constitute notice of the mortgagee's rights in the chattel. Hence, the creditor, if he wishes to protect his rights against third parties, must give public notice of his interest in the chattel. He does this by filing the chattel mortgage or a true copy of it in a prescribed public place.

The duration of a chattel mortgage is limited in some states—sometimes to three or four years, after which time it becomes void automatically unless renewed. See also CONDITIONAL SALE; RECORDING OF CONDITIONAL SALE CONTRACT.

Check. A written order drawn upon a bank by a depositor, requesting the bank to pay on demand a certain sum of money to the bearer, or to the order of some person or corporation named on the face of the check.

Post-dated check. A check is not invalid merely because it bears a date later than that on which it is drawn. The holder may transfer it before the date on which it is payable, but the drawer's bank will not honor it before that date. A post-dated check is a promise to pay rather than an order to pay; therefore, the drawer generally cannot be prosecuted criminally if the check is refused for lack of sufficient funds.

Discrepancy in amounts. The Negotiable Instruments Law provides that the amount expressed in words is the sum payable when there is a discrepancy between that amount and the amount expressed in figures. Banks generally refuse to accept checks with discrepancies in amounts. The holder may endorse it, guaranteeing the correct amount, and deposit the check for collection.

Certification. (See CERTIFIED CHECK.)

Time within which check must be presented for payment. The Negotiable Instruments Law provides that a check must be presented for payment within a "reasonable time," determined by the circumstances of each particular case. Ordinarily a check must be presented to the bank on which it is drawn during business hours of the next business day after it is received; or deposited by the payee in his own bank for collection and presented by the collecting bank on the following day. Failure to present a check for payment within a reasonable time discharges the drawer from liability to the extent of loss caused by the delay. Thus, if the bank on which a check is drawn becomes insolvent so that the drawer loses the amount he had on deposit to meet the check, the loss must be borne by the one who was lax in presenting the check for payment.

Checks that "bounce." Almost every check deposited will clear. Occasionally, however, a check will be returned to the depositor by the bank. When the bank does this, a statement of the reason will accompany the returned check. There are a great many possible reasons. For example, "lack of endorsement," which means that the depositor failed to endorse the check. When this occurs the check should be endorsed and redeposited. Or, for example, "no account," which means that the maker of the check has no account at that bank. Unless the depositor is familiar with the appropriate steps to take when a check is returned, he should consult counsel within twenty-four hours. Legally prescribed steps must be followed to preserve the rights of the depositor against the maker and all endorsers.

Insufficient funds. One of the reasons why checks "bounce" is "insufficient funds." A person who, with fraudulent intent, issues a check knowing that he has not sufficient funds for its payment is subject to criminal prosecution in many states.

Death of drawer. This revokes the authority of the bank to pay. If a bank pays a check without knowledge that the drawer has died, it cannot be held liable for the amount.

Given in full settlement of claim. When the amount of a claim is *disputed,* a check reciting that it is in full settlement, accepted or collected by the creditor without objection, discharges the debtor's obligation. A creditor cannot accept the check and then write the drawer that he does not consider it full settlement; nor can he strike out the words "in full" and avoid acceptance as full payment. It is important to indicate clearly on the check the fact that it represents payment in full. A check should be returned at once if the amount is not acceptable.

Forged or raised check. A bank is liable to a depositor for payment of a forged or raised check. The Negotiable Instruments Law provides, however, that the drawer must notify the bank within one year after return to him of the paid check that it was forged or raised.

Drawn on Sunday or holiday. Technically, a check should not be drawn on Sunday or on a holiday, but few banks refuse payment for this reason.

Endorsement. The endorsement appears on the reverse side of a check. When an endorsed check is received in payment of debts, there are two things to watch. (1) The spelling of the name in the endorsement. It should correspond exactly with the name of the payee on the face of the check. A check made payable to J. Doe should be endorsed J. Doe and not John Doe, although it may be endorsed both J. Doe and John Doe. A check made payable to a business firm should be endorsed in the firm's name and signed by the authorized person of that firm. (2) Any additional words accompanying the signature. What the endorser adds may have important legal significance; for example, his adding "without recourse," may prevent the holder from making a valid claim against the endorser if the check proves worthless. Any wording having unfamiliar legal significance should be a warning to the recipient of the check to consult his attorney.

Checking Manuscript. The process of examining a MANUSCRIPT carefully for errors before it is sent to the printer. Checking saves time and money and contributes to a better finished product. *Read the manuscript over several times,* looking for errors. Each error corrected on the typed manuscript will save the expense of resetting a line or even a whole paragraph. Here are some guides the secretary should follow when checking the copy:

1. *Be consistent.* If a word can be spelled or abbreviated in more than one correct form, choose one and use it consistently. On the first reading, make a list of selections of optional spellings to be a guide toward consistency.

2. Make *short corrections* by crossing out the incorrect word and writing the correction over it, not in the margin. The margin is used for instructions to the printer. To make *lengthy corrections,* cross out the incorrect matter and type the correct matter on a separate sheet of paper. Mark the correction as an insert and show clearly where it is to be inserted.

3. *Circle* anything on the page that the printer should not set in type. Thus, any instructions to the printer should be circled.

4. In checking the manuscript, do not indicate corrections to be made in the margins; make all changes directly on the manuscript.

5. To start a new paragraph, insert a ¶ sign; to run in material typed as a new paragraph, draw a line from the word starting the new paragraph, draw a line from the word starting the new paragraph to the last word of the preceding paragraph.

6. To separate two words typed as one, draw a vertical line between them.

7. To make deletions, use a heavy pencil and ruler and neatly and heavily cross out what is not wanted.

8. To retain material already crossed out, insert a row of dots beneath it and write the word "stet" in the margin beside it in a circle. Be sure, however, that the crossed-out material that is to be retained is legible; if there is any doubt, retype it as an insert.

9. *Number the pages* of the manuscript consecutively after all corrections and insertions have been made.

Check-Off. A system whereby the employer deducts the union dues and initiation fees from the paychecks of the employees and transfers these amounts directly to the union. The check-off saves the union time and money in collecting dues and also guarantees the union a financial security as a result of the continuing and steady payment.

Child Labor. The use of children in the labor market. The large-scale employment of children, often under dangerous and unsanitary conditions, was one of the most serious evils of early industrialization. Chiefly as a result of Federal and state regulatory legislation, the relative number of children in the nation's labor force has sharply declined over the years.

Chinese Copy. A duplicate of an original document, signed letter, quoted material, book extract, and the like (not a reproduction, such as a photostat or camera copy) that has been copied so that it follows the original faithfully. It does not correct errors, but purports to be a "true and exact" copy, including even the most obvious mistakes. Here is how the secretary should type Chinese, or exact, copy.

1. Type the word COPY in the upper left-hand corner.

2. Copy exactly, even obvious errors.

3. Indicate obvious errors copied from the original as follows: (a) Underline an incorrect letter or figure. (b) Put "sic" in parentheses or brackets after apparently or obviously incorrect words or phrases. (c) Show an omission by a caret. If the typewriter does not have a caret, use the slanting bar and underscore key (/). Below are some examples:

agreement entered into the 31st day of April. . .upon reciept. . .
I give, devise and bequest (sic) unto. . . meeting of the United/Assembly in New York. . .

4. Copy page for page and line for line as far as practicable.

Chose in Action. A right to receive or recover a debt or DAMAGES in an action on a CONTRACT, or in a TORT action. A Chose in Action is intangible personal property. Often the phrase includes not only the right of action, but also the thing that forms the subject matter of that right, e.g., contracts, stocks, bonds, bank accounts, and the like.

Circumstantial Evidence See DIRECT EVIDENCE.

Citation (Admiralty Proceeding). A written command by the United States Marshal served upon a vessel or party being sued in an ADMIRALTY action. The citation commands the party to admit or deny the assertions in the libel. [See LIBEL (IN ADMIRALTY PRACTICE.)] It is substantially the same as a SUMMONS in an action at COMMON LAW except that an action in admiralty is "commenced" by

the filing of the libel in the U.S. District Court, not by service alone. The citation, however, must be served reasonably soon after the libel is filed.

Citation (in Probate Proceeding). An official order notifying a person to appear before a probate court. See PROBATE OF A WILL.

Citation (to Legal Authorities). Reference to an authority that supports a statement of law or from which a quotation is taken. Citations most frequently occur in a BRIEF, MEMORANDUM OF LAW, and OPINION LETTERS. The lawyer speaks of *citing a case, a cited case, citing a report,* and the like. The references are principally to the following sources:

1. Constitutions, statutes, codes
2. Law reports
3. Texts and periodicals

How to take citations in shorthand. It sometimes happens that citations, particularly volume, page, and section number, are incorrectly set down when dictation is rapid. The following procedure is recommended: Write down the volume number, allow a small space, and immediately write down the page or section numbers, going back to fill in the title of the volume. The memory more readily retains the title of the volume than it does the volume and page number. In the citation of a case, it is more important to obtain the correct numbers and title of the book than the correct names of the parties. The secretary can go to the law report and easily find the title of the case.

Accuracy of citations. The importance of accuracy of citations cannot be overemphasized. Check and double-check volume and page references and spelling of names. The secretary should check against the original reports, not against her notes. Check printed briefs against the original reports, not against manuscript. A judge is annoyed if he cannot find a case cited to him because of a typographical error in the citation. Misspelling of the name of a well-known case marks the lawyer as either careless or ignorant. Errors in citations are always avoidable, and it is the secretary's responsibility to see that no reflection is cast upon the lawyer through her carelessness.

How to cite a constitution. Show the number of the article, or amendment, in Roman numerals; the section number in Arabic numerals. Give date if the constitution cited is not in force.

U.S. Const.	Art. IV, §2
U.S. Const.	Amend. VI, §2
Ga. Const.	Art. XI, §3
Ga. Const.	Art. II, §1 (1875)

How to cite statutes and codes. Whenever full reference to a Federal statute is necessary, cite date, chapter number, statute citation, and United States Code citation, thus: Section 1 of the Act of June 13, 1934, c. 482, 48 Stat. 948, 40 U.S.C. 276 b. Compilations of state statutes and codes are cited by chapter, title, or section number.

When citing statutes and codes, the secretary should observe these directions:

1. If a compilation in its preface gives the method of citing it, use that citation.

2. Where the date is incorporated in the title of the compilation, show it.

3. When statutes or codes of one state are cited outside of that state, the name of the state is always indicated for identification purposes. For example, lawyers in Kansas cite the Kansas General Statutes as "G.S." but outside of Kansas the citation is Kan. G.S.

4. When citing an act or law that has been repealed and no longer appears in the latest compilation, give the date of the compilation cited.

Ill. Rev. Stat. C. 114, §88 (1889)

How to cite cases in official reports and reporters. Cases in OFFICIAL REPORTS and reporters are cited alike. Directions for citing cases must be considered in the light of applicable court rules. Some courts lay considerable emphasis on how cases should be cited and whether citation to the NATIONAL REPORTER SYSTEM should be included. The following directions are the rules of thumb used in many law offices. *Examples of citations are on pages 109 and 110.*

Names of parties. 1. Cite the name of the case as it appears in the running head of the report, not as it appears at the beginning of the opinion. Do not abbreviate the first word.

2. When the United States is a party, do not abbreviate U.S. unless it is part of the name of a Government vessel. (See Example 1.)

3. Do not substitute the initials of a Government agency or a labor union for its full name in briefs. It may be done in other legal writings. (See Example 2.)

4. Use the first name of railways, but abbreviate the balance. (See Example 3.)

5. When *Co.* and *Inc.* are both part of a name omit the *Inc.*

6. When the names of parties change completely on APPEAL indicate that fact by the use of *sub nom.* (See Example 4.) This direction does not apply when the names of the parties are merely reversed.

Volume and page. Cite the volume and page number of the report or reporter in which the opinion is published. The reference is to the entire opinion and gives the page at which the opinion begins. A *spot page reference* follows when it is desired to call attention to a particular page, such as one from which a quotation is taken. (See Example 5.)

The designation "2d" *must* be included in the citation of a volume in a second series. A reference to 58 N.E. is not the same as a reference to 58 N.E. 2d.

Date. Show in parentheses the year the decision is handed down by the court. It appears at the beginning of the court's opinion. Both *A Uniform System of Citation* and *Practical Manual of Standard Legal Citations* place the date at the end of the citation (Example 1), but lawyers, when writing briefs, frequently place it between the title of the case and the volume reference (Example 5). Many lawyers do not show the date of the decision unless it is relevant to the argument.

Jurisdiction and court. When the name of the reporter does not indicate the JURISDICTION, show the jurisdiction in parentheses preceding the date. (See Example 6.) Also show the name of the court deciding the case if it is not the highest court in the state. (See Example 7.) This is always necessary when only the unofficial reporter is cited.

Parallel citations. Both the official

and unofficial reports should be cited if available. Cite the official report first. (See Example 8.) When the case has not been published in the official reports, but will be in the future, cite the name of the official report, preceded and followed by blanks, thus, __ Miss. __, 55 So. 2d 477. (See Example 9.)

Federal courts. When citing cases decided by the Federal courts of appeals, show the circuit in parentheses. (See Example 10.) The District of Columbia circuit is indicated by *D. C.* (See Example 11.) When citing cases decided in the Federal district court, show the district, but not the division, in parentheses. (See Example 12.)

Selective case series. In some law report series, such as *American Law Reports* and *Law Reports Annotated*, only certain cases are published. These series are cited by the year of publication, the *letter* of the volume (A, B, C, or D), and page. (See Example 13.) In parallel citations, they follow the National Reporter citation. It is customary to cite selective case series in briefs for state courts but not in those for Federal Courts.

Named reporters. Old court reports carry the name of the reporter. When citing cases in the U.S. reports prior to volume 91, always cite by the volume number and name of the reporter, not by the subsequently assigned consecutive U.S. number. To cite these volumes by the U.S. number is considered bad form. The following are the names of the old court reports and the number of volumes they reported.

4 of Dallas (cited as 1 Dall. 10)
9 of Cranch (cited as 1 Cranch 10)
12 of Wheaton (cited as 1 Wheat. 10)
16 of Peters (cited as 1 Pet. 10)
24 of Howard (cited as 1 How. 10)

2 of Black (cited as 1 Black 10)
23 of Wallace (cited as 1 Wall. 10)

When citing state cases, follow the local practice. For example, in Massachusetts the early reports are invariably cited by the name of the reporter, whereas in North Carolina a rule of court requires that they be cited by the consecutive number. When the named reporter is used, indicate the jurisdiction and date in parentheses. (See Example 14).

String citations. When several cases are cited one after the other instead of on separate lines, the citation is referred to as a *string citation.* Separate the cases with a semi-colon. (See Example 15.)

How to cite an unpublished case. When citing a case that has not been reported, cite by name, court, the full date, and the docket number if known. (See Example 16.)

How to cite slip decisions. Each opinion of the United States Supreme Court is published separately as soon as it is handed down. This form of publication is called a *slip decision.* Slip decisions are printed by the Government Printng Office and also by two unofficial publishers, Commerce Clearing House and U.S. Law Week. They are widely circulated and are frequently cited in briefs. Cite by number, court, date of decision, and source if unofficial. (See Example 17.)

How to cite treatises. Cite by volume number (if more than one volume), author, title of the publication, page or section number, and the edition in parentheses. If the editor is well known, his name follows the edition. Underscore or italicize the title of the publication. (See Example 18.)

In a few well-known works, the paging of the original edition is indicated by stars in differently paginated editions. Cite by the star page. (See Example 19.)

How to cite law reviews. Cite the volume and page number and the year. Underscore or italicize the title of the review. If an article is referred to, place it in quotation marks. Abbreviate *Law (L.), Review* (Rev.), and *Journal (J.).* (See Example 20.)

How to cite legal newspapers. When citing a case that has not been published in either the official or unofficial reports but has been published in a legal newspaper, give the name of the newspaper, the volume and page number, the column, the court, and the exact date of the decision. (See Example 21.)

Underscoring and italicizing. Underscoring and italicizing vary with the law office, but the following directions, some of which are arbitrary, are based upon the practices followed by many lawyers:

1. Underscore the names of the parties.

2. In a printed brief, the underscoring of *v.* or *vs.* is optional. Continuous underscoring gives a more even appearance on the typed page and requires less care than breaking the underscoring at the desired points. Printers usually set the *v.* or *vs.* in roman type.

3. When a previously cited case is referred to in the text of the brief by part of the title used as an adjective, italicize it.

Under the authority of the *Daoud* case the Court held...

When the reference is repeated under

the same point of the brief, do not italicize it.

4. Italicize *case* or *cases* only when it is part of the usual name of the case.

5. It is preferable not to underscore words and expressions between citations of the same case that relate to its history, such as *affirmed, certiorari denied,* and the like. (See Example 22.)

Spacing of abbreviations. In briefs the parts of an abbreviation are separated by a space, thus *N.E. 2d.* In other legal writings, the general practice is to close up the citation, thus *N.E.2d.*

Placement of citations. Unless a citation is part of a quotation, it is indented and placed on the line following the quotation. If it runs over one line, the carry-over line is indented.

"...should be denied, as proposed allegations would add nothing to the equity of the bill."
> *Volunteer Security Co. v. Dowl* (1947), 159 Fla. 767, 33 So. 2d 150, 152

When several citations are given in support of a point, list them one under the other.

Illustrations of citations. The following examples of citations illustrate the foregoing directions. Parts appearing in italics would be underscored on the typewriter. Apparent inconsistencies in the italics and in the placement of the dates in the examples demonstrate the variations in accepted practices. However, the secretary should be consistent throughout a brief.

Example   *Citation*

1. *United States v. Texas & Pacific Motor Transport Co.,* 340 U.S. 450, 71 S. Ct. 422 (1951)
2. *United States v. Congress of Industrial Organization,* 335 U.S. 106, 68 S.

Ct. 1349, 48 A.L.C. 1164, aff'g 77 F. Supp. 355, 48 A.L.C. 559 (D.C. Cir. 1948)
3. *Nashville, C. & St. L. Ry. v. Walters,* (1934) 294 U.S. 405, 55 S. Ct. 486
4. *Blaustein v. United States,* 44F. 2nd 0106163 (C.C.A. 3), certiorari denied *sub. nom. Sokol v. United States,* 283 U.S. 838, 51 S. Ct. 486
5. *Green Point Savings Bank v. Board of Zoning Appeals,* (1939) 281 N.Y. 534, 24 N.E. 2d 319, 321
6. *Harrington v. Board of Adjustment, City of Alamo Heights,* (Tex. 1939) 124 S.W. 2d 401, 404
7. *Rayl v. General Motors Corp.,* (Ind. App. 1951) 101 N.E. 2d 433 *Janice v. State,* 107 N.Y.S. 2d 674 (Ct. Cl. 1951)
8. *People v. Davis,* 303 N.Y. 235, 101 N.E. 2d 479
9. *Hughes v. Wilson,* (1961) . . . . Ohio St. . . . ., 174 N.E. 2d 789
10. *American Fruit Machinery Co. v. Robinson Match Co.,* 191 Fed. 723 (3rd Cir. 1911)
11. *Barbee v. Capital Airlines, Inc.,* (D.C. Cir. 1951) 191 F. 2d 507
12. *Standard Oil Co. v. Atlantic Coast Line R. Co.,* (W.D. Ky. 1926) 13 F. 2d 633
13. *Hanover Star Milling Co. v. Allen & Wheeler Co.,* 208 Fed. 513, 1916D L. R. A. 136 (7th Cir. 1913)
14. *Forward v. Adams,* 7 Wend. 204 (N.Y. 1831)
15. *Rubin v. Board of Directors of City of Pasadena,* (2940) 16 Cal. 2d 119, 104 P. 2d 1041; *Harrington v. Board of Adjustment, City of Alamo Heights,* (Tex. 1939) 124 S.W. 2d 401; *Green Point Savings Bank v. Board of Zoning Appeals,* (1939) 281 N.Y. 534, 24 N.E. 2d 319
16. *Roe v. Doe,* No. 152 U.S. Sup. Ct., Jan. 10, 1961
17. *Torcaso v. Watkins,* No. 40, U.S. Sup. Ct., No. 373, 1961 (29 U.S. Law Week)
18. 2 Pomery, *Equity Jurisprudence* §428 (5th Ed., Symonds, 1941)
19. 2 Bl.Comm. *358
20. 42 *Yale L.J.* 419 (1933)
21. *Marine Midland Trust Co. of N.Y.*

v. *Dow*, 146 N.Y. L.J. 9, Col. 2 (Sup. Ct. Spec. Term Sept. 8, 1961)
22. *In re Morse*, (1928) 220 App. Div. 830, 220 N.Y. Supp. 858, Rev'd on the other grounds, 247 N.Y. 290, 160 N.E. 374

Citators. See SHEPARD'S CITATIONS; FEDERAL TAX CITATOR.

Citizenship. Membership in a political community. Citizenship may pertain either to a state or to the United States or to both. Each status carries with it certain obligations of the citizen and also gives him the enjoyment of full CIVIL RIGHTS which are protected against encroachment by governmental power.

Civil Court. A body in the government delegated to administer justice in connection with *civil wrongs*, that is, wrongs arising from the relationship between individuals as such, as distinguished from wrongs against the public. (See CRIMINAL LAW.) Civil wrongs infringe on private rights and duties; remedy against them is sought by private action. TORT and BREACH OF CONTRACT are among common civil wrongs. See also CIVIL LAW.

Civil Law. A term generally used to designate Roman jurisprudence. The law of the Romans under Emperor Justinian was condensed and digested into a code known as Corpus Juris Civilis. The laws of Justinian were lost in the Western Empire during the early Dark Ages, but a complete copy was found about 1137. The laws were then revised and became the basis of jurisprudence for most of continental Europe. The present law on the Continent is therefore referred to as the Roman or civil law. See COMMON LAW; CRIMINAL LAW; CIVIL COURT; CRIMINAL COURT.

Civil Rights. Rights belonging to a person by virtue of his CITIZENSHIP in a state or community. The failure of the Constitution to guarantee many of the personal rights which the people regarded as fundamental led to the almost immediate adoption of a BILL OF RIGHTS in the form of the first ten amendments.

Civil Wrongs. See CIVIL COURT.

Claimant. In ADMIRALTY law, the term *claimant* has two meanings, each almost opposite to the other. (1) When a vessel is sued *in rem*—that is to say, no individual or corporation is sued—the owner of the ship appears, files a *claim of owner* and defends the action on behalf of the ship. In such a case, the owner is called a claimant. (2) When a steamship owner whose vessel has been in a disaster petitions to limit his liability, the parties who have claims against the limitation fund (who are really plaintiffs) file their claims against the fund and are called *claimants*.

Clean Hands. Equitable relief may be denied on ground of deceit or impurity of motive.

Clear and Present Danger. A classic test applied by Justice Holmes in determining what limitations may constitutionally be put upon FREEDOM OF SPEECH AND PRESS. The test would be applied to determine if a man should be stopped from making a speech where there appears to be a "clear and present danger" that an uncontrollable riot would occur because of it. The law cases stress that by "clear and present danger" is meant something more than public inconvenience, annoyance, or unrest. One of the functions of free speech is to invite dispute, and it may not be abridged merely because it stirs people to anger and creates a condition of unrest.

Clerk of the Court. The official recorder of all court business. He receives all court papers such as complaints, answers, amendments, motions, and appearances, assigning them numbers according to what is known as the *clerk's index system.*

The secretary's contact with the court is chiefly through the clerk of the court. Almost all correspondence is addressed to him. For the proper form of address in writing to the clerk of the court see ADDRESSING OFFICIALS. The clerk of the court answers inquiries, written or telephonic, about pending court cases, court rules, the calendar, and any other matters pertaining to his office. He and the personnel in his office can be of considerable help to the lawyer's secretary. It is frequently necessary for her to look up something in the records of his office or to telephone for information regarding a case. It behooves the secretary to maintain cordial relations with the personnel in the clerk's office at all times. Although the systems of keeping records in clerk's offices vary in detail because of statutory requirements and custom, they are fundamentally the same. For a basic explanation of how these records are kept and what the secretary's duties are in relation to them see CLERK'S INDEX SYSTEM.

Clerk's Index System. The method by which the CLERK OF THE COURT receives and records all court papers such as complaints, answers, amendments, motions, and appearances. (See CLERK'S PERMANENT RECORD BOOK.) As soon as the summons and complaint, or other first pleading is filed, the clerk assigns an index number, also called a *docket number* and an *action number,* to the case. The numbers are consecutive. In some courts, an initial is used to indicate the court in which the case is filed. For example, *S* for Superior, *C* for Circuit, *P* for Probate. In courts that have separate law and EQUITY divisions, the letter *L* or the letter *E* will be a part of the index number. In some courts, the successive numbering of cases starts over at the beginning of each year, and the number includes the year. Thus the index number might read 77S-1328, or 1328/77, or 1328-1977, indicating that the case was filed in 1977. When a clerk uses this system of numbering, the year is as important as any part of the number. The clerk keeps a cross-index of the cases, arranged alphabetically according to the name of the plaintiff, and also, in some courts, a cross-index according to the name of the defendant.

How the secretary uses the index number. 1. If she files the first pleadings, she must get the index number from the clerk of the court or from his records so that she may enter it in the office file. If an attorney in the office files the paper, he should get the number and give it to the secretary. She may ask him for it. The index number should be procured as soon as possible after it is assigned to a case.

2. After an index number is assigned to a case, the secretary *must* type that number on all papers thereafter prepared in the case in that court. Before filing a paper or giving it to an attorney to file she should check to see that the proper index number is endorsed on it, both on the paper itself and on the backing.

3. She must have the index number in order to get information about the status of a case.

Clerk's Minute Books. The books in which the CLERK OF THE COURT enters abstracts of all court orders. He does so numerically according to index number. He might have separate books for law, chancery, divorce, and the like.

How the secretary uses the minute book. If the secretary wants any information about the court's orders in a case, she can get it by consulting the minute book. She must have the index number. Usually the clerk's office will give the secretary the information over the telephone. See also CLERK'S PERMANENT RECORD BOOK; CLERK'S INDEX SYSTEM.

Clerk's Permanent Record Book. The standing register, kept by the CLERK OF THE COURT, of all records of legal papers filed in a particular case. The cases are entered consecutively according to index number, a case to a page. The permanent record book may be called also the *docket* or *register*. The clerk enters on the docket sheet the index number, the title of the case, the names and addresses of the attorneys, and the date the SUMMONS was served. He also enters on the docket sheet all subsequent proceedings.

How the secretary uses the register. Although the lawyer keeps his own record of the information in the clerk's register (See SUIT REGISTER), it is sometimes necessary to consult the court register for the purpose of checking on dates that papers were filed by opposing counsel. Besides, an attorney is frequently interested, for one reason or another, in the developments in a case in which he is not representing a litigant. He is usually interested in knowing the status of cases immediately preceding his on the court calendar, so that he can judge when his case will be reached.

If the secretary wants information on any case in court, she looks in the alphabetical index unless, of course, she already has the number. Then she turns to that page number in the docket and reads the entries made there. When the secretary wants to read the original papers on file, she gives the clerk the index number and asks him to get them for her. Sometimes he will let the secretary get them herself; if he does, she must be sure to put the papers back exactly where she found them. See also CLERK'S INDEX SYSTEM; MINUTE BOOKS.

Clients, Charges to. See BILLING CLIENT.

Clients' Telephone Calls. Clients frequently ask permission to place telephone calls. Quite often these calls are TOLL CALLS and the question of payment for them might present an embarrassing situation. The thoughtful client immediately suggests payment, but many excellent clients simply do not think about payment. Keep a record of these calls and bill the client for them, unless special circumstances make it more diplomatic for the law firm to charge the call to overhead.

Close (or Closed) Corporation. A corporate enterprise whose capital stock is held by a limited group; its shares are ordinarily not sold in the securities markets. A close relationship between ownership and management is an identifying characteristic as well as a main objective. Usually a close corporation is small. (The Ford Motor Company was an exception.)

Theoretically, there is no difference between meetings of stockholders or boards of directors of great enterprises and those of close corporations (See DIRECTOR'S MEETINGS). Statutes and judicial decisions spell out the meticulous care that must be taken in fulfilling technical requirements. In practice, however, it is a recognized fact that a CORPORATION having relatively few stockholders holds meetings without extensive advance preparation.

Closed Shop. An agreement whereby all employees must be members of a union before they can be hired by the employer. The closed shop is the strongest form of union security. See OPEN SHOP.

Closing. See CLOSING TITLE.

Closing File, Preparation for. The necessary measures taken to make a file ready for inactive safekeeping. When closing a file, the secretary should go through it carefully and remove all paperclips, pins, and the like. This procedure eliminates the possibility of storing papers that do not belong in that particular file. Quite often a misplaced paper is found, and removal of the clips reduces the size of the file. If a file has several jackets, the secretary might be able to combine the contents into one jacket. Papers and folders in a closed file may be packed more tightly than those in an active file.

See also FILING, PREPARATION OF MATERIAL FOR; INDEX TABS AND LABELS, TYPING OF.

Closing Statement. (Real estate) The provision in a CONTRACT OF SALE that contains an adjusted and prorated summation of certain charges against REAL PROPERTY and the income from it. For example, if the seller has paid the insurance for a year in advance, he is entitled to receive an adjustment from the buyer. If the seller has collected the rents for an entire month in advance, the buyer is entitled to an adjustment. This prorating or adjustment results in credits in favor of each party. A statement of the charges and credits is known as the *closing statement,* sometimes called a *settlement sheet.*

Forms of closing statements vary. Printed forms are available and are widely used. When the printed forms do not provide for all the items that must be entered on the closing statement, the statement is typed. This situation frequently arises in large, complicated deals. The statement cannot be prepared in final form until the closing is held, because all of the necessary information is not available. It is prepared on the basis of the figures agreed upon by all parties at the closing. (See CLOSING TITLE). However, the lawyer for each party usually calculates the adjustments and prepares a memorandum of them before the closing. The secretary will probably have the responsibility of calculating the adjustments. See ADJUSTMENT OF CHARGES AND INCOME.

Closing Title. A transaction in which the formalities of a sale of REAL PROPERTY are executed. When the purchaser agrees to buy, he generally pays a deposit and enters into a contract with the seller. The contract designates a certain day, and sometimes hour, when the deed and mortgages, if any, shall be delivered and the balance of the purchase price paid.

Preparations for closing. As soon as a CONTRACT OF SALE is received in the lawyer's office, the secretary should enter the date of the closing in her DIARY. The following checklists show some of the preparations that the secretary has to make prior to the closing.

Checklist of preparation by secretary to seller's attorney. (The asterisks indicate items that are to be delivered to the buyer at the closing.)

*1. Prepare the DEED.

2. Prepare the purchase money mortgage and bond or note, if any. (See MORTGAGE, *purchase money mortgage.*)

*3. Prepare, or obtain from the seller, a list of the tenants, rents paid and unpaid, and due dates.

*4. Obtain a certificate, properly acknowledged, from the holder of any mortgage that the purchaser assumes, showing payment on account or the amount actually due at the closing date.

5. Prepare memorandum of closing figures (see CLOSING STATEMENT). (A copy of the memorandum might be mailed to the attorney for the purchaser, thus saving time in adjusting figures at the closing.)

6. Prepare letter to tenants advising them to pay future rent to the purchaser.

*7. Prepare assignment of any service contracts, such as exterminator's contracts, that are to be assigned to the purchaser.

8. Notify seller of the exact time, date, and place of the closing. Tell him to bring to the closing the following papers:

    a. Receipts for last interest payment on mortgages

   *b. Insurance policies and assignment of them

   *c. Last receipts for taxes, special assessments, gas, electricity, and water

   *d. Leases and assignments

   *e. Securities or cash deposited by tenants as security for rent.

9. If seller is an individual, tell him that his wife must also be present at the closing to sign the deed.

10. If seller is a corporation, indicate

the two officers, who are to sign the deed and who, therefore, should be present at the closing. Also, advise the officers to bring the corporation's seal.

11. Notify others who might be present in behalf of seller of closing date—broker, accountant, title closer.

Checklist of preparations by secretary to purchaser's attorney.

1. Order ABSTRACT OF TITLE.

2. Type opinion of title after lawyer dictates it.

3. Prepare a memorandum of closing figures (see CLOSING STATEMENT). (This might be mailed to the seller's attorney, thus saving time in adjusting figures at the closing.)

4. Notify purchaser of the exact time, date, and place of the closing. Tell him to bring to the closing the following:

   a. Certified check for approximate amount that will be due to the seller. (The figure is in the memorandum of closing figures.)

   b. Cash for any additional amount owed the seller.

5. If purchaser is a corporation indicate the two officers who are to sign the purchase money mortgage and who, therefore, should be present at the closing. Also advise the officers to bring the corporate seal with them.

6. Notify others who might be interested in behalf of the buyer of the closing date—accountant, insurance broker, title closer.

7. Prepare for the attorney a checklist of papers that are to be delivered to the buyer at the closing. This list will include the items marked

with an asterisk in the foregoing checklist of preparations by the seller's secretary.

Code Address. An address in code registered with international telegraph carriers to obviate the expense incurred in using full address and signature in INTERNATIONAL CABLE OR RADIO messages. Code addresses may be registered with the Central Bureau of Registered Addresses, 67 Broad Street, New York; with international carriers maintaining offices at Washington, D.C. (American Cable & Radio and R.C.A. Communications) and at San Francisco (American Cable —Radio, R.C.A. Communications, and Globe Wireless); and with local Western Union offices. The addresses need be registered with only one carrier, which will supply all other carriers with each new registration.

Codes and Statutes. Compilations of the laws that have been enacted by the Congress of the United States and the various state legislatures. They are systematically sorted and arranged in chapters and subheads to facilitate their use. These compilations, known as *codes* and *statutes* usually contain also, the Constitution of the United States and of the particular state.

Every lawyer has the compilation of his own state; law firms that practice in several states have the compilations for those states; nearly all lawyers have the United States Code; law association libraries and law college libraries usually have the compilations of every state.

The majority of the compilations are kept up to date by pocket parts and supplements, but in some states the session laws for all years after the date of the compilation must be used in conjunction with the compilation. Florida and Wisconsin publish a new compilation after every session of legislature.

How to find a law. The secretary should familiarize herself with the plan of arrangement of the compilation for her state. She will find that the preface contains explanatory and useful material. All of the compilations contain a general index, and some of them also have an index in each volume. The indexes vary in their completeness and usefulness, but with a little perseverance she will be able to find the desired section of the law. After the secretary searches the compilation, she should search the supplements and pocket parts, if any, and all session laws since the date of the compilation or since the date of the latest supplement. The section of the law in which she is interested might have been amended or repealed since the compilation, or a new law on the subject might have been enacted.

When a lawsuit involves a statute, the court's judicial interpretation and construction of that statute becomes as much a part of the law as the statute itself.

Codicil. A supplement to a WILL that changes its provisions. The same procedures and formalities that are necessary to execute a will properly must be observed when making a codicil.

Coercion. Compulsion; constraint; compelling by force of arms.

Cohabitation. The act of living together in the manner of husband and wife. When a man and woman live together in a manner that makes people believe they are married, the law will presume that they are legally and validly married. In a case that seeks to disprove the existence of a valid marriage, such as one involving the legitimacy of a child, it would take very strong evidence to overcome this presumption of validity where there has been cohabitation.

Collateral. Something of value, easily converted into cash, deposited as a pledge with a lender to secure the repayment of a loan; its value is usually substantially more than the amount of the loan. If the borrower is unable to meet the loan when due, the lender is free to sell the collateral and collect the debt from the proceeds of the sale.

Collating. The process of checking a set of typed pages for correct numerical sequence. When a typing job consisting of more than one page is completed, the material must be separated and arranged in sets consisting of the original of each page, the first carbon of each page, the second carbon of each page, and so on. Each set must be checked for correct sequence of pages. The task of compiling the sets of copies and collating them is made easier by the use of a rubber finger or pencil eraser.

Collection Agency. A firm specializing in collecting overdue accounts receivable. It has no means of collection not available to the creditor, but is frequently successful in obtaining payment of past due accounts after the creditor's collection system has failed.

The agency is often successful because it has no interest in keeping the good will of the customer and can press its demands more vigorously. The customer also knows that his credit rating will suffer if he fails to respond to the agency's demand.

Claims, or accounts, are taken on a contingent basis—if there is no collection, there is no charge. Rates depend on the amount of money collected and whether the collection is made by letter or personal call.

Collection Letters. Correspondence sent to a debtor with the purpose of collecting the debt. The secretary will probably be called upon to draft collection letters. If so, she should keep these premises in mind:

1. The purpose of the letter is to collect money; therefore, do not hesitate to ask for a check.

2. Do not take the attitude that the account "probably has been overlooked," because nuumerous demands for payment are made before the account is given to the attorney.

3. Use *dated action*. That is, tell the debtor that a certain action is expected by a given date, or within a given number of days, not in the "near future."

4. The *divided urge* is a serious fault in a collection letter. Suggest only one course of action—do not mention an alternative. For example, do not tell the debtor that you expect a check by a certain date and then suggest to him that he should telephone if payment is impossible.

5. The period between letters should be short—from 5 to 10 days.

A first letter to the debtor from the attorney on May 3 might read:

Dear Sir:

Department Stores, Inc. has retained us to collect your past due account in the amount of $345.

Since this account has been delinquent for six months, it is imperative that you give it your immediate attention. Please let us have your check in full by May 13.

Very truly yours

After this letter is written, mark the file for follow-up for May 15. If the debtor does not reply by that date, another letter might be sent that reads:

Dear Sir:

We have received no reply to our letter of May 3 concerning your past due account with Department Stores, Inc. in the amount of $345. We shall be compelled, therefore, to bring suit against you for the above amount, together with costs, disbursement, and interest, unless your check in full payment is received at this office by May 20.

Very truly yours,

Collections. Past due accounts that the lawyer undertakes to collect for others. Collections may be turned over to the lawyer by local clients, or they may be forwarded to him from another town by a COLLECTION AGENCY or by another lawyer. Unless suit is filed, collections are handled on a contingent fee basis, usually at standard Commercial Law League rates. Although some commercial items involve large amounts, the majority of them are for small sums, with a correspondingly small fee. It is, therefore, desirable in the case of small items to curtail the usual office procedure as much as is consistent with efficiency. Collections are usually segregated from the other cases and are handled in a special manner. The procedure is routine and, after it has been established, the secretary can assume responsibility for the entire operation of the collection department.

Office procedures affecting collections. The office procedures affecting collections involve the following:

1. Files
2. Follow-up system
3. Acknowledgment of claim
4. Letters to debtor
5. Reports to forwarder
6. Records of collections
7. Remittance to forwarder
8. Forwarding collection items
9. Suit

How to file collection matters. As

DEBTOR'S NAME Jackson, L. E.	ADDRESS 405 South Adams, City
CREDITOR A. B. Corporation	ADDRESS 307 South Main St., Chicago
FORWARDER	ADDRESS
SENT TO	ADDRESS

AMOUNT OF CLAIM	INTEREST	DATE OF CLAIM	DATE DUE	DATE RECEIVED	LIST
NATURE OF CLAIM (Check proper space)	ACCOUNT	AFFIDAVIT	NOTE	ACCEPTANCE	DRAFT	JUDGMENT
COLLECTION RATE	COSTS ADVANCED	REGISTERED		PROOF FILED	

CORRESPONDENCE WITH — Forwarder, Debtor, General

CALLS MADE

SUIT MEMORANDA
COURT
SUIT FILED — RETURNABLE
CONTINUANCES
TRIAL — JUDG. COSTS
EXECUTION ISSUED
SUPPLEMENTARY
CITATION — COSTS
GARNISHMENT — COSTS
FINAL DISPOSITION
TOTAL — JUDG. & COSTS

CASH ACCOUNT

DATE	MEMO	REC'D	DISB.

FOLLOW UP DATES

REMARKS:

MADE IN U.S.A.—COMMERCIAL LAW LEAGUE OF AMERICA—STANDARD VERTICAL COLLECTION FOLDER, NO. 2—LETTER SIZE

Debtor's Name and Address — Jackson, L. E.

STICK GUMMED TAB ON BACK LEAF OF FOLDER OPPOSITE INDEX LETTER IN POSITION INDICATED BELOW.

1 2 3 4 5 6 7 8 9 10 11 12 13 14 15 16 17 18 19 20 21 22 23 24 25 26 27 28 29 30 31

Jackson, L. E.

Forwarder's Number — Office Number

Collections: Figure 1. Collection folder with name tab.

soon as a collection item is received, a file folder should be made for it. The folders are filed alphabetically under the debtor's name. In conformance with the policy of keeping office procedure at a minimum, file index cards are not made. If the lawyer prefers that index cards should be made, the secretary uses plain 3 by 5 inch cards and keeps them separate from her other index cards. Show on the card the name of the creditor, the name of the debtor, and the name of the forwarder.

The secretary will notice that the printed file folder in Figure 1 has space for a file number. When the numbering system of filing is used for collections, cross-reference index cards are essential.

When suit is brought on a collection, the case is transferred to a legal folder and handled like any other litigated case. Since default judgment is obtained in the majority of collection cases, considerable clerical work can be saved by not transferring the file unless the suit is contested.

Follow-up system. A desirable method of following collections is to use a file folder that has the days of the month printed on the top edge of the folder. See Figure 1. The alphabet on the folder is ignored. Folders without any printed matter except the days of the month are also obtainable. A metal tab is placed on the date that the file should come up for action, and the folder is filed alphabetically under the name of the debtor. Thus, regardless of the follow-up date, the folder is always in its proper alphabetical position in the filing cabinet. Each morning the secretary pulls all folders that have the metal tab placed on the current date. After the necessary action is taken, the metal tab is moved to the date on

which the file again should come up for action.

Another popular method of follow-up for collections is a follow-up file with the folders tabbed so that they can be located alphabetically. The folder illustrated in Figure 1 is also appropriate for this system; the dates on the top edge are ignored. Each file drawer, if more than one is necessary, is arranged as a follow-up file, with guides for the months and dates. Each drawer is operated as a separate follow-up file. How can a folder be located if it is needed before the follow-up date? The letters of the alphabet printed near the top edge of the front leaf of the folder make this possible. A small gummed tab marked with the debtor's name is pasted on the back leaf of the folder, opposite the index letter printed near the top of the front leaf. Thus, the name *Jones* is on the folder opposite *J;* the name *Smith* is opposite *S,* and so on. It makes no difference under what date the folder is filed: the *J's* are always in one line in one position in the file, and so is each letter of the alphabet. By looking at the proper line, the secretary can easily find the proper folder at any time. The folder can be returned to the correct follow-up date, because the last date in the space for follow-up dates, on the front of the folder, shows where it is to be filed. This system simplifies the task of pulling the folders each morning, because all folders to be brought up on a certain date are together. It also eliminates moving the metal tabs, which are sometimes difficult to move without tearing the folder.

Acknowledgment of claim. Simultaneously with the preparation of the folder, the claim should be acknowledged. Promptness in acknowledging the collection is very important, because the forwarder is naturally interested in knowing that the matter is receiving immediate attention. The acknowledgment might read:

Dear Sir:

Re: Department Stores, Inc. v.
J.C. Adams
Amount $345

We acknowledge receipt of the above styled claim and accept the claim for collection on the basis of the terms and regulations of the Commercial Law League of America.

You are recognized as the client's agent. We will report developments and make remittances to you.

Yours very truly,
Elwood & Adams

Reports to the forwarder. The forwarder is interested in developments. As soon as contact is made with the debtor, write to the forwarder telling him what the prospects for collection are. It is helpful to the forwarder to send reports in duplicate, especially those in which the lawyer recommends suit or some special arrangment. The forwarder can then send a copy to the client, thus saving the time and trouble in copying the report.

See also COLLECTION LETTERS; COMMERCIAL LAW LISTS; INSTALLMENT COLLECTIONS.

Collective Bargaining. The negotiation, administration, and enforcement of written agreements between employers and unions. The agreements set forth joint understandings as to policies and procedures governing wages, hours, and other conditions of employment. Collective bargaining is the principal method of determining wages and other conditions of employment for those who earn their living by working for others. By substituting group action for individual action in making and enforcing agreements, the worker has protected himself and improved his economic status. See LABOR UNION.

Collusion. A conspiracy between two or more persons for a fraudulent or deceitful purpose. In DIVORCE law, collusion is a conspiracy of the husband and wife to obtain a decree of divorce by false testimony, such as testimony of ADULTERY when none, in fact, occurred.

Combination Envelope. (See ENCLOSURE.)

Combing-back. The process of moving forward from week to week reminders of matters that require attention at an indefinite date until a definite date is established or until the matter is completed. See also DIARY; TICKLER CARD FILE.

Comity. The practice by which the courts of one state or country follow a statute or JUDGMENT of another on a like question, though not legally bound to do so. A state will not give the judgment of a foreign country comity if it contravenes its own public policy. Under FULL FAITH AND CREDIT, as contrasted to comity, the judgment of a sister state must be recognized no matter how erroneous and unjust it may seem to be.

Commercial Law Lists. Names of lawyers who handle COLLECTIONS of commercial items. It is from these lists that out-of-town lawyers select an attorney in the debtor's locality to handle the claim. It is from these lists that the lawyers in the secretary's office will select attorneys to whom to forward accounts against debtors in another jurisdiction.

Usually the FORWARDER of an item will mention the law list from which the lawyer's name was obtained. Some lists produce better results than others. The secretary, therefore, should keep a record of the items the lawyer receives through each list and the fees he earns by reason of his representation on that list. The lawyer can then determine whether continued representation on a special list is warranted. A simple record is sufficient. Keep a separate sheet for each law list and show on it the forwarder, the item (creditor, debtor, amount), and when the matter is closed, the amount of the fee. The secretary might keep these sheets in a folder in the front of the file drawer in which the collection cases are filed. See also COLLECTION LETTERS.

Commercial Lease. A binding CONTRACT, for the possession of lands and improvements to be used in the conduct of business (such as retail stores, office buildings, theaters, shopping centers, parking facilities, hotels and motels) in return for a specified rent. See also LEASE; RESIDENTIAL LEASE; COMMERCIAL PROPERTY.

Commercial Property. REAL PROPERTY used in connection with all activities of business, industry, and trade, for the purpose of producing income. These may include: (1) residential property such as an apartment house or hotel; (2) industrial property, such as a factory building or loft; (3) business property, such as a retail store, office building, gasoline station, garage, warehouse, market, motel or resort property; and (4) amusement and recreation properties, such as theaters, taverns, bowling alleys, dance halls, and skating rinks.

Common Carrier. One whose business it is to transport goods or passengers for all who may choose to employ him.

Common carriers of goods are responsible for all loss or damage of merchandise during transportation from any cause except the act of God or the public enemy. They may, however, quality this liability by CONTRACT. The responsibility of the carrier terminates after the goods have arrived at their destination and a reasonable time has elapsed for the owner to receive them. After that, the carrier may put them in a warehouse, and is only responsible for ordinary care. Carriers, both by land and water, when they undertake the general business of carrying every kind of goods, are bound to carry for all who offer; if they refuse, without just excuse, they are liable to an action at law.

Common carriers of passengers, unlike common carriers of goods, are not responsible as insurers of their cargo. Passenger-carriers, however, do have the duty to exercise a high degree of care and watchfulness to their passengers. There is no responsibility when injury results directly from the passenger's NEGLIGENCE.

Common Law. A system of law, or body of legal rules, derived from decisions of judges based upon accepted customs and traditions. It was developed in England. It is known as the *common law* because it is believed that these rules were generally recognized and were in full force throughout England. Common law is now the basis of the laws of every state of the Union, except Louisiana, which bases its laws upon the early laws of France. Statutes have been enacted to supplement and supersede the common law in many fields; the common law, however, still governs where there is no statute dealing with a specific subject. Although the common law is written, it is called the *unwritten law* in contradistinction to STATUTORY LAW enacted by the legislatures.

Common-Law Marriage. A marriage not solemnized in the ordinary way, but created by an agreement to marry, followed by COHABITATION. Most states declare a marriage to be valid only if there is a formal procedure prescribed by statute. Common-law marriages legally contracted in a state that does consider them valid, however, must be given FULL FAITH AND CREDIT by all the other states.

Common-Law Trust. See MASSACHUSETTS TRUST.

Common stock. Corporate stock characterized by the fact that it entitles its holder to a DIVIDEND only after the rights of the holders of PREFERRED STOCK have been satisfied, and, secondly, by the fact that it usually has voting rights attached.

Common stock represents the basic ownership of the CORPORATION. With only nominal exception, all corporations have common stock. Some corporations have common stock only; others have common and preferred and/or a variety of hybrids.

Upon the dissolution of a corporation, common stock entitles its owners to all that is left after allowance for claims having priority. During periods of prosperity common stockholders are in the enviable position of having an unlimited interest in the profits and assets of the corporation while the holders of preferred stock have only the right to receive dividends at a fixed

or stated rate. However, during periods of business decline the position of common stockholders is less desirable because by the time prior claimants have received their due, there may be nothing left for the holders of common stock.

Common stock generally carries with it voting rights which enable the holders to participate in the management of the corporation and thereby to exercise a certain amount of control of the corporate assets which, basically, they own. Sometimes common stock does not have the voting privilege.

Community Property. In some states a system exists whereby all earnings of either husband or wife constitute a common fund of the husband and wife. The property is known as *community property*. The central idea of the system is the same in all states where community property exists, but statutes and judicial decisions have directed the development of the system along different lines in the various states. For example, in some states only property that is acquired by the exertion or labor of either party is *common,* whereas in other states income from separate property is also considered community property. Generally, either husband or wife may have "separate" property, such as that belonging to either of them at the time of marriage, real estate acquired in a state that does not recognize community property, or property given to or inherited by either at any time. Property acquired in exchange for separate property is separate property; that acquired for community property is community property. In some states the husband may dispose of, or encumber, the community property, but the wife may not; nor may the community property be attached for the wife's debts, except for those contracted for necessities for herself and her children.

In states having community property laws, a SEPARATION AGREE-MENT should provide for the disposition of community property with sufficient exactness to avoid the implication that the question of division remains unsettled.

In community property states, the prevailing rule at the death of a spouse is that the half belonging to that spouse descends to his or her heirs, except when it has been disposed of by WILL.

To correct the inequalities in tax treatment between residents of community property states and residents of non-community property states, the Federal Government passed statutes allowing joint INCOME TAX returns, and a MARITAL DEDUCTION for the Federal ESTATE TAX and GIFT TAX.

Company Union. An organization of employees that is dominated by the employer. This type of union has been generally opposed by the labor movement because the workers have to be represented by bargaining specialists who are dependent upon the company for their livelihood. Company unions have been initiated by management when it seemed necessary to forestall outside organizing threats. See LABOR UNION.

Competent Parties. Parties who have the legal right to make a CONTRACT.

Complaint. In the practice of law, the name given to the statement of the case of the PLAINTIFF or complaining party. (See PARTIES TO AN ACTION.) It is a formal and methodical specification of the facts and circum-

stances surrounding the cause of action. Known also as the plaintiff's *first pleading* (see PLEADINGS), the *complaint* sets forth in detail the grounds upon which the plaintiff is suing the DEFENDANT, and asks the court for damages or other relief. The first pleading is called the *complaint* in the majority of states; the *petition* or the *declaration* in a few states; still other states distinguish between actions at law and in EQUITY and call the first pleading the *bill of complaint* in an action at law, or *bill in equity* in an equity case.

Regardless of the variance in terminology in the various states, a *complaint* follows a standard pattern, which consists of the following parts:

1. *Caption.* the CAPTION to the complaint designates the court in which the action is brought and lists the full names of all plaintiffs and defendants. It does not show the clerk's index number because that is not available at the time the complaint is prepared. (See CLERK'S INDEX SYSTEM.)

2. *Introduction.* The opening paragraph of the complaint simply states, "The plaintiff, by his attorney, John Jones, complaining of the defendant, alleges as follows:" or words to that effect.

3. *Body.* The body of the complaint states the facts and circumstances that are the basis for the action. The complaint may contain one or more causes of action, each of which is a separate and complete division within itself. These divisions are referred to as *counts* in some jurisdictions. A cause of action, or count, is composed of one or more *allegations.* These are statements that the plaintiff expects to prove. Complaints in certain actions must contain standard allegations, which the

JMH:p 3/30/— 1-2-1

IN THE CIRCUIT COURT OF THE ELEVENTH
JUDICIAL CIRCUIT OF FLORIDA, IN AND
FOR DADE COUNTY. AT LAW.

AUGUSTUS N. ROBERTSON and ELIZABETH
R. ROBERTSON,

                    Plaintiffs,

        -against-   COMPLAINT

JOHNSTON-DOUGLAS MANAGEMENT CORPORA-
TION, a corporation, and FREDERICK
FASHIONS, INC., a corporation.

                    Defendants.

        Plaintiffs by their attorneys, Elwood & Adams,
complaining of the defendants above named, allege:

        FOR A FIRST CAUSE OF ACTION:

        FIRST: That the plaintiffs_____

_____

_____.

        SECOND: Upon information and belief, that _____

_____.

        FOR A SECOND CAUSE OF ACTION:

        THIRD: Plaintiffs repeat, reiterate_____

(Continued on following page)

Complaint: Figure 1.

(Continued from preceding page)

WHEREFORE, plaintiffs demand judgment against defendants for the sum of Five thousand three hundred twenty-five and 36/100 dollars ($5,325.36), with interest thereon from the 20th day of December, 19—, together with the costs and disbursements of this action.

Elwood & Adams
Attorneys for Plaintiffs

Complaint: Figure 1(Continued).

lawyer dictates from memory or from a practice manual. (See FORM BOOKS.) For example, when a domestic corporation is the plaintiff, the allegation will allege the corporate status in a form similar to the following: *That at all times hereinafter mentioned, the plaintiff was and still is a domestic corporation, organized and existing under and by virtue of the laws of the State of* .... When a corporation is the defendant, the allegation is introduced by the words: *Upon information and belief . . . , etc.*

4. *Prayer.* The prayer, also called the WHEREFORE CLAUSE, is the final paragraph of the complaint and "demands" judgment against the defendant for a specified sum, or, in equity actions, "prays" for or seeks other relief to which the plaintiff believes he is entitled. The complaint will also demand interest if the action is for a definite amount of money owed by the defendant, as when the action is on a stated account or a promissory note.

5. *Signature.* Either the plaintiff or his attorney must sign the complaint. The original must be signed manually in every state except New York, where a typed signature is sufficient. In Federal courts, pleadings must be signed by an attorney in his individual name, not in the firm name.

6. *Verification.* The law in the various states specifies which complaints shall be verified, but many lawyers follow the practice of having all complaints verified. The VERIFICATION is signed before a notary public.

Figure 1 above illustrates a *complaint* as the secretary might type it.

Complimentary Close. The final phrase in a letter expressing the regard of the writer for the addressee. The form of close varies with the tone of the letter and degree of acquaintanceship between the lawyer and the client. In the interchange of letters between the lawyer and client, observe how the client closes the letter and be guided by his taste. See also SIGNATURE; ADDRESSING OFFICIALS.

Conciliation. The act of a third party helping two contending parties settle their differences. A conciliator transmits information between the parties as requested and otherwise tries to keep negotiators at their appointed tasks. He is not supposed to evaluate or to express a judgment on the merits of opposing contentions. See ARBITRATION; MEDIATION.

Concurrent Powers. Political powers exercised independently in the same field of legislation by both Federal and state governments. The concurrent power of the states is potentially subordinate to that of the Federal Government; it cannot be exercised unless Congress consents. Congressional consent may be given expressly or it may be implied. An example of concurrent power to regulate commerce is a case which held that where, in the absence of congressional legislation on the matter, a state was permitted to dam a navigable river. The theory used was that the commerce clause did not affect the power of the states where the Federal power was not exercised. See EXCLUSIVE POWERS.

Conditional Sale. An installment sale. The buyer usually gives the seller a promissory note secured by a conditional sale contract or a chattel mortgage. A *conditional sale contract* is a contract for the sale of goods under which the goods are delivered to the buyer but the title remains in the seller until the goods are paid for in full, or until the conditions of the contract are fulfilled. When a chattel mortgage is used, the seller transfers the goods to the buyer who, in turn, executes a chat-

tel mortgage in favor of the seller. This instrument gives the seller a lien on the goods.

The seller's choice of security instrument depends upon the laws in his state. He studies the laws and selects the type of instrument that provides the most protection with the least inconvenience. The instrument usually includes a provision that if an installment is not paid for when due, the entire debt becomes payable at once. This clause, called the ACCELERATION CLAUSE, is essential in any installment contract. Otherwise the seller would have to sue for the amount of each installment as it became due, or would have to wait until the debt matured. See also CONTRACT; RECORDING OF REAL ESTATE INSTRUMENTS.

Condominium. System of separate ownership of individual units in a multiple-unit building.

Condonation. The conditional forgiveness by a husband or wife of a marital indiscretion committed by the other. Condonation is a valid defense in a DIVORCE action based on ADULTERY. COHABITATION with the guilty party, with knowledge that he or she committed adultery, amounts to conclusive evidence of condonation. The cohabitation after knowledge of the adultery must be voluntary and free from duress in order to constitute the defense of condonation.

Conference Calls. Conference telephone service makes it possible for a lawyer to be connected simultaneously with a number of other stations. No special equipment is required. If the lawyer needs to discuss a contract provision, for example, with three other people (or any number up to ten) who are in different cities, by means of a conference call he and the other persons can talk back and forth over long-distance as though they were all grouped around a conference table.

If an executive so desires, he can speak to a gathering of employees in different cities at the same time. He can do this by having the telephone company install loudspeaker equipment, appropriate for the number of listeners. A control dial permits volume adjustment.

The caller asks Long Distance to connect him with the Conference Operator and explains to her the setup desired.

Confession. An acknowledgment of guilt by a person charged with having committed a crime. A judicial confession is made before a judge during a trial or preliminary examination; an extrajudicial confession is an acknowledgment of guilt elsewhere than in court or before a magistrate. See CORROBORATING EVIDENCE.

Confirmation. 1. *Of telegram.* Carbon copy of telegram which is mailed to the addressee of the telegram as corroboration of it.

2. *Of hotel reservation.* Message, by wire or letter, from hotel establishing that a requested reservation has been made. The person in whose name the reservation has been made should have the confirmation with him when he registers at the hotel.

3. *Of airline reservation.* Airline reservations should be confirmed by telephone a few days before the flight.

Conforming Documents. The writing or typing on copies of documents, the signatures, dates, recording data, and notarial data inked or stamped on the original.

In typing the signature, there is no need to type *Signed* in front of the typed copy. In a conformed copy of an executed document bearing an official or corporate seal, CORPORATE SEAL, OFFICIAL SEAL, or NOTARY'S SEAL, as the case may be, is written in brackets at the left of the official or corporate signature. Seals of individuals are indicated by SEAL unless written otherwise on the original.

When a county clerk's certificate is attached to an original document, it is sometimes sufficient to make a notation such as:

> County Clerk's Certificate for........County, State of.........attached to original.

on the conformed copies. But it is sometimes important to attach a copy of the entire certificate to the conformed copies, especially where a certified copy of an original instrument is required. The lawyer instructs the secretary on this point.

Congress of Industrial Organizations (CIO). A LABOR UNION formed in 1938 to encourage and promote organization of workers in the mass production industries. The founders of the CIO broke away from the AMERICAN FEDERATION OF LABOR because of its emphasis on craft union organization. In 1955 the CIO merged with the AFL to form the AFL-CIO.

Congressional Directory. See OFFICIAL CONGRESSIONAL DIRECTORY.

Congressional Record. A daily record of the proceedings of Congress, including a complete history of all legislation. Texts of bills are not included. Indexes give names and subjects of bills and a history of them under their respective numbers. The final index to a volume, covering one session, thus provides references to the complete history of all legislation introduced during that session.

Consequential Damages. DAMAGES resulting, not from taking any part of physical property, but as a consequence of some act in connection with the property. For example, a city may raise the grade of a street without taking any additional land but in such a way that adjoining property is left an objectionable distance below the new street grade. The property owner may be entitled to consequential damages. This is different from SEVERANCE DAMAGE, where a part of an original lot may be taken with damage to the remaining portion.

Conservator. See GUARDIAN and GUARDIANSHIP.

Consideration. The price, motive, or matter inducing a party to make a contract. See CONTRACT, *Consideration.* See also MORTGAGE STATEMENT AND CLAUSES, *Mortgage Consideration.*

Consolidation of Corporations. The unification of two or more corporations into a single new CORPORATION, which acquires the property and assets and assumes the debts and liabilities of those passing out of existence.

In a MERGER, an existing corporation absorbs one or more other cor-

porations and remains in existence, the absorbed corporations being dissolved. The distinction between a consolidation and a merger may be of great importance in such matters as tax liabilities, JURISDICTION of the courts, and special statutory privileges and exemptions. It may also be important to creditors who seek satisfaction of unpaid claims against the constituent companies.

Conspiracy. An agreement between two or more persons to commit a crime. All the conspirators must share the intention to accomplish, by concerted action, the act that they plan. The act which the conspirators agree to do need never be done; the conspiracy itself is a crime. See AIDING AND ABETTING.

Constitution, United States. The written instrument agreed upon by the people of the Union as the absolute rule of action and decision for all departments and officers of the government in respect to all the points covered by it. The Constitution has become adapted to modern times through amendment, custom, statute, and judicial interpretation. See AMENDMENT OF THE CONSTITUTION; BILL OF RIGHTS.

Constructive. In a legal sense, the term "constructive" generally applies to that which amounts in the eyes of the law to an act, although the act itself is not necessarily performed. The law presumes an act to have been performed, and applies the term to many situations to prevent a miscarriage of justice. For example, the holder of a warehouse receipt has *constructive possession* of the goods represented by the receipt, although he does not have actual personal occupancy or possession of the property.

Some of the circumstances under which the law will presume an act are indicated by the following: constructive abandonment, constructive delivery, constructive desertion, constructive eviction, constructive fraud, constructive gift, constructive notice, constructive possession, constructive process, constructive receipt of income, constructive service, and constructive trusts. A few of these are explained.

Constructive delivery. Arises when actual, or manual, delivery is impossible or undesirable. Constructive delivery includes those acts that are equivalent to actual delivery although they do not confer real possession. Acts that bar a lien or a right to stoppage in transit, such as marking and setting apart goods as belonging to the buyer, constitute constructive delivery.

Constructive notice. Notice that arises from a strictly legal presumption that cannot be controverted. The presumption is one of law and not of fact, as distinguished from implied notice that arises from an inference of facts. The presumption of constructive notice is conclusive against the actual facts. Thus, a mortgage recorded with the proper public authorities is constructive notice of the mortgagee's interest in the property.

Constructive receipt. Constructive receipt of income usually constitutes taxable income under the various tax laws. For example, any time during the year commissions may be credited on a firm's books to a salesman who may draw upon the firm to the amount of the credit. The commission is said to be constructively received. Whatever amount is credited to the salesman would have to be reported by him as income in the year the amount was credited on the books, even if the money was not drawn until the following year.

Constructive Notice. See CONSTRUCTIVE.

Contacts over the Telephone. Telephone contacts are of paramount importance in a law office. The secretary must know how to answer and make calls smoothly, how to talk into the instrument, and how to take messages for the lawyer, as well as what to say.

Placing calls for the lawyer. The correct practice to follow when placing calls for the lawyer has developed from expediency. When the secretary places the call, it is her privilege to get the person called on the wire before connecting her employer. Assume that she is calling Mr. Wilson for the lawyer, Mr. Rogers. When she gets Mr. Wilson's secretary on the wire, she says, "Is Mr. Wilson there, for Mr. Rogers?" Then Mr. Wilson's secretary will put her employer on and trust to the caller's good judgment and care to see that Mr. Rogers comes on the line promptly. (When *she* calls, the courtesy is reciprocated.) When Mr. Wilson comes on the line, say to him, "Here is Mr. Rogers, Mr. Wilson," and establish the connection between the two men at once.

The secretary must be extremely careful not to keep the person called waiting for the lawyer to take the call. On the other hand, it is her job to see that he does not hold the phone needlessly. When calling a person whose secretary is cooperative and dependable, there is no difficulty because the employers can be connected simultaneously.

There is an exception to this

procedure. If the secretary calls a close friend or a person to whom deference is due by the lawyer, she should connect him as soon as the secretary is reached at the other end of the line. She should tell the lawyer that the person he is calling will be on the line immediately and let him receive the call direct. Some secretaries follow this procedure at all times. However, the practice described above is preferred because the person making the call is alert to take it and, therefore, time for both the caller and the person called is saved in the long run.

Answering calls for the lawyer. If a secretary calls and says that her employer wants to speak with a certain lawyer in the office, ask her to wait a moment and announce the call to the lawyer. Say to the secretary, "One moment, please," and tell the lawyer that "Mr. Wilson of ABC is calling." The lawyer will then pick up the phone and

wait until Mr. Wilson is connected with him. Or perhaps the other secretary has learned that the secretary she is speaking to is cooperative and she puts Mr. Wilson on the line simultaneously.

Making notes of incoming calls. It is important that the lawyer be informed of every call that comes in for him, whether the caller leaves a message or not. Do not depend upon memory for this, but make a note immediately. If the office does not have printed forms for this purpose, it might be suggested that some be ordered. They are not expensive and are convenient, easy-to-read, and neat. Figures 1 and 2 illustrate useful forms. Keep a pad of the form on the desk—and on the desk of everybody in the office who takes telephone messages.

An irate client calls. Occasionally a client who is annoyed about something telephones while the lawyer is out. It is usually advisable to avoid making ex-

---

C & S

....19 ......

TELEPHONE MESSAGE for Mr...

Mr...called at.................o'clock

He was told that you were:

He said (left):

out...☐

no message.................................:☐

not in to-day.................................☐

he will call again.........................☐

not in your room...........................☐

he is answering your call ☐

talking on telephone.......☐

please call him..............................☐

out of town.....................................☐

please see him...............................☐

to call him back.............................☐

it is urgent.....................................☐

His telephone number is...

Additional remarks:...

....

....

....

Contacts over the Telephone: Figure 1. Telephone message memo.

planations to him. The secretary should simply tell him that she will ask the lawyer to call as soon as he returns—and make sure that she tells the lawyer about his call. No matter how good a secretary is, how tactful and diplomatic, some things must be handled by the lawyer, and annoyed clients belong at the top of the list.

Client or prospective client asks what

a fee will be. Many clients and prospective clients try to find out over the telephone what the lawyer will charge for certain services. A lawyer's secretary should *never* quote fees; that is for the lawyer to do. As a matter of fact, the lawyer himself does not like to quote fees until he is thoroughly familiar with the amount of work involved. For example, the fee for draw-

---

Form No. 30

Telephone Call Memo

Date_____.

Place this slip under telephone instrument on desk of

Mr._____

_____

Mr._____

Tel. No._____

Called you at_____M.

Message:

Refused Name

No Message

Please Call

Will Call

Please See

_____

Telephone operators are expected to report on this form **every** call which does not reach the person called, regardless of instructions from the person calling. If no message, so state.

Contacts over the Telephone: Figure 2. Telephone message memo—another form.

ing a simple WILL is not as much as the fee for drawing a will that involves a TRUST. When a client asks the secretary what a fee will be, she should offer to make an appointment for him with the lawyer. If he does not want an appointment, she should offer to have the lawyer call him.

Telephone conversation. If the secretary has to make a telephone call for the lawyer, she should plan her conversation before placing the call. Know the facts. Know the points to cover. If necessary, have an accessible outline of them while talking. Have all records and other material available. This is particularly important on out-of-town calls.

The secretary should identify herself immediately to the person to whom she is speaking, thus, "This is Miss Smith, Mr. Roger's secretary," or, "This is Miss Smith of the firm of Rogers and Williams." It is neither necessary nor desirable to give a first name.

Keep the telephone conversation brief but not to the point of curtness. Take time to address people by their names and title and to use expressions of consideration, like "Thank you," "I am sorry," and "I beg your pardon." See also TELEPHONE SERVICE; SCREENING CALLS; TOLL CALLS; TELEPHONE COURTESY.

Contempt of Court. Any act which is meant to embarrass the court or lessen its authority and dignity. Contempt of court committed in the presence of the court, and which interrupts its proceedings, may be punished immediately by order of the presiding JUDGE. Constructive contempts are those that arise from a refusal to comply with an order of the court. The punishment for contempt of court is a fine or imprisonment.

Contingent Fee. A charge for services to a client based on an agreement that the fee will be dependent on the lawyer's successful handling of the case. Contingent fees are customary in personal injury cases, especially if the client is unable to pay for the lawyer's time except out of the damages he might recover. The lawyer usually agrees to take a case for a client for a percentage of the amount recovered.

Continuation Sheets. Stationery used for second, third, etc. pages of a letter. Continuation sheets, loosely called "second sheets," should be the same size and quality of paper as the letterheads. Since comparatively few letters are more than one page, continuation sheets should be ordered in considerably smaller quantities than letterheads. The name of the addressee, the number of the page, and the date should be typed across the top of each page of a letter other than the first.

Law firms generally have continuation sheets with the firm name, but no address, engraved on them for use when a letter runs more than one page. If the office does not have engraved continuation sheets, the secretary should use a plain sheet of the same size and quality as the letterhead. Type enough descriptive matter at the top of succeeding pages to make them recognizable if they should become separated from the first page. The name of the addressee, the number of the page, and the date should be sufficient.

Contract. An agreement, between two or more parties whereby each promises to do or refrain from doing some act. A contract may be oral or in writing, sealed or unsealed, except that state statutes, designated as the STATUTE OF FRAUDS, require certain agreements to be in writing. A contract may be *express* or *implied*. An *express contract* is one in which the terms are set forth by the parties involved, either orally or in writing. An *implied contract* is a contract implied by law. For example, when a person sits down in a restaurant and orders a meal, it is implied that he will pay for it, although there is no express promise to that effect.

If a contract has been fully performed by all the parties to it, it is referred to as an *executed contract*. Sometimes a contract is *executed* on the part of one party and *executory* on the part of the other. For example, when a merchant delivers a television set to a customer who has purchased it on credit, the merchant's contract is executed. He has completed his part of the agreement. On the other hand, the customer's contract is executory, until such time as the final payment on the television set is made.

To be enforceable at law, a contract must have the following elements:

1. *Offer and acceptance.* Before a contract can be formed, there must be an offer by one party, called the offeror, to do or to refrain from doing a certain thing, and an acceptance of the proposal by another party, called the offeree.

An offer is considered open until it is revoked, rejected, or accepted, or until after the lapse of a reasonable time. The only case in which an offeror cannot withdraw an offer before acceptance is the case in which he has entered into an OPTION contract, which is an agreement supported by the payment of a sum of money, or for some other consideration, to hold an offer open for a definite period of time.

An acceptance is an indication by the offeree of his willingness to be bound by the terms of the offer. The acceptance may take the form of an act, the signing and delivery of a written instrument, or of a promise communicated to the offeror. Silence on the part of the offeree is not an acceptance unless the previous dealings between the parties create a duty upon the part of the offeree to accept or reject the offer. The acceptance must be unequivocal and must show an intention to accept all the terms of the offer. In the language frequently used by the courts, there must be a "meeting of the minds" of the offeror and the offeree.

2. *Competent parties.* All persons are presumed to have unlimited power to contract—except infants, insane persons, intoxicated persons, and corporations.

Legally, a person is in his infancy until he reaches the age of twenty-one, although some states provide that women become of age at eighteen and other states, that marriage removes the infancy status. Contracts by infants are not void, but generally they may be disaffirmed by the infant. An infant is not bound by an executory contract unless he affirms the contract after coming of age; failure to affirm implies disaffirmance. An infant may disaffirm an executed contract during infancy or within a reasonable time after he attains his majority; failure to disaffirm within a reasonable time implies affirmance. Contracts for necessities, such as food, clothing, shelter, medical care, education, and the like, may be binding upon an infant.

Like infants, insane persons are not absolutely incapable of making contracts; their contracts are voidable, not void, and they may be held liable for necessities. A person who is so drunk that he is deprived of his reason and does not understand the nature of his acts is in the same position as a mental incompetent; he may disaffirm his contracts if the disaffirmance does not injure third persons, and provided he disaffirms immediately upon restoration of his faculties.

Under the COMMON LAW a married woman has few contractual powers, but the statutes in most states have modified the common law. In

THIS AGREEMENT, entered into on the ___ day of
_____, 19—, by and between _____ CORPORATION,
a corporation organized and existing under and by virtue of
the laws of the State of _____, and having its office
at _____, _____, hereinafter referred to as
"_____," and THE _____ COMPANY, a corporation organized and existing under and by virtue of the laws of the
State of _____, and having its office at _____,
_____, hereinafter referred to as "_____,"

W I T N E S S E T H :

WHEREAS _____
_____; and
WHEREAS _____
_____
_____.
NOW, THEREFORE, in consideration of the premises
_____
_____,

IT IS AGREED:

1. _____
_____

Contract: Figure 1.   Agreement between two corporations with seals attested.

2. _____

_____.

     IN WITNESS WHEREOF the parties hereto have on the day and year first above written caused these presents to be executed in their behalf and in their corporate names respectively by their proper officers hereunto duly authorized and their respective corporate seals to be hereto attached by like authority.

(Corporate Seal)

               _____CORPORATION

ATTEST:

By _____
                President

_____·Secretary

THE _____COMPANY

(Corporate Seal)

By _____
              Vice President

ATTEST:

_____Secretary

Contract: Figure 1. Agreement between two corporations with seals attested *(Continued).*

general, a married woman may now contract as freely as a single woman, but in some states she cannot contract with her husband, enter into partnership with him, or act as surety for him.

A corporation's ability to contract is limited by its charter and by various statutes.

3. *Legality of subject matter.* A contract is illegal if it calls for the performance of an act forbidden by law or against public policy. Gambling and wagering contracts and usurious contracts (see USURY), for example, are generally held to be illegal. In some states any contract entered into on Sunday is illegal. Federal and state

laws make illegal those contracts that restrain trade, fix prices, or result in unfair practices.

4. *Consideration.* Something of benefit to the person making a promise must be given, or some detriment must be suffered by the person to whom a promise is made to make a contract binding. *Consideration* is the price, motive, or matter inducing the contract; it may consist of (a) doing some act that one is not obligated to perform; (b) refraining from doing something that one would otherwise be free to do; (c) giving some money or property; (d) giving a promise. The value of the consideration is generally immaterial.

5. *Contracts under seal.* The placing of a SEAL on a contract has lost the significance formerly attached to it, but it is still customary, and required in some states, to place a seal on contracts of major importance. Deeds, mortgages, and other conveyances of real estate are among the contracts requiring a seal.

Figure 1 on pages 134-135 illustrates an agreement between two corporations. See also DEFAULT.

The above contracts are usually bilateral contracts.

Unilateral contracts. A unilateral contract is one in which one party makes an express engagement or undertakes a performance, without receiving in return any express engagement or promise or performance from the other. For example, an offer of a reward would be a unilateral contract. There is an offer but no specific acceptance.

Rescission of Contract. To rescind a contract means to abrogate, annul, void, or cancel a contract; particularly, nullifying a contract by the act of a party to it.

Contract of Sale. (Real estate) A formal CONTRACT entered into between a seller (known as VENDOR) and a buyer (known as VENDEE) of REAL PROPERTY, setting forth in full all the terms of the agreement between them for the conveyance of title within a specified time. The contract of sale sets in motion the various investigations as to title and encumbrances, arrangements for financing, and preparation of instruments to be signed upon CLOSING TITLE. It is important that the contract of sale be prepared carefully to include all the terms of the agreement between buyer and seller and to state them clearly, for if any dispute should arise, the courts will not admit any oral testimony in variance of the written contract.

How to prepare a contract of sale. Each locality has a contract of sale form approved by the local real estate board. Printed forms of the contracts are available from stationery stores and, also, from abstract and title companies. (See ABSTRACT COMPANY.) The forms are easy to complete and require little explanation. The lawyer will provide a memorandum of the information necessary to complete the form.

Four copies should be made— original and duplicate original for the seller and buyer, a copy for the broker, and a copy for the lawyer's file. Both the seller and the buyer sign the contract and, usually, the seller's wife. Generally an acknowledgment is not necessary, because ordinarily the contract is not recorded. If the form has an ACKNOWLEDGMENT printed on it, it should be completed. The form will also indicate whether it should be witnessed.

Checklist of information necessary to fill in form.

1. Date of contract
2. Name and residence of seller
3. Name of seller's spouse if spouse must join in deed that is to be delivered
4. Name and residence of the buyer
5. Description of property to be conveyed (See LAND DESCRIPTION)
6. Purchase price, the exact amount being named
7. Amount to be paid when contract is signed (EARNEST MONEY)
8. Amount to be paid at closing, when DEED is delivered
9. Whether existing mortgage, if any, is to be assumed or property purchased subject to it
10. How balance is paid, and when
11. Name of trustee in those states where a deed of trust is the security instrument
12. Unpaid taxes and assessments
13. Fire insurance data
14. Name of broker
15. Closing date
16. How long offer is open
17. Evidence of title. Whether abstract of title, title insurance or certificate of title.
18. Possession date.

Contributory Negligence. Lack of care by the person suing in a NEGLIGENCE action, which, concurring with the defendant's negligence, was a PROXIMATE CAUSE of his injury. Most courts hold that if the complaining party in any way negligently contributes to his own injury, he may not collect DAMAGES. See also LAST CLEAR CHANCE.

Conventional Mortgage. See FORMS OF MORTGAGES, MORTGAGE.

Conversion. The unlawful taking or possession of the CHATTEL of another. When, for example, title to the goods has passed on a sale, but the seller has refused to deliver the goods to the buyer, the buyer may sue for conversion. Conversion may also take the form of an unauthorized destruction or alteration of another's property.

Copy. Manuscript to be sent to the printer and set in type. The MANUSCRIPT becomes "copy" after the copy editor has prepared the manuscript for the printer by marking it for type and attending to other numerous details necessary for the production of the manuscript. (See CHECKING MANUSCRIPT.)

Copyholder. A stand-like device, usually made of metal, that holds material to be copied in a semi-upright position, so that the typist may read and follow the material with ease. The copy holder has an adjustable line-spacing attachment that decreases the possibility of skipping or repeating lines when the secretary is doing copy work. The attachment is operated by depressing a lever with the right little finger. This movement soon becomes as automatic as depressing the space bar on a typewriter. Some copyholders may be placed back of the typewriter, so that the paper is in front of the secretary as she works. This eliminates the strained position necessary when copying from material which is placed flat on the side of the desk. There are copyholders on the market that accommodate magazines, directories and even thick law books in addition to single sheets.

Copyright. A protection granted by national governments through statutory enactment covering the production, publication, and sale of the content and form of literary and artistic work, and advertisements.

When a person creates a book, song, or picture, he has a COMMON LAW right to the exclusive ownership of his creation. He need not publish his work and may prevent others from doing so. Once he does publish, however, the common law right is lost. Upon publication he must obtain a *statutory copyright* in place of the common law right or he loses his right in the published work forever.

In order to obtain a statutory copyright, a sufficient inscription or notice of claim must be on the published work. Promptly after publication, 2 copies of the published work must be filed in the Copyright Office, accompanied by application for copyright and statutory fee.

In 1976, the old copyright law was changed drastically. The old law provided for copyrights to be granted for a term of 28 years, renewable for an additional period of 28 years.

Under the new law passed in 1976, copyrights are now granted for a period of 50 years after the author's death. This will permit heirs to collect royalties for a period of 50 years after the author's death.

A copyright may be assigned, given away, or mortgaged by an instrument in writing signed by the owner of the copyright, or may be bequeathed by WILL. The ASSIGNMENT should be recorded by the assignee in the Copyright Office within three months after its execution in order to protect his rights if there is any subsequent as-signment or mortgage by the original owner.

Corporate Mortgage Bond. A written promise, under seal, to pay a specific sum of money at a fixed time in the future, usually more than ten years after the promise is made. It is generally one of a series of similar bonds, all of which usually carry interest at a fixed rate, covered by a TRUST DEED or MORTGAGE in which the corporation's property is mortgaged to the trustee for the benefit of the bondholders. These bonds are evidence of indebtedness on the part of the borrower to the lender; the lenders, however, may not enforce the mortgage covenants directly as in the case of individually owned mortgages, but must have the trustee act in their behalf to enforce mortgage convenants or to carry out FORECLOSURE. See also BOND ISSUE; DEED OF TRUST.

Corporate Seal. An engraved symbol used by a corporation to make an impression upon its business papers. The seal usually recites the name of the corporation and the year and state of incorporation. The BYLAWS of a corporation usually provide that any instrument signed on behalf of the corporation shall be impressed with the corporate seal. An officer of the corporation impresses the seal on the instrument at the time it is signed. In many cases the corporate secretary must bear witness or *attest* to the fact that the imprint on the paper is the seal of the corporation. See AT-TESTATION.) When the document recites that the seal is to be attested, the following is typed on the left-hand side of the page, opposite the signature lines:

ATTEST

. . . .
Secretary

Corporation. A collection of persons who act together in order to accomplish some monetary, ideal, or governmental purpose. A corporation is a legal entity separate and apart from the persons who are interested in and control it. The state authorizes its existence and gives it certain powers. It also has certain powers that it gives itself, within the limits prescribed by the state, when it goes through the formalities of organization. A corporation has fundamental characteristics that make it the most popular form of business organization. Probably the most favorable aspect of the corporate form is the assurance of limited liability to the persons who put capital into the business.

Corporations may be classified as public corporations, corporations not for profit, and corporations for profit, each class being organized under different statutes.

Public Corporations include all the subdivisions of the state, such as cities, tax districts, and irrigation districts. They also include Government-owned corporations, such as the Commodity Credit Corporation.

Corporations not for profit are those organized for purposes other than the pecuniary gain of their members. Nonprofit corporations do not have CAPITAL STOCK or pay a DIVI-DEND. Those who are interested in and control the corporation are referred to as its members, rather than its stockholders or shareholders as in a corporation for profit. These corporations include religious, civil, social, educational, fraternal, charitable, and cemetery associations.

Corporations for profit, or *business corporations,* are corporations with capital stock that carry on an enterprise for profit. Business corporations fall into three groups: (1) banks and insurance companies, which are known as *moneyed corporations;* (2) corporations that furnish public utility services to the public, such as transportation and electricity, which are known as *public service corporations;* and (3) corporations engaged in ordinary business pursuits, such as manufacturing, which are known as *private corporations.* The first two classes are subject to stricter governmental control than the private corporation.

The organization procedure herein described relates to a private business corporation, but it is adaptable to other corporations.

Incorporating procedure. To organize a corporation means to bring it into existence. Each state designates a specific department and official through which the lawyer must work. Certain steps are necessary. These involve routine procedure that the secretary can follow at the lawyer's direction without detailed instruction.

The usual steps in the organization of a corporation are:

1. RESERVATION OF CORPORATE NAME

2. Preparation of incorporating papers
3. Execution of papers
4. Filing of papers
5. First meeting of INCOR-PORATORS
6. First meeting of directors (see BOARD OF DIRECTORS).

See also CERTIFICATE OF INCORPORATION; STATE OF INCORPORATION; DE JURE CORPORATION; DE FACTO CORPORATION; SUBSIDIARY CORPORATION; CLOSE (OR CLOSED) CORPORATION.

Corpus Juris Secundum System. A complete statement of the body of American law in encyclopedic form. The Corpus Juris Secundum and Corpus Juris are broken down into approximately 430 titles. The text of Corpus Juris Secundum supersedes the corresponding text of Corpus Juris. Each title of the Secundum brings down to date the same title in Corpus Juris. The authorities cited in the notes in the Secundum are the cases decided since that title in Corpus Juris was written. If there are earlier cases on the point, footnote references in Corpus Juris Secundum direct the searcher to the precise page and note in Corpus Juris where they will be found. The absence of a footnote reference to Corpus Juris is conclusive evidence that there are no earlier cases. Thus, although the text of Corpus Juris is superseded by Corpus Juris Secundum, Corpus Juris remains a vital part of the law library because of the footnotes.

The titles embraced by the system are alphabetically arranged. Judicially defined words, phrases, and maxims are alphabetically interspersed through the titles. The backbone of each volume shows the first and last words in that volume and also the volume number. Volume 72 of Corpus Juris is a complete DESCRIPTIVE WORD INDEX to all volumes of Corpus Juris. Each volume of the Secundum has an index to the titles contained in that volume.

How to use Corpus Juris Secundum System. There are three methods of finding the discussion and supporting authorities in the Corpus Juris Secundum System.

1. *The fact, or descriptive, word index.* Find the descriptive word in the index to the title in the back of the volume. For example, if looking for the extent of an implied agency, the title would be *Agency*. In the index "Implied agency" shows the section and page number where implied agency is discussed. At the head of the section is an analysis of points covered in the section, which enables the search to be narrowed.

Each volume of Corpus Juris does not contain an index. If the pertinent title has not been published in the Secundum, look for the descriptive word in Volume 72, "Descriptive-word Index and Concordance," of Corpus Juris.

2. *The general analysis preceding each title.* At the beginning of each title is an analysis, or breakdown, of the contents of the title. The topics are in boldface capitals and are numbered with roman numerals. Each of the topics has a subanalysis. Judge which topic should cover the point and then look at the subanalysis for the specific point. "III Creation and Extent of Relation" should cover implied agency. In the subanalysis of that topic will be found, "§24. Implied Agency— p. 1045."

If it cannot be determined which topic should cover the problem, look at each of the subtopics, but this, of course, is a slower method of research.

3. *Words and phrases alphabetically arranged throughout the set.* If an important word or words in the problem can be picked out, refer to those words in CJS and find cross-references to related topics in which the words have meaning or importance.

How to cite. Cite by volume number, title, and page and section number.

57 C.J., Set-Off and Counterclaim, p.476, § 22

24 C.J.S., Criminal Law, p. 147, § 1606

Corroborating Evidence. Evidence supplementary to that already given and tending to strengthen and confirm it. Under certain circumstances the testimony of a witness, even though uncontradicted, is not sufficient to establish the truth of a certain fact unless his testimony is corroborated. Examples of this are the provision in the Federal Constitution (see CONSTITUTION, UNITED STATES) that the crime of TREASON can be proved only by the testimony of two witnesses to the same overt act, and the statute found in about half the states that an accused cannot be convicted by the uncorroborated testimony of an ACCOMPLICE.

Counterclaim. A cause of action set up by a DEFENDANT, to be tried at the same time as an original cause of action alleged by a plaintiff. The defendant takes advantage of the suit against him to ask the court for relief against the plaintiff, when otherwise he would be compelled to institute an action of his own. For example, the maker of a note might claim that the payee is indebted to him for certain sums in connection with a matter not related to the note.

Counterfeiting. See FORGERY AND COUNTERFEITING.

County Court. See COURTS OF SPECIAL JURISDICTION.

Court. In the legal sense *court* relates to the law in these commonly used senses:

1. *Court* refers to the *persons* assembled under authority of law, at a designated place, for the administration of justice. These persons are the JUDGE or judges, clerk, marshal, bailiff, reporter, jurors, and attorneys, and they constitute a body of the government. Thus, the lawyer's secretary says that her employer "is in court this morning," meaning that he is appearing before this duly assembled body in the interest of a client. It is not necessary that all of these persons be present to constitute a court—court is frequently held without a jury.

2. The word refers to the authorized *assembly* of the persons who make up the court. Thus, we say, "Court will be held . . ." meaning that the judge, clerk, attorneys, etc. will gather together to administer justice. Or we say, "Judge Smith's court . . . ," meaning the clerk, attorneys, jurors, etc. over which Judge Smith presides.

3. *Court* refers to the judge or judges themselves, as distinguished from the counsel or jury. Thus, we have the expression, "In the opinion of the Court . . . ," "May it please the Court, . . . ," "The Court stated. . . ." In this sense, the word is written with a capital, because it is personified when it stands for the judge.

4. The word *court* is used occasionally to refer to the chamber, hall, or place where court is being held. Thus, a spectator is present "at court," in the courtroom, but the defendant is

"in court" because he is part of the assembly.

5. The name of a specific court always includes the word *court,* which is capitalized; for example, Probate Court, Essex County. Neither probate nor court is capitalized if reference is made to probate courts generally; for example, "Petitions for letters of administration are filed in probate courts."

Court Bond. Litigants at law are required many times to file a bond or other security guaranteeing that, if unsuccessful in litigation, they will pay to the other party the monetary DAMAGES awarded by the court. These bonds are known as *court* or *judiciary* bonds. Another class of court bonds is known as *probate bonds.* They are issued to executors, administrators, and other fiduciaries to guarantee the faithful performance of their legal duties.

Court of Appeal. See APPELLATE COURT.

Court of Last Resort. The final tribunal in the APPELLATE COURT structure to which a case may be taken for APPEAL. Each state has its highest court; the court of last resort in the Federal judiciary system is the SUPREME COURT OF THE UNITED STATES.

Court Packing. An approach to changing the complexion of the Supreme Court championed by President Franklin D. Roosevelt in his message to Congress in February, 1937. He proposed an enlargment of the Supreme Court through the appointment of new younger appointees to match members of the Court who had

reached a specified age limit. The President's plan created much opposition and was not adopted by Congress.

Court Procedure. The method by which the COURT operates. All court proceedings are conducted for and on behalf of the litigants (see PARTIES TO AN ACTION) by attorneys at law. It is permissible for a party to a law suit to represent himself in court, but a layman seldom has the required technical knowledge. Court actions consist of a series of written statements of the claims and defenses of the parties to a court action. These written statements are known professionally as PLEADINGS.

Court Register. See CLERK'S PERMANENT RECORD BOOK.

Courts of Intermediate Review. Courts that are established to relieve congestion in a state's highest APPELLATE COURT. See Table II, AMERICAN COURT SYSTEM. These courts exercise appellate jurisdiction only, except that in some states they have original jurisdiction to issue writs of MANDAMUS, CERTIORARI, HABEAS CORPUS, and the like. They have jurisdiction of matters of appeal from the final judgments, orders, or decrees of superior courts (see DECREE), usually in both law and chancery matters. (See CHANCERY COURT.) The appellate jurisdiction of intermediate courts is frequently restricted. For example, the Georgia Court of Appeals, which is a court of intermediate review, does not have jurisdiction over appeals involving the Constitution of Georgia or of the United States. The appellate courts of Illinois do not have jurisdiction over criminal appeals other than misdemeanors. In New Jersey and New York, divisions of the superior court (New York's equivalent of superior courts is called Supreme Court) exercise intermediate jurisdiction. See also the AMERICAN COURT SYSTEM; APPELLATE COURT; SUPERIOR COURT; INFERIOR COURT; COURTS OF SPECIAL JURISDICTION.

Courts of Record. Judicial organized tribunals where acts and proceedings are permanently enrolled. Courts of record may be Federal or State. For a listing of Federal and State courts of records in the United States, see AMERICAN COURT SYSTEM.

Courts of Special Jurisdiction. Tribunals of ORIGINAL JURISDICTION to administer justice in certain restricted matters. Some states have courts of special jurisdiction in some fields; other states, in other fields. The most common courts of special jurisdiction are probate courts, criminal courts, chancery courts, juvenile courts, county courts, and municipal courts in large cities.

Probate courts, sometimes called Surrogate Courts, have jurisdiction over the probate of wills, administration of a decedent's estate, and guardianship of minors and insane people.

Criminal courts have jurisdiction over criminal cases. Criminal trial courts may be called *oyer & terminer* (hear and determine).

Chancery courts have original jurisdiction over criminal cases. See CHANCERY COURT.

Juvenile courts usually have exclusive original jurisdiction over all neglected, dependent, or delinquent children under eighteen.

County courts have widely diverse jurisdictions in the different states. For example, in Alabama they are courts of criminal jurisdiction; in Colorado, they have jurisdiction over probate matters, over delinquent children in some counties, and in civil actions if the amount involved is not over $2,000; in Mississippi, they have concurrent jurisdiction with circuit and chancery courts if the amount involved does not exceed $2,000.

Municipal courts in large cities are frequently courts of record and have concurrent jurisdiction with superior courts, if the amount involved does not exceed a stated sum, usually $3,000. See also INFERIOR COURTS; SUPERIOR COURTS; the SUPREME APPELLATE COURTS; the APPELLATE COURT; AMERICAN COURT SYSTEM.

Covenant Against Encumbrances. See COVENANTS OF TITLE.

Covenants of Quiet Enjoyment. See COVENANTS OF TITLE.

Covenant of Seizin. See COVENANTS OF TITLE.

Covenants. Agreements of legal validity between two or more persons to do or to refrain from doing some act, or that a given state of facts exists or does not exist. Covenants may arise by implication of law or from the conduct of the parties and may be divided into two classes: (1) personal covenants, and (2) covenants running with the land, known as restrictive covenants. See COVENANT OF TITLE.

Covenants in Deeds. Promises made by the GRANTOR and GRANTEE in the sale of REAL PROPERTY. The usual covenants by the grantor, which are printed in the deed, relate to the TITLE to the property and to its quiet and peaceful enjoyment by the grantee. The grantor might make special promises not included in the usual printed form, such as agreeing to construct and maintain roadways. Covenants by the grantee are less common than covenants by the grantor. The most frequent use of covenants by the grantee is in connection with the sale of lots in subdivisions; they usually relate to the type of structure that may be erected on the premises. These covenants are not included in the usual printed form of deed, but special deeds that contain them are usually printed for the sale of lots in a specific subdivision.

Example of covenant by grantee:

And the said grantee does hereby for himself, his heirs and assigns, covenant with the said grantor, his heirs, executors, and administrators, that he will not, at any time hereafter, erect, or cause, or suffer, or permit, to be erected upon the hereby granted premises, or any part thereof, any building other than a brick or stone private dwelling house, not less than three stories in height.

See also COVENANTS OF TITLE.

Covenants of Title. Guarantees or assurances by the GRANTOR contained in a WARRANTY DEED that the DEED conveys a good and unencumbered TITLE. These guarantees differ in scope in various localities, but generally the covenants guarantee the following:

1. *Covenant of Seizin.* That the grantor is seized of the property in FEE SIMPLE and has good right to convey. If the grantor owns only part of the title conveyed, or if he has only a LIFE ESTATE, he has violated the covenant of SEIZIN and is liable to the GRANTEE for DAMAGES caused by such violation.

2. *Covenant of Quiet Enjoyment.* That the grantee shall quietly enjoy the premises. The purpose of this warranty is to make certain that the possession of the grantee after he takes title will not be disturbed by anyone having a better title or LIEN.

3. *Covenant Against Encumbrances.* That the premises are free from encumbrances, other than those mentioned in the deed. Such encumbrances may include a MORTGAGE, tax lien, judgment lien, restriction on the use of the land. Even if the grantee knew of the ENCUMBRANCE, the grantor is liable if any encumbrance not indicated in the deed exists.

4. *Covenant of Further Assurance.* That the grantor will execute or procure any further necessary assurance of title. Additional instruments needed to confirm title to the premises are usually executed at the purchaser's expense. Requests for further assurance must, of course, be reasonable.

5. *Covenant of Warranty.* That the grantor will forever warrant the title to the premises conveyed. This imposes a personal obligation upon the seller to defend the title of the purchaser and, in effect, includes the covenant of quiet enjoyment and the covenant of further assurance.

Craft Union. See LABOR UNION.

Credibility. That quality in a witness which makes his evidence worthy of belief. Whether a witness' testimony is to be accepted as true is normally a question for the jury to decide.

Credible, credulous, creditable. *Credible* means believable *credulous* means easily imposed upon, believing too easily; *creditable* means praiseworthy.

He is not a *credible* witness.

The readers are indeed *credulous* if they believe the editorial completely.

His summation of the case was *creditable*.

Crime. An act that a government regards as injurious to the public. One charged in court with the commission of a crime is prosecuted by the state or Federal government, depending on whether the act violates a state or Federal criminal statute. In the United States the law of crimes is covered solely by statute. A TORT, on the other hand, is an infringement on the rights of an individual rather than the community as a whole and is prosecuted by the injured party. See also FELONY; MISDEMEANOR.

Criminal Court. A government tribunal empowered to administer justice in connection with public wrongs, that is, crimes of *treason, felony,* or *misdemeanor.* Criminal trial courts may be called *oyer & terminer* (hear and determine). See CRIMINAL LAW; CIVIL COURT.

Criminal Law. The statutes and general dicta that forbid certain actions or conduct as detrimental to the welfare of the state and that provide punishment therefor. Criminal acts are prosecuted by the state, whereas civil wrongs (see CIVIL LAW), are prosecuted by a private individual. A wrong may be both a criminal wrong and a civil wrong; for example, ASSAULT AND BATTERY. A crime may be a *treason,* a *felony,* or a *misdemeanor.* The Constitution of the United States states that treason "shall consist only in levying war against them or in adhering to their enemies, giving them aid and comfort." Felonies

are crimes punishable by death or by imprisonment in a Federal or state prison. They include murder, GRAND LARCENY, ARSON, and RAPE. Misdemeanors are crimes of lesser importance than felonies and are punishable by a fine or imprisonment in the local jail. They include petty larceny, drunkenness, disorderly conduct, and vagrancy. Violation of traffic ordinances, building codes, and similar city ordinances are not crimes but are termed "petty offenses," "public torts," or *mala prohibita.* See TORT; CRIMINAL COURT; CIVIL LAW.

Cross-examination. The interrogation of an adverse witness after he has testified on DIRECT EXAMINATION for the party who called him. Cross-examination of unfriendly witnesses is a matter of right in every trial of a disputed issue of fact and is recognized as the best means of discovering truth.

Cruelty. A ground for DIVORCE and SEPARATION in many states. If one is claiming physical cruelty it is wise to produce medical testimony and, if possible, photographs of bruises and lacerations.

Mental cruelty is more difficult to prove because the insults made by husband and wife are often in private and rarely result in sufficient proof. The classic example of successfully proving mental cruelty is evidence of the subjection of the innocent spouse to ridicule, humiliation, and scorn in the presence of friends, relatives, or members of the community.

Cul de Sac. (French for the bottom of a sack): a blind alley; a street which is open at one end only.

145

Cumulative Preferred Stock. A class of PREFERRED STOCK, which, if dividends are not paid in any given year or DIVIDEND period, entitles the owner to the arrearage in subsequent years. Ordinarily, if the CERTIFICATE OF INCORPORATION does not specify whether the stock is to be cumulative or not, the law will hold the preferred stock to be cumulative. See NON-CUMULATIVE PREFERRED STOCK.

Cumulative Voting. A system of voting for directors of a CORPORATION under which each stockholder is entitled to a number of votes equal to the number of shares he owns multiplied by the number of directors to be elected. He may cast all the votes for one candidate—cumulate them—or he may distribute his votes among the candidates in any way he sees fit. This system enables the minority stockholders to elect one or more of the directors. The right to cumulative voting cannot be claimed unless provided for (1) by statute, (2) by the corporation's charter or bylaws, or (3) by contract among all the stockholders, provided the agreement is not otherwise illegal.

Curtesy. The right of the husband to enjoy during his life and after his wife's death any land that his wife might own during marriage, provided she had legitimate children born to her during the marriage. This is a COMMON LAW right that has largely been abolished by statute. See DOWER.

Custody of Children. The care and control of infants as determined by a court. The court's basic consideration when it gives orders and directions concerning the custody of children is the welfare of the particular child. Courts will often consult a child to find out with which parent he prefers to live. A child may be taken away from a parent or legal guardian, a charitable agency or welfare commissioner, or even from one to whom the court itself had given custody.

Customs. The Government agency concerned with collecting duties and enforcing the rules and regulations that govern the export and import of merchandise. The United States Customs Service is under the jurisdiction of the Treasury Department; it maintains staffs in all American ports of entry and has representatives in many important foreign ports.

Imported goods must be "entered" upon arrival with customs officials either by the importer or his authorized agent, the broker, regardless of whether the goods are dutiable or duty free. See also CUSTOMS COURT.

Customs Court. A tribunal delegated to hear appeals in connection with the tolls and levies upon merchandise, exported or imported, that have been imposed by the customs appraisers and are payable by law.

Cut. An engraving, line cut, or halftone, used by printers to reproduce art work. The art work is sent to the engraver to have a cut made. The cut, in turn, is sent to the printer and becomes a part of a PLATE. See LINE CUTS AND HALFTONES.

Cutoff Button. See TELEPHONE SERVICE, *exclusion button.*

Cy Pres Doctrine. (French for "as near as.") An ancient doctrine applicable to the construction of instruments in EQUITY, whereby the intention of the party making the instrument is carried out as nearly as possible when it is impossible to carry out his precise intention. The doctrine, though ancient, is especially useful in modern times as a device to render charitable trusts useful. For example, if funds left to a charitable trust are insufficient to carry out the provisions of the testamentary trust, the fund does not necessarily revert to the estate, but may be used for a charitable purpose similar to that provided for in the trust. The doctrine is not accepted in all states.

D

Daily Call. See CALENDAR CALL.

Daily Time Sheet. The record that is kept of the amount of time the lawyer spends on particular tasks, for the purpose of arriving at an estimated cost of each job. Figure 1, page 149, illustrates a Daily Time sheet.

Many offices prefer to combine the daily time sheet with the DIARY. See Figure 2, page 150.

Still another method of posting the time the lawyer spends for each job is the system used in keeping the *lawyer's diary.* Figure 3, page 151, shows a page from a lawyer's diary.

Damages. A monetary compensation that may be recovered in the courts by any person who has suffered loss or injury because of the unlawful act or NEGLIGENCE of another.

General damages are presumed by the law to have stemmed from the wrong because they necessarily result from the injury; they do not refer to the special character, condition, or circumstances of the plaintiff. General damages include compensation for physical injury, physical pain, and mental anguish.

Special damages are the natural, but not the necessary, result of the injury. Unlike general damages, special damages can generally be computed exactly. In a negligence action they usually consist of reasonable amounts spent for hospital, medical, and related services.

Day Letter. See TELEGRAPH SERVICES.

De Facto Corporation. An organization started in good faith by people who attempted to organize a CORPORATION under a valid statute and have failed in some minor particular, but have thereafter exercised corporate powers. Failure to have incorporators' signatures on applications for CERTIFICATE OF INCORPORATION notarized is an illustration of noncompliance with statutory requirements. The decided weight of authority is that a *de facto* corporation can do everything that a properly organized corporation can do. See also DE JURE CORPORATION.

De Jure Corporation. A CORPORATION that has complied with the letter of the law governing incorporating procedure. A *de jure* corporation is distinguished from a DE FACTO CORPORATION in that a *de facto* corporation has done something that less than fully complies with the state's incorporating procedure. A *de jure* corporation exists in law as well as in fact.

Dead Freight. See FREIGHT.

Debentures. Bonds issued without security and therefore not protected by any specific LIEN upon property. They are simply the promise of the borrower to pay a certain sum of money at a stipulated time and place, with interest

HALL and DOBB

DAILY SERVICE REPORT OF

DATE

CLIENT	CASE	CHARACTER OF SERVICES	TIME
			HOURS	TENTHS

Key

T. T. telephone to
T. F. telephone from
L. T. letter to
L. F. letter from

S. L. study of law
P. F. preparation of facts
M. T. memorandum to
M. F. memorandum from

Ct. T. court trial
Ct. M. court motion
Ct. A. court argument
C W. conference with

Ex. examination of title
P. P. passing papers
R. P. recording papers
R. T. reviewing title

Daily Time Sheet: Figure 1.

149

HOUR	PLACE	SUBJECT
9:00	Office	C. L. Schum - Drafting lease
10:00	Probate Court	Williams Estate - Hearing
11:30	Office	Conference re income tax
12:00	Office	Hugh Bailey - Auto accident
12:45	Biltmore Hotel	Luncheon with Clemens
2:30	Mathews' office	Community Chest Committee, meeting
3:30	Office	Henry Fowler - Escrow agreement

HOUR	CASE NUMBER	✓	CLIENT	NATURE AND CLASSIFICATION	NEW	ESTIMATED FEE	TIME	CHARGE EXPENSE	FEE
8 00									
8 30									
9 00	3		C. L. Schum	Drafting lease			1		
9 30									
10 00			Williams Estate	Hearing					
10 30									
11 00									
11 30	4		Rogers	Conference re income tax			.50		
12 00			Hugh Bailey	Auto accident	X	50	.75		
12 30									
12:45 1:00			Luncheon	Clemens - Biltmore					
1 30									
2 00									
2 30									
3 00				Community Chest					
3 30	3	✓	Henry Fowler	Conference	2	200	1.25		
4 00									
4 30									
5 00									
5 30									
EVENING	9:00			Churchill Dinner - Waldorf					

FORM A 11 COLWELL PUBLISHING COMPANY CHAMPAIGN ILLINOIS

Daily Time Sheet: Figure 2. Daily time sheet combined with diary.

Saturday, APRIL 21   112th Day

9:45 - Dept. 2 - King V. Smith - Trial

11:00 - Mr. S. A. Murray (Tr. 7491)

(ax. - 7230 - chg. Smith V. City)

4:30 - Harbor Committee Meeting

Last day to file Op. Br. - Allen V. City
Pay jury fee Deposit - Linn V. Fall

Clients Name and Address	Work Done	Time
King (Arthur L.)	Briefing	2 hrs.
207 Sunset Ave.	Trial	4 hrs.

Daily Time Sheet: Figure 3. Page from the Lawyer's diary.

at a fixed rate. The bonds are issued under a trust indenture, which distinguishes them from ordinary notes. Debentures are issued by corporations that (1) have a relatively small percentage of tangible assets, which prevents them from issuing secured bonds, (2) have unquestionable credit ratings and can readily market unsecured bonds, or (3) have mortgaged all of their tangible assets and therefore must resort to debentures to raise funds.

Trust indentures under which debentures are issued usually contain provisions or restrictions designed to protect the investment of the unsecured bondholders. The most common types of provisions are (1) covenants regarding future mortgages or pledges of property, (2) restrictions against additional indebtedness, and (3) dividend restrictions while debentures are outstanding. See also DEED OF TRUST; CORPORATE MORTGAGE BONDS.

Decedent's Estate. The property left by a deceased person. See WILL; PROBATE OF A WILL; LETTERS OF ADMINISTRATION; LEGACY.

Decentralized Filing. See CENTRALIZED FILING.

Declaratory Judgment. An edict of the COURT which simply states the rights of the parties or expresses an opinion on a question of law. For example, a party would want a *declaratory judgment* to determine who has TITLE in a piece of property when there is another claimant.

Decree. The judicial decision of a litigated cause by a court of EQUITY. See also JUDGMENT; INTERLOCUTORY DECREE.

Deed. A formal written instrument by which TITLE to REAL PROPERTY is conveyed from one person to another. The legal effect of the deed is to transfer ownership from the seller to the purchaser, taking away from the seller the use and enjoyment of the property and relieving him of its burdens. The deed is usually prepared by the seller's attorney, and is signed and delivered upon CLOSING TITLE.

The parties to a deed are the *grantor*, who conveys his interest in the property, and the *grantee*, to whom the conveyance is made. The grantor is the seller, and the grantee is usually the purchaser, but not necessarily. The purchaser may buy the land for the grantee. Only the grantor signs the deed, unless the grantee makes special covenants.

Bargain and sale deed. A deed in general use for the transfer of title when there are no warranties made by the grantor. The deed transfers whatever interest the grantor has in the property at the time of its execution.

Warranty deed. A deed under which the GRANTOR (seller) agrees that he will forever guarantee title to the premises conveyed. It assures that he is the true owner and has the right to pass title; guarantees that there are no encumbrances on the property, such as a MORTGAGE or tax lien, except those that have been specifically mentioned; and guarantees that the grantee will have quiet possession, that neither he nor his heirs shall be dispossessed because of defect of title. The grantor further agrees to obtain and to give to the grantee and his successors any legal documents that may be necessary (such as a quitclaim from the heir of a deceased previous owner) to perfect the title. Most important, the grantor guarantees the title. If a flaw in the title should develop later, the grantee or his successor is entitled to recover up to the full value of the property at the time of the sale.

Figure 1, page 153, is a printed form for a Warranty Deed and Figure 2, page 154, is an endorsed back.

Quitclaim deed. A deed which merely releases the grantor's interest in the property and nothing further.

Deed of gift. A deed of gift is given in consideration of the "love and affec-

---

WARRANTY DEED   Form 1001   Published by Tennessee Title Company

For and in consideration of the sum of $ 1.00 -
- - - - - - - - - - - - - - ONE AND NO/100 - - - - - - - - - - - - - - DOLLARS
cash in hand paid by the grantees herein, and other good and valuable considerations,

the receipt of which is hereby acknowledged,

We, John Albert Green and wife, Ellen Blake Green,

_____have bargained and sold, and by these presents do transfer and convey unto the said
ROBERT COLE BROWN and wife, MARY HOWARD BROWN
_____heirs and assigns, a certain tract or parcel of land in Davidson County, State of Tennessee, described as follows to wit:

Land in Davidson County, Tennessee, being Lot No. 26 on the Plan of a Resubdivision of Part of Royal Oaks Subdivision, as of record in Book 1424, page 31, Register's Office for said County.

Said Lot No. 26 fronts 165 feet on the northerly side of Sunnybrook Drive and runs back 271.3 feet on the easterly line and 262.8 feet on the westerly line, to a dead line in the rear, measuring 182.8 feet thereon.

Being the same property conveyed to John Albert Green and wife, Ellen Blake Green, by deed from Royal Highland Land Company, of record in book 2063, page 25, said Register's Office.

To have and to hold the said tract or parcel of land, with the appurtenances, estate, title and interest thereto belonging to the said Robert Cole Brown and wife, Mary Howard Brown, their_____heirs and assigns, forever.

And we do covenant with the said Robert Cole Brown and wife, Mary Howard Brown, _____that we are lawfully seized and possessed of said land in fee simple; have a good right to convey it. and the same is unencumbered.

And we, John Albert Green and wife, Ellen Blake Green
do further covenant and bind ourselves, our heirs and representatives, to warrant and forever defend the title to the said land to the said Robert Cole Brown and wife, Mary Howard Brown, their_____heirs and assigns against the lawful claims of all persons, whomsoever.

Witness our hands this 15th day of December , 19

_____   *John Albert Green*

_____   *Ellen Blake Green*

STATE OF TENNESSEE }
Davidson County

Personally appeared before me, James D. White , a Notary Public in and for said County and State, the within named John Albert Green and wife, Ellen Blake Green

the bargainor s , with whom I am personally acquainted, and who acknowledged that they executed the within instrument for the purposes therein contained. Witness my hand and official seal at
Nashville , Tennessee, this 15th day of December , 19

Commission expires May 1, 19   *James D. White*
                                   Notary Public

Deed: Figure 1. Warranty deed from husband and wife.

tion" that the GRANTOR has for the GRANTEE. A deed of gift passes TITLE as completely as a deed for which there is a monetary consideration.

Statutory deed. A short form of deed approved by some states to save the space required for recording deeds. By statute, certain covenants and warranties are made part of the deed and, although not set forth in the deed, are binding on the grantor and his heirs. Since the statute is actually part of the deed and a state statute is not effective outside of the state enacting it, a statutory form of deed can be used only in the specific state that makes statutory provision for it.

See also DEED, CONTENTS OF; DEED, PREPARATION OF; RECORDING OF DEED.

Fiduciary Deed. A fiduciary deed may have a grantor as an executor, administrator, trustee, guardian, receiver, or commissioner. Some states permit a statutory form to be used, wherein the main difference between the fiduciary deed and a general warrant deed is that the fiduciary must state his source of authority.

Sheriff's Deed. A deed usually

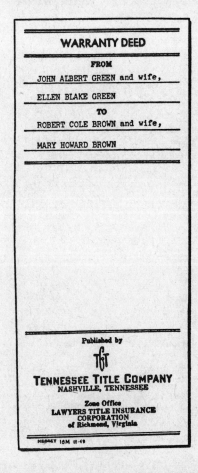

Deed: Figure 2. Back of warranty deed endorsed by husband and wife.

prepared by the sheriff for real estate sold at public sale.

Tenancy by the Entirety. See TENANCY BY ENTIRETY.

Deed, Contents of. Regardless of the type or form of DEED the secretary should be sure the instrument contains the following:

1. Date of execution.

2. Whether grantor is an individual, a partnership, or a corporation.

3. Full name of grantor who has fee simple. (See FEE SIMPLE) as determined by abstract, title insurance or deed, residence of Grantor.

4. Marital status of grantor.

5. Full name of spouse if spouse must join in the conveyance.

6. Full name and residence of GRANTEE.

7. Description of property. See LAND DESCRIPTION.

8. Whether deed is to be a warranty, bargain and sale, quitclaim, or gift deed. If printed form is used, the type of deed will be printed on the form.

Printed forms come for corporation to individual, corporation to corporation and individual to corporation.

9. Consideration to be expressed in deed. Consideration is the price given for the property or the motive for giving it.

10. A recital of any MORTGAGE or other ENCUMBRANCE on the property. The statement of encumbrances, if any, follows the description of the property.

11. HABENDUM CLAUSE. States that the grantee is to have the property transferred to him.

12. COVENANTS. Promises made by the grantor and grantee. The most usual ones, such as the grantee's right to quiet enjoyment of the property, and the assurance that the grantor has the right to pass title, are printed in the forms for deeds. The lawyer will dictate any unusual covenants.

13. TESTIMONIUM CLAUSE. Closing clause immediately preceding the signature. The introductory words to the testimonium clause, *in witness whereof, in testimony whereof,* and the like, are usually typed in solid caps. The word following begins with lower case unless it is a proper name. A comma usually follows the introductory words.

See also DEED; DEED, PREPARATION OF; DEED OF TRUST.

Deed of Trust. An instrument in use in some of the states and the District of Columbia by which legal title to real estate is conveyed to a *third party* to be held in trust for a lender until the debt secured by the instrument is paid. It is, in effect, a MORTGAGE with three parties, the borrower, the lender, and the trustee. This security instrument is also known as a TRUST DEED, but the term *trust deed* is more generally applied to the security for a corporate bond issue.

Deed, Preparation of. The following are general directions the secretary may use in preparing a DEED. She should:

1. Make 3 copies—the original for the GRANTEE, a copy for the GRANTOR, and a copy for the lawyer's files.

2. Use LEGAL CAP, if a printed form is not used.

3. Remember the *responsibility and distribution line* (see TYPING COURT PAPERS) at the top of the first page.

(This goes on the office copy only of a printed form.)

4. Double space.

5. Type the LAND DESCRIPTION.

6. Number all pages of typed deed.

7. If a printed form is used, be sure the "Z" appears after the land description. See "Z" Ruling, PRINTED LAW BLANKS.

8. Make sure there are at least two lines of typing on the signature page.

9. Prepare signature line for the GRANTOR. The GRANTEE does not sign a deed except in special circumstances.

10. In the case of an individual grantor, type *L.S.* in caps at the end of the signature lines. In the case of a corporate grantor, be sure that the authorized officer, usually the corporate secretary, affixes the seal.

11. Type witness lines and ATTESTATION when required.

12. Prepare certificate of ACKNOWLEDGMENT.

13. Collate (see COLLATING).

14. Check and double-check spelling of names.

15. Have someone compare the land description with her.

16. Endorse back of printed form. If deed is typed, prepare LEGAL BACK.

17. Arrange for the grantor to come in and sign the deed and acknowledge it.

18. Get the lawyer's approval of the instrument *before* it is signed. Have the grantor sign the original only. Make sure that the grantor's signature agrees with name typed in the deed.

19. Have the deed notarized. If the secretary is the notary, she should take the acknowledgment.

20. Affix documentary stamps if they are required by the state.

21. Conform copies to original upon completion of signature and acknowledgment.

22. Get the lawyer's approval and then have the deed recorded. The secretary makes a notation that the deed is to be returned to the lawyer's office. (The secretary to the lawyer for the grantee attends to the recording.)

23. When the deed is returned by the recorder, send it to the grantee with a covering letter, or have the grantee call for it.

Defamation. See LIBEL AND SLANDER.

Default. The failure to perform what is required by duty or law.

1. In litigation, a plaintiff or defendant is in default when he does not appear at court within the time prescribed by law to prosecute his claim or prosecute his defense. The JUDGMENT entered when the defendant does not appear is called a *judgment by default*. When the plaintiff defaults he may be non-suited.

2. A *borrower* is in default when he fails to meet his obligation to pay. If security has been given for the debt and the borrower defaults the lender has a right to look to that security for the satisfaction of the debt. See BOND AND MORTGAGE; PLEDGE.

Defeasance Clause. A provision in a MORTGAGE that if the indebtedness is paid in accordance with the terms of the mortgage agreement, the mortgage shall be null and void.

Defendant. In a law suit, the party against whom action is brought. He is the person required to make answer in

156

the action or suit. See also PARTIES OF AN ACTION.

Del Credere. (Italian.) A term applied to an agent who, for a higher commission, guarantees his principal that he will pay for goods sold on credit if the buyer does not. Del credere agencies are common in businesses that employ commission merchants or agents whose relatively independent financial status enables them to guarantee their customers' accounts.

Demand. A formal requisition or request that the party under obligation do a particular thing specified under a claim of right on the part of the person making the request. For example, where property is sold to be paid for on delivery, a *demand* would have to be made before an action for failure to deliver the goods might be instigated.

Demand for Bill of Particulars. A demand by one of the PARTIES TO AN ACTION for more definite information from the other party. A BILL OF PARTICULARS is usually desired when PLEADINGS have been served which do not give *details* as to time, place or circumstance of what is to be proved. For example, some of the particulars that may be required in a personal injury action are date and time of day of the occurrence, its approximate location, a general statement of the acts constituting the NEGLIGENCE claimed, a statement of injuries, and medical expenses. A party demands this statement of details within a specified time. He may request the court for an order for the bill of particulars, in which case the procedure is like that in any other MOTION. The demand for the bill of particulars is addressed to opposing counsel. No VERIFICATION of a demand is necessary.

Parts of demand for bill of particulars. The demand for bill of particulars consists of the following parts: (1) caption; (2) salutation; (3) introduction; (4) details demanded; (5) date line; (6) signature of attorney demanding the bill; (7) name and address of attorney on whom demand is made.

How the secretary prepares the demand for bill of particulars. Usually the lawyer dictates the demand for bill of particulars. Unless otherwise instructed, the secretary follows Figure 1 on pages 158-159 for style.

The secretary should check the following points:

1. Make an original for the court (some courts require an extra copy), copy to serve on each opposing counsel, and a copy for the file.

2. The caption is the same as that on the complaint; the title of the case may be shortened.

3. The salutation is to opposing counsel. It is typed in solid caps, and reads:

SIRS: (if to a law firm)
SIR: (if to one lawyer)
or TO . . . .,
ATTORNEY FOR . . . . . . :

In some jurisdictions the demand for bill of particulars is addressed to the party *and* his attorney.

4. Number consecutively and indent the details demanded.

5. Type the date line at the left margin, three spaces beneath the last numbered paragraph.

6. Type a line for signature of attorney demanding the bill. Beneath the

JMH:p 8/23/— 1-2

SUPREME COURT OF THE STATE OF NEW YORK

COUNTY OF RICHMOND

---x
:
AUGUSTUS N. ROBERTSON and ELIZABETH
R. ROBERTSON,
:
                                    Plaintiffs,   DEMAND FOR BILL
                                                    OF PARTICULARS
:
                        -against-
:
JOHNSTON—DOUGLAS MANAGEMENT CORPORATION,
and FREDERICK FASHIONS, INC.
:
                                    Defendants.
---x

SIRS:

        PLEASE TAKE NOTICE that the above named defendants
hereby demand that the plaintiffs serve upon the attorneys
for the defendants within ten days a Bill of Particulars
showing in detail the following:

        (1) The date and the time of day of the occur-
rence as closely as the plaintiffs can fix it.

        (2) Its location, identifying as closely as pos-
sible the display counters and the place on the floor
between them as described in paragraph FIFTH of the
complaint.

(Continued on following page)

Demand for Bill of Particulars: Figure 1.

(Continued from preceding page)

> (3) A statement of the injuries and a description of those claimed to be permanent.
>
> Dated, New York, August 23, 19—,
>
> Yours, etc.,
>
> JONES & SMITH,
> Attorneys for Defendants,
> 14 Mall Street,
> New York, N. Y.
>
> TO:
>
> ELWOOD & ADAMS,
> Attorneys for Plaintiffs,
> 18 Broad Street,
> New York, N. Y.

Demand for Bill of Particulars: Figure 1 *(Continued).*

signature line, indicate the party he represents.

7. Type name and address of counsel to whom the demand is addressed at the left margin, several spaces beneath the signature. If the attorney's name is given in the salutation, this is not necessary.

8. There is no verification to a demand for bill of particulars.

9. Endorse legal back for original and all copies except the office copy.

10. Collate and staple in backs.

What the secretary does about the demand for bill of particulars.

1. Prepare the demand for bill of particulars

2. Ask attorney to sign.

3. See that copy is served on opposing counsel.

4. Be sure that receipt or certificate of service is endorsed on back of original.

5. Conform the office copy.

6. *Make diary entry* of date bill of particulars must be served.

7. File original in court.

8. Make entry in suit register of service and filing.

9. The secretary to the attorney on whom the demand is served makes a notation on back of the copy of date and hour of service. *Enter in diary date by which bill of particulars must be served.* Also make entry in suit register.

Demise. Verb. In conveyancing. To convey or create an estate for years or life; to lease. The usual and operative word in leases: "have granted, *demised,* and to farm let, and by these presents do grant, *demise* and to farm let."

Demise Charter. See CHARTER-PARTY.

Demurrage. In ADMIRALTY law, the money allowed to a shipowner whose vessel has been held by a charterer or shipper beyond the number of days allowed by the CHARTER-PARTY or BILL OF LADING for loading and unloading or for sailing. The term is sometimes used to refer to the period of time during which demurrage accrues.

Demurrer. A pleading that raises an issue of law, not of fact. It objects to defects that are apparent from the pleading itself. Instead of denying facts alleged in the COMPLAINT, as an ANSWER does, a demurrer to a complaint takes exception to the complaint because it is *insufficient on some legal ground*. For example, a defendant may demur to a complaint on the ground that the plaintiff does not have legal capacity to sue. The defendant may also demur to the plaintiff's reply. But a demurrer is not a pleading to be used by the defendant only. A plaintiff may demur to the defendant's answer, or to a cross-complaint. Each cause of action (count), or each defense, is demurred to separately. Many states have abolished demurrers, but they are still permitted as a pleading in some states.

A demurrer consists of the following parts:
1.. Caption
2. Introduction
3. Grounds of demurrer, each stated separately
4. Signature of attorney
5. Attorney's certificate of good faith when required
6. Points and authorities

The statutes name the grounds for demurrer. These grounds usually include, among others, the following: (1) that the court has no jurisdiction; (2) that the plaintiff has no legal capacity to sue; (3) that the complaint (or answer) is ambiguous, unintelligible, uncertain. A demurrer is supported by legal points and authorities sustaining the grounds of demurrer.

How to prepare the demurrer. The statement of a specific ground for demurrer usually follows a standard form, with which the secretary quickly becomes familiar. Although the lawyer ordinarily will dictate the demurrer, he might ask her to follow a form. Unless otherwise instructed, the secretary types the demurrer in a style similar to that illustrated by Figure 1, pages 161 and 162. Figure 2, page 163, illustrates the points and authorities supporting a demurrer. The secretary might use the following guide:

1. Type on legal-size paper.
2. Make an original for the court, a copy for the opposing party's counsel, and a copy for your file.
3. The caption is the same as that on the complaint, but the title of the case may be shortened.
4. The index number must appear on the demurrer, at the right of the box.
5. The title of the document is "Demurrer to Complaint," or Demurrer to Answer," as the case may be.
6. Number the grounds of demurrer to each cause of action or count (or each defense) consecutively, beginning with "I."

8   IN THE SUPERIOR COURT OF THE STATE OF CALIFORNIA

9   IN AND FOR THE COUNTY OF LOS ANGELES

10

11   MARY JANE DOE,   No. 14788

12   Plaintiff,

13   vs.   DEMURRER
                                      TO

14   JOHN W. DOE   COMPLAINT

15   Defendant.

16 _____

17   Comes now the above named defendant, JOHN W.

18 DOE, and demurs to Count One of the Complaint on file herein

19 upon the following grounds and each of them:

20   I

21   That Count One of said complaint fails to state

22 facts sufficient to constitute a cause of action against

23 this defendant.

24   II

25   That Count One of said complaint fails to state

26 facts sufficient to constitute a cause of action against

27 this defendant in this, that it affirmatively appears there-

28 from that the purported cause or causes of action therein

29 set forth are barred by the provisions of §§ 339(1), 343

Demurrer: Figure 1. First page.

1	IV
2	That Count One of said complaint is ambiguous
3	for each of the reasons heretofore set forth for its uncer-
4	tainty.
5	
6	That Count One of said complaint is unintelli-
7	gible for each of the reasons heretofore set forth for it's
8	uncertainty.
9	DEMURRER TO COUNT TWO
10	Defendant demurs to Count Two of said complaint
11	upon the following grounds and each of them:
12	I
13	(Continue as in the demurrer to Count One.)
14	WHEREFORE, this demurring defendant prays that
15	this demurrer be sustained without leave to amend and that
16	he be dismissed with his costs.
17	EMMETT BROWN Attorney for Defendant
18	I hereby certify that this demurrer is filed in
19	good faith; that it is not filed for the purpose of delay,
20	and in my opinion the grounds are well taken.
21	EMMETT BROWN Attorney for Defendant

Demurrer: Figure 1. Last page.

<u>POINTS AND AUTHORITIES</u>

<u>POINT ONE</u>

A PARENT IS NOT BOUND TO COMPENSATE THE OTHER PARENT FOR THE VOLUNTARY SUPPORT OF HIS CHILD WITHOUT AN AGREEMENT FOR COMPENSATION.

Civil Code § 208

<u>POINT TWO</u>

AS BETWEEN THE PARENTS OF MINOR CHILDREN, THEIR RESPECTIVE OBLIGATIONS OF SUPPORT OF EACH OTHER AND TO THE MINOR CHILDREN MUST BE DETERMINED IN THE PROCEEDING FOR DIVORCE, AND IN THE ABSENCE OF SOME SPECIFIC PROVISION TO THAT EFFECT, THE FATHER WHO HAS BEEN DEPRIVED OF THE CUSTODY OF THE MINOR CHILDREN IS NOT OBLIGATED FOR THEIR SUPPORT.

<u>Calegaris v. Calegaris</u>, 4 Cal. App. 264, 87 Pac. 561;

<u>Ex Parte Miller</u>, 109 Cal. 643, 42 Pac. 428;

<u>Lewis v. Lewis</u>, 174 Cal. 336, 163 Pac. 42.

Respectfully submitted,

_____
EMMETT BROWN
Attorney for Defendant

Demurrer: Figure 2. Points and authorities supporting demurrer.

7. Type a line for the attorney's signature.

8. There is no verification because a demurrer does not allege or aver facts.

9. Type the attorney's certificate of good faith in jurisdictions where it is required by the court rules. The certificate reads:

I hereby certify that this demurrer is filed in good faith and not for the purpose of delay. In my opinion the grounds are well taken.

Attorney for ....

10. Begin the points and authorities on a separate page.

11. Endorse a legal back for each copy except your file copy. The endorsement is similar to the endorsement on the back of the answer in that it shows the index number and the name of opposing counsel on whom a copy of the demurrer is served.

What the secretary does about a demurrer.

1. Prepare the demurrer and points and authorities.

2. Staple original and copies in endorsed legal backs.

3. Get attorney to sign original and copies, and also certificate of good faith if required.

4. Serve copy on attorney for opposing party.

5. See that admission of service is endorsed on back of original.

6. Conform the office copy.

7. File original in court, with fee if required.

8. Make entry in SUIT REGISTER of service and filing.

9. The secretary to the counsel *on whom the demurrer is served* makes a notation on the back of that copy, of the date and hour the demurrer was served, and an entry in the SUIT REGISTER. See also PLEADINGS.

Depletion. An exhaustion or gradual reduction of an asset. Depletion in the Federal income tax law applies to the exhaustion of such assets as oil, gas, timber, mineral deposits, and other natural resources. To compensate for the wasting away of the taxpayer's assets, an annual depletion deduction is allowed when computing INCOME for the Federal INCOME TAX. See also DEPRECIATION.

Deponent. A person making an AFFIDAVIT.

Depositary, Depository. *Depositary* applies to the person or authority entrusted with something for safekeeping. It may also be used to apply to the place where something is deposited or stored. *Depository* applies only to the place where something is deposited or stored.

Deposition. Testimony of a witness under oath taken in writing to be introduced at a trial, hearing, investigation, or arbitration proceedings.

Many occasions arise when the secretary in a law office is required to take the testimony of a person under oath. The testimony is usually in question and anwer form and is referred to as a *depositon.* Counsel for both sides are present at the examination.

The secretary takes the testimony verbatim and transcribes it verbatim, without editing even glaring grammatical errors. If the exchange of questions and answers is too rapid and the secretary falls behind in her notes, she should raise her left hand as a signal to the attorney conducting the examination to slow down. It is essential that every word of the testimony be reported accurately.

The secretary should use a notebook that has a vertical line down the center of the page. She divides each half of the page into three columns by lightly penciled vertical lines in the positions shown in Figure 1 below. (It is assumed she customarily writes only to the dividing line, treating each column as a separate page.)

Notes of the questions by the examining attorney are placed on the page in the same position as notes are ordinarily placed. Each question begins at the extreme left of the page, extends to the center line, and, if it takes more than one line, continues at the extreme left of the next horizontal line.

Notes of the witness' answers begin at the right of the first vertical line and extend to the center line. If more than one line is necessary, the answer continues on the next horizontal line at the right of the first vertical line. The witness' answers never extend to the left of that line.

Notes of the interpolations by opposing counsel begin at the right of the second vertical line and extend to the center line. If more than one line is necessary, the interpolation continues on the next horizontal line at the right of the second vertical line. Remarks by opposing counsel never extend to the left of that line.

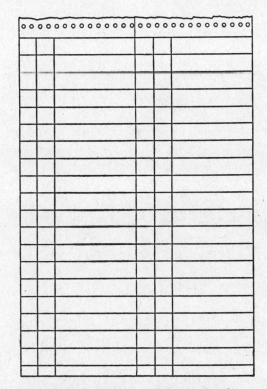

Deposition: Figure 1. Notebook rulers for question and answer testimony.

RICHARD C. JONES

DIRECT EXAMINATION BY MR. SMITH:

Q. Mr. Jones, what is your full name?

A. Richard C. Jones.

Q. What is your address? A. 226 Clinton Avenue, Mamaroneck, New York.

Q. Where are you employed, sir? A. Robert S. Still, Inc., 607 Tenth Avenue, New York, N. Y.

Q. How long have you been employed there? A. Since 1943.

Q. What is your position at Still's? A. Salesman.

Q. Do you know Mrs. Mary Jackson, the plaintiff in this action? A. Not too well; I know her as a customer.

Q. In April, 19—, did you see her when she brought in the necklace to Still's? A. No.

Q. What officer or employee did see her? A. Another salesman.

Q. What is his name? A. William A. Nelson.

Q. You don't know what he said to her concerning

(Continued on following page)

Deposition: Figure 2. Transcription of question and answer testimony.

Continued from preceding page)

the work to be done?

     MR. HOWARD: I object to the form of that question.

     A. No, only from our records.

     Q. What records do you have with you that show the delivery of the necklace to Still's?

     [Mr. Jones produces record and Mr. Smith studies it.]

     MR. SMITH: I offer that in evidence.

     MR. HOWARD: Can I see that?

     MR. SMITH: Certainly, I thought you had already seen it.

     MR. HOWARD: It should not be admitted in evidence but should be marked for identification.

     [Marked Plaintiff's Exhibit 1 for Identification.]

     Q. Mr. Jones, with reference to plaintiff's exhibit marked Exhibit 1 for identification on your examination, do you recognize the handwriting in pencil on the notations on that exhibit? A. Yes, sir, that's Mr. Nelson's.

     MR. SMITH: I have no further questions at this time. Mr. Benjamin, would you like to cross-examine?

Deposition: Figure 2. Transcription of question and answer testimony *(Continued)*.

Notes of actions that must be indicated, such as marking exhibits for identification, are enclosed in brackets, thus distinguishing them from notes of the testimony. They are written in the same position as notes of the questions by the examining attorney.

Notes are written on the right half of the page in the same manner as on the left half, the center vertical line representing the left edge.

The preceding method of arranging the shorthand notes on the page of the notebook increases your speed by eliminating the writing of "Q" and "A," punctuation after the questions and answers, and the name of the opposing counsel when he makes an objection. It also facilitates reading back.

Figure 2 illustrates a transcription of testimony (pages 166-167).

Court Stenographers. If the secretary feels she cannot take shorthand fast enough, she may arrange for a professional court stenographer to be present. Many of the court stenographers use shorthand machines (Stenotype) which are much speedier. They will furnish a transcribed copy of the deposition with as many additional copies as desired. Many attorneys use court stenographers regularly for depositions and do not call on their secretaries for this purpose.

Depreciation. The decline in value of an asset caused by wear, tear, and obsolescence. A corporation may deduct depreciation as an expense on its Federal income tax return. An individual may take a deduction for depreciation of income producing property from his adjusted gross income. (See INCOME.) The depreciation allowance that is taken during the

useful life of the property should be part of a reasonably consistent plan (not necessarily the same rate each year) authorized under Federal income tax law. The total depreciation deductions may not exceed the difference between the cost (or other basis) and the salvage value of the property.

Derivative Action. A suit brought by a shareholder on behalf of the CORPORATION in order to compel management to act properly for the protection of the corporation's rights. The relief, if granted, is in favor of the corporation. The suit may involve restitution from the directors who have misappropriated assets, or who, by their NEGLIGENCE have brought a loss upon the corporation. Before a stockholder may maintain a derivative suit he must make a demand to the BOARD OF DIRECTORS that they act properly and redress any wrongs, and the directors must refuse to do so. See also REPRESENTATIVE ACTION.

Description of Property. See LAND DESCRIPTION.

Descriptive Word Index. An alphabetical list of topics with references to the place these topics are found in multivolume reference works such as AMERICAN DIGEST SYSTEM and CORPUS JURIS SECUNDUM SYSTEM.

Desertion. A voluntary separation from a spouse without justification and with the intention of not returning. In some states, desertion is a ground for DIVORCE; in others, for SEPARATION. The courts hold that a justified absence does not constitute desertion. As an example, a wife is justified in leaving her husband's home if she fears bodily injury from him. This is not an act of desertion even though she does not intend to return to him. Desertion is sometimes also known as *abandonment*.

Devise. A gift of real property by WILL. One who receives a devise is a *devisee*. See also LEGACY.

Diary. A daily record of what is accomplished and also of future appointments and work to be done. Diaries instead of calendars are usually kept by lawyers because they want a record of time devoted to a specific client so that the client may be charged for the time. The diary has a separate page for each day in the year. Many standard yearbooks are satisfactory. The important thing is that they should have space for work performed and the time consumed doing it, as well as space for appointments and matters to be attended to. A diary is prepared originally in the same manner as are calendars. Entries of time consumed on each task are made from day to day after the work is completed.

Diaries that the secretary should keep. Two diaries are required, one for the lawyer and one for the secretary, but the entries are not completely duplicated. In the lawyer's diary, the secretary will enter all of his appointments and important days he should remember, such as his wife's birthday. If the important days are not noted, he may inadvertently make conflicting engagements. The secretary does not enter in the lawyer's diary items that are merely reminders to herself, such as

days on which checks should be written. She watches his diary closely for appointments he makes without telling her.

In the secretary's own diary, she enters notations of her own business activities and appointments, as well as the lawyer's appointments and the things that she will have to remind him about.

If the secretary is responsible for following court cases for more than one lawyer, as well as being responsible for personal matters for a member of a firm, it will be less confusing to keep all court matters in a separate diary.

How to make up diaries. The secretary keeps a list of items that go in the diary year after year (see checklist, page 171). As soon as diaries for the forthcoming year are available, she enters all the recurring items, events, and appointments under the appropriate date. In preparing the diaries, she works from the list, not from the previous year's diary, because dates for events change. For example, if the board meetings of a corporation client are held on the first Monday of every month, the actual dates vary from year to year. In making an entry, she should be certain that the date is not Sunday or a holiday. She enters notations of additional appointments and things to do as soon as she learn about them.

The secretary should enter time-consuming tasks that must be done by a certain date sufficiently *in advance* to permit the work to be finished on time. She also makes an entry under the date on which the action must be taken. The practice of making advance entries is very important and will save the secretary and the lawyer the strain of having to prepare material on short notice. It is not usually necessary to make advance entries in the lawyer's diary—the secretary can remind him of work to be done. She underlines important due dates and deadlines in red.

When dates call for presents or cards, the secretary enters a reminder in her diary, about ten days before the date, as well as on the date. Christmas presents and card lists should be brought up about six weeks before Christmas, the exact time depending upon local shopping conditions.

Advance notice of payments of large sums should also be entered in the diary. The lawyer's funds might be low, or he might want to negotiate a renewal of a loan.

How to make entries about legal work. Under the date upon which a step must be taken, make an entry setting forth (1) the title of the matter, (2) the time and place for the step, and (3) the nature of the act to be performed, fully described. If a secretary keeps the diary for more than one lawyer, she should also include the initials of the lawyer or lawyers interested. The third example of entries, below, indicates that a BRIEF must be prepared. This entry should also be made under an advance date (see above), with a notation of the date the briefs must be ready. A secretary should form the habit of making entries in the diary immediately upon learning that they should be made. *No telephone calls or other interruptions should interfere.*

Examples of entries:

Joan Wilson Estate—pay on account New York Estate Tax to obtain benefit of 5% discount.   RSF

International Jones Co.—Clerk's Office, U. S. Court House, Foley Square— Order to show cause returnable why cer-

tain claims should not be compromised.   NEL

Richards v. Rogers (both actions)—Last day to serve and file reply briefs.
RSF:NEL

How to obtain information for entries. Information necessary to make these entries is obtained in various ways:

1. Observe the dates and the places mentioned in papers that the firm prepares and in those served on it by opposing counsel. For example, an order in the International Jones Co. case would read, in part:

"ORDERED that the plaintiff or his attorney show cause, . . . at the office of the Clerk of the United States District Court for the Southern District of New York in the United States Court House, Foley Square, Borough of Manhattan, City of New York, on the 18th day of July, 19. ., at 10:30 o'clock in the forenoon . . . ."

Obviously, a diary entry should be made under date of July 18 and that the place is the Clerk's Office, U. S. Court House, Foley Square.

2. Observe the date a notice is served on the office, or the office serves a notice on another concern.

3. Calculate the time prescribed by law or rules of law for answering, replying to, or moving to dismiss or correct a pleading when a pleading is served on the office. The secretary can get this information from the practice rules of the court.

4. Calculate the time for taking any step when the time limit for that step runs from some other act of which there is notice.

It would be impossible to set forth here all of the instances and time limits that affect litigation; not only are they numerous, but they vary with the state. Knowledge of them is gained by experience and study. The lawyer is responsible for knowing them and instructing the secretary accordingly; the secretary is responsible for making notations in the diary in accordance with his instructions and for asking him to give her those instructions. A few diaries have an appendix of timetables of procedure and court rules for specific states, which are very helpful to the legal secretary.

Checklist of entries to make in diary. Here is a checklist of the items that the secretary usually enters in the appropriate diary:

Appointments
   Clients, in and out of office
   Doctor and dentist
   Social, evening and daytime

Court Work
   Return dates on summons
   Deadlines for filing pleadings and serving copies on opposing counsel.
   Deadlines for serving notices in probate court
   Hearings
   Pre-trial conferences with court and opposing counsel
   Trial dates

Family Dates
   Anniversaries
   Birthdays
   Mother's Day
   Father's Day

Holidays
   Christmas
   Easter
   Election Day
   Independence Day
   Labor Day
   Religious holidays
   Thanksgiving
   Valentine's Day

Meetings
   Board meetings
   Club meetings
   Committee meetings
   Stockholders' meetings
   Bar Association meetings

Payment Dates
   Bar Association dues
   Contributions
   Insurance premiums
   Interest on notes payable and maturity dates
   Periodic payments, such as salaries, rent, allowances to children, tuition. and the like

Renewal Dates
   Automobile license
   Hunting and fishing licenses
   Subscriptions to periodicals

Tax Dates
   Federal income tax returns and payment dates for clients and for the lawyer's personal tax
   Federal estate tax returns for clients
   Social Security tax returns and payments

Checklist of entries of work accomplished. The purpose of making entries in the diary of work accomplished and time consumed is to charge the client for the work. Therefore, any time consumed in behalf of a client should be entered unless a separate time sheet is kept. This time includes:

   Dictation
   Appointments
   Conferences
   Closings
   Interviewing witnesses
   Trials
   Hearings
   Arguments
   Research
   Some telephone calls
   Some stenographic work

Dictum. An opinion expressed by a court that is not necessary in deciding the question before the court. When, in additon, such opinion does not relate to the question before the court, it is called *obiter dictum* (Latin for "remark by the way"). Dicta carry legal weight in courts deciding subsequent questions but not to the extent that court decisions do. Court decisions are binding precedents; the dicta expressed in the opinion are not.

Digest. (Law) An index arranged by subject matter to the rules of law raised or discussed in reported cases. A digest is the most important and necessary single tool of the lawyer for getting at the law as stated in judicial opinions.

The digest is a collection of separate paragraphs, each of which is related to the others only because they belong in the same subject grouping. There is no editorial comment on the case, no statement as to jurisdictional rules, historical developments, majority and minority views. Each rule is there on its own. The lawyer must be constantly on the alert, therefore, to the law's changes, both by decision and statute.

Digests vary in scope. The AMERICAN DIGEST SYSTEM, covering all printed opinions in all American jurisdictions, from 1658 to date, is the most comprehensive.

Direct Evidence. Sworn testimony by a person that he saw the acts done, or heard the words spoken, that are in question and have to be proven.

On the other hand, *circumstantial evidence* consists of facts introduced that tend to prove indirectly a point in dispute. For example, a person's reputation for honesty or dishonesty may be shown where he is on trial for LARCENY.

Direct Examination. The first interrogation or examination of a witness by the attorney for the party on whose behalf he is called. Direct examination is followed by CROSS-EXAMINATION, which is conducted by the adverse party.

Director. See BOARD OF DIRECTORS.

Direct Taxes. Levies borne directly by the taxpayer; opposed to "hidden" or *indirect taxes* which are often included in the price of goods and are thus borne indirectly by the purchaser rather than directly by the taxpayer. The individual INCOME TAX is a clear example of direct taxation, and the EXCISE TAXES on alcohol, tobacco, automobiles, and the like, are examples of indirect taxes.

Directors' Meetings. Formal meetings or assemblies of the individual directors of a CORPORATION for the purpose of taking joint action on business of the corporation. The BOARD OF DIRECTORS, acting as a body, has sole authority to manage the corporation in those matters which are not reserved for action by stockholders. The stockholders cannot take this authority from the board and give it to an individual.

Notice of directors' meetings. The legal secretary should follow the provisions of the BYLAWS in sending notices of meetings to directors. Even if notice of a regular meeting is not required by the bylaws, it is advisable to notify the directors of the meeting. If a special meeting is to be called, telephone or telegraph the directors to determine whether the time is convenient for all of them. Send a written notice after the time of the meeting is definitely fixed.

Notices of directors' meetings are usually typewritten on the corporation's letterhead. Printing or multigraphing the notice on cards or paper slips, with blanks for the date, time, and place of the meeting, is a timesaving expedient. A light stock for card notices is preferable, since heavy stock is not suitable for insertion in the typewriter to fill in necessary information.

The notice is sent in the name of the corporate secretary. It should specify the date, the place, and the hour at which the meeting is to be held. It is advisable, though not obligatory unless required by statute or bylaw, for the notice of a special meeting to state the purpose for which it is held.

Quorum at directors' meeting. A directors' meeting cannot be held unless a QUORUM is present. Consult the bylaws for the number of directors necessary to constitute a quorum. A quorum at a directors' meeting differs from a quorum at a stockholders' meeting in that the representation is based upon the number of directors and not upon the amount of stock owned by them.

If you learn that a quorum will not be present, telephone those directors who expect to attend and arrange, with approval of the person calling the meeting, to have the meeting postponed. This is particularly important if the directors are coming from a distance.

A director cannot give a PROXY for a directors' meeting.

Preservation of notice. Keep a copy of every notice of meeting, with the date of mailing noted on it. If the notice has been published in the newspapers, keep a clipping of the published notice and the name of the publication and dates of publication.

The agenda. The agenda consists of an itemized list of matters to be brought up at a meeting. The secretary lists them from the accumulated material in the current meeting folder. The agenda should follow the order of business as set forth in the bylaws.

Here is a typical agenda prepared for a director's meeting:

1. Read minutes of last meeting. (Attach a typewritten copy of the minutes of the previous meeting to the corporate secretary's copy of the agenda.)

2. Submit the following statements: (Here enumerate the reports of officers and committees to be presented to the meeting. Copies of the reports may be attached to the agenda.)

3. Adopt resolution approving minutes of executive committee meetings. (If minutes are long, copies may be made and attached to the agenda.)

4. Business of the meeting. (Here enumerate business to be acted upon indicating each item by a summary of the resolution that is required.)

Begin preparation of the agenda several days before the meeting. Have it completely in order the evening before the meeting. Prepare a copy for each director. Attach to the agenda the exhibits, supporting papers, reports, and the like that contain the information necessary to supply the groundwork for discussion.

Reservation and preparation of the meeting room. If a meeting is to be held in a room that is used for other purposes, notify the person who is responsible for the room to have it available at the time of the meeting. When entering the date of the meeting in the corporation's calendar, also enter at an earlier date a reminder to reserve the room. This should be done in ample time to avoid conflict, the time of the advance notice depending upon the demand for the room.

In preparing the room for the meeting, have it dusted, properly heated, and ventilated. See that sufficient costumers and coat hangers are available. Provide stationery, memorandum pads, pen and ink, and pencils for each person who is expected to attend the meeting. Have a supply of clips, pins, rubber bands on the table, and put an ashtray and matches at each place.

Directors' fees. The fee payable to directors for attendance at a meeting is usually fixed by resolution adopted by the board of directors. When preparation for the meeting is the lawyer's responsibility, payment of the fees might be his responsibility also. In this case, arrange with the treasurer of the corporation to have the money at the meeting. If any money is left over because of nonattendance, return it to the treasurer. Give the money to the directors after the meeting, preferably enclosed in an envelope.

Material to take to meetings. Take the following material to directors' and stockholders' meetings:

1. Pamphlet copy of the corporation laws of the state in which the corporation is organized.

2. Copy of the CERTIFICATE OF INCORPORATION, with marginal notations of amendments and copies of them.

3. Copy of the bylaws, with marginal notations of amendments and copies of them

4. Separate sheet for order of business

5. Rules and regulations of the cor-

poration, if any, governing the conduct of meetings

6. Proof of the mailing of notices of the meeting and, where necessary, of publication

7. The original call for the meeting and, if there has been a demand for a call, the original of the demand

8. The minute book

9. The corporate seal

10. Current papers pertaining to the meeting

11. Blank affidavits, oaths, and the like

Directory of Post Offices. A manual published by the U. S. Government Printing Office which lists the post office and zip code number of every city or town in the United States that has a post office. However, the most valuable feature of this manual is that it gives the county in which each post office is located. This may be used in typing acknowledgments on deeds which will be acknowledged out of the community in which the law office is located. The manual may be ordered by sending $4.25 to the United States Government Printing Office, Washington, D.C. 20402. See POSTAL SERVICE.

Disaffirmance. The act by which a person who has entered into a voidable contract indicates that he will not abide by the contract. For example, an infant may refuse to honor a contract by disaffirmance when he reaches majority.

Disbarment. Expulsion of a lawyer from the legal profession or from the bar of a particular court. Although the disbarment of an attorney is not a conviction for crime, disbarment may result from such a conviction.

Discharge of Contract. The release of the parties to a contract from their obligations under it. Contracts may be discharged by the following methods: (1) *Performance,* or the carrying out of the terms of the contract. (2) *Agreement.* The parties may agree to discharge one another from further liability under the contract. There must be sufficient consideration for the agreement. (3) *Impossibility of performance.* When a contract is based on an implied condition that certain factors shall continue to exist and performance is impossible, the contract is discharged. (4) *Operation of law.* A change in the law in effect at the time the contract was made may bring about a discharge of the contract, or a law itself may operate as a discharge. Thus, a contract to build a garage on a certain site would be discharged by a zoning ordinance forbidding the erection of a garage within that zone. (5) *Breach.* If one party breaches a contract the other may be discharged. (See BREACH OF CONTRACT.)

Disclosure. See PATENT.

Discovery. A procedure designed to obtain facts known by the defendant, or referred to in papers in his possession. The information is obtained by means of a *bill of discovery.*

Discovery and Inspection. A procedure whereby an attorney may obtain information contained in books, papers, documents, photographs, or other articles of property which are under control of the adverse party. This procedure is extremely helpful in preparing a case for pleading or for trial. See also DEPOSITION.

Dishonor. Refusal to pay a NEGOTIABLE INSTRUMENT when due. Notice of dishonor is usually given to endorsers and drawers, who, in addition to the maker, are liable on the instrument. Notice of dishonor may be given orally or in writing. If it is not given, endorsers and drawers are discharged from liability. See also PROTEST.

Dismissal. 1. An order or judgment finally disposing of an action, suit, motion, etc. by sending it out of court, though without a trial of issues involved.
2. A release or discharge from employment.

Disorderly Conduct. A term of indefinite meaning (except when occasionally defined in statutes), but signifying generally any behavior that is contrary to law and tends to cause a BREACH OF THE PEACE or to shock the public morality. One who commits a breach of the peace is guilty of disorderly conduct, but not all disorderly conduct is necessarily a breach of the peace. Soliciting by a prostitute is an example of disorderly conduct which is not a breach of the peace.

Dispossess. To take legal action to exclude an occupant from REAL PROPERTY. A dispossess action (summary proceeding) is a comparatively simple and short legal procedure that should be distinguished from the more lengthy and complicated action of EJECTMENT. The dispossess action may be brought where, under the terms of the LEASE, a breach of a covenant by the tenant automatically terminates the lease (known as, *conditional limitation*). The ejectment action is required where the breach of a covenant merely gives the landlord a right of re-entry and does not automatically terminate the lease (known as a condition).

Dissolution. *In Contracts.* The dissolution of a contract is the cancellation or abrogation of it by the parties themselves, with the effect of annulling the binding force of the agreement, and restoring each party to his original rights. In this sense it is frequently used in the phrase "dissolution of a partnership."

In Practice. The act of rendering a legal proceeding null, abrogating or revoking it; unloosing its constraining force; as when an injunction is dissolved by the court.

Of Corporations. The dissolution of a corporation is the termination of its existence as a body politic. This may take place in several ways; as by act of the legislature, where that is constitutional; by surrender or forfeiture of its charter; by expiration of its charter by lapse of time; by proceedings for winding it up under the law, by loss of all its members or their reduction below the statutory limit.

Of Marriage. The act of terminating a marriage; divorce; but the term does not include annulment. See DIVORCE *(No-Fault)*.

Distraint for Rent in Arrears. A statutory proceeding, allowed in some states, under which the landlord may seize the tenant's goods and chattels for rent in arrears, hold it as security, and sell the property to satisfy tenant's debt. The right does not exist until there has been a DEFAULT in rent, but the landlord can bring the action the day after the rent is due. When a landlord takes distraint proceedings to collect back rent, he cannot then oust the tenant from possession (see DISPOSSESS). Distraint amounts to a technical waiver of FOREITURE OF LEASE. A landlord who has habitually indulged a tenant and accepted rent after the due date fixed in the lease cannot suddenly insist upon punctual payment and institute distraint proceedings. He is estopped from doing so, and must first give the tenant notice that he will be held to punctual payment of rent in the future. See also ATTACHMENT; ESTOPPEL; LIEN.

District Courts. See AMERICAN COURT SYSTEM.

Ditto Marks. The punctuation (") which indicates that the material typed directly above the marks should be repeated. Such punctuation saves the time of retyping exactly the same words. Ditto marks are *not permissable* in a legal document. They may be used in exhibits and schedules but not in the document to which the exhibits and schedules are annexed. Ditto marks may sometimes be used in drafts, to save time, but the language is always repeated in full in the final instrument.

Divided Damages Rule. A doctrine developed by ADMIRALTY that divides DAMAGES equally where two vessels collide and both are at fault. Most of the leading maritime nations have adhered to an international convention, the Brussels Collision Convention of 1910, under which damages are proportioned in accordance with the party's degree of fault, i. e., a party 20 percent at fault bears 20 percent of the resulting loss while the party 80 percent at fault would be taxed for 80 percent of the loss. Under the COMMON LAW rule, recovery would be barred to both parties because of each one's CONTRIBUTORY NEGLIGENCE.

Dividend. That portion of the profits and surplus funds of a CORPORATION that has actually been set aside by a valid act of the corporation for distribution among the stockholders of record on a fixed day, in proportion to their holdings. The declaration of a dividend and the fixing of the amount, time, and terms of payment rest generally in the discretion of the BOARD OF DIRECTORS.

Divorce. The legal separation of man and wife, founded on matrimonial wrong, by the JUDGMENT of a court disolving the marriage. A divorce may be granted by the state where the parties have their legal DOMICILE. A decree of divorce must be given FULL FAITH AND CREDIT in every other state. There has been much abuse in divorce practice because of the different standards in each state as to what constitutes grounds for divorce. Fradulent claims of domicile are often made in order to obtain a divorce in a state with less strict standards.

Divorce *(No Fault).* In more recent times, consideration of the problem of no-fault divorce began with a 1965 report of the Special Committee on Uniform Divorce and Marriage Laws to the National Conference of Commissioners on Uniform State Laws.

The study indicated that the traditional conception of divorce based upon fault had failed to prevent marriage dissolution and had engendered perjury as an avoidance technique, resulting in loss of respect for the law and its processes. (*Handbook of the National Conference of Commissioners on Uniform States Laws* 1970, pp. 176-179.)

On August 6, 1970, the National Conference adopted a proposed uniform act which included a provision for divorce founded upon an irretrievably broken marriage. *Sec. 305.*

California acted in advance of the uniform act with its Family Law Act of 1969 which provided for termination of marriage based upon irreconcilable differences resulting in the irremediable breakdown of the marriage. *Civil Code, Sec. 4506.*

It replaced the traditional fault concept in which the grounds of adultery, extreme cruelty, willful desertion, willful neglect, habitual intemperance, conviction of a felony, and incurable insanity were recognized. *Civil Code Sec. 92.*

With the no-fault basis, incurable insanity has been retained as a second basis for dissolution of marriage in California.

Florida adopted the Uniform Act basis in 1971. Iowa adopted a dissolution of marriage law based on the breakdown of the marriage relationship to the extent that the legitimate objects of matrimony have been destroyed and there is no likelihood that the marriage can be preserved.

Indiana replaced the fault system with a dissolution of marriage proceeding which recognized the grounds of: (1) irretrievable breakdown, (2) conviction prior to marriage of an infamous crime, (3) impotency, and (4) incurable insanity for at least two years.

In 1973 Washington adopted a dissolution of marriage law using the Uniform Act concept of irretrievable breakdown.

The uniformity in approach has been the recognition of the need to deal with the problem of evasion and avoidance so rampant under the fault law with the recognition of the reality of *de facto* termination of the marriage contract, all the while preserving the interests of the state by requiring approval of the action and the meeting of standards in the matters of property, custody, support and alimony. It is against this developing change across the country that the Ohio law emerged. The Ohio law provides for a dissolution of marriage, providing an agreement is reached between the parties with regard to alimony, child support and property division.

(Reprinted by permission of Ohio Legal Center Institute, who own the copyright, from their manual, "Reference Manual for Continuing Legal Education Program.")

See also ANNULMENT; SEPARATION.

Docket. (Court) A formal record of all the important acts done in court in the conduct of each case from its beginning to its end. *Trial docket* is the name sometimes given to the list of causes set to be tried at a specified term and prepared by the clerks for use of the court and bar. See also CLERK'S PERMANENT RECORD BOOK.

Docket Number. See CLERK'S INDEX SYSTEM.

Domestic Corporation. A CORPORATION doing business in a state in which it was incorporated. See also FOREIGN CORPORATION; ALIEN CORPORATION; STATE OF INCORPORATION.

Domestic Postal Service. See POSTAL SERVICE.

Domicile. That place where a man has his true and permanent home and to which, whenever he is absent, he has the intention of returning. A man who goes away temporarily on business or for a vacation does not change his domicile. A person can have only one domicile at any one time. Domicile is important for purposes of taxation and JURISDICTION. See also RESIDENCE; VENUE.

Donee. One who is given a POWER OF APPOINTMENT. The recipient of a GIFT or LEGACY is also known as a donee.

Double Jeopardy. The situation where a person is twice put in danger of punishment for committing the same offense. The Fifth Amendment bars a second prosecution where a party has already been put in jeopardy. For a plea of double jeopardy to be valid, the offense charged in the second indictment (see GRAND JURY INDICTMENT) must be the same as that charged in the first, and both prosecutions must take place within the same JURISDICTION. See also BILL OF RIGHTS.

Dower. An allowance the law gives a widow from the real estate of her deceased husband for her support and the care of the children. Whether or not a widow is entitled to dower depends on the law of the state where the real estate is situated. See CURTESY.

Dower by Common Law. The ordinary kind of dower in English and

American law, consisting of a life interest in one third of the lands which the husband or wife was seized in fee at any time during the coverture. The dower interest must be released by the spouse signing the Warranty Deed if the real estate is conveyed to a new party, or the title is defective to the new party.

Drafts in Typing. A first copy of material that is to be revised. The word *Draft* should be written across the top of every page of a draft to avoid mistaking it for the final copy. Drafts should be triple-spaced for convenience in making changes. In retyping a draft, the following should be carefully noted: (1) portion marked for omission, (2) additional material to be inserted, (3) transpositions, and (4) corrections in spelling, punctuation, and the like.

Dress for the Office. See PERSONAL IMPRESSIONS.

Due Process of Law. Provisions in the Fifth and Fourteenth Amendments to the Constitution that prohibit the Federal Government and states from depriving any person of his life, liberty, or property without *due process of law*. The clauses have been interpreted by the courts as protecting the individual from arbitrary government activity and the unreasonable use of POLICE POWER.

Dummy. In publishing terminology, blank sheets cut and assembled to look like a proposed book or booklet. Layouts are generally drawn and copy stripped into the dummy to give the general appearance of the finished product. A *cut dummy* consists of plain sheets of paper on which engraver's proofs of cuts have been pasted, one cut to a page. Beneath each proof the corresponding label and credit lines are typed. A *page dummy* also called a "paste-up," is made by cutting GALLEY PROOFS to size and pasting them on the blank sheets, allowing spaces at the appropriate places for illustrations, tables, and the like.

How to make a page dummy. Mark off on 8 ½ by 11 inch sheets of paper the depth of the actual type page. For instance, if the type page, including RUNNING HEAD, is 46 PICAS deep, deduct 2 picas for running head and space, and place guide lines on the sheet for a type page 44 picas deep. (Be sure to allow extra space for sinkage on the opening pages of chapters.) Use a duplicate set of galleys for the page dummy. On each galley, mark every paragraph with the number of that galley. For example, each paragraph of galley 5 will be marked "5." Next, cut and paste onto the guide sheets the marked duplicate set of galleys, at the same time placing the cuts and captions in the proper position on each page. Try to allow proper spacing before and following cuts. It is a good plan to experiment with the placing of cuts and type on a page before actually pasting them down.

A page dummy should contain no type corrections, additions, or deletions. All such changes, even those that are necessary to lengthen or shorten pages to make them come out right, should be made on the master set of galleys.

Long or short pages must be

remedied. In the case of a long page, the editor can generally find a line at the end of a paragraph on that page that is very short. By shortening the sentence of which that line is a part, he is able to save a line. If the page is short, he looks for a full line at the end of a paragraph, and by adding a word or two to the sentence he makes an additional line. If the page is long or short by several lines and the editor is unable to remedy the situation, he asks the author to delete or add a few lines. If both facing pages (that is, an even and an odd page) are one line long or short, they are allowed to stay that way.

There should be at least three lines of type between a center heading and the bottom of a page. A paragraph with a BOLDFACE side heading should not begin at the bottom of a page. A page must not begin with a WIDOW.

Dun & Bradstreet, Inc. The only agency in existence that gathers and distributes credit information about persons and firms engaged in all lines of trade, in contradistinction to special agencies that limit their fields of operation to special trades.

Dun & Bradstreet "rates" a business on the basis of information gathered by reporters and correspondents about the owners and managers, giving consideration to character and ability to make good on obligations. The ratings cover capital and credit. They are condensed conclusions that show, by means of symbols, (1) the range of a concern's estimated financial strength, and (2) its grade of credit, reflecting past record, ability, and business prospects. Letters, from Aa to L, denote the estimated financial strength,

numbers, from $A1$ to E, denote the composite credit appraisal.

Duplicate Original. A carbon copy that is to be signed and treated in all respects as though it were an original or ribbon copy.

In the law office, an original, an office file copy, and a varying number of carbon copies of all legal documents are necessary. Frequently, one or more of the carbon copies must be used in the same manner as the original. When an original and two copies are needed for use in exactly the same way as the original, the term used becomes *triplicate original*.

The dictator tells the secretary how many copies to make. Instructions are usually given in this manner: "Two and four," meaning an original, a duplicate, and four copies; or, "One and five," meaning an original and five copies, no duplicate original being necessary.

Paper. Use heavyweight paper for the original or ribbon copy, and lightweight for the carbons, the weight depending on the number of copies. Duplicate and triplicate originals are usually typed on paper of the same substance as the ribbon copy. Some offices follow the practice of making the last carbon copy, which is the office copy, on heavy paper because it is more durable.

The kind of paper used depends upon the document that is being typed and also varies with the office.

Duress. Coercion causing action or inaction against a person's will through fear. Duress may take the form of physical force, imprisonment, bodily harm, improper moral persuasion, or the threat of any of these. Threat of criminal prosecution constitutes duress, but threat of civil prosecution does not. A contract made under duress is avoidable at the option of the party subjected to duress.

Duties. The tax imposed on the export or import of goods. The term *duty* is distinguished from the term *tariff* solely by the fact that the *duty* is the *actual tax* imposed or collected, while the *tariff,* technically speaking, is the *schedule* of duties. However, in practice the words are often used interchangeably.

Dying Declaration. A statement by a dying person, who has been injured by another and is aware of his impending death, about the person who inflicted the fatal injuries. This statement is admissible at the trial for HOMICIDE where the killing of the declarant is the crime charged to the defendant. This is an exception to the rule that would ordinarily exclude such a statement as HEARSAY. The reasons for this exception are the declarant's death and the probability of the trustworthiness of a declaration made by someone when he feels his death is imminent.

E

Earnest Money (Real estate). The payment of part of the purchase price to bind a sale. The cash deposit made by the buyer is an element of all contracts of sale, and is the indication that he intends to go through with the purchase if the seller furnishes good title to the property. The deposit is also referred to as the *binder*, although this term is more frequently applied to a deposit made under informal agreements than to deposits made in connection with formal contracts of sale drawn up by the lawyer. If the buyer fails to consummate the deal, the earnest money is retained by the seller; if he does perform his part of the contract, the earnest money is applied as part payment of the purchase price. If the seller cannot convey good title to the property, the deposit is returned to the buyer. The amount of earnest money depends upon the agreement between the parties. It is ordinarily sufficient to cover the broker's commission, expenses of the title search, and compensation to the seller for the loss he might sustain should the buyer fail to go through with the deal.

Easement. A right or privilege by one owner of land to use the land of another for a specific purpose. For example, *A* owns adjoining lots. He constructs a driveway on the common boundary line between the lots and sells one lot to *B. B* has an implied easement to use the driveway. An ease-

ment may be created by express grant, reservation, or agreement, or as a right acquired by lapse of time.

Ejectment. A form of action brought to regain possession of real property and to obtain DAMAGES for its unlawful retention. The action of ejectment is used to test or establish TITLE to REAL PROPERTY. See also DISPOSSESS.

Emancipation. The act whereby one is set free from the control of others. When a child is emancipated from his parents the duty of care is renounced along with the right to the custody and earnings of such child.

Embezzlement. The fraudulent appropriation of property or money by a person to whom it has been entrusted lawfully. In embezzlement the original taking of the property was lawful or with the consent of the owner, while in LARCENY the felonious intent must have existed at the time of the taking.

Eminent Domain. The power of Federal, state, and local governments to appropriate property for public use or the public welfare. When such property is taken, the owner is reimbursed according to a fair appraisal, and has the right to sue for a greater amount. PUBLIC UTILITY corporations are also given the power of eminent domain.

Enclosure. Material referred to in a letter and placed in the same envelope as the letter. (See also ENCLOSURE MARK.)

IN OUTGOING MAIL

When it is necessary to fasten enclosures together or to a letter, staples should be used. The Post Office Department objects to pins or metal clips.

1. *Enclosures the size of the letter.* If the enclosure consists of two or more sheets, they should be stapled together but not fastened to the letter. The enclosure and the letter should be folded separately and the enclosure slipped inside the last fold of the letter.

2. *Enclosure larger than the letter.* Enclosures too large to fit into a commercial envelope of ordinary size may be handled in one of several ways.

(a) The letter is inserted with the enclosure in the large envelope, which is sealed. First-class postage is charged for both the letter and the enclosure. The material will be dispatched as first-class mail.

(b) A letter may be enclosed with a parcel if postage is paid for the letter at the first-class rate and for the package at the parcel-post rate. The postage for the letter may be placed on the parcel separately or included with the postage for the parcel. The material will be dispatched as fourth-class mail. Beneath the postage and above the address, "First-Class Mail Enclosed" is written. If practical, the letter should be placed on top of the other items that make up the parcel.

(c) A *combination envelope* is used. This is a large envelope with a flap that is fastened by a patent fastener of some kind, *but not sealed.* A smaller envelope of commercial size is affixed on the front of this envelope in the process of manufacture. The letter is inserted into the small envelope and the flap is sealed. Postage is affixed to the large envelope at third-class rate and to the small envelope at first-class rate. The mail will be dispatched as third-class mail.

3. *Enclosures smaller than the letter.* Small enclosures should be stapled to the letter in the upper left-hand corner, on top of the letter. If two or more such enclosures are sent, the smaller one should be placed on top.

IN INCOMING MAIL

When an incoming letter contains an enclosure, the enclosure should be fastened to the accompanying letter. If the enclosure referred to is missing, a notation to that effect should be made on the letter and the omission called to the attention of the sender of the letter.

Enclosure Mark. The notation on a letter indicating that the letter contains other material. (See ENCLOSURE.) When a letter contains enclosures, type the word *Enclosure* or the abbreviation *Enc.* flush with the left-hand margin one or two spaces beneath the identification line. If there is more than one enclosure, indicate the number. If the enclosures are of special importance, identify them. If an enclosure is to be returned, make a notation to that effect.

```
RPE:es                      RPE:es
Enclosure                   Enc. 2
RPE:es
Enc. Cert. ck. $2,350
   Mtge,—Nelson to Jones
RPE:es
Enc. Policy 35 4698-M (to be returned)
```

The secretaries in a well-known law firm in the East follow the practice of placing an asterisk in the margin of the letter opposite the line that refers to the enclosure. This eliminates the possibility of forgetting to indicate at the bottom of the letter that there are enclosures.

Encumbrance. A burden or charge on property, either REAL PROPERTY or PERSONAL PROPERTY, consisting of a legal right or interest in favor of a person other than the owner. Frequently there is an indebtedness against real property that is being sold, or taxes or assessments are owed on it. These are *encumbrances* against the property, and the deed recites the agreement between the parties regarding them. The person who holds the encumbrance is the *encumbrancer.* The statement of encumbrances, if any either follows the property description (see TYPING PROPERTY DESCRIPTIONS) or is made a part of the HABENDUM CLAUSE. It is usually dictated by the lawyer.

The said premises are conveyed subject to a mortgage in the sum of Ten Thousand Dollars ($10,000), with interest, made by Roger L. Thompson to Edgar N. Wilson, dated the fifteenth day of January, 19.., and recorded in Book 27 or Conveyances, page 359, in the office of the Clerk of said county.

Subject to a purchase money mortgage made by the Grantee to the Grantor delivered and intended to be recorded simultaneously herewith.

Endorsed Legal Back. The manuscript cover of a legal instrument or court paper, on which has been written certain data referred to as the *endorsement.* See LEGAL BACK.

Endorsement. Writing one's name, either with or without additional words, on a NEGOTIABLE INSTRUMENT or on a paper (called an ALLONGE) attached to it. By an endorsement, the endorser becomes liable to all subsequent holders in due course for payment of the instrument if it is not paid by the maker when properly presented, and if he is given notice of dishonor. (See DISHONOR.)

Blank endorsement. The writing of one's name on an instrument, or an allonge, without any additional words, is a blank endorsement. Its effect is to make the paper payable to the bearer. Thus, a finder or thief might transfer the note to a third party for a consideration, and the third party may then enforce payment against the maker or the endorser.

Special endorsement. The designation of a certain person to whom the instrument is payable is a special endorsement. Thus, if an instrument is endorsed "Pay to John Jones," or "Pay to the order of John Jones," followed by the endorser's signature, no one but John Jones can receive payment for the instrument or transfer it.

Restrictive endorsement. An endorsement that transfers possession of the instrument for a particular purpose is a restrictive endorsement. Examples: "Pay to John Jones only. Sam Brown." "Pay to National City Bank for collection. Sam Brown." A restrictive endorsement terminates the negotiability of the instrument.

See also HOLDER IN DUE COURSE.

Enoch Arden Law. A statute that terminates the marriage because of the continuous absence of one of the spouses. The law proceeds upon the theory that, where a spouse has absented himself from his mate for a fixed period of time and where diligent effort has been made to locate him, without success, the court should declare the marriage to be at an end.

This type of law gets its name from *Enoch Arden,* a poem by Tennyson. Enoch Arden, the hero, is a sailor. He is wrecked on a desert island, and returns after many years to find his wife happily remarried. He takes up his abode near by, but self-sacrificingly conceals his identity, and dies of a broken heart.

Envelopes. The address on the envelope is the same as that on the letter's INSIDE ADDRESS. Figures 1 and 2, page 190, show acceptable and commonly used styles of address. They also show the correct placement of the ATTENTION LINE and MAILING NOTATIONS.

If there is no street address, put the name of the state on a separate line from the name of the city. Write the name of a foreign country in capitals on the envelope; use initial capitals in the inside adress.

CONNELLY, KARTER & MARTIN
627 Ingraham Building
Miami, Florida

SPECIAL DELIVERY

Mr. R. S. Jackson, President
Northern Manufacturing Company
25 West 79 Street
Milwaukee, Wisconsin

Envelopes: Figure 1 Indented style of address with special delivery notation.

CONNELLY, KARTER & MARTIN
627 Ingraham Building
Miami, Florida

Northern Manufacturing Company
25 West 79 Street
Milwaukee, Wisconsin

Attention Mr. R. S. Jackson

Envelopes: Figure 2. Block style of address with correct placement of attention line.

185

EQUAL PROTECTION OF THE LAWS

The U. S. Postal Service has issued an acceptable list of abbreviations for the name of states, and territories. They are as follows:

Alabama	AL	Nebraska	NE
Alaska	AK	Nevada	NV
Arizona	AZ	New Hampshire	NH
Arkansas	AR	New Jersey	NJ
California	CA	New Mexico	NM
Canal Zone	CA	New York	NY
Colorado	CO	North Carolina	NC
Connecticut	CT	North Dakota	ND
Delaware	DE	Ohio	OH
District of	DC	Oklahoma	OK
Columbia		Oregon	OR
Florida	FL	Pennsylvania	PA
Georgia	GA	Puerto Rico	PR
Guam	GU	Rhode Island	RI
Hawaii	HI	South Carolina	SC
Idaho	ID	South Dakota	SD
Kansas	KS	Tennessee	TN
Kentucky	KY	Texas	TX
Louisiana	LA	Utah	UT
Maine	ME	Vermont	VT
Maryland	MD	Virginia	VA
Massachusetts	MA	Virgin Islands	VI
Michigan	MI	Washington	WA
Minnesota	MN	West Virginia	WV
Mississippi	MS	Wisconsin	WI
Missouri	MO	Wyoming	WY
Montana	MT		

Personal notation. A letter or envelope should not be marked "Personal" or "Confidential" as a device to insure its delivery to a busy man. These words should be used only when no one but the addressee is supposed to see the letter. The word *Personal* or *Confidential* is typed, in solid caps underlined, on the envelope, two spaces above the address.

Equal Protection of the Laws. A guarantee made by the Fifth and Fourteenth Amendments that neither Congress nor the states may impair equal protection and security to all in their enjoyment of their personal and CIVIL RIGHTS. The clause refers to rights already in existence; it does not create any new rights.

Equitable Title. A person's right to obtain absolute ownership of property to which another has TITLE at law.

Equity. 1. *Courts.* A branch of remedial justice by and through which relief is afforded to suitors in CHANCERY COURT, or a court of equity. The word *equity* in the legal sense means "fair dealing," and that is the purpose of the system of legal rules and procedures known as equity.

Remedies at the COMMON LAW in England were frequently inadequate to give the wronged party a fair deal. He would then take his case to the King's Chancellor, who tempered the strict letter of the law with fairness. As a result of this practice, *chancery courts,* in which equity is practiced, were established, presided over by a chancellor instead of a judge. A few states still have chancery courts. See Table II, AMERICAN COURT SYSTEM.

In the course of its development, equity has established certain fundamental principles or maxims, which the lawyer frequently uses in dictating a BRIEF. Among these are the following:

1. *He who seeks equity must do equity.* If I seek the return of property that I was induced to sell through fraud, I must offer to return the purchase price.

2. *He who comes into equity must come with clean hands.* If I induce you to breach a contract and to make one with me instead, and then you breach the contract with me, a court of equity will not compel specific performance of your contract with me.

3. *Equity will presume that to be done which should have been done.* If I unlawfully take possession of your cow, a calf from that cow will belong to you, because a court of equity will presume that I was holding the cow for you.

4. *Equity aids the vigilant, not those who slumber on their rights.* Where the STATUTE OF LIMITATIONS has not run, but a claimant has delayed unreasonably in bringing suit, a court of equity may bar the claim by reason of such delay.

5. *Equity follows the law.* Except where the common law is clearly inadequate, equity follows the precedents of the common law and the provisions of the statutes. Thus, if a deed is void by common law or statute, the mere fact that a holder has given valuable consideration for it will not make the deed valid in equity.

6. *Equity regards substance rather than form.* Common law is normally governed by legal forms. Corporations, for example, are regarded in law as artificial beings, separate from their stockholders, directors, and officers. To accomplish justice, equity may disregard the corporate fiction and examine the substance of the dispute. For example, several men sold out a fish business and agreed not to go into the fish business in the same locality. They immediately formed a corporation to carry on a fish business in competition with the purchaser. The Court ignored the corporate entity and granted an injunction against this violation of the agreement not to compete.

Equity. 2. In accounting and finance. The value of the owner's interest in property in excess of all claims against it. Examples: (a) An owner's equity in his home is its present value less the amount of the mortgage. (b) The equity of the stockholders of a business is its net worth; hence, the interest of the stockholders as measured by capital and surplus, or the value of the assets of the business in excess of its liabilities. Sometimes, however, equity refers to the unlimited interest of common stockholders. (The equity of a person who has bought securities on margin is the present market value of the securities less the sum borrowed from the broker to make the purchase.

Erasures and Corrections on Typed Material. Most legal secretaries are familiar with the best methods for making erasures and corrections on the typed material they produce. The following is a review of standard methods and a briefing on new devices for erasing that are now on the market:

Standard method of erasing. Use two erasers—a hard one and a soft one. They may be combined into one eraser. Move the carriage as far to the side as possible so that paper and eraser fragments will not fall into the typewriter mechanism. Start with the soft eraser to remove the excess surface ink. Then change to the hard eraser to remove the imbedded ink. Finally, use the soft eraser again, to smooth off the surface. When erasing, rub with short, light strokes. A sharp razor blade may be used on a good grade of paper to remove punctuation marks and the tails of letters.

Insert a steel eraser guard between the carbon paper and the copy. The eraser guard is heavy enough to protect the other copies under it and is easy to handle. Or use a celluloid eraser shield but *do not use pieces of paper.*

Corrections on carbons. Corrections on carbon copies are often much fainter than the rest of the typing. To avoid this, make the correction as follows: After the necessary erasure has been made, adjust the ribbon control indicator to stencil position. Put the carriage in the proper position and strike the proper key. This will leave the impression on the carbon copies, but the original will still be blank. Then switch the control indicator back to the ribbon, place the carriage in position, and again strike the proper key. This procedure permits a perfect match of the typing on the original and will leave the typing on the carbon copies with an equal density of color.

Erasures near the bottom of the page. To erase on a line near the edge of the page, feed the sheet back until the bottom of the paper is free of the platen. Erase, and turn the page back into position for typing.

Corrections on bound pages. Corrections can be made on pages that are bound at the top. Insert a blank sheet of paper in the typewriter, as though for typing. When it protrudes about an inch above the platen, insert between it and the platen the unbound edge of the sheet to be corrected. Turn the platen toward you until the typewriter grips the sheet to be corrected. You can then adjust the bound sheet to the proper position for making the correction. Correction cannot be made on pages that are bound at the side without unstapling them.

New methods of erasing. New methods of erasing are being developed all the time. The secretary can investigate the following time-saving devices:

1. An eraser made of glass fibers is on the market. It will permit the secretary to erase on the original without the impression of the erasure going through to the carbon. (The carriage should always be moved to the right or left when using this eraser, and the glass part of the eraser should not be handled.)

2. There is available on the market a battery-operated electric eraser.

3. An eraser made of special paper is now being marketed. The special paper erases a mistake by covering it with a white, chalk-like chemical. All the secretary has to do is backspace to the point of the mistake, whether it is a single letter or a complete word, place the erasing paper in front of the error, and retype the error. This results in a blank space in which the correct word or letter may now be typed. There is also a companion product for erasing carbon copy mistakes. Also on the market is a liquid which paints the error white to match the paper. Then

the correction can be typed over the error. The most well known of these is "Liquid Paper." It is now on the market also in colors to match colored papers. These products are available at the stationers.

Escheat. The return of land to the state if the owner dies without legal heirs. Unclaimed personal property may also go to the state. Escheated personal property is called *bona vacantia.*

Escrow. A conditional delivery of something to a third person to be held until the happening of some event or the performance of some act. To place an instrument or fund in escrow is to deliver the instrument or fund to a person charged with its custody and disposition under the terms of a specific agreement, known as the *escrow agreement.* For example, a grantor may deliver a deed in escrow to a trust company until the grantee makes certain payments on the purchase price, at which time the trust company delivers the deed to the grantee.

Necessary components of escrows for the sale of REAL PROPERTY are:

1. A valid and enforceable contract for the sale of land.

2. An escrow agreement.

3. A disinterested third party, usually a bank, to act as escrow holder (*escrowee*). Neither buyer nor seller, nor their agent or attorney can act as escrowee.

Many banks, trust companies, building and loan associations, and title companies maintain special departments for escrow transaction.

Escrow upon exchange of property.

Placing the transaction "in escrow" is particularly helpful in a deal involving the exchange of real estate in one city for property in another city. When TITLE on both properties has been cleared and all the details attended to, arrangements can be made by telephone between the escrow agent in one city and the correspondent in the other city for simultaneous recording of the deeds.

Estate by the Entirety. See TENANCY BY THE ENTIRETY.

Estate Tax. A Federal or state excise tax, usually levied on a graduated basis, on the right to transfer property from the dead to the living. It includes transfers taking effect at death and certain other transfers that are defined by the law as having been made in "contemplation of death."

Estate taxes should not be confused with INHERITANCE TAXES, which are EXCISE TAXES levied by all of the states, except Nevada, on the right of the living to receive property from the dead. Inheritance taxes are payable by the heirs and not by the estate of the deceased, or must be paid by the estate if so directed in the decedent's Last Will and Testament. See also MARITAL DEDUCTION.

Estoppel. A barrier raised by law preventing a person from taking a position, denying a fact, or asserting a fact, in court, inconsistent with his previous conduct or statements. Example: *A* sells *B* a house that he (*A*) does not own, giving *B* a covenant and warranty deed, in which he warrants that he has title to the house. Later, *A* obtains title from the actual owner and attempts to eject *B* on the ground that *A* is now the true owner and *B* is not. *A* would be estopped from disputing what he formerly warranted, namely that he was the true owner when he sold the house.

In real estate, an *estoppel certificate* is the legal instrument commonly used when a mortgage is assigned. It shows the unpaid principal and interest due on a MORTGAGE. It is executed by a mortgagee or holder of a LIEN and bars the signer from making a claim inconsistent with the instrument.

Estoppel Certificate. See ESTOPPEL.

Ethics of the Legal Secretary. The professional standards of conduct to which a legal secretary must conform. The law secretary is bound by the same code of ethics as her employer. She cannot solicit business for him; she must regard everything she knows about a client or a case as confidential. She never divulges the contents of a written document in the office, without permission from the lawyer. It is a cardinal sin for a law secretary to talk outside of the office about a case, even if the talk is merely an anecdote. Frequently she is tempted to entertain her friends with interesting tidbits about socially prominent clients, but she always resists the temptation. Irreparable harm can result from mentioning anything about what is transpiring in a case. For example, suppose a lawyer dictates an application for injunction against removal of certain property from the county, so that he can levy upon it. If the secretary should mention this, the owner of the property, especially in a small town, might hear about it and remove the property before the judge signs the injunction. Facts and information received from clients by a secretary in the course of her work are PRIVILEGED COMMUNICATIONS.

Euthanasia. Practice of causing death painlessly to end suffering. This practice is very controversial. The controversy is over what is called brain death. The Harvard Medical School has drawn up guidelines to define brain death. These guidelines have been incorporated into laws passed by Maryland, Oregon, Michigan, California, Virginia, Kansas, Georgia, and New Mexico.

Eviction. The dispossession of tenant from the use and possession of REAL PROPERTY.

There are two forms of eviction: (a) actual eviction, by which the landlord forces the tenant to quit the property in advance of the termination of the lease; and (b) constructive eviction, where the tenant is forced to leave the property because it has become uninhabitable or not useful for the purpose for which leased (destruction by fire, for example).

Both types of eviction are subject to widely varied laws and to specific agreements written into the contract. See also DISPOSSESS; FORCIBLE ENTRY AND DETAINER; EJECTMENT.

Evidence of Title. See TITLE.

Ex Post Facto Law. Any retroactive legislation that has the effect of substantially prejudicing the rights of the accused or convicted party in a criminal proceeding. An example of an ex post facto law is one that designates an act as criminal after it has been committed. Another example is the passage of a law that would increase the penalty for a crime already committed. The Constitution denies to both Congress and the states the right to pass ex post facto laws.

Examination Before Trial. See DEPOSITION.

Excise Taxes. Federal, state, and local taxes imposed on acts rather than on property. For example, excise taxes are levied on the sale of gasoline and tobacco rather than on the items themselves.

Excise taxes may be levied either against the seller or the purchaser. Manufacturers' excise taxes are levied against persons who sell various articles, but admissions taxes and communications taxes are borne by the consumer. However, excise taxes paid by the consumer are usually collected by the seller and remitted by him to the taxing authority.

Federal excise taxes are deductible for Federal INCOME TAX purposes only when paid or incurred as an ordinary and necessary expense of carrying on a trade or business, or incurred as "non-business" expense. *Nonbusiness expenses* are ordinary and necessary expenses paid or incurred by an individual in connection with (1) the production and collection of income, or (2) the management, conservation, or maintenance of property held for the production of income, or (3) the determination, collection or refund of any tax.

State excise taxes are deductible as such for Federal income tax purposes. Since these taxes are deductible as such and not as expenses, the deductibility

does not depend on whether the tax is connected with the taxpayer's business or "non-business" activities. State excise taxes are deductible by the person on whom it is imposed. However, a state tax separately stated may be deducted by the buyer even it if is imposed on the seller. The person on whom the tax is imposed depends on state or local law.

Whether Federal and state excise taxes are deductible for state income tax purposes depends on the tax law of the particular state. See also DIRECT TAXES.

Exclusions. See INCOME.

Exclusive Powers. Those powers delegated by the Constitution solely to Congress. Powers are exclusive with Congress and denied to the states either by express provision in the Constitution or where exercise of a similar power by the states would be inconsistent with Congressional action. Congress is given exclusive powers to do such things as coin money, declare war, provide and maintain a navy, and to establish post offices and post roads.

The Tenth Amendment provides that the powers neither delegated nor prohibited by the Constitution to the states are "reserved to the states respectively or the the people." See STATE'S RIGHTS; CONCURRENT POWERS.

Execution. 1. *Of judgment.* A legal writ directing an officer of the law to carry out a judgment is an execution of judgment.

2. *Of an instrument.* The signature and delivery of a written instrument constitutes execution of the instrument. In law office parlance, *execution* more frequently refers merely to the signing

of an instrument by the party or parties described in it. See ATTESTATION CLAUSE; TESTIMONIUM CLAUSE.

Execution of Lease. See LEASE.

Executor. The person or corporation named by a testator in his will to administer his estate. The testator may name as many executors as he desires. Often a man names his wife and a bank as co-executors—his wife because he wants her to have a voice in the administration of the estate; the bank, to advise his wife and to relieve her of the considerable amount of work involved in the administration. (A woman is an *executrix*.)

Exhibit. *In Trial.* A document or any other tangible item that has been received in evidence at a trial. The general rule in civil cases is that a jury is permitted to take exhibits into the jury room at the court's discretion. In criminal cases, permission may be granted for the jury to have exhibits in the jury room only upon the consent of the defendant and the counsel for the prosecution.

Of an Instrument. Attachment to a legal instrument which is too lengthy to be typed in the body of the document itself or is further explanatory of the document. Usually marked "Exhibit A" or "B" etc.

Expense Account. A statement of an individual's costs incurred for a specific period and purpose, usually for a particular assignment on behalf of his company. Sometimes a lawyer's firm will advance money to him and he returns the unused portion, or the lawyer uses his own funds and the company reimburses him.

If the lawyer accounts to his firm for expenses incurred on its behalf, he need not report on his income tax return those expenses that are charged to the company or those for which he was reimbursed. The expenses and reimbursements balance, thus having no effect on his income. However, he must state on his return that reimbursements did not exceed expenses, or if they did that the excess was included in income.

If the lawyer does *not* account to his firm for expenses, he must report them on his return. He must also attach a statement showing the total of all amounts received from the firm including the amounts charged to it.

The lawyer's secretary should keep a record of expenses incurred by him on behalf of the firm. The record shows the company the amount spent for each item and also serves as a record for income tax purposes. Any form of record that shows the date, description and amount of the expenditures is satisfactory. If the lawyer takes many trips, a columnar sheet similar to that illustrated in Figure 1 is appropriate.

Mo.	Day	Description	Fares	Meals	Lodging	Tips	Automobile Expenses	Misc.

Expense Account: Figure 1. Record of expenses of business trip.

Expert Witness. A person selected because of his knowledge or skill to examine, estimate, and ascertain things, and to make a report of his opinion at trial. An expert can draw from facts inferences that a layman could not make, and in this way he aids the jury. The facts upon which his opinion is based may have been personally observed by the expert or incorporated in a hypothetical question put to him. Whether a witness is qualified to speak as an expert is a preliminary question of fact to be determined by the trial court. A few examples of specialized fields where an expert's testimony would be necessary are medicine, ballistics, chemical analysis, psychiatry and engineering.

Extortion. The wrongful act of compelling payments by means of threats of injury to a person, his property, or his reputation. Extortion is distinguished from ROBBERY in that the intimidation can be done at one place and the money taken at another. See also BLACKMAIL.

Extract. A printer's term for quoted material or an excerpt that is to be set in a smaller size of type than the rest of the text. The printer uses the term "extract" because the copy that is to be set in smaller type is "extracted" from the other copy and is set on a different typesetting machine. Quotation marks are omitted. Lists, examples, problems, and quotations of over four lines are generally set in smaller type.

Extradition. The surrender by one state to another state of a party who has fled in order to escape prosecution. The state desiring extradition must be competent to try him and must demand the surrender.

F

False Imprisonment. The substantial restraint of a man's freedom of movement, without authority of law and against his will. Arresting the wrong person under a WARRANT is an example of false imprisonment. An action for DAMAGES may be had against the offender.

Featherbedding. Payment by an employer for services which are not performed or not to be performed. Legislation bans featherbedding, but the problem exists in particular cases as to whether an employee is needed or just on the payroll for doing nothing. An example of what management considers featherbedding is the employment of stand-by musicians.

Federal Court. See AMERICAN COURT SYSTEM.

Federal Reporter. See NATIONAL REPORTER SYSTEM.

Federal Rules Decisions. See NATIONAL REPORTER SYSTEM.

Federal Supplement. See NATIONAL REPORTER SYSTEM.

Federal Tax Citator. A loose-leaf publication that gives a complete judicial history of every Federal tax case and ruling. It shows where to find everything that has been said about any Federal tax case or ruling in all succeeding cases or rulings. The Federal Tax Citator covers all standard court reporting systems, and other official sources, such as TAX COURT, Appeal and Review Memoranda, Revenue Rules, Treasury Decisions, Income Tax Unit Rulings, Mimeograph Rulings, and Internal Revenue Bulletins.

The cases are arranged in alphabetical order. Cross references insure that the title under which each CITATION is listed may be readily found. In those cases in which the Government, the Commissioner, or the collector is a party, the citations are listed under the name of the taxpayer. The names of companies are listed as court decisions without reference to initials or first names of parties.

The Federal Tax Citator is the only CITATOR system on Federal taxes that indicates the *exact page* in the *exact volume* of whatever reporter system is being used. It is standard equipment in the offices of leading tax practitioners. Supplements are mailed approximately once a month to subscribers.

It is published by Prentice-Hall, Inc., Englewood Cliffs, New Jersey.

Fee Simple. The absolute ownership of REAL PROPERTY. It gives the owner and his heirs the unconditional power of disposition and other rights.

Fees (lawyer's). Compensation for the legal services rendered to clients.

The fees that a lawyer charges usually depend on a number of factors. When fixing fees the lawyer considers the amount of money involved in the controversy, the time spent, the difficulty and importance of the questions of law and fact involved, the ability of the client to pay, and the results accomplished. See FORWARDING FEE; CONTINGENT FEE.

Felony. A crime punishable by death or by imprisonment in a state prison. See MISDEMEANOR.

Felony-Murder. The act of killing in the perpetration or attempted perpetration of a FELONY. Felony-murder is a crime that may be punishable by death. The offender's intent in felony-murder is his intent to commit the underlying felony and not his intent to kill. Killing someone while in the act of burglarizing a house is an example of felony-murder.

Fictitious Names. Names (either imaginary or only partly accurate) that are used temporarily in preparing legal papers in an action, with the express intention that the true names be substituted as soon as they are learned.

Since someone frequently has an interest that the plaintiff (see PARTIES TO AN ACTION) does not know about, or someone whose name is unknown has an interest in the suit, several fictitious names are added as defendants can be brought into the action without the necessity of serving an amended complaint on all defendants. Perhaps an interested party's last name is known but not his first; a fictitious first name is given to that defendant thus:

"Richard" Neilson, first name "Richard" being fictitious, defendant's first name being unknown to the plaintiff.

The complaint usually alleges that the names are fictitious. The true name is substituted for the fictitious name as soon as it is learned. In all subsequent papers filed in the case, the caption reflects the substitution.

Fiduciary. A person, or organization such as a CORPORATION, holding a position and acting in the capacity of trust and special confidence, so that he or it is obliged to act with the highest degree of good faith, and to place ahead of his or its own interests the interest of those represented; as an adjective—having the nature of a trust. Attorneys, guardians, directors of corporations, and public officers are fiduciaries.

Fiduciary Account. An accounting of receipts and disbursements made to the Probate Court by a guardian for his ward, or an executor, or an administrator for a decedent. Accounts are usually numbered "First Account," "Second Account," and "Third, Final and Distributive" Account, when an estate is closed or the guardianship is terminated.

File Folders, Arrangements of Papers in. There is a definite way in which the legal secretary arranges all papers within the folders before they are filed. A file in a law matter consists of at least two parts: correspondence and formal documents, whether they be court papers or legal instruments such as agreements, leases, and the like. Each file must have a correspondence folder and a document folder, both of which are kept together in the file jacket. It does not matter what kind of "folder" is used, as long as it has enough firmness to serve as a backing sheet to which the papers may be fastened with a brad or other fastener that permits removal when desired. Correspondence and papers are both filed in their respective folders according to date, usually with the latest on top, although some lawyers prefer the reverse order. Always keep the correspondence folder on top of the document folder in the jacket.

A file might consist of more than two parts. Separate folders are required for briefs and law memoranda; drafts; extra copies; miscellaneous memoranda, such as interoffice memos, notes made by the lawyer, etc. If a file contains both legal instruments (agreements, contracts, and the like) and court papers, a separate folder is made for each. If a case has papers filed in more than one court, a separate folder is made for each court. A law file might also contain a folder for "hold papers," that is, papers belonging to the client other than those kept in the safe. The "hold papers" should not be fastened in the folder. Always indicate on the index card the folders that are made up in each case.

As a file grows, it is broken down into volumes, with all letters together in one or two folders, all court papers together, and so on. Law files frequently become so voluminous that two or more jackets are required. All of the jackets in a particular case have the same number. On each jacket, write the classification of the contents of that jacket—that is, the folders that are in the jacket—so that you will not have to open more than one jacket to find the desired papers. Some offices make a separate index card for each jacket.

For a matter that will not become sufficiently voluminous to warrant separate folders and a jacket, use a legal size folder and fasten the documents to the right side, and the cor-respondence to the left. Either an Acco or a Kompact fastener is useful for this purpose. Some offices do not put the file folders in a jacket, but simply file them together. This eliminates having to open a jacket in order to get out the folder that is needed.

Write the title of the case, the client's name, and the number of the file on each folder and on the jacket. Figure 1 on page 197, shows a properly labeled jacket.

Filing (in a law office). A methodical laying away of important papers and material in such a way that the lawyer may have access to specific folders, papers, or letters promptly.

No matter what system of filing the secretary uses it is the accuracy with which she files that determines whether or not she is able to find desired material without extended searching and fumbling. It is one of the secretary's most important duties to produce papers promptly so that neither she nor the lawyer is caused embarrassment. Mislaid papers may even mean a lost client. It is expedient to segregate files pertaining to clients' business from files pertaining to personal and office administration matters. The following classification is appropriate for the typical law office.

1. *Clients' business.* Files in this category include all matters relating to clients, with the exception of commercial collections when handled in volume. Some offices separate the material into litigation and non-litigation matters. Other offices segregate files relating to a particular field of law if a large part of the practice is in a specific field. Still other offices segregate matters relating to a retainer client with a large volume of business. The least confusing method,

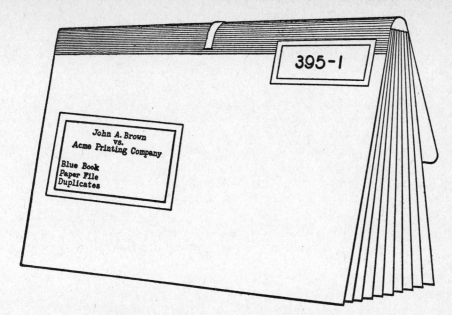

File Folders: Figure 1. File jacket properly labeled.

however, is to keep all the files of each client together.

Since clients' files constitute by far the major part of the files in a law office, the detailed explanations in this book of the numerical and alphabetical systems of filing relate to clients' files.

2. *Commercial collections.* Where a fair volume of commercial collections is handled, the files are segregated from other clients' business because of the close follow-up on these cases. (See COLLECTIONS, *How to file collection matters.*)

3. *Personal files.* The lawyer's personal file contains material relating to the lawyer's personal business matters, correspondence, and outside activities, such as bar association committees. (See PERSONAL FILE.)

4. *General correspondence files.* This is the miscellaneous or "catch-all" file. It contains all material not relating to clients' business or to the lawyer's personal matters. Office administration material, such as personnel applica-

tions and records, correspondence about office equipment, correspondence with law book publishers, and the like would be placed in this file. Correspondence about a case that the lawyer does not accept would be filed here.

5. *Periodicals, bulletins, etc.* Every office accumulates pamphlets, booklets, periodicals, and the like that contain information likely to be needed in the future. (See PERIODICALS, BULLETINS, ETC., FILING OF.)

See also FILING, PREPARATION OF MATERIAL FOR; ALPHABETICAL FILING, LAW OFFICE; NUMERICAL FILING SYSTEM (APPLIED TO CLIENTS' FILES); CLOSING FILE, PREPARATION FOR; FOLLOW-UP FILING SYSTEM.

Filing Loose-leaf Publications. The great complexity and ever changing rules and regulations of modern business have brought about the development of the specialized loose-leaf publications (also known as "services"). Most businesses and professional advisers subscribe to one or more loose-leaf services. These publications usually contain an explanatory text (compilation) and report on new laws, regulations, administrative interpretations, judicial decisions, and other developments affecting the subjects covered. Lawyers, tax consultants, accountants, and other businessmen use these services.

The original compilation is furnished in a large loose-leaf binder. Periodically, loose-leaf report bulletins are sent to the subscribers to highlight recent developments and furnish new pages that bring the compilation up to date. This material is numbered by page and paragraph, and is filed in the loose-leaf binders. With loose-leaf binders it is easy to remove pages as they become obsolete, and replace those pages with new ones giving up-to-date information. It is the secretary's job to file these new pages *immediately and accurately*.

The loose-leaf services the lawyer finds most helpful are Prentice-Hall's *Wills, Estates, and Trusts* and *Corporation* services and Federal and state tax services. Each week, the secretary receives in the mail report bulletins and new pages for the services. She follows the enclosed directions *carefully and promptly*, because she knows that it is just as important to discard the old pages indicated on the directions sheet, as it is to file correctly the new pages of each bulletin. Here is one of the instruction sheets she received recently and an illustration of how it works. (The superior figures and explanations do not appear on the instruction sheet but are used in the illustration below to explain how the service works.)

CONTENTS[1]

Report No. 5

Pages not required[2]	Pages in this report[3]	Reason for change[4]
9293-9294[5]	9293-9294	Reference added in ¶ 9217
12,201-12,208[6]	None	Obsolete Regulations removed
None[7]	28,801-28,806	New Regulations added
30,101-30,107[8]	30,101-30,104	Editorial Revision to conform with new law provisions
36,201-36,208[9]	36,201-36,218	Annotations added

Explanations:

[1]*Contents* means these are the items in the report which must be replaced, added to, or removed from the volume.

[2]*Pages not required* means that the pages in this column are to be replaced or removed.

[3]*Pages in this report* means that the pages in this column contain the latest information and are to be inserted.

[4]*Reason for change*

[5]*9293-9294   9293-9294*   In this case pages 9293-9294 are being replaced by the same number of new pages, which have new information.

[6]*12,201-12,208   None*   The secretary removes these pages and nothing is to take their place.

[7]None$28,802-28,806		There are no comparable pages in the volume to be removed. The addition is inserted in the numerical sequence of pages already in the volume.
[8]30,101-30,107	30,101-30,104	The obsolete material removed is larger than the new material to be inserted.
[9]36,201-36,208	36,201-36,218	The material to be removed is replaced with a larger amount of material.

Warning: From the above, it is easy to see that short cuts in filing are dangerous. Only through consecutively performing the step in the first column, followed by the step in the second column, can one be sure of accuracy. Unless this is done, there is danger of removing too little or too much.

Filing, Preparation of Material for. The process of organizing and making ready for filing all office papers that are to remain on record. To prepare material for filing the secretary will do the following:

1. Segregate papers belonging in different files: clients' matters; personal; general correspondence.

2. Check to see if the lawyer has initialed the paper for filing. (In offices with more than one attorney, there should be a hard and fast rule that no paper is to be filed until the responsible attorney has initialed it.)

3. Check through all papers that are clipped or stapled together to see whether they should be filed together.

4. Remove all paper clips.

5. Mend torn papers with Scotch tape.

6. See that all legal documents have been conformed.

7. Mark on all court papers the date they were filed with the CLERK OF THE COURT or served upon opposing counsel. (This information is stamped by the clerk of the court on the back of the paper and is not evident when the paper is fastened to the folder unless noted on the face of the paper.)

8. Note on the paper where it is to be filed. For numerical files, write the key and identification numbers in the upper right-hand corner; for a name file, underline the name in colored pencil; for a subject file, write the subject in colored pencil in the upper right-hand corner, or underline it in colored pencil if it appears on the paper.

9. Punch a hole or holes in the *exact* place where the paper should be fastened to the folder. An electric gadget that punches holes in the paper is a valuable time saver when thick documents must be stapled into folders.

10. When fastening the paper in the folder, check the number and name on the paper being filed with the number and name on the folder.

For any filing problem, write:

System Service Department
Oxford Filing Supply Co., Inc.
East Stewart Avenue
Garden City, New York 11530

See FILE FOLDERS, ARRANGEMENT OF PAPERS IN; CLOSING FILE, PREPARATION FOR; INDEX TABS AND LABELS, TYPING OF; FOLLOW-UP FILING SYSTEM.

Filling-in Law Blanks. See PRINTED LAW BLANKS.

Findings of Fact and Conclusions of Law. A statement of the facts and the applicable rules of law in a particular jurisdiction, prepared by the attorney at the direction of the court. At the trial of a case, certain facts are determined from the pleadings and evidence. Certain rules of law are applicable to those facts. After the trial of a case by the court without the jury, the court directs the attorneys to prepare a statement of the facts and applicable rules of law. This statement is designated *findings of fact and conclusions of law.* In other jurisdictions, the court directs counsel for both sides to prepare findings of fact and conclusions of law. In some jurisdictions, the court directs counsel for only one party to prepare the statement; opposing counsel then has a specified time within which to file objections and submit his proposed findings. The secretary's duties are the same in either situation.

How to prepare findings of fact and conclusions of law. The lawyer dictates the findings of fact and conclusions of law.

1. Make an original for the court, a copy for each counsel, and a copy for the file.

2. The caption is the same as on the complaint.

3. The document is entitled "Findings of Fact and Conclusions of Law."

4. The findings of fact are enumerated, beginning with FIRST, or I.

5. The conclusions of law are enumerated, beginning with FIRST, or I.

6. The date line is typed below the last conclusion of law, at the left margin.

7. Type a line for the judge's signature.

8. Endorse legal backs and all copies except office copy.

What the secretary does about findings of fact and conclusions of law.

1. As soon as the court directs counsel to prepare findings of fact and conclusions of law, *enter in diary* the date by which the statement must be prepared.

2. See that copy is served on opposing counsel.

3. See that receipt of copy is acknowledged, or make an affidavit of service by mail.

4. *Enter in diary* date by which opposing counsel must file objections and submit his proposed findings.

5. The original, with proof of service on opposing counsel, is submitted to the judge who tried the case.

6. Make entry in suit register of service, submission to judge, signing, and filing.

First-class Mail. See POSTAL SERVICE.

First Pleading. See PLEADING.

Flight Number. Number assigned for convenience by an airline to a specific plane flight to distinguish the flight from other flights, Instead of identifying a flight by time of departure and route, the airlines identify it by number.

Flotsam. See JETTISON.

Follow-up Filing System. A method of filing material whereby it will be brought to the attention of the interested person on a certain date. The follow-up file is a check on whether correspondence has been answered or any other desired action has been taken.

If all matters in a law office that had to be followed were entered in the DIARY, it would become so cluttered it would lose its usefulness. Therefore, follow-up, or tickler files are a useful supplement to the diary. A notation or reminder, usually a carbon copy, is placed in the tickler file while the material itself remains in its proper place in the regular files. If the material itself is placed in the follow-up file instead of in the regular file, it cannot be located if it is needed before the follow-up date.

Checklist of material to be placed in follow-up files. Court cases are preferably followed through the DIARY, or SUIT REGISTER, but the following matters are generally followed through follow-up files rather than through the diary:

1. Matters that are referred to other lawyers or law clerks in the office for information, comment, or action.

2. Correspondence or memoranda awaiting answer.

3. Collection letters.

4. Covering letters enclosing documents sent by registered mail, until receipt is received.

5. Requests for acknowledgments of documents, etc.

6. Receipts for documents left with court clerks or other officials for recording.

7. Letters of Register of Deeds, or other officials, enclosing papers for recording, to be kept until papers are returned and delivered to client.

8. Letter to ABSTRACT COMPANY.

Equipment for follow-up system. Numerous styles of equipment for follow-up purposes are on the market, but many secretaries to busy lawyers have found the follow-up file system described here to be practical, efficient, and time saving.

The only equipment necessary is a file drawer and file folders. Make a set of file folders consisting of (a) 12 folders labeled from January through December, (b) 31 folders labeled from 1 through 31, and (c) 1 folder marked, "Future Years." If you have a heavy volume of follow-up material, it is advisable to have two sets of folders labeled by days—one for the current month and one for the succeeding month.

Tabbed guides marked 1 through 31 and removable separators tabbed with the months will make it easier to locate a particular folder, but these are not necessary to the efficient functioning of the system.

Arrangement of folders for follow-up. Arrange the folders labeled by days in numerical order in the front of the file. Place in these the follow-up material for the current month. The folder labeled for the current month is at the back of the other monthly folders ready to receive any material to be followed up in the same month next year. Immediately following the numerical daily folders is the folder for the coming month, followed by the folder for the succeeding month, and so on.

Operation of the follow-up system.

1. Make an extra copy of correspondence or memoranda that require a follow-up, preferably on paper

of a different color. Mark on the extra carbon the date on which it is to be followed up. When there is no carbon copy of material for follow-up, write a brief memo for the tickler file. For example, if your employer gives the secretary a newspaper clipping and tells her to bring it to his attention on the 30th of the month, she prepares a tickler memo (on the same color paper as the follow-up carbon copy of correspondence) for follow-up on the 30th, but she files the clipping so that she can put her hands on it if her employer wants it before the 30th. The memo should indicate where the material is filed. File any pertinent papers in the regular files.

2. Place material that is to be followed up in the current month in the proper date folders. Each day transfer the empty daily folder back of the folder for the coming month. Thus there are always 31 daily folders for follow-ups, part of them for the remaining days in the current month and part of them for the first part of the coming month. Place material that is to be followed up more than 30 or 31 days in the future in the proper month folder, regardless of the day of follow-up. See Figure 1 which is a diagram of the arrangment of folders on April 15. On that day, material to be followed up from April 16 through May 15 is placed in daily folders; material to be followed up after May 15 is placed in the proper month folder.

3. On the first of each month, transfer the material from the folder for that month into the folders labeled by days. To avoid filing material for follow-up on Saturdays (if the office closes), Sundays, or holidays, reverse the folders for those days so that the blank side of the label faces the front of the file. Note in Figure 1, page 203,

that the folders for April 16, 17, 23, 24, 30 and 31 (since April has only 30 days), and May 1, 7, 8, and 14 are blank. The empty folder for the current month is then transferred to the rear of the other month-by-month folder.

How to handle material in the daily follow-up file. Each day when examining the follow-up file the secretary will find that a large part of the material has been answered without a follow-up. She should destroy these carbons or memoranda. If a heavy schedule keeps her from giving attention to all the material in the daily folder, she marks the less important items for follow-up at a later date.

Move indefinite follow-ups forward from week to week until a definite date is established or until the matter is completed. This procedure is often referred to as "combing-back."

Follow-ups on a small scale. When the secretary has only a small amount of correspondence or other matters to follow up, a set of follow-up file folders is not necessary. She marks the carbons with the follow-up date and files them chronologically in one folder, with those marked for the earliest follow-up on top.

Tickler card file for follow-up. A TICKLER CARD FILE is as useful as follow-up file folders for any type of material except correspondence. The secretary can type a notation for herself on a card and place it in a tickler card file as easily as she can type a memorandum and put it in a file folder. But it is a waste of time to make a card notation of correspondence when she can make an extra carbon at the time of transcription. Therefore, unless she has only a small amount of correspondence to follow up and handle as described in the preceding paragraph, use follow-up file folders instead of a tickler card.

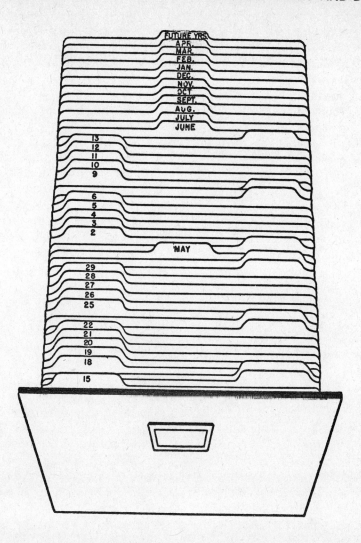

Follow-up Filing System: Figure 1. Diagram of follow-up files.

Force Majeure (French). Superior or irresistible force. Corresponds in a general way to "Act of God"; for example, an earthquake, or the sudden death of a person. If a party to a contract is prevented from executing it by a *force majeure,* he may not be held liable for damages. If the vendor of a contract for the sale of real estate dies before the contract is completed and the contract states that it includes his executors, administrators, heirs and assigns, the decedent's executor or administrator may bring an action for the completion of the contract.

Forcible Entry and Detainer. A remedy provided by statute in some states to enable the lessor (landlord or owner) to recover possession of his property, upon one or more of the following violations by the lessee (tenant):

(1) Holding over after termination of the LEASE. (2) Failure to pay rent a fixed number of days after it is due, after specified notice has been given by the lessor. (3) Violating other terms of the lease. (4) Committing waste.

Foreclosure. A proceeding against property securing a debt, brought upon DEFAULT, to cut off the mortgagor's equitable right to redeem the property (see REDEMPTION). The most common method is by *foreclosure suit* in a court of EQUITY. In a few states foreclosure may also be effected by exercise of a power of sale given in the mortgage (Colorado, for example), by cntry and posscssion (New Hampshire, for example), or by writ of entry (Maine, for example). The mortgage may provide that the holder of the mortgage is entitled to the appointment of a receiver in any action to foreclose it. See also FORECLOSURE PROCEDURE.

Foreclosure Procedure. The legal action taken by a lawyer on behalf of a creditor against a debtor who has defaulted in payment on a secured debt or MORTGAGE.

The first steps in the foreclosure proceeding are (1) the preparation of the notice of LIS PENDENS; (2) the preparation of the SUMMONS and COMPLAINT, which are prepared like the summons and complaint in any civil action. Because the foreclosure action generally has numerous defendants, the secretary usually types the summons instead of using a printed form.

Filing and service of Lis Pendens, Summons and Complaint. After the Lis Pendens, Summons and Complaint are prepared, the procedure is the same as in any civil action. The notice of *lis pendens* must be filed with the proper county official (The official varies with the jurisdiction); the summons is issued for service and the complaint is filed with the CLERK OF THE COURT. The summons and complaint must be served on the defendants within a specified time after the *lis pendens* is filed.

The secretary must not forget to make DIARY *and* SUIT REGISTER *entries accordingly.*

Follow-up of process service. Follow-up of process service is necessary in all civil actions, but is particularly important in foreclosure actions because of the number of defendants. Numerous foreclosure actions are delayed because service of process is lax. It is the secretary's responsibility to see that the process server makes every effort to effect service expeditiously on all defendants. (See also *Service on opposing counsel,* NOTICE OF APPEAL.)

Other steps in foreclosure proceedings. After the summons, complaint, and *lis pendens* have been filed and served, the procedure in foreclosure litigation varies. The following steps are among those that will have to be taken, depending upon the jurisdiction and the circumstances of the case.

1. Application for receivership. If the property involved is income producing, the plaintiff will ask for the appointment of a receiver to collect the income and make the necessary disbursements.

2. Application for appointment of guardian *ad litem*. If the parent of an infant defendant will not ask for the appointment of a guardian *ad litem*, the plaintiff does.

3. *Ex parte* motion to obtain leave to sue "arm of court," such as a trustee in BANKRUPTCY.

4. Entry of DEFAULT judgment.

5. Reference to compute or reference to master in chancery.

6. Hearing before referee or master. The lawyer will want the following papers to take to the hearing:

   a. Referee's oath

   b. Referee's report ready for signature

   c. Bond or note

   d. MORTGAGE or DEED OF TRUST

   e. Assignments

   f. True or photostatic copies of (c), (d), and (e), so that the originals may be withdrawn when the hearing is over

   g. Receipted bills for taxes, assessments, water rates, penalties or interest, if any, paid by mortgagee

   h. Receipt for payment of insurance if paid by mortgagee

   i. Summons with affidavit of service

   j. Check to order of referee

7. Judgment or DECREE of foreclosure and sale.

8. Publication of notice of sale.

9. Sale.

Checklist of what to do in foreclosure action. Here is a checklist of what the secretary will have to do when her officer handles a foreclosure action.

1. Make file and process as any other new matter.

2. *Keep diary entries* and progress record.

3. Order ABSTRACT OF TITLE continuation.

4. Prepare all papers, as directed by the attorney.

5. See that summons, complaint, and *lis pendens* are filed and served.

6. Follow process server closely.

7. Have copies (typed or photostatic) made of mortgage or deed, trust, bond or note, and assignments.

8. Prepare party sheet and keep it up to date.

9. If a receiver is appointed, keep after him for regular reports.

10. Gather together papers for the lawyer to take to the hearing (see preceding paragraph).

11. Make bookkeeping entries of all disbursements and receipts, just as in any case.

Foreign Corporation. A CORPORATION transacting business in a state other than the one in which it is incorporated is known as a foreign corporation in that state. A foreign corporation is obliged to observe all the requirements of the state in which it seeks to do business with respect to right of admission, service of process, taxation, etc. See also ALIEN CORPORATION; DOMESTIC CORPORATION; STATE OF INCORPORATION.

Foreign Travel. When a lawyer plans a business or pleasure trip to a foreign country, it is advisable to make arrangements through an accredited travel service (see TRAVEL AGEN-

CY). Travel agents offer a complete service in all matters pertaining to travel throughout the world. Since it is their business constantly to keep in touch with air, rail, and steamship lines everywhere, as well as commercial and resort hotels, they are able to make advance arrangements for clients. In addition, travel bureaus have circulars and booklets describing foreign countries and each part of this country.

A travel agent who is asked to arrange a trip should be told the number in the party, names, ages, sex, and, if the trip includes a foreign country, citizenship. Also, he should be told where the party wants to go, dates of departure and return, mode and class of travel, and, if the expense of the trip is important, the approximate amount that can be spent. The travel agent will be able to advise about the classes of travel and rates on a particular steamship or airline and on the trains in the foreign countries and recommend hotels to conform to a budget.

What the travel service will do. The following is some of the assistance that travel agents are able to give:

1. Prepare and submit tentative itinerary, which can be changed or adjusted.

2. Make all travel, hotel reservations, and sight-seeing arrangements for the entire trip.

3. Tell what documents are necessary, such as passport, health and police certificates, and how to get them. The travel service will get them for a client unless a personal appearance is necessary.

4. Supply, in exchange for dollars, a small amount of currency of the country to be visited, for tips, taxi fares, and the like. It will also help the traveler get a letter of credit or traveler's checks and to arrange insurance.

5. Advise as to all regulations, such as restrictions on currency and customs requirements.

6. Have a foreign correspondent meet the traveler on arrival, take care of his baggage, and see him through the customs.

When unable to decide upon a definite itinerary. It sometimes happens that it is impossible for the traveler to know where he will be able to go, and when. If his plans are uncertain, he may give the travel agent the names of the places in which he expects to need hotel reservations, approximate dates, and how much per day he will spend for hotel expenses. The agent will do the following things:

1. Send him the name of a desirable hotel in each place.

2. Give him a card of introduction to the manager of each of those hotels and to the agent's foreign correspondent.

3. Write to each of the recommended hotels asking them to give the traveler's requests their best attention.

4. Advise the agent's foreign correspondent in each city of the approximate date of arrival.

Passports. An applicant for a passport must appear in person in order to get it. The person going abroad should apply to the nearest agent of the Passport Office, Department of State, or to a clerk of a Federal court or a state court authorized by law to naturalize aliens. The passport applicant must take with him:

1. Proof of United States citizenship. This could be his birth cer-

tificate, baptismal certificate, previous passport, or a certificate of naturalization if he is not a native citizen.

2. Any previous passport.

3. Two duplicate photographs, 3 by 3 inches.

4. Proof of identity. This could be a previous United States passport, naturalization certificate, driver's license, a Federal, state, or municipal government identification card or pass, or an industrial or business identification or pass. If the applicant cannot supply any of these, he must have an identifying witness complete the affidavit on the application form. The witness must be one who has known the applicant at least two years. The witness must state under oath that the applicant is the person he represents himself to be.

5. Passport fee. The fee is $13.00 for a new passport. State courts may charge $2.00 for executing the application. A passport is renewable every 5 years at a fee of $10.00.

6. A list of the countries the applicant plans to visit.

At least two weeks should be allowed for processing by the State Department.

Applications of persons who are going abroad on business must be accompanied by a letter from the head of the firm, or, in his absence, from the person in charge, showing the countries to be visited and the necessity for travel in them. The following is a form letter to the Department of State that is appropriate for this purpose:

Gentlemen:

This is to certify that Kenneth M. Ross, a member of this firm, will make a trip to the Philippine Islands and Australia on company business, within the next five months.

It is requested that Mr. Ross' passport be renewed so that this and other foreign trips may be undertaken.

Yours sincerely,
John G. Benson
President

The former rule requiring a certificate of smallpox vaccination for travelers returning to the United States has been eliminated.

Visas. After the traveler gets his passport, his next step is to get visas for the countries that require them. The travel agent will tell him whether or not a visa is required, or he can inquire at the consulates of the countries in which he is interested. Generally, the passport must be presented at the consulate and a visa form filled out. Sometimes personal appearance of the applicant is required. The various countries have a number of special requirements, such as additional photographs, police and health certificates, vaccinations, and inoculations. Usually there is a visa fee. The length of time required for processing a visa varies with the country.

Customs information. Anyone going to a foreign country should know in advance what the United States customs laws and regulations are with regard to purchases made in a foreign country and brought into the United States. A competent travel agent will usually supply this information, as well as details about customs requirements in countries to be visited.

Whether or not a travel service is used, it is advisable to send for *United States Customs Information for Passengers from Overseas.* If the traveler is going to visit Western Hemisphere nations, he should send for *Customs Hints for Returning Americans—Visitors from Canada, Cuba, Mexico and Other*

Western Hemisphere Nations. These pamphlets, available from the United States Treasury Department, Bureau of Customs, Washington, D.C., furnish the traveler with the general information he needs about United States customs laws and regulations.

Forfeiture of Lease. The right of a landlord to terminate the LEASE if the tenant fails to pay rent or commits any other violation of the terms of the lease. Practically all leases provide that the lease may be forfeited and the tenant evicted for nonpayment of rent or for any other violation of the terms of the lease. Some leases require the landlord to give the tenant both notice of intention to forfeit and a period of grace. Upon forfeiture, the landlord has the right to enter and take possession of the property, unless he has waived the violation. *Waiver* may be implied if the landlord accepts rent with knowledge of the violation.

Where the landlord evicts a tenant because of the latter's DEFAULT, the tenant's liability for future rent is ended unless the lease contains a *survival clause,* providing for continuance of such liability after EVICTION. Landlord's remedies, under a survival clause, are much the same as in the case of abandonment of the premises by the tenant. See ABANDONMENT OF LEASED PREMISES; DISPOSSESS; DISTRAINT FOR RENT IN ARREARS.

Forgery and Counterfeiting. The act of copying or altering a writing with the intent to defraud. Although a forgery and a counterfeit are frequently regarded as the same, there is a distinction. A forgery is a false object of which there is no genuine original; a counterfeit is a false object of which there is a genuine original.

Form Books. A term that refers to (1) practice manuals, (2) books of legal forms.

1. *Practice manuals* are books that contain forms of pleadings, which the lawyer usually follows when dictating. Since the wording of pleadings differs with the state, a practice manual is used only in the state for which it is prepared. With the aid of a practice manual a secretary can draft many pleadings without dictation. The forms always indicate by italics, by parentheses, or in some other manner the wording that must be changed with each case, such as names, dates, and various clauses applicable to a particular situation. In addition to the complete forms, the manuals contain many clauses applicable to various circumstances, which may be substituted for the clauses contained in the complete form.

2. *Books of legal forms* are books that contain forms of instruments and documents as distinguished from litigation papers. Although the statutes prescribe the wording of many instruments, books of legal forms are generally useful for all states. They call attention to statutory requirements and often give forms for each state. For example, *Jones Legal Forms Annotated,* published by Bobbs-Merrill, Indianapolis, one of the best known books of legal forms, gives forms of acknowledgments, deeds, mortgages, and wills that meet the requirements of

each state. Some form books cover only forms in one particular field. For example, *Corporation Forms,* a service published by *Prentice-Hall, Inc.,* contains forms covering every conceivable situation relating to the management of a corporation. Numerous clauses, as well as complete forms, enable the user to pick out the appropriate clause to suit his purpose. In giving instructions for the preparation of a legal instrument, the lawyer frequently tells the secretary to copy certain forms or clauses from a form book.

Forms of Mortgages. The forms of mortgages most commonly used are the form that might be termed the *conventional mortgage* and the form variously called a *trust deed, deed of trust, trust indenture* or *trust mortgage.*

A conventional mortgage is essentially a deed from the borrower to the lender, which contains a provision, known as the *defeasance clause,* that the mortgage shall be void on payment of the debt. The additional provisions, which appear in fine print in the printed form, vary with the state.

A deed of trust conveys the land to a third party instead of direct to the lender. The third party holds the property in trust for the lender until the debt is paid in accordance with the terms of the trust deed. In the District of Columbia and the following states, the deed of trust is more commonly used than the conventional mortgage: Alabama, California, Colorado, Illinois, Mississippi, Missouri, Montana, New Mexico, Tennessee, Texas, Virginia, West Virginia, and Wisconsin. In the other states, a deed of trust is seldom used.

Some states have short statutory forms of mortgages, which save space when recorded. The brief statutory forms are amplified by statute and therefore are not used outside the state of origin. Many careful conveyancers feel that the short statutory form does not protect the mortgagee sufficiently.

First Mortgage. The first (in time or right) of a series of two or more mortgages covering the same property and successively attaching as liens upon it; also, in a more particular sense, a mortgage which is a first lien on the property, not only as against other mortgages, but as against any other charges or incumbrances.

Second Mortgage. One which takes rank immediately after a first mortgage on the same property, without any intervening liens, and is next entitled to satisfaction out of the proceeds of the property.

Purchase money mortgage. A mortgage given in part payment of the purchase price of the property. For example, if the purchase price is $10,000, the purchaser might pay $6,000 cash and give the seller a purchase money mortgage for $4,000. The deed and the purchase money mortgage are executed simultaneously, The grantee in the deed is the mortgagor; the grantor in the deed is the mortgagee. All names and descriptions of property in the purchase money mortgage must agree with those in the deed. A purchase money mortgage has certain priorities that other mortgages do not have. It also has priority over existing judgments and other debts of the mortgagor. On the other hand, as a rule, the mortgagee cannot get a deficiency decree against the mortgagor when he forecloses a purchase money mortgage, which he cannot usually get under other mortgages.

Open End Mortgage. A mortgage contract (it may be a purchase money mortgage) allowing the borrower to re-borrow up to the amount of the original loan. For example, when a loan has been reduced several thousand dollars, at the lender's option the borrower may re-borrow up to the amount that has been paid ahead. See also MORTGAGE, PREPARATION OF.

Forwarder. One who refers a legal action to an attorney. See COLLECTIONS, *Reports to the forwarder;* COMMERCIAL LAW LISTS.

Forwarding Fee. Payment to a lawyer for referring a client to another attorney. Frequently a case is referred to a lawyer by an out-of-town firm. Often, though not always, a percentage of the fee earned is sent to the forwarding attorney.

Forwarding Mail. See POSTAL SERVICE.

Fourth-class Mail. See POSTAL SERVICE.

Franchise Tax. A tax imposed on corporations by most of the states. Franchise taxes are also called qualification taxes, corporation fees, license fees, and privilege taxes. They are all taxes on the privilege of operating as a CORPORATION and apply to a domestic and foreign corporation alike. Franchise taxes must be paid before a corporation can do business within the state. See also EXCISE TAXES.

Fraud. A false representation of a fact, whether by words or by conduct, which deceives and is intended to deceive another so that he shall act upon it to his legal injury. For example, if a jewelry salesman tells a customer that a piece of glass is a diamond, he is committing fraud.

Freedom of Speech and Press. A guarantee, provided by the First and Fourteenth Amendments, against governmental restrictions upon public speeches and publications. The Constitution, however, has not been interpreted as granting an absolute right to speak without responsibility whatever one chooses. As Mr. Justice Holmes stated in one of his opinions, "The most stringent protection of free speech would not protect a man in falsely shouting fire in a theater and causing a panic." When deciding free speech and press cases, the courts are faced with difficult questions of degree, questions involving the balancing of the public protection and an individual's CIVIL RIGHTS. See also CLEAR AND PRESENT DANGER; BILL OF RIGHTS.

Freight. In ADMIRALTY law, the money paid to a shipowner for transporting goods; the term is sometimes used by laymen to refer to the goods themselves.

Dead freight is the amount paid by a shipper or charterer for that part of the vessel's capacity which he has reserved but fails to occupy.

Full Faith and Credit. A clause in the Constitution (Art. IV, §1) providing that "Full faith and credit shall be given in each state to the public acts, records, and judicial proceedings of every other state." Thus, the JUDG-MENT of a state court that has proper JURISDICTION over the person or subject matter is conclusive in the courts of every other state no matter how erroneous in law or in fact such judgment may be. See also COMITY.

Future Files. See FOLLOW-UP FILING SYSTEM.

G

Galley Proof. A galley is a shallow metal tray into which each line of type is deposited as it comes from the typesetting machine. When a galley is filled (it holds enough lines to make about three pages in an average book) it is removed and another put in its place until the entire book is set. Proof of each galley is pulled on a small proof press. This proof contains no illustrations, is not broken up into pages, and contains no RUNNING HEAD. Each footnote appears directly beneath the reference to it in the text. Chapter titles are not necessarily set in the type in which they will finally appear. The paper on which the galley proofs are pulled is no indication of the paper that will actually be used in the book. A galley proof is also called a *galley*, for short.

Garnishment. A legal proceeding by a JUDGMENT CREDITOR to compel a third party owing money to, or holding money for, a judgment debtor to pay the money to the creditor instead of to the debtor. The third party against whom the proceedings are brought is called the garnishee. Not only wages and salaries, but trust funds, insurance disability payments, and the like, may be garnished. The laws that govern the right of garnishment and the procedures in effecting garnishment differ greatly in the various states.

Collecting a judgment by garnishment is particularly useful to a retail creditor whose customers are composed largely of salaried people or wage earners.

General Average Loss. A loss arising out of voluntary sacrifice made, or extraordinary expense incurred, for the joint benefit of a ship and its cargo when both are imperiled by a common danger. When the property of one is sacrificed to save the property of all, it would be unfair to make the owner of the sacrificed property bear the entire loss with no right of contribution from the owners of the property saved. Consequently, from the earliest times, ADMIRALTY has required that a loss occasioned for the benefit of all must be made good by the contribution of all. See also JETTISON; PARTICULAR AVERAGE LOSS; YORK-ANTWERP RULES.

General Correspondence File. The alphabetically kept records of all routine office letters, general in nature, separate from the clients' files and the lawyer's PERSONAL FILE. The file is operated in the same manner as the personal file. In a law office the secretary always keeps it alphabetically according to the name of the correspondent The division of the alphabetical guide needed will depend upon the volume of miscellaneous material. No card index is necessary.

The secretary closes and transfers these files periodically by the same method used to transfer the lawyer's personal file.

See also FILING (IN A LAW OFFICE).

General Damages. See DAMAGES.

General Strike. See STRIKE.

Gift. A voluntary transfer of property made gratuitously, and not for any CONSIDERATION.

A *gift inter vivos* is perfected when there is an intent of the donor to make a gift, a delivery of the gift, and an acceptance by the DONEE. Control over the subject of the gift is lost by the donor upon delivery, and the gift takes effect immediately. There can be no revocation of such a gift by the donor.

A *gift causa mortis* is made by the donor in comtemplation of his death from some existing ailment or some other impending peril. If the donor does not recover, the gift takes effect at his death; the gift is void if he does recover. It has been held that real estate cannot be the subject of a *gift causa mortis*. The gift may be revoked by the donor any time until his death.

Gift Causa Mortis. See GIFT.

Gift Inter Vivos. See GIFT.

Gift Tax. A tax that applies to gratuitous transfers of property during the taxpayer's life. The purpose of the gift tax law is to impose a tax on the donor that measurably approaches the ESTATE TAX that would have been payable on the donor's death if the GIFT had not been made, and if the property given as a gift was part of the donor's estate at his death. The value of property for gift tax purposes is determined as of the date the gift was made. See also MARITAL DEDUCTIONS.

Good Will. An intangible asset arising from the reputation of a business and its relations with its customers. When an established business is offered for sale, good will has a marketable value.

Government Publications. First, send for the publication "How to Keep in Touch with U.S. Government Publications," which describes 47 categories. Write:

> Superintendent of Documents
> U. S. Government Printing Office
> Washington, D.C. 20402

Since there are new publications being issued continually, the secretary should send for the free bi-weekly list of "Selected U. S. Government Publications," or for $6.00 per year she can subscribe to *Monthly Catalog* which describes all publications issued by the various departments and agencies of the U. S. Government.

Government Survey. See LAND DESCRIPTION, *Section and township*.

Graduated (progressive) Taxes. Taxes for which the rate increases as the income, or some other taxable base, increases. Graduated tax rates are found in taxes on individual incomes, corporation incomes, estates and inheritances. See INCOME TAX; ESTATE TAX; INHERITANCE TAXES.

Grand Jury Indictment. An accusation in writing found and presented by a jury charging that a person therein named has done some act which is a public offense.

The Fifth Amendment requires that criminal cases in Federal courts be instituted with a grand jury indictment. The Constitution imposes no such restriction on the states.

Grand Larceny. The unlawful appropriation of property whose value is above a certain statutory amount. If the value of the stolen property is below the amount, the crime is classified as *petit larceny*. Many states have abolished the distinction between grand and petit larceny in their statutes. The states that do maintain the distinction provide for a harsher penalty when the amount stolen classifies the crime as grand larceny. See LARCENY.

Grantee. (Real Estate) The person to whom REAL PROPERTY is conveyed by DEED. A deed must have a grantee in order to be valid. The grantee may be a minor (see INFANT) or an insane person. A misspelling of the grantee's name does not render the deed invalid if his identity is apparent. A grantee may even take TITLE in an assumed name, but a deed to an entirely fictitious person is void. The name of the grantee should appear in the body of the deed correctly and in full. The deed should state the address of the grantee,

otherwise it may not be accepted for recording.

The grantee is often designated in the deed as the "party of the second part," but he does not sign the deed.

Grantor. (Real estate) The person who conveys his REAL PROPERTY to another by DEED. The grantor is often designated in the deed as the "party of the first part." The grantor must be of legal age and of sound mind. If the grantor is a corporation, EXECUTION of the deed must be duly authorized by the directors or stockholders as required by state law. If the grantor is a trustee or executor, the trust instrument or WILL must be examined to determine whether or not he has power to convey real estate. The marital status of the grantor is usually stated in the deed—for example, bachelor, widow, spinster (or unmarried), married, or divorced and not remarried. Whether or not the grantor's spouse must join in the deed depends upon the law of the state where the land is situated. See also GRANTEE.

Gross Income. See INCOME.

Guaranty. (The term is used interchangeably with *suretyship* by courts and lawyers as well as laymen.) A contract of guaranty or of suretyship is a contract whereby one person agrees to be responsible to another for the payment of a debt or the performance of a duty by a third person. It must be in writing and is not enforecable if made orally.

The term guaranty (or *guarantee*) is often loosely used in the sense of WARRANTY. In a strict legal and commercial sense, it is of the essence of a contract of guaranty that there should be a principal, liable directly to perform some act or duty. An agreement by a third party guaranteeing the honest and faithful performance of a contract of sale is a contract of guaranty; an agreement in a sales contract "guaranteeing" the efficient performance of a product for a certain number of years is a contract of warranty.

The words *guarantee* and *guaranty* are frequently used incorrectly. For the verb, always use *guarantee*. Business convention has established a specialized use of *guaranty* as a noun, as illustrated above. However, *guarantee* is never wrong, even in these expressions. A safe rule to follow is: When in doubt, use *guarantee*.

Guardian. The person appointed by a Probate Court to act for and guard the property of a minor, or an incompetent person, known as the "ward."

Guardian Ad Litem. See *Ad litem* in the list of LATIN TERMS.

Guardianship. Guardianships may be created for minor children or mentally or physically incompetent persons. A suitable guardian is appointed by the Probate Court after serving notice upon the "ward" and his mother and father or next of kin, and Letters of Guardianship are issued to the Guardian. The guardian then gathers together all of the assets of his ward and files an Inventory with the

Court which lists all of the ward's property, real or personal. The property might consist of real estate or monthly income from the Veterans Administration, Social Security or Railroad Retirement or other retirement benefits such as annuities. The guardian opens a checking account at the bank to handle the funds of his ward. The account is in the name of the guardian and the guardian signs the checks. The guardian must make regular accountings to the Probate Court (usually once a year or sometimes once every two years, depending on the State) of receipts and disbursements which come into his hands and show the balance left in the estate. He must make an itemized statement in the account of all funds, i.e., checking account balance, savings account balance, certificates of deposit, etc. He pays all of the debts of his ward and banks all the income.

What the Secretary Does. If the guardian is the attorney, the secretary may receive and deposit all income and type out checks for bills as they come in, keeping an accounting sheet of all receipts and disbursements and balance as she goes. The secretary may note in her diary when an accounting is due and prepare the account for the guardian's signature. If V.A. funds are coming into the guardianship, an extra copy of the account should be filed with the Court for the V.A. Office. A file copy should be made and fastened down in the file when the account is filed in Court with the date of filing shown on the file copy.

H

Habeas Corpus. (Latin for "You have the body.") A writ commanding the person having custody of another to produce the person detained at a certain place and time in order that the court may determine if the detention is lawful.

A provision in the U. S. Constitution puts it beyond the power of the Government to abolish this procedure and the powers of the courts in relation to it, except in case of war when the "public safety shall require it." The provision does not bind the states, but there is commonly a similar provision in state constitutions.

Habendum Clause. The clause in a DEED or MORTGAGE which states that the GRANTEE is to have the property transferred to him. The habendum clause derives its name from the Latin phrase *habendum et tenendum* and, accordingly, begins with the words *to have and to hold*. Its purpose is to define the extent of the interest conveyed. When special circumstances surround the transfer of the property, the lawyer dictates a substitute habendum.

Examples:

TO HAVE AND TO HOLD the premises herein granted unto the Party of the Second Part, his heirs and assigns, forever,
TO HAVE AND TO HOLD the granted premises, with all the rights, easements, and appurtenances thereto belonging, to the said John L. Thompson, his heirs and assigns, to his their own use forever,
SUBJECT, HOWEVER, to all rights of the lessees, tenants and occupants of, or in said granted premises, or in any part, or parts, thereof.

Habitual Criminal. A description given in many states to a person who is convicted of a FELONY, having been previously convicted of any crime. It has been held that an offender is not put in DOUBLE JEOPARDY for one crime when, upon conviction for a second crime committed later, his punishment is increased because a statute categorizes him as an habitual criminal.

Halftone. See LINE CUTS AND HALFTONES.

Heading. The designation of the jurisdiction, the VENUE, the title of the case, index number, and title of the pleading, which appear on a legal document or court paper. See CAPTION.

Hearsay. Written or oral evidence that seeks to establish the existence of a fact based not on the witness' own personal knowledge or observation, but on what someone else said. Hearsay evidence is generally excluded at a trial because there is no opportunity for CROSS-EXAMINATION of the

216

declarant in order to lay bare whatever weakness there may be in the witness' story. See DYING DECLARATION.

Heir. One who inherits, or is entitled to inherit. See WILL; LEGACY.

Hereditaments. Things capable of being inherited, whether corporeal or incorporeal, real or personal, or mixed, and including not only lands and everything thereon, but also heirlooms, and certain furniture, which, by custom, may descend to the heir together with the land.

Holder in Due Course. The transferee of a NEGOTIABLE INSTRUMENT who acquires the instrument under the following conditions: (1) The paper must be complete and regular on its face. (2) It must be purchased before maturity. (3) The purchase must be in good faith for a valuable consideration. (4) The purchase must be made without notice of defects in the title or of defenses against payment to the transferor. A holder in due course may enforce collection of the instrument against prior parties regardless of their claims, defenses, and offsets against one another. A transferee may acquire the rights of a holder in due course without being one himself. For example: *A,* the holder in due course of a note procured by the payee through fraud, endorses the note to *B,*, who knew of the fraud and hence was not a holder in due course. *B,* however, acquires *A's* right as a holder in due course to collect the note regardless of the fraud, provided *B* has no part in the fraud. See NEGOTIABLE INSTRUMENT.

Holding Company. A CORPORATION organized for the purpose of owning and holding the stock of one or more other corporations. The term is generally applied to a corporation that owns enough of the voting stock of another corporation to have working control over it. Companies that conduct a business of their own in addition to owning the controlling stock of another company are called *holding-operating companies.* Companies that do not operate a business but merely direct the activities of their subsidiaries are called *pure holding companies.* The holding company is the *parent* and the companies whose controlling stock it owns are *subsidiaries.* See SUBSIDIARY CORPORATION. The assets of the holding company consist mainly of stocks of the the subsidiaries and from these stocks the holding company derives its income. Holding companies may be vulnerable to prosecution under ANTI-TRUST LAWS when used as a device to suppress competition or to create a monopoly.

Holographic Will. See WILL.

Homicide. The act of one human being killing another. Homicide is a necessary ingredient of the crimes of MURDER and MANSLAUGHTER. It is possible, however, to kill someone without criminal intent and without subsequent criminal prosecution. For example, killing in self-defense, or as the only means of arresting an escaping felon.

Hotels. *Reservations.* Information necessary to make a hotel reservation includes the name of the person for whom the reservation is to be made, the time of arrival and approximate time of departure, and the type of accommodations required. The reservation can be made by telephone, telegraph, or letter depending upon how soon it is needed. See RESERVATIONS, LETTERS MAKING, for form of letter requesting a hotel reservation. The type of accommodation desired should always be given in the request for a reservation. If the lawyer is attending a group convention or seminar it is wise to so state, as often group rates are given by the hotel. The usual hotel accommodations are single bedroom and bath, double bedroom and bath, and a suite consisting of a sitting-room and one or more bedrooms and baths. The location preferred may also be given in the request. Confirmation of a hotel reservation in writing or by wire should always be requested; a confirmation by wire is usually sent collect. The confirmation should be attached to the copy of the ITINERARY that the lawyer takes with him. If for any reason a lawyer learns that he must cancel his hotel reservation, his secretary should notify the hotel immediately. It is not necessary to wire, but if the letter will not reach the hotel before the time of the lawyer's expected arrival, courtesy requires a cancellation by wire.

Sources of information. Detailed information about hotels is available in the latest editions of *Leahy's Hotel Guide and Travel Atlas of the United States, Canada, and Mexico,* published by American Hotel Register Company, Chicago, and the *Official Hotel Red Book and Directory,* published by the American Hotel Association Directory Corporation, New York. The number of rooms and the price enable a person to judge the class of the hotel. Information is also available at local hotel associations or the Chamber of Commerce in the city of destination.

House Agency. A fictional collection establishment created by a creditor to convey the impression that it is an independent and bona fide COLLECTION AGENCY. It is but a name and address used by the creditor for its final collection effort. The advantage is that by use of the "agency's" stationery the creditor can press with all the vigor of a regular collection agency. See also COLLECTIONS; COLLECTION LETTERS.

I

Identification Line. See RESPONSIBILITY OR IDENTIFICATION LINE.

Illegitimate Child. See BASTARD.

Impleader. The process of bringing into an action a third party who may be liable to the defendant. See also PARTIES TO AN ACTION. The purpose of impleader is to avoid a multiplicity of actions and to encourage a determination of all the controversies existing between the parties in one suit. For example, if a housewife gets sick from tainted meat she bought, she can sue the butcher. The butcher can then, in the same action, implead the meat packer and the rights of all the parties will be determined in the single action.

Impotency. The inability to engage in the physical act of sexual intercourse. As a ground for DIVORCE or ANNULMENT the impotency must exist at the time of the marriage and be incurable.

Sterility is not to be confused with impotency. If the spouse can have intercourse, there is no ground for a matrimonial action merely because such intercourse will not result in the production of children.

Imprest Fund. See PETTY CASH FUND.

Incest. The crime of sexual intercourse between a man and a woman who are related to each other within the degrees where marriage is prohibited by law. In other words, whether or not a state allows marriage between cousins will determine whether sexual intercourse between cousins is a crime in that state. In New York State marriage of cousins is valid and therefore their relationship is not incestuous. New York law makes a marriage incestuous and void if contracted between ancestor and descendent, brother and sister (whole or half-blood), uncle and niece, or aunt and nephew. Children of these incestuous marriages are legitimate. A marriage which is void in the state where it is contracted is void everywhere.

Inchmaree Clause. The portion of an ocean marine insurance contract that covers against such perils as bursting of boilers, breakage of shafts, damage through any latent defects in the machinery, hull, or appurtenances, or from faults or errors in navigation and/or management of the vessel by the master, mariners, mates, engineers, or pilots.

Inchoate. Begun but not completed, as a contract not executed by all parties. An instrument that the law requires to be recorded is an *inchoate in-*

219

strument until it is recorded, in that it is good only between the parties and privies (see PRIVITY). A wife's interest in her husband's lands that becomes a right of dower upon his death, is an inchoate right of dower during his lifetime. An interest in real estate that may become a vested interest unless barred is an *inchoate interest*. Other phrases are *inchoate equity, inchoate lien, inchoate title*.

Income (Federal tax law). The return in money, property or services from one's business, labor, or invested capital.

Gross income. To determine gross income, subtract from income the income that is exempt from taxes. Items of income that are exempt from Federal INCOME TAX are called *exclusions*. Some examples of exclusions are gifts, inheritances, and interest on state bonds.

Adjusted gross income. Gross income less business expenses of the taxpayer. Adjusted gross income is computed by individuals only, not by corporations.

Taxable income. Gross income less deductions allowed by law. For individuals, adjusted gross income less additional deductions for personal expenses and personal exemptions is the taxable income. Individuals may take a standard deduction in lieu of itemizing deductions for personal expenses. The standard deduction is *in addition to* deductions for adjusted gross income, but *instead of* deductions for personal expenses. In every case, the amount of the standard deduction depends on the amount of the taxpayer's adjusted gross income.

For corporations, taxable income is gross income less deductions. Many expenses incurred by corporations are deductions.

Prepaid income. Income that is received before it is earned. See also WITHHOLDING; CAPITAL GAIN AND LOSS.

Income Tax. A federal, state, or local tax that is levied on the INCOME of individuals and corporations, estates, and some trusts. The Federal income tax is expressly authorized by the Sixteenth Amendment to the Constitution.

Under the Federal pay-as-you-go income tax collection system, most individuals pay all or a substantial part of their income tax during the year in which they receive their income. The tax is withheld from their wages (see WITHHOLDING) or is paid in quarterly installments based on a declaration of estimated tax, or both.

Most income taxes are GRADUATED TAXES. The rates increase as the amount of income reported increases. See also INTERNAL REVENUE SERVICE.

Incompatibility. Incapability of existing together. Incompatibility is not ordinarily grounds for DIVORCE, although in some states it is.

Incorporating Procedure. See CORPORATION.

Incorporators. Those who unite for the purpose of forming a CORPORATION. They tell the lawyer the kind of business the corporation will engage in and other details that are necessary for the lawyer to know before he commences the legal organization procedure. They also put up the capital for the corporation. Only natural persons may incorporate, although they may actually be representing a corporation or a PARTNERSHIP.

A large majority of the states require three or more incorporators. Many states also require that one or more of the incorporators shall be a resident of that state, or that the organization meeting of the corporation shall be held in that state. For these reasons, and for convenience, the incorporators are frequently *dummies*. They are not the principals who are actually interested in the organization of the corporation, but merely act for them until the organization meeting. Secretaries frequently act as dummy incorporators. See also CERTIFICATE OF INCORPORATION.

Indemnity. An undertaking, either express or implied, to compensate another for loss or damage, or for expenses or trouble incurred, either in the past or in the future. Under a contract of indemnity, the indemnity is the obligation or duty resting upon a particular person or company to make good any loss or damage another has suffered, or may suffer, upon the happening of a specific event. The person giving the indemnity (agreeing to indemnify) is the *indemnitor,* corresponding to the insured. The term *indemnity* also applies to the sum paid as compensation or remuneration in the event of loss or damage to the indemnitee. The indemnity may be payable to the indemnitee or to someone else in behalf of the indemnitee. For example, the payments that are made to an injured workman under workmen's compensation insurance are indemnities. They are payable to the workman in behalf of his employer, who is the indemnitee.

Indented Style. See LETTERS, STYLE AND SETUP.

Indenture. A formal written instrument between two or more parties, involving reciprocal rights and duties—for example, a lease. In ancient times, the practice was to write two or more copies of the instrument on the same piece of parchment. The copies were then separated by tearing the parchment in irregular fashion so that the indentations of each torn part would fit the other. Hence, the term *indenture.*

Independent Contractor. A person who is hired to perform services and is responsible for the end results of his labor. The hirer has no control over the method of performance or details of the independent contractor's work. The general rule is that a hirer is not liable for a TORT committed by an independent contractor.

Index Number. See CLERK'S INDEX SYSTEM.

Index Tabs and Labels, Typing of. The best results in typing tabs, guides, and folder labels will be obtained if the secretary observes the following suggestions.

Use the briefest possible designations. Abbreviate, omitting punctuation whenever possible. Index tabs need to be legible only a normal reading distance. Guide labels should be legible at two or three feet. File drawer labels should be legible at six feet.

Use initial caps whenever needed. Full caps, especially in elite and pica type, do not increase the legibility of label designations; they decrease the amount of light background around the letters and make reading more difficult. Do not underline.

Folder labels. The most important part of a folder label is the eighth of an inch immediately below the scoring (the place at which the label is folded when it is pasted on the folder tab). Frequently this space is the only part visible in the file. Therefore, start at the first typing space below the scoring. Typing should begin in the first or second typing space from the left edge of the label, except for one or two character designations. If this is done, all folder labels in the file drawer will present an even left margin.

Use initial caps and indent the second and third lines so that the first word of the first line will stand out.

In typing labels for a numbered subject or name file, leave space between the number and first work; type the subject in block form. Avoid exceptionally long file numbers if possible.

Guide labels. For file guide labels, use the largest type available. Begin the typing as high on the label as the guide tabs will permit. Center one- and two-character designations. Start all other designations in the second typing space from the left edge. Use abbreviations or shortened forms and omit punctuation, except for large numbers such as 10,000.

File drawer labels. In preparing labels for file drawers, use the largest type available. Center the typing on the label and leave a double space above and below detailed reference information. It is better to print file drawer labels because typing is not legible at a distance.

Index To Foreign Legal Periodicals. An index to legal periodicals used as a "secondary" source by the lawyer. It was started in 1960 as a quarterly with annual cumulations.

Index To Legal Periodicals. An index to legal periodical publications by law schools and professional associations used as a "secondary source" by the lawyer.

Indictment. An accusation in writing found and presented by a grand jury, legally convoked and sworn, to the court in which it is impaneled, charging that a person therein named has done some act, or been guilty of some omission, which, by law, is a public offense, punishable on indictment.

Indirect Taxes. See DIRECT TAXES.

Industrial Union. See LABOR UNION.

Infant. One who is not yet twenty-one years old or in some states such as Ohio, now eighteen. The state gives protection to minors by setting up separate rules and laws for their benefit. As an example, a CONTRACT made with an infant may be enforced or avoided by him on his coming of age.

The protection that the law gives an infant is said to act as a shield to protect him from unfair contracts, but not as a sword to do injury to others. An infant is, therefore, responsible for NEGLIGENCE, SLANDER, or any other TORT he might commit. An infant usually may not manage his own trial. He is represented by a "next friend," or a guardian.

Infant's Contract. See CONTRACT.

Inferior Courts. Judicial tribunals that have limited jurisdiction and powers. The most common inferior courts are justice of the peace courts, small claims courts, and a class of courts whose jurisdiction is confined to violations of city ordinances. Courts of this class are variously called *police, magistrate's, municipal,* or *recorder's courts.* All inferior courts have a narrow jurisdiction. In criminal matters, they are restricted to preliminary hearings or inquiries except in minor matters. In civil actions, they have jurisdiction over actions involving small amounts only, the amount varying with the state. For example, in Alabama, justice of the peace courts have jurisdiction over claims of $100 or less; in Illinois, of $500 or less. Inferior courts are usually courts not of record, but their proceedings may be recorded. Frequently the judge of an inferior court is not a lawyer. The decisions of these courts are subject to review or correction by higher courts. Actually, circuit and district courts are "inferior" to appellate or supreme courts, but the term is usually applied to the courts not of record described here. See also SUPERIOR COURTS; COURTS OF SPECIAL JURISDICTION; COURTS OF INTERMEDIATE REVIEW; AMERICAN COURT SYSTEM.

Ingress, Egress and Regress. These words express the rights of a lessee to enter, go upon, and return from the lands in question.

Inheritance Taxes. Levies by some of the states on the right of the living to receive property from the estate of the deceased. Inheritance taxes are EXCISE TAXES payable by the heirs and not by the estate of the deceased unless decedent specifies in his Last Will and Testament that the estate pay the inheritance taxes, in which case it is mandatory that the estate pay the taxes. See ESTATE TAXES.

Injunction. A writ restraining a person or corporation from doing or continuing to do something that threatens or causes injury, or requiring the defendant to do a particular act. The writ may be granted by the court to which the case is brought, or by a judge of the court. Injunctions may be classified as *prohibitory* and *mandatory.* A prohibitory injunction restrains the commission or continuance of an act. Thus, a prohibitory injunction may restrain a board of elections from placing a certain candidate's name on the ballot. A mandatory injunction commands acts to be done or undone. For example, a mandatory injunction may compel a property owner to open a road that he had closed by constructing a fence across it, thus depriving another property owner of the use of the road.

Injunctions may also be classified as (1) restraining orders, (2) temporary injunctions, and (3) permanent injunctions. A restraining order may be granted without notice to the opposite party, for the purpose of restraining the defendant until the court has heard an application for a temporary injunction. A temporary injunction is granted on the basis of the application, before the court has heard the case on its merits. It restrains the defendant during the litigation of a case, and may be either dissolved or made permanent when the rights of the parties are determined. Temporary injunctions are also called preliminary, interlocutory, or injunction *pendente lite* (see LATIN TERMS). Permanent injunctions are granted on the merits of the case. They are often called "Final Injunction." See PROVISIONAL REMEDIES.

Insanity. A lack of reason, intelligence, and memory that prevents a man from understanding the nature of his acts or from distinguishing between right and wrong conduct. This legal definition is to be distinguished from the medical idea of insanity, which has to do with a prolonged departure of the individual from his natural mental state. Insanity in law covers nothing more than the relation of the person and the particular act which is the subject of judicial investigation.

A few examples of legal proceedings where insanity may be shown are a criminal proceeding where insanity is alleged as a defense, a proceeding to defeat a WILL on the ground of the insanity of the maker, and a suit to avoid a CONTRACT.

Inside Address. The address on the letter itself as distinguished from the address on the envelope. (See ADDRESS ON LETTERS.)

Insolvency. The inability to pay debts as they mature. The word is used in two senses: (1) A debtor whose assets exceed his liabilities but who is temporarily unable to meet his obligations as they mature because his assets are not readily convertible to cash is insolvent in the *equitable* sense. (2) A debtor whose total assets are less than his liabilities is insolvent in the *bankruptcy* sense.

Installment Collections. Receipt of partial payments of debts. Litigation as a means of collecting a small sum should be a last resort; it is expensive, and the JUDGMENT may be as difficult to collect as the debt. For this reason, attorneys will "play along" with the debtor and accept partial payments from him. Usually the arrangement is that the debtor shall pay a certain amount at regular intervals. An arrangement of this type is often made after judgment is obtained against the debtor. It is the secretary's responsibility to bring up the file for attention on the dates that payments are due. If a payment is not made as promised, upon instruction from the lawyer, she should communicate with the debtor, either by telephone or mail. The file folder illustrated on page 118 has space for these data.

Installment Contract. An agreement in which credit is extended upon the promise to pay a certain part of a particular debt at certain regular times. The credit may be granted as a loan of money. For example, a person may borrow money from a bank or a personal finance company on his personal credit with an agreement to repay a certain portion of it each month, or each week. Or the credit may be extended upon the sale of goods. For example, a person buys furniture and agrees to pay a certain part of the price at regular intervals instead of paying the entire price immediately. See also CONDITIONAL SALE.

Installment Credit. That form of credit that involves the repayment or amortization of an obligation by payments of fixed portions at regular intervals. Installment credit is granted as a loan of money or extended upon the sale of goods. When extended for consumer goods, the credit is known as *consumer* or *retail installment credit;* when extended for commercial or business use, the credit is known as *productive* or *mercantile installment credit*. See also ADD-ONS.

Instructions to Jury. See CHARGE TO THE JURY.

Insurable Interest. A person has an insurable interest if he might be financially injured by the occurrence of the event insured against. Under American law if an insurable interest is not present, the contract is a mere wager and is not enforceable.

In property. Insurable interest must exist at the time the loss occurs. Title to the property insured is not necessary; an owner, lessee, mortgagee, or purchaser has an insurable interest. Thus, the interest (1) may be contingent, as the interest of a purchaser under contract of sale; (2) may be conditional, as the interest of a purchaser under a contract of CONDITIONAL SALE until the conditions of the sale have been met; (3) may arise from possession as in the case of a bailee (see BAILMENT).

In life. Insurable interest must exist at the time the policy is written but need not exist at the time death occurs. Every person has insurable interest in his own life and may name anyone he chooses as beneficiary. Other examples of relations giving rise to an insurable interest are those of (1) employer and valued employee; (2) several partners of a partnership; (3) creditor and debtor; (4) corporation and its officers; (5) wife and husband; (6) dependent children.

Insurance. A social device designed to eliminate pure risk. Almost everything is insurable, if a person wants to pay the premium. General classifications of insurance are Fire and Extended Coverage, Casualty, Accident and Health, Life, and Marine. Also available to the home owner is the Home Owner's policy which covers a number of perils. Available to the business man and attorney are special multi-peril policies which cover fire, extended coverage, burglary, personal injury and other liability perils. Insurance companies are controlled by State Insurance Departments and the statutes of the state in which they operate. The contracts or policies are written, but an agent may place an oral binder on property to obtain immediate coverage.

Insurance Records. *Life insurance.* The secretary should keep two classes of life insurance records: (1) a reminder of premium dates and (2) a description of the policies. A premium distribution record might also be desirable.

1. A TICKLER CARD FILE should be kept as a reminder of premium dates. The card should show (1) due dates of the premiums; (2) amount of premium; (3) to whom the premium is payable (checks are made to the company, agent, or broker who bills the lawyer); (4) where to mail the check; (5) policy number; (6) name of company issuing the policy; (7) name of insured. If dividends are to be applied as part payment of the premium, a note to that effect should be made on the tickler card. If the secretary handles more than one bank account, the tickler card should also show the name of the bank account on which the payment check should be drawn. Some secretaries note on the tickler card the dates the premiums are paid.

2. The secretary should maintain a record describing the life insurance policies carried by her employer and by each member of his family if she is responsible for those policies. A

POLICY RECORD										
COMPANY	NUMBER	AMOUNT	TYPE	DATE OF ISSUE	AGE AT ISSUE	GROSS YEARLY PREMIUM	DISABILITY		DOUBLE INDEMNITY	BENEFICIARY
							PREMIUM WAVER	MONTHLY INCOME		

Insurance Records: Figure 1. Sheet record of life insurance policies.

desirable form for this purpose is a sheet record, which shows at a glance the entire life insurance program. (Figure 1.) A separate record should be kept of policies carried by each person.

3. Professional men and business executives who carry a heavy life insurance program are interested in knowing how the premiums are distributed throughout the year. Figure 2 is a form that may be used for that purpose. The day of the month on which the premium is due is entered in the "Day of Mo. Due" column, and the amount of the premium is entered opposite the policy number in the column for the appropriate month. The record shows the totals for each month and for the year.

This record may be used in either of two ways: (1) to show the distribution of premiums for the forthcoming year, or (2) to enter payments as they are made, thus providing a running record of all premiums paid in a given year. This record is kept in addition to, and not as a substitute for, the reminder of premium dates and description of the policies.

Insurance other than life. The records that the secretary should keep for insurance other than life are determined by the extent of the insurance program. A reminder of expiration dates must be

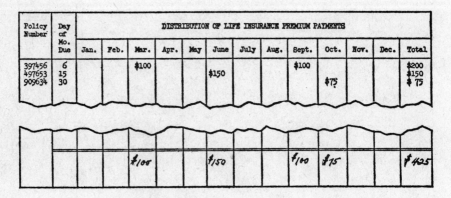

Policy Number	Day of Mo. Due	DISTRIBUTION OF LIFE INSURANCE PREMIUM PAYMENTS												
		Jan.	Feb.	Mar.	Apr.	May	June	July	Aug.	Sept.	Oct.	Nov.	Dec.	Total
397456	6			$100						$100				$200
497653	15						$150							$150
909634	30										$75			$ 75
				$100			$150			$100	$75			$425

Insurance Records: Figure 2. Life insurance premium distribution record

Insurance Records: Figure 3. Detailed description of policies other than life insurance.
(Courtesy, Trussel Manufacturing Co., Poughkeepsie, N.Y.)

227

kept. The other records described below are desirable.

1. Whenever a policy or certificate is received, whether as a first contract or as a renewal of an expiring contract, the secretary should make up a 3 by 5 inch tickler card as a reminder of the expirations date. Entries on the card will vary with the type of policy. The following, however, are the minimum essentials to be noted: (1) type of coverage and expiration date; (2) identification by company and policy number; (3) agent's name; (4) insured; (5) property covered; (6) amount of premium. There is no need for a tickler card for the premium due date because a bill ordinarily accompanies the new policy. The bill is the reminder that a premium payment is due.

2. The form in Figure 3 (page 227) provides for a *detailed description* of policies other than life insurance policies. A separate sheet is kept for each kind of insurance on each piece of property. The entry showing value of the property is particularly useful for reference when market values fluctuate and the insured wants to check on whether he is fully insured or overinsured.

3. A form similar to Figure 2 on page 226 for distribution of life insurance premiums may be used to show a distribution of premiums for general insurance. The premium distribution for all general and life insurance may be kept on the same sheet.

Insured Mail. See POSTAL SERVICE.

Inter Vivos Trust. See TRUST.

Interference Proceeding. A hearing instituted by the Patent Office to determine, from evidence, the prior inventor entitled to the PATENT when two or more applicants claim the same invention. The priority question is determined by a board of three *interference examiners* on the evidence submitted. From the decision of the Board of Patent Interferences, the losing party may appeal to the Court of Customs and Patent Appeals or file a civil action against the winning party in the appropriate United States district court.

Interim. In the meantime.

Interlocking Directorates. Boards of directors of two or more corporations having one or more directors in common. Through this method of control, the will of the common dominant stockholders is executed. See BOARD OF DIRECTORS.

Interlocutory Decree. An intermediate or preliminary finding of a court. It is not conclusive and does not determine the suit, but directs some further proceedings preparatory to the final DECREE. For example, in an action for *partition* (division of property among co-owners), an interlocutory judgment must first declare what is the right, share, or interest of each party in the property. A final decree of partition is thereafter given based on the interlocutory finding. See also JUDGMENT.

Intermediary Appellate Courts. Tribunals to which cases are brought from courts of ORIGINAL JURISDICTION for appeals. They exist in those states where a large volume of cases makes it necessary to relieve the congestion that might develop if all cases for appeal were brought only to the highest appellate court. See COURTS OF INTERMEDIATE REVIEW; APPELLATE COURT; AMERICAN COURT SYSTEM; COURTS OF SPECIAL JURISDICTION.

Internal Revenue Service. A Federal agency that administers the nation's tax laws.

Information as to the applicability of internal revenue laws may be obtained from the principal and local offices of District Directors of Internal Revenue. Requests for extensions of time for filing returns and requests for information as to cases in their charge, offers in compromise, and claims for abatement, credit, or refund of taxes may be submitted to District Directors. See INCOME TAX.

International Cable or Radio. Method of transmitting messages to foreign countries. A message may be sent to any foreign country over either cable or radio facilities by filing the message directly with any of the international telegraph carriers or at any Western Union office. If it is desired that a message go by any specific carrier, the name of the desired route should be typed on the message immediately after the destination. Classes of international messages are (1) full-rate messages [FR—standard fast service for messages in plain or secret (code or cipher) language]; and (2) letter telegrams [LT—sometimes called Cable Letters or Radio Letters], an overnight service designed for messages of some length that are not of sufficient urgency to warrant full-rate dispatch. Letter telegrams may be written only in plain language; however, a registered CODE ADDRESS or signature may be used. The charge for a letter-telegram is approximately one-half of the charge per word for a full-rate message.

How charges are counted. A charge is made for the name and address of the *addressee.* The place of destination, including the name of the country when it is necessary, is counted as one word regardless of the number of letters it contains. The names of persons or street may be run together and counted as 15 letters, or fraction thereof, to the word. As as example, STJAMES-STREET is one word, but St. James Street is counted as three words. Registered code address may be used. A charge is made for each word in the signature and address of the *sender,* but the message need not be signed or it may be signed with a code signature.

In *plain-language* messages each word containing 15 letters or less is counted as one word; each word containing more than 15 letters is counted at the rate of 15 letters to the word. *Secret language words* (code or cipher) are counted at the rate of five characters or fraction thereof, to the word. A *mixed group of figures,* or of figures and letters, is counted at the rate of five, or fraction therof, to the word. A *dollar or cents sign* or a pound sterling mark counts as a separate word, but the fraction bar, commas, and decimal points may be grouped with the figures and letters. They then count as one character in the group of which they are part. Thus, 8,976, 18,54, or 74/5 are counted as one word each, but $3.25 and 25¢ are counted as two words each. Commercial *abbreviations,* such as *FOB* and *CIF,* are counted at the rate of one word for each five figures or letters or fraction thereof. Abbreviations contrary to common usage may not be sent. *Punctuation marks,* hyphens, and apostrophes are not transmitted except when expressly requested, and then they are charged for as one word each. A charge is also made for the telegraph company's code word.

International Mail. Mail deposited for dispatch to points outside continental United States and its territories and possessions. See POSTAL SERVICE. International mail is classified as (1) letters and letter packages, (2) postcards, (3) printed matters, (4) samples, (5) commercial paper, (6) small packets, and (7) parcel post. Detailed postal regulations covering international mail can be obtained from *A Directory of International Mail Rates and Conditions of Mailing.* The publication is available from the Superintendent of Documents, Government Printing Office, Washington, D.C. 20025

International Metered Communication. A service inaugurated by Western Union Cables providing a direct teleprinter connection between the New York and London offices of the subscriber, over which keyboard conversations are carried on as desired. This service is paid for on a per character basis. Other services of this type are offered on a time basis.

Interstate Commerce. Any business transaction conducted directly or indirectly across state boundaries.

The U. S. Constitution gives Congress the power to regulate interstate commerce, and forbids the states to regulate, restrict, or interfere with it.

Interstate commerce includes the following:

1. Any interchange of commodities, both tangible and intangible.

2. All facilities of transportation across state lines.

3. Transmission of power, and communication—radio, television, telephone, and telegraph.

4. All persons who work in, or in connection with, interstate movements.

The power to regulate interstate commerce also includes the power to regulate any business that "affects" interstate commerce. This means that a business being conducted locally and not across state lines may still be regulated under some circumstances. See INTRASTATE COMMERCE; CONCURRENT POWERS.

Intervenor. See PARTIES TO AN ACTION.

Intervention. A procedure a person uses to become one of the PARTIES TO AN ACTION in order to protect his interests. A person has a right to intervene if he may be bound by a JUDGMENT in an action where he is not represented.

Intestate. Without making a WILL. The word is also often used to designate the person, himself, who has died without making a will. See also TESTATOR; LETTERS OF ADMINISTRATION; PROBATE OF A WILL.

Intra. (Latin) Within; inside.

Intrastate Commerce. Business conducted entirely within a state and not part of an interchange or movement of tangible or intangible commodities across state boundaries.

A firm that manufactures, sells, and uses a product entirely within one state is engaged in intrastate commerce.

Isolated cases of engaging in INTERSTATE COMMERCE will not affect the standing of an intrastate firm.

A state can prohibit a foreign CORPORATION from doing intrastate business within its borders unless it meets certain qualifying conditions. Of course, these conditions must be reasonable.

It is important to differentiate between intrastate and interstate commerce under most of the Federal regulatory laws. Any business (even though intrastate in nature) that "affects" interstate commerce, may be subject to Federal regulation. For example, the Wage-Hour Law regulates labor conditions in industries engaged in the production of goods for commerce. Thus, employees of a local linen supply company that services the needs of customers engaged in interstate commerce are rendering services necessary for the production of goods for interstate commerce, and are therefore covered by Federal law. See also INTERSTATE COMMERCE; CONCURRENT POWERS.

Invitee. A person on the premises for a purpose of mutual benefit concerning the business of the owner, e.g., a shopper in a store. A social visitor is not an invitee. The owner of the premises has the legal duty towards the invitee of reasonable care to keep the premises in a safe condition of repair. There is also the duty to give notice of any latent unsafe condition. See LICENSEE; TRESPASSER; NEGLIGENCE.

Issue of Execution. When a judgment is obtained by one party against another, the successful party is known as a *judgment creditor* and the other party as a *judgment debtor.* If the judgment debtor does not pay the judgment, the attorney for the judgment creditor may get the CLERK OF THE COURT to issue execution to a designated officer of the law, usually the sheriff, constable or marshal. The

			EST			
FROM	TO	VIA	DATE & TIME	ARRIVE	ACCOMMODATION	HOTEL
N.Y.	Boston	New Haven	5/6 -11:30P	5/6/50-5:15A	Car 106 Room M Train 467	Parker House
Boston	N.Y.	Eastern	5/8 - 3:30P	5/8/50-4:45P	Flight #633	Home
N.Y	Washing.	Eastern	5/13 - 8:30A	5/13 -9:47A	Flight #431	Shoreham
Washing.	Atlanta	Eastern	5/15 - 2:50P	5/15 -7:32P	Flight #565	Atlanta-Biltmore
Atlanta	Cleveland	Eastern	5/19 - 5:50P	5/19 -10:32P	Flight #732	Carter Hotel
Cleveland	Chicago	United	5/22 - 6:10P	5/22 - 7:10P	Flight #501	Stevens Hotel
Chicago	New York	United	CST 5/28 -12:00N	5/28 - 4:00P	Flight #622	Home

All Standard Time one hour earlier than Daylight Time.

Checking Out Time - 3:00 P.M.

Itinerary: **Figure 1.** Travel itinerary.

execution is a printed form, easily filled out upon the basis of the information in the file. If the officer to whom the execution is issued can find no property of the judgment debtor against which to levy, he returns the execution "unsatisfied." The lawyer may then commence a SUPPLEMENTARY PROCEEDING.

Italic. A style of type characterized by letters that slope up, *as in these words.* Italic type is used principally for emphasis and side headings. In typing, material that is to be set in italic type should be underlined. Although *italic* is derived from a proper name, it is usually written with a LOWER CASE *i*.

Itinerary. Outline or schedule of a traveler's route or journey. The itinerary of a business trip shows (1) point of departure, (2) points of arrival, (3) name of railway or airline, (4) date and time of departure from each point, (5) date and time of arrival at each point, (6) train or flight number, and (7) hotels at which he is stopping. The itinerary should be prepared similar to Figure 1 (on page 231). It should be typed on durable paper in triplicate: a copy for the employer, a copy for his family, and a copy for his secretary. Additional copies should be made if anyone else in the organization needs the information shown by the itinerary.

J

Jason Clause. A clause in a BILL OF LADING that requires cargo owners to contribute in GENERAL AVERAGE LOSS in cases of damage resulting from navigation errors or faulty equipment. In order for the Jason clause to operate, the ship owner must have exercised diligence to make the vessel seaworthy (see SEAWORTHINESS) and have it properly manned, equipped, and supplied.

Jeopardy. See DOUBLE JEOPARDY.

Jetsam. See JETTISON.

Jettison. The act of throwing part of the cargo overboard in order to lighten a ship that is in a storm or other emergency. The cargo thrown overboard is called *jetsam;* the loss incurred is a GENERAL AVERAGE LOSS.

Goods that float upon the sea when a ship sinks, or otherwise perishes, are called *flotsam.*

Joint Adventure (Venture). An association of two or more persons for a given, limited purpose, without the usual powers, duties, and responsibilities that go with a PARTNERSHIP. Thus, if two people buy a specific piece of real estate for resale at a profit, they become parties to a joint adventure; but if they enter into an agreement whereby each contributes money and services in establishing and carrying on a real estate business, they become members of a partnership.

Joint and Several. An obligation or liability incurred, under contract or otherwise, by two or more parties together and separately is said to be *joint and several.* The parties may be held jointly responsible or severally responsible. Thus a bond may be joint and several, in which case the obligors are liable either individually or together, at the option of the obligee.

Joint Bank Account. A checking, savings, or thrift account opened in the names of two or more people. The deposit agreement and the designation of the account should be specific as to whether the depositors are tenants in common or joint tenants.

When two depositors are tenants in common, either party can make deposits, but the signatures of both are required for withdrawal. At the death of one of them, the survivor is entitled to his own interest in the account only. The heirs of the deceased are entitled to the decedent's interest. Where two depositors are joint tenants, either party can deposit or withdraw. At the death of one of the depositors, the survivor is entitled to the balance of the account. The same principles apply where there are more than two depositors.

233

Joint Stock Company. A form of business organization created by an agreement of the parties. This agreement is commonly called *articles of association.* This type of company is similar to the CORPORATION in the following respects: (1) the ownership is represented by transferable certificates; (2) management is in the hands of a board of governors or directors elected by the members (shareholders); (3) the business continues for its fixed term notwithstanding the death or disability of one or more of the members. It is unlike the corporation and like the PARTNERSHIP in that each shareholder is personally liable for the company's debts.

Joint Tenancy. An estate held by two or more persons at the same time, under the same TITLE or source of ownership, in which each has the same degree of interest and the same right of possession. The chief characteristic of a joint tenancy is that upon the death of one of the joint tenants, his interest automatically passes to the other joint tenants still living. The courts do not favor joint tenancies, and many jurisdictions permit joint tenants to defeat the right of surviving joint tenants in the state of MORTGAGE or conveyance to other persons.

Some of the states have gone so far as to pass retroactive statutes making existing undivided interests *tenancies in common* unless the survivorship element is expressly provided for in the DEED or WILL that created the interest. See also TENANCY IN CONMON; TENANCY BY THE ENTIRETY.

Joint Tortfeasors. People whose separate wrongs unite in producing a single injury, e.g., NEGLIGENCE of two drivers causing a collision. If the defendants are treated as joint tortfeasors, each one is liable for the plaintiff's injuries and either one or both may be sued.

Judicial Notice. The knowledge that a judge will officially take of a fact, although no evidence to prove that fact has been introduced on trial. It is a judicial shortcut, a doing away with evidence because there is no real necessity for it. The court will generally take judicial notice of facts that are so notorious that a production of evidence would be unnecessary. It is not necessary, for example, to produce evidence to show the laws of the state, international law, historical events, and main geographical features of the community.

Judicial Review. The power of the courts to declare an act of the legislature invalid as a violation of the Constitution.

The United States Supreme Court will refuse to pass upon the validity of a statute unless it is involved in an actual case or controversy presented to it for decision. The Court, in other words, will not render "advisory opinions" upon constitutional questions. A statute that is held to be unconstitutional is as inoperative as though it had never been passed. See AMERICAN COURT SYSTEM; APPELLATE COURT.

Judge. An officer of the court invested with authority to administer justice. In so far as power, authority, and duty are concerned, there is no distinction between a judge and a justice. The law in each state specifies whether the members of each court in that state shall be designated as judges or justices. In the majority of states the members of the highest appellate courts are called justices, whereas the members of the trial courts are judges. See Table II, AMERICAN COURT SYSTEM, starting on page 48, for the technical designation of the various courts listed there.

The lawyer prepares orders and decrees (see ORDER; DECREE) for the Court's approval. It is important that the secretary know whether the technically correct designation of the Court is *judge* or *justice,* because these papers always contain the Court's title, either in the heading or in the signature. Almost all of them commence with a heading similar to the following:

EXAMPLE 1.
  Present:
    HONORABLE JOHN E. SMITH,
                                Justice.
EXAMPLE 2.
  Present:
    HONORABLE JOHN E. SMITH,
              United States District Judge.

The proper form should always be used in writing or speaking to or about court members. See ADDRESSING OFFICIALS.

Judgment. An official decision of a court, based on a jury's verdict or, in absence of a jury, on the law and facts as found by the judge. Broadly speaking, any adjudication by a court of law or of equity is considered a judgment, but technically an adjudication by a *court of equity* is a *decree*. The words *judgment* and *decree* are often used synonymously, especially since many courts now combine both law and EQUITY jurisdiction.

A decree usually directs the defendant *to do or not to do some specific thing,* as opposed to a judgment for DAMAGES in a court of law. For ex-

ample, an owner of real property can obtain an INJUNCTION to prevent his tenant from changing the character of his property, such as by razing a barn and erecting a dwelling house in its place. The injunction is a *decree* of the court.

A decree or judgment is *final* when it disposes of the case, leaving no question to be decided in the future. (See INTERLOCUTORY DECREE.) The parties, however, may appeal to a higher court from a final judgment or decree. The execution of the judgment is *stayed* pending the higher court's decision.

A judgment is sometimes entered "on the pleadings" upon motion of counsel (see PLEADINGS), before trial of the cause is reached. For example, the plaintiff moves the Court to strike the ANSWER of the defendant and direct judgment for the plaintiff (the party who brings a law suit). More frequently, however, the judgment is not entered until the case has been tried and FINDINGS OF FACT AND CONCLUSIONS OF LAW have been made.

How to prepare a judgment or decree. In a few jurisdictions, the CLERK OF THE COURT prepares the judgments, but usually the prevailing lawyer does. The lawyer will dictate the judgment or decree to the secretary. A judgment is similar in style to a court ORDER. Figure 1 (pages 236-237) illustrates the style of a decree.

Number of copies. It might be necessary to prepare extra copies, in addition to the usual original for the court, copy for each opposing counsel, and an office copy. The number of copies will depend upon the following factors:

1. Number of copies to be certified for delivery to the parties.

2. Whether service of copy is made

JUDGMENT

IN THE DISTRICT COURT IN AND FOR THE CITY AND COUNTY

OF DENVER AND STATE OF COLORADO

CIVIL ACTION NO. 3-504, Div. 7

MARY FRANCES HINES,

               Plaintiff,

        -vs-   INTERLOCUTORY DECREE IN
                                      DIVORCE.

CHARLES WILLIAM HINES,

               Defendant.

THIS CAUSE, coming on to be heard on this 9th day of
January, 19--, upon its merits, the plaintiff being represented by Elwood & Adams, attorneys of record, and the defendant appearing by Ames & Thomas, attorneys of record,
and the Court having examined the full record herein, finds
that it has jurisdiction herein; and having heard the evidence and the statements of counsel, the Court now being
fully advised

DOTH FIND that a divorce should be granted to the
plaintiff herein upon the statutory grounds of_____

_____

IT IS ORDERED, ADJUDGED and DECREED by the Court, that
an absolute divorce should be granted to the plaintiff, and
an Interlocutory Decree of Divorce is hereby entered, dis-
solving the marriage of plaintiff and defendant six months
after the date of this Interlocutory Decree.

IT IS EXPRESSLY DECREED by the Court that during such
six months period after the signing of this Interlocutory

Judgment: Figure 1. Interlocutory decree of divorce.

Decree the parties hereto shall not be divorced; shall still be husband and wife, and neither party shall be competent to contract another marriage anywhere during such period, and the Court during all of said period does hereby retain jurisdiction of the parties and the subject matter of this cause and upon motion of either party; or upon its motion, for good cause shown, after a hearing, may set aside this Interlocutory Decree.

It is further ORDERED, ADJUDGED and DECREED by the Court that defendant shall pay into the Registry of the District Court on the_____

_____

It is further ORDERED, ADJUDGED and DECREED by the Court that the sole care, custody and control of the minor children, Steven Robert Hines and Marion Linda Hines, is hereby awarded to the plaintiff as a suitable person to have such care and custody until the further order of the Court, with the defendant to have reasonable visitation rights.

The Court FURTHER DECREES that after six months from the date hereof this Interlocutory Decree shall be and become a Final Decree of Divorce and the parties shall then be divorced, unless this Interlocutory Decree shall have been set aside, or an appeal has been taken, or a writ of error has been issued.

Done in open Court this 9th day of January, 19—.

BY THE COURT,

Judge.

Judgment: Figure 1.   Interlocutory decree of divorce (Continued).

on opposing counsel with notice of entry after judgment is entered, as well as before the judgment is submitted to the court.

3. Kind of action.

Judgment by Default. After a SUMMONS has been served and returned to the court, the court has JURISDICTION over the defendant (see PARTIES TO AN ACTION). If the defendant fails to defend a civil case by filing proper PLEADINGS, or fails to appear within a definite time, a judgment is given against him in his absence. This judgment is called judgment by default.

It is important for the secretary to the lawyer for the defendant to remember to enter in the DIARY, the *return day of summons*. Failure to do so may lead to a failure to answer by that date resulting in a default judgment.

How the secretary prepares a judgment by default. A printed form is generally available. The secretary can get the necessary information from the office file. She should:

1. Make an original and two copies.

2. Calculate the interest at the legal rate, from the date indicated in the summons.

3. Itemize the cost disbursed by the office and include the total in the amount of the judgment.

4. Get the CLERK OF THE COURT to sign the original and file it in court.

5. Conform the two copies. (See CONFORMING DOCUMENTS.)

6. Fill in the notice of entry of judgment in the space provided on the back of the judgment.

7. Mail one copy to the defendant. The other copy is for the office file.

After judgment by default is entered, the plaintiff is known as a *judgment creditor* and the defendant as

a *judgment debtor*. If the judgment debtor does not pay the judgment, the attorney for the judgment creditor may ask the clerk of the court to issue execution. Should the execution be returned unsatisfied, the attorney will commence supplementary proceedings, if he believes the judgment debtor has any assets out of which the judgment may be collected.

Judgment Creditor. One who has obtained a JUDGMENT against his debtor. For example, when a seller wins a suit against a customer who has failed to pay his debts, the seller is given a judgment against the debtor. The judgment officially declares that the debtor owes the seller the amount stated in the judgment, and that the seller shall recover that amount from the debtor. Frequently, however, a debtor refuses to pay a judgment or insists that he cannot pay it. The creditor can then instruct his attorney to apply to the court for an order, or WRIT, directing the sheriff to seize the debtor's property. This is called applying for a *writ of execution*. In some states an attorney can issue the writ without applying to the court. The property is sold and the creditor is paid out of the proceeds of the sale. Only property in the state where the suit is brought can be seized to satisfy the judgment. If the property is located out of the state, another suit, technically known as *suit on the judgment*, must be brought in that state.

Jurat. The clause in an official certificate attesting that the AFFIDAVIT or deposition was sworn to at a stated time before an authorized officer. It is often referred to as the "sworn to" clause. The form of jurat varies slightly in the different states. In a few states, the jurat recites the title of the officer and the state, or state and county, in which he is authorized to act. In a few other states, the name of the affiant is repeated in the jurat. The most common form of jurat is:

Subscribed and sworn to before me this day of   , 19...

....

Notary Public

Signature of notary. The notary signs immediately beneath the jurat. He also affixes his seal and the expiration date of his commission.

Jurisdiction. The authority of a court to hear a particular cause of action and to render a binding decision. The laws of our country provide that certain causes of action (law suits) must be brought in one court, others in another. It is the lawyer's problem to determine in which court his client's case should be brought—which court has *jurisdiction* over it.

In order to hear a case, a court must have jurisdiction *in personam* (of the person) or *in rem* (of the matter).

In personam jurisdiction. This means that a court must have jurisdiction over litigants (the person or persons bringing the suit and those defending it; see PARTIES TO AN ACTION). For example, if the litigants live in different cities in the same county, the county court, rather than a city or municipal court, has jurisdiction. A New York court does not have jurisdiction over a citizen of Mississippi in a suit brought by a New York citizen.

In rem jurisdiction. This means that the court must have jurisdiction over the subject matter in controversy. *In rem* jurisdiction depends upon several factors: nature of the case, amount involved, location of the property. For example, a magistrate's court has jurisdiction over a traffic violation but cannot try a person for murder. A suit for damages caused by an automobile collision cannot be brought in a probate court (see COURTS OF SPECIAL JURISDICTION). Foreclosure actions can be brought only in the county where the property is located. See also ORIGINAL JURISDICTION; APPELLATE COURT; AMERICAN COURT SYSTEM.

Jurisdictional Dispute. (Labor) A disagreement between two or more labor unions as to whose members have the right to do a particular kind of work. This dissension has always been a major problem of organized labor because of the existence of unions whose jurisdictions overlap.

Jury. *In Practice.* A certain number of men or women, selected according to law, and *sworn* (jurati) to inquire of certain matters of fact, and declare the truth upon evidence to be laid before them. This definition embraces the various subdivision of juries, as *grand jury, petit jury, common jury, special jury, coroner's jury, sheriff's jury.*

Justice. Broadly speaking, the maintenance or administration of that which is just, or the administration of law according to the rules of law or EQUITY. See also JUDGE.

Juvenile Court. See COURTS OF SPECIAL JURISDICTION.

K

Kidnapping. The act of carrying away a person against his will by unlawful force or by FRAUD. While the kidnapper usually has a further intention, such as holding for RANSOM, the only intent necessary to constitute the crime of kidnapping is the intent to detain the victim against his will. Kidnapping may be punishable by death.

Kin. Relation or relationship by blood or consanguinity. The nearness of *kin* is computed according to the civil law.

Kiting. The unethical and sometimes illegal practice of issuing checks against a bank account in which there are not sufficient collected funds to cover the check, with the expectation that before the check drawn is presented for payment funds will be deposited to make good the withdrawal. A bank may close the account of a depositor who is detected in this practice.

L

Labor Union. An organization of employees seeking favorable wages, improved labor conditions, better hours of labor, and the righting of grievances against employers.

The *craft union* is an organization of employees engaged in a single occupation. Such a union is based upon skill in the performance of one task or of a number of closely allied tasks or crafts. An example of a craft union is an association of barbers or plumbers.

The *industrial union* is organized on the basis of the industry rather than the craft. It unites into one group all the workers in a given industry, skilled and unskilled, without regard to craft or occupation. The Amalgamated Clothing Workers of America is an example of an industrial union. See AFL-CIO; AMERICAN FEDERATION OF LABOR; CONGRESS OF INDUSTRIAL ORGANIZATIONS; COLLECTIVE BARGAINING.

Laches. Unreasonable tardiness in bringing suit or seeking remedy in an EQUITY court. For a defendant (see PARTIES TO AN ACTION) to plead *laches* as a defense to a suit, he must show that he suffered from the plaintiff's delay in bringing suit.

Land Description. Identification of a tract of land contained in a DEED, MORTGAGE, LEASE, or other instrument. To avoid dispute and litigation, land should always be described according to one of the following methods, known as a "record description":

1. Section and township (Government Survey)
2. Metes and bounds
3. Lot and block identification

Section and township description (Government Survey). In the 18th century, when the United States began to sell public lands, it was necessary to adopt some conventional method of describing the tracts that were sold. A rectangular system of surveys was devised. The survey divided the public lands into rectangular tracts, located with reference to base lines running east and west, and *prime* or *principal meridians* running north and south. The prime meridians are numbered, as Third Prime Meridian, or named, as San Bernadino Meridian. The rectangular tracts are divided into six-mile squares, known as *townships.* A row of townships running north and south is called a *range,* and the ranges are numbered east and west from the prime meridians. The townships are divided into 36 sections, each one mile square or 640 acres. (Figure 1 on page 242). The sections are numbered from 1 to 36, beginning with the section in the northeast corner of the township, proceeding west to boundary of the township; the next row is numbered from west to east, and so on. (See Figure 2.) The sections in turn are divided into half and quarter sections, and the quarters into quarter-quarter sections, designated by their direction from the center as northwest, southwest, northeast, and southeast.

The description of a given five acres of land identified by the section and township (Government Survey) description might read:

The East Half of the Northeast Quarter of the Northeast Quarter of the Northeast Quarter of Section One, Township 39 North, Range 12 East of the Third Prime Meridian.

The small shaded portion of the diagram in Figure 2 on page 243 represents the parcel described above, as-

suming that the diagram is Township 39 North, Range 12 East.

Land identification in the 29 public land states in which Government Survey description is used is precise and orderly; it is possible to designate any plot of land as small as five acres with perfect accuracy; no two parcels are described in exactly the same terms because they are identified with reference to a specific prime meridian.

Metes and bounds description. Prior to the Government Survey the land in the area comprising the thirteen colonies (18 states) was held under original grants given by the Crown to

Land Description: Figure 1. A section of land.

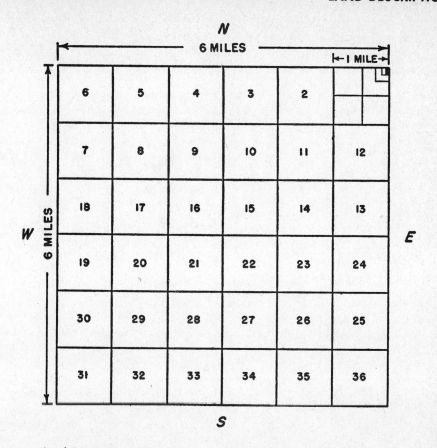

Land Description: Figure 2. Diagram of township divided into sections.

the Colonists. In these states and in Texas[1], each parcel of land is different in size and shape and is described by metes and bounds. A metes and bounds description is not correlated to any system of meridians and base lines, but each tract of land is described by the lines that constitute its boundaries. A natural landmark, such as a tree or river, or an artificial landmark, such as a fence, stake, railroad, or street, often marks the corners and angles. These marks are known as *monuments*. A description by courses and distances constitutes part of a metes and bounds

[1]The United States never had original title to the land in Texas because it was annexed by the United States as an independent republic.

description. The direction from the starting point in which the boundary line runs in a *course*; the length of the line is a *distance*.

The following is an example of a metes and bounds description:

ALL that lot or parcel of land, situate, lying and being in the Town of Oyster Bay, County of Nassau, State of New York, bounded and described as follows:

BEGINNING at a point in the center line of Buena Vista Avenue distant two hundred sixty-one and thirty-one hundredths (261.31) feet southerly from the point of intersection of said line with the center line of Jones Road; running thence along the center line of Buena Vista Avenue South twenty-five (25) degrees thirty-three (33) minutes East four hundred fifty-two and seventy-eight one hundredths (452.78) feet to a point; running thence North sixty-eight (68) degrees thirty-two (32) minutes East three hundred ten and eleven one hundredths (310.11) feet to a point in the center line of a driveway; running thence generally along the center line of said driveway the following courses and distances:

A. North forty-five (45) degrees forty-two (42) minutes West, 50 feet;

B. North thirty-nine (39) degrees two (02) minutes West, 50 feet;

C. North thirty-four (34) degrees sixteen (16) minutes West, 50 feet;

D. North twenty-eight (28) degrees fifty-eight (58) minutes West, 50 feet;

E. North twenty-six (26) degrees seventeen (17) minutes West, 100 feet;

F. North thirty-two (32) degrees six (06) minutes West, 50 feet;

G. North forty-five (45) degrees thirty-four (34) minutes West, 50 feet;

H. North sixty-one (61) degrees thirty-two (32) minutes West, 50 feet;

I. North eighty (80) degrees thirty-three (33) minutes West, 50 feet;

J. South seventy-nine (79) degrees eleven (11) minutes West, 50 feet;

K. South sixty-five (65) degrees thirty-two (32) minutes West, 50 feet; and

L. South sixty-four (64) degrees forty-seven (47) minutes West, 77 feet, to a point in the center line of Buena Vista Avenue, the point or place of beginning;

Containing, in area, approximately two and seven hundred seventy-four thousandths (2.774) acres;

Being and intended to be all of Plot No. 5, as shown on a map entitled "Plot Plan, Property of John Doe Estate, Town of Oyster Bay, Nassau County, New York, made by James Brown, Surveyor, November 1, 19. ., as revised January 13, 19. ., and December 31, 19. . ."

Lot and block description. Property is described by lot and block number when land has been surveyed and subdivided into parcels. A map of the subdivision is recorded in the appropriate county office. A lot and block description might read:

Lot ten (10), Block Eight (8) Bay Shore Subdivision, as recorded in Volume 5 of Plats, Page 39, records of Blank County, State of. . . . .

Style in preparing descriptions. Descriptions of land to be included in an instrument are usually copied from some earlier document or from a survey or an ABSTRACT OF TITLE. These should be transcribed exactly. It is permissible, however, and sometimes desirable to write out words which have been abbreviated and to correct capitalization. The following general rules should be observed in preparing descriptions for real estate instruments:

1. Single space, with double space between paragraphs.

2. Do not abbreviate Street, Avenue, Road, Boulevard, in the text.

3. Write the words *North, Northeast, South, West, Southwest,* and the like with initial capitals, but do not capitalize the words *northerly, northeasterly,* and the like.

4. Capitalize *Quarter, Township, Section,* and *Range,* and the name or number of a *Prime Meridian.*

5. Write courses as follows: "South twenty (20) degrees, thirty-three (33) minutes, forty-five (45) seconds West."

6. Write distances as follows: "One hundred thirty-three and twenty-nine one hundredths (133.29) feet."

7. When several courses and distances are given in succession, introduced by a phrase such as ". . .the following three courses and distances. . ." each of the courses and distances is written separately, indented and single spaced, separated one from the other by a double space, and each course and distance is ended with a semicolon. The sentence after the last course and distance is flush with the left-hand margin of the text preceding the itemized courses and distances.

8. It is preferable not to use figures, symbols, and abbreviations, but it is sometimes necessary to use them because of the limited space on a printed form. A description would then be written: "South 20° 33' 45″ Wes , 50 ft." In offices with considerable rea estate practice, a special key is placed on the typewriter for the symbol of the word *degrees;* otherwise, the symbol is made by turning the platen back a half space and striking the small *o.*

Checking land descriptions. An error in the description of land can cause considerable trouble and even result in a law suit. The importance of checking the description cannot be over-emphasized. It is easy to make an error in copying that is not always discernible from merely reading the description. For example, the section and township description shown above contains the phrase "of the Northeast Quarter" three times. It would be easy to omit the phrase once, but difficult to realize the omission in reading over the description; yet the omission would double the amount of land conveyed by the deed. Nor is it advisable for one person to compare the description line by line. The safest method of checking the typographical accuracy of land description is to have one person read aloud to another the original copy, slowly enough to permit him to follow the typed copy carefully.

Larceny. The act of wrongfully taking and carrying away the personal goods of another. The physical act of carrying away the property is called *asportation.* Asportation, when done with the intent to steal the thing asported, is the crime of larceny. State laws divide the crime of larceny into degrees, with the severity of punishment depending on the value of the property stolen, whether the act was committed during the night or day, and whether the property was stolen from the victim's person or house. See also EMBEZZLEMENT; ROBBERY.

Last Clear Chance. A doctrine that permits a plaintiff to recover in spite of his own CONTRIBUTORY NEGLIGENCE. The doctrine applies when the plaintiff is in a position of peril and the defendant knows that the plaintiff cannot act to save himself. If the defendant has such knowledge in sufficient time to enable him to avert the injury by the exercise of reasonable care, but he thereafter fails to exercise due care, the plaintiff may recover.

As an example, the Last Clear Chance doctrine would be applied in a case where a boy is trespassing on railroad tracks and the engineer of a train realizes that the boy cannot get out of the way of his moving train. The engineer would be held liable if he had sufficient time to stop his train, but did not. The doctrine of last clear chance permits recovery even though the boy was contributorily negligent by being on the tracks.

Last Resort. A Court from which there is no appeal is called the "court of last resort."

Latin Terms. The following is an alphabetical list of Latin words and phrases most likely to be used in the law office. (A few French terms that are in legal usage are included also.) Those words or phrases now considered to be a part of everyday English language are in Roman type instead of italics.

a fortiori. With stronger reason; much more.

a mensa et thoro. From bed and board.

LATIN TERMS

a priori. From what goes before; from the cause to the effect.

a rendre. (French, to render, to yield). That which is to be rendered, yielded, or paid. *Profits a rendre* comprehend rents and services.

a vinculo matrimonii. From the bonds of marriage.

ab initio. From the beginning.

actiones in personam. Personal actions.

ad faciendum. To do.

ad hoc. For this; (for this special purpose).

ad infinitum. Indefinitely; forever.

ad litem. For the suit; for the litigation. (A guardian *ad litem* is a person appointed to prosecute or defend a suit for a person incapacitated by infancy or incompetency.)

ad quod damnum. To what damage; what injury. (A phrase used to describe the plaintiff's money loss or the damages that he claims.)

ad respondendum. To answer.

ad satisfaciendum. To satisfy.

ad valorem. According to value. (See also AD VALOREM TAX.)

aggregatio mentium. Meeting of minds.

alias dictus. Otherwise called.

alibi. In another place; elsewhere.

alii. Others

aliunde. From another place; from without (as evidence outside the document).

alius. Another.

alter ego. The other self.

alumnus. A foster child.

amicus curiae. Friend of the court.

animo. With intention, disposition, design, will.

animus. Mind; intention.

animus furandi. The intention to steal.

animus revertendi. An intention of returning.

animus revocandi. An intention to revoke.

animus testandi. An intention to make A testament or will.

anno Domini (A.D.). In the year of the Lord.

ante. Before.

ante litem motam. Before suit brought.

arguendo. In the course of the argument.

assumpsit. He undertook; he promised.

bona fide. In good faith.

bona vacantia. Vacant goods. (Personal property that no one claims, which escheats to the state.)

capias. Take; arrest (A form of writ directing an arrest.)

capias ad satisfaciendum (ca. sa.). Arrest to satisfy. (A form of writ.)

causa mortis. By reason of death.

caveat. Let him beware; a warning.

caveat emptor. Let the buyer beware.

cepit et asportavit. He took and carried away.

certiorari. To be informed of; to be made certain in regard to something.

cestui que trust. He who benefits by the trust.

cestui que use. He who benefits by the use.

cestui que vie. He whose life measures the duration of the estate.

civiliter mortuus. Civilly dead.

Consensus, non concubitus, facit nuptias. vel matrimonium. Consent, not co-habitation, constitutes nuptials or marriage.

consortium (pl. consortia). A union of lots or chances (a lawful marriage).

contra. Against

contra bonos mores. Against good morals.

contra pacem. Against the peace.

coram non judice. In presence of a person not a judge. (A suit brought and determined in a court having no jurisdiction over the matter is said to be *coram non judice,* and the judgment is void.)

246

corpus. Body.

corpus delicti. The body of the offense; the essence of crime.

corpus juris. A body of law.

corpus juris civilis. The body of the civil law.

Cujus est solum, ejus est usque ad coelum. Whose the soil is, his it is up to the sky.

cum testamento annexo (c.t.a.). With the will annexed. (Describes an administrator who operates under a will rather than in intestacy.)

damnum absque injuria. Damage without injury. (Damage without legal wrong.)

datum (*pl.* data). A thing given; a date. (See also DATA.)

de bonis non administratis. Of the goods not administered. Frequently this is abbreviated to *de bonis non.*

de bono et malo. For good and ill.

de facto. In fact; in deed; actually. (See also DE FACTO CORPORATION.)

De minimis non curat lex. The law does not concern itself with trifles.

de novo. Anew; afresh.

de son tort. Of his own wrong.

dies non. Not a day (on which the business of the courts can be carried on.

doli incapax. Incapable of criminal intention or malice; not of the age of discretion and intelligence to distinguish between right and wrong to the extent of being criminally responsible for his action.

donatio mortis causa. A gift by reason of death. (A gift made by a person in sickness, under apprehension of death.)

duces tecum. You bring with you. (A term applied to a writ commanding the person upon whom it is served to bring certain evidence with him to court. Thus, we speak of a *subpoena duces tecum.*)

dum bene se gesserit. While he shall conduct himself well; during good behavior.

durante minore aetate. During minority.

durante viduitate. During widowhood.

Eate inde sine die. In criminal practice. Words used on the accquittal of a defendant, or when a prisoner is to be discharged, *that he may go thence without a day,* i.e. be dismissed without any further continuance or adjournment.

e converso. Conversely; on the other hand.

enlarger l'estate. A species of release which inures by way of enlarging an estate, and consists of a conveyance of the ulterior interest to the particular tenant; as if there be tenant for life or years, remainder to another in fee, and he in remainder releases all his right to the particular tenant and his heirs; this gives him the estate in fee.

eo instanti. Upon the instant.

erratum. (*pl.* errata). Error.

et alii (et. al.). And others.

et alius (et. al.). And another.

et cetera (etc.). And other things.

ex cathedra. From the chair.

ex contractu. (Arising) from the contract.

ex delicto. (Arising) from the tort.

ex gratia. As a matter of favor.

ex necessitate legis. From the legal necessity.

ex officio. From office; by virtue of his office.

ex parte. On one side only; by or for one party.

ex post facto. After the act.

et uxor (ex ux.). And wife.

et vir. And husband.

felonice. Feloniously.

feme covert. A married woman.

feme sole. A single woman (including one who has been married but whose marriage has been dissolved by death or divorce).

ferae naturae. Of a wild nature.

fiat. Let it be done. (A short order or warrant of a judge, commanding that something shall be done.)

fieri. To be made up; to become.

fieri facias. Cause to be made. (A writ directed to the sheriff to reduce the judgment debtor's property to money in the amount of the judgment.)

filius nullius. The son of nobody; a bastard.

filius populi. A son of the people.

flagrante delicto. In the very act of committing the crime.

habeas corpus. You have the body. (See also HABEAS CORPUS.)

habere facias possessionem. That you cause to have possession. (A writ of ejectment.)

habere facias seisinam. That you cause to have seisin. (A writ to give possession.)

honorarium (*pl.* honoraria). An honorary fee or gift; compensation from gratitude.

idem sonans. Having the same sound (as names sounding alike but spelled differently).

Ignorantia legis neminem excusat. Ignorance of the law excuses no one.

illicitum collegium. An unlawful association.

Impotentia excusat legem. Impossibility is an excuse in law.

in bonis. In goods; among possessions.

in esse. In being; existence.

in extremis. In extremity (in the last illness).

in fraudem legis. In circumvention of law.

in futuro. In the future.

in loco parentis. In the place of a parent.

in pari delicto. In equal fault.

in personam. A remedy where the proceedings are *against the person,* as contradistinguished from those against a specific thing.

in praesenti. At present; at once; now.

in re. In the matter.

in rem. A remedy where the proceedings are *against the thing,* as contradistinguished from those against the person.

in rerum natura. In nature; in life; in existence.

in specie. In the same, or like, form. (To decree performance *in specie* is to decree specific performance.)

in statu quo. In the condition in which it was. (See *status quo.*)

in terrorem. In terror.

in toto. In the whole; completely.

in transitu. In transit; in course of transfer.

indebitatus assumpsit. Being indebted, be promised, or undertook. (An action in which plaintiff alleges defendent is indebted to him.)

indicia. Marks; signs.

infra. Below.

innuendo. Meaning.

inter. Among; between.

inter vivos. Between the living.

interim. In the meantime.

intra. Within; inside.

ipse dixit. He himself said (it). (An assertion made but not proved.)

ipso facto. By the fact itself.

ita est. So it is.

jura personarum. Rights of persons.

jura rerum. Rights of things.

jure divino. By divine right.

jure uxoris. By his wife's right.

jus (pl. jura). Law; laws collectively.

jus accrescendi. The right of survivorship.

jus ad rem. A right to a thing.

jus civile. Civil law.

jus commune. The common law; the common right.

jus gentium. The law of nations; international law.

jus habendi. The right to have a thing.

jus proprietatis. Right of property.

levari facias. Cause to be levied; a writ of execution.

lex loci. Law of the place (where the cause of action arose).

lex loci rei sitae. The law of the place where a thing is situated.

lex mercatoria. Mercantile law.

lis pendens. Litigation pending; a pending suit.

locus delicti. The place of the crime or tort.

locus in quo. The place in which.

locus sigilli (L.S.). The place for the seal.

mala fides. Bad faith.

mala in se. Wrongs in themselves (acts morally wrong).

mala praxis. Malpractice.

mala prohibita. Prohibited wrongs or offenses.

malo animo. With evil intent.

malum in se. Evil in itself.

mandamus. We command. (See also MANDAMUS.)

manu forti. With a strong hand (forcible entry).

mens rea. Guilty mind.

nihil dicit. He says nothing. (Judgment against defendant who does not put in a defense to the complaint.)

nil debet. He owes nothing.

nisi prius. Unless before. (The phrase is used to denote the forum where the trial was held as distinguished from the appellate court.)

nolle prosequi. To be unwilling to follow up, or to prosecute. (A formal entry on the record by the plaintiff or the prosecutor that he will no further prosecute the case.)

nolo contendere. I will not contest it.

non compos mentis. Not of sound mind.

non est factum. It is not his deed.

non obstante. Not withstanding.

non prosequitur (non pros.). He does not follow up, or pursue, or prosecute. (If the plaintiff fails to take some step that he should, the defendant may enter a judgment of *non pros.* against him.)

nudum pactum. A nude pact. (A contract without consideration.)

nul tiel record. No such record.

nul tort. No wrong done.

nulla bona. No goods (Wording of return to a writ of *fieri facias.*)

nunc pro tunc. Now for then.

obiter dictum. Remark by the way.

onus probandi. The burden of proof.

opus (pl. opera). Work; labor.

ore tenus. By word of mouth; orally.

pari delicto. In equal guilt.

particeps criminis. An accomplice in the crime.

paterfamilias. The father (head) of a family.

peculium. Private property.

pendente lite. Pending the suit; during the litigation.

per annum. By the year.

per autre vie. For another's lifetime. (See also *pur autre vie.*)

per capita. By the head; as individuals. (In a distribution of an estate, if the descendants take per capita, they take share and share alike regardless of family lines of descent.)

per centum (percent). By the hundred.

per contra. In opposition.

per curiam. By the court.

per diem. By the day.

per se. By itself; taken alone.

per stirpes. By stems or root; by representation. (In a distribution of an estate, if distribution is *per stirpes,* descendants take by virtue of their representation of an ancestor, not as individuals.)

post-mortem. After death.

post-obit. To take effect after death.

praecipe or *precipe.* Command. (A written order to the clerk of the court to issue a write.)

prima facie. At first sight; on the face of it.

pro. For.

pro confesso. As confessed.

pro forma. As a matter of form.

pro hac vice. For this occasion.

pro rata. According to the rate or proportion.

pro tanto. For so much; to that extent.

pro tempore (pro tem.). For the time being; temporarily.

prochien ami. Next friend. Also may be spelled *prochien amy, prochain ami* and *prochain amy.*

publici juris. Of public right.

pur autre vie. For, or during the life of another. (See also *per autre vie.*)

quaere. Query; question; doubt. (This word indicates that a particular rule, decision, or statement that follows it is open to question.)

quantum. How much; the amount.

quantum meruit. As much as he deserved.

quantum valebant. As much as they were (reasonably) worth (in absence of agreement as to value).

quare. Wherefore.

quare clausum fregit. Wherefore he broke the close. (A form of trespass on another's land.)

quasi. As if; as it were. (Indicates that one subject resembles another, but that there are also intrinsic differences between them. Thus, we speak of quasi contracts, quasi torts, etc.)

quid pro quo. What for what; something for something. (A term denoting the consideration for a contract.)

quo warranto. By what right or authority. (See also QUO WARRANTO.)

quoad hoc. As to this.

quod computet. That the account.

reductio ad absurdum. Reduced to the absurd.

res. A thing; an object; the subject matter.

res gestae. Things done; transactions. itself.

res judicata. A matter adjudicated.

scienter. Knowingly.

scilicet (SS, or ss.) To wit. (sc. is not used in legal papers)

scintilla. A spark; the least particle.

scire facias. Cause to know; give notice.

(A writ used to revive a judgment that has expired.)

se defendendo. In self-defense; in defending oneself.

semper. Always.

semper paratus. Always ready. (A plea by which the defendant alleges that he has always been ready to perform what is demanded of him.)

seriatim. Severally; separately.

sigillum. A seal.

simplex obligato. A simple obligation.

sine die. Without day. (Without a specified day being assigned for a future meeting or hearing.)

situs. Situation; location.

stare judice. To abide by decided cases.

status quo. State in which (the existing state of things at any given date.) See *in statu quo.*

sub judice. Under a consideration.

sub modo. Under a qualification; in a qualified way.

sub nom. Under the name.

subpoena duces tecum. See SUBPOENA.

sui juris. Of his own right; (having legal capacity to act for himself).

supersedeas. That you supersede. (A writ commanding a stay of the proceedings.)

supra. Above

terminus a quo. The starting point.

ultra vires. Without power; beyond the powers of.

venire facias. That you cause to come; (a kind of summons).

Verba fortius accipiuntur contra proferentem. Words are to be taken most strongly against the one using them.

versus (vs., v.). Against.

vi et armis. By force of arms.

via. A road; a right of way; by way of.

vice versa. On the contrary; on opposite sides.

videlicet (viz.). (contraction of *videre* and *licet*). It is easy to see; (that is to say; namely).

virtute officii. By virtue of his office.

vis major. (Latin) A superior force. In law, the term signifies "an inevitable accident"—as in common law, "an act of God."

A loss by *vis major* is one that results from some natural cause without the intervention of man, and that could not have been prevented by the exercise of prudence, diligence, and care. The term is sometimes used in certain types of contracts. For example, a motion-picture distributor would be likely to include in his contracts with lessees, a section that renders him not liable for loss or damage occasioned by wars, delays in transportation, acts of God, or accidents considered to be the result of a *vis major.*

viva voce. By the living voice; by word of mouth.

voir dire. To speak the truth. (Denotes a preliminary examination to determine the competency of a witness.)

Law Degree. A rank to which law scholars are admitted by a university, in recognition of their legal attainments. The law degrees obtainable and the abbreviations of them follow. Notice that in some cases the abbreviation of the Latin *juris,* meaning law, is used.

Bachelor of Laws	LL.B.;B.L.
Bachelor of Civil Law	J.C.B.;B.C.L.
Master of Laws	LL.M.;M.L.
Doctor of Laws	LL.D.;J.D.

Doctor of Law	Jur. D.
Doctor of Civil Law	J.C.D.;D.C.L.
Juris Civilis Doctor	J.C.D.
Doctor of Jurisprudence	J.D.
Juris Doctor	Jur. D.
Jurum Doctor	J.D.
Doctor of Juristic Science	J.S.D.
Doctor of Both Laws	J.U.D.

Law School Reviews. Scholarly publications sponsored by law schools. Law reviews serve as outlets for legal articles by teachers, practitioners, and judges. Editorial work and some writing are done by the best students from the sponsoring school. CITATION (TO LEGAL AUTHORITIES). See *How to cite law reviews.*

Lawyer's Edition. See AMERICAN LAW REPORTS.

Lawyers' Incorporated. The Internal Revenue Service has made provisions for incorporating professional persons with possible large tax advantages to the individual. All fifty states and the District of Columbia have made provision for professional corporations, but the provisions may or may not include lawyers. Following is an example of the mechanics of forming a professional corporation in the State of Ohio. The procedure varies from state to state.

Professional Association Act—in general.—Ohio adopted its Professional Association Act in 1961 and amended the statute in 1969. Here are some highlights of the statute:

Type of organization. Ohio calls them professional associations. But the act refers to incorporation and corporation as well as association. The entity is a mixture of corporation and association in concept; there are elements of both.

Statutory purpose: An Ohio professional association is organized for the sole purpose of rendering one professional service.

What professions are included: Ohio's professional association act is specific, it names the professions that are involved. These are: certified public accountants, licensed public accountants, architects, attorneys, dentists, pharmacists, optometrists, physicians and surgeons, professional engineers, veterinarians and practitioners of limited branches of medicine or surgery as defined in the Ohio Code (chiropractice, naprapathy, spondylotherapy, mechanotherapy, etc).

Incorporators: One individual or a group of individuals may organize a professional association and may incorporate their practice. Each individual must be licensed to practice the same kind of professional service in Ohio. The organizers become shareholders, so apparently you can't use accommodation parties as incorporators.

Stockholders: Any number of persons may own stock in an Ohio professional association; there's no specific limitation in the Ohio professional association statute. However, only persons duly licensed to practice the same professional service as the association may be shareholders. Apparently there's no reason why a stockholder in an Ohio professional association must also be an employee of that association.

Directors. The Ohio professional association statute doesn't make any mention of directors or governors. It refers to officers and employees and agents but is silent about a board of directors. There apparently is no reason why an Ohio professional association can't use a board of directors composed of individuals who are not licensed to practice the particular profession and who are not shareholders in the professional association. The incorporating dentists' attorney, for example, could serve as a member of the board of directors. Officers also apparently don't have to be licensed professionals, so the dentist's wife, for example, might serve as an officer of the professional association.

Association name: The Ohio Professional Association Act places no limitations on the name used. The statute is silent concerning the association's name. However, attorneys must abide by the Supreme Court Rules and one of these rules is that the corporate name must end with the words "Co., L.P.A." (for "legal professional association"). The rules also require that the corporate name must consist only of the surname of one or more of the active shareholders. Most other states do have specific provisions saying, for example, that the name must contain the words "professional association" or similar wording. In Ohio, the association selects a name that is permissible under the rules of the particular profession and without other restrictions.

Certificates and reports: An Ohio professional association is not obligated by statute to file, in or with the agreement to associate, or the articles of association, any independent evidence that its shareholders are duly licensed professionals. No certificate from regulating boards is required. But, annually, an Ohio professional association must furnish a statement to the Secretary of State, certifying that all shareholders are duly licensed to render professional service in Ohio. The form of such annual statement is prescribed by the Secretary of State and it must be furnished within 30 days after each June 30th.

Investments: Again, the Ohio professional association statute has no direct provision. Many other states' laws do. It seems that an Ohio professional association may invest its funds in all the usual types of investments, without restriction that these investments be necessary or related to the rendering of professional service.

Other applicable laws: The Ohio General Corporation Law applies to professional corporations, except when its provisions may conflict with the Professional Association Act. In that event the Professional Association Act takes precedence. (From "Professional Corporation Guide" by Prentice-Hall.)

For the procedure in your state see your local law library.

Layout. (Printing). A design of the job to be printed, showing, page by page, margins, blocks or columns of type, illustrations, heading, captions, and the like, each drawn to exact size. Every item, even page numbers and credit lines, is carefully identified for size. See DUMMY.

Layout of Law Office. The physical setup and arrangements that facilitate a smoothly operating law practice.

The ideal suite of law offices consists of a reception room, a workroom, a library, a file room, a conference room, and a series of private offices. The reception room, workroom, and file room may be combined as a general office; the law books may be in various offices; there may be no conference room, but each lawyer *always* has a private office. The confidential nature of legal matters and the desire of clients for privacy demand this. Glass partitions so common to business offices are not used in law offices because they do not insure privacy. Large law offices usually have a series of private suites consisting of an office for the lawyer and an office for the secretary who is assigned to him. Lawyers sometimes share an office suite, each lawyer conducting his practice as a sole practitioner.

Here are some suggestions the secretary can make about the layout of a suite of law offices when she is asked for ideas:

1. If the workroom is also the waiting room, separate the waiting room from the work portion with a rail. At least arrange the furniture so that it is not necessary for people passing in and out of the general office to enter the part used as a workroom. A cabinet with filing facilities is also appropriate for separating the work space from the waiting room.

2. The secretary should be located as near as possible to the lawyer to whom she is assigned.

3. A private exit from the lawyer's private office is desirable so that a client does not have to leave through the waiting room where other clients are waiting. It also affords the lawyer an opportunity to go and come without being observed.

Leading. The white space between the lines of type. See also POINT.

Lease. A binding CONTRACT, written or oral, for the possession of lands and improvements on the one side, and the recompense by rent or other compensation on the other side. When the lease is evidenced by a written instrument which binds the parties to fulfill certain covenants or agreements, that instrument is known as a *lease.* It is sometimes called an INDENTURE. Leases range from the letting of an apartment for one year to a 99-year lease on vacant property. They may cover real property, personal property, or both, but a lease of real property is most common. Leases of realty give the lessee a *leasehold estate in the premises.*

Parties to a lease. The parties to a lease are the *lessor,* who owns the property, and the *lessee,* who rents it. The lessor, or owner, leases the property *to* the lessee, or tenant; the lessee leases the property *from* the lessor.

A party to a lease may be a natural person, or a partnership, or a CORPORATION. Leases on behalf of minors or insane persons should be made by a guardian. The officers of a corporation enter into a lease on its behalf pursuant to authorization of the board of directors or stockholders. An administrator cannot make a lease because his function is to wind up the estate, not to lease real property. An executor or testamentary trustee must have specific authority given to him by the will in order to make a lease.

Classification of leases. Duration. Leases may be classified according to their duration as *short-term* or *long-term leases.* Although there is no definite duration that takes a lease out of the short-term class into the long-term class, a lease of 10 or more years is generally considered a long-term lease. The fundamental distinctions are in the responsibilities assumed by the lessee, and in the bond and security requirements. Under a short-term lease, the lessor usually requires the lessee to deposit with him one, three, or six months' rental at the time the lease is executed, whereas under a long-term lease the lessee is required to furnish a bond or collateral in an amount equal to about three-years' rental. The most common practice is for the lessee to deposit with a bank or other financial institution negotiable securities of the required amount.

A special type of long-term lease is the 99-year lease, which has been utilized extensively for the purpose of developing business districts in large cities. These leases are made on parcels of valuable real estate strategically located for business expansion. They contemplate the erection or improvement of buildings upon the property by the lessee.

Type of property. Leases may be classified as *commercial* or *residential,* according to the type of property covered by the lease. (See COMMERCIAL LEASE; RESIDENTIAL LEASE.) The secretary in a law office is more likely to prepare commercial leases than residential leases. Short-term leases may be either commercial or residential leases, but long-term leases are almost exclusively commercial leases.

Rental. The majority of leases call for the payment of a definite amount of rental, which continues at a uniform rate throughout the term of the lease. The amount is called a *flat rental.* Other leases, especially long-term leases, provide that the rental shall start at a comparatively low figure and gradually increase. A rental provision of this type is called a *graded rental.* Another method of fixing the amount of rental is to require the tenant to pay a specified percentage of the gross income from sales made upon the premises. A lease with this requirement is called a *percentage lease.* These leases generally cover premises occupied by retail businesses, such as chain stores and department stores. Percentage leases generally run for ten or more years.

Printed forms. Printed forms of leases covering almost any kind of property are available and are frequently used for short-term leases. Many concerns print their own leases, in a form prepared by the lawyer. The lawyer's secretary is more likely to be concerned with the drafting and printing of a form than with filling in the run-of-the-mill lease, such as a lease on an apartment. (See CHECKING MANUSCRIPT.)

Figures 1 and 2 on pages 256-257 illustrate the first and last pages of a commercial lease covering a loft. The back of the lease contains a proper endorsement and forms of acknowledgment for an individual and for a corporation.

Standard lease clauses. Usually the lawyer dictates both the short-term and long-term leases that are prepared in his office. Although many of the clauses are standard (see below), a variety of other clauses is necessary to express the agreement between the parties, especially in long-term leases. Ninety-nine year leases and many other long-term leases are extremely technical legal instruments, their

205—Blumberg's Mercantile Lease.   JULIUS BLUMBERG, INC., LAW BLANK PUBLISHERS

This Indenture, made the   day of

in the year one thousand nine hundred and

Witnesseth, That

as Lessor, does grant, demise and let to

and to   legal representatives, as Lessee.

with the appurtenances, for the term of

beginning the   day of

and ending the   day of

The Said Lessee, for   and   legal representatives, do covenant with

the said Lessor and   legal representatives, as follows:

FIRST:—To pay the annual rent of

Dollars, in equal   payments in advance on the

day of

in each year during the continuance of the said term.

SECOND:—To pay whenever called upon such proportion of all the charges of water, as the number of lofts occupied by the Lessee shall bear to the total number of tenanted lofts in the building, during the term of this lease, in accordance with the bills produced from the Department of Water Supply, Gas and Electricity, or other Municipal Authority, and if not so paid, the same shall be added to the rent due or to become due.

THIRD:—Not to use or permit to be used the roof of said building, nor cut, drill into or otherwise disfigure, nor permit the disfigurement of the iron, marble or stone of said building, nor obstruct, nor permit any obstruction of any lights or skylights, nor injure, nor deface the premises, nor without the written consent of the Lessor, make any alterations therein, nor use, nor suffer to be used, the whole or any part thereof for any purpose other than

FOURTH:—To make all necessary repairs on said premises, including plumbing, window chains, radiators and locks, as well as other repairs, without expense to the Lessor, except damage by fire and damage to the roof. Such repairs shall only be made to restore and keep said premises in their ordinary good condition, and to be equal to the original in class and quality.

FIFTH:—That the Lessor is exempt from any and all liability for any damage or injury to person or property caused by or resulting from steam, electricity, gas, water, rain, ice or snow, or any leak or flow from or into any part of said building, or from any damage or injury resulting or arising from any other cause or happening whatsoever, unless said damage or injury be caused by or be due to the negligence of the Lessor.

SIXTH:—To permit the Lessor and   agents at all times to enter the premises or any part thereof for the purpose of inspection and repair; and to show them to persons wishing to hire or purchase, and during six months next preceding the expiration of term, to permit the usual notice "To Let" or "For Sale" to be and remain posted upon the premises.

SEVENTH:—This lease shall not be assigned or encumbered, and the said premises, or any part thereof, shall not be let or underlet, nor used or permitted to be used, for any purpose other than above mentioned, nor by any other person without the written consent of the said Lessor.

EIGHTH:—Upon the determination of this demise to peaceably surrender the premises in as good order and condition as at the beginning of the term, reasonable wear and damage by fire only excepted.

NINTH:—To promptly execute and comply with all rules, orders, ordinances and regulations of the City and State Governments, and all other authorities, and of any and all their Departments and Bureaus, applicable to said premises, for the correction, prevention and abatement of nuisances or other grievances, in, upon or connected with premises during said term, and shall also promptly comply with and execute all rules, orders and regulations of the New York Board of Fire Underwriters for the prevention of Fires, at their own cost and expense; also all rules and regulations, as well as suggestions of the New York Fire Insurance Exchange and also to comply with the rules and regulations hereinafter set forth and made part hereof.

Lease: Figure 1. First page of commercial lease form.

Electric Current   *TWENTY-FIFTH:*—The Lessee hereby agrees, that at the option of the Lessor, the Lessee will purchase from the Lessor, or from any person or corporation designated by Lessor such electric current as may be required by the Lessee at the terms, classification and rates charged to such consumers by the public utility corporation serving the part of the city where the building is located. That the current consumed by the Lessee be measured in the same manner as is current furnished direct by the public utility, and that the service, in general, shall be at least equal to that furnished direct by the public utility. Such electric current shall be paid for monthly and the amount thereof shall be added to the rent for the month next following, and the Lessor shall have the same rights and remedies upon non-payment of any such charges as upon non-payment of rent.

Security   *TWENTY-SIXTH:*—The Lessee has this day deposited with the Lessor the sum of .... Dollars as security for the full and faithful performance by the Lessee of all of the terms, covenants and conditions upon the Lessee's part to be performed, which said sum shall be returned to the Lessee after the time fixed as the expiration of the term herein, provided the Lessee has fully and faithfully carried out all of the terms, covenants and conditions on the Lessee's part to be performed.

War   *TWENTY-SEVENTH:*—This lease and the obligation of Lessee to pay rent hereunder and perform all of the other covenants and agreements hereunder on part of Lessee to be performed shall in nowise be affected, impaired or excused because Lessor is unable to supply or is delayed in supplying any service expressly or impliedly to be supplied or is unable to make, or is delayed in making any repairs, additions, alterations or decorations or is unable to supply or is delayed in supplying any equipment or fixtures if Landlord is prevented or delayed from so doing by reason of governmental preemption in connection with the National Emergency declared by the President of the United States or in connection with any rule, order or regulation of any department or subdivision thereof of any governmental agency or by reason of the condition of supply and demand which have been or are affected by the war.

In Witness Whereof, the parties have inter-changeably set their hands and seals (or caused these presents to be signed by their proper corporate officers and caused their proper corporate seal to be hereto affixed) the day and year first above written.

Signed, sealed and delivered in the presence of }

_____   _____
       As to Lessee

                              _____

_____   _____
       As to Lessee

                              _____

Lease: Figure 2. Last page of commercial lease form.

preparation requiring a lawyer who is a specialist in the field. The secretary will probably have to type several drafts before the lawyer and his client are satisfied.

If the lawyer's practice involves drawing commercial leases, he will probably have a work folder, or loose-leaf notebook from which he dictates the lease. This folder will consist of each of the standard lease clauses in the form that the lawyer prefers. (If the lawyer does not have a work folder of this kind, the secretary might compile one for him.) Each clause will be pasted on a separate sheet, or half-sheet, and the lawyer will probably have written comments for his guidance beneath the form. The folder, or notebook, will also contain clauses that are not standard, or that do not appear in all leases. It occasionally happens that the lawyer overlooks one of the standard clauses, even when he is using the notebook for guidance. The secretary should become familiar with the standard clauses in commercial leases so that she will be able to call the omission to his attention. Furthermore, in dictating he might tell her to insert the usual insurance, or liability clause, or some other standard clause, and she should be able to select the proper clause without further instruction from the lawyer.

Checklist of standard clauses in commercial leases. Here is a list of the standard clauses that appear in almost all commercial leases. Although each clause might not be in a separate paragraph, in all probability the lease will contain words covering each of these subjects.

1. Term of duration
2. Rent
3. Water, electricity
4. Alterations
5. Repairs
6. Damage or liability—that is, the provision fixing the liability for injury to persons or property
7. "To let" sign prior to expiration of the lease
8. Assignment of the lease
9. Surrender of the premises upon expiration of the lease
10. Rules and ordinances
11. Fire—that is, the agreement about the respective rights of the parties if the building should be destroyed by fire or "other action of the elements"
12. Elevators and heat
13. Insurance
14. Default in payment of rent
15. BANKRUPTCY of lessee
16. Peaceful possession or quiet enjoyment of the premises
17. No waiver—that is, the provision that the consent of the lessor to a variation of the terms in one instance is not a waiver of terms and conditions of the lease
18. Subordination to mortgages
19. Sprinkler system
20. Condemnation or eminent domain proceedings—that is, the rights of the respective parties if the city, county, state, or Federal authority should condemn or take possession of the premises
21. Security deposited by lessee
22. War—that is, the provision that the lessee is not exempt from payment of rent if lessor, because of shortages caused by war, is unable to supply ser-

vices or equipment called for by the lease

Execution, acknowledgment, and recording of lease. A lease of land or commercial property is executed with the formalities of a deed. The state statutes vary, but generally the following apply:

1. Both the lessor and lessee sign the lease.

2. A lease is sealed unless the state statute does not require a deed to be witnessed.

3. A lease is witnessed unless the state statute does not require a deed to be witnessed.

4. If the duration of the lease is more than one year (longer in some states), the lessor and lessee acknowledge it, and the lessee should have it recorded.

5. A lease may be signed by an agent with written authority.

The execution of the run-of-the-mill short-term lease, such as a lease on an apartment, is not so formal. Both the lessor and lessee sign, and usually the signatures are witnessed. Otherwise there are no formal requirements. The directions about acknowledgments and recording apply only to leases that must be recorded. (See RECORDING OF LEASE.)

Style of typed lease. When a lawyer drafts a lease, he simplifies the location of specific provisions by the order in which he groups them. In planning the style in which to type the lease, the secretary's object should be to simplify further the location of specific provisions. She can do this by indicating the subject of each provision in the margin, as in the printed form illustrated in pages 256-257. Another style of type-

ing the lease is to make side headings of the subjects and underscore them. Still another style is to center the numbered subjects. Usually the clauses are numbered consecutively throughout the lease. The numbereing may be any of the following styles: I, II, FIRST, SECOND; ONE, TWO; 1., 2.; (1), (2).

"Do's" and "dont's" in the preparation of a lease. Unless otherwise instructed, the secretary should follow these directions in the preparation of a lease of realty or commercial property. Obviously some of them apply to typed leases, some to printed forms, and some to both.

1. Make 4 copies—an original for the lessee, a duplicate original for the lessor, a triplicate original for the other attorney, and a copy for the files.

2. Use legal cap.

3. Follow carefully the directions for filling in a printed form. (See PRINTED LAW BLANKS.)

4. Don't forget the RESPONSIBILITY AND DISTRIBUTION LINE at the top of the first page. (This goes on the office copy only of a printed form.)

5. Double space.

6. Number all pages.

7. Type the land description in accordance with directions. (See LAND DESCRIPTION)

8. If using a printed form, be sure and make the "Z" after the land description. (See PRINTED LAW BLANKS.)

9. Don't forget to have at least two lines of typing on the signature page. (See TESTIMONIUM CLAUSE).

10. Prepare signature lines for the lessor and lessee.

11. If the state statute requires that a deed be sealed, affix seals to the lease in accordance with directions.

12. Type witness lines and AT-TESTATION clause if the statute requires that a deed be witnessed. (See SEAL.)

13. Prepare certificate of ACKNOWLEDGMENT for lessor and lessee.

14. Collate (See COLLATING.)

15. Get someone to compare the LAND DESCRIPTION with her.

16. Check and double check spelling of names.

17. Endorse legal backs. (If printed forms are used, no LEGAL BACK is necessary.)

18. Staple in backs.

19. Arrange for lessor and lessee to come in and sign.

20. *Get lawyer's approval of the lease before it is signed.*

21. Have lessor and lessee sign three copies, including broker's copy.

22. Make sure the signatures agree with the names typed in the lease.

23. Have the lease notarized if it is to be recorded. If the secretary is the notary she should take the acknowledgments. (See NOTARIZE.)

24. After signature and acknowledgment conform the office copy to original.

25. *Get the lawyer's approval of the executed lease,* and then have the lease recorded. (See RECORDING OF LEGAL INSTRUMENTS.) Don't forget to put a notation on the back of the lease asking that it be returned to you. (The secretary to the lawyer for the lessee attends to the recording.)

26. Make an entry in the DIARY to follow the recorder within ten days or two weeks.

27. When the lease is returned, send it to the lessee. (See also RECORDING OF DEED.)

Legacy. A testamentary gift of personal property. Legacies (also known as *bequests*) are of three kinds: specific, general, demonstrative.

A *specific legacy* is a bequest of a particular part of a testator's estate, described so as to be distinguished from all other property in his estate. Examples of specific legacies are testamentary gifts of identified bank deposits, or clothing, jewelry and other personal effects. If the subject matter of the gift does not form part of testator's estate at his death, the legacy is lost; if it is in existence, the specific legatee has priority over other legatees and is assured of getting his share of the estate.

A *general legacy* is a bequest that cannot be traced to a specific source within the estate. Thus, a testamentary gift of money, payable out of the testator's general assets and not from a particular bankbook or account, is a general legacy. A general legatee will receive under a WILL only if the specific and demonstrative legatees (see below) have received the specific property designated for them. A general legatee has priority over a residuary legatee (see below).

A *demonstrative legacy* is a bequest of a certain sum of money, stock, or the like, payable out of a particular fund or security. If the fund does not exist at testator's death, the demonstrative legacy is paid from the general estate. Demonstrative legacies are entitled to the same preference as specific legacies so far as they may be satisfied out of the particular property or fund designated for their payment.

However, if this property has disappeared from testator's estate, demonstrative legacies then rank with general legacies for purposes of priority.

A *residuary legacy* is a bequest, general in nature, of all of testator's estate not otherwise effectively disposed of; it is the remainder after other legacies are distributed.

Legal Assistant. (See PARALEGAL.)

Legal Back. A manuscript cover which comprises a backing in which to

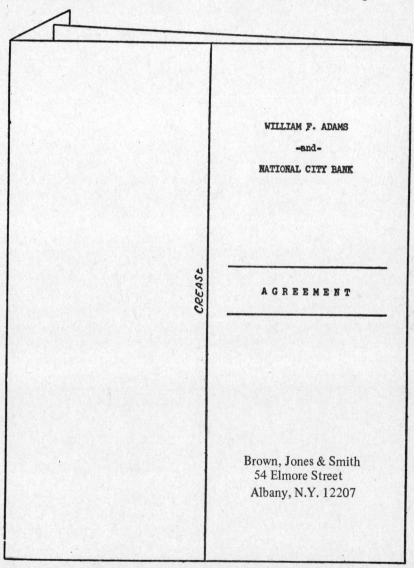

WILLIAM F. ADAMS

-and-

NATIONAL CITY BANK

A G R E E M E N T

Brown, Jones & Smith
54 Elmore Street
Albany, N.Y. 12207

CREASE

Legal Back: Figure 1. Endorsed legal back of agreement.

bind a legal instrument or court paper. It is of thick paper, 8½ or 9 inches by 15 inches. This cover is called a *back* because it covers only the back of the papers that are bound in it. Certain data, referred to as the *endorsement*, are typed on the back of the cover. The endorsement varies with the instrument and the names of the parties to it; but it must be typed in a definite position on the backing sheet and the sheet must be folded in a special manner so that the typing will appear in the proper position.

Court papers usually have a printed panel in which the endorsement is typed; some backs have the name and address of the law firm engraved on them; other are plain. Figure 1 on page 261 illustrates an endorsed legal back for an Agreement.

To type the endorsement:

1. Lay the backing sheet on the desk as though for reading.

2. Bring the bottom edge up to approximately one inch from the top and crease.

3. Bring the creased end (which is now at the bottom) up to approximately one inch from the top. (There is now a fold with about one inch of the top edge of the backing sheet protruding beyond the fold.)

4. The surface of the folded sheet that is uppermost is the surface on which the endorsement is to be typed.)if the backing sheet has a printed panel or the firm's name on it, that portion of the sheet will be the uppermost surface.) Put a small pencil check in the upper *left*-hand corner of that surface.

5. Partially unfold and insert in typewriter so that the pencil mark is on the upper *right*-hand corner of the surface when you type on it.

6. Do not type to the left of the crease (see Figure 1). After typing the endorsement, turn down the top edge of the backing sheet about an inch (see step 3), crease, insert document in the crease, and staple. Fold the document and the backing sheet, creasing the document to fit the creases in the backing sheet.

Legal Cap. The regulation paper used for court papers and for legal instruments such as agreements and contracts. It is white paper, 8 by 13 inches or 8½ by 14 inches, with a wide ruled margin at the left and a narrow ruled margin at the right. Substance 16 is generally preferred for the original or ribbon copy, but substance 20 is preferable for the original of wills; substance 13 for the carbon copies. In some states, legal cap has numbers along the left margin.

Bond or onion skin legal cap is used for the carbon copies, substance 13 or 9 if no more than 8 copies are made; substance 9, for more than 8 copies. Some offices use substance 16 (same as ribbon copy) for the office copy.

Typing should *never* extend beyond the lines marking the margins. See TYPING LEGAL DOCUMENTS.

Legal Dictionaries. A dictionary of legal terms. Most commonly used are *Black's,* or *Ballentine's.*

Legal Instrument. A formal, written document, such as a deed, bill of sale, lease, or will. It gives formal expression to a legal act or agreement.

Although both legal instruments and court papers are referred to as legal documents, a legal instrument is not to be confused with a court paper. A court paper or *pleading,* as it is called professionally, constitutes a step in bringing or defending a law suit and is prepared and filed for the information of the court, whereas a *legal instrument* is designed for the use of the parties who sign it and constitutes evidence of the agreement between them. A legal instrument is not a step is a court action, but it is frequently the basis of one. If one of the parties to a legal instrument does not abide by its provision, the other party may sue to enforce the provisions of the instrument. Copies of a legal instrument are used frequently as exhibits in court actions.

Parties to an instrument. Those who acquire a right or give up a right, as evidenced by a written instrument, are the parties to the instrument. A party may be an individual, a partnership, or a corporation. Almost all instruments have two or more parties, but there are some—for example, assignments and powers of attorney—that have only one party. All parties who have a common interest in the subject matter of the document are grouped together and are usually referred to throughout the instrument by a descriptive identification, instead of by name. An expression frequently used is "party (parties) of the first part," "party (parties) of the second part." Or the term may be a description such as *contractor, seller,* or any term appropriate to the party's interest in the subject matter of the instrument. There may be more than one party in a group designated by a descriptive term. Notice that the instrument illustrated in Figure 1 has two parties of the first part but only one of the second part.

Execution of an instrument. Technically, execution of an instrument is doing that which is required to give effect or validity to the instrument

and, therefore, includes signing the delivery. In law office parlance, *execution* more frequently refers merely to the signing of an instrument by the party or parties described in it. Legal instruments must be executed with a certain formality. Some or all of the following formalities attach to the execution of various instruments: sealing, ATTESTATION, ACKNOWLEDGMENT and notarization. See also ATTESTATION CLAUSE; NOTARY'S SEAL, and TESTIMONIUM CLAUSE.

Signatures on a legal instrument. An instrument recites who will sign it. As a general practice, lines are typed for signatures. Type the first line of signature four spaces below the body of the instrument, beginning it slightly to the right of the center of the page. Type a line for the signature of each person who must sign the instrument. There are no special requirements for the spacing of signature lines, except that sufficient space should be allowed for the average-size handwriting and the lines should be evenly spaced. Three or four spaces between lines are practical.

Frequently the descriptive identification of the parties signing is placed under the signature lines, for example, "First Party," "Parties of the First Part," or whatever identification was used in the instrument. The lawyer usually instructs the secretary as follows: "Two signature lines for parties of the first part, and one for the party of the second part," but the secretary knows from the content of the instrument what signature lines are necessary. Figure 1 on page 264 illustrates signature lines and identification of parties.

When a corporation is a party to an instrument, the instrument is signed in

IN WITNESS WHEREOF, the parties hereto have hereunto set their hands and seals, the day and year first above
written.

In the Presence of:

_____L.S.

_____/

_____L.S.
                    Parties of the First Part

_____

_____L.S.
                    Party of the Second Part

Legal Instrument: Figure 1. Testimonium clause,
signature and seal for individuals, witnessed.

the name of the corporation by the officer or officers authorized to execute it. The secretary types the name of the corporation in solid caps, leaving sufficient space beneath it for signature, and types "By" and a line for signature. Under the signature line, she types the title of the corporate officer who is going to sign the instrument. The testimonium clause usually recites the title of the officer who is supposed to sign the instrument. The COR-PORATE SEAL is placed at the left margin, parallel to the signature.

When a partnership is a party, the secretary types the name of the partnership in solid caps, leaving sufficient space beneath it for signature, and types "By" and a line for signature. Since partnerships do not have officers, there will be no title under the signature line.

How to fit the signatures on the page. Arrange the body, or text, of the instrument so that at least two lines appear on the page with the signatures. The signatures must all be on the same page unless there are so many that they require more than a full page. To comply with these requirements the secretary must gauge carefully the length of the material to be typed. This is not difficult when copying from a draft; otherwise, it might be necessary to make a test copy and adjust the spacing accordingly. Here are methods by which to lengthen or shorten the available typing space in order to fit the signatures on the page:

1. Leave wider or narrower top and bottom margins.

2. On paper without ruled margins, leave wider or narrower left and right margins.

3. If the last line of a paragraph is full-length, adjust the right margin of that paragraph so that at least one word carries over to another line, thereby taking up an extra line. Or, if a paragraph ends with one word on a line, adjust the margin so that it is not necessary to carry over the one word, thereby saving a line of space.

4. Triple space between paragraphs.

5. Leave less space between the text of the instrument and the signatures.

6. Leave less space between the signatures.

See also CONTRACT; DEED; BILL OF SALE; WILL; AFFIDAVIT; MORTGAGE.

Legatee. One who is bequeathed a LEGACY.

Letterpress. A printing process in which the printing surface (the actual design or letter) is raised *above* the base level of the type or plate, just as lettering on a rubber stamp is raised above the rubber plate. This process is also known as the *relief* process.

Letters of Administration. The formal instrument of authority and appointment given a person by the proper court, empowering him to enter upon the discharge of his office as an administrator of an estate. They correspond to letters testamentary granted to an executor. See PROBATE OF A WILL.

When someone dies without leaving a WILL, a person who is over 21, of sound mind, and entitled by law to share in his estate, may ask to be appointed adminstrator of the estate. He does this by applying to the probate court for *letters of administration.*

Parties. The person who files an application for letters of administration is known as the *petitioner.* There are no plaintiffs and defendants—the petitioner does not bring a suit against someone else—but there are other necessary and interested parties. Those nearer of kin to the deceased than the petitioner have a prior right to be appointed; those of an equal degree of kinship have an equal right to be appointed. The kin of the decedent in these two categories are, therefore, necessary parties to the proceeding and are made parties to it by the service of a citation, unless they waive citation.

All of those who are entitled by law to share in the intestate's estate—the distributees—are interested parties to the proceedings, although they may not be entitled to letters of administration. For example, a minor child of the deceased, or a minor child of his prior deceased child, are distributees of the estate and are interested parties. They are not served with citations because they cannot serve as administrators, but they are given notice of the application for letters of administration.

Necessary papers in application for letters of administration. Printed forms of papers that must be prepared by the attorney and filed in an application for letters of administration are usually available, and the courts prefer that they be used. The forms are not uniform, varying even from county to county within state, but they are similar. In every state, there is a petition for letters of administration, an oath of administrator, and a notice in some form to interested parties. In New York County, the papers consist of the following:

1. Petition for letters of administration

2. Oath of administrator (Frequently combined in one paper).

3. Designation of the clerk of the court as a person on whom service of process may be made. (Sometimes combined with petition and oath.)

4. Renunciation, if any.

5. Citation.

6. Notice of application for letters of administration, if necessary.

Renunciation. The Surrogate's Court Act of New York provides that a person who is entitled to letters of administration may renounce his right. He does this by signing a simple printed form entitled, "Renunciation of Rights to Letters of Administration and Waiver of Citation." The waiver reads:

I, ...,
do hereby renounce all rights to letters of administration on the estate of the said deceased and hereby waive the issuance of a citation in the above-entitled proceeding.

The *I* may be changed to *We* and several distributees may sign the same waiver. It is acknowledged in the presence of a notary. The renunciation makes it unnecessary to serve a citation on those who renounced.

Citations. All interested parties must be notified of the application for letters. The method of notifying them varies. In New York State, parties who have a prior or an equal right with the petitioner to letters of administration are made parties to the proceeding by the service of a *citation,* except those who waive citation by renunciation of their right to letters of administration. The writ is signed by the clerk of the probate court (surrogate's court in New York), but is prepared by the attorney for the petitioner. It cites the person or persons upon whom it is served to appear before the court on a certain date and show cause why letters of administration should not be granted to the petitioner. The person cited does not have to appear in court or reply in any way unless he opposes the appointment of the petitioner. Service is had in the same manner as service of citation in a proceeding to prove a will. Printed forms of citations are available. They are similar to, but not the same as, the form used in a proceeding to prove a will. The secretary should be sure of the following points:

1. The citation does not have a caption.

2. Address the citation to those distributees who have a right prior or equal to that of the petitioner to letters of administration. The names and addresses of those to whom the citation is to be addressed are listed in the petition.

3. Make an original for the court, a copy for each person to whom the citation is addressed, and an office copy.

4. Find out the return date of the citation under the court rules. In some jurisdictions the date is set by the clerk of the court when the petition in filed.

5. Get the court clerk to sign the original.

6. Conform the copies and serve.

7. Make affidavit of service.

8. *Enter return date in diary.*

9. Make entry in suit register, and follow the court calendar just as in a contested action.

Notice of application for letters of administration. In New York State distributees who do not have a right to letters of administration equal to that of the petitioner are not served with a citation but are notified of the application. Printed forms are available. The secretary should:

1. Make an original for the court, a copy for each distributee entitled to the notice, and an office copy.

2. Date the notice of application at any time subsequent to the filing of the petition and before the issuance of the letters.

3. Have the petitioner sign the notice.

4. Mail copies of the notice to each distributee entitled to it at the address given in the petition.

5. Make affidavit that notice was mailed.

6. Conform office copy and file original in court.

7. Enter in suit register.

Issuance of letters of administration. If there is no opposition to the appointment of the petition as administrator, the court enters a decree directing that letters of administration issue to the petitioner. The letters of administration serve the same purpose for the administrator as letters testamentary do for the executor. The attorney for the petitioner prepares the decree and the letters in the same manner as when a will is admitted to probate and letters of testamentary are granted.

As soon as letters of administration are granted, notice to creditors must be published. Be sure and make appropriate *diary entries* and suit register entries.

Administrator de boni non. Administrators *de boni non administratis* are, as the term signifies, persons appointed by the court of probate to administer on the effects of a decedent which have not been included in a former administration.

Administrator with the Will Annexed. One appointed administrator of deceased's estate after executors named in the will refused to act.

Letters, Style and Setup. The physical arrangement of the various parts of a letter. The styles in which letters are usually set up in the law office are the full-block style (Figure 1), semi-block style (Figure 2) and the indented style (Figure 3). Law offices have been slow to adopt the more modern styles used extensively in business offices. The official style (Figure 4) is used frequently for informal letters written to personal acquaintances. (See figures on pages 268-271.)

Full-block style. All structural parts of the letter, including the first line of each paragraph, and complimentary close, are flush with the left-hand margin.

Semi-block style. The distinguishing feature of the semi-block style of letter is that all structural parts of the letter begin flush with the left-hand margin, but the first line of each paragraph is indented ten spaces. Carry-over lines in the address are indented three spaces. All lines of the typed signature are aligned with the complimentary close. The date is typed in the conventional position.

Indented style. The distinguishing feature of the indented style of letter is that each line of address is indented five spaces more than the preceding line. The first line of each paragraph is indented ten spaces, which aligns the paragraphs with the third line of address. Each line of the typed signature is indented three or four spaces from the beginning of the COMPLIMENTARY CLOSE.

```
                        CONNELLY, KARTER & MARTIN
                            627 Ingraham Building
                            Miami, Florida  33131

        Charles E. Connelly
        Theodore B. Karter
        Christopher A. Martin
        Walter W. Ore
        Lewis T. Kobbe
        Walter R. Schwenker


                    November 29, 19--


                    Messrs. Smith Jones Nelson
                    35 Fifth Avenue
                    New York, NY  10003

                    Gentlemen:

                    Re:  Full-Block Style of Letter

                    This is an example of the full-block style of letter.
                    Some law firms prefer it to the semi-block style.
                    It is faster to type as it does not require setting
                    tabs.

                    As you can see, everything is flush with the left
                    margin, including the date, the name and address,
                    the salutation, the re clause, the complimentary
                    close, and signature line.

                    Very truly yours,


                    Robert E. Adams
```

Letters—Style and Setup: Figure 1.   Full-block style. Everything is flush with the left-hand margin, including the date and complimentary close.

Official Style. The distinguishing feature of the official style of letter is that the inside address is placed below the signature, flush with the left-hand margin, instead of before the SALUTATION. The address may be blocked or indented. The identification line and ENCLOSURE notations, if any, are typed two spaces below the last line of the address.

Subject line. In any letter, a subject line makes it unnecessary for the writer to devote the first paragraph of the letter to a routine explanation of its subject. In correspondence about law matters the subject line is a necessity as well as a convenience. The correspondence is filed according to the subject and not according to the name of the correspondent, and, frequently, it is dif-

```
                    CONNELLY, KARTER & MARTIN
                       627 Ingraham Building
                       Miami, Florida  33131

Charles E. Connelly
Theodore B. Karter
Christopher A. Martin
Walter W. Ore
Lewis T. Kobbe
Walter R. Schwenker

                                                April 23, 19--


        Messrs. Smith Jones Nelson
        35 Fifth Avenue
        New York, NY  10003

        Dear Sirs:

                    Re:  Semi-Block Style of Letter
                    This is an example of the semi-block style of letter.
        Many law firms prefer it to the indented style because it com-
        bines utility with an attractive appearance.

                    As you can see, the inside address is blocked.  The
        first line of each paragraph is indented ten spaces.  As in all
        letters, there is a double space between paragraphs.

                    The date line is flush with the right margin, two or
        four spaces below the letterhead.  The subject line is two
        spaces below the salutation and is centered.  The complimentary
        close begins slightly to the right of the center of the page.
        All lines of the signature are aligned with the complimentary
        close.  Open punctuation is used in the address.

                    No identification line is used in this example.  As
        the dictator's name is typed in the signature, his initials are
        not necessary.  The typist's initials are shown on the carbon
        copy.

                            Very truly yours,


                            Robert E. Adams
```

Letters — Style and Setup: Figure 2. Semi-block style. (The distinguishing feature of this style is that all structural parts of the letter begin flush with the left-hand margin, but the first line of each paragraph is indented five or ten spaces. All lines of the typed signature are aligned with the complimentary close. The date is typed in the conventional position. Open punctuation is used.)

ficult to deduce from the letter the matter to which it refers. Since the subject is actually part of the body of the letter, it should follow the salutation. Preferably, it is centered two spaces below the salutation, and is preceded by *Re* or *In re,* which may be followed by a colon, or not, as desired.

How to type the date line. 1. Date the letter the day it is dictated, not the day it is typed, unless instructed otherwise. If the secretary dates the letter the day

```
                    CONNELLY, KARTER & MARTIN
                       627 Ingraham Building
                       Miami, Florida  33131

     Charles E. Connelly
     Theodore B. Karter
     Christopher A. Martin
     Walter W. Ore
     Lewis T. Kobbe
     Walter R. Schwenker

                                                    April 23, 19--


     Mr. N. E. Edwards, Office Manager,
        Elwood & Adams,
           35 Fifth Avenue,
              New York, NY  10003

     Dear Mr. Edwards:

              In re:  Indented Style of Letter

                   This is an example of the indented style of letter.
          I am enclosing three sheets from our Correspondence Manual
          that describe the other forms in which you are interested.

                   Many conservative law firms still use the indented
          style as they prefer it to new forms.  The indented style is
          correct, however, for any type of organization.

                   Each line of the address is indented five spaces
          more than the preceding line.  The beginning of each para-
          graph is indented the same as the third line of the address,
          which is ten spaces.  The complimentary close begins a few
          spaces to the right of the center of the page.  Each line
          of the signature is indented three spaces from the begin-
          ning of the complimentary close.  Close punctuation is used
          in the address but not in the signature.

                                        Sincerely yours,


                                        John E. Marsh

          jmh
          Enclosures 3
```

Letters — Style and Setup: Figure 3. Indented style. (The distinguishing feature of this style is that each line of the address is indented five spaces more than the preceding line. The first line of each paragraph is indented ten spaces. If the name is typed in the signature, it is typed flush with the complimentary close, but each additional line is indented three spaces.)

it is transcribed, she adjusts references to time made in the dictation, such as "today" or "yesterday."

2. Type the date conventionally, all on one line.

3. Do not use *d, nd, rd, st,* or *th* following the day of the month.

4. Do not abbreviate or use figures for the month.

5. Do not spell out the day of the month or the year, except in very formal letters, such as invitations to formal dinners.

```
                        CONNELLY, KARTER & MARTIN
                           627 Ingraham Building
                           Miami, Florida  33131

     Charles E. Connelly
     Theodore B. Karter
     Christopher A. Martin
     Walter W. Ore
     Lewis T. Kobbe
     Walter R. Schwenker


                                                    April 23, 19--


     Dear Mr. Edwards:

              This letter is an example of the official style.  It
     is used in many personal letters written by executives and pro-
     fessional men, and looks unusually well on the executive-sized
     letterhead.

              The structural parts of the letter differ from the
     standard arrangement only in the position of the inside address.
     The salutation is placed two to five spaces below the date line,
     depending upon the length of the letter.  It establishes the
     left margin of the letter.  The inside address is written in
     block form, flush with the left margin, from two to five spaces
     below the final line of the signature.  Open punctuation is
     used in the address.

              Letters written in this style do not usually have a
     subject line.  The identification line, if used, should be placed
     two spaces below the last line of the address, and the enclosure
     mark two spaces below that.  As the dictator's name is typed in
     the signature, it is not necessary for the letter to carry an
     identification line.  The typist's initials are on the carbon
     copy of the letter, but not on the original.

                              Very truly yours,


                              Thomas E. Richards

     Mr. N. E. Edwards, Office Manager
     Elwood & Adams
     35 Fifth Avenue
     New York, NY  10003
```

Letters — Style and Setup: Figure 4. Official style. (The distinguishing feature is that the inside address is placed below the signature, flush with the left-hand margin, instead of before the salutation. The identification line and enclosure notations, if any, are typed two spaces below the last line of the address. Open punctuation is used. This style is especially appropriate for the lawyer's personal letters.)

RIGHT:
    November 15, 19. .
WRONG:
    November 15th, 19. .
    9/15/ . .   Nov. 15, 19 . .
    November fifteenth, Nineteen
       hundred and . . . .

See also ATTENTION LINE; SALUTATION; COMPLIMENTARY CLOSE; RESPONSIBILITY OR IDENTIFICATION LINE; CARBON COPY DISTRIBUTION NOTATION; POSTSCRIPT.

Letters Testamentary. See PRO-
BATE OF A WILL.

Libel and Slander. That which tends
to injure the reputation of a living
person or the memory of a deceased
person, and to expose him to public
hatred, disgrace, ridicule, or contempt,
or to exclude him from society, is
known as *defamation. Slander* is *oral*
defamation of one person by another in
the presence of a third person or
persons; *libel* is *written* or *printed*
defamation of one person by another,
published before a third person or
persons. A corporation is a person in
this sense. For a slanderous statement
to be actionable, it must be false and
must cause injury to the person to
whom the statement refers. In libel actions, no injury need be proved,
although, of course, proved injury will
affect the amount of damages awarded.
See also, LIBELOUS LETTERS;
LIBEL (IN ADMIRALTY PRAC-
TICE).

Libel (in admiralty practice). The initial pleading on the part of the complainant in an ADMIRALTY action,
corresponding to the COMPLAINT in
a COMMON LAW action.

Libelant. The complainant or party
who files a LIBEL (see LIBEL (IN
ADMIRALTY PRACTICE) in an
ADMIRALTY case, corresponding to
the plaintiff in an action at law.

Libelous Letters. For a letter to be
libelous it must have been read by
someone other than the person
defamed. The reader may be a
stenographer who takes the libelous
writing by dictation and transcribes the
notes, although some courts have taken

the view that publication to a
stenographer does not subject the
writer to liability unless the letter was
prompted by actual malice.

License, Business. Federal, state, or
city approval and permission are necessary to engage in certain businesses
that are of sufficient concern to the
public to justify regulation. Permission
and approval are issued in the form of
a license, for which a fee is charged.

Licensee. One on the premises with
the permission of the owner, for a purpose beneficial only to himself, e.g., a
passenger in an automobile or a dinner
guest. The duty of the owner of the
premises is to warn the licensee of a
known dangerous condition. There is
no duty to use reasonable care to keep
the premises in a safe condition. See
INVITEE; TRESPASSER; NEG-
LIGENCE.

Lien. A charge imposed on property,
by which the property is made security
for the discharge of an obligation. (See
also ENCUMBRANCE.) The holder
of the lien gives notice of his claim by
recording it in some designated public
office. Here are some of the most common liens against REAL PROPERTY:
1. Landlord's lien.
2. Mortgage lien.
3. Mechanic's lien.
4. Judgment lien.
5. VENDEE'S LIEN.
6. VENDOR'S LIEN.
7. TAX LIEN.
Landlord's lien. In many states, the
statute gives the landlord a lien upon
the property of the tenant for unpaid
rent. The landlord may seize such
property, hold it as security, and sell it
within a fixed time to satisfy the ten-

ant's debt. In some states, the lien is enforceable in distraint proceedings (see DISTRAINT FOR RENT IN ARREARS); in others it is enforceable in ATTACHMENT proceedings.

Mortgage lien. In a majority of the states ("lien theory" states), a MORTGAGE on REAL PROPERTY given as security for a debt is a lien on the property. It becomes a lien upon recording of the mortgage. All persons who thereafter acquire any interest in the property, such as subsequent purchasers or mortgagees, take the property subject to the mortgage lien. Even in "title theory" states, anyone dealing with land on which a mortgage has been given is bound by the mortgage. (See ESTOPPEL certificate.)

Priority as between successive mortgage liens. The general rule is that mortgage liens have priority according to the time they attach to the land. Recording may be required to give the lien effect.

Example: The owner of land gives a mortgage to *X* in 1976 and another mortgage on the same property to *Y* in 1977. If *X*'s mortgage is valid and properly recorded, it has a lien prior to the lien of *Y*'s mortgage. Even if *X*'s mortgage is not recorded, it may be prior to *Y*'s mortgage if *Y* has knowledge of the earlier mortgage.

Mechanic's lien. A person who furnishes certain kinds of labor or materials in the construction of improvements on land may, on failure of the owner of the land to pay him, acquire a lien on the land and improvements by complying with certain formalities. This is known as a mechanic's lien, and is governed by state statutes. The statutes vary from state to state. In some states, the mechanic must have been hired by the owner of the land or

his agent in order to establish his lien; in other states, the consent of the owner is sufficient. The statutes distinguish between a *contractor* hired by the owner to construct an improvement and a *subcontractor* hired by a contractor. In some states the subcontractor's lien is dependent upon the amount that the owner owes to the contractor (New York system); in other states, the subcontractor's lien is a direct lien independent of the indebtedness from the owner to the contractor (Pennsylvania system). The subcontractor may be required to serve notice of his claim on the owner within a fixed time. Both contractor and subcontractor may be required to file notice of their claims within a specified time after the work is completed. Steps must be taken to enforce the lien by FORECLOSURE within a fixed time after the claim is filed. A mechanic's lien may be released or waived, just like a mortgage.

Priority of mortgage lien over mechanic's lien. The state statutes vary as to when a mechanic's lien attaches to the land. The time it attaches is most important in determining which has priority, a mortgage lien or a mechanic's lien. In a few states (New York and Vermont, for example), a notice is filed in the proper public office, and a mortgage recorded prior to the filing of the lien has priority over the lien. In other states (Illinois and Massachusetts, for example), the mechanic's lien attaches on the date the owner of the land orders the work to be done, and the mechanic's lien has priority over the lien of a mortgage made after the date the work was ordered. In a majority of the states, no mechanic's lien may attach, so far as purchasers and mortgagees are concerned, until actual commencement of the improvements.

Where a mortgagee is required to advance funds for *construction* of a building on the land, a different rule prevails. In most states, the mortgage lien is prior to a mechanic's lien for work or materials furnished in constructing the building. To protect the mechanic's lien, however, the mortgagor is required under the terms of the mortgage to apply the advances first to the payment of the cost of improvement before using the funds for any other purpose.

Protection of mortgage against mechanic's liens. To protect themselves against mechanic's liens. (particularly on construction loans) owners and mortgagees adopt various measures:

1. The mortgagee may insist that the original construction contract contain a WAIVER of all mechanic's liens. In some states, this is effective and is binding on all subcontractors if the contract is recorded or the subcontractor knows of this provision at the time he furnishes the labor or material. Such a waiver is, in substance, a voluntary release or relinquishment of the lien, the contractor electing to rely solely on the personal responsibility of the party ordering the erection of the building. This arrangement hampers the contractor in obtaining credit from subcontractors.

2. The owner or mortgagee may withhold payout to the contractor of an amount ample to protect against subcontractors' liens until the time for the giving of notice of subcontractors' liens has expired.

3. Under some statutes, an owner or mortgagee is protected in paying out to subcontractors named on a verified list furnished by the contractor. As each payout is made to subcontractors named in the list, each subcontractor is required to furnish a lien waiver. If the general contractor claims that he has paid a particular subcontractor and produces the subcontractor's lien waiver, payment may be made to the contractor, though to protect against forged waivers the check is sometimes made payable to the contractor and subcontractor.

4. When final payment is made to the contractor, he is required to furnish a full lien waiver.

5. The arrangement between mortgagor and mortgagee is such that the mortgagee is obligated to pay out the loan as the work progresses.

6. A surety BOND may be required by the mortgagee to protect against mechanic's liens. In some states, the posting of the proper surety bond discharges all mechanic's liens that have attached to the property.

7. To protect himself when making a loan other than a construction loan, the mortgagee inspects the premises to make sure that no recent repairs or improvements have been made, and requires an AFFIDAVIT from the mortgagor that no such repair or improvements have been made or ordered. If traces of recent work are apparent, lien waivers are required.

8. Since some laws provide that the interest of the owner shall be subject to liens for any work done with his knowledge (even on the order of a tenant, for example) unless he posts in a conspicuous place on the building a notice that he will not be responsible, some owners keep such a notice posted on their buildings at all times.

Judgment lien. In most states, a

JUDGMENT for money becomes a lien on all the land of the judgment debtor in some other county by filing an official copy of the judgment in the proper office of such county. The judgment may also become a lien on real estate which the judgment debtor acquires after the judgment is entered. The duration of the lien depends upon the governing state statute; ten years is most common. The judgment lien is enforced by issuance of EXECUTION and levy. When the judgment is paid, the judgment debtor files a formal declaration known as a *satisfaction*.

Purchasers of property and mortgages must make a search of judgment records to ascertain whether there are any judgment liens affecting the property about to be purchased or mortgaged.*

See MARITIME LIEN.

Life Estate. An interest in property, real or personal, that lasts only for the duration of the owner's life. A life estate may also be for the duration of another's life, or may terminate with the happening of a certain contingency. For example, a life estate may terminate upon the marriage of the owner. This estate may be created by an act of the parties, as by deed, will, or gift; or by operation of law, as by dower or curtesy. The owner of a life estate (called the *life tenant*) has the current use of the property and is responsible for its maintenance, including taxes and carrying charges. He also gets the income from the property, but cannot ordinarily sell the property or do anything to impair its permanent value. However, the life tenant may be allowed to sell or consume property to support himself if the deed or will so provides. He cannot dispose of the property at his death. The person, or persons, to whom the estate passes upon termination of the life estate is determined when the life estate is created. The estate that is left at the termination of the life estate is called a *remainder*; the person to whom it passes is a *remainderman* (plural, *remaindermen*).

Life Insurance. A CONTRACT under which the insuring company agrees, in consideration for the payment of premiums, to pay a stipulated sum of money to a designated beneficiary upon the death of the insured.

The flexibility of the modern life insurance contract makes it possible for insurance to perform a number of useful functions in estate planning. Life insurance gives financial security to dependents. It can serve as a savings program, affording a plan involving the growth of cash value over the years without INCOME TAX liability. Finally, life insurance can assure estate liquidity by making a cash fund available to the insured's legal representatives for the payment of debts, expenses and taxes, which will eliminate or reduce the need for the forced sale of non-liquid assets.

Lightface. (l.f.) Any type face with lines fine enough to give a light impression when printed, in contrast to BOLDFACE. Lightface, in which this book is set, is the type seen in print generally. On flight schedules, lightface indicates AM and **boldface, PM.**

*Acknowledgment: Robert Kratovil, *Real Estate Law*, 6th ed. New York, Prentice-Hall, Inc., 1974.

Limited Partnership. A partnership in which the liability of one or more special partners for debts of the firm is limited to the amount of his investment in the business. Special partners have no voice in the management of the partnership. They merely invest money and receive a certain share of the profits. There must be one or more general partners who manage the business and remain liable for all its debts.

A limited partnership is organized under state statutes, usually by filing a certificate in a public office and publishing a notice in a newspaper. The statutes, codified in many states as the Uniform Limited Partnership Law, must be strictly observed. A limited partnership is regarded as a general partnership in states other than the state in which it is organized; therefore, it must register and form a limited partnership with the same firm members under the laws of each state in which it wishes to do business.

Line Cuts and Halftones. Methods of reproducing illustrations in a book. Line cuts are made of those illustrations (drawings, charts, graphs, pictographs) that consist only of lines and areas of black and white. A halftone must always be used to reproduce gradations or shadings of tone between black and white found in photographs, paints, and wash drawings.

Liner. A vessel sailing in accordance with a fixed schedule along a line of certain ports at advertised times. See also TRAMP.

Linotype. A method of printing, used for almost all printed matter, in which an entire line of type is set and cast in metal in one continuous machine operation. The result is known as a "slug." If a mistake is made in setting the line the slug cannot be corrected without resetting and recasting a complete new line.

Liquidated Damages. An amount that the parties to a contract have agreed upon shall be paid in satisfaction of a loss resulting from a BREACH OF CONTRACT. The amount must be in proportion to the actual loss; otherwise the agreement is unenforceable.

Lis Pendens. Litigation pending; a pending suit. Whenever a law suit involving real property is commenced, a notice of *lis pendens* or "pendency of action," is filed. A notice of *lis pendens* gives constructive notice to the world that the property described therein is involved in a law suit. The notice is filed with the proper official, such as the county clerk, recorder, or register of titles under the TORRENS SYSTEM, at the time the COMPLAINT is filed.[1] The filing of the notice of *lis pendens* is a vital step in actions involving REAL PROPERTY, such as foreclosures, actions to quiet title, condemnation proceedings, and partitions. If a defendant disposes of an interest in the property after suit is commenced but before notice is filed, the plaintiff's suit is defective. On the other hand, any claim against, or interest in, the property arising subsequent to the filing of the *lis pendens* is

---

[1] In New York Supreme Court, notice of dependency is filed before complaint because in that court no pleadings are filed until issue is joined.

276

IN THE DISTRICT COURT OF THE STATE OF IOWA

IN AND FOR POLK COUNTY

ROBERT COLE BROWN and MARY HOWARD
BROWN,

Plaintiffs,	No. 4896
vs.	NOTICE OF LIS PENDENS

JOHN ALBERT GREEN and ELLEN BLAKE GREEN,
husband and wife, PAUL NELSON, DOE ONE,
DOE TWO, DOE THREE, and DOE FOUR,

Defendants

NOTICE IS HEREBY GIVEN, That an action has been commenced and is pending in this Court upon a complaint of the above named plaintiffs against the above named defendants for the foreclosure of a mortgage, bearing date the twenty-first day of September, one thousand nine hundred and ...., executed by John Albert Green and wife, Ellen Blake Green, to Robert Cole Brown and wife, Mary Howard Brown, to secure the sum of Five Thousand Dollars ($5,000), and recorded in Liber 2063 of Mortgages, at page 25, in the office of the Recorder of Deeds of the County of Polk, on the twenty-second day of September, one thousand nine hundred and .... at ten o'clock in the forenoon;

AND NOTICE IS HEREBY GIVEN, That the mortgaged premises affected by the said foreclosure action, were, at the time of the commencement of said action, and at the time of the filing of this notice, situate in the County of Polk

(Continued on following page)

Lis Pendens: Figure 1.   Notice of Lis Pendens.

(*Continued from preceding page*)

in the State of Iowa, and are described in the said mortgage
as follows, to wit:

(Insert description that appears in mortgage)

....
Elwood & Adams
Attorneys for Plaintiffs

To THE CLERK OF THE DISTRICT COURT OF POLK COUNTY:

You will please index the above notice to the name
of each of the following defendants: John Albert Green,
Ellen Blake Green, and Paul Nelson.

Dated: May 7, 19—.

....
Elwood & Adams
Attorneys for Plaintiffs

Lis Pendens: Figure 1. Notice of Lis Pendens (*Continued*).

subordinate to the interest of the plaintiff as determined by the law suit.

Preparation of notice of lis pendens. As soon as the secretary receives the certification of defendants, or FORECLOSURE report, from the title company (see ABSTRACT COMPANY), she can prepare the notice of pendency without waiting for the lawyer to give her instructions about the complaint. He will not dictate the notice; the secretary will be expected to follow a form. The only parts that change are the names of the defendants, the description of the mortgage, and the description of the property. Figure 1 illustrates a notice of pendency of action or *lis pendens*, but the wording varies with the state.

The secretary should observe these points

1. Use the same kind of paper that is used for any court paper (see TYPING COURT PAPERS).

2. Make an original and a file copy. Also make an extra copy for the looseleaf notebook. Copy of the notice is not served on the defendants.

3. The caption is the same as the caption in the complaint. The secretary may shorten the title by the use of *et al.*, unless the wording of the notice makes this inadvisable. See 6 below.

4. The title of the document is "Notice of Lis Pendens," or "Notice of Pendency of Action."

5. Have someone compare the description with you against the description in the original mortgage. *This is most important.*

6. The notice in Figure 1 contains a direction to the county clerk to the ef-

fect: "Your are hereby directed to index the foregoing notice of pendency
against the names . . . ." Insert
the name of every *known* defendant as
listed in the certification of defendants,
but do not include fictitious names. If
the form of notice that you follow
refers to the defendants without listing
them, the title of the case must contain
the name of every known defendant
and cannot be shortened by the use of
et al. A *lis pendens* is no good unless it
is indexed against each defendant, in-
sofar as that defendant has an interest
in the property.

7. Staple the original in an endorsed
LEGAL BACK.

8. The attorney for the plaintiff
signs the notice.

Lithographic. See OFFSET.

Litigants. See PARTIES TO AN
ACTION.

Litigation Blanks. See PRINTED
LAW BLANKS.

Litigation Lists. Listings of local
businessmen who were served with
summonses during the preceding day.
Publishers of court records and other
legal materials in several large cities
publish these lists daily.

Lockout. The refusal of an employer
to furnish work to his employees.
Sometimes there is a tactical advantage
for management in closing the plant
before the men have a chance to go out
on STRIKE. A lockout, like a strike, is
a drastic step because it curtails
business and thereby stops profits and
wages.

Long-term Capital Gain. See
CAPITAL GAIN AND LOSS.

Long-term Lease. See LEASE, Classification of leases.

Lot and Block. See LAND
DESCRIPTION.

Lower Case. Pertaining to small letters of the alphabet, as opposed to
capital (upper case) letters. To *lower
case* a letter is to change it from a
capital to a small letter.

Lynching. The infliction of punishment for suspected crime by an unlawful assembly known as a mob. The mob
takes over the judicial process and
deprives the victim of his right to a fair
trial. Lynching is generally made a
severely punishable FELONY by
statute.

M

Magistrate's Court. A judicial tribunal that has limited jurisdiction and powers. See INFERIOR COURT.

Majority. Full age; the age at which, by law, a person is entitled to the management of his own affairs and to the enjoyment of civic rights. The opposite of minority.

Mailing Notation. Writing placed on envelope and letter when the letter is sent by any method other than regular mail. The method of mail, such as air mail or special delivery (see POSTAL SERVICE), is typed four spaces above the INSIDE ADDRESS, or it may be typed flush with the left margin two spaces below the RESPONSIBILITY OR IDENTIFICATION LINE. It is also typed on the envelope in the space below the stamps and above the address. See TELEGRAPH SERVICE.

Majority Vote. The number greater than half of any total.

Malicious Mischief. The intentional destruction of someone's property because of resentment or ill will towards its owner. Where the act of destruction is by fire, statutes will define the crime as ARSON rather than malicious mischief.

Malicious Prosecution. A lawsuit started out of ill will without reason to believe that the charges would be upheld in court. If the malicious prosecution was a criminal proceeding, suit for DAMAGES may be brought against the prosecuting officer; if a civil action, against the plaintiff. The question of whether there was actual malice is one that a jury answers.

Mandamus. (Latin for "We command.") A writ issued by a court of superior jurisdiction to a public or private corporation, or an official thereof, or an inferior court, commanding the performance of an official act, which the person or body named in the writ had failed or refused to perform. It is an extraordinary WRIT, which is issued in cases where the usual and ordinary procedures do not afford remedies to the party aggrieved. The writ of mandamus is known as a remedy for official inaction. It was introduced to prevent disorder from a failure of public officials to perform their duties and is still an important legal remedy for the protection of the public and of individuals against exploitation and abuse by official inaction. Mandamus is frequently applied for in order to control the letting of public contracts.

A mandamus may also enforce a private right. It compels the performance by a corporation of a variety of specific acts within the scope of the corporations's duties. For example, a stockholder may institute a mandamus proceeding to compel a corporation to submit to an inspection of its books and records.

The writ is either peremptory or alternate. The peremptory mandamus compels the defendant to perform the required act; the alternate mandamus compels him to perform the act or show cause on a certain day why he should not perform it. The alternate writ is usually issued first.

Mansion. A dwelling-house or place of residence, including its appurtenant outbuildings. Commonly used to refer to the principal place of residence of a deceased person.

Manslaughter. The unlawful killing of another without malice. If death is the result of recklessness and NEGLIGENCE, manslaughter would be the crime charged against the offender; for example, death resulting from reckless driving. Killing in the heat of passion amounts to manslaughter. It is the lack of malice that makes a killing manslaughter and not MURDER.

Manuscript. Written material that is to be sent to the printer for setting in type and publication. The manuscript is also called COPY. (See TYPING MANUSCRIPT; CHECKING MANUSCRIPT.)

Margins. (*On legal documents*) The white space (frame) that is left around the typewritten material of legal documents. See TYPING LEGAL DOCUMENTS; LEGAL BACK.

Marital Deduction. The Tax Reform Act of 1976 makes many changes in Federal and Gift Tax Laws. The entire area has been drastically overhauled. Thnks to the changes, starting in 1977, most estates will not pay federal estate tax. But those that must pay will probably pay more.

Federal estate tax. A tax deduction that the estate of a deceased may take for the value of certain property that passes at death to a surviving spouse. The marital deduction has been increased under the Tax Reform Act of 1976 from half of the adjusted gross estate (gross estate minus the estate's debts and expenses) to the larger of $250,000 or half of the estate.

Federal gift tax. The $3,000 annual gift-tax exclusion is retained. However, the $30,000 lifetime exemption is done away with. Gifts to a spouse up to the first $100,000 are tax-free; from $100,000 to $200,000, the gifts are fully taxed; beyond that a 50% marital deduction applies.

Some more of the major changes are:*

* The present separate structures for estate and gift taxes are changed into a single unified tax setup designed to insure that, whether a taxpayer gives away all of his assets during his life or waits until he dies, the eventual tax payable will be approximately the same.

* The present $60,000 estate-tax exemption is replaced by a credit which will gradually rise from $30,000 in 1977 to $47,000 in 1981. The net impact here is that for 1977 the credit will be equivalent to an exemption of $120,000 which will rise to $175,000 by 1981.

* The stepped-up-date-of-death basis for assets received from a decedent is out. Basically, from 1977 on it will be the decedent's cost or the fair market value of the asset on December 31, 1976, whichever is higher.

* New limits and restrictions have been placed on the use of the so-called "grandfather" or "generation-skipping" trusts.

The marital deductions give substantial tax advantages to married couples and have revolutionized many estate planning concepts. Through their judicious use, it is possible to effect tremendous tax savings, often amounting to a major part of what the tax would have been without the marital deduction. The marital deduction in the *ESTATE TAX* and *GIFT TAX* has brought about the equalization of taxes between residents of COMMUNITY PROPERTY states. The concept of divided ownership of property by husband and wife is now on a national basis.

Maritime Lien. A right against a vessel arising out of certain maritime contracts and maritime torts. Claims that are subject to maritime liens include the wages of a SEAMAN, a BOTTOMRY LOAN, a RESPONDENTIA loan, repairs and supplies to vessels, AFFREIGHTMENT CONTRACTS, TORT and collision claims, TOWAGE, WHARFAGE, stevedore services, SALVAGE, GENERAL AVERAGE LOSS, and PILOTAGE.

One having a maritime lien can sue the ship itself *in rem* and, if successful in the litigation, can cause the ship to be sold and the purchase moneys applied to his claim. The proceeding *in rem* is begun by the seizure of the vessel by the marshal of the district in which the suit is brought.

_____
*From *Concise Explanation of the Tax Reform Act of 1976,* Copyright by Prentice-Hall, Inc.

Unlike the common law LIEN, the possessor of a maritime lien does not have to retain possession of the object (the vessel or cargo) in order to retain his claim. The lien on a ship and the right to proceed against it will remain even if the ship is sold to another. Only a sale by a United States Marshal will strip the vessel of its liens.

Maritime Tort. An injury to an individual or to property which occurs on navigable waters.

Marked Copy. Manuscript that is marked with instructions to the printer. When the secretary marks COPY of a BRIEF, for example, she should remember that she gets what she asks for and that she must mark clearly and accurately. She instructs the printer by doing the following:

1. Underline all words or sections to be set in italics.

2. Draw a wavy line under the words or sections to be set in BOLDFACE, or type them in red.

3. Indicate what is to be set in capital letters and what in small capitals or a combination of capitals and small capitals.

4. Mark all headings in the desired size and style of type.

5. In the left-hand margin, mark the size and name of the body type and the PICA width of the type area, thus: $\frac{11 \text{ on } 13}{18}$ Caslon, which calls for 11 point Caslon type, leaded 2 points, set 18 picas wide. The printer may use a numerical code instead of names for his types. If the code number for Caslon were 97, you could write your instructions thus:

11/13
18/97

In marking copy, use PROOFREADERS' MARKS whenever possible. These marks are a shorthand system that will save time and be perfectly clear to the printer.

Martindale-Hubbell Law Directory. A four-volume annual directory of lawyers and a DIGEST of the laws of all the states.

In Volumes I through III, lawyers' names are listed alphabetically by state and town. If the legal secretary is looking for the name of a lawyer in Laurel, Montana, for example, she searches Volume II covering states alphabetically from Kansas through North Carolina. Within the pages devoted to Montana lawyers, she will find alphabetical breakdowns by city. The secretary will find lawyers in the city of Laurel listed by name with appropriate symbols indicating the date of birth, college and law school graduation, and of admission to the bar, together with membership in the American Bar Association, and a "confidential" rating. A key to the symbols and explanatory notes appears at the beginning of each volume. Ratings are based on the standard of ability for the place where the lawyer practices. Age, practical experience, nature and length of practice, and other relevant qualifications are considered. There might also be a reference to the firm with which the lawyer is associated. Law firms are listed in the second half of these volumes alphabetically by state and city, with the partners' names, bank references, the nature of the practice, and sometimes the names of some clients. In addition, there is a listing of foreign lawyers. A special listing is made of lawyers admitted to practice before the United States Patent Office.

Another section is devoted to the American Bar Association, its organization, officers, activities, and canons.

Volume IV of the directory contains a digest of the laws of all states and territories of the United States. There are eighty-nine principal subject headings and numerous subheadings all included in the Topical Index at the beginning of the volume. Suppose the lawyer is interested in knowing the usury law in California and instructs the secretary to look it up for him. She looks up *usury* in the Topical Index. Under the term *usury* there is the cross-reference, "see Interest." Within the section devoted to the law of California, the secretary looks under the *I*'s and finds a sub-heading *usury* within the major heading Interest. The uniform arrangement of the material, supported by abundant citations, presents the law in an organized and quickly accessible form. Statutory forms (see PRINTED LAW BLANKS) are frequently a part of the text.

Part II of Volume IV is a section confined to digests of United States copyright, patent, tax, and trademark laws. Part III contains digests of the laws of the Federal government of Canada and of each of her ten provinces. Part IV of Volume IV contains digests of the laws of fifty-two foreign countries. In the case of Australia there is a digest of the laws of the States of that Commonwealth with the digest of its Federal laws. Part V carries the court calendars of the Federal judicial system of the United States and of the territories of Puerto Rico and the Virgin Islands. The calendars classify the courts and define their JURISDICTION. In Part VI the complete texts of thirty-three Uniform Acts and three Model Acts are presented. Thus the user of this volume has at hand the full texts of these important enactments which cover so many fields of the statutory law of a large number of the states.

Massachusetts Trust. A business association formed under a deed of trust, which is really a contract between the trustees and beneficiaries. It is also known as a *business trust* or a *common-law trust*. Its structure closely resembles that of a CORPORATION. The interests of the beneficiaries are represented by certificates, frequently called certificates of stock, which may be divided into several classes of common and preferred stock and may be listed on stock exchanges. The trustees correspond to the directors and the certificate holders to the stockholders. The trustees manage the property and pay dividends out of the profits. They usually appoint and remove the officers. Unlike a corporation, the management is permanent. The trustees are personally liable in dealing with outsiders unless they clearly indicate that they are acting as trustees and that the creditors shall look only to the trust property for all payments.

Massachusetts trusts are regarded as corporations under many taxing statutes and Federal acts.

The duration is limited by statute in most states, but the parties interested at the time the trust expires can agree to another trust.

Mechanic's Lien. See LIEN.

Mediation. The act of a third person who intervenes between two contending parties with a view towards reconciliation. In a labor dispute, mediation procedures cannot force labor and management to agree. In guiding the parties to mutual agreement, the mediator may only suggest compromises and solutions. See ARBITRATION; CONCILIATION.

Memorandum of Law. A document prepared by the attorney before trial to acquaint the judge with the legal theory of the action and the authorities relied upon in support of that theory. The memorandum also presents a general outline of the facts of the case. It should not assist the opposing party by going into details of evidence, the names of witnesses, or a discussion of the admissibility of evidence.

Invariably the judge is gratified to discover that his task has been made lighter at the very outset of the trial by the lawyer who has prepared his case well and has clarified all the issues involved. The lawyer should make his argument clear and unequivocal. Not too many authorities should be cited. An ancient precedent should never be cited if there is anything more recent on the subject. See CITATION (TO LEGAL AUTHORITIES).

There is no such thing as a standard memorandum of law. It will vary in accordance with the tastes of the lawyer and the court. Generally speaking, however, it is safe to assume that a brief, concise trial memorandum, which the judge can read in minutes, is preferable to the kind that would require hours to wade through, sometimes with little gain.

Merger. The fusion of one interest into another.

1. *Corporate.* The absorption of one or more corporations by another existing CORPORATION. The latter corporation retains its identity and takes over all the rights, privileges, franchises and properties of the absorbed companies, and assumes their obligations. (See also CONSOLIDATION.)

2. *Criminal law.* the absorption of a lesser crime into a greater one. As examples, the crime of ATTEMPT disappears once the attempted act is completed; when a person commits a FELONY and also a TORT against someone by the same act, some states merge the tort into the felony and thereby prevent the civil suit.

3. *Contracts.* Oral agreements and proposals merge in a subsequent written CONTRACT that deals with the same subject matter.

Metes and Bounds Description. See LAND DESCRIPTION.

Microfiche. A process by which pages of printed material are reduced and placed on a card which can be read through a viewer. The cards with the reduced images have much greater accessibility through the viewer than the rolls of film used in the microfilm process. Many of the Reporter volumes are now being placed on Microfiche to save space.

Microfilming. A process of photographing records on motion picture film (16 or 35mm), thus making it possible to keep the contents of a four-drawer filing cabinet on about three 200-foot rolls of film that require only 48 cubic inches of storage space.

Minority. The state or condition of a minor; infancy. The smaller number of votes of a deliberative assembly; opposed to majority.

Minute Books. The record books in which the CLERK OF THE COURT enters abstracts of all court orders. He records them numerically according to index number. He might have separate books for law, chancery, divorce, and the like.

If the secretary wants any information about the court's orders in a case, she can get it by consulting the minute book. She must have the index number. Usually the clerk's office will give her the information over the telephone. See also, CLERK'S PERMANENT RECORD BOOK.

For Corporation The book that contains records of minutes of shareholders' and directors' meetings, copy of the incorporation procedures, by-laws and sometimes a register of stock issued.

Misdemeanor. An offense lower than a FELONY and generally punishable by fine or imprisonment in a place other than a state penitentiary.

Mistrial. A declaration of the COURT that a trial is to be ended because for some reason justice may not be done if the trial continues. Disqualification of the judge or a juror or the inability of the jury to agree upon a verdict may result in a mistrial. The court will declare a mistrial if a matter has been brought to the jury improperly and could possibly prejudice the verdict. The declaration of a mistrial ends the trial, but the action, itself, continues. In other words, the defendant will not be put into DOUBLE JEOPARDY if he is again brought to trial on the same charge.

Mobile Telephone Service. This service makes it possible to interconnect mobile units, such as cars, trucks and passenger trains, with the general telephone system. Direct telephone communication with mobile units eliminates mileage and time required by special trips, thus saving operational costs. Radio equipment is installed on the mobile unit. At present, the equipment may be rented from the telephone company or provided by the owner of the mobile unit.

Moody's Manuals. A comprehensive source of information on American businesses. The manuals, covering industrial, transportation, public utility, and bank and finance companies, are valuable to the investor, analyst, business executive, and banker. Included in the manuals are financial statements, a listing of the officers, and highlights of outstanding bond and stock issues.

Annual Dividend Yield. A publication by Moody of the annual yield of various stocks, useful in preparing intangible tax returns.

Mortgage. A *conditional conveyance.* A mortgage is given by a borrower or debtor (the *mortgagor*) to secure the payment of a debt, with a provision that the conveyance will become void on the payment of the debt by the date named. In early English times the debtor actually turned over his property to the lender (the *mortgagee*) who would keep the income and profits from it. The land was "dead" to the

owner and gave him no return; hence the word *mort-gage,* meaning *dead pledge.* A mortgage may be given on real estate or on personal property, but a mortgage on personal property is referred to as a *chattel mortgage,* whereas a mortgage on real estate is referred to simply as a *mortgage.* Some *mortgages* cover both real and personal property, for example, a mortgage on a furnished apartment building.

The word mortgage also refers to the instrument used to make the conveyance. The debt is evidenced by promissory notes; the mortgage is the security instrument that secures payment of the notes. In some states, New York for example, the debt is evidenced by a bond instead of a promissory note. The bond takes the place of the note. Frequently, the bond and mortgage are combined in one instrument, which is referred to as a BOND AND MORTGAGE.

Mortgage Consideration. A statement reciting the consideration for which the mortgage was given. See MORTGAGE STATEMENT AND CLAUSES, *Mortgage consideration.*

Mortgage, Preparation of. In preparing a mortgage, the secretary will find the following general directions helpful: (Some of the directions apply only to typed mortgages, some to printed forms, and some to both.)

1. Make an original for the mortgagee, a copy for the mortgagor, and a copy for the lawyer's files.

2. Use LEGAL CAP paper.

3. Follow carefully the directions for filling in a printed form. (See PRINTED LAW BLANKS.)

4. Be sure the RESPONSIBILITY

AND DISTRIBUTION LINE is at the top of the first page. This goes on the office copy only of printed form.

5. Double space.

6. Type the LAND DESCRIPTION. Accuracy is essential.

7. If using a printed form be sure to make the "Z" after the land description. See Z RULING.

8. Number all pages of a typed mortgage.

9. Have at least two lines of typing on the signature page.

10. Prepare signature line for the mortgagor. If the mortgagor is an individual, his wife will probably have to sign. The mortgagee does not sign a mortgage.

11. Affix the SEAL when required.

12. Have proper officer affix corporation seal.

13. Type witness lines and ATTESTATION CLAUSE when required.

14. Prepare certificate of ACKNOWLEDGMENT.

15. Collate.

16. Check and double check spelling of names. If the mortgage is a purchase money mortgage, compare names of mortgagor and mortgagee with names of GRANTOR and GRANTEE. Extreme care should be exercised to see that the name of the mortgagor appears exactly as it appears in the instrument under which he claims title to the property; otherwise, the mortgagee's TITLE might be defective if it becomes necessary for him to foreclose.

17. Endorse back. If the mortgage is typed, prepare LEGAL BACK.

18. Compare LAND DESCRIPTION with someone to insure accuracy.

19. Arrange for the mortgagor to sign the mortgage.

20. Get the lawyer's approval of the instrument before it is signed.

21. Have the mortgagor sign the original only. Be sure that the mortgagor's signature agrees with the name, exactly as it is typed in the mortgage.

22. Have the mortgage notarized. The secretary can take the acknowledgment if a notary.

23. After signature and acknowledgment, conform copies to original.

24. Get the lawyer's approval of the executed mortgage and have it recorded. Put a notation on the back to have it returned to the office. (The secretary to the lawyer for the mortgagee attends to the recording.)

25. When the mortgage is returned by the recorder, send it to the mortgagee.

Printed mortgages. Printed forms are used extensively. The forms for the ordinary mortgage and deed of trust usually can be filled in without dictation from the lawyer. He will dictate any special clauses needed. Following is a checklist of information needed to fill in a mortgage or deed of trust. (The information can be obtained from the files, the lawyer, or, with his permission, from the client.)

1. Full name of mortgagor and mortgagee; also of trustee in the case of a trust deed.

2. County and state of residence of mortgagor and mortgagee; in a large city, their street address; also residence of trustee in the case of a trust deed.

3. Full description of the mortgagor's office and authority if he is conveying in a representative capacity.

4. Marital status of mortgagor.

5. Full name of spouse if spouse must join in the conveyance.

6. If purchase money mortgage, is wife to join?

7. Date of mortgage.

8. Amount of mortgage.

9. Period of time that the mortgage is to run; as well as its maturity date.

10. Rate of interest and when payable.

11. Description of property.

12. Date and place mortgage is to be acknowledged.

13. If mortgagor is corporation, name and title of officers signing and acknowledging.

14. If mortgage contains power of sale, number of days notice to be given in newspaper (this is determined by statute) and where newspaper is published.

15. If there is to be an AFFIDAVIT OF TITLE, who is to make it?

See also MORTGAGE CONSIDERATION; MORTGAGE STATEMENT AND CLAUSES; PARTIES TO A MORTGAGE; TRUST DEED; CORPORATE MORTGAGE BOND.

Typed mortgages; deeds of trust; trust deeds. The lawyer will dictate a mortgage or a DEED OF TRUST or a TRUST DEED when the printed form is inadequate for the special conditions of the transaction. Trust deeds that are given to secure a bond issue are long and involved and are printed especially for a specific bond issue. The secretary follows the general style of the printed form. See also MORTGAGE STATEMENT AND CLAUSES; LIEN, FORMS OF MORTGAGES.

Mortgage Statement and Clauses. The written summation that identifies precisely the debt and all of the conditional terms of a particular MORTGAGE agreement. The statement and clauses set forth:

1. *Description of debt.* A mortgage is given to secure a debt, and the mortgage instrument must describe and identify the debt with preciseness. The description includes the rate and time of payment of interest and clearly states the time of payment of the debt. Some forms call for a copy of the note secured by the mortgage to be copied in the body of the instrument.

Example:

...an indebtedness in the sum of fifteen thousand (15,000) dollars, lawful money of the United States, to be paid on the first day of April, 19. ., with interest thereon to be computed from April 1, 19. ., at the rate of nine (9) per centum per annum, and to be paid semi-annually thereafter, according to a certain note bearing even date herewith. ...

2. *Defeasance clause.* The provision in the mortgage that if the indebtedness is paid in accordance with the terms of the mortgage agreement, the mortgage shall be null and void.

Example:

Provided always, that if said mortgagor, ... shall pay ... a certain promissory note, a copy of which is on the reverse side hereof, and shall perform and comply with each and every stipulation, agreement and covenant of said note and of this mortgage, the estate hereby created shall be void, otherwise the same shall remain in full force and virtue.

... provided that if I shall punctually pay said notes according to the tenor thereof, then this mortgage shall be void.

3. *Mortgage consideration.* A mortgage recites the consideration for which it was given. Statement of the consideration might name the amount of the indebtedness, or it might recite a nominal consideration.

Examples:

... for and in consideration of the aforesaid debt of five thousand dollars

($5,000), and the better securing the payment of the same with interest . . .

. . . for the better securing the payment of the sum of money mentioned in the said bond, or obligation, with the interest thereon, and, also, in consideration of One Dollar ($1.) paid by the Second Party, the receipt whereof is hereby acknowledged . . .

4. *Acceleration clause.* See ACCELERATION CLAUSE.

5. *Description of property.* See LAND DESCRIPTION.

6. Prepayment privilege. A clause giving the mortgagor the right to pay off the mortgage, or part of it, before maturity. Mortgages and mortgage notes frequently provide that the debt shall be payable on or before the maturity date, or they contain a specific clause giving the mortgagor the right. A comparable provision in trust deeds securing issues of bonds permits redemption of the bonds prior to maturity dates. The privilege enables a mortgagor to refinance his debt when money is cheaper, or to sell the property free and clear of any mortgage. Printed forms do not usually include the prepayment privilege.

Example:
The mortgagor is hereby authorized and permitted to pay the debt hereby secured, or any part of it, not less than . . . . dollars at any one time, whenever and at such time and times as he may choose, and the mortgagee hereby agrees to accept such payment or payments, and thereupon the interest shall cease upon such part of the debt as may be so paid; and upon the full payment of said debt, with all interest up to the date of actual payment, he will discharge this mortgage.

7. *Partial release clause.* This clause permits the mortgagor to sell part of the land, permitting the release of a specified portion of the premises covered by the mortgage upon payment of a specified sum.

Example:
Said mortgagor reserves the right to release all or any part of the said land from the operation of this mortgage, in case said land is subdivided, upon payment to mortgagee of a sum of money to be agreed upon for each lot, the sum to be determined according to the size and location of the lot as soon as the said land is subdivided.

Said mortgagee has agreed to sign a plat of said premises prepared by mortgagor.

See also MORTGAGE; MORTGAGE, PREPARATION OF; MORTGAGE CONSIDERATION, FORMS OF MORTGAGES.

Motion. The application for an order addressed to the COURT or to a judge in his chambers by the lawyer for a party to a law suit. For example, when an attorney wants the court to take a particular action in a pending case, he "moves" the court to take that action. Unless a motion is made during a hearing or trial, it is in writing.

Motions are numerous and varied. Some of the motions more frequently addressed to the court include: (1) Motion for Change of Venue (2) Motion to Strike (3) Motion for New Trial (4) Motion for Leave to Amend (5) Motion to set for Trial.

Some jurisdictions have special terms of court at which all motions are heard. In crowded jurisdictions, the contested motions are heard in one part and *ex parte* motions of which opposing counsel has no notice, are heard in another part. The secretary must acquaint herself with the part in which they are heard, if there is a distinction in any of the courts in her locality. See also NOTICE OF MOTION.

Municipal Court. See COURTS OF SPECIAL JURISDICTION.

Muniments of Title. Written evidence

by which title to real property may be defended. The word *muniments* is derived from the Latin verb *munio,* meaning *to fortify.* Hence, muniments of title fortify or strengthen rights in property. The expression as generally defined refers to deeds of conveyance, wills, legislative grants, and other documents relating to the title land.

Murder. The unlawful killing of someone by deliberate design. In many states, legislative enactments have divided murder into degrees. First degree murder is generally defined as the act of killing another with deliberate and premeditated design, or as killing another while in the act of committing a FELONY (see also FELONY-MURDER). Murder in the second degree occurs where there is no deliberately formed design to kill; the idea of killing occurs instantaneously with the act. See also MAN-SLAUGHTER.

Mutiny. An insurrection by military or naval personnel, or seamen against the authority of their commanders. Seamen who by force, intimidation, or trick deprive the vessel's captain of his authority, or resist or prevent his exercise of authority, may be guilty of the crime of mutiny.

N

Nasciturus. Future issue of a marriage.

National Association of Legal Secretaries. Legal secretaries and attorneys recognize that the successful legal secretary must now be more than a proficient stenographer and typist. Not only must her skills include a working knowledge of every type of work that is done in either a large or small law office but she must, in addition, be an expert in human relations, law office ethics and etiquette, and law office procedures and management. The National Association of Legal Secretaries now plays a vital role in assisting and educating the legal secretary to attain these goals. Through the association's nationally sponsored program for certifying legal secretaries by special examination, the rating of a Professional Legal Secretary may be earned.

The PLS as it is known is awarded to any legal secretary who is a member of NALS, who has at least five years' legal experience, and who successfully completes a two-day examination covering six parts, to wit: Part I, Written Communication, Skill and Knowledge; Part II, Human Relations; Part III, Secretarial Procedures and Office Management; Part IV, Secretarial Accounting; Part V, Legal Terminology; and Part VI, Legal Secretarial Skills. The examinations are conducted twice a year in various test centers across the country. When the examination is completed and passed the secretary is given a PLS certificate.

Preparation for the examination can be worth the time and effort, even if it is not passed on the first attempt. Each part passed need not be repeated. Only the parts failed need be taken over, and the subject areas covered are useful to any legal secretary.

For information about the PLS program or about membership in NALS, write to:

National Association of Legal Secretaries
3005 E. Skelly Drive
Tulsa, Oklahoma 74105

National Labor Relations Board (NLRB). A panel of men appointed by the President with the advice and consent of the Senate. The board is given the power by the National Labor Relations Act (Wagner Act) to establish procedures for the settlement of questions of union representation and to prevent persons from engaging in unfair labor practices.

National Reporter System. The published opinions of the Federal courts and the courts of every state, those of several states being publishd in the same bound volume. This system of reports, published by West Publishing Company, covers the entire country. Table I shows the names of the reporters, how they are cited (see CITATION TO LEGAL AUTHOR-

ITIES), and the courts covered by each. Some of the reporters are designated "Second Series." The designation is for numbering purposes and indicates that the numbers of the volume have started over with 1.

Table I

REPORTERS OF NATIONAL REPORTER SYSTEM

Name of reporter	Cite as	Courts covered
Supreme Court Reporter	S. Ct.	United States Supreme Court
Federal Reporter	F.	United States Circuit Courts of Appeals and the District Courts
Federal Reporter, Second Series	F. 2d	United States Courts of Appeals, United States Court of Customs and Patent Appeals, United States Emergency Court of Appeals
Federal Supplement	F. Supp.	United States District Courts, United States Court of Claims
Atlantic Reporter Atlantic Reporter, Second Series	A. A. 2d	Connecticut Delaware Maine Maryland New Hampshire New Jersey Pennsylvania Rhode Island Vermont District of Columbia
New York Supplement New York Supplement, Second Series	N.Y. Supp. N.Y.S. 2d	New York Court of Appeals Appellate Division of the Supreme Court Miscellaneous Courts
Northeastern Reporter Northeastern Reporter, Second Series	N.E. N.E. 2d	Illinois Indiana New York Massachusetts Ohio
Northwestern Reporter Northwestern Reporter, Second Series	N.W. N.W. 2d	Iowa Michigan Minnesota Nebraska North Dakota South Dakota Wisconsin
Pacific Reporter Pacific Reporter, Second Series	Pac. P. 2d	Alaska Arizona California Colorado

TABLE I
REPORTERS OF NATIONAL REPORTER SYSTEM

Name of reporter	Cite as	Courts covered
Pacific Reporter	Pac.	Hawaii
Pacific Reporter	P. 2d	Idaho
		Kansas
		Montana
		Nevada
		New Mexico
		Oklahoma
		Oregon
		Utah
		Washington
		Wyoming
Southeastern Reporter	S.E.	Georgia
Southeastern Reporter, Second		North Carolina
Series	So. 2d	South Carolina
		Virginia
		West Virginia
Southern Reporter	So.	Alabama
Southern Reporter, Second		Florida
Series	S.W. 2d	Louisiana
		Mississippi
Southwestern Reporter	S.W.	Arkansas
Southwestern Reporter, Second		Kentucky
Series	S.W. 2d	Missouri
		Tennessee
		Texas

These reporters, which are "unofficial" reports of the courts' opinions, are published much sooner than the OFFICIAL REPORTS, especially those in some states. Some states have doscontinued the publication of state reports and use the appropriate reporter of the National Reporter System as the official report.

Before the opinions are published in bound volumes of the National Reporter System, they are published in weekly pamphlets known as *Advance Sheets*. (Some official reports also have advance sheets.) Thus, the lawyer is informed immediately of the decisions of courts in which he is interested. The page numbers in the advance sheets correspond with the page numbers that will appear in the bound volumes.

Negligence. The failure to use reasonable care in order to avoid injury to another. The standard of care that should be used is that degree of care that would have been used by a reasonable man in the light of all the circumstances of the case. For example, a doctor in treating a patient must act with the skill of the average member of the profession.

If the defendant's negligence is the PROXIMATE CAUSE of injury to the plaintiff, and the plaintiff is free from CONTRIBUTORY NEGLIGENCE, he is entitled to DAMAGES.

Negotiable Instrument. A written instrument, signed by a maker or drawer, containing an unconditional promise or order to pay a certain sum of money, which can be passed freely from one person to another in a manner that constitutes the transferee as the holder. If payable to bearer, the instrument may be negotiated simply by delivery; if payable to order, it is negotiated by endorsement of the holder, completed by delivery.

The Uniform Commercial Code, which has been adopted by all of the States, governs negotiable instruments. See UNIFORM ACTS. The law states the manner in which a negotiable instrument shall be transferred, and it fixes the rights and duties of the maker, the payee, the holder and the endorser. For example, under the law an indorser of a negotiable instrument vouches for its genuineness. If it is a forgery, the endorser if liable to a HOLDER IN DUE COURSE of the instrument after delivery.

Strictly speaking, documents of title (such as order bills of lading, warehouse receipts, and stock certificates) are not negotiable instruments because they do not contain an order to pay a sum of money. However, various statutes have given certain documents of title the quality of negotiability. These are known as quasi-negotiable instruments.

Negotiation. The transfer of a written instrument in a manner that makes the transferee the holder of the instrument. If payable to order, an instru-ment is negotiated by endorsement and delivery; if payable to bearer, by delivery alone. An instrument is not negotiated until it is transferred by the person to whom it is issued. Thus, *A* makes a note payable to *B* and delivers it to him. Subsequently, by negotiation, *B* transfers the note to *C*, and *C* to *D*, and so on. As opposed to transfer by ASSIGNMENT, the innocent transferee by negotiation takes the paper free of defenses that are good against the transferor. See also NEGOTIABLE INSTRUMENT.

Necessaries. An article which a party actually needs, such as food, clothing, and shelter. Infants may be held liable for contracting for necessaries; also mentally incompetent persons. See PROVISION OF NECESSARIES.

New Case Report. A systematically kept record of all the pertinent information on a new matter received in the law office in which it will act for a client. In any well organized law office, a report is made immediately on every matter received. The lawyer who interviews the client obtains from him the following information: (1) name, address, and telephone number of the client; (2) name of opposing party, and his address and telephone number, if known; (3) attorney for opposing party, if any. Occasionally these data are given to the secretary by the client as he leaves the office, but it is usually more diplomatic for the lawyer to make a note of the information during the interview.

What the secretary does. The secretary's job is to get the information from the lawyer as soon as the client leaves the office, so that she can make up a new case report. The reports also call for one or more of the following items of information, which the lawyer should indicate to the secretary.

1. The general nature of the case, whether general litigation, probate, foreclosure, etc.
2. Whether the case is on an annual retainer basis or is a single case. This affects the bookkeeping.
3. Whether the client is new or old.
4. Whether stenographic services are to be billed separately or included in the over-all fee.
5. Name of the junior partner or associate, if any, to be assigned to the case.

Printed forms are provided for new case reports, or they may be mimeographed. Frequently the lawyer himself makes out the reports, because they call for very little writing. Two types of forms are illustrated in Figures

1 and 2. Notice that the form illustrated in Figure 2 even has a space in which the attorney indicates whether or not the client is to be added to the firm ANNOUNCEMENT CARD list.

When the report is filled out, it is ready to be routed.

Routing of new case report. The routing procedure varies with the office, but the following order or routing is practical and can be adapted to the requirements of any office. When a secretary works in a small office, instead of routing the new case report she will take the steps indicated by this procedure.

1. File department. File number is assigned and a file opened. File clerk initials. See FILING (IN A LAW OFFICE).
2. Accounting department. Ledger sheet for the client and case is opened, after which disburse-

MORGAN, BURBANK & CHAMBERS
REPORT OF NEW CASE OR MATTER
MUST BE TYPEWRITTEN

Date:
Name of Client:

Address:
Title of Case or Matter:

Court:
Member in Charge:
Assistant:

CLASSIFICATION

☐ General Litigation
☐ Corporate and Financial
☐ Indiv. Pers., Trust
☐ Estate and Litigation as to Estate

REAL ESTATE

☐ General
☐ Certiorari
☐ Dispossess
☐ Foreclosure

(CHECK AND RETURN PROMPTLY)
1. Charge Register:............... 2. Managing Clerk:............... 3. Bookkeepers:...............
4. Budget Committee:............... 5. Files:...............

New Case Report: Figure 1.

ments may be made for and charged to the case. Bookkeeper initals.

In an extremely large firm, there might be other departments or committees to which the report whould be routed.

The new case is then returned to the filing department and filed. The mechanics of processing the case have been completed, and the attorney and his secretary are ready to work on it. The matter might consist of drawing an instrument, in which event the file will

---

HALL and DOBB
NEW CASE REPORT

File No. _____

Received by _____

For Credit of _____ Date _____

Attorney receiving a new case will fill out this blank, sign it, and then send it to Files.
Files will assign the file number, index under the names given in 1 to 4; note any instructions as to filing in 5; initial

here _____ and send to Assistant Managing Partner.

Assistant Managing Partner will assign attorneys, initial, etc. and send to the Accounting Department.
Accounting Department will see that the report is properly filled out, service ledger cards made, open a service ledger

account, and initial here _____ Submitted by _____ Verified by _____

Accounting Department will list on weekly summary and initial here _____

Estimated Value of Case $ _____

Nature of Case

Add to Firm Announcement List   Yes ☐   No ☐

Billing: Retainer or Continuing ☐   Single Cases ☐

Client: New ☐   Old ☐

1. Name of Client _____

    Address _____

    _____

2. Title of Case _____

    _____

3. Opposing Party _____

    Address _____

    _____

4. Additional Names (if any) _____

    that should be indexed _____

    (Additional names should be given where the name of the person referring the case or the name of a person with whom there is to be much correspondence does not appear in 1, 2, or 3 above.)

5. Filing Instructions (if any) _____

6. Remarks _____

Received by Assistant Managing Partner _____ Date _____ at _____

Attorney Responsible _____

Assistant Assigned _____

Junior Assigned _____

Will case be litigated?

No ☐

Yes ☐

Doubtful ☐

New Case Report: **Figure 2.** Another form.

soon be closed; or it might involve litigation that extends over a period of years; or it might be a matter in a specialized field of law, such as organizing a corporation. Regardless of the nature of the case, the secretary will have dictation and typing about it, and, very probably will have contact with the client either in person or by telephone. See also CONTACTS OVER THE TELEPHONE; SUIT REGISTER.

Next Friend. One acting for the benefit of an infant, or other person not *sui juris,* without being regularly appointed guardian.

Night Letter. See TELEGRAPH SERVICE.

No-par Stock. Stock without any nominal or designated value in money. Such stock may be either COMMON STOCK or PREFERRED STOCK.

It was originally considered necessary for the CERTIFICATE OF STOCK to show the amount in dollars for which the stock was issued, whether that amount was actually received by the CORPORATION or not. See PAR VALUE STOCK. The actual value of the stock might change from day to day but the value stated in the stock certificate, the nominal or par value, always remained the same. Thus, rather than being a statement of the actual or book value of the stock evidenced by the stock certificate, the statement of par value in the certificate was more often than not no indication at all of the actual or book value of the stock. This fact, in large measure, accounts for the substitution of no-par stock for stock expressing a par value. No-par stock tends to relieve the necessity for, or embarrassment of, explanation of discrepancy between the book or market value and the face value of corporate stocks.

Nonage. Under the proper age to be able to do a particular thing. For example, an action for the ANNULMENT of a marriage may be brought where one or both of the parties have not attained the legal age of consent. Whether the marriage of an INFANT may be annulled for nonage depends upon the age of consent in the place of marriage.

Nonbusiness Expenses. See EXCISE TAXES.

Noncumulative Preferred Stock. A class of stock characterized by the fact that unpaid dividends do not accumulate as arrearages, which must be eliminated before dividends may be paid on COMMON STOCK. See also CUMULATIVE PREFERRED STOCK; PREFERRED STOCK; DIVIDEND.

Nonsuit. A dismissal of the plaintiff's COMPLAINT by the court because he failed to establish a good cause of action. Defendant makes a motion for a nonsuit after the close of plaintiff's evidence. Defendant's motion should be specific and should indicate the particular defects or failures in plaintiff's proof. In determining the motion, the court will assume that all plaintiff's evidence is true and will draw every reasonable inference in plaintiff's favor.

Nonsupport. The failure of a husband to furnish to his wife and children support consistent with his means. Withholding of such support is a ground for SEPARATION in most states and for DIVORCE in some.

Notarize. To acknowledge or attest a document as a NOTARY PUBLIC. The notary public exercises special care to see that documents that he notarizes are executed correctly. If the papers are not in conformity with the requirements of the office where they are to be recorded, they will be rejected. The notary does not read an instrument that he notarizes but he should read the ACKNOWLEDGMENT and also glance over the instrument. He observes the following details when taking an acknowledgment.

1. If the instrument recites that it is "under seal," the notary should be sure that the signature to the instrument is followed by "L.S."

2. When a corporation is a party to an instrument, the notary should be sure the CORPORATE SEAL is impressed on the instrument if required; seals are usually required on corporate instruments.

3. The notary should fill in all blanks in the instrument and in the certificate of ACKNOWLEDGMENT or the JURAT.

4. The notary should show the date of the expiration of his commission when required.

5. The notary should be sure to impress his notarial seal on the certificate when required. Some states do not require a notary's seal on papers acknowledged within the state, but all states require a seal on papers acknowledged in another state.

6. The notary should be sure that rubber stamps used by him make legible imprints. A black stamp pad is preferable because the black ink photostats more distinctly than other inks.

Following the letter of the law when notarizing a paper. A commission as a notary public is a trust; it confers certain powers upon the notary as well as requiring that he perform certain duties. In exercising these powers and duties, he should observe punctiliously the "letter of the law." In a law office the principal duty as a notary public will be taking acknowledgments.

Notice that all of the certificates of acknowledgments illustrated in Figures 1 to 4 under ACKNOWLEDGMENT recite that the person making the acknowledgment "personally appeared" before the notary. This is true of all forms of acknowledgments in every state. Therefore, when the secretary acts as notary she should never take an acknowledgment without the actual appearance of the individual making the acknowledgment. In fact, it is illegal to do so. If a client's wife signs an instrument at home and wants to acknowledge it over the telephone, politely but firmly decline to take the acknowledgment and state the reason for your refusal.

Acknowledgments also recite that the individual "acknowledged" that he signed the instrument. The notary does not administer an oath to a person making an acknowledgment, but asks him: "Do you acknowledge that you signed this instrument?" or, "Do you acknowledge that you executed this instrument as attorney-in-fact for Edward R. Stevens?" or a similar question, depending upon whether the acknowledgment is being made by an individual in his own behalf, an officer of a corporation, a partnership, or an attorney-in-fact.

Acknowledgments also recite that the notary knows, or has satisfactory evidence, that the person making it is the person "described in and who executed" the instrument. The notary must have satisfactory evidence of the identity of a person whose acknowledgment is taken. Of course, in taking acknowledgments made by clients, he is not likely to have difficulty in this respect. A notary who willfully makes a false certificate that an instrument was acknowledged by a party to the instrument is guilty of forgery.

A certificate of acknowledgment also shows the date it is signed by the notary. The notary should never postdate or ante-date a certificate. To do so constitutes FRAUD and deceit in the exercise of his powers.

Notary *Public*. (Pl., notaries public.) A commissioned officer of a state, whose powers and duties consist, among others, in administering oaths, certifying to the genuineness of documents, and taking acknowledgments. In some states a notary is authorized to act only in the county in which he is commissioned; in others, he is qualified to act throughout the state. Almost all law offices have a notary public, and frequently the secretary is the notary. Lawyers in New Jersey and New York have DE FACTO notarial authority, but they must qualify, register and have a notarial seal or stamp (see NOTARY'S SEAL). The eligibility requirements are not stringent, relating primarily to age and residence. If the secretary's office wants her to be commissioned as a notary, she writes to the official in her state who appoints notaries for an application blank. Some states require a bond; stipulate that the notary public must keep a record of all his official acts; require that the application be endorsed by a member of the legislature, a judge, or some other designated official. The secretary must meet the requirements of the state in which she resides.

After the commission is received, the secretary orders a notary's seal and stamp. She registers her commission with the CLERK OF THE COURT (or other designated official) in her county, so that the officer can authenticate her certificate of ACKNOWLEDGMENT on papers that are to be recorded in another state. The secretary who becomes a notary must follow the letter of the law. Notary Commissions are renewable at intervals, except that in some states lawyers are given lifetime commissions. (see NOTARIZE).

Notary's Seal. The stamp or imprint that is placed upon a legal instrument, certificate or paper by an authorized NOTARY PUBLIC. The notary's seal (also called the *notarial seal*) is required by some states when acknowledgment is made within the state. *All* states require a seal on papers acknowledged in another state.

Note of Issue. See NOTICING A CASE FOR TRIAL.

Notice of Appeal. Under the rules of a typical state, the filing of a *notice of appeal* with the CLERK OF THE COURT whose order is appealed from gives the appellate court jurisdiction, and an appeal is deemed to have commenced. It is the appellant's notice of his intention to appeal a decision rendered by a lower court. (See APPELLATE COURT.) The time usually allowed for filing a notice of appeal is 30 days after receipt of a copy of the judgment with NOTICE OF ENTRY.

IN THE CIRCUIT COURT OF THE ELEVENTH
JUDICIAL CIRCUIT OF FLORIDA, IN AND
FOR DADE COUNTY.   IN CHANCERY

———————————————————————x

JOHN JONES,   :   No. 13,670–C

             Plaintiff,   :

        vs.   : AFFIDAVIT OF SERVICE

ALBERT SMITH,   :

             Defendant.   :

———————————————————————x

STATE OF FLORIDA,)
               : SS.
DADE COUNTY.   )

      Before the subscriber personally appeared MARY ED-
WARDS, who, being first duly sworn, deposes and says that
she is employed by Elwood and Adams and was so employed on
January 8, 19—; that on said date she personally placed in
an envelope addressed to J. W. Brown, Jr., Esq., a true
copy of the foregoing Notice of Appeal; that said envelope,
having been properly addressed and sealed, with sufficient
postage affixed thereto, was deposited by her on said date
in the United States Mails at Miami, Florida.

_____

Subscribed and Sworn to Before Me
This 8th day of January, 19—.

_____
Notary Public, State of Florida
at Large.
My commission expires: 5/8/—.
(SEAL)

Notice of Appeal: Figure 1. Affidavit of service by mail.

The secretary can get the wording of the notice of appeal from the court rules or from FORM BOOKS, or the lawyer will dictate it to her or give her a form to follow. The secretary sets it up in the same manner and on the same kind of paper as for other court papers. (See TYPING LEGAL DOCUMENTS.) She will (1) make an original, a copy for each appellee, and a copy for her own files (but see 5 below); (2) see that the caption is the same as that on the PLEADINGS; (3) bind the notice in a legal back, properly endorsed; (4) see that the attorney for the party who appeals signs the notice of appeal; (5) serve a copy on counsel for appellee, and file the original, with proof of service, with the clerk of the court. In some states the rules do not require service of notice of appeal on opposing counsel. In other states the rules require that the notice be filed in duplicate, on containing the proof of service.

Service on opposing counsel. Service of all papers and notices required by the rules of an appellate court may be made by leaving the same in the office of the opposing counsel during regular office hours with a person in charge of the office. Service may also be made by depositing papers and notices securely sealed and post paid, in the post office directed to such attorney at his usual post office address. *Proof of service* is made by affidavit, when service is had by mail. Placing the properly sealed and addressed document in an "outgoing basket" to be dispatched by the mail clerk in the office is not compliance with the statutes.

The secretary must actually do what the *affidavit of service* says. Figure 1, page 300 illustrates an affidavit of service by mail. If the wording of the affidavit used in an office differs, the secretary should make an extra copy for the office form book. Notice that the affidavit is preceded by the caption of the case. When this affidavit is copied into the RECORD ON APPEAL, the caption will be omitted, but the recital of venue will be included.

See also AFFIDAVIT.

Notice of Appearance. A written statement by the attorney for the defendant, *that the defendant appears* in a particular action or jurisdiction. Thereafter, copies of all pleadings will be served on the attorney appearing for the defendant, if such service is required. In some jurisdictions the notice of appearance is addressed to the attorney for the plaintiff; in others to the CLERK OF THE COURT. Figures 1 and 2 illustrate notices of appearance in (1) a common law case and (2) in an equity case (pages 302 and 303).

How to prepare a notice of appearance. A printed form of the notice of appearance is available, but the notice may be typed on legal-size paper.

1. Prepare an original for the court, a copy to be served on opposing counsel, and a copy for your office file.

2. The caption is identical with that on the SUMMONS. If the title of the case is long, you may shorten it (see CAPTION).

3. Type signature line for attorney, with his address underneath. When a printed form is used, it is advisable to type the attorney's name in parentheses underneath the line for signature so that the opposing counsel will have no difficulty in deciphering the signature.

4. Endorse the back. If you type the

SUPREME COURT OF THE STATE OF NEW YORK
COUNTY OF NEW YORK

———————————————————————————x

JOHN ROBERTS,   :

                              Plaintiff, :

            —against—   :

THOMAS SMITH,   :

                            Defendant. :

———————————————————————————x

S I R:

      PLEASE TAKE NOTICE that the defendant Thomas Smith
hereby appears in the above entitled action and that we are
retained as attorneys for him therein, and hereby demand
that a copy of the complaint and of all other papers in this
action be served on us at the office below designated.

Dated, New York, July 25, 19—.

                              Yours, etc.,

                              RANDOLPH & PETERS,
                                Attorneys for Defendant,
                                80 Towers Avenue
                                New York, N. Y.

To:

      HAROLD B. WRIGHT, ESQ.,
        Attorney for Plaintiff,
         14 Hale Street,
         New York, N. Y.

Notice of Appearance: Figure 1. Notice of appearance in commmon law case.

UNITED STATES DISTRICT COURT

EASTERN DISTRICT OF NEW YORK

————————————————————————————x

RAY SMITH,   :

                     Plaintiff,   :

          –against–   :   E 87–20

JACKSON & COMPANY,   :

                    Defendant.   :

————————————————————————————x

TO THE CLERK OF THE ABOVE COURT:

      We hereby enter our appearance as attorneys and solicitors for the defendant JACKSON & COMPANY in the above entitled suit.

Dated, New York, July 5, 19—.

                          Yours, etc.,

                          ELWOOD & ADAMS
                            Attorneys for Defendant
                            Jackson & Company,
                            36 Mall Street,
                            New York, N. Y.

To:

    JOHN ELLIS, ESQ.,
      Attorney for Plaintiff,
      150 Brown Avenue
      New York, N. Y.

THE CLERK OF THE UNITED STATES DISTRICT COURT,
  Eastern District of New York,
    Post Office Building,
    Brooklyn, N. Y.

Notice of Appearance: Figure 2. Notice of appearance in equity case (Federal Court).

notice, put a properly ENDORSED LEGAL BACK on it.

What the secretary does about the notice of appearance. A notice of appearance is never verified, because it contains no statements of fact. Otherwise, the secretary's responsibilities with respect to the notice of appearance are the same as with respect to the ANSWER. In some jurisdictions the notice of appearance is not served on opposing counsel; he learns from the court record that the appearance has been filed.

Notice of Entry. Written notification given to opposing counsel by the prevailing attorney, stating that a JUDGMENT is being entered against him in the court of record. The right to APPEAL or to make MOTIONS affecting the judgment date from the time notice is given.

Notice of Motion. A warning in writing to the opposing counsel concerning a particular action that an attorney wishes the COURT to take in a pending case.

The notice of motion states the papers and proceedings upon which the motion will be brought and also the grounds of the motion. The supporting papers usually include an affidavit that is attached to the notice of motion.

Return day of motion. All notices of motion give the date the attorney will move the court for entry of the desired order. This date is the *return day* of the motion; the motion is *returnable* on that day. The practice rules provide that the notice shall be served on opposing counsel a specified number of days, or a reasonable time, before the return day of the motion. Some jurisdictions that do not have special terms of courts for motions set aside certain days in the month as motion day, on which days all motions are returnable. You will become familiar with (1) the motion days in the various courts and (2) how many days of notice are required.

Information needed to prepare a notice of motion. Notices of motion are prepared like other notices. The lawyer will dictate some notices of motions, but the secretary should be able to prepare many of them upon instructions from him without dictation. She will need the following information:

1. Style of case. Get this from the complaint or other papers in the file.

2. Papers and proceedings upon which the motion will be based. The lawyer usually dictates this.

3. Grounds upon which the motion will be made. The lawyer will dictate these, except when they are standard. For example, a motion to strike is always on the ground that portions of the pleadings are "sham, irrelevant and redundant." (The standard wording of the clause varies with the court.)

4. Return day of motion. If the secretary does not know how to calculate the return day, she asks the lawyer.

5. Time motion will be heard. Usually court practice rules set aside a certain hour at which motions will be called. If the secretary is not familiar with this time in the various courts, she asks the lawyer or consults the rules. The notice will read "at . . . o'clock in the . . . . . . noon, or as soon thereafter as counsel can be heard."

6. Where the motion will be heard. Motions are usually heard in the court where the case is pending. In some

jurisdictions specific terms, parts, departments, or divisions are set aside for motions.

7. Name of affiant and date of supporting affidavit, if the motion is based on an affidavit, as it usually is. The lawyer will give the secretary this information. Very probably he will dictate the affidavit before he instructs her about the notice.

What the secretary does about the notice of motion and affidavit. A motion is frequently based upon an affidavit, as appears from the wording of the notice. When this is the case, the secretary's responsibilities, after preparation of the notice and affidavit, are the following:

1. Endorse a legal back "Affidavit and Notice of Motion" and staple the papers together, placing the notice on top.

2. After approval by the lawyer, see that copy is served on opposing counsel.

3. See that receipt of service is on back of original. If the papers are served by mail, prepare certificate of service by mail.

4. *Enter return day of motion in the diary.*

5. Conform the office copy.

6. File original, with proof of service in court.

7. Make entries in SUIT REGISTER of service and filing.

8. The secretary to the attorney on whom the papers are served, makes a notation on back of that copy of date and hour of service. *Enter in diary return day of motion.* Also make entry in suit register.

Notice of Trial. See NOTICING A CASE FOR TRIAL.

Noticing a Case for Trial. The procedure by which a case is placed on the trial calendar of the court.

A material point, raised by the PLEADINGS, about which there is a controversy between the parties is an *issue*. The issue may be an *issue of fact* or an *issue of law*. When an issue is raised, it is said to be *joined,* and the case is *at issue.* Issue is deemed joined the date the last pleading is served.

At any time after issue is joined, either party may have the case *noticed for trial.* (In the New York Supreme Court no papers are filed in court until issue is joined—the court does not even know a law suit is pending.) In some jurisdictions a case is noticed for trial by the filing of a *note of issue* or *memorandum setting for trial;* in others, by the filing of a *notice of trial.* Some jurisdictions require both. In still other jurisdictions, a case is set for trial on MOTION of counsel. Regardless of the procedure, or the particular name of the notice used, its purpose is to place the case on the trial calendar.

Noticing a case for trial does not mean that it will be brought up for trial on that date or even at that term of court, but that it will be placed on the trial calendar to await its turn.

When the notice must be served. Note of issue or notice of trial must be served on opposing counsel a designated number of days before the TERM OF COURT at which the case will be placed on the trial calendar. The requirement varies with the jurisdiction. Suppose a new term of court commences on the first Monday of the following month, which, let us say, is May 5. Practice rules require that the note of issue or notice of trial shall be served 12 days, for example, before the commencement of the term. Therefore, the notice must be served by April 23. Service after that date will not give counsel 12 days' notice. Thus, if on April 25 the lawyer tells the secretary to prepare a notice of trial, she should know that it will have to be for the June, not the May, term of court.

It is important that she become familiar with this particular practice requirement; otherwise, she will not be able to prepare the note of issue or the notice of trial.

Note of issue—preparation. Note of issue is a printed form that can be easily completed without directions from the lawyer. (Figure 1 illustrates a completed form.)

These suggestions will guide the secretary:

1. Make an original for the court, a copy to serve on each opposing counsel, and a copy for the file.

2. Telephone numbers of attorneys should be included in the note of issue and *must* be included in some jurisdictions.

3. Each sentence is a separate paragraph.

4. Do not staple in legal back, but endorse on printed form.

5. The back of the printed note of issue has forms for affidavit of personal service and of service by mail. After service is made, fill in the appropriate form. Figure 2 illustrates the back of a note of issue with affidavit of service by mail completed. (See page 307.)

Notice of trial—preparation. The lawyer does not usually dictate a notice

Courtesy Julius Blumberg Inc.

Noticing a Case for Trial: Figure 1. Note of issue.

Noticing a Case for Trial: Figure 2. Back of note of issue.

of trial. The secretary can get the wording from a practice manual in the office. (See FORM BOOKS.) The wording varies slightly with the jurisdiction, and, in some jurisdictions, notice given by the plaintiff differs from notice given by the defendant. Notice of trial given by the plaintiff recites an intention to take an "inquest," whereas notice by the defendant recites that a motion to dismiss the complaint will be made. Memorize the wording in your jurisdiction to save time in the preparation of notices. (Figure 3 (page 308) illustrates a notice of trial.) The secretary should:

1. Make an original for the court, a copy to serve on each opposing counsel, and a copy for the office file.
2. Endorse legal backs.
3. Have attorney sign it.

What the secretary does about the notice of trial or note of issue.

MUNICIPAL COURT OF THE CITY OF NEW YORK
BOROUGH OF MANHATTAN: FIRST DISTRICT

LAWRENCE ADAMS,	No. 7834/—
Plaintiff,	
—against—	NOTICE OF TRIAL
LUCIUS WEBB and ABC COMPANY, INC.,	
Defendants.	

S I R S:

　　　　　PLEASE TAKE NOTICE that the issues in this action will be brought to trial and an inquest taken therein at Part II of this Court, to be held at the Court House situated at No. 8 Reade Street, Borough of Manhattan, City of New York on the 24th day of November, 19—, at 10 o'clock in the forenoon of that day or as soon thereafter as counsel can be heard.

Dated, New York, November 8, 19—.

　　　　　　　　　　　　　　　Yours, etc.,

　　　　　　　　　　　　　　　ELWOOD & ADAMS
　　　　　　　　　　　　　　　　Attorneys for Plaintiff,
　　　　　　　　　　　　　　　　48 Mall Street,
　　　　　　　　　　　　　　　　New York, N. Y.

To:

　　　　JONATHAN EDWARDS, ESQ.,
　　　　　Attorney for Defendant,
　　　　　120 Dew Street,
　　　　　New York, N. Y.

　　　　CLERK OF THE MUNICIPAL COURT OF
　　　　　THE CITY OF NEW YORK—
　　　　　Borough of Manhattan,
　　　　　First District.

Noticing a Case for Trial: Figure 3.　Notice of trial given by plaintiff.

1. Prepare the note of issue or notice of trial, as the case may be.

2. After the lawyer approves it, see that it is served on opposing counsel by the required date.

3. Be sure that receipt of service is endorsed on back or that the printed form provided is properly completed.

4. Conform the office copy.

5. File original in court.

6. *Make diary entry.* See DIARY.

7. Make appropriate entry in SUIT REGISTER.

8. The secretary to the counsel on whom notice is served notes on her copy the date and hour of service; *makes an appropriate diary entry;* enters it in suit register.

Novation. An agreement to replace an original party to a contract with a new party. The substitution must be agreed to by all parties. For example, *A* has a contract to repair certain machinery for *B*. *A*, finding himself overloaded with work gets *C* to agree to do the repairs for *B*. Once *B* has agreed to the substitution and released *A* from the contract, a novation has been completed and *A* is discharged from liability on the contract.

Numerical Filing System (applied to clients' files). In the law office, under the numerical system of filing, each file is given a number, and the folders are arranged in numerical sequence. This is an *indirect* filing system since it must be used in connection with a cross-index. The subject and number of each file are put on an index card, and the cards are arranged alphabetically. The advantages of the numerical system are the rapidity and accuracy of refiling and the maintenance of the auxiliary card index and the necessity of making two searches, one of the index and one of the files, whenever papers or folders are withdrawn.

How to use the numerical system in a law office. A method of numerical filing used successfully in law offices is to give a key number to a client instead of to a case. Each case for that client is given the client's key number plus an identifying number or letter. An explanation of how the secretary should set up and maintain a filing system of this kind follows:

1. Assign a key number to the client in numerical sequence. His general file has this number. Then assign an identifying *number* to each matter that is litigation and an identifying *letter* to each matter that is not litigation. For example, Client Brown & Rogers, Inc. has a file of general correspondence, a profit-sharing plan for employees, and a suit against Ellis & Lewis Co. You give the general file the number 85, the profit-sharing file the number 85-A, and the suit number 85-1. The next suit will be 85-2. (If the secretary prefers she might identify all files by number or letter instead of using numbers for the suits and letters for the non-suit files, but the number and letter system segregates the client's court matters from the non-litigation matters in the file cabinet and in the card index.)

2. Make index cards under each name that appears in connection with the matter. In some instances, for example estate matters, the client's name does not appear in the subject of the file; nevertheless a card should be made in the client's name.

Type on the card the title of the case, the number assigned to it, and the client's name if it does not appear in the title. In a matter of litigation the card under the defendant's name will read *defendant ads. plaintiff,* instead of plaintiff vs. defendant. If the matter is not a suit or claim, type on the card, in addition to the client's name, an identifying description of the subject matter.

For example:

> Brown & Rogers, Inc.
> Profit-sharing Plan

It is not necessary but the secretary might also make a card under the subject, which would read:

> Profit-sharing Plan
> Brown & Rogers, Inc.

Make index cards and cross-index cards freely, and be liberal in the information that you type on them. They are the key to the filing system and eventually justify the time consumed in typing them. Figures 1, 2, and 3 il-

Doe, John ads Thomas Green (Client)			
Document File	**Correspondence File**	**Printed Papers**	**Storage**
152-1	152-1		

Numerical Filing System: Figure 1. File index card.

Jones, John v. Smith, Allen				81-5
Correspondence	DOCUMENTS	PRINTED PAPERS	GENERAL SAFE	
81-5	81-5	Cabinet 2		
Cabinet #2 - Extra copies of Briefs, case on appeal, etc.				

Numerical Filing System: Figure 2. File index card—another form.

Brown, John A.	395-1
vs Acme Printing Company Blue Book Paper File Duplicates	

Numerical Filing System: **Figure 3.** File index card—another form.

lustrate three types of index cards. Figures 1 and 2 are printed especially for law offices.

3. File the index cards alphabetically. When there is more than one card under a client's name, place them in this order: general card, non-litigation cards arranged alphabetically according to subject, litigation cards arranged alphabetically according to opposing party. Suppose a client has a general file and five other files. The cards will be arranged as follows:

Brown & Rogers, Inc.	52
Brown & Rogers, Inc.—Arbitration	52-B
Brown & Rogers, Inc.—Legislation	52-C
Brown & Rogers, Inc.—	
Profit sharing Plan	52-A
Brown & Rogers, Inc. vs. Jones	52-2
Brown & Rogers, Inc. ads. Matthew	52-1

If the client's cases are numerous, the secretary might put a guide card between the litigation and non-litigation cards to facilitate locating the desired card.

4. File the folders in numerical sequence according to key number. If there is more than one file for a client, arrange those bearing identifying letters in alphabetical sequence; follow with those bearing identifying numbers in numerical sequence. Thus, in the cabinet, all files pertaining to one client are together; all of his non-litigation matters are together, and all suits and claims are together.

5. Keep a card showing the key number to be assigned to the next client in front of the index box.

6. When a client brings a case to the office, give the client a key number and assign the case an identifying letter or number. Reserve the key number, without identifying letters or numbers, for the client's general correspondence should it become desirable to have a file of that nature for him.

7. Reserve a key number for miscellaneous clients, who might want a letter written for them or have some small matter involving only one or two papers. These matters can be filed un-

der the same key number, but all necessary index cards should be made.

Assigning numbers according to type of case. When files are separated according to type of case, a group of numbers is set aside for each category. For example, cases involving litigation will be numbered 1 through 199; probate cases, 200 through 399, and so on. The client does not have a key number. A list of available numbers is kept for each category, and the number of a closed file is placed on the appropriate list and used again.

Another method of numbering when files are separated according to type of case is for each category to have a separate sequence of numbers. There might be, for example, a Claim 485 and a Probate 485. Different colored labels or folders should be used for each category.

Transferring numerical files. Apparently it is against the lawyer's conscience to destroy a file. Consequently all available space in the office is used for retired files, and the overflow is sent to a warehouse, or to the attic, or to any place where space is available. The procedure followed by many firms is to retain in the office as many closed files as space permits; and from time to time to send the oldest closed files to outside storage, replacing them in the office with more recently closed files. When there are retired files in the office, the active files might be kept in the top drawers of the filing cabinets and the retired files in the lower drawers. The retired files are referred to only occasionally, and by using the top drawers for active files, stooping and bending are eliminated. We use the words *closed* and *retired* interchangeably here.

Law files are not retired periodically but are closed when the matter is presumably completed. A file opened in 1976 might be completed and ready for retirement in 1977, whereas a case opened in 1975 might remain active until 1985, or longer.

Ideally the secretary should process a file for retirement as soon as she is informed that the matter has been completed, without permitting an accumulation. But this is a job that secretaries are inclined to postpone until there is a lull in the work. As soon as she is informed that the matter has been completed she should stamp the file jacket "Closed." Then when time permits, she can go through the filing cabinets and withdraw all closed cases and process them for retirement. Use old jackets for storage files.

Here are the steps in processing a file for retirement or storage.

1. Withdraw from the active index all cards relating to the closed case. Stamp the cards "Closed" with a small rubber stamp. If the secretary wishes she might also stamp the date on the card. Notice that the index card illustrated in Figure 1 has a column for this purpose, and the card shown in Figure 2 has a column that can be designated *storage*.

2. Withdraw from the active files all jackets or folders holding papers that relate to the completed case. The index card will indicate whether there are extra copies or printed papers that have been removed from the regular filing cabinet. (See Figure 2.) The documents in the safe will not be sent to storage. They will be returned to the client, or other appropriate disposition will be made of them.

3. Keep the index of closed files

separate from the index of active files.

4. File the index cards in the closed card index, alphabetically, just as they were filed in the current index.

5. File the closed files in the transfer cabinets numerically just as they were filed in the active files.

Terminal digit filing. The numerical sequence follows the terminal digits. This system is used often by insurance companies for filing dailies.

See ALPHABETICAL FILING, LAW OFFICE; FILING (IN A LAW OFFICE).

O

Objection to Title. A ground for questioning the validity of a TITLE to REAL PROPERTY. See CLOSING TITLE; *Subject clauses* under CONTRACT OF SALE; TITLE INSURANCE.

Offense. A crime or misdemeanor; a breach of the criminal laws.

Offer and Acceptance. See CONTRACTS, 1.

Officer of a Corporation. A person who has the power and the duty to manage and carry out the business of the CORPORATION. An officer is created by the CERTIFICATE OF INCORPORATION or BYLAWS of the corporation, and the officer is elected by the BOARD OF DIRECTORS.

Most states designate by statute what officers are required. These usually include a president, vice-president, a secretary, and a treasurer.

In the absence of express provisions in the bylaws, directors of a corporation have the inherent right to remove any officer for cause, even if he is employed for a definite term. In the absence of cause, however, directors cannot remove an officer elected for a specified term.

Official Congressional Directory. A listing of the names and addresses of officials associated with the Federal Government, including members of the press. The directory, published by the Government Printing Office, also contains biographical data on each member of Congress and maps of Congressional Districts. The directory is issued normally at least once during each session of Congress.

Official Register of the U.S. Government. A publication that appears approximately annually, listing, by agency, all persons holding administrative or supervisory positions in the legislative branches of the Federal Government and the District of Columbia. It gives the person's name, title, legal residence, and in most cases, his salary. The book is indexed by agency and by name.

Official Reports. The opinions of a court prepared by an appointed reporter and published under authorization of statute. All written U.S. Supreme Court decisions are printed in the official United States Reports. There is also statutory provision for official reporting and publication of judicial appellate decisions in all of the states.

The largest group of *unofficial* reports is the NATIONAL REPORTER SYSTEM. See also CITATION (TO LEGAL AUTHORITIES).

Official Seal. An authorized stamp by an officer other than a notary public, who has been empowered to authenticate an executed document. See also CORPORATE SEAL; NOTARY'S SEAL; CONFORMING DOCUMENTS.

Official Style. See LETTERS, STYLE AND SETUP.

Offset. A printing process in which the printing is done from a very thin zinc plate on which the letters are not raised above the surface of the plate. This plate is prepared by a photographic process. The matter to be reproduced is photographed and transferred to the plate. The impression on the plate never comes in direct contact with the paper, but it is inked and the inked impression is transferred to a "rubber blanket," which in turn comes in contact with the paper on which the book is printed. Offset printing is also known as *planographic* or *lithographic* printing.

Offset is used chiefly to print from typewritten copy without incurring the expense of setting type; to reprint a book the type of which has been destroyed and for which no electrotypes have been made; and for heavily illustrated books with a great many photographs and drawings.

Olograph. See WILL, Holograph.

Omnibus. A term applied to that which contains two or more independent matters. The term is applied, for example, to a legislative bill that relates to two or more subjects.

Open-end Mortgage. See FORMS OF MORTGAGES.

Open Policy. An insurance agreement where the value of the insured property is not fixed, but is left to be definitely determined after the loss occurs. The term is also used to refer to a "floating" insurance agreement which covers all goods of the assured as and when acquired. See also VALUED POLICY.

Opening Statement of Counsel. Outline of anticipated proof.

Open Shop. An arrangement whereby the employer is free to hire whomever he chooses, but all employees must join the union within a specified period. All employees must remain in good standing of the union where such an agreement exists. See CLOSED SHOP.

Opinion Letters. Formal correspondence giving a professional opinion to a client on some legal question. Each law firm has its own method of setting them up, usually in the style that is used for ordinary letters. These letters are generally signed manually with the firm name, because they represent advice from the firm, not merely from the lawyer who dictated the letter. Usually the dictator's initials do not show on the original but do show on the office copies.

See also OPINION OF TITLE.

Opinion of Title. An attorney's written summation of his opinion as to the validity of TITLE to REAL PROPERTY. When the attorney receives the ABSTRACT OF TITLE, he examines it and prepares his *opinion* as to the legal strength of the title. If he finds any difficulty, such as a deed that was improperly acknowledged, or a discrepancy in the description of the property, he states the defects in his opinion. They constitute *clouds* upon the seller's title and must be removed by affidavits, quitclaim deeds, or court procedure to quiet title. The attorney also sets forth in his opinion any LIENS and MORTGAGES on the property, because the title is subject to them. Usually the CONTRACT OF SALE mentions the liens and mortgages and provides for their disposition.

The lawyer dictates the opinion of title, which is usually in the form of a letter. If there are no defects in the title, the secretary might be asked to draft a routine opinion of title letter. Below is a sample of such a letter.

July 21, 19 . .

Mr. and Mrs. John Duane
R. R. #1
Niles, Michigan 49120

Dear Mr. and Mrs. Duane:

We have examined the abstract of title continued by the Benton Harbor Abstract and Title Company of Benton Harbor, Michigan to date of June 15, 19 . . at 8:00 A.M., for the following described premises:

The west three (3) rods of Lots Thirty (30) and Thirty-one (31), Jacob Beeson's Addition to Niles, Berrien County, Michigan, according to the recorded plat thereof.

From such examination, we find the title thereto to be in Phyllis Franz, subject to the following:

1. There are ancient and minor errors in this title, but we do not consider any of them sufficiently important to affect the merchantability of the title.

2. There are no liens or encumbrances against said premises.

3. The abstract shows no unpaid taxes for 19 . . and prior years. The summer taxes for 19 . . will be due July 1. 19 . . and may be checked with the City Treasurer, as may also special assessments.

It is therefore our opinion that a merchantable title exists in said above named title holder, subject to the exceptions above noted. This opinion is based upon the abstract continued as aforesaid, and does not cover rights of persons in possession, line fences, location of buildings, or any other matter or thing not contained in said abstract.

Respectfully submitted,

JC:F

Option. An agreement, usually in consideration for the payment of a certain sum of money by the offeree, to hold an offer open for a definite period of time. The offer ceases to be an offer and becomes a contract of option; it cannot be withdrawn until the option period expires. Although an option is generally based upon a consideration, a few states require no consideration if the contract is in writing. Others recognize an option under seal as binding because a seal, at COMMON LAW, indicates consideration. The consideration for an option is not returnable to the optionee if he fails to take up the option; it is, however, usually applied to the purchase price if the offer is accepted.

Oral Argument. The spoken presentation by counsel of his client's case before an APPELLATE COURT. In some cases the lawyer feels that his BRIEF is sufficient and does not choose to argue the case up on APPEAL. If he does want to appear before the appellate court, he makes application for oral argument at the same time the brief is filed. A copy of the application is served on opposing counsel in the same manner that the brief is served.

Ordinance. A law or statute. The word is commonly used to apply to enactments of a municipality.

Original Jurisdiction. An initial authority on the part of a judicial tribunal to hear a particular cause of action in order to render a decision. Some courts have original jurisdiction, whereas others have appellate jurisdiction. See APPELLATE COURT. Suits are commenced and tried first in courts of original jurisdiction, which are usually the lower courts. After a case has been decided in a court of original jurisdiction, it may be brought to a higher court having appellate jurisdiction for another decision. Appellate courts have original jurisdiction over some matters. See also JURISDICTION; COURTS OF SPECIAL JURISDICTION; AMERICAN COURT SYSTEM; INFERIOR COURTS; SUPERIOR COURTS.

Out File Control. A regulation process that assures a systematic check and return of material taken from office files. To control folders removed from the files, the secretary uses guides that are the same height as the file folders but of different-colored stock, with the word *out* printed on the tab. The *out* guide provides space on which to make an entry of the date, the material taken, who has it, and date it should be returned. The secretary should place the guide in the files where the removed material was located.

A secretary in a private office does not put an *out* guide in her file every time she withdraws material for the lawyer. She uses the guide under these circumstances: (1) Someone outside her immediate office wants the material. (2) The lawyer expects to take the material out of the office, say, when he goes on a trip. (3) She expects her employer to keep the material a week or so, say, to prepare a BRIEF.

When a paper is removed from a folder, the secretary makes a note of the removal and inserts it in the folder. Many law offices have a rule (and it is a good one) that no one may remove a paper from a folder except the person responsible for the filing.

Ozalid. A duplicating process frequently used in law offices for making copies of documents. (A print made by this process is frequently called an "ozalid.") The process makes prints the same size as the original document by passing light through the item to be copied onto sensitized paper. The Ozalid is fixed in ammonia fumes so that it does not become wet; it also maintains its original dimensions. See also MICROFILMING.

P

Page Numbers. The numbers that designate the sequence of arrangement of legal documents or court papers. The preferable method of numbering the pages of legal documents and papers is to place the numbers one-half inch from the bottom of the page, in the center of the line. The number should be preceded and followed by a hyphen, thus: -4-. If the first page is not numbered, the numbering begins with -2-. Be exact in placing the number; when the pages are collated the numbers should overlie one another.

Page Proof. When the GALLEY PROOF is returned to the printer, with corrections indicated by the publisher and the author, and with the positions of all illustrations indicated, the printer makes the corrections, places the illustrations in the the proper places, and breaks the type up into pages, just as it will appear in the final book. He then pulls a proof of these pages, and that proof is known as *page proof.*

Pain and Suffering. A result of an injury, for which a person may be compensated when suing for DAMAGES.

Paralegals. The Paralegal (or Legal Assistant) assists the attorney in those procedural matters that do not fall within the exclusive, deliberative province of the attorney. Specific duties will vary depending on the lawyer's preference, but the following functions are within the general scope of the Paralegal's responsibilities:

- Searching and checking public records
- Attending departmental meetings
- Developing research data in specific subject areas assigned by the Lawyer
- Conducting pre-interviews with clients
- Preparing probate inventory
- Assisting with inheritance, federal and state tax returns
- Contacting clients for information relative to their case
- Indexing documents
- Preparing legal digests

Paralegal's may also be assigned to those areas of law that involve litigation, estate administration, corporate law, and real estate law.

Additional information can be secured by writing to:

American Paralegal Association
P.O. Box 35233
Los Angeles, California 90035

Parcel Post (fourth-class mail). Packages to be mailed that weigh sixteen ounces or more. See POSTAL SERVICE.

Parent Corporation. See SUBSIDIARY CORPORATION.

Parentheses and Brackets. Parentheses are used to mark off an interjected explanatory or qualifying remark. Brackets are used to enclose extraneous and incidental matter. The secretary should follow these rules:

(1) *Brackets.* If the typewriter has a bracket key, use brackets to enclose comments or explanations in quoted material, to rectify mistakes, and to enclose parentheses within parentheses; otherwise, use parentheses for these purposes. If necessary, brackets can be made by using the virgule and dash.

2. *Explanatory expressions.* Use parentheses to enclose parenthetical or explanatory expressions outside the general structure of the sentence. Parentheses indicate a stronger separation than do commas or dashes.

The place at which an incorporators' meeting (sometimes called the first meeting of the stockholders) is to be held is determined by statute in most states.

(3) *Figures.* Enclose a figure in parentheses when it follows an amount that has been written out in words, and when the American equivalent of foreign currency is given.

Under the will he received £100,000 ($280,000).
Seven thousand five hundred (7,500) dollars.
Seven thousand five hundred dollars ($7,500).

NOTE: If the figure is written before the word "dollars," do not use the dollar sign; if the figure is written after the word "dollars," use the dollar sign. This rule also applies to the percent sign.

(4) *Questions and answers.* In testimony (question and answer material) use parentheses to enclose matter describing an action and, also, to indicate a person who has not previously taken part in the questions and answers.

Q. (By M. Smith) Will you identify this handkerchief? (handing the witness a handkerchief)

(5) *Enumerations.* Enclose in parentheses letters or numbers if enumerations run into the text.

Stock may be divided broadly into two kinds: (1) common stock and (2) preferred stock.

(6) *Single (closing) parentheses.* Parentheses are usually used in pairs, but a single closing parenthesis may be used instead of a period to follow a letter or small roman numeral in outlines and in lettering and numbering paragraphs.

(7) *Punctuation in parentheses.* Commas, periods, and similar punctuation marks belong within the parentheses if they belong to the parenthetical clause or phrase. They are outside the parentheses if they belong to the words of the rest of the sentence.

The boy ran as if a ghost (and, indeed, he may have been right) were following him.

He reported the action at once. (He has a strong civic sense of responsibility.)

Parol Evidence Rule. A regulation that makes a written agreement, when finally executed, supersede all prior negotiations between the parties Evidence of conversations or negotiations before or at the time of EXECUTION of the instrument may not be admitted to vary its terms. Courts wish to consider a written CONTRACT as they find it and pass on its validity in that form. The general rule protects against FRAUD, PERJURY, infirmity of memory, and death of witnesses.

Parole. The release of a convict from imprisonment on certain conditions to be observed by him, with his sentence suspended during the time of his liberty.

Partial Release Clause. A clause in a MORTGAGE agreement that permits the mortgagor to sell part of his land. See *Partial release clause,* MORTGAGE STATEMENT AND CLAUSES.

Particular Average Loss. A property loss borne entirely by the party suffering it. A particular average loss is distinguished from a GENERAL AVERAGE LOSS in that in the latter there is a right of contribution from others, so that the party does not bear the loss alone. Unlike the general average loss, the particular average loss is not voluntary and is not incurred for the common benefit; it is the result of accident or NEGLIGENCE. Examples of particular average loss are damage to a ship by fire, storm, or collision.

Parties to a Deed. The parties to a deed are the GRANTOR, who conveys an interest in property, and the GRANTEE, to whom the conveyance is made.

Parties to a Foreclosure Action. Those persons involved in the legal proceedings against property securing a debt, brought upon DEFAULT, to cut off the mortgagor's equitable right to redeem the property. The persons involved are known as:

Parties plaintiff. The owner of the mortgage—the mortgagee, or his beneficiary or assignee—is the plaintiff in a foreclosure action. The suit must be brought in the name of the actual owner of the mortgage. For example, if the morgage is held by Richard Barth as Trustee for Thomas Jones, the action is brought by *Richard Barth, Trustee for Thomas Jones,* not by Richard Barth. If the mortgage is owned jointly, say by husband and wife, the action is brought in the name of both owners.

Parties defendant. Every person who has any interest in the property covered by a mortgage is made a party defendant to the foreclosure action. These might include the mortgagor; the mortgagor's heirs, devisees, or legatees; wife of the mortgagor; *cestui que trustent* (see LATIN TERMS, *cestui que trust*); persons in possession as tenants or occupants; the People of the State; and others.

See also FICTITIOUS NAMES.

Parties to a Mortgage. The parties to a conventional MORTGAGE are the *mortgagor,* who is the debtor or borrower, and the *mortgagee,* who is the lender. The mortgagor owns the property that is being mortgaged and gives a mortgage to the mortgagee, usually in return for a loan; he is frequently referred to in the instrument as the party of the first part. The mortgagee is frequently referred to as the party of the second part.

The parties to a DEED OF TRUST are the mortgagor, party of the first part, and the trustee, party of the second part. Some states, Colorado for example, have designated officials, known as public trustees, to whom the estate is conveyed under a deed of trust.

Designation of the parties. Extreme care should be exercised to see that the name of the mortgagor appears exactly as it appears in the instrument under which he claims title to the land; otherwise, the mortgagee's title might be defective if it becomes necessary for him to foreclose. The mortgagor's name should be exactly the same in the body of the mortgage, in the signature, and in the acknowledgment. If the mortgage is a *purchase money mortgage* (see MORTGAGE), the names of both parties should be given precisely as they appear in the deed from the mortgagee to the mortgagor.

The requirements relative to the GRANTOR and the GRANTEE in a DEED apply generally to the mortgagor and mortgagee.

Parties to an Action. The principals involved in a particular lawsuit or litigation. These may be described as follows:

Party bringing a lawsuit. The party who brings a lawsuit—the one who has a cause of action—is the *plaintiff.* He is the one who complains. (See also COMPLAINT.) In Alabama, Mississippi, Rhode Island, Tennesssee, and Virginia, the party bringing the action is called the *complaintant* when the suit is an action in equity. In Massachusetts, the practice is not uniform; it varies with the court and with local custom. In all the other states, the party who brings an action in equity is no longer called the complaintant, but is known as the plaintiff, just as in actions at law.

Party defending a lawsuit. The party against whom suit is brought is the *defendant.* In Alabama and Rhode Island, the person defending an equity action is known as the *respondent.* In Massachusetts and Virginia, he is referred to as either defendant or respondent. In all other states, the party defending an equity action is no longer called the respondent but is referred to as the defendant, just as in actions at law.

Parties to a cross action. In some cases, defendant's interests cannot be defended properly by answering the plaintiff's complaint or by a counterclaim. For example, an airline and an airplane manufacturer were codefendants in a death action. The complaint alleged that the plane was improperly designed and was not safe for its intended use. The airline claimed that if defective and hazardous conditions existed in the plane, they were caused by the failure of the airplane manufacturer to keep his guarantee that the plane would be free from defect in design.[1]

Under these circumstances, in almost all states the defendant (airline here) files a cross-complaint and is called the *defendant and cross-complainant,* or *cross-claimant,* or *cross-plaintiff,* or *cross-petitioner,* the designation varying with the state. The party against whom a cross-complaint is brought (airplane manufacturer here) is the *cross-defendant.* The plaintiff or a co-defendant in the initial action may be the cross-defendant and is then referred to as the *plaintiff and cross-defendant,* and *defendant and cross-defendant,* respectively. A party who was not a party to the original action may be brought into the case, also, as a cross-defendant.

Party intervening. A lawsuit sometimes affects adversely a third party who is not a party to the litigation. If the Court permits, that person may become a party to the action by filing a *complaint in intervention,* and is called an *intervenor,* or in some states, the third-party plaintiff. For example, while negotiations for a contract were in progress, the employee who was negotiating the contract as agent for his employer suddenly quit the employer

---

[1] Blue et al. v. United Air Lines, Inc., et. al., 98 N.Y.S. (2d) 272.

and closed the contract in his own behalf. The former employee later sued to enforce the contract. His former employer claimed that the former employee was his agent, and was permitted to intervene to assert his interest in the contract. He became a party to the actions as an *intervenor*.[2]

Amicus curiae. An *amicus curiae* (Latin for "friend of the court") is not strictly speaking a party to the lawsuit. He is a person who has no inherent right to appear in the suit but is allowed to participate to protect his own interests. Leave to file a brief as *amicus curiae* is frequently granted to a lawyer when he has another case that will be affected by the decision of the Court in the pending case. An *amicus curiae* might also volunteer information for the benefit of the judge. For example, in adoption proceedings the guardian of a child might seek permission to appear as *amicus* for the purpose of presenting evidence about which the Court should be informed and which might lead the Court to refuse the order of adoption.

Who may be parties to a lawsuit. A party to a lawsuit may be an individual, a partnership, a corporation, or an association.

Minors and incompetents. An individual ordinarily sues on his own behalf, but minors (frequently referred to as infants) and incompetents (persons of unsound mind or habitual drunkards) are legally incapable of bringing a legal action. If the minor or incompetent has a legally appointed guardian, the suit is often brought by him. Otherwise, depending upon the state, a suit is brought on behalf of a minor or incompetent by his "next friend," or by a guardian *ad litem* appointed by the Court for the special purpose of the litigation. The fact that the plaintiff sues by his guardian or next friend is indicated in the caption of the case and is alleged in the pleadings. If a minor or an incompetent is defendant in a suit, he answers by a guardian *ad litem* or next friend. In Louisiana a minor is represented by a *Tutor,* and a mentally incompetent person, by a *Curator.*

The expressions commonly used follow:

JAMES JONES, a minor, suing by his father and next friend, TOM JONES

JOHN JONES, guardian ad litem of JAMES JONES, an incompetent

MARY ANN JONES by her next friend, GEORGE G. JONES

JOHN BROWN by ROBERT BROWN, guardian by appointment of Orphans' Court of Baltimore City

Executors, administrators, trustees. Often a plaintiff has a cause of action, not for a wrong against him in his individual capacity, but for a wrong against him in his representative capacity as executor, administrator, or trustee. The action is then brought by the plaintiff in that capacity. The capacity in which the action is brought is indicated in the caption and is stated in the introductory sentence of the pleadings. An executor (executrix, if a woman) sues "as executor of the last will and testament of Mary Jones, deceased." An administrator (administratrix, if a woman) sues "as trustee under will of Mary Jones," or "as trustee under trust created by Mary Jones." Actions are also brought against, and defended by, executors, administrators, and trustees of estates and trusts.

Husband and wife. In some actions if a married person sues, the spouse joins

---

[2]Patterson v. Pollock, et al., 84 N.E. (2d) 606.

in the complaint. The caption indicates, and the first paragraph of the pleading declares, the relationship. If the husband has the cause of action, the suit is brought by Thomas W. Jones and Mary R. Jones, his wife; if the wife has the cause of action, the suit is brought by Mary R. Jones and Thomas W. Jones, her husband. The same practice is followed when a married person is sued. In the CAPTION of all PLEADINGS, except the complaint, and in the endorsements on the back of a court paper (see LEGAL BACK), the Latin phrase *et uxor,* or *et ux.,* may be substituted for "and Mary R. Jones, his wife"; *et vir* may be substituted for "and Thomas W. Jones, her husband."

Partnerships. When a party to an action is a partnership, that fact is indicated in the caption and declared in the first paragraph of the pleading.

Expressions similar to the following are used in the caption.

JOHN JONES and HENRY A. BROWN, doing business as a partnership under the name of JONES AND BROWN.

JOHN JONES and RICHARD ROE d/b/a JONES & ROE, a partnership

See PARTIES TO AN APPEAL.

Parties to an Appeal. The litigants in a legal action when the decision of a lower court is brought to a higher court for review. In almost all of the states the party appealing is referred to as the *appellant,* and the party opposing the APPEAL is referred to as the *appellee* or the *respondent.* When the defendant in the lower case is the appellant the title of the case is reversed in the majority of the states. Thus, *John Smith v. Alfred Jones* becomes *Alfred Jones v. John Smith.* But this is not the practice in all of the states. Eight methods of designating parties on appeal in the

CAPTION are shown on page 324. Table I, following them, lists the states and indicates the style followed in each state, assuming that the title of the case in the lower court was *John Jones v. Albert Smith* and the defendant brings the appeal to the highest state court. In cases where review is by petition for a WRIT, the party appealing is designated as the petitioner, and the other party as the *respondent.*

Although the designation of the parties changes in the title of the case, the briefs sometime refer to the parties by their designation in the lower court. (Some rules require this designation.) Or the BRIEF might refer to a party by the lower court designation on one page and by the APPELLATE COURT designation on the other. The change in designation is very confusing, and the lawyer might inadvertently refer to the defendant-appellant when he means plaintiff-appellant, or to the plaintiff when he means plaintiff-in-error. Before the lawyer commences to dictate a brief to his secretary, she should fix firmly in her mind the designation of the parties in both the trial and appellate courts so that she can observe any error in designation of parties.

Partnership. A business owned by two or more persons, each of whom is legally responsible for the total liabilities of the business, unless this responsibility is limited, as in a LIMITED PARTNERSHIP.

Partnerships are governed by fairly uniform laws, which are codified in many states by the Uniform Partnership Law. A partnership may carry on business in any state without paying greater taxes than residents of the state pay.

STYLES OF DESIGNATION OF PARTIES ON APPEAL BY DEFENDANT TO HIGHEST STATE COURT WHEN TITLE OF CASE IN LOWER COURT WAS

John Jones, Plaintiff vs. Albert Smith, Defendant

Style 1 (Names reversed)
Albert Smith,
      Appellant,
  vs.
John Jones,
      Appellee.

Style 5 (Names not reversed)
John Jones,
      Appellee,
  vs.
Albert Smith,
      Appellant.

Style 2 (Names not reversed)
John Jones,
      Plaintiff and Respondent,
  vs.
Albert Smith,
      Defendant and Appellant.

Style 6 (Names not reversed)
John Jones,
      Respondent,
  vs.
Albert Smith,
      Appellant.

Style 3 (Names not reversed)
John Jones,
      Plaintiff and Appellee,

Albert Smith,
      Defendant and Appellant.

Style 7 (Names reversed)
Albert Smith,
      Appellant and Defendant,
  vs.
John Jones,
      Respondent and Plaintiff.

Style 4 (Names reversed)
Albert Smith,
      Plaintiff-in-Error,
  vs.
John Jones,
      Defendant-in-Error.

Style 8 (Names reversed)
Albert Smith,
      Defendant Below, Appellant,
  vs.
John Jones,
      Plaintiff Below, Appellee.

TABLE I

DESIGNATION OF PARTIES ON APPEAL TO HIGHEST STATE COURT

State	Designation	State	Designation
Alabama	Style 1	Kentucky	Style 1
Alaska	Style 1	Louisiana	Style 3
Arizona	Style 1	Maine	Style 5
Arkansas	Style 1	Maryland	Style 1
California	Style 2	Massachusetts[2]	
Colorado	Style 4	Michigan	Style 3
Connecticut	Style 3	Minnesota	Style 2
Delaware	Style 8	Mississippi	Style 1
Florida	Style 1	Missouri	Style 6
Georgia	Style 4	Montana	Style 2
Hawaii	Style 1	Nebraska	Style 3
Idaho	Style 2	Nevada	Style 7
Illinois	Style 3	New Hampshire[1]	
Indiana	Style 1	New Jersey	Style 2
Iowa	Style 1	New Mexico	Style 3
Kansas	Style 5	New York	Style 2

State	Designation	State	Designation
North Carolina[2]		Utah	Style 2
North Dakota	Style 2	Vermont[1]	
Ohio	Style 3	Virginia	Style 1
Oklahoma	Style 4	Washington	Style 6
Oregon	Style 6	West Virginia	Style 1
Pennsylvania	Style 5		(Equity)
Rhode Island[1]			Style 4
South Carolina	Style 2		(Law)
South Dakota	Style 6	Wisconsin	Style 7
Tennessee	Style 1	Wyoming	Style 2
Texas	Style 1[3]		

[1]Title in both trial court and appellate court: John Jones vs. Albert Smith. There is no designation.
[2]Not reversed. Designation the same as in the trial court.
[3]Except that in the Supreme Court the person seeking relief is called the "Petitioner" and the other party is the "Respondent."

Each partner of a general partnership is fully liable personally for all partnership debts regardless of the amount of his investment. All types of capital produced or acquired by the partnership become partnership property. Real estate is generally acquired in the individual names of the partners or in the name of one partner who holds the property in trust for the partnership.

In absence of a specific contract, partners share profits and losses equally. It is customary, however, to provide in the partnership agreement that profits and losses shall be distributed pro rata according to the amount of capital contributed by each, or in any other ratio to which they agree. Partners have no right to salaries unless they are agreed upon, even though one partner may devote all of his time to the business and another may devote little or none. The agreement may provide for the division of profits after allowing each of the partners an agreed-upon salary.

Partnerships are dissolved without violation of the partnership agreement by (1) withdrawal of one of the members under some circumstances; (2) operation of law through death or bankruptcy of one of the partners or a change in the law that makes the partnership's business illegal; (3) court decree granted because of incapacity or insanity of one of the partners, gross misconduct, or neglect or breach of duty. See also JOINT ADVENTURE (VENTURE).

Party Sheet. A special record of the dates of service on, and appearance by, each defendant in a FORECLOSURE action. (This record is not to be confused with the party sheet of paper for the record, with the following heading:

PARTY SHEET
Action No.... Plaintiffs ... Premises ... (brief description) ... Office No....

Rule the sheet into vertical columns, with the following columnar headings:

Defendants (specify legal status, such as infant, CORPORATION, trustee)

Interest in premises (owner, tenant, etc.)

Address where served

When served

How served

By whom served

Affidavit of service made before . . . (*notary's name*)

Last day to answer

Appeared by . . . *(name of defendant's attorney)*

Address and telephone number of attorney

Date appearance entered

Remarks

A glance at the party sheet will tell the lawyer the status of service and appearance of each defendant.

Par Value Stock. Stock with face or nominal value. There is no necessary relation between the par value and the real value of the stock. The par value is an amount predetermined by the corporation and remains the same regardless of how many times the share of stock changes hands or how much is paid for it. The real or actual value of stock is the price which it can command in the market. Par value is a fixed amount. Emphasis is placed on the distinction because too often the concepts of par value and actual value are confused. See NO-PAR STOCK.

Patent. An exclusive right granted by the Federal Government for a fixed period of time, to make, use, and sell an invention. For example, a person who perfects a new machine, process, or material, or any new and useful improvement of them, or who invents or discovers and reproduces a distinct and new variety of plant, may make application to the government for a patent for it. The person to whom a patent is granted is called the *patentee.* Patent rights are issued in the form of letters and run to the patentee, his heirs and assigns, generally for a period of 17 years. A *design patent,* which is an ornamental design to be placed upon an article of manufacture, runs for three and one-half, seven, or fourteen years, according to the application made by the patentee. A patent is not renewable. Anyone using a patented product without the owner's consent may be compelled to pay damages.

How to apply for a patent. When a client wishes to obtain a patent, he brings or sends, the details of his invention or discovery to the lawyer in the form of a disclosure. The disclosure may be a picture, a sketch, or a working model. An idea is not patentable; only the device for carrying out an idea can be patented.

The Patent Office will not respond to inquiries about the novelty of an alleged invention, so the patent lawyer must make a *search* to learn what patent or patents have already been issued on that idea. The copies of other patents issued on an idea are called *prior art,* and they may be inspected at the Patent Office. The patent lawyer studies the art prior to preparing the application. Copies of patents may be obtained from the Patent Office for 25 cents; copies of trademarks, for 10 cents.

There are various divisions in the United States Patent Office, each of which handles applications for certain types of patents. The patent lawyer sends the application to the Commissioner of Patents, who sends it to the appropriate division; the next step will be an *official action.* The official action may be an *allowance,* which means that the Patent Office deems the application ready to issue into a patent. In almost every case, however, the official action is a response by the Patent Office in which the Patent Office Examiner points out the items in the application he considers objectionable for one reason or another. Some of the divisions in the Patent Office are so overloaded with applications that it may take two years or more to get an official action. After receipt of the official action, the attorney has six months in which to file an amendment. In the amendment the lawyer takes each point objected to by the examiner and either deletes it from the application or argues for it. There is no definite time by which the Patent Office responds to the amendment, the time depending upon the volume of work in the particular division. If the first amendment does not make the application ready for allowance, then there must be another amendment and so on until the examiner states that the next amendment must be final. The average number of amendments is three or four. If the patent lawyer does not think the examiner has a clear view of the whole idea, he may go to Washington and interview the examiner. Sometimes this facilitates the allowance.

Parts of the application. The application consists of:

1. *Specification.* This is a written description of the invention or discovery and the manner and process of making it.

2. *Claims.* These are the assertions made for the invention. Each individual part of the invention is written up as a claim. A design patent has only one claim, but other patents may have many claims. These claims are numbered 1, 2, 3 and so on. A patent application might begin with 40 claims and have only 15 when it is finally allowed. Some claims will be "stricken" because the claim has been covered by a prior invention.

3. *Drawings of the invention.*

4. *Petition.* This gives the name, residence, and post office address of the inventor and the title of the invention sought to be patented.

5. *Oath or affirmation.* The applicant swears or affirms that he believes himself to be the first inventor or discoverer of the invention sought to be patented.

6. *Power of attorney.* The applicant usually gives his lawyer POWER OF ATTORNEY to transact all business in the Patent Office connected with the patent.

What the secretary does. 1. The lawyer will dictate the specification and claims. The secretary makes an original, a copy for each inventor, and a file copy on plain legal-size paper.

2. The oath, power of attorney, and petition are printed forms that can be easily filled in. They are frequently combined in one document. Make an original and the same number of copies as were made of the specification and claims.

3. The applications must be signed and verified before a notary public by the inventor, or inventors if there is more than one. When there is more than one inventor, there must be a separate verification for each if the in-

ventors do not sign the application at the same time, or if they are at different locations when signing.

4. Have photoprints made of the drawings of the invention, send one copy to the inventor (or a copy to each inventor) and keep one for the files. The originals made by a draftsman accompany the application to the Patent Office for filing.

5. The Patent Office issues rules about how the papers are arranged, the backing, and the like.

6. As soon as the application is typed and assembled, the secretary sends it to the applicant for signature and verification. If there is more than one inventor, the application will have to be sent to each in turn for his signature and verification.

7. The secretary makes diary or calendar entries with reference to any action that must be taken at a future date. Although an application for a patent is not a legal action, it is advisable to keep a progress record sheet (See SUIT REGISTER). The sheet can be kept in the file folder. If litigation develops from the application, the same records are kept as in any litigated matter.

Assignment of application for patent. Frequently an inventor agrees to assign his patent rights before he applies for the patent. When he does, he makes an *assignment of application* simultaneously with his application. A printed form is usually used. The secretary makes an original, a copy for each applicant, and a copy for the office file. She sends the original to the inventor (or inventors) for signature and acknowledgment before a NOTARY PUBLIC. When the original has been executed by each inventor, forward it to the Patent Office to be recorded. The Patent Office will return the assignment after it has been recorded. It is forwarded to the assignee.

Covering letters that the secretary writes. Whenever the lawyer sends papers to the client or to the Patent Office the secretary can usually write the covering letters without dictation. Here are three sample letters.

Letter forwarding application to Patent Office.

The Commissioner of Patents
United States Patent Office
Washington, D.C. 20013
Sir:

We are enclosing, for filing, the application of . . . . (inventor or inventors) . . . . for Letters Patent covering an improvement in . . . . . (title) . . . . ., Case . . . . . We are also enclosing our check for $. . . . . to cover the first government fee.

Very truly yours,

Letter forwarding assignment to Patent Office for recording.

The Commissioner of Patents
United States Patent Office
Washington, D.C.
Sir:

We enclose for recording assignment of . . . . . (patentee or patentees) . . . . transfering unto . . . . (assignee) . . . . ., a (an) . . . . (name of state) . . . . corporation, all right title and interest in and to his (their) application for . . (title) . . ., Case . . . ., executed . . . . and transmitted for filing of even date herewith.

Our check for $3.00 to cover the recording fee is also enclosed.

Very truly yours,

Letter sending issued patent to patentee.

Dear Mr. . . . .:

We are enclosing original United States Letters Patent No. . . . ., issued to you on . . . (date) . . ., covering an improvement in . . . . (title) . . . . .

Please acknowledge receipt of the patent.

Yours very truly,

Patent Infringement. The act of making, using, or selling, without authority, any patented invention within the United States, while the PATENT is in effect. The legal remedy for patent infringement is INJUNCTION and DAMAGES. A patent is said to be infringed when "the accused device does the same work in substantially the same way and accomplishes the same result."

Pecuniary. Monetary; relating to money; financial; consisting of money or that which can be valued in money.

Perils of the Sea. Most commonly the risk of damage to a ship or its cargo from unexpectedly violent action of wind and waves, but it also refers to the danger from icebergs, rocks, shoals and (in former times) pirates. Ocean marine insurance usually covers perils of the sea.

Periodicals, Bulletins, etc., Filing of. The keeping in systematic fashion of reading material that is of interest to the lawyer. Magazines, bulletins, law journals are generally filed alphabetically according to subject. The filing cabinet used for them need not be fireproof, and a twenty-five division alphabetical guide is usually sufficient. This material often consists of government bulletins, advertisements, catalogues, announcements of changes in law firms, announcements from law schools, any other material of this nature that the lawyer wishes to keep. Periodically the secretary should go through the file and discard material that is out of date.

Perjury. The act of deliberately making a false statement under oath.

Punishment for perjury, by fine or imprisonment, is provided for by Federal and state statutes.

Willful inducement of another to commit perjury is called *subornation of perjury* and is punishable by law.

Personal File. In the law office, the personal file is a combination name and subject file, and the alphabetical system of filing is used for it. (See ALPHABETICAL FILING, LAW OFFICE.) The file relates to matters of direct personal concern to the lawyer and is separate from those matters that relate to his clients and the legal work of the office. A twenty-five division alphabetical guide is probably sufficient; no cross-index is needed. To set up this file the secretary can use the following guide:

Make a folder for each letter of the alphabet. File the correspondence under the first letter of the correspondent's last name, according to date. Thus, correspondence with Mr. Moss and with Mr. Matthews will be in the same folder. If the lawyer has prolific correspondence with a certain person, make a separate folder for that correspondent. Also make a separate folder for each separate business matter and outside activity. Thus, if the lawyer is on the Grievance Committee of the American Bar Association, there will be a folder labeled, "American Bar Association—Grievance Committee," and the folder will be filed under the letter *A*. Should the material for any particular subject become voluminous withdraw it from the alphabetical file and file it under a guide of its own.

Close these files periodically by moving them to another drawer in the office where they will be available for reference if necessary. The correspondence folders can probably be transferred intact, or several letters of the alphabet combined in one folder to save space. However, it will probably be necessary to go through the subject folders, such as the "American Bar Association—Grievance Committee" folder, and extract material that is pertinent to the forthcoming year. Transfer the closed files from the office to storage when they are several years old, to make room in the office for the more recent personal files.

See also GENERAL CORRESPONDENCE FILE.

Personal Impressions. The legal secretary is in constant contact with professional people and clients whose first impressions are often formed when greeted by the secretary of the lawyer they plan to retain. Her standards of dress must be appropriate and, while not necessarily costly, they should be tasteful.

Personal Notation. See ENVELOPES.

Personal Property. A right or interest, protected by law, in something that is not land or anything permanently attached to land (see REAL PROPERTY). Personal property is movable. It may be tangibles (also called *chattels*), such as money, gold, merchandise, or any movable object susceptible to physical possession. It may be intangibles, such as contracts, stocks, and the like (see CHOSE IN ACTION). Personal property may be an interest in land: a 99-year lease is personal property. Products of the soil become personal property when severed from the land: trees and crops that are sold while attached to the land

constitute real property, but when severed from the land they constitute personal property.

Title to personal property may be acquired by the following methods: (1) Appropriation or original possession: although almost all property today belongs to someone, there are still some kinds of property, such as wild game and fish, that may be appropriated. (2) Discovery: the finder of lost property acquires a title that is good against everyone except the rightful owner. (e) Creation: a person is entitled to that which he produces by his physical or mental labor, unless the product is produced during the course of his employment or under some other contract; then it belongs to his employer or the party for whom he is contracted to create the property. (4) Gift. (5) Sale or exchange. (6) Will. (7) Operation of law: when a person dies without making a will, his property passes by operation of law to certain relatives. Or, if a person becomes bankrupt, his property, with certain exceptions, passes to a trustee for the benefit of creditors. A person's property may also be taken from him by legal process (see EXECUTION).

Personal Service. See SERVICE OF SUMMONS.

Petition. A written plea brought before a court so that it may redress some wrong or grant some favor. In some states, the initial pleading is called a "petition" instead of a COMPLAINT.

Petition in bankruptcy. BANKRUPTCY proceedings are commenced by the filling of a petition, asking that the court declare some person a bankrupt. In *voluntary bankruptcy* the petitioner asks that he himself be adjudged a bankrupt. In *involuntary bankruptcy* the petitioner requests that some person other than the petitioner or petitioners be adjudged a bankrupt.

Petitory Action. A proceeding in which a party seeks to establish his title to land or other property in dispute. A petitory action is distinguished from a *possessory* action where the right to the possession is the point in issue. The term is used in ADMIRALTY to describe an action to determine title to a ship.

Petty Cash Fund. An amount of cash on hand used for disbursements that are too small to justify the use of checks. The purpose of the fund is to expedite the payment of any incidental expenses that may arise, such as RECORDING FEES and collect messages. The size of the fund will vary according to the demands made upon it, but it should be large enough to last about a month. The secretary should keep the money in a safe place because she is usually responsible for it. She must never mix this money with her own funds; never make change from it unless she can make the exact change; and *never* borrow from it.

Petty cash record. The secretary should keep a running record of expenditures made from the fund. As each expenditure is made, no matter how small, she enters the date, the amount, purpose for which spent, and the client and case to which it is chargeable. When the petty cash fund gets low, she adds up the expenditures and writes a check, payable to herself, for the total—that is, the amount necessary to bring the petty cash fund

up to its original figure. She attaches the record to the check when she gives it to her employer for his signature. Then she marks the record "Paid—(date)—, Ck. No. _____," initials, and files it. Then she starts a new running account for future expenditures from the fund.

A petty cash fund is also called an *imprest fund* because it is restored periodically to a given level.

Pica. (pronounced pi'kah) 1. A printer's measure. There are approximately six picas to an inch and 12 POINTS to a pica.

2. A size of type used on typewriters, slightly larger than elite type. Measured horizontally, 10 spaces of pica type measure one inch, whereas 12 spaces of elite type measure an inch.

Picketing. The practice of placing employees at or near the entrances of an industrial plant suffering from a STRIKE in order to make the strike more effective. Picketing, often accompanied by statements on placards, informs other unionists and the public of the union's grievances. The unwillingness of workers and customers to cross a picket line will, of course, paralyze the operations of a stricken plant. The Supreme Court has upheld peaceful picketing as a form of free speech.

Pilotage. The compensation given to a pilot for conducting a vessel, usually in or out of a port or dock or through waters unknown to the vessel's master.

Plaintiff. The party who commences a personal action or suit to obtain a remedy for an injury to his rights. See also PARTIES TO AN ACTION.

Planographic. See OFFSET.

Plat. A plan or map of land showing its subdivision into smaller parcels or lots, used in LAND DESCRIPTION.

Plate. A flat or curved sheet of metal or plastic used in printing; also the impression made from such a plate. All printing is done from a master surface of some sort. The type is etched on the surface and a printed impression is made from that master surface or plate. A plate may consist entirely of text or of text and a CUT. It is inaccurate to refer to a cut as a plate.

Pleadings. Written statements of the *claims* and *defenses* of the parties to a court action.

In almost all states a legal proceeding is commenced when the *first pleading* is filed with the CLERK OF THE COURT by the person bringing the suit. The plaintiff—the person bringing the suit—makes a written statement in clear and concise language of the facts that caused him to bring the suit. The designation of this first pleading varies with the court; it might be called a complaint, a declaration, a libel, or a PETITION. In some states the first pleading in an EQUITY action is designated as a *bill in equity* or a *bill of complaint*. (See COMPLAINT.) A SUMMONS, or its equivalent, is then issued and served upon the person against whom the action is brought— usually called the DEFENDANT. The defendant answers the summons and complaint, defending himself by raising legal arguments or by denying the facts stated by the plaintiff in the complaint. When the case is finally submitted to the court for a decision, the judge decides controversies about legal points; a jury, or a judge acting in place of a jury, decides questions of fact. See PRACTICE AND PROCEDURE.

Pledge. The placement of personal property by the owner with a lender as security for a debt. Pawned articles and stocks and bonds put up as collateral for a loan are the most common pledges. Essentials of a pledge are (1) a debt or obligation to be secured; (2) the thing pledged; (3) the pledgor (the one who gives the pledge) and the pledgee (the one who receives the pledge); (4) transfer of possession of the property (if actual physical possession is practically impossible, the pledgee may acquire CONSTRUCTIVE possession); (5) retention of title in the pledgor; (6) the pledgor's right to redeem the pledge; (7) a contract, express or implied, covering the transaction.

When stock is pledged as collateral, the pledgee has the right and is bound to collect the dividends and apply them to the loan, in the absence of an agreement to the contrary between the pledgor and the pledgee. This is the legal theory. As a matter of practice, the stockholder makes an assignment of the stock in blank and the stock is not transferred on the books of the corporation unless the pledgor defaults; the stockholder-pledgor therefore continues to collect the dividends.

PLS Certificate. See NATIONAL ASSOCIATION OF LEGAL SECRETARIES.

PLS (Professional Legal Secretary). See NATIONAL ASSOCIATION OF LEGAL SECRETARIES.

Point. A type measurement. A point is one-twelfth of a PICA. Type and the space between lines (leading) are measured in points.

Police Court. See INFERIOR COURT.

Police Power. That power which any governmental body has to protect the property, life, health, and well-being of its citizenry by legislation. State minimum wage laws have been held by the United States Supreme Court (see AMERICAN COURT SYSTEM) to be a proper exercise of the states' police powers. Under police powers, states license doctors and lawyers, barbers and beauticians, and the like, and only those who obtain a license are authorized to practice their profession or trade. City ordinances that require certain standards of cleanliness in restaurants, or that impose building restrictions, are regulations issued under police power. The extent of a governing body's police power is limited by the state constitutions and by the Fourteenth Amendment to the Constitution of the United States, which protects personal liberties and freedoms. The power of Congress to regulate and control business activities is not a police power but is a power expressly granted by the Constituiton. See also DUE PROCESS OF LAW.

Poor's Register of Directors and Executives. A national listing of corporate executives and directors.

Postal Service. *Sources of information.* Postal information which might at times be needed in the law office can be obtained from the following sources:

(a) The Directory of Post Offices: an annual publication with quarterly supplements, used in identifying post offices and computing parcel post rates.

(b) The Postal Manual, Chapters 1 and 2, explaining the services available, and the rates, fees, and conditions.

(c) A Directory of International Mail Rates and Conditions of Mailing. (See INTERNATIONAL MAIL.)

All three publications are available from the Superintendent of Documents, Government Printing Office, Washington, D.C. 20013. Chapters 1 and 2 of the Postal Manual may be purchased either in Postal Manual format or as a volume of the Code of Federal Regulations.

DOMESTIC POSTAL SERVICE

Classes of mail. There are four classes of mail: first, second, third, and fourth. Each class may involve some special form of handling: airmail, special delivery, and the like. First-class mail consists of sealed matter and also of certain items that the U.S. Postal Service considers first-class matter whether they are sealed or not (see the following list). Second-class mail consists of newspapers and periodicals; third-class mail, of unsealed matter weighing less than 16 ounces; fourth-class mail, or parcel post, or packages weighing sixteen ounces or more. For details about rate basis, weight limit, preparation for mailing, and postal instructions and regulations, consult the local post office.

Mailable items and how to dispatch them. The list on pages 334-335 shows the class of mail by which the items mentioned are ordinarily sent.

First-class mail. The rate is based on the ounce or fraction thereof, without regard to zone.

ITEM	HOW TO SEND
Birth announcements.	First-class
Bonds (negotiable)	Registered first-class
Bonds (nonnegotiable)	First-class or certified first-class
Books	Third- or fourth-class

(Special rates apply to books. The book may be autographed. Mark the package "Book or Books.")

Catalogues	Third- or fourth-class

(Special rates apply to printed catalogues individually addressed, consisting of 24 pages or more and not weighing over 10 pounds. Each piece must be clearly marked "Catalog.")

Checks, filled out	First-class
Cancelled	First-class
Certified	Registered first-class
Endorsed in blank	Registered first-class
Circulars	Third-class
Currency	Registered first-class
Documents with no intrinsic value	Certified mail
Documents with intrinsic value	
Signed originals	Registered first-class
Copies	First-class
Drawings	Third-class
Form letters	Third-class

(To be mailable as third-class matter, these must be deposited in the post office, unsealed, in quantities of 20 or more. They must be identical except for the date and the name and address of the addressee. The name, address, and handwritten signature of the sender may be filled in on the form. Correction of obvious typographical errors may be made.)

Greeting cards	First-class
In unsealed envelopes	Third-class

(If the greeting cards bear written messages, they must be sent first-class, even though unsealed.)

Jewelry	Registered first-class

(Limit of liability is $10.000—$1,000 if commerical or other insurance is also carried.)

Letters	
Carbon copies	First-class
Duplicate copies	First-class
For delivery to addressee only	Registered first-class
Form (see Form Letters)	
Handwritten or typed	First-class
Magazines	Second-class
Manuscript	Registered first-class
Accompanied by proof-sheets	Third- or fourth-class depending on weight

(Corrections on proof sheets may include insertion of new matter, as well as marginal notes to the printer. The manuscript of one article may not be enclosed with the proof of another unless the matter is mailed at the first-class rate.)

Merchandise (see Packages)	
Money orders	First-class
Newspapers	Second-class
Packages	
Less than 16 ounces	Third-class
16 ounces or more	Parcel post
Containing personal messages (See *First-class mail*.)	

(Packages may be sealed if they bear an inscription authorizing inspection by the postmaster. Packages containing articles valued at not more then $200 may be insured, but if

ITEM   *HOW TO SEND*

they contain articles valued at more than $200, they should be sealed and registered. First-class postage will then apply and the liability limit is $10,000.)

Item	How to Send
Periodicals	Second-class
Photographs	Third-class

(Wrap with a cardboard protection and mark the envelope "Photograph—do not bend." Photographs may be autographed.)

Item	How to Send
Postal cards	First-class
Post cards	First-class

(In order to be mailed at post card rates, cards cannot be smaller than 2¾ by 4 inches or larger than 3 9/16 by 5 9/16 inches. If the card is enclosed in an envelope, it cannot be mailed at the post card rate. Cards carrying a statement of a past-due account cannot be mailed at the card rate because they must be enclosed in an envelope.)

Item	How to Send
Plants, seed, cutting, scions, bulbs	Third-class or parcel post
Printed matter	Depending on weight
Less than 16 ounces	Third-class
16 ounces or more	Fourth-class
Stock certificates (negotiable)	Registered first-class
Stock certificates (nonnegotiable)	First-class or certified
Typewritten material (see Manuscript	First-class

Seal the envelopes. Mark oversized or odd-shaped envelopes "First-Class." If the envelope flap is not gummed, seal with glue or mucilage. Do not seal with strips of gummed paper or Scotch tape.

When first-class mail is enclosed with second-, third-, or fourth-class, first-class rate is required for the letter. (See *Fourth-class mail,* page 336.)

Second-class mail (publishers). The rate basis varies with the weight, percentage of advertising, and zone to which mailed. Only newspapers and periodicals bearing a printed notice of second-class entry are admissible as second-class matter for mailing to established lists of paid subscribers. Publications produced by stencil or hectograph methods are not admissible as second-class matter. The entire newspaper or periodical must be mailed; otherwise, the *higher* third-class rate applies on material weighing up to 16 ounces.

Second-class mail (transient). The rate is based on each two ounces or fraction thereof, without regard to zone. When sent unsealed by other than publishers or registered news agents, address an envelope, slit the ends, and wrap the newspaper or periodical in it. Write "Second-Class matter" above the address, "to" in front of the address, and "From" in front of the return address. To call attention to a special passage in the text, mark with symbols, *not words,* in colored pencil. Write "Marked Copy" on the wrapper.

Third-class mail. The rate is based on a minimum of two ounces with an increase for each ounce or fraction thereof, without regard to zone. The rate for bulk lots is based on the pound, with a minimum charge per piece. The weight limit is up to sixteen ounces. The material becomes fourth class or parcel post when mailed in packages weighing 16 ounces or over. Do not seal. Writing, except something in the nature of an autograph or inscription, is not permitted to appear on third-class matter. "Do not open until Christmas," or a similar legend may be written on the wrapper; other directions or requests may not. Corrections of typographical errors may be made. Invoices can be enclosed.

Fourth-class mail (parcel post). The rate is by the pound, according to distance or zone. A fraction of a pound is computed as a full pound. To find the zone of the place of destination, telephone the post office, or consult *Directory of P. O.* and a zone key.

Pack contents solidly. If they are crushable, pack in an extra heavy cardboard box. Twine may be used but do not seal the package unless it bears an inscription that it may be opened for postal inspection. No communications may be enclosed, except invoices and customer's orders that relate entirely to the articles enclosed. When articles are being returned for repair, exchange, or credit, no communication, such as "Please credit my account," may be included, but the sales slip may be enclosed.

Seasonal greetings may be enclosed.

A letter may be sent with a parcel by enclosing the letter in an addressed envelope and attaching it securely to the address side of the package, but not covering the address on the package. Postage must be paid on the letter at the letter rate and on the package at the parcel-post rate. They will be dispatched as fourth-class matter.

A letter may also be enclosed with a parcel if postage is paid for the letter at the first-class rate and for the package at the parcel-post rate. The postage for the letter may be placed on the parcel separately or included with the postage for the parcel. The mail will be dispatched as fourth-class matter. Beneath the postage and above the address, write "First-Class Mail Enclosed." If practical, the letter

should be placed on top of the other items that make up the parcel.

Special handling postage entitles fourth-class mail to the most expeditious handling, transportation, and delivery possible, but not to immediate delivery by the office of destination. Nor does special handling insure the safe delivery of the mail. Fourth-class mail can be insured.

Air mail and air-mail parcel post. Any mailable matter except that liable to damage by freezing or from high altitudes may be sent by air mail. The rate on air mail for matter not over 8 ounces is based on the ounce or fraction thereof, without regard to distance. The rate on matter over 8 ounces is based on the pound or fraction thereof, according to the distance or zone.

Air mail may be sealed or left unsealed without affecting the air rate. Air mail should be conspicuously marked in the space immediately below the stamps, above the address, "Via Air Mail." Articles for dispatch overseas via air mail should bear the blue label "Par Avion—By Air Mail," which may be secured without expense at postoffices. Letters or other mail bearing special-delivery air-mail stamps should be conspicuously marked "Special Delivery—Air Mail." Parcels should be stamped "Air Mail" on the top, bottom, and sides.

Air mail may be registered, insured, or sent C.O.D. or special delivery if the charges for these services are paid in addition to the regular air-mail rate. The fees for these services are the same on air mail as on ordinary mail.

Registered mail. This service offers additional safeguards for the transmission of valuable mail. The sender must declare the full value of the mail presented for registration. The fee is determined by the declared actual value, not by the indemnity desired. The U.S. Postal Service will pay an indemnity *not exceeding* $10,000, if no commercial or other insurance is carried. The limit is $1,000 if commercial or other insurance is carried.

All registered mail, except second- and third-class mail valued at not more than $100, must be sealed with glue or mucilage. Indicate the value on the face of the matter being mailed, near the space for the stamps.

Air mail may be registered. Registered mail may be sent C.O.D. Registered mail may not be mailed in a mail box; it must be deposited at the post office.

Certified mail. First-class mail without intrinsic value may be sent by *certified* mail. This class of mail is handled in transit like first-class mail. There is no indemnity, but the sender can request a return receipt. Certified mail can be dropped into any mail box. Blank certified mail coupons and return receipt coupons may be obtained from the Post Office. The fee is about half the fee for registered mail.

Insured mail. Third- and fourth-class mail may be insured. First- and second-class mail cannot be insured; such matter should be registered. The indemnity limit on insured mail is $200. The insurance fee depends upon the declared value.

Do not seal, but wrap securely. Under the return address write "Return Requested." All insured mail is sent with the understanding that forwarding or return postage is guaranteed.

The air-mail system handles insured mail if it is sent at the air-mail rate of postage plus insurance fees.

Return receipt may be had for an extra fee if insured for more than $10.

Insured mail must be mailed at the post office; it cannot be deposited in a mail box.

Special delivery. For the payment of a fee any class of mail may be sent *special delivery*. Special delivery postage provides immediate delivery by the office of destination. See also *special handling* of fourth-class mail.

C.O.D. mail. Domestic third- and fourth-class mail and sealed matter of any class bearing postage at the first-class rate may be sent C.O.D. (collect on delivery). The sender must pay the postage and the C.O.D. fee, but may include these in the price of the article that is to be collected upon delivery. The maximum amount that may be collected on any single C.O.D. parcel is $200. The collections are sent to the sender by the post office in the form of a money order.

The sender of a C.O.D. parcel must guarantee return and forwarding postage. C.O.D. mail may be sent special delivery or special handling if fees applying to those services are paid in addition to postage and C.O.D. charges. The air-mail system handles C.O.D. mail if it is sent at the air-mail rate of postage plus C.O.D. charges.

How to reduce postage costs. Money can be saved by knowing how and when to use the various types of mail service. Here are a few suggestions to reduce postage costs.

1. Use business-reply envelopes, not stamped self-addressed envelopes.

2. Consider the use of metered mail.

3. Eliminate special delivery if let-

ters will reach destination in time for the first mail delivery.

4. Economies are possible if the mailer knows how and when various classes of mail can be used.

5. If there are several letters for the same person, put them in one envelope.

6. Send all material to the same branch in one envelope. Postage is paid on so much per ounce or fraction and combining fractions saves ounces, and a saving is also made on envelopes.

7. Write communication to branch offices on memo paper. This reduces the weight of the mail going to branch offices.

8. Use lightweight paper for air-mail.

9. Give thought to weight of paper and envelopes used for normal correspondence. Reduced weight need not mean sacrifice of quality.

10. Do not send paper clips through the mail.

11. When you send a letter with material that does not require first-class postage, use specially constructed envelopes that have one part for the first-class letter and another part for the lower-class material.

Postscript. An additional thought or appendage to an original letter. When it is necessary to add a postscript to a letter, type it two spaces below the identification line or the last notation that is on the letter. See RESPONSI-BILITY OR IDENTIFICATION LINE. The left margin of the postscript should be indented five spaces from the left margin of the letter itself. The secretary may include or omit the abbreviation "P.S." She types the dictator's initials after the postscript.

Power of Appointment. Testamentary authorization to a DONEE to determine to whom testator's property shall be distributed.

If the donee is given an unrestricted power to dispose of property to any person or persons he may choose, the power is *general*. When the donee's power is restricted in favor of a particular person or class, such as only to members of the family of testator, he has a *special* or *particular* power of appointment.

Power of Attorney. A written instrument in which the principal (the person giving the power of attorney) authorizes another to act for him. The instrument may be a blanket authorization, as in the case of a person embarking on an extended voyage. More often it authorizes the agent to represent the principal in one specific transaction, as the closing of a real estate deal; or to do a particular act continuously, as the signing of checks, or the collecting of money on behalf of the principal, or authority to institute suit, or collect dividends.

The appointed person is commonly called an *attorney in fact*. The power of attorney may be revoked at the will of the principal, unless it was given to the agent for a consideration. See also PROXY.

Directions for the preparation of a power of attorney. Unless otherwise instructed, the secretary should follow these directions when typing a power of attorney.

1. Make an original for the attorney in fact, a copy for the principal, and a copy for the files.

2. Use legal cap.

3. Place the responsibility marks on the office copy only.

4. Double space.

5. Have at least two lines of typing on the signature page.

6. Prepare signature line for principals or principals only.

7. If the powers granted relate to the conveyance of real estate, the instrument must be prepared with the formalities required for a DEED.

8. If the powers granted do not relate to real estate, ask the lawyer if the power of attorney is to be witnessed and acknowledged.

9. Collate (see COLLATING).

10. Endorse LEGAL BACK.

11. Check to see that the principal's signature agrees with the name typed in the instrument.

12. After the instrument is signed, and acknowledged if necessary, conform copies to original. See CONFORMING DOCUMENTS.

13. If a power of attorney relates to real property, it is recorded like any conveyance. However, sometimes it is not recorded until the attorney in fact exercises the power granted. Ask the lawyer for instructions as to recording.

14. The lawyer will tell the secretary whether the original of the power of attorney is to be delivered directly to the attorney in fact, or to the principal.

15. Make a notation on the office copy of the distribution of the original and copy.

Practice and Procedure. The procedure in law actions is highly technical and is the lawyer's responsibility. He will dictate many pleadings in their entirety because their wording must be precise to meet statutory requirements. The secretary's responsibilities might consist in (1) keeping an accurate calendar and record of the proceedings; (2) preparing the pleadings in a workmanlike manner; (3) relieving the lawyer of details.

Variations in practice and procedure. The rules of civil practice and procedure vary in detail not only in the various states but, to a lesser extent, in various jurisdictions within a state. A fundamental variation of interest to the secretary is the requirement with respect to the service and filing of pleadings. The jurisdictions may be grouped in respect to service and filing as follows:

A. In the majority of jurisdictions, a copy of every pleading and supporting paper must be served on opposing counsel, and the original filed in court. When a copy of the initial pleading is served with the summons, as is often the case, it is served on the defendant, because there is no counsel of record at that time.

B. In a few jurisdictions copies of pleadings and supporting papers do not have to be served on opposing counsel, but *a copy as well as the original must be filed in court.* Counsel withdraws the duplicate from court in order to learn the contents of the papers filed by opposing counsel. (All jurisdictions require service of the summons on the defendant.)

C. In a few jurisdictions, for example in New York Supreme Court, copies of pleadings are served on opposing counsel, but the originals are not filed in court until the case is at issue. The court has no indication that a law suit is pending until the case is ready to be set for trial. This procedure does not apply to municipal courts.

D. In some jurisdictions a copy must be served on opposing counsel, and an original and a copy filed in court. Opposing counsel refers to the counsel for each adverse party. Thus, if the rules require service on opposing counsel and there is more than one adverse party, sufficient copies of the paper are prepared to permit service of a copy on counsel for each party.

Practice Manual. See FORM BOOKS.

Prayer. See WHEREFORE CLAUSE; COMPLAINT.

Pre-emptive Rights. In corporation law, the shareholder's right to subscribe pro rata to additional new shares of stock before such new shares are offered to outsiders. A pre-emptive right, if exercised, will guarantee a shareholder's proportionate interest in the CORPORATION.

Such rights provide a safeguard which operates in favor of the original investor, protecting him against the dilution of voting power and his equities in the surplus and earnings of the corporation. A stockholder should determine whether he has pre-emptive rights by examining the CERTIFICATE OF INCORPORATION. If he has the rights and they are violated, he may bring action against the BOARD OF DIRECTORS and may also bring action to cancel the issue if shares are held by persons who took them with knowledge that pre-emptive rights were being violated.

Preferred Stock. Stock that is given a preference over other stock of the same

CORPORATION primarily with respect to DIVIDEND payments, but preferences with respect to asset distribution upon liquidation and other matters, as well as limitations, may also exist.

Preferred stock gives its owner a claim on income either in a fixed amount or at a fixed rate, unlike COMMON STOCK which entitles its owner to a residual share of the corporate income. In the event of dissolution, the preferred stockholder is entitled to a stipulated sum for his principal claim before anything is paid to common stockholders.

Preferred stock has certain features that are of particular advantage to the issuing corporation. The issuance of preferred stock makes financing possible without sharing profits and control in the unlimited fashion required by common stock. Also, preferred stock has the advantage, generally, of being redeemable at the option of the corporation, thus enabling refinancing with a new security paying a lower dividend.

Preferred stock, like common stock, may have the right to participate in the management of the corporation through its voting power, but ordinarily preferred stock does not carry the general voting privilege. However, preferred stock is frequently given vetoing power or the right to vote as a class on particular questions and the general voting privilege under particular circumstances. See also CUMULATIVE PREFERRED STOCK; and NON-CUMULATIVE PREFERRED STOCK.

Prentice-Hall Loose-leaf Services. (For lawyers). Compilations of *all* pertinent material in specific fields of law.

A compilation includes all statutes, administrative regulations, executive orders, rulings, court decisions, and interpretations affecting a specific field of law. In addition, the service gives editorial analysis, comments, and recommendations.

When a court hands down a decision within a field of law covered by a service, a copy of the decision is immediately sent to Prentice-Hall, and the subscriber to the service receives it in his next current supplement. For example, court decisions in the *Prentice-Hall Federal Taxes* are regularly in the hands of subscribers a few days after their issuance by the judges. Accompanying each current supplement is a Report Bulletin that highlights all new laws, decisions, and rulings. In addition, the Report Bulletin gives law notes on important recurring problems on the subject with which it deals. See FILING LOOSE-LEAF PUBLICATIONS.

Prepaid Income. See INCOME.

Prepayment Privilege. A clause giving the mortgagor the right to pay off the mortgage, or part of it, before maturity. See MORTGAGE STATEMENT AND CLAUSES.

Presumption. An inference as to the existence of one fact from the existence of some other fact, founded upon a previous experience of their connection.

Presumption of law requires that a particular inference *must* be drawn from an ascertained state of facts. For example, a child of seven is, under the COMMON LAW rule, conclusively presumed to be incapable of committing a crime.

Presumption of fact is a term used to describe a logical inference which the court is authorized, but not required, to draw from the evidence in the case. As an example, it might be inferred that a person in possession of a murder weapon committed the murder.

Prima Facie Evidence. Evidence deemed by law to be sufficient to establish a fact if the evidence is not disputed. For example, the placement of a CORPORATE SEAL on an instrument is prima facie evidence that the instrument was executed by authority of the corporation.

Prime Meridian. See LAND DESCRIPTION, *Section and township.*

Principal. 1. A sum loaned, borrowed, or invested; the sum of money on which interest is paid.

2. One who authorizes another, called an agent or broker, to act for him in dealings with third persons. A *principal* may be an individual, a partnership, or a CORPORATION acting through its authorized officers.

Principal Meridian. See LAND DESCRIPTION, *Section and township.*

Printed Law Blanks. Commercially prepared legal instruments which are set up in printed form, with blank spaces to be filled in with specific information. For example, a printed law blank of a MORTGAGE or DEED will need only to be filled in with the necessary information to complete the document, such as the names of the parties and the description of the property being mortgaged or sold.

Printed law blanks are widely used in drawing up legal instruments. Law blank printers publish a catalogue showing the numbers and titles of the blanks that they print. Each law blank has its title and, usually, the printer's catalogue number, printed in small letters on it. The blanks are obtainable at almost any stationery store. Frequently the secretary can fill in these blanks without any dictated instructions. When it is necessary to dictate the material to be inserted in the blanks, the usual manner of giving instructions is as follows:

The dictator numbers in pencil the spaces to be filled in——1, 2, 3, etc. He then dictates the material that should be typed in each numbered blank, thus eliminating any confusion about where each dictated insertion should be typed.

Observe the following suggestions about filling in law blanks, so that the completed form will be neat and accurate:

Typing on ruled lines. Make certain that the typing is adjusted so that the bases of letters with tails that extend below the line of type (g, p, and y) just touch the ruled line.

Date of printing. Printed forms bear a printer's mark showing the number of copies printed and the date of the printing. When filling in more than one copy, use forms that were printed at the same time, because a change might have been made in the form.

Registration of printing. Before attempting to fill in more than one blank form at a time by using carbon paper, make sure that the printing on all copies registers exactly. To do this, place the edges of the forms together and hold to the light. The printed matter in one copy should be exactly over corresponding material in the other copy. After the forms and carbon are inserted in the typewriter, if the forms are not perfectly aligned, loosen the typewriter platen and adjust the edges of the forms. They must be exactly even or the typing will not be properly spaced on the copies.

Fill-ins on both sides of sheet. When making carbon copies of a form that has fill-ins on both sides of the sheet, take particular care to avoid having one side the ribbon copy and the other side the carbon copy, thus rendering the form unfit for execution. Double sheet forms are particularly apt to cause trouble in this respect.

Small blanks. When the blanks on the form are small, fill in each form individually; do not use carbons. Be careful not to overlook any of the small blanks. In many forms they are not indicated by underlining, but only by a small space. Many of them call only for letters identifying the person or persons signing the document. For example, a printed mortgage form might include the following: "Said mortgagee__, ___h___ heirs or assigns." If there is more than one mortgagee, s is added to *mortgagee* and ___h___ becomes *their*. If there is only one mortgagee, the first blank is not filled in, and __h__ becomes her or his.

"Z" ruling. Frequently the material typed on a printed form does not fill the space provided. To protect the instrument from alteration draw a "Z" ruling, as illustrated here, with pen and ink in the unused space.

Printed Mortgage Form. See MORTGAGE.

Privilege Against Self-incrimination. A provision in the Fifth Amendment stating that no person shall be compelled to be a witness against himself in a criminal case in a Federal court. No inference of guilt may be drawn from his failure to take the stand or to call witnesses in his own behalf. The Supreme Court has held that the due process clause of the Fourteenth Amendment does not require state courts to give accused persons the protection against self-incrimination stated in the Fifth Amendment. Most states, however, do have similar provisions in their own constitutions and statutes.

Privileged Communications. Any information which one person derives from another by reason of a confidential relationship existing between the parties. The parties to such communications are, under certain circumstances, not allowed to testify in COURT as to what was said. Relationships that most states recognize are those of (1) attorney and client, (2) clergyman and penitent, (3) physician and patient, and (4) husband and wife.

When the statute so provides, the attorney-client privilege may be extended to include the attorney's secretary if the communication is spoken to the lawyer in her presence.

Privity. Mutual or successive relationship to the same right of property, or the power to take advantage of and enforce a promise or WARRANTY. Identity of interest is essential. There must be a connection or bond of union between parties as to some particular transaction. Thus, privity of contract exists between a lessor and lessee, because the parties are mutually interested in the lease. Privity of contract also exists between a lessor and an assignee of the lease, because the assignee succeeded to the rights of the lessee. Heirs, executors, and assigns succeed to the rights and liabilities of a contract whether it so states or not. They are thus *privies* to the contract.

Privity affects legal rights and duties and, in many cases, determines whether a party may sue or be sued. Thus, a privy has the same right to relief against mistake of fact as the original party to a contract. A stranger to a contract has no right to sue for fraud, but a privy does. An injunction extends to all persons in privity with the parties enjoined. Evidence may be admissible or inadmissible because of privity. Privity may be an element in an action for negligence, or in the substitution of parties in a legal action.

Prize. In ADMIRALTY law, property of the enemy and its nationals captured at sea under the authority of a belligerent power. Ships and cargoes are the usual prizes.

Probate Court. See COURTS OF SPECIAL JURISDICTION.

Probate of a Will. A judicial act or determination of a COURT having competent JURISDICTION establishing the validity of a WILL.

In most states, a will has no effect until it has been admitted to probate by a probate court. (See COURTS OF SPECIAL JURISDICTION.) Probate is essential in order to establish power in the executor to administer. Probate may be dispensed with, however, if all persons interested in the will so agree. Family settlements are favored by the law and will be upheld. By such a CONTRACT the parties may agree upon a distribution of the estate different from that provided for in the will, or they may agree to carry out the provisions of the will without probate.

Where there is a proceeding to probate a will, the attorney for the estate generally prepares and submits to the executors the necessary papers in the proceeding. The probate proceeding is initiated by the filing of the will itself, together with a copy of it, certified to be a correct and true copy. (Figure 1 shows entries made in the SUIT REGISTER record in a probate proceeding.) A *petition* for the probate of a will is also filed with the will and the copy. Simultaneously, a transfer tax affidavit is filed. The inheritance tax is not based upon the AFFIDAVIT. A special proceeding must be had for that. Legal notice of the probate proceeding must be served upon all interested parties, and affidavit of service (or waiver of service) filed with the court. Sworn depositions of witnesses to the will must also be filed (see DEPOSITION). If there are no objections to the admission of the will within the time specified, the will is admitted to probate by a DECREE of the court to that effect. The person named as executor in the will then files a bond (unless waived in the will) and an oath, and *letters testamentary* as executor issue to him. A corporate fiduciary named as executor does not file a bond.

Parties to a probate proceeding. The proponent of the will, that is, the person or corporation seeking to have the will probated, is the *petitioner*. The petitioner is usually the person or corporation named in the will as executor. There are three groups of interested parties who must be informed of the probate proceeding so that they may protect their interests:

1. The surviving spouse and the distributees. These are the heirs-at-law of the deceased who would have inherited if the decedent had died intestate. This group of distributees includes the heirs-at-law who are also named in the will as legatees, because they might take less by the will than they would have inherited if there had been no will.

2. The executors and trustees named in the will who do not sign the petition.

3. Legatees or devisees who are not distributees. These are the legatees or devisees named in the will who would not have inherited if the decedent had died intestate. They are interested in the proceeding because they lose their legacies if the will is not admitted to probate.

Copy of will and affidavit. A copy of the will is filed in the probate court with the original will. In some jurisdictions a photographic or photostatic copy may be filed. In the administration of a large, complicated estate, where numerous copies of the will are needed, the will is sometimes mimeographed, printed or Xeroxed. The secretary should follow these instructions:

1. Make as many legible copies as can be made in one typing.

2. Copy the will exactly, typing also the signature and data that are written in ink.

3. Have two adults (the secretary may be one of them) compare one copy with the original and make an affidavit

SURROGATE'S COURT—COUNTY OF NEW YORK

In the Matter

of

CHARLES RAY DOE,   Deceased,

Proving the Last Will and Testament of

As a Will of Real and Personal Property.

          X
          :
          :
          :
          :
          :
          :
          :
          :
          :
          X

FILE NO. P 1277 – 19——

PROBATE PROCEEDING

Date of death: March 28, 19——
                105 East 37th Street, NYC.

Elwood & Adams, Esqs.,
Attorneys for Petitioners
            Partner in Charge: Mr. Rey
            Principal Assistant: Mr. Blank

19——

April 23 Mr. Blank filed original and sworn copy of will dated February 25, 19—— and petition of
          Charles T. Doe, John T. Roe and Barbara S. Roe, and their oaths and designations as execu-
          tors and trustees and filed waiver of citation executed by Beatrice S. Roe.

24 M. J. Ryan mailed 31 copies of notice of probate to legatees, etc. named therein.
25 Filed original notice of probate with proof of mailing.
25 Depositions of the subscribing witnesses Mary Roeman and Anthony J. Maurman were sworn to
          before John A. Killoran, Probate Clerk.
25 Decree signed, Collins, S., and filed, admitting will to probate and directing that letters
          testamentary and letters of trusteeship be issued to the executors and trustees who may
          qualify thereunder.
25 Letters Testamentary issued to Charles T. Doe, John T. Roe and Barbara S. Roe, Liber 633,
          Page 434.
26 Letters of Trusteeship issued to Charles T. Doe, John T. Roe and Barbara S. Roe, in Liber
          51, Page 842.

Probate of a Will: Figure 1. Progress record.

to that effect. They must both compare the same copy. Figure 2 on page 347 illustrates the affidavit.

4. Fill in the blanks on the back of the affidavit. If the secretary does not use a printed form of affidavit, she should make a legal back endorsed like the printed form on page 348, Figure 3.

5. Staple the affidavit to the compared copy of the will, placing the affidavit beneath the copy.

Petition for probate of will. The petition sets forth certain factual data about the testator, his heirs, legatees, and devisees, and prays that the will be admitted to probate and that letters testamentary be issued to the executor. If trustees are named in the will, the petition also prays for letters of trusteeship. The secretary should follow these instructions:

1. Make an original for the court and a copy for the office file.

2. Be especially careful about names, addresses, and values of legacies and devises.

3. The lawyer will give the secretary a memorandum of (a) the name and address of the petitioner of petitioners; (b) the name of the testator, his residence at the time of his death, and the time and place of his death; (c) the names, addresses, ages, and degree of kinship to the decedent of the heirs-at-law and of those interested in the will; (d) the addresses of the other legatees and devisees. This memorandum and the copy of the will give the secretary the information necessary to fill in the form, unless the will is complicated. If so, the lawyer will dictate the necessary information.

4. The executors and trustees, if any, named in the will are listed with the distributees.

5. Delete from the form of petition unnecessary allegations. The relationship of the distributees indicates the allegations that should be deleted. A surviving spouse always shares in a decedent's estate. The distributees, other than the surviving spouse, take in the following order:

Children and issue of deceased children

Father, mother

Brothers, sisters, and issue of deceased brothers and sisters

Uncles, aunts, and issue of deceased uncles and aunts

There is no need to make an allegation concerning relatives of a deceased who are not entitled to inherit. Thus, in the illustration, surviving children are listed as distributees. There is no need to make an allegation about a surviving mother or father, or others, because in this case they cannot inherit. If there were no surviving children or issue of a predeceased child, and no surviving mother or father, the brothers and sisters would be listed as distributees. It would then be necessary to allege that there were no surviving children or issue of a deceased child, and no surviving mother or father. It would not be necessary to allege that there were no surviving aunts or uncles and no issue of a deceased aunt or uncle, because they could not inherit, unless specifically named in the will.

6. The secretary can always get the names of the legatees and devisees from the copy of the will.

7. The petition indicates the kind of legacy, as well as its value. This information can be taken from the will. Thus, the testator might leave the residue of his estate in trust for his widow, the remainder to go to his children upon the death of his widow.

Surrogate's Court
County of New York

In the Matter of Proving the Last Will and
Testament of

EDGAR BROWN

Deceased

Affidavit Proving a Correct Copy
of the Will Filed for Probate

P_____ 19 __

County and State of New York, ss.:

We___PAUL BELL_____

and___MARY WILLIAMS_____, being duly and severally sworn,

say, each for himself, that he has carefully compared the foregoing paper S   with the original thereof

dated the ___23rd_____ day of ___November_____, 19___

_____

about to be filed for probate, and that the same___are___in all respects a true and correct copy of

said instrument   and of the whole thereof.

Paul Bell

Mary Williams

Sworn to before me this 5th day of

___June_____, 19 __

Leslie Nash

(Notary Stamp)

Probate of a Will: Figure 2. Affidavit proving a correct copy
of will filed for probate.

The petition would show that the widow was the "beneficiary of a residuary trust," and that the children were given a "remainder interest in the residuary trust."

If the testator does not place the residue of his estate in trust but leaves it outright to someone, the petition indicates that the person is the "residuary legatee."

When specific personal property, rather than a sum of money, is be-

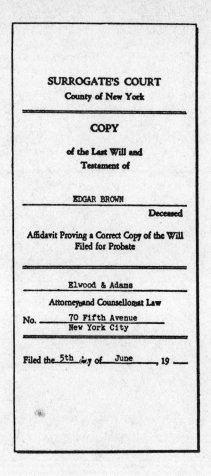

> SURROGATE'S COURT
> County of New York
>
> **COPY**
>
> of the Last Will and
> Testament of
>
> EDGAR BROWN
>
> Deceased
>
> Affidavit Proving a Correct Copy of the Will
> Filed for Probate
>
> Elwood & Adams
>
> Attorneys and Counsellors at Law
>
> No. 70 Fifth Avenue
> New York City
>
> Filed the 5th day of June , 19 ___

Probate of a Will: Figure 3. Back of affidavit
proving a correct copy of will filed for probate.

queathed, the bequest is indicated in the petition as a "specific legacy." Thus, as in the example, the widow and James Wilson received specific legacies. The exact nature of the widow's specific legacy is not indicated because it consisted of numerous items—the testator's jewelry, his household effects, automobiles, wearing apparel, and the like.

8. Arrange for the petitioners to come in and sign the petition.

9. Have the petitioners verify the petition. The illustrated petition has a form of verification by an individual printed on it. When the petitioner, or one of them is a corporation, type a **VERIFICATION** by a corporation on the form if there is space. If there is no space, type it on plain paper the width of the printed form and paste on the form immediately following the individual verification.

10. Conform the office copy.

11. File the original of the petition, the original and certified copy of the will, and the transfer tax affidavit (see below) in the probate court.

12. Mark on the office copy the date the petition was filed.

13. Make entry in suit register.

Transfer tax affidavit. A transfer tax affidavit is filed with the petition. This is a sworn statement as to the totals of realty and personalty affected by the will and of the names, amounts of legacies, residences, and relationship of those who receive gifts under the will. The affidavit supplies the state taxing authorities with data to be used by them for taxing purposes. It is typed on a printed form supplied by the taxing commissioner.

Citation and waiver in probate proceeding. The Surrogate's Court Act of New York provides that the surviving spouse, distributees, and executors and trustees named in the decedent's will shall be given notice of the petition for probate by service of a *citation.* Probate acts of other states have similar provisions. The citation is a legal writ citing those to whom it is addressed to appear in court on a certain date and show cause why the will should not be admitted to probate. It does not *command* an appearance as a summons does. Those who do not wish to contest the will need not appear in court. A citation is issued by the clerk of the court, but is prepared by the petitioner's attorney.

Any person over eighteen may serve a citation. Service is made by delivering a copy to the person upon whom it is served. If an infant is a distributee, the citation is addressed to him, but is served upon the parent with whom he resides or upon his guardian. If an infant is over fourteen, service is made upon him, as well as his parent or guardian.

Service of citation by publication and mailing. If any of the distributees live outside the state, or if there are any heirs or next of kin whose names and place of residence are unknown, service is had upon them by publication and mailing. The procedure is similar to that in a civil action. See SERVICE OF SUMMONS.

Adults may waive the issuance and source of a citation in the matter of proving the last will and testament of the deceased, but infants may not. Thus, before the citations are prepared, waivers are secured.

How to prepare a waiver of citation. Figure 4 on page 350 illustrates a properly completed form of waiver. The secretary should:

1. Make an original for the court and an office copy.

2. Have those who waive citation sign the original in the presence of two witnesses.

3. Take the acknowledgment of those signing the waiver.

4. Conform office copy, marking on it the date the original is filed.

5. File original in court.

6. Make entry in suit register.

How to prepare a citation. Figure 5, on page 351, illustrates a properly completed form of citation in probate proceedings. The secretary should:

1. Make an original for the court, an office copy, and a copy for each person to be served. In the illustrated case 5 copies must be made—an original for the court; an office copy; a copy for service upon Robert Brown, an infant over fourteen; a copy for service upon his mother in his behalf; a copy for service upon the mother of Irene Brown, an infant under fourteen. The adult distributees waived citation.

2. Find out the last return date allowed by the court rules.

Form 9 · · · (L.S.) · · · ·

Surrogate's Court, County of New York

In the Matter of Proving the Last Will and Testament of

EDGAR BROWN
Deceased,
As a Will of Real and Personal Property

Waiver of Citation in Probate Proceeding

P. 11,235 , 19 –

We, ELIZABETH R. BROWN, JOHN BROWN, and MARY BROWN,

_____

_____

_____

the undersigned, _____ being _____ heirs at law and next of kin of

EDGAR BROWN _____ deceased, do hereby

_____ appear in person and waive the issuance and service of a citation in the matter

of proving the last will and testament of said deceased, bearing date November 23, ____

and consent that the said instrument be admitted to probate.

Dated, New York
June 6 , 19 –

Elizabeth R. Brown
John Brown
Mary Brown

Signed in the presence of

John Blank
Susie White

State of New York
County of New York } ss.:

On the 6th day of June , 19 –, before me personally came

ELIZABETH R. BROWN, JOHN BROWN, and MARY BROWN,

to me known and known to me to be the individuals described in and who executed the foregoing instrument, and they duly acknowledged that they executed the same.

Mary W. Williams
(Notary Stamp)

NOTE—Outside the State of New York use the certificate printed on the reverse page.
(OVER)

Use BLACK ink only, as this sheet will be photographed.

Probate of a Will: **Figure 4.** Waiver of citation in probate proceeding.

Form A

CITATION

P. 11,235 _____, 19 _.

The People of the State of New York
By the Grace of God Free and Independent,

To

ROBERT BROWN, IRENE BROWN

the above   next of kin and heirs at law of   EDGAR BROWN

, deceased, send greeting:

Whereas, Thomas Nelson and The City Trust Company of New York, residing

at 52 Gramercy Park, North, New York City and having its principal ,

place of business at 70 Fifth Avenue, New York City, respectively ,
have
lately applied to the Surrogate's Court of our County of New York to have a

certain instrument in writing bearing date November 23, 19 ,

relating

to both real and personal property, duly proved as the last will and testament of EDGAR BROWN

, deceased, who was at the time of his death a resident of

214 East 17 Street, New York City   , the County of New York,

Therefore, you and each of you are cited to show cause before the Surrogate's Court of our

County of New York, at the Hall of Records in the County of New York, on the 18th

day of June   , one thousand nine hundred and -------- , at half-past ten o'clock

in the forenoon of that day, why the said will and testament should not be admitted to probate as a

will of real and personal property, and why letters of testamentary and letters of trusteeship should not be issued to the executors and trustees who may qualify there-
under.

In testimony whereof, we have caused the seal of the Surrogate's Court of the said County of

New York to be hereunto affixed.

Witness, Honorable John Doe

Surrogate of our said County of New York, at said county, the

(L.S.)   6th   day of   June   in the

year of our Lord one thousand nine hundred and

Richard Roe

Clerk of the Surrogate's Court

NOTE.—The original citation must be returned to the Probate Clerk before one o'clock p.m. on the day preceding the Return Day,
with sworn proof of service.

Use BLACK ink only, as this sheet will be photographed.

Probate of a Will: Figure 5.   Citation in probate proceeding.

351

3. Get the clerk of the court to sign the original.

4. Conform copies and give original and copies (except office copy) to person who is to serve the citation.

5. Prepare affidavit of service, which is usually printed on the back of the citation (Figure 6), and have the person who served the citation sign and swear to the affidavit in the presence of a notary.

6. Conform office copy, marking on it the date the original is filed in court.

7. File original in court.

8. *Enter in diary* return date of citation.

9. Make entry in suit register.

Preparations for hearing. The hearing in an uncontested probate proceeding is rather informal. The lawyer for the petitioners appears before the clerk of the court with the witnesses to the will. The date of the hearing is the return day indicated in the citation. (In some jurisdictions the clerk of the court sets the date for hearing at the time the petition is filed.) The secretary will have to make certain preparations prior to the hearing. She will:

1. Prepare deposition of witnesses.

2. Notify witnesses to the will.

3. Prepare and mail notice of probate.

4. Prepare oath of executor.

5. Prepare decree.

6. Prepare letters testamentary; also letters of trusteeship if the petition prays for them.

Notice of probate. The legatees and devisees who are not heirs-at-law must be given notice that the will has been offered for probate. The printed form of notice calls for the name and address of the proponents (the petitioners) and for a list of the names and addresses of

the legatees, devisees, and beneficiaries who have not been cited or have not waived citation. The secretary should follow these instructions:

1. Make an original for the court, an office copy, and a copy for each person listed in the notice.

2. Send the notices by mail if directed to do so by the attorney. The attorney for the petitioners makes affidavit of service by mail on the back of the notice.

3. Notarize the affidavit made by the attorney.

4. Conform the office copy.

5. Place the original with the papers that the lawyer will take to the hearing.

6. Make entry in suit register that the notices were mailed.

Deposition of witnesses to the will. As soon as the date of the hearing is known, notify the witnesses to the will of the time and place of the hearing. Their names and addresses can be gotten from the will. If the witnesses are not available, the lawyer will have to take other legal steps to prove the will. Make an entry of the notice in the suit register. In some states, such as Ohio, wills no longer have to be proved with deposition of witnesses, except in the case of Contest of Will.

Printed forms of deposition are available. The secretary should:

1. Prepare an original and an office copy for each witness. Thus, if there are two witnesses, prepare two sets of depositions.

2. Make sure not to date the depositions. They are signed and sworn to before an officer of the court, who dates them at that time.

3. Place the originals with the papers that the lawyer will take to the hearing.

4. Draw checks to witnesses for fee

Surrogate's Court, County of New York

In the Matter of Proving the Last Will and
Testament of

EDGAR BROWN

Deceased,

As a Will of Real and Personal Property

Note—*Outside the State of New York* a certificate must be procured from the proper official. Such certificate must show that the officer taking the acknowledgment is an officer of the state where it is taken and is authorised by the laws thereof *to take the acknowledgment of deeds*; that said official is well acquainted with such officer's handwriting and believes the signature to the original certificate is genuine.

**AFFIDAVIT OF SERVICE
OF CITATION**

State of New York

County of New York ss.:

Mathew Davis

of 33 West 10 Street, New York City, being duly sworn, says that he is over the age of eighteen years; that he made personal service of the within citation in the above-entitled special proceeding on the persons named below, whom deponent knew to be the persons mentioned and described in said citation, by delivering to and leaving with each of them personally a true copy of said citation, as follows:

On the 7th day of June, 19 --, at 214 East 17 Street, New York City, on Robert Brown.

On the 7th day of June, 19 , at 214 East 17 Street, New York City, on Elizabeth R. Brown, in behalf of Robert Brown, an infant.

On the 7th day of June, 19 , at 214 East 17 Street, New York City, on Elizabeth R. Brown, in behalf of Irene Brown, an infant.

On the day of 19 , at

On the day of 19 , at

Specify clearly time and place of service of each party served.

Mathew Davis

Sworn to before me on the

8th day of June 19 -

Mary Williams

(Notary Stamp)

Probate of a Will: **Figure 6.** Affidavit of service of citation.

allowed by law. The lawyer will probably take the checks to the hearing and pay the witnesses at that time; otherwise mail the checks after the depositions are taken. In some states Deposition of Witnesses is prepared by the Probate Court, acknowledged by the Court, and the fees are paid by the Court out of the costs placed on deposit with the Court at the time the Will is filed.

Oath of executor. In some states, an executor must take an oath that he will faithfully perform his duties as executor. Printed forms are available.

1. Prepare an original and an office copy for each executor. Thus, if there are two executors, prepare two sets of oaths.

2. Each executor signs the original of his oath in the presence of a notary.

3. Conform the office copies.

4. Place the originals with the papers that the lawyer will take to the hearing.

5. Make an entry in the suit register that the oaths have been executed.

Decree admitting will to probate. A decree in a probate proceeding serves the same purpose as an order or judgment in a civil action. A favorable decree admits the will to probate and directs that letters testamentary be issued to the executor nominated in the will. The probate judge (the surrogate in New York) signs the decree, but the petitioner's attorney prepares it. Printed forms are available.

1. Make an original for the court and a copy for the office file.

2. Do not date the decree. It will be dated when the judge signs it.

3. Place the original with the papers that the lawyer will take to the hearing.

4. The decree might not be signed for several days after the hearing. *Make a follow-up entry in the diary* for a few days after the hearing and inquire of the clerk of the court if it has been signed.

5. Mark on the office copy the date the decree was signed.

6. Make entry in the suit register.

Letters testamentary. After the judge signs the decree, the CLERK OF THE COURT issues letters testamentary to the executor. In some courts, the attorney for the executor prepares the letters. They are the evidence of the executor's authority to act. Anyone dealing with the executor as the representative of the estate will require a certificate to the effect that letters have been issued and are still in force. Certificates are available from the clerk of the court for a small fee.

1. Prepare an original or duplicate original for each executor, an office copy, and a sufficient number of copies to be certified by the clerk of the court. Thus, if there are two executors, prepare three copies in addition to the copies that are to be certified. There must be a certified copy for each bank account, each security issue, each safe deposit box, and the like.

2. If there are two or more executors, all of them are named in the letters.

3. Do not date the letters. The clerk of the court will date them when he issues them.

4. Place the original and duplicate original with the papers that the lawyer will take to the hearing. The clerk will sign a copy for each executor named in the letters and return them to the office.

5. Conform the office copy.

6. Deliver a signed copy to each executor. If the lawyer is an executor, he will retain one of the signed copies.

7. Make entries in suit register.

Notice to creditors. As soon as letters testamentary are issued, notice to creditors should be published in a local newspaper. Creditors of the decedent are given a certain length of time in which to file any claims they may have against the decedent. *Enter in diary* the last day the creditors have to present claims.

Newspapers usually have an appropriate printed form of notice to creditors that can be filled in without any difficulty. Within a specified time after the last publication, affidavit of publication is filed with the clerk of the court. The publisher makes the affidavit of publication and delivers it to either the clerk of the court or the attorney. *Enter in diary* the date by which the affidavit must be filed; also make entries in the suit register.

Procedural Law. See SUBSTANTIVE LAW.

Procedure. See PRACTICE AND PROCEDURE.

Proctor. The term used to designate an attorney in an ADMIRALTY proceeding.

Progressive Taxes. See GRADUATED TAXES.

Prohibition. The name of a writ issued by a SUPERIOR COURT, directed to the judge and parties to a suit in an INFERIOR COURT, commanding them to cease from the prosecution of the suit, because the original cause of action (or some matter arising from it) belongs to the jurisdiction of another court. See also MANDAMUS; HABEAS CORPUS; STAY; QUO WARRANTO; CERTIORARI; REVIEWING COURT.

Promoter of a Corporation. A person who undertakes to form a new CORPORATION, to procure for it the rights and money by which it is to carry out the purposes set forth in its CERTIFICATE OF INCORPORATION, and to establish it for the prosecution of its business.

A promoter occupies a FIDUCIARY relationship, or a relationship of trust and confidence toward the corporation that he promotes. The utmost good faith is required of him in his dealings with it. He also occupies a position of trust and confidence toward the persons induced to subscribe for shares to be issued by the corporation. Ordinarily a promoter's activities are over when the corporation is fully formed—that is, when the real stockholders in interest have elected a permanent and independent BOARD OF DIRECTORS that undertakes the management of the corporation.

Proof of Service. See NOTICE OF APPEAL.

Proofreaders' Marks. Standard symbols and abbreviations that are used for marking errors on printer's proof. They save time and are understood by the printer. Fig. 1, page 356, shows standard proofreaders' marks; Figure 2, page 357, a page of corrected proof. Here are some guides to follow:

(1) Place all marks in the margin of the proof, left or right, whichever is nearer, on the same line as the error. (2) Separate corrections on the same line (*e.g.*, lc/tr) and arrange them in order so that they read consecutively from left to right. (3) If the same correction is to be made in two places in the line, with no intervening correction, write the correction only once and follow it with two slant lines. (4) When material is to be added to the line, place a caret ( ) in the text at the point of insertion and write the addition in the margin. (5) When material is to be deleted and none added in its place, cross out the

PROOFREADERS' MARKS

∧	Make correction indicated in margin.	⌐	Raise to proper position.
Stet	Retain crossed-out word or letter; let it stand.	∟	Lower to proper position.
....	Retain words under which dots appear; write "Stet" in margin.	////	Hair space letters.
Stet		*w.f.*	Wrong font; change to proper font.
✗	Appears battered; examine.	*Qu?*	Is this right?
≈	Straighten lines.	*l.c.*	Put in lower case (small letters).
ⱽⱽ	Unevenly spaced; correct spacing.	*s.c.*	Put in small capitals.
//	Line up; i.e., make lines even with other matter.	*Caps*	Put in capitals.
run in	Make no break in the reading; no ¶	*C+s.c.*	Put in caps and small caps.
no ¶	No paragraph; sometimes written "run in."	*rom.*	Change to Roman.
out see copy	Here is an omission; see copy.	*ital.*	Change to Italic.
¶	Make a paragraph here.	≡	Under letter or word means caps.
tr	Transpose words or letters as indicated.	=	Under letter or word, small caps.
ℐ	Take out matter indicated; dele.	—	Under letter or word means Italic.
ℐ	Take out character indicated and close up.	⁓	Under letter or word, bold face.
¢	Line drawn through a cap means lower case.	⸴/	Insert comma.
⊘	Upside down; reverse.	;/	Insert semicolon.
⊃	Close up; no space.	:/	Insert colon.
#	Insert a space here.	⊙	Insert period.
⊥	Push down this space.	/?/	Insert interrogation mark.
⊡	Indent line one em.	(!)	Insert exclamation mark.
[	Move this to the left.	/=/	Insert hyphen.
]	Move this to the right.	∜	Insert apostrophe.
		⸢⸣	Insert quotation marks.
		ℓ	Insert superior letter or figure.
		⊓	Insert inferior letter or figure.
		[/]	Insert brackets.
		(/)	Insert parenthesis.
		⸺/m	One-em dash.
		⸺/m/m	Two-em parallel dash.

Proofreaders' Marks: Figure 1.

HOW TO CORRECT PROOF

It does not appear that the earliest printers had any method of correcting errors, before the form was on the press. The learned correctors of the first two centuries of printing were not proofreaders in our sense; they were rather what we should term office editors. Their labors were chiefly to see that the proof corresponded to the copy, but that the printed page was correct in its latinity; that the words were there, and that the sense was right. They cared little about orthography, bad letters or purely printers errors, and when the text seemed to them wrong they consulted fresh authorities or altered it on their own responsibility. Good proofs, in the modern sense, were impossible until professional readers were employed, men who had first a printer's education, and then spent many years in the correction of proof. The orthography of English, which for the past century has undergone little change, was very fluctuating until after the publication of Johnson's Dictionary, and capitals, which have been used with considerable regularity for the past 80 years, were previously used on the miss or hit plan. The approach to regularity, so far as we have, may be attributed to the growth of a class of professional proof readers, and it is to them that we owe the correctness of modern printing. More errors have been found in the Bible than in any other one work. For many generations it was frequently the case that Bibles were brought out stealthily, from fear of governmental interference. They were frequently printed from imperfect texts, and were often modified to meet the views of those who published them. The story is related that a certain woman in Germany, who was the wife of a printer, and had become disgusted with the continual assertion of the superiority of man over woman which she had heard, hurried into the composing room while her husband was at supper and altered a sentence in the Bible, which he was printing, so that it read Narr instead of Herr, thus making the verse read "And he shall be thy fool" instead of "And he shall be thy lord." The word not was omitted by Barker, the King's printer in England in 1632, in printing the seventh commandment. He was fined £3,000 on this account.

Proofreaders' Marks: Figure 2. A page of corrected proof.

unwanted characters and place a delete sign in the margin. (6) When material is to be substituted for a deletion, do not use the delete sign; just cross out the unwanted material and write the substitution for it in the margin. (7) Use ink or pencil of a different color from any of the markings already on the proof.

Proofreading. Reading proof for errors. It is not enough to read for sense and accuracy of facts, dates, and statistics. Each word and each mark of punctuation should be examined. The proof should be read word for word against COPY, preferably by having one person read aloud from the copy of each word and mark of punctuation as another person follows the proof. Certainly all tables, equations, statistics, and the like should be read against copy. (See PROOFREADERS' MARKS for standard proofreaders' marks and a piece of corrected proof.)

Property Descriptions. See LAND DESCRIPTION.

Property Exempt. Property Exempt is property allowed in some states to the surviving spouse of a decedent, which is paid after costs of administration and funeral expenses and before other debts. It may consist of PERSONAL PROPERTY or cash.

Proprietorship, Sole. One of the three most common forms of business organization. Ownership of the business is vested in one proprietor. The other two common forms of business organization are PARTNERSHIP and CORPORATION.

Protest. A formal certificate attesting the DISHONOR of a NEGOTIABLE INSTRUMENT after NEGOTIATION. A protest is usually made by a NOTARY PUBLIC but may be made by a responsible citizen, in the presence of two witnesses. The certificate states that the instrument was duly presented for payment, at the proper time and place, that payment was refused for the reason given, and that the holder intends to hold the drawer and endorser responsible for payment. The protest is attached to the dishonored instrument or copy of it. Notice of protest is then sent to the parties who are secondarily liable (drawer and endorser). Protest is required only when a bill of exchange or check drawn in one state (or country) and payable in another is dishonored, but as a matter of business practice domestic instruments are often "protested." The word protest is loosely applied to the process of presenting an instrument for payment, demanding payment, and giving notice to the drawer or endorser.

Example:

Buyer accepts a trade acceptance drawn by Seller. Seller endorses and discounts the acceptance at Doe Bank, which sends it to Roe Bank for collection. Roe Bank's notary public (usually an employee) presents the instrument to Buyer for payment, which is refused. The notary then *protests* (using the term loosely): he makes out the certificate, attaches it to the instrument and sends notice of protest to Seller, who is secondarily liable, through Doe Bank. In this case, Seller is the drawer and the endorser.

Provision of Necessaries. The supply of food, clothing, medical services, and household supplies that a husband is legally bound to provide for his wife. If a third person, *e.g.,* a doctor or grocer, provides these necessaries, the husband may be sued for their cost if he has failed to provide for them. Where the wife has breached her marital obligations, such as by committing ADULTERY, the husband is no longer legally bound to support her.

Provisional Remedies. Methods provided by law to make judgments more effective. The provisional remedies of arrest, temporary injunction, attachment, and receivership prevent the defendant from placing himself or his property beyond reach, or from doing damage to the very property the action was brought to protect.

The provisional remedy of *arrest* insures the court's control over the defendant. Restraining a person's liberty can be effective in coercing the performance of an act to be done, such as the payment of ALIMONY. A defendant may also be arrested, in some actions, where he is a nonresident or there is good reason to believe that he is about to depart from the state.

A *temporary injunction* can be granted by a court where there is an action seeking a permanent INJUNCTION, if the applicant will be immediately and irreparably injured unless the defendant is restrained *immediately*. A temporary injunction can also be granted when the defendant in any type of action is about to destroy, damage, or get rid of the subject of the action.

Attachment is a means of security for the plaintiff. The property of defendant that is attached is held by the court to secure payment of any judgment the plaintiff may obtain.

The provisional remedy of *receivership* puts property that is the subject of an action in the hands of a representative of the court, or "receiver." By taking custody of the property, the receiver prevents the defendant from taking it out of the court's JURISDICTION or materially injuring or destroying it.

Proximate Cause. That which, in a natural and continuous sequence, unbroken by any intervening cause, produces an injury, and without which the injury would not have occurred. For example, the failure to repair a faulty brake in an automobile may be the proximate cause of a subsequent collision.

Proxy. An authorization to vote at a meeting in place of an absent stockholder. The term is also applied to the person or persons holding the authority. Although the statutory provisions concerning voting by proxy vary throughout the states, the usual provisions are (1) that the proxy shall be in writing; (2) that the person giving it can revoke it at any time; (3) that it will expire after a certain number of months or years from its date unless the stockholder executing the proxy indicates the length of time it is to continue in force; and (4) that the term of the proxy shall be limited to a definite period.

As a meeting generally cannot be held unless a QUORUM (a certain portion) of stock is represented, it is usually necessary to get proxies when the stockholders are widely scattered. The Securities and Exchange Commission regulates the solicitation of proxies in respect to registered securities. A proxy need not be in any particular form, as long as it meets statutory requirements and requirements of the SEC. It need not be witnessed, but a witness can prove the authenticity of the signature.

Public and Private Law. Public law is the law that relates to the public as a whole, rather than to a specific individual. It involves the authority of the Federal and state governments to make laws and of Federal and state executives to issue orders, as well as ADMINISTRATIVE LAW and CRIMINAL LAW. Private law is that body of the law that pertains to the relationship between individuals as such. It includes laws regulating to contracts, sales, agency, NEGOTIABLE INSTRUMENTS, and business organizations.

Public Utility. A private corporation that renders service to an indefinite public, which has a legal right to demand and receive the service or commodities of the corporation. Public utilities are subject to special laws that do not apply to other corporations, and they are closely supervised by governmental agencies. They owe a duty to the public that they may be compelled to perform. For example, a railroad company cannot abandon part of its route without authority from the Interstate Commerce Commission. On the other hand, public utilities are given certain powers of a public nature, for example, the power of EMINENT DOMAIN. Public utilities include railroads, bus lines, airlines, gas and electric companies, hydroelectric, water, and irrigation corporations.

Publici Juris. (Latin) Of public right.

Purchase Money Mortgage. See MORTGAGE.

Q

Quadriennium Utile. In Scotch law. The term of four years allowed to a minor, after his majority, in which he may by suit or action endeavor to annul any deed to his prejudice granted during his minority.

Quash. To overthrow; to abate; to vacate; to annul; to make void.

Query. An interrogation point (?) used as the sign of a question or indicating doubt. A query on a MANUSCRIPT, a GALLEY PROOF, or a PAGE PROOF indicates doubt about a detail and is a request to the editor or author to clarify or supply the detail. For example, when a page number is missing, the proofreader places a query on the proof where the page number should be. The query is carried on the proof through each stage of printing until the editor or author is able to supply the missing detail.

Quiet. Adj. Unmolested; tranquil; free from interference or disturbance. Often used in leases.

Quiet Title, Action to. An EQUITY proceeding to establish the plaintiff's title to land by bringing into court an adverse claimant and compelling him either to establish his claim or to be estopped from asserting it. Whenever a deed or other instrument exists that may throw a cloud over the complainant's title or interest, a court of equity will clear the title by directing that the instrument be canceled, or by making other decrees required by the rights of the parties. For example, when a real estate mortgage is valid on its face but has ceased to be a LIEN, it may be canceled as a cloud on the title by an action to quiet title.

Quitclaim Deed. See DEED.

Quo Warranto. A WRIT of inquiry as to the warrant or authority for doing the act complained of. The writ tests the right of a person to hold an office or franchise or to exercise some right or privilege derived from the state. Quo warranto affirms an existing right to an office, or it sets aside wrongful claims of a pretender. An information in the nature of a quo warranto has replaced the old writ, but the terms *information in the nature of a quo warranto* and *quo warranto* are used interchangeably and synonymously and have substantially the same purpose. The power to file a quo warranto is incident to the office of the attorney general, but the privilege of instituting the proceeding upon the refusal of the attorney general to act has been granted to private individuals in their capacity as taxpayers and citizens.

Quorum. The number of persons who must legally be present at a meeting to transact corporate business or the business of any assembly of persons. When the membership of the assembling group or body consists of a *definite* number of persons as required by law—for example, a board of directors or the United States Senate—a majority (more than half) of the members is required to make a quorum, unless the controlling law expressly states that another number constitutes a quorum. At COMMON LAW, when the membership of the assembling body consists of an *indefinite* number of persons (that is, the law requires no definite number)—as the stockholders of a corporation—any number constitutes a quorum; however, the BYLAWS, and frequently the statutes or charter, customarily make an express provision concerning a quorum. In the case of a stockholders' meeting, the designated quorum usually relates to the amount of stock represented at the meeting, and not to the number of stockholders.

Quotations and Indented Material, Typing. Passages (words of another) or recessed material that is typed in such a manner as to be set apart from regular text by the leaving of blank space or margins.

HOW THE SECRETARY TYPES QUOTATIONS AND OTHER INDENTED MATERIAL

Margins and paragraphs. The left margin of quotations and other indented material should be five spaces to the right of the principal left margin; the beginning of a paragraph within the material should be indented an additional five spaces. If a quotation begins in the middle of a paragraph, the paragraph indentation is omitted.

The right margin of indented material may be even with the principal right margin or about five spaces to the left of it.

Short lines of indented material should be indented about fifteen spaces, thus:

The American Bar
The Bar Register
The Lawyer's List

Line spacing. Quotations are usually single spaced, but this does not apply to all indented material. Triple space before and after each quotation or other indented material; double space between paragraphs of single-spaced indented material.

Quotation marks. Place double quotation marks at the beginning and end of the quotation and at the beginning of each new paragraph within the quoted material. Change double quotation marks in material that you quote to single quotation marks, thus conforming to the rule that quotations within quotations should be enclosed in single quotation marks. Change single quotation marks in quoted material to double quotation marks.

Errors. Copy quotations exactly, even obvious errors. Indicate errors in the same way that you do in making an exact copy of any material. (See CHINESE COPY.)

Italics. If words in the original are in italics, underscore them. If words that are not in italics in the original are underscored at the direction of the dictator, the words "Italics ours" in parentheses are added at the end of the quotation. It frequently happens that part of a quoted passage is italicized and that the dictator wishes to emphasize another part of it. In that case, put "Italics theirs" in parentheses immediately following the italicized matter, and add the words "Emphasis ours" in parentheses at the end of the quotation. In Figure 1, page 363, the word *records* was italicized in the original. The rest of the underscoring was added by the dictator for emphasis.

How to show omissions. Omissions of part of a quotation are indicated by the use of ellipses. They may be points (dots) or asterisks (stars) and are usually in groups of three. Preferably, there is a space between asterisks, but not between points. Some law offices that formerly used asterisks now use points, probably because they eliminate the necessity of using the shift key and, also, they look neater if the material contains many omissions. The secretary will be guided by the practice in her office.

In using either points or asterisks, simply remember that they take the place of words, and place them accordingly. Thus, if a quotation begins in the middle of a sentence, there is no space between the quotation mark and the first ellipsis, but there is a space between the final ellipsis and the following word. If an entire sentence is omitted, two spaces precede and follow the ellipses, just as they would the sentence. Punctuation is placed in the same relation to the ellipses as if they were words.

Indicate omission of one or more entire paragraphs by a line of ellipses, five spaces apart. Some law offices use a single group of three asterisks in the center of the line instead of a full line.

Figure 1 illustrates a quotation with points showing omissions. (It also shows errors that were in the material being copied.) Note that the first

```
        The pertinent part of the opinion rendered by the
Copyright Office at our request reads as follows:

        "The Copyright Office does not undertake to pass
        upon his [the author's] rights, leaving the ques-
        tion to the courts in case of dispute.  It simply
        records (italics theirs) his claims, and by this
        recording gives him certain rights provided his
        claims can be substantiated.

            .   .   .   .   .   .   .   .   .   .   .

            "... this [copyright] is taken out in the
        name of the publisher rather than of the author,
        as the contract itself is really a license to sell
        from the publisher to the author [sic].  It is
        also the duty of the publisher to take all neces-
        sary steps to effect renewals... .

            "An auther should be 'guided' by his pub-
        lisher in all questions of copyright."  (Emphasis
        ours.)

        We contend that this opinion strongly supports the
contention of the petitioner.
```

Quotations and Indented Material—Typing: Figure 1.
Exact (Chinese) copy of quoted material.

paragraph begins in the middle; that there are one or more paragraphs omitted; the next paragraph begins and ends in the middle of a sentence; the last paragraph is quoted in full. Note also in Figure 1 that there are four points at the end of the second paragraph. The fourth one is a period, indicating the end of the sentence.

See also TAKE-IN.

R

Radio Photo. A service covering the transmission of photographs by radio. Among the types of material suitable for transmission are financial statements, machine drawings, production curves, fashion designs, architectural designs, typewritten matter, printed matter, affidavits, contracts, signatures, and business and legal papers of all kinds. Photo service is available to the public through Mackay Radio and R.C.A. Communications, Inc.

Rand McNally Bankers Directory. A semiannual publication, with a monthly supplement, giving the latest statement, official personnel, transit number, check routing symbol, and other data on every bank in the United States. Similar, but less inclusive, data are included on every Canadian bank. Latest statements and names of officers are given for all foreign banks of any importance. U. S. banking and commercial laws are discussed. Directors of all banks are listed geographically, and there is a list of discontinued bank titles for the five years preceding each issue.

Range. 1. In real estate, a row of *townships* (rectangular tracts of land divided into six-mile squares) running north and south. See LAND DESCRIPTION.

2. In stock market parlance, *range* refers to the price fluctuations that occur at the *beginning* of a trading session (opening range); or to the price fluctuations that occur at the *end* of a trading session at the close of the day's market (closing range).

Ransom. The money demanded for the release of a person from captivity. See KIDNAPPING.

Rape. The carnal knowledge of a woman taken forcibly and against her will by a man who is not her husband. Carnal knowledge has been interpreted by most courts and statutes as penetration to any degree.

Most statutes have created an offense commonly known as *statutory rape* where the crime consists in having sexual intercourse with a female under statutory age. The offense may be either with or without the female's consent.

Ratification. The approval of an act that had not been binding previously; ratification, or *affirmance,* reverts and becomes effective as of the date the act was performed. An infant may ratify, or affirm, his contracts after he reaches his majority; a principal may ratify, or affirm, the unauthorized acts of an agent; a corporation may ratify, or affirm, the unauthorized acts of its officers. A corporation cannot ratify or affirm the acts of its promoters before the corporation was formed because it was not in existence and could not possibly have entered into a contract at that date. It may, however, *adopt* the acts of the promoters.

Real Property. The land, appurtenances, and any man-made improvement attached to it. (All other property is PERSONAL PROPERTY.) Thus, in addition to the land, real property includes the buildings, natural growth, minerals, and timber, that *have not been separated from the land.* For example, apples on the tree constitute real property, whereas harvested apples become personal property.

Real Property Description. A written representation contained in a LEGAL INSTRUMENT of a particular piece of land, the appurtenances and any man-made improvement attached to it. Such representation is usually made from other documents or from an ABSTRACT OF TITLE. The secretary must be exceptionally accurate in preparing the instrument that describes REAL PROPERTY. Property is never identified solely by street and number because the names and numbers of streets might change. For details on how to prepare real property descriptions, see LAND DESCRIPTION.

Rebate. A deduction from a fixed payment, charge, or rate. The amount is not taken out before payment, but like a refund, is "rebated" to the payer after he has remitted the full amount due.

Rebates are frequently paid to taxpayers because of tax overpayments that may result from miscalculation, a change in the rates by which the original calculation was made, or excessive amounts withheld from income at the source. Each law contains its own particular provisions for rebates, and stipulates the procedure that must

be complied with to be able to obtain it. See WITHHOLDING.

Receiver. *In real estate,* a court-appointed custodian who holds property for the court and attends to the details of management pending final disposition of the matter before the court. While the receiver holds the property, no person can proceed against it without the consent of the court. Thus, a receivership effectively prevents the dissipation of property though haphazard seizures.

The receiver appointed by the court in which the proceeding is instituted has JURISDICTION only within the territorial limits of the court as prescribed by law. An ANCILLARY *receiver* is one appointed in a foreign jurisdiction for the purpose of taking charge of the assets in the jurisdiction where he is appointed.

A MORTGAGE may provide that the holder of the mortgage is entitled to the appointment of a receiver in any action for FORECLOSURE or the mortgage. See also DEFAULT.

Receiver of Stolen Property. One who knowingly obtains goods that are stolen. The act of receiving stolen property is an offense that involves a criminal intent as a material element of the crime, such as an intent to aid the thief, or to obtain a reward for returning the goods to the owner, or in some way to derive profit from the act. A person who receives and passes stolen goods is sometimes known as a "fence."

Receivership. See PROVISIONAL REMEDIES.

Record on Appeal. A copy of the pleadings, exhibits, orders or decrees filed in a case in the lower court, and a transcript of the testimony taken in the case. The purpose of the record is to inform the APPELLATE COURT of what transpired in the lower court. The rules specify that the record shall be abbreviated as much as possible, so that the judges will not have to wade through a mass of extraneous material. The appellate court does not need to be informed about matters that are not pertinent to the decision of the questions before it. The larger the record, the more expensive it is.

Assignment of errors and instructions to the clerk. Within a certain number of days after the NOTICE OF APPEAL is filed, the number being specified by the *rules of the reviewing court* (see APPEAL), the appellant files assignments of error and directions to the CLERK OF THE COURT for making up the transcript of record on appeal. The assignments of error and directions to the clerk may be combined in one document.

The purposes of the assignment of errors are to apprize the appellate court of the specific questions presented by the appellant for consideration, and to inform the opposite party of the matters of error relied on, so that discussion may be limited and concentrated on those points.

The directions to the clerk designate the portion of the proceedings and evidence to be included in the transcript of record—those portions pertinent to the questions before the appellate court. The appellee might consider that other portions of the record will throw light on the questions to be reviewed by the court. If so, the appellee files additional directions and cross-assignments.

In lieu of directions to the clerk the parties may file written stipulations with the clerk designating the contents of the record.

Preparation. The directions for preparing the notice of appeal apply also to assignments of error and instructions to the clerk. The originals are filed with the clerk of the court, and copies are served on counsel for the appellee. Proof of service of these documents on opposing counsel is filed with the clerk and included in the transcript of record.

Who prepares the record. The clerk of the court or the appellant prepares the record from the directions to the clerk filed by the parties. The common practice is to employ a court reporter to make up the transcript, but sometimes preparation of the record is the task of the secretary to the attorney for the appellant.

How to prepare the record. The instructions to the clerk will indicate to the secretary the documents and evidence that are to be included in the record. She will copy them from the papers in the court file, which may be obtained from the clerk of the court. The following directions are applicable to the preparation of records in any state:

1. Omit formal parts of documents.
2. Copy pleadings in the order of filing.
3. In the center of the page, just above the pleading, put in solid caps the nature or kind of document, such as "Demurrer to Amended Complaint" (not simply "Demurrer").
4. Do not copy the caption of the pleadings.
5. Indicate the filing date of each pleading by typing "Filed" and the date at the end of the pleading. This information is

usually stamped on the back of the document.

6. The first page in the record is a complete index that gives in chronological order the date of the filing of each instrument in the court below, the name or character of the instrument, and the page of the record where the same may be found. The index is prepared last.

Format and make-up of record. Consult the rules. They provide whether the record shall be printed or typewritten, or either. They also specify the kind of paper, size of type, folio size, and the like. Here are the requirements in a typical state that permits a record to be either printed or typewritten. The following requirements also apply to briefs.

1. Black and distinct lettering
2. Type no smaller than small pica
3. Double spaced (this requirement is stated in terms of leading for a printed brief)
4. Margin no less than one inch
5. Quoted material indented and single spaced (for a printed record this requirement is stated in terms of ems)
6. Opaque, white, unglossed paper
7. Legal cap if typewritten; 6 by 9 inch folio if printed

Binding, volumes, and title. The record is bound in pamphlets. If typewritten, the pamphlets are securely fastened; if printed, they are stitched. If the record consists of more than 200 pages, it should be bound in two or more volumes. The cover of each volume contains the style of the cause, the title of the appellate court, the title of the court from which the cause is appealed, and the names and addresses of counsel, and, if more than one volume, the number of the volume.

Certification, filing, and service. The record is certified by the clerk of the lower court, and also verified by him if he does not prepare it. A copy (or copies) is served on opposing counsel, and the original and required number of copies (see the rules) filed with the clerk of the appellate court, together with proof of service. The record must be filed within the time specified by the rules. A filing fee is required at the time the record is filed.

Record Sheet. See SUIT REGISTER.

Recorder's Court. A tribunal of limited jurisdiction. See INFERIOR COURTS.

Recording Fee. The fee which is fixed by state statutes for recording a legal document in an official recording office. See RECORDING OFFICE.

Recording of Conditional Sale Contracts. The official registration with the proper authorities of a written document which establishes the terms and conditions of the CONTRACT made between buyer and seller in a CONDITIONAL SALE.

In some states (Delaware, Massachusetts, New Jersey, New York, and Wisconsin, for example), a conditional sale contract may be filed or recorded in the *land records,* with a description of the land on which the articles have been installed; subsequent purchasers or mortgagees of the REAL PROPERTY are bound by the recorded conditional sale contract, and the conditional seller may remove the article in the event of nonpayment. If a conditional sale contract is not recorded, subsequent purchasers or mortgagees are not bound by it unless they knew of the conditional sale contract. As in the case of prior recorded chattel mortgages, some states do not require subsequent purchasers or mortgagees to search the records for conditional sales contracts. They are bound only if they know of the prior conditional sale.

Recording of a Deed. Filing of a DEED in a public office designated by state statute, generally the county or town clerk's office or Recorder's office where the property is located. A person desiring to record a deed deposits with the proper official the original signed instrument, properly acknowledged. It is now *filed for record* and is deemed to be recorded. All persons have CONSTRUCTIVE notice of the existence of the deed. The official copies the document in his record books, indexes it, and returns the original, with suitable notations as to recording, to the person who presented it for recording. An unrecorded deed, while valid and effective as between the parties, is ineffective so far as subsequent bona fide purchasers or mortgagees of the same property are concerned.

The usual practice is for the purchaser's attorney to attend to the recording and for the purchaser to pay the recording fees. The attorney also sees that the proper revenue stamps, known as documentary stamps, are affixed to the deed, if required by his state. Federal documentary stamps are no longer required. The attorney also sees that the proper transfer tax is withheld from the seller at closing and paid by check or cash to the proper court official, if his state requires no documentary stamps. See TRANSFER TAX. Where there is a TITLE INSURANCE company representative at the closing, he may take the deed, at-

tend to the recording, and return it to the attorney. Eventually the recorded deed is returned to the owner of the property by his attorney or mailed to him directly by the recorder's office.

Recording of Lease. Filing a copy of the LEASE with the proper official of the county where the leased property is located. State laws differ as to the necessity for recording a SHORT-TERM LEASE. As a practical matter, regardless of statute, a lease on property or space of any importance should be recorded by the lessee. Recording serves notice to the world that lessee holds possession of the premises for a specified term; it assures him of possession against another leasing of the premises by the same owner and protects lessee's possession if lessor sells the property.

For recording purposes, a skeleton form of lease may be used. This serves the dual purpose of saving recording fees (which are generally based on the number of words, or the number of pages, in the document recorded) and of avoiding publicity as to the terms of the lease.

Recording of Legal Instruments. The official registration with the proper authorities of written documents for the purpose of establishing legally, some act or agreement. The purpose of recording the instrument is to protect the interests of all persons. For example, *A* wants to purchase some property from *B*. He learns from the public record that *C* holds a mortgage on the property. *A* purchases the property, but he makes legal arrangements that will protect not only his own interests but those of *C* as well.

What the secretary does. When the lawyer asks his secretary to have an instrument recorded, she should know not only what official is to record it, but also *where* it is to be recorded. For example, although the lawyer's office is located in Adams County and the client signs the paper there, if the instrument relates to property located in Brown County, the instrument will be recorded in Brown County, not Adams County. The firm's name and address will probably appear on the legal back in which the instrument is bound. Some Recorders require that the attorney's name as preparer and address be typed on the document to be recorded before it will be accepted for recording. Before having the instrument recorded, write immediately above it, "Please record and return to:" If the firm's name and address are not printed on the legal back, type them on it.

If the instrument is to be recorded in a place located near the office, take it in person to the office of the proper official. He will receipt for it and return it to the lawyer's office when he has recorded it.

Pay the *recording fee,* which is fixed by state statutes. Unless the photostat method of recording is used, the fee is usually based on the number of folios (groups of 100 words) in the instrument. Pay the fee out of petty cash, or take a blank check to the recording office and fill in the amount when you are told what the recording fee will be. When the photostat method is used, the fee is usually charged per page.

When it is necessary to mail the instrument to the recording office, send it by registered mail, return receipt requested with a covering letter. The letter should be addressed to the designated official and should describe the instrument sufficiently to identify it. Enclose a check for the fee or re-

quest that a bill be forwarded. The official will not record the instrument until the fee is received. The model below illustrates how such a letter might be worded:

REGISTERED
RETURN RECEIPT REQUESTED
November 14, 19..

John R. Blank Esquire
Clerk of the County Court
Starkville, Mississippi (ZIP)
Sir:

We are enclosing for recording lease, dated November 14, 19.., between Edgar S. Norris and Robert T. Ellis.

If you will tell us the correct amount of your fee for recording this instrument, we shall forward a check to you promptly.

> Very truly yours,
> ELWOOD & SMITH
> By
>   S. R. Elwood

Enclosure

A blank check may be sent with the words "not over Five Dollars" typed on the check, and the recording official asked to fill in the proper amount and notify the attorney of the amount when he returns the instrument.

Recording of Real Estate Instruments. The official registration with the proper authorities to those written documents that establish ownership or the right to possess and use certain land, appurtenances, and any man-made improvement attached to it. (See REAL PROPERTY.) Real estate instruments are usually recorded in a public office so that the record is available to any one who is interested. The purpose of the record is to protect the interests of all persons concerned. See (1) RECORDING OF DEED; (2) RECORDING OF LEASE; (3) RECORDING OF CONDITIONAL SALE; (4) RECORDING OF LEGAL INSTRUMENTS.

Recording Office. A public office where legal instruments are officially recorded so that they may be available to anyone who is interested. See RECORDING OF LEGAL INSTRUMENTS.

Redemption. 1. *Of real estate.* The recovery of property given as security for a debt by paying off a note, BOND or MORTGAGE. *Equity of redemption* is the right of a mortgagor to recover (redeem) the property and obtain legal TITLE thereto by paying the amount due in full, with interest.

2. *Of securities.* The exchange of corporate stocks or bonds for cash. Common stock is never "redeemed"; preferred stock may be redeemable; bonds are frequently issued subject to redemption.

Redemption Tables for Series E Bonds. A series of tables showing the current value of E bonds published by the United States Government. A single copy is 60¢ and is for a six-month period. Or a two-year subscription released semi-annually, may be ordered for $2.20. Write

Superintendent of Documents
U. S. Government Printing Office
Washington, D.C. 20402

Re-entry. The act of resuming the possession of lands or tenements in pursuance of a right which party exercising it reserved to himself when he quit his former possession. See FORCIBLE ENTRY AND DETAINER.

Refund on Unused Travel Ticket, Letter Requesting. A brief statement giving the necessary facts is the best way to secure a prompt refund for unused travel tickets. Here is a recommended pattern to follow in returning a ticket, after cancellation has been made by phone.

1. Enclose and describe the ticket, giving ticket number, accommodation, travel points, time, and date.

2. Tell when canceled.

3. Ask for refund, stating amount if it is known.

4. State to whom refund should be made.

Gentlemen:

I enclose unused ticket #1576 for Roomette 6, Car 758, on train leaving Los Angeles for San Francisco at 9:00 P.M. on October 29, 19___.

This ticket was canceled on October 28, as indicated on the back.

Please arrange to have refund in the amount of $70.00 made to:

Mr. R. S. Adams
Adams, Woods & Miller
Eastern, Connecticut 06101

Very truly yours,

If the lawyer is traveling at the firm's expense and wants the refund made to the firm and sent to his attention, it is better to write the letter in his name. The last two paragraphs of the letter should then read:

The ticket was canceled on October 28, as indicated on the back. I, therefore, shall appreciate receiving your refund in the amount of $70.00.

Please make the refund check payable to Adams, Woods & Miller but send it to my attention.

Yours truly,

R. S. Adams

Register. See CLERK'S PERMANENT RECORD BOOK.

Registered Mail. See POSTAL SERVICE.

Relict. The survivor of a pair of married people; whether the survivor is the husband or the wife; it means the relict of the united pair, (or of the marriage union) not the relict of the deceased individual.

Relief Printing. See LETTERPRESS.

Reminders to the Lawyer. It is advisable for a secretary in a new job to ask the lawyer if he likes to be reminded of things to be done and if he has a preference as to the method. His diary shows his appointments and the things he has to do. For many lawyers, placing the diary, open at the current date, in a conspicuous place on his desk is sufficient.

Suggestions for other methods of reminding the lawyer of things to do follow.

How to remind the lawyer of appointments. In the later afternoon, or the first thing in the morning, place on the lawyer's desk a typed schedule of his appointments, giving him all the pertinent information. Memorandum paper about 6 by 9 inches is desirable for this purpose. Before the time of the appointment give the lawyer the file and other material that he will need for it.

Reminders showing appointments for a month. Many lawyers like to see the month's engagements at a glance. There are calendars designed for this purpose, usually on cardboard about 9 by 11 inches. Figure 1 is an illustration of such a calendar. Note that under the arrangement of dates on this calendar, every Sunday in the month is on the top row, every Monday on the next row, and so on.

How to remind the lawyer of things to be done. To remind the lawyer of a task that he should do, place the file on his desk, with a memorandum if necessary. For example, if a real estate closing is scheduled for the 29th and papers must be drawn for it, the secretary puts the file on his desk about the 27th with a memo that the closing is scheduled for the 29th.

If the lawyer told her that he wants to do a certain thing in connection with a matter, she attaches a reminder to the file. For example, suppose he told her, "If we do not receive that information from Robinson by Friday, I want to obtain a stipulation postponing his case another week." On Friday, if the information has not been received, the secretary types a memo, "You wanted to obtain a stipulation to postpone this case," and attach it to the Robinson file before placing it on the lawyer's desk. It might be even better for the secretary to type the stipulation and give it to him with the file. This procedure would depend on the secretary's experience and the lawyer's wishes in connection with delegating such duties to her.

Some lawyers make a practice of calling their secretaries into their office the first thing every morning to dispose of the correspondence and to discuss pending matters and things to be done. This is the ideal arrangement. For the discussion, she takes with her a list of things to be done and any material pertaining to them, as well as a notebook.

How to remind the lawyer of court work. In a large office a diary of court cases is maintained by the managing clerk under the supervision of the managing attorney. Although each lawyer in charge of a matter is presumed to know its status, it is the duty of the managing clerk to follow

NOVEMBER

	Sunday, 6th	Sunday, 13th	Sunday, 20th	Sunday, 27th
	Monday, 7th	Monday, 14th	Monday, 21st	Monday, 28th
Tuesday, 1st	Tuesday, 8th	Tuesday, 15th	Tuesday, 22nd	Tuesday, 29th
Wednesday, 2nd	Wednesday, 9th	Wednesday, 16th	Wednesday, 23rd	Wednesday, 30th
Thursday, 3rd	Thursday, 10th	Thursday, 17th	Thursday, 24th Thanksgiving Day	
Friday, 4th	Friday, 11th	Friday, 18th	Friday, 25th	CALENDAR 19...
Saturday, 5th	Saturday, 12th	Saturday, 19th	Saturday, 26th	

Reminders to the Lawyer: Figure 1. Appointments calendar for a month.

the status of the matter, to furnish information regarding the status, and to aid in securing prompt and orderly disposition of court matters. In a comparatively small office, the secretary to the senior partner or to the managing partner, will probably have this responsibility.

From diary records, the secretary sends a written notice to the lawyer in charge, sufficiently in advance to permit him to make preparations necessary to take the indicated step. Figure 2 on page 374 is a printed form, filled out, used for this. Mimeographed or typed slips would serve the purpose. The lawyer in charge of the matter should return the written notice to the secretary with a notation of the action taken.

Another method of reminding the lawyers in the office about pending court work is to type the entries from the diary each week for two weeks in advance, making as many copies as necessary to circulate among the lawyers. In an office with numerous attorneys, the list would be mimeographed. Each lawyer then checks the cases in which he is interested. Note that the diary entries include the initials of the interested lawyers.

When the secretary to a lawyer receives a notice from the managing clerk, or from the secretary to the managing partner, she checks her DIARY and sees that preparations necessary to take the required action are made.

MORGAN, BURBANK & CHAMBERS
Managing Clerk's Department

To Mr. Edwards

Reference Wilson vs. Green

Time: October 22,   19 -- . at 10 AM.

Place: County Court House, Department B

Action

　　　　Last day to

　　　　Motion for order dismissing complaint

　　　　Settlement of

　　　　Examination of

　　　　Hearing

　　　　Trial

　　　　Argument

　　　　　　　　　　　　　　　　　　　　　　ESR
　　　　　　　　　　　　　　　　　　　　Managing Clerk

Dated October 19   , 19 --

(Please note below disposition of matter and return to
Managing Clerk.)

Attended and argued in support of motion.
Decision reserved.

　　　　　　　　　　　　　　　J. T. E.

Reminders to the Lawyer: Figure 2. Notice of diary entry.

Remainder. The remnant of an estate in the land, depending upon a particular prior estate created at the same time and by the same instrument, and limited to arise immediately on the determination of that estate, and not in abridgement of it. For example, a mother deeds her real estate to her daughter, but reserves a life estate for herself. The daughter is the remainderman. Upon the death of her mother she will hold a fee simple in the real estate. See LIFE ESTATE.

Remise. To remit or give up. A formal word in deeds of release and quitclaim; the usual phrase being "remise, release, and forever quitclaim."

Remittitur. The power of a judge to decrease the amount of an excessive award made by a jury verdict. The award is decreased, with the consent of the plaintiff, as condition for the denial of defendant's motion for a new trial because of the excessiveness.

Remittitur is a means of giving a just award without the expense and trouble of a new trial. See ADDITUR.

Replevin. A court action to recover possession of property unlawfully taken or detained. Title to the property must be in the person bringing the action. Thus, if title passes to the buyer and the seller refuses to deliver the goods, the buyer may bring an action in replevin to get possession of the goods. Or the seller, under a conditional sale contract by which he retains title to the goods until payment is made, may recover the goods by an action in replevin if the buyer does not make the payments called for by the contract.

Representative Action. In corporate law, a suit brought to redress injury to the stockholders rather than to the CORPORATION. (See DERIVATIVE ACTION.) Types of injury that would give a stock holder the right to start a representative action would be wrongful deprivation of the right to vote, to transfer stocks, to share in dividends, or to exercise PRE-EMPTIVE RIGHTS. One stockholder may bring the action on behalf of himself and all other stockholders who may be similarly damaged.

Res Ipsa Loquitur Doctrine. The *res ipsa loquitur* doctrine means that certain occurrences contain within themselves a sufficient basis to infer NEGLIGENCE. Where the instrument causing the accident was in the exclusive control of the defendant, and the accident is one which would not ordinarily happen without negligence, the facts are sufficient to justify an inference of negligence and to force the defendant to explain it. For example, if a building collapses and injures a man passing by, it may be inferred that the injury is a result of negligence. The injured party is not forced to show at the trial the specific negligent act of the defendant that caused the building to fall. It becomes the duty of the *defendant* to prove that he was *not* negligent.

Rescission. An action in equity whereby a court is asked to annul a contract entered into through fraud, misrepresentation, or excusable error. For example, if a person enters into a contract of partnership and then discovers that material facts were misrepresented, he brings an action in rescission. Rescission may be absolute or qualified. Thus, in rescission of a contract of sale, the seller resumes title and possession of the goods as though he had never parted with them, but he has no claim for damages. In qualified rescission he resumes title and possession but does not rescind the entire contract because he reserves the right to sue for damages. A contract may also be rescinded by mutual consent.

Reservations, Letter Making.

1. *Plane reservation.* A letter making a plane reservation should cover the following points: (1) name and position of person desiring reservation; (2) flight and date on which space is desired; (3) schedule of flight; (4) air card (see TRAVEL CARD) number (if any); (5) confirmation.

Mr. Robert J. Jones, partner in the law firm Hamilton, Jones & Adams, would like to reserve space to Los Angeles on Flight 26 out of Chicago on Saturday, November 24. Our schedule shows this flight leaves at 9:45 A.M., Central Standard Time, for Los Angeles and arrives at 2:45 P.M., Pacific Standard Time. Mr. Jones is holder of air travel card 72910.

Please confirm reservation by wire immediately.

2. *Train reservation.* A letter making a train reservation should cover the following points: (1) name and position of person desiring reservation; (2) accommodation desired; (3) point of departure and destination; (4) date and time; (5) name of train, if known; (6) arrangement for delivery of tickets; (7) confirmation; (8) arrangement for payment.

Please reserve a drawing room for Mr. Robert J. Jones, partner in the law firm Hamilton, Jones & Adams, on the Rosebowl from Chicago to Los Angeles, leaving Chicago Saturday, November 27, at 3:00 P.M. Mr. Jones will call for the tickets at the Chicago station on November 24.

Please confirm reservation as soon as possible.

If you will send the invoice for the tickets to this office, we shall remit at once.

3. *Hotel reservation.* A letter making a hotel reservation should cover the following points: (1) accommodations desired; (2) name of person for whom reservation is requested; (3) date and time of arrival; (4) probable date of departure; (5) request for confirmation; (6) Purpose of registration such as attending a convention or seminar.

Please reserve for Mr. Robert J. Jones, partner in the law firm of Hamilton, Jones & Adams, a corner bedroom and bath, preferably a southeastern exposure, beginning Monday, December 14. Mr. Jones will arrive early in the evening of the 14th and plans to leave the morning of December 20. Mr. Jones will be attending the Practising Law Institute Seminar.

Please confirm this reservation by wire.

Reservation of Corporate Name.

Deciding on a corporation's name is a serious matter, to which the incorporators and the lawyer give careful consideration. All of the states require that a corporation's name should indicate that it is a corporation by the use of *company, association, incorporated,* or similar words or abbreviations of them. Also, the majority of the states will not permit the use of the word *bank* or *trust* in a name of a corporation unless it is a banking institution. The chief importance of a name to the incorporators is that, as a business develops, its name acquires a value in itself, representing to a great extent the GOOD WILL of the company. The state laws and the courts generally protect the corporation's exclusive right to the use of its name. The state official will not accept for filing a CERTIFICATE OF INCORPORATION, if the name of the proposed corporation so closely resembles that of a corporation existing in the state that deception or confusion might result. Therefore, the lawyer will tell his secretary to find out if the choice of name is available, and, if so, to reserve it.

What the secretary does to clear the name. The secretary writes to the designated state official and asks if the chosen name is available. She ascertains if the proposed name is available not only in the STATE OF INCORPORATION, but also in any states in which the corporation expects to qualify. If the organization of the corporation must be completed quickly, the secretary might wire, or at least ask the state official to answer by wire collect.

In some states the state official will reserve a name for a specified period of time for the payment of a fee or as a courtesy. In the states that require a fee enclose a check when asking to have the name reserved. When the secretary wires, she should send the check to the designated official as soon as she gets a reply.

The letter might read as follows:

The Honorable John R. Blank
Secretary of State of Delaware
Dover, Delaware 19901
Sir:

    Joseph A. Smith, Inc.

Will you please advise us whether the above styled name is available for a domestic corporation, which we are about to organize under the laws of your state.

If so, will you be good enough to reserve it for us for the statutory period. Enclosed is check for $____ in payment of reservation fee.

    Please reply by wire, collect.
          Very truly yours,
          Hamilton & Jones

If the incorporators expect to qualify as a foreign corporation in another state, the first paragraph will be changed to read: ". . . foreign corporation, which we are about to qualify to transact business in your state."

If the secretary wires, the telegram might read: "Wire collect if Joseph A. Smith, Inc. is available for corporation."

Reserved Powers. See EXCLUSIVE POWERS.

Residence. A particular locality where a person lives. He need not intend to make his residence a fixed and permanent home, which is what distinguishes a residence from a DOMICILE. Although a person may have only one domicile, he may have many residences.

Residential Lease. A binding CONTRACT for the possession of lands and improvements to be used for dwelling purposes. These may be single-family homes and two- to four-family houses. See also COMMERCIAL LEASE; LEASE.

Residuary Legacy. See LEGACY.

Resolution. A formal expression of the opinion or will of an official body or a public assembly, adopted by vote, as a legislative resolution.

Respondent. 1. The opposing party in an APPEAL.
2. The defending party in EQUITY and ADMIRALTY cases (corresponding to the DEFENDANT in a case at law).

Respondentia. A loan usually made to the master of a ship in a foreign port in cases of emergency for which the cargo aboard the ship is pledged as security. If the cargo is lost in the course of the voyage, the lender loses his money; if the cargo arrives safely at its destination, the borrower pays the sum borrowed plus the agreed interest. Like BOTTOMRY LOAN, respondentia bonds are becoming obsolete.

The term *bottomry loan* is used when the ship, rather than its cargo, is used as security for a loan.

Responsibility and Distribution line. In a legal paper, a notation of the number of copies made, the date, the dictator's initials and the secretary's initials. These should be typed in the upper left-hand corner.

Example:

3-3
10/9/..
JTB:sp

This indicates that an original and two duplicate originals and three copies, one of which is for the files, were typed on October 9, 19 .. and that the document was dictated by *JTB* to *sp*. The binding covers the notation. It is not necessary to put the notation on any page except the first one. If a page of the document is retyped subsequent to the date shown, a new responsibility line should be put on that page. The identification data should appear on the *file copy only* of wills, minutes, proxies, and statistical statements.

The distribution should be indicated in the upper right-hand corner of the file copy, thus:

1 orig. to ACC
1 orig. to ETB
1 orig. to HPM

1 copy to MST
1 copy to JFP

The third copy is the file copy.

Responsibility or Identification Line. The typed notation that shows who dictated a letter, and who typed it. The only purpose of the identification is for reference by the firm *writing* the letter. It does not belong on the original of a letter, but many firms have the line typed on the original because it saves time.

The usual position of responsibility marks is on a line with the last line of the signature, flush with the left margin. If the dictator's name is typed on the letter, there is no need for his initials to appear in the responsibility marks.

Restatements of the Law. A presentation by the American Law Institute of the "best rules" of law applied in the United States.

While the Restatements are not primary authority of the law, they have proved to be extremely persuasive. The Restatements are presumed by many to state the COMMON LAW rule, and the party opposing them has the burden to prove the contrary. This does not make the Restatements mandatory on the court, but it does indicate that they are becoming accepted as the authoritative statement of the common law in the United States.

Most of the work of compiling the Restatements was done by reporters for each topic, men eminent in their respective fields, helped by staffs of advisers. After each group of specialists determined for itself the proper statement of the "best rule" of law in each case, the tentative draft or parts of it were submitted to the Council of the

American Law Institute for debate and final approval.

Restraint of Princes and Rulers. A clause in a maritime contract that excuses the shipper for delay in delivery of goods when the vessel carrying cargo is captured or detained by the force of a sovereign nation.

Restrictive Covenant. A stipulation in an agreement limiting or restricting the action of one of the parties to an agreement. Thus, a seller of a business may agree not to engage in the same business within a certain number of years. Or a deed may contain a covenant restricting the type of building that may be placed upon the property. A restrictive covenant of this type is said to "run with the land"— subsequent purchasers are bound by the covenant whether or not it is expressly set forth in the deed to them.

Return Day of Motion. See NOTICE OF MOTION.

Return Day of Summons. The final date that a DEFENDANT must answer a SUMMONS or file a NOTICE OF APPEARANCE in accordance with civil practice and procedure codes and statutes. Thus, if the defendant is required to answer "within 20 days" from the service of the summons, the 20th day is the *return day*. In some jurisdictions certain days, designated as *return days* or *rule days*, are set aside for filing papers in court. In these jurisdictions the rules provide that the defendant shall appear "by the *next rule day*," if the summons is served on him a certain number of days before RULE DAY; otherwise, he shall appear on the following rule day. Thus, the return date is always a rule day.

These return dates are very important and the secretary should always *enter them in her diary,* whether her office is serving the summons or has received a summons for a client.

How to compute the time. The statutes and codes also provide how the time shall be computed. The usual method is to *exclude* the date from which the period of time begins to run, but to *include* the last day of the period of time. If it falls on Sunday or a legal holiday, the next business day is the return date. Intermediate Sundays or holidays are included in the computation, unless the period of time allowed is less than seven days. The period of time begins to run the day the summons is served, not the day it is dated. This method of computation of time applies to the time for filing all pleadings as well as to the return day of the summons. See also ALIAS SUMMONS.

Revocation of a Will. The act of invalidating instructions concerning the disposition of one's property after death. The maker (testator) may change or revoke his WILL at his pleasure at any time prior to his death, unless he has renounced or retracted his right of revocation by CONTRACT.

An effective revocation requires an intent to revoke plus an outward manifestation of that intent. For example, a will that is intentionally destroyed by the maker is revoked. A will may also be revoked by making a subsequent will or CODICIL that expressly revokes prior wills or that is inconsistent with any prior wills.

Right of Assemblage and Petition. A provision in the First Amendment to the Constitution that says Congress cannot deny the right of the people to assemble peaceably and to petition the Government for a redress of grievances. The Fourteenth Amendment has been interpreted by the Supreme Court as placing the same restriction on the states. See CIVIL RIGHTS; BILL OF RIGHTS.

Right to Religious Liberty. A guarantee of the First Amendment to the Constitution stating that "Congress shall make no law respecting an establishment of religion, or prohibiting the free exercise thereof. . . ." The Fourteenth Amendment has been interpreted by the Supreme Court as placing the same restrictions on the states. See CIVIL RIGHTS; BILL OF RIGHTS.

Right-to-work Laws. Legislation specifying that no person shall be denied or excluded from employment because of membership or non-membership in a labor organization. Proponents of the laws say they are necessary for the maintenance of basic freedoms being challenged by union autocracy. Labor spokesmen contend that the purpose of the laws is to weaken and destroy unions. Legislative popularity of the right-to-work laws has been limited almost exclusively to rural or southern states where union membership is small.

Robbery. The act of taking property in the possession of another, from his person or immediate presence, against his will by force or threat of injury. An example of robbery is the act of taking a wallet from a person whom the taker has knocked out; taking a sleeping man's watch, however, is LARCENY.

The greater the violence that accompanies the robbery, the more severe is the punishment.

Royalties. Payments or rentals made to the owner of a PATENT for the privilege of manufacturing or using the patented device. The term is also used to designate payments made to an author or composer under a COPYRIGHT, as well as payments under oil, gas, mining or mineral leases.

Rule Days. The particular dates that have been designated as the day or days a defendant is required to answer a SUMMONS. See RETURN DAY OF SUMMONS.

Rules of Navigation. Regulations adopted by shipping nations to govern the steering and management of ships at sea so as to avoid the danger of collision. Rules of navigation are commonly called *rules of the road*.

Compliance with the rules of navigation is considered so essential that any deviation resulting in a collision may be construed as automatic fault. To mitigate this harsh rule the doctrine of *in extremis* was developed. A violation of the rules of the road is excused under this doctrine if a vessel, through no fault of her own, is placed in a position where collision is imminent.

Rules of the Reviewing Court. See APPEAL.

Running Head. The line that runs across the top of every page of a book, magazine, pamphlet, and the like, giving the title or chapter title. In some books the running heads change with center headings.

S

Salutation. Expression of courtesy to the addressee of a letter.

Forms of salutation. See ADDRESSING OFFICIALS for the correct salutation to use in letters to people in official or honorary positions. The form of salutation varies with the tone of the letter and the degree of acquaintanceship between the lawyer and the client. The trend today is toward the less formal salutation.

1. If the letter is addressed to an individual, make the salutation singular, for example, *Dear Sir.* If the letter is addressed to a company or group, make it plural, for example, *Gentlemen* or *Dear Sirs.* The latter is preferable when addressing a firm of lawyers.

2. Never use a designation of any kind after a salutation.

Right
Dear Mr. Roberts:

Wrong
Dear Mr. Roberts, C.P.A.:

3. The salutation in a letter addressed to an organization composed of men and women is *Gentlemen* or *Ladies and Gentlemen;* to a man and woman, *Dear Sir and Madam;* to a married couple, *Dear Mr. and Mrs. Marsh.*

4. Never use a *business* title or designation of position in a salutation. (Honorary and official titles are frequently used in salutations. See the chart in ADDRESSING OFFICIALS.)

Right
Dear Mr. Adams:

Wrong
Dear Secretary:
Dear Secretary Ames:

5. If a letter addressed to a firm of lawyers is to the attention of an individual lawyer, the salutation is to the firm, not to the individual.

6. Follow a title with the surname.

Right
Dear Professor Ames:

Wrong
Dear Professor:

Forms of salutation in letters addressed to women. 1. Do not use *Miss* as a salutation unless it is followed by a name.

Right
Dear Miss Brown:
 (preferred)
Dear Madam:

Wrong
Dear Miss:

2. If the letter is addressed to a firm of women, the salutation is *Ladies* or *Mesdames.* Do not use "Dear" or "My dear" with either of these salutations.

3. The salutation to two women with the same name is:

My dear Mesdames Smith (if married)
My dear Misses Smith (if unmarried)

When in doubt as to whether the addressee is a man or woman, use the salutation appropriate for a man. *For the correct form of salutation in letters* addressed to women holding official or honorary positions, see ADDRESSING OFFICIALS.

How to type the salutation.

1. Capitalize the first word, the title, and the name. Do not capitalize *dear* unless it is used as the first word of the salutation.

2. Use a colon following the salutation. A comma is used only in social letters, particularly in those written in longhand.

3. *Mr., Mrs., Ms.,* and *Dr.* are the only titles that are abbreviated.

Salvage. A reward for saving property at sea. The principle of salvage has been developed by ADMIRALTY. On land, one who goes to the rescue of his neighbor's property receives no remuneration for his efforts.

Essentially there are three elements to a valid salvage claim:

1. The ship or property must have been so imperiled that without the salvager's aid it could not have been rescued.

2. A voluntary act on the part of the salvager is essential. There must be no pre-existing duty to give assistance, as there might be, for example, under a CONTRACT, or as there is between a vessel and its own crew.

3. The salvager must successfully save, or assist in the saving of, the property at risk.

It is interesting to note that salvage is the factor that often compels captains to remain on board their imperiled vessels, for once a ship is abandoned anyone may salvage her. If not under a pre-existing duty, the salvager will thus be entitled to a bounty. Remaining on ship, the captain may be able to overcome the peril or negotiate a reasonable salvage contract. He may

also be awaiting assistance from his own company, assistance he knows to be on the way.

Savings Bank Trust. Money deposited in a savings bank "in trust for" another person. A savings bank trust may be revoked by the depositor at his will unless he acts in a way that clearly shows his intent to make the trust irrevocable. Such an intent will be evidenced by unconditional delivery of the passbook to the beneficiary or by notice to the beneficiary or bank that the trust is absolute. A savings bank trust is also called a *Totten trust,* the name being derived from the precedent-making case *Matter of Totten* which was decided in New York.

Screening Calls. Protecting the employer from the inconvenience of answering unimportant or undesirable telephone calls. A lawyer usually expects his secretary to screen his calls; otherwise his calls do not go through the secretary but are put through directly to him.

A polite way of asking who is calling is, "May I tell Mr. Rogers who is calling?" Or, "May I ask who is calling?" A legitimate caller seldom objects to giving his name.

If the caller does not want to give his name, the secretary has the right to insist, politely but firmly, that he do so. As a matter of fact, she has no right to put through calls without first screening them, when this is expected of her, and without learning that the lawyer is willing to talk. If the caller insists upon withholding his name the secretary might say, very politely, "I'm very sorry, but Mr. Rogers has someone with him at the moment. If you cannot tell me who is calling, may I suggest that you write to him and mark your letter 'personal'? I'll be glad to see that he gets it promptly."

Finding the purpose of a call. A secretary is usually expected to find out why a person wants an appointment with her employer. This frequently poses a delicate problem in the law office, because the callers are often reluctant to disclose the nature of their legal business. However, knowledge of what the client wants frequently enables the secretary to save considerable time, not only for the lawyer but also for the prospective client. This situation is illustrated by the following conversation between a secretary and Mr. Wilson, the caller:

Secretary: Rogers & Williams. (The practice in answering the telephone varies. In some offices, the practice is to answer the telephone with the number.)
Mr. Wilson: This is James Wilson. I'd like an appointment to see Mr. Rogers, please.
Secretary: I am Mr. Rogers' secretary, Mr. Wilson, and I'll be pleased to arrange an appointment for you. Approximately what date and time would you like to see Mr. Rogers?

Informing the caller that the party he is speaking to is the lawyer's secretary gives him an opening to tell the nature of his business. But this caller did not respond in the manner the secretary desired.

Mr. Wilson: I would like to see him on Tuesday afternoon, say around 2 o'clock.
Secretary: Mr. Rogers will be busy part of the afternoon on Tuesday, Mr. Wilson. About how long will you require for your appointment?

This gives the caller another opportunity to state the nature of his business, but Mr. Wilson is rather elusive.

Mr. Wilson: I will not require more than an hour of his time. How about two to three?

Now comes the difficult part. The secretary must find out what he wants and she must do it diplomatically. The "voice with a smile" is especially important here.

Secretary: In connection with a client's visit, Mr. Wilson, it is often necessary for Mr. Rogers to have certain forms or information available. In order that I may have everything in readiness for your appointment on Tuesday, could you give me a general idea about the nature of your business? I do not need to know any of the details, of course, just a brief statement.

By giving him a good reason for the inquiry and assuring him of not being interested in details, the secretary has asked him, in a gracious and courteous manner, for a statement concerning his appointment.

Perhaps he says he wants a divorce. The secretary knows that Mr. Rogers will not handle the case but that it will be turned over to a junior member of the firm.

Secretary: Mr. Davis of this office usually handles matters of that kind and confers with Mr. Rogers regarding them when necessary. It would really be better for you to see Mr. Davis on Tuesday. If agreeable to you, I'll arrange the appointment with Mr. Davis instead of Mr. Rogers.

Or perhaps Mr. Wilson says that he has a small collection matter he would like Mr. Rogers to handle. The office does not handle collections except for retainer clients.

Secretary: I'm sorry, Mr. Wilson. As much as Mr. Rogers would like to help you, he does not handle collections. However, Mr. Robert Ames, a young member of the Bar located in this building, would be pleased to handle the matter for you. Would you like his telephone number?

There are innumerable situations, but by exercising discretion and diplomacy the secretary will soon be able to handle them all. See also

TELEPHONE COURTESY; CONTACTS OVER THE TELEPHONE; TOLL CALLS; TELEPHONE SERVICE.

Scrivener. A writer; scribe; conveyancer. One whose occupation is to draw contracts, write deeds and mortgages, and prepare other species of written instruments.

Seal. An impression upon wax or wafer, or some other substance capable of being impressed. The practice of affixing a seal to an instrument originated in the days when only a few people could write their names. Written instruments were marked with sealing wax, which was impressed with a ring or other device. This seal was the mark of the person making the instrument and took the place of his signature. Today, any material affixed to an instrument and intended as a seal, or the writing of the word *Seal* or *L.S.* (*locus sigilli,* Latin for "place of the seal") after the signature is considered a seal. The process of affixing the seal is referred to as *sealing* the instrument, and the instrument, then becomes a *sealed* instrument. Today, the sealed instrument has a twofold significance: (1) Under the statutes of limitations, the time during which suit may be brought on a sealed instrument is longer than on an unsealed instrument. (2) Suit on a contract cannot be defended on the basis that it was without consideration, because the consideration of a sealed instrument cannot be questioned. If an instrument is to be sealed, the TESTIMONIUM CLAUSE will so indicate. See also CORPORATE SEAL.

Seaman. A person who assists in the conduct, service, or maintenance of a ship. Seamen are today protected by numerous statutes which were passed to correct poor conditions and abuses that developed in the shipping industry. Seamen are also regarded as wards of the courts.

Search and Seizure. The act of probing for information or evidence on a person or his property. The Fourth Amendment to the Consitution guarantees the security of the individual against searches and seizures that are unreasonable and arbitrary. To assure a citizen his constitutional rights, the courts will give a police officer a search WARRANT only for a good reason supported by oath and describing the place to be searched and the persons or things to be seized.

Seaworthiness. That state of a seagoing vessel when it is in fit condition to withstand the perils of an ordinary voyage. In addition to the ship's structure and appliances, the fitness of the crew has been made a condition of the seaworthiness of the vessel.

The doctrine of seaworthiness has developed into a rule of absolute liability—a liability without fault. Unless a statute or contract should provide otherwise, no amount of care or diligence on the part of the shipowner relieves him of his obligation to provide a seaworthy ship, appliances, and crew. The owner's ignorance of the condition of his ship is not a valid defense when a SEAMAN sues because of injuries resulting from the vessel's unseaworthiness. ADMIRALTY, however, has developed the rule that allows DAMAGES to be diminished in proportion to the amount of NEGLIGENCE attributable to the injured seaman. This is contrary to the COMMON LAW rule that bars recovery when there is CONTRIBUTORY NEGLIGENCE.

Secondary Boycott. See BOYCOTT.

Second-class Mail. See POSTAL SERVICE.

Second Mortgage. See FORMS OF MORTGAGES.

Section and Township. See LAND DESCRIPTION.

Security Deposit Under Lease. A deposit by tenant with the landlord of money or securities, at the time a LEASE is signed, to secure the landlord against loss upon failure of the tenant to pay rent due. The lease may contain various provisions with regard to the security deposit:

1. That interest will be paid to the tenant on such deposit.

2. That upon reletting the premises, damages sustained by the landlord may be collected from the security deposit, and the balance returned to the ousted tenant.

3. That the security deposit shall be retained by the landlord as liquidated damages if the landlord terminates the lease because of the tenant's DEFAULT. Courts in some cases have compelled the landlord to return the deposit to the tenant, less rent due up to the time of termination of lease.

Bonus. In lieu of a security deposit, the tenant may, at the time the lease is signed, pay a sum of money as a "bonus" for receiving the lease. This amount becomes the property of the landlord upon payment, and no part of it is recoverable by the tenant even if

default occurs early in the life of the lease.

Advance rental. In lieu of a security deposit, the tenant, at the time of signing the lease, may pay the landlord a sum of money to be applied in payment of the rent for the last months of the lease. Upon default, the landlord is generally allowed to retain the advance. In a few states (Illinois, for example), the "advance rental" is treated as a "security deposit," and landlord must return the amount to the tenant, less the amount of delinquent rent.

Effect of assignment of lease. A tenant's right to refund of a security deposit or advance rental does not automatically pass upon an assignment of the lease. It passes to the assignee only if the assignment specifically so provides, or if it is assigned by a separate instrument.

Effect of sale of leased property. The landlord is not relieved of his liability to return the tenant's deposit by a sale of the leased property. The fact that he turned the deposit over to the purchaser is no excuse.

Seizin. Actual possession of LAND. A COVENANT in a WARRANTY DEED that the seller is "seized" of the premises in FEE SIMPLE and has good right to convey, means that at the time of execution and delivery of the DEED, he is in lawful possession of the fee estate in the property, and has lawful TITLE. If the seller does not have lawful title, the purchaser cannot get title; but under the *covenant of seizin* the seller becomes personally liable to the purchaser for any expenses incurred up to the time of delivery of the deed. A covenant of seizin does not run with the land but is personal to the

GRANTEE. A certification of title by a title company that the seller has a good and marketable title to the premises in fee, and that he has the right to convey, may furnish better protection to the purchaser than a covenant of seizin. See also COVENANTS OF TITLE.

Semi-block Style. See LETTERS, STYLE AND SETUP.

Seniority. The principle of granting employees preference in certain phases of employment in accordance with the length of service.

Separate but Equal. A system that was used to maintain legally segregation of Negroes and whites. In 1896 the Supreme Court held that a statute requiring "separate but equal" accommodations for the white and colored races did not constitute a denial of EQUAL PROTECTION OF THE LAWS in violation of the Fourteenth Amendment. This remained the law until 1954 when the court, in the famous school segregation cases, ruled that the "separate but equal" doctrine was not valid and that segregation, itself, was illegal.

Separation. A discontinuance of COHABITATION by mutual agreement of a husband and wife or by the DECREE of a court. In an action for separation, the complaining party must establish the existence of a valid marriage and then must prove the wrongdoing by the other party that constitutes grounds for separation. In New York State, an action for separation may be maintained by either spouse on the grounds of CRUELTY, conduct making it unsafe to cohabit with the defendant, DESERTION, or ADULTERY. See also SEPARATION AGREEMENT.

Separation Agreement. A CONTRACT between a husband and wife, who are not living together as such, that provides for the division of property, support, and the CUSTODY OF CHILDREN. The agreement can be enforced in the same way as any other contract. In order to enter into a separation agreement, there does *not* have to be a SEPARATION action pending in court. A separation agreement will become void upon the resumption of COHABITATION with the intent to reconcile or resume marital relationships.

Separation of Powers. The doctrine that forbids one branch of the Government from interfering with another by usurping its powers. In order to maintain the separation of legislative, executive, and judicial functions, the courts have at times had to clarify the extent of each branch's power. For example, it has been held that the separation of powers protects the President in the exercise of his power to remove executive officers appointed by him, but it also prevents him from removing officers who are not essentially executive and whose removal has been restricted by Congress.

Sequestration. The seizure and maintenance of the property of a defaulting party in a matrimonial action. Sequestration is a method of enforcing the provisions of a JUDGMENT against him to pay ALIMONY or support.

Service by Publication. See SERVICE OF SUMMONS.

Service of Summons. The manner in which JURISDICTION is given to the courts by the PARTIES TO AN ACTION. A SUMMONS served on the defendant is also a means of giving him notice that an action is being brought against him and that his failure to appear or answer will cause a JUDGMENT to be entered against him by DEFAULT.

Personal service is the most direct way of letting the defendant know he is being sued. The summons must be served personally within the territorial limits of the court's authority.

Substituted service can be used when personal service upon a resident defendant cannot be accomplished. The plaintiff may see that a summons is left with someone at the defendant's home, or can attach it to his door and mail a copy to him.

Service by publication is allowed in certain types of actions where neither personal service within the state nor substituted service is possible. Service is made by actual newspaper publication of the summons or by personal service outside the state.

Service by Mail. In some states where new civil rules have been adopted to conform to Federal Civil Rules, service may be made by mail and the attorney signs a statement on the Complaint that the service was made by mail on a certain date.

Whether service should be personal, substituted, or by publication depends on the type of action, where the party to be served resides, and ultimately, the rules of the state. Use of the correct means of service is vital for a court to obtain jurisdiction. If a court is to give a judgment affecting the status of property it must be given jurisdiction over the property (jurisdiction *in rem*); if it is to give a judgment against a person, it must be given jurisdiction over the person (jurisdiction *in personam*). Generally, personal and substituted service gives *in personam* jurisdiction while service by publication gives *in rem* jurisdiction.

Session Laws. The laws enacted by a State Legislature are published as "Session Laws" before they are codified.

Sessions. See TERM OF COURT.

Settlement. An agreement by which disputing parties ascertain what is coming from one to the the other. A person who has suffered an injury because of someone's NEGLIGENCE would desire, more than likely, a settlement immediately so that he may be reimbursed for his injuries promptly. He is advised, however, not to institute settlement negotiations until he knows the full extent of his injuries; he might be asking too little.

Settlor. See TRUST.

Severance Damage. The damage that property sustains when a portion of it is taken in condemnation, and the remaining property becomes less valuable owing to change in size, shape, and utility. An award of severance damage is allowable only if there is unity of ownership and unity of use. In some states contiguity is also a requisite; that is, the remaining parcel must be contiguous (in actual contact or adjoining) with the part taken. When a parcel is totally absorbed in condemnation proceedings, no severance damage exists. Speculative and doubtful DAMAGES are compensable.

In estimating the amount of severance damage, the appraiser must determine the highest and best use to which the property may be put. The damage cannot be greater than the full value of the property. Special and direct benefits to the property are generally considered as an offset against the amount of severance damage.

Shepard's Citations. A service that tells the lawyer whether statutes and cases to be cited by him as authority are in fact valid for that purpose. The law is constantly changed by legislative or judicial action. The careful lawyer, therefore, checks upon the present value of each authority sought to be used by him. By far the most complete American citator system, in both geographical scope and fullness of treatment, is *Shepard's Citations*, covering all states and units of the National Reporter series and a special Labor Law Citator.

Purpose of Shepard's Citations. To prove his point, the lawyer cites a decision contained in a published opinion. Before citing the case he wants to know something of its history and subsequent treatment. He is interested in knowing whether the case has been appealed to a higher court; whether it was affirmed or reversed; whether it has been followed in many other cases; and whether it has been overruled in a subsequent case. *Shepard's Citations* is designed to give the lawyer this information. It is quite easy to "Shepardize" a case, and the secretary will probably be asked to assist the lawyer with this research. A lawyer never cites a case as authority without first "Shepardizing" it.

Abbreviations used. The following abbreviations are used by Shepard for the purpose of indicating the "Judicial History of Case."

History of Case

a	(affirmed)	Same case affirmed on appeal.
cc	(connected case)	Different case from case cited but arising out of same subject matter or intimately connected therewith.
D	(dismissed)	Appeal from same case dismissed.
m	(modified)	Same case modified on appeal.
r	(reversed)	Same case reversed on appeal.
s	(same case)	Same case as case cited.
S	(superseded)	Substitution for former opinion.

Treatment of Case

c	(criticised)	Soundness of decision or reasoning in cited case criticised for reasons given.
d	(distinguished)	Case at bar different either in law or fact from case cited, for reasons given.
e	(explained)	Statement of import of decision in cited case. Not merely a restatement of the facts.
f	(followed)	Cited as controlling.
h	(harmonized)	Apparent inconsistency explained and shown not to exist.
j	(dissenting opinion)	Citation in dissenting opinion.
L	(limited)	Refusal to extend decision of cited case beyond precise issues involved.

o	(overruled)	Ruling in cited case expressly overruled.
p	(parallel)	Citing case substantially alike or on all fours with cited case in its law and facts.
q	(questioned)	Soundness of decision or reasoning in cited case questioned.

How to use Shepard's Citations. An explanation of how to use the Shepard's Federal Reporter Citations will enable the secretary to use the other Shepard's Citations. Figure 1, page 390, illustrates a page from the Federal Reporter Citations.

ILLUSTRATIVE CASE

(Acknowledgment is made to Shepard's Citations, Inc., for this explanation.)

Let us assume that by reference to a digest, encyclopedia, textbook or other unit of legal research, you have located the case of *Hanover Star Milling Co.* v. *Allen & Wheller Co.,* reported in Volume 208 of the Federal Reporter on page 513 dealing among other things with the property right which a complainant has in a trademark.

Figure 1 is a reproduction of a page from Shepard's Federal Reporter Citations. Note the volume of reports to which the citations apply, "Vol. 208," in the upper right-hand corner of the page.

An examination of the heavy face type numbers within the page locates the page number "—513—" in the seventh column of citations. This is the initial page of the case under consideration. Following this page number you will find the citation "sLRA1916D 136" indicating that the same case "s" is also reported in 1916D Lawyers Reports Annotated 136.

In obtaining the history of this case you will observe that upon appeal to the United States Supreme Court, it was affirmed "a" in 240 United States Reports "US" 403, 60 Lawyers Edition of United States "LE" 713, 36 Supreme Court Reporter "SC" 357, 1916 Decisions of the Commissioner of Patents '"16 CD" 265. Wherever there are parallel sets of reports covering the same citing case these citations immediately follow each other.

It is also to be observed that by examining the abbreviations preceding the citations, this case has been followed "f," explained "e," and harmonized "h" in subsequent cases in the Federal Reporter.

The next citation covers the reference "215F¹495." The small superior figure "¹" in advance of the citing page number 495, indicates that the principle of law brought out in the first paragraph of the syllabus of the cited case is also dealt with in 215 Federal Reporter 495.

Assuming that you are primarily interested in the principle covered in paragraph one of the syllabus, we find that the additional citations which contain the superior figure "¹" in advance of the citing page number include numerous other cases that deal with this particular point of law and that are reported in the Federal Reporter; Federal Reporter, Second Series "F2d"; Federal Supplement "FS"; Appeal Cases District of Columbia "ADC"; Decisions of the Commission of Patents and United States Patents Quarterly "PQ."

In addition to the citations in point with paragraph one of the syllabus, there are several citations to other

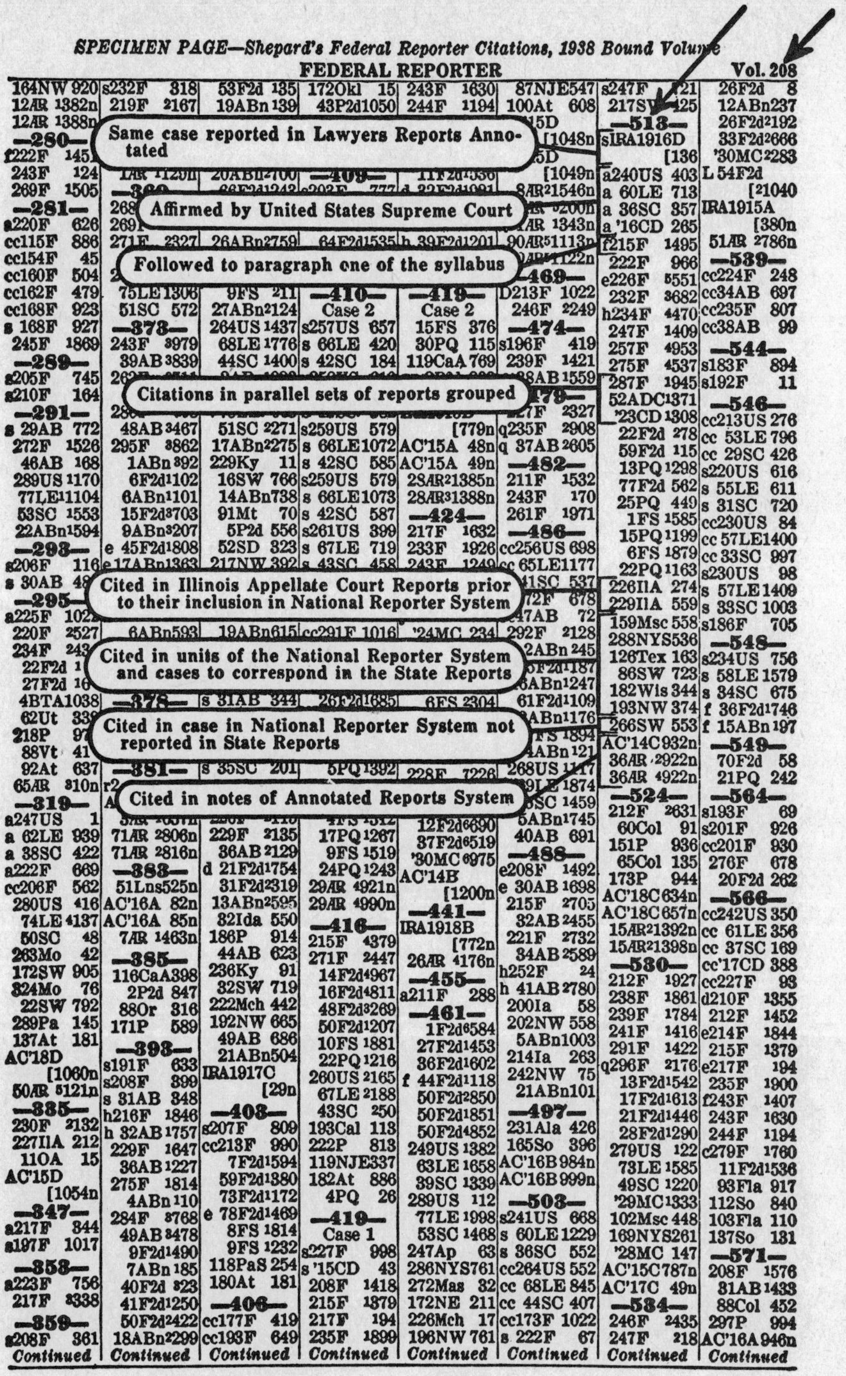
SPECIMEN PAGE—Shepard's Federal Reporter Citations, 1938 Bound Volume
FEDERAL REPORTER
Vol. 208
Same case reported in Lawyers Reports Annotated
Affirmed by United States Supreme Court
Followed to paragraph one of the syllabus
Citations in parallel sets of reports grouped
Cited in Illinois Appellate Court Reports prior to their inclusion in National Reporter System
Cited in units of the National Reporter System and cases to correspond in the State Reports
Cited in case in National Reporter System not reported in State Reports
Cited in notes of Annotated Reports System

Shepard's Citations: Figure 1. Page from Shepard's Federal Reporter Citation. (Courtesy—Shepard's Citations, INC.

paragraphs of the syllabus of this case in cases reported in the Federal Reporter, Federal Reporter, Second Series, and in the notes "n" of the American Law Reports "ALR." Thus, the citations dealing with a point of law in any particular paragraph of the syllabus may be referred to instantly without examining every citation to the case.

It will be noted that this case has been cited by the courts of Illinois, New York, Texas, and Wisconsin. These citations are arranged alphabetically by the state reports with the corresponding reference in the National Reporter System. The citation 266 Southwestern Reporter (SW) 533 is a case decided in the Court of Civil Appeals of Texas and not reported elsewhere. This case has also been cited in the notes of 1914C Annotated Cases 932 (AC'14C932n).

By examining this same volume and page number in the 1953-1961 Bound Supplements, and the latest issue of the Cumulative Supplement, and intervening Advance Sheet, all subsequent citations to this case will be found.

In a similar manner, constructions and references to the statute under consideration may be obtained by referring to the appropriate Shepard edition.

Short-term Capital Gain. See CAPITAL GAIN AND LOSS.

Short-term Lease. See LEASE, *Classification of leases.*

Signature. Firms of attorneys frequently sign letters manually with the firm name, particularly if the letter expresses a professional opinion or gives professional adivce. In some offices the firm name is typed on the letter and the lawyer who dictated it signs his name, thus:

BLACK, WILLIAMS & LOWE
By *Edgar R. Black*

A letter signed in the firm name, whether manually or typed, is written in the first person plural, not the singular.

Many letters are signed by the dictating attorney or by a partner without having the firm name appear in the signature. The purpose of typing a signature is to enable the recipient of the letter to decipher a difficult signature. There is no need, therefore, for the lawyer's name to be typed in the signature if it appears on the letterhead.

If a firm has alternate forms of signature, the dictator will indicate his preference.

How to type the signature. 1. Type the firm name in capitals exactly as it appears on the letterhead.

2. If the signature of the dictator is typed, type it exactly as he signs his name.

Right

Richard P. Miller
Richard P. Miller

Wrong

Richard P. Miller
R. P. Miller

3. The typed signature should never extend beyond the right margin of the letter.

4. No title except *Miss* or *Mrs.* precedes either the written or typed signature.

391

See also ADDRESSING OF-FICIALS for the correct forms of written address, SALUTATION, and COMPLIMENTARY CLOSE in letters to government and court officials, and others holding official or honorary titles.

Silent Partner. A partner who has no voice in the management of the partnership business. Unless he is also a special partner (see LIMITED PARTNERSHIP), a silent partner is equally responsible with the other partners for the debts of the partnership.

Simplex Obligatio. A simple obligation.

Simplified Letter. Style of letter in which the SALUTATION and COMPLIMENTARY CLOSE are omitted. The name of the addressee is always mentioned in the first line of the letter, thus compensating for the salutation. All structural parts are flush with the left-hand margin. The subject line (see LETTERS, STYLE AND SETUP) is placed between the address and the body of the letter. "Copy to" is also omitted before the names of persons to whom carbon copies are to be sent.

Single Retainer. A fee charged by the lawyer for a specific service that he renders to a client. Frequently part of the retainer is paid in advance. See also YEARLY RETAINER.

Sit-down Strike. See STRIKE.

Skip-tracing. The act of locating or tracing a debtor who has moved from one place to another without leaving a forwarding address. Skip-tracing may be done by (1) retail credit bureaus which offer this service to their members, (2) concerns organized for this special purpose. Usually skip-tracing is done on a contingent fee basis, but in some cases a flat fee is charged whether the skip is located or not; in other cases, a small recording fee is charged in every case and a larger fee in successful cases.

Slander. See LIBEL AND SLANDER.

Slip Decision. See CITATION (TO LEGAL AUTHORITIES), *How to cite slip decisions.*

Slip Laws. The laws enacted by Congress are first published officially as "slip laws." Later they are reprinted in a bound volume of *Statutes at Large.*

Small Claims Court. A court designed to handle claims of a small amount, i.e. claims under $100. A citizen may represent himself and does not need to hire a lawyer. The court is designed to relieve the caseload of the larger courts.

Social Security Taxes. Taxes on wages and salaries, as well as on the earnings of self-employed persons, in order to finance the benefits provided under the Social Security Act. The provisions of the Act include old age benefits paid to workers and their families on retirement, survivor benefits paid to the families of deceased workers, and benefits paid to certain disabled workers and their families. The taxing provisions are found in the Federal Insurance Contributions Act and in the Tax on Self-Employment Income section of the Internal Revenue Code.

Both employers and employees are taxed on the employee's salary at the same rate. The employer withholds the employee's contribution and remits it to the Government. Self-employed persons are taxed at a rate half again as large because the self-employed person does not have an employer contributing to help pay for his benefits.

Participation in a company's private pension plan does not excuse an employee from payment of the tax.

Spacing. *In legal documents.* Legal documents are double spaced with a triple space between numbered articles or items and between paragraphs with side headings. Quoted material (see TAKE-IN) and description of land may be single-spaced. See also TYPING LEGAL DOCUMENTS.

Between typewriter characters. Usage has established the following standard rules for spacing between typewriter characters:

One space:
    After a comma
    After a semicolon
    After a period following an abbreviation or an initial but not between initials forming a single abbreviation
    After an exclamation mark used in the body of a sentence
    Before and after "x" meaning "by," for example, 3 x 5 inch card
Two spaces:
    After a colon
    After every sentence
    After a period following a figure or letter at the beginning of a line in a list of items
No spacing:
    Before or after a dash, which is two hyphens

Before or after a hyphen
Between quotation marks and the matter enclosed
Between parentheses and the matter enclosed
Between the initials that make up a single abbreviation—for example, C.O.D.
Before or after an apostrophe, unless it begins or ends a word

Punctuation should never be separated from the word it follows—for example, a dash should never be placed at the beginning of a line.

Special Damages. See DAMAGES.

Special Delivery Mail. See POSTAL SERVICE.

Special Partner. See LIMITED PARTNERSHIP.

Specific Performance. The performance of a contract according to its exact terms. A court of EQUITY will enforce specific performance, whereas a court of law awards damages to the injured party to a contract. Specific performance is never enforced in contracts for personal services. It is usually confined to sales of REAL PROPERTY and unique personal property, for example an antique.

Spendthrift Trust. See TRUST, *Spendthrift.*

Star Page. The line and word at which the pages of a first edition of a law book begin are frequently indicated by a star in differently paginated later editions. The original page number is indicated in the margin. In citing a few well-known works, the edition is left out and the star page is referred to, thus, 1 Bl. Comm. *150.

State of Incorporation. A state in which a CORPORATION is organized. A corporation is not necessarily incorporated under the laws of the state in which its executive office is located, especially if it is to carry on business in more than one state. Each state has a corporation law under which private business corporations for profit are organized. The laws of some states are more favorable to corporations generally than those of other states. The lawyer recommends the state whose laws are most favorable to the proposed corporation. The cost of incorporating and the tax laws in each state are taken into consideration. Therefore, the lawyer might organize a corporation under the laws of a state far removed from his office. Delaware is the leading incorporating state.

In the state of incorporation, a corporation is known as a DOMESTIC CORPORATION; in all other states, as a FOREIGN CORPORATION. (Corporations organized outside the United States are referred to as *alien corporations*.) Thus, a corporation incorporated in Delaware is a domestic corporation there, but in New York and California it is a foreign corporation. A corporation is sometimes incorporated in more than one state, but generally if it wants to carry on its business in another state, it qualifies to do business in that state as a foreign corporation.

States' Rights. A theory of government that advocates more power and independence to the individual states rather than to a strong central government. The conflict between the two points of view when our government was being organized led to the present distribution of power in our Federal Government. The conflict has continued to this day in the courts and in politics.

Stationery Supplies. The stationery supplies used for various purposes in a typical law office follow.

"Legal cap" is white paper, 8 by 13 inches or 8½ by 14 inches, with a wide ruled margin at the left and a narrow ruled margin at the right. It is used for court papers and for legal instruments, such as agreements, contracts, and the like. Substance 16 is used for the original or ribbon copy. Legal cap, substance 20, is preferable for the original of wills; substance 13 for the carbon copies. In some states legal cap has numbers along the left margin.

Bond or onion skin legal cap is used for the carbon copies, substance 13 or 9 if no more than 8 copies are made; substance 9, for more than 8 copies. Some offices use substance 16 (same as ribbon copy) for the office copy because it is more durable.

"Legal-size" paper, plain without the ruled margins, same substance as the legal cap, is also used for legal instruments of various kinds and for court papers in some jurisdictions.

Short white paper, approximately 8 by 10½ inches, or 8½ x 11, with ruled margins, substance 16, is used for the ribbon copy of briefs and law memoranda; substance 9 or 13 for the carbon copies.

Short white paper, approximately 8 by 10½ inches, or 8½ x 11, plain without ruled margins, is used for legal documents that are not written on long paper. The choice varies with the office.

"Manuscript covers" are of a heavy colored paper, usually blue, about 25 per cent cotton fiber. Legal instruments and court papers can be bound in them.

Legal-size covers, with or without the firm name, are used for binding legal instruments and court papers. Legal-size covers with a printed panel are frequently used for binding court papers. These covers are referred to as *backs,* because they cover only the back of the paper bound in them.

White covers, with or without the firm name engraved on them, are used for binding wills.

Short covers, with or without the firm name, are used for binding briefs, law memoranda, and legal instruments that are typed on short paper. They are double and are bound at the side.

Legal-size yellow manifold is used for drafts.

Legal scratch pads are pads of 8½ by 12½ inch yellow paper, with ruled margin and lines. See that there is always one on the lawyer's desk and one in his brief case. He uses the pads for making notes, writing drafts in longhand, and the like.

"Firm letterheads," 8½ by 11 inches, substance 24, 20, or 16, are used for the original of firm correspondence. Some firms also have an 8½ by 7½ inch letterhead for short letters.

"Continuation sheets," loosely called second sheets, of the same substance as the letterheads are used for additional pages of a letter. They do not have a letterhead on them but usually have the firm name engraved or printed on them.

"Firm letterheads," marked "copy," on unglazed onion skin, substance 9, are used for copies of correspondence.

Colored onion skin or yellow manifold is used for the file copy of correspondence.

"Executive letterheads," 6 by 7 in-

ches, engraved with the attorney's name, are used for the attorney's personal correspondence. This paper frequently has a kid finish.

"Monarch" size envelopes, 3⅞ by 7½ inches are used with the executive stationery. No. 6¾ (3⅝ by 6½ inches) and No. 10 (4⅛ by 9½ inches) envelopes fit the 8½ by 11 inch letterheads.

Envelopes of heavy manila stock (about 40 pounds), 3½ inches bottom flap, 3½ inches top flap gummed solid, with a ¾ inch scored shoulder also gummed, are used for mailing bulky documents and papers that can be folded.

Statute of Frauds. An ordinance, enacted with variations in all the states, providing that certain contracts cannot be enforced unless they are in writing signed by the party against whom the contract is sought to be enforced. The writing need not be a formal document signed by both parties—a written note or memorandum of the transaction signed by the party to be bound by the agreement is sufficient. The laws in the various states are fairly uniform in requiring the following contracts to be in writing:

1. A special promise to be responsible for the debt, default, or miscarriage of a third person.

2. An agreement by an executor or administrator to become liable out of his own property for the debts of the estate.

3. A contract, the consideration for which is marriage. Engagement contracts are not included.

4. Contracts for the sale of real estate or any interest therein.

5. Contracts that cannot be performed within one year.

6. Contracts involving the sale of

personal property in excess of a certain amount (which varies in the different states), when no part of the property has been delivered and no part of the purchase price has been paid.

In addition, many states require the following contracts to be in writing:

1. An agreement to bequeath property or to make any provision for someone by will.

2. An agreement to pay upon attaining legal majority a debt contracted during infancy.

3. The creation of a trust.

4. The promise to pay a debt that has been outlawed by the STATUTE OF LIMITATIONS or barred by BANKRUPTCY.

5. An assignment of wages to be earned in the future.

6. A mortgage of personal property.

Statute of Limitations. A state ordinance that limits the time within which legal action may be brought, either upon a CONTRACT or TORT. State and Federal statutes also limit the time within which certain crimes can be prosecuted. The purpose of the time limitation is to make it impossible to bring suit many years after a cause of action originates, during which time witnesses may have died or important evidence may have been lost. When a debt is involved, it is possible to interrupt (or "toll") the running of the statute—that is, to lengthen the period in which action may be brought—by obtaining a payment on the debt or a promise to pay. A promise to pay a debt that has been barred by the statute of limitations does not require new consideration but many states require such a promise to be in writing. The statutes often differentiate between oral and written contracts.

Statutes at Large. A bound volume of "slip laws" or laws enacted by Congress. See SLIP LAWS. *The Statutes at Large* have been codified into the *United States Code,* of which there are two unofficial editions—the *U. S. Code Annotated* and the *Federal Code Annotated.*

Statutory Deed. See DEED.

Statutory Law. Rules that have been formulated into law by legislative action. The Constitution of the United States and the constitutions of the various states are the fundamental written law. All other law must be in harmony with the constitutions, which define and limit the powers of government. State constitutions must be in harmony with the Constitution of the United States. Congress, cities and towns, and other governmental units find in the constitutions their authority, either express or implied, to enact certain laws. These legislative enactments are called statutes and constitute the greater part of the written or statutory law. Statutory law supplements and supersedes COMMON LAW.

Stay. The legal procedure of stopping a judicial proceeding by the order of a court. The proceeding may be stopped under the authority of the various stay laws that have been enacted by legislation. These stay laws are applicable in legal proceedings in both civil and criminal cases if the situation covered by the legislation exists.

For example, in a criminal case, when a woman is capitally convicted and she is proved to be with child there shall be a stay of execution till after her delivery. In a civil case concerning legal remedies against debtors, a moratorium may grant a term of suspension of certain of these legal remedies during times of financial distress.

Sterility. See IMPOTENCY.

Stipulation. Agreements concerning certain phases of a law suit made by attorneys for opposing parties by mutual consent. The agreement might be an accommodation to opposing counsel, such as an extension of the time in which to file a pleading; or it might be an agreement that will save time in court, such an agreement admitting certain facts. Usually the stipulation is an agreement among the attorneys for all PARTIES TO AN ACTION. However, it may be simply an agreement between the attorney for the plaintiff and the attorney for *a* defendant, the other defendants not being interested in the particular stipulation. Although stipulations are filed in court (except in those few jurisdictions where no papers are filed until note of issue), approval of the court to the stipulation is not usually required.

A stipulation consists of the following parts:
1. Caption
2. Body
3. Date line
4. Signatures of attorneys for all interested parties.

How to prepare a stipulation. The wording of all stipulations about a particular step in the litigation is substantially the same. The lawyer does not usually dictate the simple stipulations. He will say, "Draw up a stipulation in the Jones case extending our time to answer until March 10"; or, "Draw up a stipulation in the Smith case to set for trial on March 18." The secretary gets the wording from a practice manual or her form file. Whenever she prepares a stipulation of a different kind she makes an extra copy for her form file. She memorizes the short forms to save time in preparing them. The lawyer will dictate some stipulations, such as those admitting certain facts.

It is customary for the attorney seeking the stipulation to prepare it. When typing it, the secretary follows the style shown in Figure 1 (page 398). She will:
1. Type on legal-size paper.
2. Make an original for the court and a copy for all interested attorneys.
3. Make the caption the same as that on the complaint, except in those cases where the style of the case may be shortened.
4. Type "IT IS HEREBY STIPULATED AND AGREED" in solid caps.
5. When there is more than one stipulation in the same document, type each in a separate paragraph.
6. Type a signature line for each attorney or firm of attorneys who are stipulating. Indicate the party represented by the stipulating attorney, thus: "Attorney for Defendant Richard Brown."
7. Endorse legal back for each copy of stipulation, including the copy for the office, unless instructed to back only the court copy, for purposes of economy.

What the secretary does about stipulations. The secretary's responsibilities about the stipulation are the following:
1. Prepares the stipulation.
2. Staples original and all copies in endorsed legal backs.

WGR:MH 9/25/— (2)

IN THE COURT OF COMMON PLEAS OF ALLEGHENY COUNTY,

PENNSYLVANIA

AUGUSTUS N. ROBERTSON and
ELIZABETH R. ROBERTSON,

        Plaintiffs,

        vs.   No.. 223 October Term, 19—

JOHNSTON-DOUGLAS MANAGEMENT
CORPORATION and FREDERICK
FASHIONS, INC.,

        Defendants.

S T I P U L A T I O N

IT IS HEREBY STIPULATED AND AGREED by and between the undersigned attorneys that the time for defendant Frederick Fashions, Inc. to answer or otherwise plead to the Second Amended Complaint herein, filed the 22nd day of September, 19—, be and the same hereby is extended to and including the 13th day of October, 19—.

                    ———————————————
                    (Elwood & Adams)
                    Attorneys for Plaintiff

                    ———————————————
                    (Jones & Smith)
                    Attorneys for Defendant
                    Frederick Fashions, Inc.

Dated: September 25, 19—.

Stipulation: **Figure 1.** Stipulation extending time to answer.

3. Asks the attorney to sign the original and all copies.
4. Delivers them to opposing counsel who is stipulating and asks for his signature on the original and her office copy, giving him a copy that was signed in her office.
5. If the stipulation sets a date for future action, *she makes an entry in the diary*. See DIARY.

Stock. See CAPITAL STOCK.

Stock Book. A record of stockholders that contains their names alphabetically arranged, the residence of each stockholder, and number of shares he owns. Also included is the date each stockholder became an owner and the amount paid for his shares.

The stock book must be open for inspection to all stockholders. This right to inspect the stock book is valuable to stockholders who want to change the existing management. They can promptly learn the names and addresses of those entitled to vote for directors and try to influence them into voting for their slate.

Stock Certificate. See CERTIFICATE OF STOCK.

Stoppage in Transit. The act of stopping the delivery of goods while they are aboard a carrier.

When a seller, after having shipped goods to a buyer at a distance, learns that the buyer is insolvent, he has the right to stop the goods at any time before they reach the buyer. This right is called the right of stoppage *in tran-*situ (in transit). The right continues until the goods are actually delivered to the buyer, or until the carrier tells the buyer that it holds the goods for him. If the seller stops the goods when there is no evidence of the buyer's insolvency, he may be compelled to deliver the goods and, in addition, he will be held liable for any damage caused to the buyer by the delay.

No special form of notice is necessary to exercise the right of stoppage in transit. The seller simply notifies the carrier of his claim, requests it to hold the goods, and forbids their delivery to the purchaser. The seller may sue the carrier for breach of CONTRACT or for DAMAGES if the carrier delivers the goods to the buyer after notice of the seller's claim.

Street Address, How to Type. See ADDRESS ON LETTERS, *How to type the street address*.

Strike. The act of workmen quitting their employment in a body. The strike and threat of one are the union's most powerful weapons in getting its demands from management.

A *sympathetic strike* is a work stoppage by men not directly involved in the controversy, but willing to help out another group of workers already on strike.

A *general strike* goes a step further than a sympathetic strike by getting all organized workers within all occupations to go out on strike.

In a *sit-down strike* the workers remain inside the plant instead of walking out. The continual physical control of the factory by the workers prevents management from hiring replacements.

String Citation. See CITATION (TO LEGAL AUTHORITIES), *String Citations.*

Subject Line. See LETTERS, STYLE AND SETUP.

Subordination. An instrument signed by one having an interest in, or LIEN upon, property declaring that such interest or lien is placed in a lower order or rank than another interest or lien, such as MORTGAGE or LEASE.

Subordination of lease to mortgage. Placing an existing lease in an order or rank lower than that of a new mortgage on the leased property. It sometimes becomes necessary for the owner of leased property to obtain a loan secured by a mortgage on the property. The lender may be unwilling to accept the property as security burdened with the prior lease. The usual procedure is to obtain from the holder of the lease (lessee), for a consideration, a WAIVER of his priority in favor of the new mortgagee. This waiver is known as a "subordination agreement." The agreement may be made between the lessee and the lender (mortgagee); the owner (lessor) is not a necessary party, although in many instances he joins in the agreement as a matter of formality.

Subornation. The crime of procuring another to commit perjury. In legal circles the expression *"suborning* witnesses" is frequently heard.

Subpoena. The process a COURT uses to assure a person's attendance before it. A subpoena that requires the production of books, papers or docu-ments is called a *subpoena duces tecum.* If a person served with a subpoena fails to obey it without reasonable excuse, he may be punished for CONTEMPT OF COURT and is liable for the DAMAGES sustained by the aggrieved party.

Subrogation. The substitution of one person in another's place. For example, *A*'s car is insured by an insurance company against collision. *A*'s car is negligently damaged by *B*. The insurance company pays $150 for repairs to *A*'s car. The insurance company is subrogated to *A*'s position and may prosecute the claim for damages against *B*.

Subscribing Witness. See ATTESTATION.

Subsidiary Corporation. A company in which another CORPORATION (called the *parent corporation*) owns at least a majority of the shares, and thus has control.

When a parent corporation appears to have complete control over its subsidiary, the subsidiary is called the parent's *alter ego.* When the *alter ego* doctrine is applied, the dominant corporation may be held liable for the subordinate corporation's NEGLIGENCE.

Substantive Law. The part of the law that creates, defines and regulates rights and duties. Substantive law is opposed to *adjective* or *procedural* law, which provides the method of administering and protecting the rights, duties, and obligations created by substantive law. All statutes of a general nature are substantive law. All CASE LAW, except the decisions interpreting administrative regulations, codes of procedure, and court rules are substantive law. For example, the right of administration of an estate is substantive; the procedures by which the estate can be administered are adjective law. The line of distinction between the two is narrow and often hard to define.

Substituted Service. See SERVICE OF SUMMONS.

Suit on the Judgment. See JUDGMENT CREDITOR.

Suit Register. The record that a law office keeps of the progress of all of its matters pending in court, whether the matter is a litigated case, a foreclosure, an estate administration proceeding, or a special proceeding. The record saves time that would be required to examine all of the papers in the file. A quick examination of the suit register shows the status of a particular matter, acts as a double check on things to be done in relation to pending cases before term time (see TERM OF COURT).

Physical features of a suit register. The progress record of an action is typed or written on forms designed for the purpose, or on plain paper. The form or sheet used depends on where the records are kept. The records are commonly kept in (1) a loose-leaf binder, (2) the file folder, or (3) a portable tray or cabinet.

Loose-leaf binder for the suit register. Either an ordinary three-ring, letter-size binder or a post binder may be used for keeping the suit register. If the record is typed, the former is probably more expedient because the sheets are more easily removed for the purpose of typing the entries. Numerous types of forms for keeping the record are printed by various office supply houses and are on sale at local stationers. These forms are usually designed to fit a special loose-leaf binder, also manufactured by the supply house. Printed forms are not necessary, unless a special binder is used. In an ordinary loose-leaf binder, punched paper of durable quality, with reinforced edges is adequate.

File folder used for progress record. Some offices keep progress records in the file folder, either by writing the entries on the folder itself or by typing them on a sheet that is placed in the front of the folder. If the record is kept on a loose sheet, a colored sheet is desirable because it is more easily distinguished from the other papers in the folder. Figure 1, page 402, illustrates a sheet appropriate for this purpose.

Portable tray or cabinet for the suit register. A portable cabinet or tray with a visible index is probably the most advantageous facility for keeping the record. The cabinet may be fireproof with a lid that may be locked when the record is not being used. The visible index shows the name of the case, the attorney handling it, and the court INDEX NUMBER. Celluloid tabs may be used to flag specific cases. The manufacturer of the cabinet or tray also manufactures strips for the index and sheets for typing the record. The sheets are designed for numerous uses and have no printing on them except a ruled space at the left for the dates. They are of heavy stock paper and come in various sizes. Unless a wide carriage machine is available for typing the record, the sheets should be small enough to fit the carriage of a standard machine. The sheets are loose in the pocket provided for them in the cabinet and thus are easily removed for typing entries or for reference. The portable cabinets hold a large number of cases and, therefore, are not appropriate for offices with a light docket unless they are also used to house other records.

How to file the record sheets. The

COURT	HALL and DOBB	OFFICE NAME
	10 SLATE STREET	
	BOSTON, MASS.	
DOCKET NO.		OUR FILE NO.
SERVICES		ATTACHMENTS
	VS.	

RESPONSIBLE ATTY.
ATTY. TO BE NOTIFIED.
PLAINTIFFS ATTY.
DEFENDENT ATTY.
TRUSTEE ATTY.

DATE OF WRIT.
RETURN DAY.
FORM OF ACTION.
AD DAMNUM.
NATURE OF CASE.

COPY WITHIN	DATE FILED	DESCRIPTION	TRIAL LIST

Suit Register: Figure 1. Progress record sheet.

preferable method of filing the record sheets is alphabetically according to the first-named plaintiff, or the decedent in the case of an estate, or the principal corporation or individual named in a special proceeding. In offices with a heavy docket, the estates and special proceedings might be segregated from the litigated cases. Some offices with extremely heavy dockets separate the records according to the court in which the case is pending. When a visible index is used, celluloid tabs of various colors can designate specific courts, if it is desirable to be able to select quickly the cases pending in a particular court.

When and how to open a case in the suit register. A suit register sheet is not opened on every matter in the office—it is opened only on court matters. Therefore, the record is opened when the first paper is filed in court, or when a paper is served on the office for whom the secretary works, indicating that the case is pending in court. In opening the record, the secretary enters on the sheet (1) the court in which the action is pending; (2) the full title of the case, as it appears on the summons and complaint or other first paper filed; (3) nature of the proceeding, that is, "Suit on note," "Divorce," "Petition for letters of administration," and the like, as indicated by the new matter slip (see NEW CASE REPORT); (4) amount, if any, sued for; (5) names, addresses, and telephone numbers of all opposing counsel; (6) name of the attorney in the secretary's office who is handling the matter; (7) court index number as soon as available; (8) calendar number, as soon as available. (See CALENDAR CALL.)

All of the above information is put at the top of the record sheet. The entries follow, and each entry is dated at the left side of the sheet. Figure 2, page 404, illustrates a detailed suit register record.

What to enter. Some offices record only court papers and orders in the suit register. The office record is then actually a duplicate of the court docket kept by the clerk of the court; hence, the name "office docket." Many offices enter all written, formal steps in connection with an action. It is often a matter of practice and judgment as to what to enter. The secretary would not enter, "Received phone call from plaintiff's attorney asking when we thought case would be reached: told him we had no definite estimate." That does not affect the progress of the case. But she would enter, "Served NOTICE OF TRIAL for October 19. . . Term," just as soon as the notice of trial was served on the opposing counsel. The best rule is that the secretary use her own judgment as to what actually affects the progress of the action and to enter too much rather than too little. If she is in doubt as to the advisability of making an entry, she asks the lawyer in charge.

Form and sufficiency of record. In making entries in the suit register give complete information. Describe the matter entered with particularity, but not in great detail. Observance of the following directions will help to make complete and accurate entries:

1. Date all entries.
2. Avoid abbreviations.
3. When an action is commenced by the service of a summons only, open the record sheet immediately, but the nature and substance of the action cannot be entered until the complaint is received. Enter this information opposite the title as soon as the complaint is received.
4. When an ANSWER or NOTICE OF APPEARANCE is

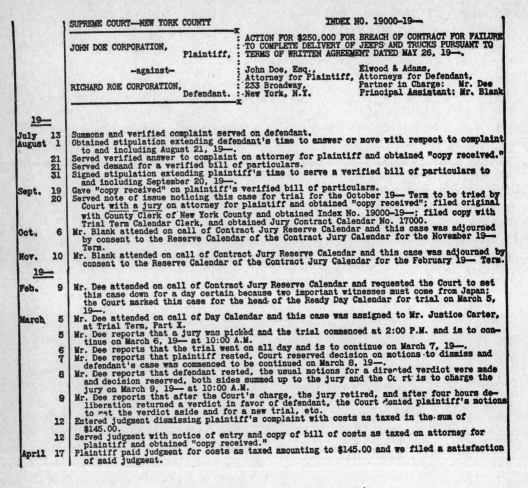

SUPREME COURT—NEW YORK COUNTY   INDEX NO. 19000–19—

JOHN DOE CORPORATION,   : ACTION FOR $250,000 FOR BREACH OF CONTRACT FOR FAILURE
                                         : TO COMPLETE DELIVERY OF JEEPS AND TRUCKS PURSUANT TO
                              Plaintiff. : TERMS OF WRITTEN AGREEMENT DATED MAY 26, 19—.

      —against—   : John Doe, Esq.,   Elwood & Adams,
                                         : Attorney for Plaintiff, Attorneys for Defendant,
RICHARD ROE CORPORATION,   : 233 Broadway,   Partner in Charge: Mr. Dee
                              Defendant. : New York, N.Y.   Principal Assistant: Mr. Blank

19—

July 13 Summons and verified complaint served on defendant.
August 1 Obtained stipulation extending defendant's time to answer or move with respect to complaint to and including August 21, 19—.
21 Served verified answer to complaint on attorney for plaintiff and obtained "copy received."
21 Served demand for a verified bill of particulars.
31 Signed stipulation extending plaintiff's time to serve a verified bill of particulars to and including September 20, 19—.
Sept. 19 Gave "copy received" on plaintiff's verified bill of particulars.
20 Served note of issue noticing this case for trial for the October 19— Term to be tried by Court with a jury on attorney for plaintiff and obtained "copy received"; filed original with County Clerk of New York County and obtained Index No. 19000–19—; filed copy with Trial Term Calendar Clerk, and obtained Jury Contract Calendar No. 17000.
Oct. 6 Mr. Blank attended on call of Contract Jury Reserve Calendar and this case was adjourned by consent to the Reserve Calendar of the Contract Jury Calendar for the November 19— Term.
Nov. 10 Mr. Blank attended on call of Contract Jury Reserve Calendar and this case was adjourned by consent to the Reserve Calendar of the Contract Jury Calendar for the February 19— Term.
19—
Feb. 9 Mr. Dee attended on call of Contract Jury Reserve Calendar and requested the Court to set this case down for a day certain because two important witnesses must come from Japan; the Court marked this case for the head of the Ready Day Calendar for trial on March 5, 19—.
March 5 Mr. Dee attended on call of Day Calendar and this case was assigned to Mr. Justice Carter, at Trial Term, Part X.
5 Mr. Dee reports that a jury was picked and the trial commenced at 2:00 P.M. and is to continue on March 6, 19— at 10:00 A.M.
6 Mr. Dee reports that the trial went on all day and is to continue on March 7, 19—.
7 Mr. Dee reports that plaintiff rested, Court reserved decision on motions to dismiss and defendant's case was commenced to be continued on March 8, 19—.
8 Mr. Dee reports that defendant rested, the usual motions for a directed verdict were made and decision reserved, both sides summed up to the jury and the Court is to charge the jury on March 9, 19— at 10:00 A.M.
9 Mr. Dee reports that after the Court's charge, the jury retired, and after four hours deliberation returned a verdict in favor of defendant, the Court denied plaintiff's motions to set the verdict aside and for a new trial, etc.
12 Entered judgment dismissing plaintiff's complaint with costs as taxed in the sum of $145.00.
12 Served judgment with notice of entry and copy of bill of costs as taxed on attorney for plaintiff and obtained "copy received."
April 17 Plaintiff paid judgment for costs as taxed amounting to $145.00 and we filed a satisfaction of said judgment.

Suit Register: **Figure 2.** Suit register record.

served on the office, enter the name of the attorney, his address and telephone number, and the party he represents.

5. As soon as the court index number is known, enter it opposite the title. Also enter it on the index tab if a visible index record is kept.

As a condition precedent to proper filing, the court index or docket number must be placed on every paper that is filed. The individual who files the paper on behalf of the office must get the index number from the clerk of the court or from his docket and give it to the secretary so that she can enter it on the record. She should make a practice of checking the suit register weekly for any missing index numbers.

6. Keep the entries opposite the title up to date, including index number, substitutions of attorneys, changes of addresses, office file number, and the like.

7. In describing petitions, orders,

and STIPULATIONS, enter a notation as to when they were verified, signed, entered, or dated, respectively, and by whom.

8. When entering stipulations, enter, "Obtained stipulation . . ." if the office is granted something by it; enter "Signed stipulation . . ." if the office gives a right. For example, if the office represented the plaintiff, the entry of the stipulation illustrated in Figure 1, STIPULATION, page 398, would be:

Signed stipulation with Land & Frank, dated September 25, 19. . extending time of Frederick Fashions, Inc. to answer to October 13, 19. .

If the office represented the Fox Fashions, Inc., the entry would read:

Obtained stipulation from Green & Ryder, dated September 23, 19. ., extending time to answer to October 13, 19. .

Some stipulations, for example a stipulation of discontinuance, are both "obtained" and "signed."

9. Enter the name of the attorney from the office who attends motions, calls of calendar at trials, hearings, arguments of appeals, and the like, and the disposition of the respective matters.

10. Enclose in quotation marks any entry from a law journal or similar publication with a reference to the date and page of the publication, because the date of the event is often different from the date upon which the event is announced in the publication.

11. When cases are settled out of court, enter the amounts paid, dates of payment, data concerning exchange of general releases, if any, and the like.

12. When judgment is entered, enter the amount of the judgment, the amount of costs, and payment received, if any.

13. Examine the DIARY each day for the day just past, to be certain that a report and entry has been made for everything listed there.

Closing the record of a case. Do not close the record of a case in the suit register until reasonably certain that no further steps, such as appeal, collecting on a judgment, moving to vacate a judgment, recording a satisfaction, levying execution, and the like, are to be taken by either party. The time to appeal should always have elapsed before the case is closed.

As soon as a case is closed, remove the sheet on that case from the record file and place it in the designated place. This might be another loose-leaf book, or a file cabinet. File the sheets alphabetically according to the first-named plaintiff, or the decedent in the case of an estate, or the principal corporation or individual named in a special proceeding. The closed sheets are kept indefinitely; some law offices have them bound from time to time.

Summary Judgment. An award of victory granted by the COURT to one of the parties without waiting for trial. MOTION for summary judgment must be supported by AFFIDAVIT, a copy of the PLEADINGS, and other available proof to show that there is no issue of fact worthy of trial. The motion for summary judgment will be denied if any party has presented issues that require a trial for settlement. The power to resolve summarily a law suit without the expense and trouble of a trial makes summary judgment one of the most practical and useful tools in modern procedure.

Summary Proceeding. A form of legal proceedings in which the established procedure is disregarded, expecially in the matter of trial by jury. The term is applied to the process by which a landlord may dispossess a tenant instead of having to resort to eviction, which is a long drawn-out proceeding.

Summons. The first paper that is served on the DEFENDANT, sometimes being served before the preparation of the COMPLAINT. It notifies the person named in the summons that suit is being brought against him and commands him to appear in court or answer the complaint by a certain date. Although the secretary to the plaintiff's attorney prepares the summons, it is generally issued and signed by the CLERK OF THE COURT. The summons consists of the following parts:

1. Caption.
2. Body. This commands the defendant to answer the complaint within the time specified.
3. Signature and seal of the clerk of the court. (In New York the plaintiff's attorney signs the summons.)

How to prepare the summons. A printed form of summons (see Figure 1, page 407) is used, unless there are numerous parties plaintiff or parties defendant.

1. If the name of a court is printed on the form, make certain that it is the court in which the action is being filed.
2. Make an original for the court, a copy for each defendant, and a copy for your file. An extra copy of the summons must be filed in court in those jurisdictions that require an extra copy of pleadings to be filed.
3. The caption is exactly like that of the complaint. List names of all parties in full.
4. If there are numerous parties, type on legal-size paper instead of using a printed form. Copy the printed form exactly, making sure that all punctuation is included, because usually the statutes direct the form of a summons.
5. Put a legal back on a typed summons, so that the affidavit of service can be filled in.
6. Endorse the back of the original summons and of each copy unless the summons is stapled to the complaint. The endorsements need not list all the parties. It is sufficient to show the name of the first plaintiff and the name of the first defendant, with appropriate words indicating that there are others. (See CAPTION.)

What the secretary should do about the summons and complaint.

1. Prepare the complaint, and verification when required.
2. Have original complaint signed and verified, after approval by the lawyer.
3. Conform the copies.
4. Prepare summons.
5. Attach copy of summons to each

copy of complaint. Place the complaint against the inside of the cover so that the VERIFICATION printed on the inside cover shall read as a continuation of the complaint. Put

---

In The Circuit Court of Duval County, Florida At Law

RICHARD JONES AND MARY JONES, his wife,
                                        Plaintiff s.

vs.

SMITH & DOUGLAS, INC., a corporation,
                                        Defendant.

Civil Action -
Damages $ 5,000

No.   L

Summons at Law

The State of Florida -

To   SMITH & DOUGLAS, INC.

You are hereby summoned and required to serve upon   Allen S. Brown

plaintiff's attorney, whose address is   321 Main Street, Jacksonville, Florida,

an answer to the complaint which is herewith served upon you within 20 days after service of this summons upon you, exclusive of the day of service. If you fail to do so, judgment by default will be taken against you for the relief demanded in the complaint.

Witness *my hand and the seal of said Court, at Jacksonville, Florida, this*   Sixth   *day of*   November   *A. D. 19*

Clerk Circuit Court

By

Deputy Clerk

Sheriff's Return of Service

Summons: Figure 1. Printed form of summons.

the summons on top of the complaint. Do not attach original summons to original complaint.

6. Open case in SUIT REGISTER and make appropriate entry.

7. File original complaint in court, have clerk of court issue (sign, seal, and date) original summons, and pay required fee.

8. Conform copies of summons, by filling in date, name of clerk, and seal of court.

9. Make a note of the INDEX NUMBER assigned by the clerk and put it on all subsequent papers prepared by you in that particular case.

10. Give original of summons, together with copy of summons and copy of complaint for each defendant, to process server for service on defendants. (In some jurisdictions, the copies are given to the clerk of the court at the time the original summons is issued, and he, in turn, delivers them to the sheriff for service.)

11. The summons illustrated in Figure 1 has a space for the sheriff's return, which the sheriff fills in after he serves the summons. If a process server is employed to make service, he should be instructed to get in touch with the attorney employing him as soon as he serves the summons and complaint, for the purpose of making affidavit of service. The affidavit should be made on the same day that service is made. If affidavit of service is on a separate sheet, it should have a regular caption, like that on the complaint, but if the affidavit is made on the back of the summons, no caption is necessary.

12. File original summons and proof of service in court. If the summons is not filed within the time permitted by the practice rules, a new summons must be served.

13. Mark on office copy the date service is made, and by whom.

14. *Enter in diary* RETURN DAY OF SUMMONS. The period of time begins to run the date the summons is served, not the date it is prepared.

15. The secretary to the lawyer for defendant must, *enter in the diary* the return day of summons, This is very important. Failure to answer by that date might mean a JUDGMENT BY DEFAULT. See also ALIAS SUMMONS.

Superior Courts. The highest state courts of ORIGINAL JURISDICTION. These courts are usually designated as circuit, district, or superior courts. (In New York the highest court of original jurisdiction is called the Supreme Court.) They have original jurisdiction in the first instance and are the courts where cases not within the jurisdiction of inferior courts are tried originally. They also have appellate jurisdiction over matters arising in inferior courts and, in many states, over probate matters. They control or supervise the lower courts by WRITS OF ERROR, APPEAL, or CERTIORARI.

In some states, superior courts have one or more departments or divisions that have jurisdiction over special matters. For example, the Superior Court of New Jersey has a law division for the trial of actions at law and a chancery division for hearing EQUITY matters; in California, a department of each superior court acts as a probate court.

Other states have COURTS OF SPECIAL JURISDICTION to probate matters.

Supplementary Proceeding. When an execution of judgment is returned unsatisfied, the judgment creditor has the right to force the judgment debtor to submit to an examination for the purpose of discovering any assets that may be applied to the payment of the debt. The legal procedure by which the judgment creditor exercises this right is known as a *supplementary proceeding*— it is supplementary to the execution of judgment (see ISSUE OF EXECUTION).

Supreme Appellate Courts. There is only one supreme APPELLATE COURT in each state. These courts are courts of last resort in their respective states. (In Oklahoma, the Criminal Court of Appeals, and in Texas, the Court of Criminal Appeals, are courts of last resort in criminal cases.) The jurisdiction of these courts is appellate (see APPELLATE COURT), their original jurisdiction, if any, being limited to the issuance of writs of MANDAMUS, CERTIORARI, HABEAS CORPUS, and the like.

The highest court in 42 states is designated as the *Supreme Court*. The designations in the other 8 states are as follows:

Connecticut	Supreme Court of Errors
Kentucky	Court of Appeals
Maine	Supreme Judicial Court
Maryland	Court of Appeals
Massachusetts	Supreme Judicial Court
New York	Court of Appeals
Virginia	Supreme Court of Appeals
West Virginia	Supreme Court of Appeals

See AMERICAN COURT SYSTEM; COURT OF INTERMEDIATE REVIEW; COURTS OF RECORD; COURTS OF SPECIAL JURISDICTION; INFERIOR COURTS; SUPERIOR COURTS; PARTIES TO AN APPEAL.

Supreme Court of the United States. The highest judicial tribunal in the Government. Every state also has its highest appellate court. For the precise designation of these courts in the 50 states see SUPREME APPELLATE COURTS.

Supreme Court Reports. The opinions of the Supreme Court are published officially in the United States Reports and unofficially in *Lawyers' Edition* and *Supreme Court Reporter*. CCH also publishes the *U.S. Supreme Court Bulletin*. Supreme Court opinions are also reported in the *United States Law Week*.

Suretyship. See GUARANTY.

Surrender of Lease. An agreement between the landlord and the tenant to terminate the LEASE prior to its expiration date, followed by delivery of possession of the premises to the landlord. A surrender releases the tenant from liability for rent accruing thereafter. It is the *agreement* between landlord and tenant that distinguishes a surrender from an ABANDONMENT OF LEASED PREMISES by tenant. The agreement need not be in writing, nor need it be in any particular form. No consideration is required to make the agreement binding; the advantage accruing to both parties is sufficient. If the tenant merely abandons the premises, the fact that the landlord accepts the keys does not constitute a surrender.

If the landlord, with tenant's consent, gives a new lease to a stranger during the term of the lease, this is considered a surrender. The making of a new lease between landlord and tenant operates as a surrender of a prior inconsistent lease.

Survey. The process by which the dimensions of a parcel of land are measured and its boundaries, geographical position, and physical details are ascertained. The result is reduced to a pictorial delineation called a map, drawing, or survey. The survey shows the lengths and directions of the boundary lines of the tract surveyed, the location of all buildings and other improvements, and the existence of any encroachment at or above the surface of the land either by or upon adjacent property.

Upon a sale of property, it is always the safer course for the purchaser to obtain a survey. A survey of the land should always be obtained if construction of a building is planned, to make certain that the structure will be built within the lot lines of the property and within the set-back lines fixed by ZONING regulations. Even if a previous survey has been made of the property, a new survey is advisable to show conditions existing at the date of sale. A survey may be obtained through a TITLE INSURANCE company.

If a CONTRACT OF SALE provides that the seller may deliver TITLE "subject to survey," or "subject to a state of facts that an accurate survey may show," the purchaser may have to take title even if the survey reveals an encroachment which may render the title unmarketable. A careful purchaser will insist that such a "subject" clause contain the qualifying words "provided the same does not render the title unmarketable." The words "state of facts" refer to any encroachments or projections by or on the property surveyed, such as wall, fences, hedges, cornices, and chimneys, outside of property lines.

A contract of sale may provide that the sale is made subject to a particular survey identified by name of surveyor and date. The purchaser should insist on seeing the survey and have it examined by his attorney before accepting the "subject" clause. See also LAND DESCRIPTION.

Sweat Shop. A plant whose employees are overworked and paid low wages in unsanitary or otherwise unfavorable conditions.

"Sworn-to" clause. See JURAT.

Sympathetic Strike. See STRIKE.

Syndicate. An association of individuals formed to conduct and carry on some particular business transaction, usually of a financial character. A syndicate more nearly resembles a JOINT ADVENTURE than any other business organization. Syndicates in general are temporary associations or firms. They usually terminate automatically when the purpose for which they were formed has been accomplished.

In the securities trade, a syndicate is an association of investment bankers formed for the purpose of underwriting the distribution of a new security issue or a block of securities outstanding.

Tabulated Material. *Text.* When text is tabulated or itemized in the body of a letter, the items are usually preceded by a number or letter in parentheses or followed by a period. Each line of the tabulated text should begin two spaces to the right of the number. Preferably, the punctuation and capitalization should be the same as if the tabulated material were written without breaks, in regular lines (see Figure 1), but this style is not followed in all law offices.

dictation just as if it were original dictation instead of a take-in. See also QUOTATIONS AND INDENTED MATERIAL, TYPING.

Tax adjustment in Real Estate. See ADJUSTMENT OF CHARGES AND INCOME.

Tax Court. A judicial tribunal empowered to hear appeals and render decisions involving asserted tax

```
         I have revised the affidavit that you returned,
I hope in accordance with your recommendations.  If you
find it satisfactory as now drawn, may I ask you

     (1)   to swear to it before a notary and have him affix
           his seal and notarial stamp;

     (2)   to fill in the last column of Schedule B as to the
           months for which payments are in default on each
           vehicle; and

     (3)   to return the affidavit with five forms of the
           conditional sale contract.
```

Tabulated Material: Figure 1. Tabulated textual material.

Take-in. In legal work, a dictator will tell the stenographer to "take-in" certain material, meaning for her to copy it. The "take-in" might be quoted material, from a text or testimony, in which case the take-in is indented and quoted. Or the take-in might be a portion of a printed form or other document, the wording of which is applicable to the document that is being dictated. When the take-in is material of this kind, it follows the rest of the

deficiencies on the part of taxpayers. The court acts as an independent agency of the Executive Branch of the Government. It decides tax controversies, leaving the *enforcement* of its decisions to the Treasury Department.

Tax Court Practice. All papers filed with the Tax Court, including petitions, motions, briefs, and replies, should conform to the following standards (references are to "Rules of Practice, Tax Court of the United States," published by the Government Printing Office in Washington.)

1. PRINTED OR TYPEWRITTEN. All papers shall be either printed or typewritten (Rule 4 (a)).

2. PRINTED PAPERS (Rule 4 (b)).
   a. *Type.* Use 10- or 12-point type.
   b. *Paper.* Use good, unglazed paper, 5⅞ inches wide by 9 inches long.
   c. *Margin.* Inside margin not less than one inch.
   d. *Spacing.* Double-leaded text and single-leaded quotations.
   e. *Citations.* Italicize citations (Rule 4 (d)).

3. TYPEWRITTEN PAPERS.
   a. *Typing.* Type on one side only (Rule 4 (c)).
   b. *Paper.* Use plain white paper, 8½ inches wide by 11 inches long, weighing not less than 16 pounds to the ream (Rule 4 (c)), except for copies which may be on any weight paper (Rule 4 (h)).
   c. *Covers.* Attach no backs or covers. (Rule 4 (a)).
   d. *Citations.* Underscore citations (Rule 4 (d)).
   e. *Copies.* Copies shall be clear and legible (Rule 4 (h)).

4. FASTENING. Papers shall be fastened on the left side only. (Rule 4 (a)).

5. CAPTIONS. All papers shall have the proper caption. In the case of an individual petitioner, the caption shall set forth the full given name and surname, without any prefix or title, such as "Mrs.," "Dr.," and so forth. In the case of a fiduciary, the caption shall set forth the name of the estate, trust, or other person for whom he acts,

followed by his own name and pertinent title, for example:

THE TAX COURT OF THE
UNITED STATES

Estate of John Doe, deceased, Richard Roe, Executor, Petitioner,
    v.
Commissioner of Internal Revenue, Respondent.

Docket No. . . . . . .

(Rule 4 (e)).

6. SIGNATURES
   a. Original Copy. The original of all pleadings, motions, and briefs shall be signed in writing by either the petitioner or his counsel.
   b. Firm name. The signature shall be in the individual and not in the firm name, except that in the case of a petitioner that is a corporation, its signature shall be in the name of the corporation by one of its active officers, for example:

   John Doe, Inc.
   By /s/ Richard Roe,
   President

   c. Name and address. The name and mailing address of the signatory petitioner or counsel shall be typed or printed immediately beneath the written signature (Rule 4 (f)).

7. NUMBER OF COPIES.
   a. Except in cases of papers filed in more than one preceeding, the number of copies to be filed is tabulated below. Rule 4 (g) provides for an original and four conformed copies, except as provided otherwise in the Rules; but the exceptions are numerous, as the following tabulation of the more common papers filed by taxpapers indicates:

PAPER	NUMBER TO BE FILED	RULE NO.
Petition	"original and four complete, accurately conformed, clear copies"	7(a)(1)
Reply	"original and four conformed copies"	15
Request for Place of Hearing	"original and two copies"	26(b)
Brief (Typewritten)	"original and two copies"	35(d)
Brief (Printed)	"20 copies"	35(d)
Stipulation of Facts	"in duplicate"	31(b)
Computation of Entry of Decision Under Rule 50	"original and two copies"	50
Entry of Appearance	"in duplicate"	24
Application for Subpoena	"only the original"	
Application to Take Depositions	"verified application and two conformed copies"	44(b) 45(a)
Interrogatories and Cross-Interrogatories	"original and five copies"	46(a)
Motions (generally)	"four conformed copies with the signed original"	4(g)
Motion for Changing Place Designated for Hearing	"motion with four copies"	26(d)

Whenever a copy is required, it is advisable to submit conformed copies. Of course, if the papers are to be submitted "in duplicate," both the original and cuplicate should be executed.

    b. Where papers are to be filed in more than one proceeding, add to the number of copies otherwise required one additional copy for each such additional proceeding. For example, in the case of a motion to consolidate two proceedings, it is necessary to file a signed original and *five* conformed copies. (Motions generally require *four* conformed copies and the original. See above.) After the proceedings have been consolidated, all papers subsequently filed in the consolidated proceedings should be filed with the signed original and five conformed copies. (Rule 4 (g)).

See TAX COURT.

Tax Evasion. The intentional nonpayment of taxes. Unlike most crimes, it can be committed wholly by omission. A person is not in DOUBLE JEOPARDY if he is tried for committing a crime and later tried for not declaring the profits of the crime as taxable income.

Tax Lien. A claim against REAL PROPERTY that accrues to the taxing agency (municipality, township, city) from taxes that are assessed against the property. If the LIEN is not paid when due, the taxing agency sells the property at a tax sale.

Taxes, the Secretary's Duties. The legal secretary's duties might involve the following Federal INCOME TAX matters: (1) keeping income tax files; (2) keeping records of all income received by the lawyer; (3) keeping records of all expenditures that may be taken as deductions when the lawyer computes his income tax; (4) keeping a calendar of dates on which returns are to be filed and payments made.

Telegram. See TELEGRAPH SERVICE.

Telegraph Service. Classes of domestic telegraph service are (1) *fast telegram*—fastest class of service; charge based on minimum of 15 words, with additional charge for each word in excess of 15; (2) *day letter*—deferred service, transmission being subordinate to that of a fast telegram; charge of approximately 30 per cent more than that of a fast telegram is based on minimum of 50 words with additional charge for each group of five words or less in excess of 50; (3) *night letter*—delivery made on the morning of the first business day following the day the telegram is sent; charge, based on minimum of 50 words with an additional charge for each group of five words or less in excess of 50, is less than the cost of a 15 word fast telegram.

Mailgram. A Mailgram may consist of 100 words or less. The cost is $2.50 and the message must be in the telegraph office before 7:00 in the evening to deliver next day.

Telegraph companies also provide errand service and telegraph money orders.

How charges are counted. No charge is made for the name and address of the addressee or for the name of the sender, but a charge is made for the address of the sender.

The message itself, names of states, counties, and cities are counted according to the number of words they contain. For example, "New York City" is three words; "United States," two. Running the words together as "Newyork," does not affect the count. If the names are abbreviated, they count as one word. Thus, NYC is one word.

Abbreviations that do not contain more than five letters are counted as one word. They should be written without spaces or periods—COD, UN, FOB.

If separated by a space, initials are counted as separate words, but if written without spaces, they are counted as one word for each five letters or fraction thereof. Thus R L is counted as two words, but RL is one word.

Personal names are counted in accordance with the way they are usually written. Thus, Van der Gren is counted as three words; Van Dorn, as two words; and O'Connell, as one word.

Mixed groups of letters, figures, affixes, and the characters $, /, &, #, ' (indicating feet or minutes) and " (indicating inches or seconds) are counted at the rate of five characters, or fraction thereof, to the word in messages between points in continental United States and points in Mexico. Thus, "one hundred" is counted as two words, but 100 is counted as one word; $34.50, as one word (the decimal is not counted); 44B42, as one word, but 1000th (six characters) is counted as two words.

In messages sent to Canada and Saint Pierre and Miquelon Islands, each figure, affix, bar, dash, and sign in a group is counted as a word, in determining the charge for the telegram.

Punctuation marks are not charged for, but the words "stop," "comma," and the like are counted.

Compound words that are hyphenated in the dictionary are counted as one word. Thus, "son-in-law" is one word.

Paragraphing. Telegrams written in paragraphs are transmitted in paragraphs at no extra cost.

Economies in the use of telegraphic service may be made by considering the urgency of the message and thus the class of service to be used, the time zone in which the addressee is located, and the wording of the message.

How to type a telegram. 1. The number of copies depends upon the requirements of the secretary's office. Four is the usual number.

a. The original for pickup by the telegraph messenger.

b. A carbon copy for confirmation by mail.

c. A carbon copy for the file.

d. A carbon copy for the telegraph account file against which the charges may be checked.

2. Check the class of service—whether straight telegram, day letter, or night letter—in the form provided on the telegraph blank. Also type the class of service two spaces above the address.

3. Type the date and hour in the upper right-hand corner.

4. Omit the salutation and complimentary close.

5. Double space the message.

6. Do not divide a word at the end of a line.

7. Use caps and small letters and punctuate just as you would any other material.

8. In the lower left-hand corner type:

a. The dictator's initials and the secretary's initials.

b. Whether the message is to be sent "Charge," "Paid," or "Collect."

c. Address and telephone number of the firm, unless printed on the blank.

9. If the telegram is to be charged, type the name of the charge account in the space provided on the blank.

How to send the same message to multiple addresses. If the firm wants to send the same message to a number of people, the secretary types the telegram only once. List the names and addresses on a special sheet obtainable from Western Union (or on a plain sheet). Above the list type "Please send the attached message to the following 12 (whatever the number is) addresses."

How to type a telegram when work is in the machine. Always transcribe a telegram as soon as it is dictated. Often a rush telegram will be given when the secretary has other work in the typewriter, but it is not necessary to remove the work to type the telegram. Follow this procedure:

1. Back feed the paper and carbons that are in the machine until the paper shows a top margin of about two inches.

2. Insert the first sheet of the telegram behind the material you are typing, against the paper table, just as if nothing were in the typewriter.

3. To make carbons of the telegram, insert the second sheet of the telegram against the coated side of the carbon paper that is already in the machine. Thus, the second sheet of the telegram is between the carbon and the second sheet of your letter. Do the same for each carbon that is in the typewriter. (A sheet for each carbon in the machine must be inserted to prevent the typing from showing on the carbon copies of the work.) For additional copies add carbon sheets in the usual manner.

4. Turn the platen knob until the telegram blanks are in position for typing.

5. After typing the message, back feed until the telegram can be removed from the machine.

6. Forward feed to the point at which the letter or other work was interrupted and continue with the typing.

Telephone Contacts. See CONTACTS OVER THE TELEPHONE.

Telephone Courtesy. The following simple rules that the secretary should follow constitute the basis of courteous and efficient telephone usage:

1. Answer calls promptly.

2. When the secretary leaves her desk, she should arrange for someone to take her calls.

3. Keep pad and pencil handy.

4. In asking a caller to wait, the secretary should say, "Will you please hold the line while I get the information," and wait for the reply. When she returns to the telephone, she thanks the caller for waiting. If it will take her some time to get the information, she offers to call back.

5. When the secretary has finished talking, she should say, "Thank you, Mr. Smith," or "Good-by," pleasantly and replace the receiver gently. She should let the caller hang up first. See also SCREENING CALLS; CONTACTS OVER THE TELEPHONE; TOLL CALLS; TELEPHONE SERVICE.

Telephone List. A register of frequently called telephone numbers that the secretary keeps in a small directory on her desk. She should keep an up-to-date directory of the name, address, and telephone number of the following:

Law Business Numbers
Attorneys associated in current cases (temporary listing)
Attorneys available for various kinds of matters that your office does not handle
Attorneys on opposite side of current cases (temporary listing)
Auctioneers
Bonding companies
Collection agencies
Consuls
Court reporters
Courts
Custodians
Deputy sheriffs
Detectives
Engineers
Engravers
Investigators
Law journals
Law stationers
Libraries
Marshals
Mimeographers
Newspapers
Photographers
Printers
Process servers
Translators

Office Administration Numbers
Airlines
Building manager or superintendent
Emergency calls (Fire, Police, Ambulance, etc.)
Express office
Messenger service
Post office
Railroads
Residence of employees in your office
Stationer (officer supplies)
Telegraph office
Time of day
Travel Agency
Typewriter repairs
Weather

Lawyer's Personal Telephone Numbers
Bank
Dentist
Doctors
Family (residence and business)

Florist
Friends whom he calls frequently
Garage
Organizations to which he belongs
Services (dry cleaners, tailor, etc.)
Stores that he trades with
Theater ticket agency

Telephone Service. The legal secretary should have knowledge of the services and telephone aids available for maintaining peak efficiency in all office communication procedures. Then when the occasion arises she may suggest those improvements that can be of assistance to the attorney for whom she works. There are numerous types of services for local and long distance calls as well as equipment for interoffice communication systems and convenience aids that can be installed on telephone equipment for a nominal charge.

The *button telephone* has become indispensable to all modern offices and is particularly suited to the law office. Often there is more than one line connected to the office telephone so that the secretary may handle calls for more than one lawyer. Some of these lines may be outside lines; others may be inter-communication lines within the firm. Button telephones make such systems easy to use. Button telephones are furnished in one, four, and six button sets.

When there is more than one line connected to the telephone, the secretary can select the particular line on which she wishes to speak by depressing the proper button. An arrangement can be made that will cause the button for any of the lines to light up intermittently when the line is ringing. These lights can be wired to glow steadily when the secretary is talk-ing so that other persons having the same line will know that that particular line is in use. These buttons can also be used to switch calls from one telephone to another when both instruments are connected to the same line.

A *hold button* will hold a call on one line while the secretary uses the same telephone to place or receive a call on another line. The caller on the first line cannot hear the secretary's conversation on the second line after the hold button has been depressed.

A *signal button* can be wired so that when the secretary presses it, it signals another person on another phone to pick up the call she has received. Signal buttons may also be installed on a separately mounted panel, either consisting of a single button or of four or eight buttons. Signals can be either audible or visible. Visual signals can be obtained in various colors to indicate which line a call is on. Separately mounted signal buttons and signal lamps can be attached to the secretary's desk, the wall or any flat surface.

An *exclusion button* (sometimes called a *cutoff button*) can be used to cut out other telephones connected to the line on which the secretary is talking. This arrangement assures privacy for important calls. (See also CONTACTS OVER THE TELEPHONE.)

Similarly, through key or button operation, signals or telephone bells may be cut off temporarily, so that the lawyer who does not wish to be disturbed during conferences or special meetings with clients may indicate his wishes to the secretary. Contrariwise, he may want to have *his* bell ring and have the extension of his bell and line to the secretary cut off.

Wats Line. Direct line between different areas of the country. There are two types, the in-dial (800 numbers) and out-dial (regular 7 digit number). There is no charge to the calling party on 800 numbers. The telephone company bills the subscriber on a monthly basis for this service.

The secretary who has suggested telephone improvements to her employer and has received a "green light" to draft a memo concerning them may seek advice and assistance in planning for new equipment and preparing a statement of costs involved, by consulting the telephone company.

Temporary Alimony. See ALIMONY.

Temporary Injunction. See PROVISIONAL REMEDIES.

Tenancy by the Entirety. An estate held by husband and wife by virtue of TITLE acquired by them jointly after marriage. Upon the death of either spouse, his or her interest automatically passes to the other by survivorship. A tenancy by the entirety cannot be terminated without the consent of both parties. Thus, neither spouse can defeat the right of survivorship by MORTGAGE or conveyance without the consent of the other. The courts do not look with disfavor upon a tenancy by the entirety as they do upon a JOINT TENANCY. Not all states recognize tenancy by the entirety, or "tenancy by the entireties," as it is sometimes called. See also TENANCY IN COMMON.

Tenancy in Common. If two or more persons hold an estate by separate and distinct titles, with unity of possession only, the estate is called a *tenancy in common*. The tenants in common may acquire their TITLE at different times, from different sources, and have different degrees of interest in the estate, but their right of possession is common. Upon the death of one of the tenants in common, his interest passes to his heirs and legatees, and not to the other tenants in common. See TENANCY BY THE ENTIRETY; JOINT TENANCY.

Term of Court. The designated period of time prescribed by law during which a court may sit to transact business. This period may also be called *term time*. The periods during the term when the court actually sits are known as *sessions*. The terms are usually designated by the time they commence, for example, *November Term*. A term of court is also referred to in various jurisdictions as *general term* or *trial term,* meaning the term during which cases are tried.

Termination of Lease. The dissolution of a LEASE by (1) *performance,* that is, expiration of the lease at the end of its term; (2) *agreement* (see SURRENDER OF LEASE); or (3) *breach* (see EVICTION and FORFEITURE OF LEASE). The tenant usually watches the termination date of his lease so that he may not be a holdover tenant. He removes all his property by the time the lease expires. The landlord, as a rule, makes a careful physical examination of the premises when the lease terminates. He checks to see if the premises have been left in good order, if there has been unusual damage, and if the utilities work. Some leases specifically allow the landlord to inspect the premises before termination, and to show the premises to prospective tenants. See also ABANDONMENT OF LEASED PREMISES.

Testacy. The state or condition of leaving a Will at one's death Opposed to "intestacy." See INTESTATE.

Testamentary Capacity. The possession of sound mind, disposing memory, and proper age to make a WILL disposing of real and personal property. Each state has its own minimum age requirement to make a will.

Testator. A person who leaves a WILL that is in force at his death. Having left a will, he is said to have died *testate*. See also INTESTATE; PROBATE OF A WILL; LETTERS OF ADMINISTRATION.

Testatrix. Feminine form of TESTATOR.

Testimonium Clause. The closing declaration by the parties to a legal instrument that their signatures are attached in testimony of the preceding part of the instrument. The testimonium clause, which is at the close of the instrument, should not be confused with the ATTESTATION

IN WITNESS WHEREOF, the parties hereto have hereunto set their hands and seals, the day and year first above written.

In the Presence of:

_____L.S.

_____

_____L.S.

_____   Parties of the First Part

_____L.S.

Party of the Second Part

Testimonium Clause: Figure 1. Signature and seal for individuals, witnessed.

CLAUSE. The testimonium clause relates to the parties themselves, whereas the witness or attestation clause relates to those who sign the paper as witnesses, not as parties to the instrument.

Quite often, the testimonium clause guides the secretary in setting up the signature lines. It will indicate (1) what parties are to sign the instrument; (2) what officer of a corporation is to sign; (3) whether the instrument is to be sealed; and (4) whether a COR-PORATE SEAL is to be attested. For example, from the following clause, which is a form commonly used, it is evident that the president of the cor-poration is to sign, that the SEAL is to be affixed, and that the secretary of the corporation is to attest the seal.

IN WITNESS WHEREOF, Alvin Cor-poration has caused its corporate seal to be hereto affixed, and attested by its secretary, and these presents to be signed by its presi-dent, the 21st day of September, 19. . . .

On the other hand, from the follow-ing clause, also commonly used, it is evident that the instrument is not to be sealed.

IN TESTIMONY WHEREOF, the par-ties hereto have hereunto set their hands the day and year first above written.

Figure 1, page 419, is an illustration of a testimonium clause, signature and seal for individuals, witnessed.

Testimony. Evidence given by a witness under oath. See also DEPOSI-TION.

Third-class Mail. See POSTAL SER-VICE.

Tickler Card File. A small card file that acts as a reminder system. The tickler card file has a tabbed guide for each month of the year and 31 tabbed guides, one for each day of the month. The daily guides are placed behind the current month guide. Memoranda are made on cards or slips, which are filed behind the daily guide according to the date on which the matter is brought up.

Use of tickler file with diary. Generally secretaries in law offices do not like to depend upon tickler cards as reminders for deadlines, hearings, trial dates, and other legal work. It is too easy to lose or misplace a small 3 by 5 inch card or slip, and the resulting damage might be irreparable. Further-more, tickler cards do not constitute a permanent record of the day's activities as a DIARY does.

Tickler cards can be used in conjunc-tion with a diary very satisfactorily. They reduce the work necessary in making diary entries. Recurring items can be put on one card, and the card can be moved from week to week, month to month, or year to year. Thus if a certain check is made out each Fri-day, the secretary can make one card and move it each week, instead of mak-ing 52 entries in her diary. Also, she can put all necessary information on the card so that she or anyone else can attend to the task without referring to any other material. Tickler cards are also particularly useful for indefinite date follow-ups. Suppose the lawyer has told the secretary he wants to do a certain job sometime within the next few months. She makes a card and moves it from time to time if he does not do the task when she first brings it to his attention.

A tickler card file *does not* take the place of a diary for noting appoint-ments. All appointments, even regular-ly recurring ones, should be entered in the diary; otherwise, whenever the secretary wants to make an appointment she will have to look not only in the diary but also at the tickler.

The secretary should refer to the diary every afternoon for the following day and to the tickler each morning. See also FOLLOW-UP FILING SYSTEM.

Time Charter. See CHARTER PARTY.

Time Differentials. Variations in standard time in different parts of the world. If one time zone is on Daylight Savings Time, the normal differential that exists between that zone and another when both are on Standard Time is increased or decreased by one hour.

Time Table on an Appeal. A record that the legal secretary maintains of the dates certain steps must be taken by the lawyer when a case is up on APPEAL. The rules of the APPELLATE COURT require that an appeal shall be perfected according to a strict time table. It is the secretary's duty to make DIARY entries of the schedule so that there will be no slip-up on the part of her office. She should also note the progress of the appeal in the SUIT REGISTER. The rules of some courts provide for return days of appeals, just as they do for PLEADINGS. Other courts consider the date upon which the RECORD ON APPEAL is filed as the date from which the time for filing motions and briefs shall run. The secretary can get the appropriate time table from the reviewing court's rules, or the lawyer will give it to her. Dates by which the following steps must be taken should be entered in the diary:

1. Filing notice of appeal by appellant

2. Assignment of errors and instructions by appellant for making up the transcript of the record

3. Filing of additional instructions by appellee

4. Filing of record on appeal in reviewing court

5. Appellee's motion to quash or dismiss an appeal

6. Hearing of motions

7. Filing of appellant's BRIEF

8. Filing of appellee's brief

9. Filing of appellant's reply brief

Title. All of the elements that prove ownership, Title to REAL PROPERTY is the means whereby a person's right to the property is established, the means whereby the owner has the legal and just possession of his property.

Equitable title. A person's *right* to obtain absolute ownership of property to which another has title under the laws. (See MORTGAGE.)

Evidence of title. Proof that a seller has good title to property to be conveyed may be evidenced in any one of the following ways: (1) TITLE INSURANCE, (2) ABSTRACT OF TITLE, (3) CERTIFICATE OF TITLE, and (4) TORRENS SYSTEM. Local custom generally determines which kind of evidence of title will be required upon a sale of REAL PROPERTY. Title insurance is customary in urban centers. An abstract of title and opinion is widely used in rural areas in the middle west. The certificate of title is popular in the southern states. The Torrens system is used in a few localities throughout the United States.

Broker's duties with respect to title. In many states (New York included) a BROKER is under no obligation to ascertain whether his PRINCIPAL has good title to the property. When the principal employs the broker to sell his property, it is implied that the principal will furnish a good and marketable title to the property. The broker is entitled to his commission even if the transaction is not consummated because of a defect in title, unless the broker's contract of employment makes his commission dependent upon consummation of the transaction.

A broker may apply for title examination and insurance in behalf of his principal or his prospect and direct that the "title report" be delivered to him directly. When the report is delivered, the broker should examine it at once and see that the seller clears any OBJECTION TO TITLE disclosed in the report; otherwise CLOSING TITLE may be delayed, or the deal may fall through completely. See also OPNION OF TITLE.

Title Closing. See CLOSING.

Title Insurance. A CONTRACT by a title insurance company guaranteeing to make good to the beneficiary any loss, up to a fixed amount, sustained through defects in TITLE TO REAL PROPERTY. Title insurance is also known in some localities as "title insurance policy," "title guaranty policy," and "guaranty title policy." A title company issuing its policy of insurance agrees to indemnify the beneficiary against any loss he may sustain by reason of any defects in title not enumerated as "exceptions" in the policy. These defects may be (1) discoverable defects that are disclosed by the public records, or (2) hidden defects, such as forgery of a DEED in the chain of title. Some title insurance also guarantees that the title is marketable, and the title insurance company agrees to defend, at its own expense, any action attacking the title based on a defect in the title insured.

Title Search. A thorough investigation of the documented ownership of property, and liens or encumbrances against the property, as listed in the public records. It is customary to have a title search whenever real property is sold, mortgaged, or involved in litigation. For example, title should be searched between the date of the contract of sale and the date of closing title. This gives the seller enough time before the closing to clear up any objections raised by the title searcher. The seller, for example, may have to clear the record of an old mortgage that had been paid; procure a correction deed to correct an error in a previous deed; prepare an AFFIDAVIT that he is not a person with a similar name against whom there is a judgment of record, and so on.

A title search need not go back beyond the previous point of title guarantee, since the title company making the previous search guarantees good title up until that point. See also TITLE INSURANCE; ABSTRACT OF TITLE; CERTIFICATE OF TITLE; TORRENS SYSTEM; TITLE.

Toll Calls. A record must be kept of every long distance or toll call that is placed from the office. These calls are usually made on behalf of a client and are charged to his account. Always ask the operator to tell the amount of the charge and make a memorandum immediately. Figure 1, page 423, illustrates a useful printed form. After the details are filled in, give it to the lawyer who made the call so that he can initial it. The secretary may have the authority to initial it for him. The il-

```
┌──────────────────────────────────────────────────┐
│                                                    │
│  C & S                                             │
│            TELEPHONE TOLL CALL                     │
│                                                    │
│                    June 18  19 —                   │
│                                                    │
│  Mr. Elwood                                        │
│  Called Jones and Smith                            │
│        Chicago               No.                   │
│  Charge R. J. Edwards                              │
│  Re: National Trust, Inc.      $ 7.80              │
│                                                    │
│  New  Matter                  R. S. E.             │
│  Yes ☐ No ☒            (Lawyer's Initials) M       │
│                                                    │
└──────────────────────────────────────────────────┘
```

Toll Calls: **Figure 1.** Record of toll telephone call.

lustration shows that the secretary initialed the form for the lawyer and placed her own initial beneath his initials. The form is then sent to the bookkeeper. If the secretary keeps the books, she should have a folder for telephone call memoranda, against which she can check the bill and make the charges to clients' accounts. See also CLIENTS' TELEPHONE CALLS.

Torrens System. A system of registering TITLE to REAL PROPERTY, so called because Sir Robert Torrens devised it. Under the system, a person or persons in whom the FEE SIMPLE is vested, either in law or in EQUITY, may apply to have the land placed on the register of titles. After certain legal formalities are complied with, a certificate of registration is issued, and the registered owner has good title to the property. The object is to have a system of registration that accurately determines the ownership of land and every LIEN and claim upon it; the title registered is absolutely conclusive. It is not necessary to go behind the registry to effect transfer after the first registration. Many states permit registration of title in the Torrens system, but in only a few states is the system used to any extent.

Tort. A civil wrong inflicted otherwise than by a BREACH OF CONTRACT. Elements of tort are (1) a wrongful act or omission to obey the law, and (2) an injury to some person. Tort gives the injured party the right to sue for any resulting damage. Persons (including minors) and corporations are liable for torts. Some of the more common torts are NEGLIGENCE, ASSAULT AND BATTERY,

CONVERSION, FALSE IMPRISONMENT, and LIBEL AND SLANDER. *Example of tort*: A visitor to a department store (even one having no expressed intention to make a purchase but intending merely to examine the merchandise) can recover damages from the proprietor for injuries caused by the negligent maintenance of the store premises. See also CIVIL LAW; CIVIL COURT.

Totten Trust. See SAVINGS BANK TRUST.

Towage. The pulling or pushing of one vessel by another. Ore and grain are commonly transported in barges pulled or, in some cases, pushed by towboats, also called tug boats.

Township. See Section and township, LAND DESCRIPTION.

Trade Secrets. The formulas, manufacturing processes, and ideas used by a particular business in order to give it an advantage over its competition. The court reads into every contract of employment an implied term that the employee will not disclose to another, or use for his own benefit, trade secrets learned in the course of his employment. If the employer feels that his trade secrets are in danger of being appropriated, he may ask the court to issue an INJUNCTION to forbid the disclosure and use of these trade secrets.

Trademark. A mark, symbol, or design that is used to distinguish a particular make of merchandise or an individual service. Registration of a trademark with the United States Pat-ent Office is not obligatory, for a trademark rightfully belongs to the first person who has used it.

Registration does not automatically protect the owner from litigation. Once the trademark has been registered, the Patent Office is empowered to refuse the registration of infringing ideas, but the owner himself has to bring suit to restrain the use by another who has unlawfully appropriated his trademark.

Certificates of registration covering trademarks remain in force for twenty years, subject to cancellation at the end of six years unless the registrant, within one year preceding the expiration of such six-year period, files an AFFIDAVIT showing that the mark is still in use, or showing that the non-use is due to special circumstances, and not due to any intention to abandon the mark.

Tramp. A vessel which does not follow a fixed itinerary or schedule and is available to carry cargo to any port. See also LINER.

Transfer Tax. A tax imposed by some states on the conveyance of real estate. The tax is paid by the seller. Some states require documentary stamps to be placed on the warranty deed to show evidence that the tax has been paid. At one time the Federal Government imposed a Revenue Tax on real estate conveyances which required that documentary stamps be purchased and placed on the deed. The Federal Government no longer collects this tax. Transfer tax is usually based on the sale price, for example, 10¢ per hundred dollars of the sale price.

Transferring Numerical Files. A method of retiring files after the records are closed. See NUMERICAL FILING SYSTEM.

Travel Agency. An agency offering complete service in all matters pertaining to travel. A travel service is indispensable in making plans for FOREIGN TRAVEL. Many large firms have an agency make all travel reservations for domestic business trips as well as foreign trips. A firm may open an account with an agency and be billed once a month, thus avoiding the nuisance of paying for numerous tickets throughout the month.

The American Society of Travel Agents, Inc., familiarly known as ASTA, has members in the principal cities of the United States and Canada. The members may be recognized by the ASTA emblem, which they are permitted to display if they are in good standing. The name of a nearby ASTA member may be found in the telephone directory yellow pages or by writing to the association offices at 501 Fifth Ave., New York, N. Y. 10301. There are, of course, many reliable agents who are not members of ASTA, but the code of ethics of this association is high and its members, therefore, are dependable and efficient.

Travel Card. A credit card that allows the holder to be billed for travel arrangements and services, obviating the necessity for payment in cash. The charge for travel tickets, hotel accommodations, car rental, and many other travel services are billed by itemized monthly statement. Where services are involved, the statement is accompanied by a *record of charge* made at the time the service is completed. This record of charge shows the date and items of purchase, the signature of the purchaser, and the name and address of the service establishment.

The secretary should check the items of the record of charge signed by her employer against the itemized monthly statement received. She should also make certain that any travel ticket cancellations have been properly credited to her employer's account.

Treaties. Treaties and international agreements prior to 1950 were published in *Statutes at Large.* After 1950 they can be found in a series of volumes entitled *United States Treaties and other International Agreements,* cited U.S.T. Treaties may also be ordered in slip form.

Trespasser. One on the premises without the permission of the owner. There is no duty owed to the trespasser to keep the premises safe or to warn him of defects. Of course, there is a duty to refrain from willful, wanton harm. See INVITEE; LICENSEE; NEGLIGENCE; ATTRACTIVE NUISANCE.

Triplicate Original. A carbon copy that is to be signed and treated in all respects as though it were an original or ribbon copy. The term *triplicate original* is used when an original and two copies to be treated as originals are needed. The term *duplicate original* is used to designate that just one additional copy will be needed for use in the same manner as the original. For details on how the dictator usually gives instructions as to the number of copies to make, see DUPLICATE ORIGINAL.

Trust. A holding of property subject to the duty of applying the property, the income from it, or the proceeds for the benefit of another, as directed by the person creating the trust. A trust is created when *A* transfers property to *X*, the trustee, and *X* undertakes to apply the property and income from it for the purposes and in the manner directed by *A*. The elements of an ordinary trust are (1) the trustor (also called settlor, donor or grantor), who furnishes the property to be put in trust; (2) the subject matter or property that is put in trust (called the trust principal, corpus, or res); (3) the trustee, who holds the property and administers the trust; and (4) the beneficiaries, for whose benefit the trust exists. A trust may be created by will (testamentary trust) or by deed (*inter vivos* or living trust). A man may put property in trust, the income to go to his wife while she lives, the principal to go to their children upon the wife's death. In these situations the wives would be *income beneficiaries* (or "equitable life tenants") and the children would be remaindermen. (See LIFE ESTATE.)

Trust Deed. An agreement (sometimes called "trust agreement" or "trust indenture") between a *corporation* and a *trustee* who serves as a "guardian" of bondholders' interests. It sets forth all the terms and conditions of a bond issue, and the rights, powers, and duties of the parties to the BOND ISSUE. These parties are the corporation that borrows the money, the trustee through whom the corporation deals with the bondholders, and the bondholders. The bond and the deed of trust constitute the bondholders' contract with the corporation. See also INDENTURE; CORPORATE MORTGAGE BOND; DEED OF TRUST.

Trust Indenture. See TRUST DEED.

Trustee. See TRUST; BANKRUPTCY.

Trustee in Bankruptcy. See BANKRUPTCY.

Trust Funds. See ACCOUNTING.

Trust, Spendthrift. A trust created to provide a fund for the maintenance of a beneficiary, and at the same time to secure it against his improvidence or incapacity.

Type Face. The design of a style of type letter. Type faces are usually known by the name of the men who designed them as, for example, Baskerville and Granjon. This text is set in 10 point Times Roman.

Following are the better-known type faces and their characteristics:

This type is BASKERVILLE
THIS PARAGRAPH IS SET IN BASKERVILLE. Baskerville is a very legible, useful face for both display and text purposes. *Baskerville italic is illustrated by this sentence.*

This type is BODONI
THIS PARAGRAPH IS SET IN BODONI BOOK. Some of the types illustrated in this section—Caslon, Baskerville, Garamond, Electra, and Cloister—are so-called Old Style faces. Bodoni is a so-called Modern face. Bodoni comes in a number of varieties; this is Bodoni Book. The headline is set in Bodoni Bold. *Bodoni italic is illustrated by this sentence.*

This type is CALEDONIA
THIS PARAGRAPH IS SET IN CALEDONIA. Caledonia, like Bodoni, is a Mod-

ern type face. Designed in 1940, it has since become one of today's most widely employed book and advertising text faces. *Caledonia italic is illustrated by this sentence.*

This type is CASLON
THIS PARAGRAPH IS SET IN CASLON. Caslon is warm and sympathetic, yet impersonal. It is one of the most serviceable of all types, one of the most easily read, and one of the most widely used. There are a number of varieties of Caslon; this is Caslon Old Style. *Caslon Old Style italic is illustrated by this sentence.*

This type is CLOISTER
THIS PARAGRAPH IS SET IN CLOISTER BOLD. Cloister is a good type for the body matter of advertisements, and it also gives excellent results when used for display. The headline is set in Cloister Old Style. *Cloister bold italic is illustrated by this sentence.*

This type is ELECTRA
THIS PARAGRAPH IS SET IN ELECTRA. Electra, like the Caslon Old Style face illustrated above, combines beauty of form with a high degree of legibility. *Electra italic is illustrated by this sentence.*

This type is GARAMOND
THIS PARAGRAPH IS SET IN GARAMOND. Garamond is one of the most useful and beautiful of type faces, and is one of the faces most frequently used by advertisers. Its grace and beauty make it suitable for use where the beauty of the product itself is one of the points featured in the advertisement. *Garamond italic also has a good appearance; the italic is illustrated by this sentence.*

This type is MEMPHIS
THIS PARAGRAPH IS SET IN MEMPHIS. Memphis comes in a number of weights; this is Memphis light.

This type is METRO
THIS PARAGRAPH IS SET IN METRO. Metro should be used sparingly. Metro comes in a number of weights; this is Metro light. *Metro italic is illustrated by this sentence.*

This type is FUTURA
THIS PARAGRAPH IS SET IN FUTURA MEDIUM.

Futura may be used as either a body or a display type. However, although it is a good looking type, it is not very easily read, and hence should not be used except where only a few lines have to be set. Futura comes in a number of weights; this is Futura Medium. *Futura italic is illustrated by this sentence.*

Typing Court Papers. All pleadings and supporting papers, except those for which PRINTED LAW BLANKS are used, are typed on legal size paper except in Massachusetts. In some states LEGAL CAP is used for court papers; in others, plain legal size paper, without ruled margins, is used; in some states either may be used. In a few states, the legal cap has numbers in the left margin.

All court papers have a heading, or caption, consisting of various parts, which is written on every separate document, although several documents might be bound together. For the proper way to type all parts of the heading, see CAPTION. See also TYPING LEGAL DOCUMENTS.

Typing Legal Documents. To type legal documents in a craftsmanlike manner, the secretary should observe the following general suggestions:

Paper. Legal documents are generally typed on LEGAL CAP or on legal-size paper 8 or 8½ inches by 13 or 14 inches. Letter-size paper may be used, but in most cases the longer paper is preferable.

Margins. Documents typed on legal cap or legal-size paper are bound at the top; those on letter-size or short paper, at the left. Therefore it is necessary to leave a margin of at least 1½ inches for binding. Allow for proper margins this way:

TYPING LEGAL DOCUMENTS

Top margin. Begin typing either five or six double spaces from the top of the paper, but make a habit of always allowing the same number of spaces. By following this practice, you know that every page of a document starts at the same place on the paper and has the same number of typed lines.

Bottom margin. Leave a margin of approximately one inch at the bottom. With a margin of five double spaces at the top and an inch at the bottom, each legal-size page of typing will have 32 lines double spaced; each letter-size page (8½ by 11 inches), 24 lines.

In a neatly typed legal document, the typing on every page of manuscript ends exactly the same number of spaces from the bottom of the page. Carbon paper with a numbered margin, or a backing sheet with a numbered margin, will insure an even bottom margin. If the carbon paper does not have a numbered margin, or if there are too many copies to use a backing sheet, mark lightly the place where the typing should end, before inserting the paper in the typewriter.

Left margin. Leave a margin on the left of approximately 1¼ or 1½ inches if the paper is to be bound on the left. On legal cap, begin typing one space to the right of the colored line that indicates the left margin.

Right margin. Leave a right margin of approximately one inch. On legal cap, this will place the margin approximately ⅝ inch to the left of the colored line that indicates the right margin. This allows a leeway of seven spaces between the right margin and the line. Avoid excessive hyphenation and also a ragged right margin.

Under no circumstances should the typing extend beyond the colored lines that indicate the margins.

Spacing. Legal documents are double spaced, with a triple space between numbered articles or items and between paragraphs with side headings. Quoted material and description of land may be single spaced.

Paragraphs. Paragraphs should be indented ten spaces. A legal document should *never* be typed in block style. The margins of indented material should be five or ten spaces from the margins of the document itself, with an indentation of an additional five spaces for paragraphing the intended material. The right margin of an indentation may be flush with the margin of the document instead of being indented.

A paragraph should never end with the last line of the page. At least one or two lines should be carried over to the next page. This is particularly important in typing wills as a check against omission of pages.

Numbering pages. Pages should be numbered at the bottom of the sheet, in the center, or Page 1 of 10.

Signature. The line for signature should never be on a page by itself. At least one line, preferably two, of the document in addition to the TESTIMONIUM CLAUSE should appear on the page with the signature. An ACKNOWLEDGMENT or an ATTESTATION clause following the signature does not obviate this requiremen..

Carbon copies. DUPLICATE ORIGINALS (carbon copies that are signed) are typed on the same kind of paper as the original. Other carbon copies may be made on onion-skin paper. After the original and duplicate originals are signed, the carbon copies are conformed (see CONFORMING DOCUMENTS).

Erasures and interlineations. If an error is made involving more than a few letters of a word, the page should be retyped. The signer of the document must initial interlineations.

Backing. A legal document should be bound in a LEGAL BACK.

Numbers. Numbers are written in words and repeated in numerals in parentheses—for example, five thousand (5,000).

Amounts of money. Amounts of money are spelled out and repeated in parentheses, the figures in parentheses following the word "dollars." Each word except conjunctions begins with a capital—for example, Eight Hundred Fifty and 80/100 Dollars ($850.80.).

Dates. Dates may be expressed in figures or spelled out. Even if the day of the month is spelled out, the year may be written in figures, thus—the twenty-first day of August, 1965. See also PRINTED LAW BLANKS; SPACING.

Typing Manuscript. Manuscript should be typed neatly and legibly, on sheets of uniform size, preferably 8 ½ by 11 inch white bond, the sheet commonly used in offices. A carbon copy should be made for reference purposes but the original is always sent to the printer. The following suggestions should be followed in typing the MANUSCRIPT:

1. Keep the typewritten line down to six inches.

2. Use double or triple spacing.

3. Keep the right-hand margin as even as possible; this will help you in estimating the length of the copy.

4. Indicate paragraph indentions clearly. Five or six spaces are sufficient, but there should be consistency throughout the manuscript in whatever number of spaces is adopted.

5. Type headings and subheadings in the position they are to occupy on the final printed page, and be uniform in capitalizations.

6. Use one side only of the sheet.

7. Leave a margin of at least one inch on all four sides.

8. Keep the pages as nearly uniform in length as possible, to help in estimating the length of the copy.

9. If references are made to material appearing in other parts of the manuscript, instruct the printer (on the manuscript) to carry a QUERY on each successive proof as a reminder to put in the correct page reference numbers when the final page proofs are received.

10. Type any EXTRACT or quoted material just like the main text, double spaced, FULL MEASURE. To indicate that it is to be printed in a smaller size of type, draw a vertical line in the left margin, beginning exactly where the extract begins and ending where it ends.

11. Indicate that lists, examples, problems, and other material of subordinate importance are to be set in smaller type by drawing a vertical line in the left margin.

12. Draw a double vertical line in the left margin to indicate that material is to be set in a third size of type.

U

Ultra Vires. Without power; beyond the powers of. A term used to apply to a contract or act beyond the powers of a CORPORATION as expressed or implied in its CERTIFICATE OF INCORPORATION or by statute. For example, if a corporation contracts a debt in excess of the maximum allowed by statute, the CONTRACT is *ultra vires*—beyond the power of the corporation. If neither party to the contract has performed, either the corporation or the other party may declare the contract void. After both parties have performed, the courts will not rescind the contract; the weight of authority is to the effect that after one party has performed the other party cannot repudiate the contract by claiming that it was *ultra vires*. Directors may be held personally liable for loss to the corporation occasioned by an *ultra vires* act.

An *ultra vires* contract made by a municipal corporation is not binding upon the municipality, although the other party has performed.

Unauthorized Practice of Law. *Black's Law Dictionary* defines the Practice of Law as follows:

"Not limited to appearing in court, or advising and assisting in the conduct of litigation, but embracing the preparation of pleadings, and other papers incident to actions and special proceedings, conveyancing, the preparation of legal instruments of all kinds, and the giving of all legal advice to clients."

However, the American Bar Association, through the Standing Committee of Professional Ethics, Opinion No. 316, dated January 18, 1967, further clarifies the matter by concluding:

"A lawyer can employ lay secretaries, lay investigators, lay detectives, lay researchers, accountants, lay scriveners, nonlawyer draftsmen or nonlawyer researchers. In fact, he may employ nonlawyers to do any task for him except counsel clients about law matters, engage directly in the practice of law, appear in court or appear in formal proceedings as a part of the judicial process, so long as it is he who takes the work and vouches for it to the client and becomes responsible for it to the client. In other words, we do not limit the kind of assistants the lawyer can acquire in any way to persons who are admitted to the Bar, so long as the nonlawyers do not do things that lawyers may not do or do the things that lawyers only may do."

Canon 3 of a proposed Code of Professional Responsibility states with regard to the unauthorized practice of law:

430

"A lawyer often delegates tasks to clerks, secretaries, and other lay persons. Such delegation is proper if the lawyer maintains a direct relationship with his client, supervises the delegated work, and has complete professional responsibility for the work product. This delegation enables a lawyer to render legal service more economically and efficiently."

Actions charging unauthorized practice of law are usually brought by local bar associations.

Guidelines for the secretary for avoiding practicing law.

1. The secretary should never give "advice" to a client either over the telephone or in person. She should firmly inform the client that she is not an attorney and thus may not give advice. The secretary may ask, "What constitutes advice?" Advice might be defined as anything upon which a client might rely, act upon, and be injured as the result.

2. The secretary may be trained by the lawyer to draft such documents as deeds without his help, to prepare accountings for estates and guardianships, to prepare documents for transferring real estate in an estate, selling personal property in an estate, divorce pleadings from pre-dictated forms, etc. as long as the documents are supervised and reviewed by the attorney.

3. The secretary should never discuss clients' affairs with such persons as representatives of Internal Revenue Service, or authoritative tax men of various branches of the government. They may have the right to the information, but it is up to the attorney to decide what to divulge.

4. The secretary should never release documents or copies of information in files to anyone without the direction of the attorney, even though the original documents may be the property of the client, and he requests them. If the client insists on having his documents, the secretary should tell him that she must have the attorney's permission to release them, as the attorney may be holding them for payment of a fee or other reason.

5. The secretary should never discuss the client's affairs with the opposing counsel. She may reveal something that the attorney does not wish revealed at that time.

6. The secretary should never try to advise friends and relatives on legal matters, even though she may "know what she is talking about."

Thus, if the secretary applies the foregoing rules and exercises extreme care in her relationship with clients and the public both in person and over the telephone, she will avoid practising law.

Underscoring. Underscoring, or underlining, in typed material is equivalent to italics in printed material but is used less freely, probably for appearance sake. For example, the title of a book is italicized in print but, preferably, is enclosed in quotations in typed material. Generally, the underlining is continuous and not broken at the spacing between words, but may be broken in report headings and title pages for a decorative effect. The following uses of underscoring are recommended:

1. Underscore for emphasis. The dictator indicates when underscoring is to be used for emphasis.

2. Underscore material that is in italics in the original.

3. Underscore to indicate foreign words and phrases, or abbreviations of them.

Exceptions. Do not underscore foreign words that have become part of the English speech through continuous use. If in doubt, consult Webster. Parallel bars ‖ precede foreign words that occur frequently in speech and print in English but that are not yet completely Anglicized, as is shown by their being printed generally in italic type. Some words are in Roman when standing alone but are in italics when used in certain phrases. For example, the word "caveat" is not italicized, but the phrase *caveat emptor* is.

Unemployment Insurance. A form of social security that pays a weekly income to workers while they are unemployed. All states have established unemployment insurance funds, which are supported by a payroll tax. Benefit payments usually start after a fixed "waiting period" and continue for a number of weeks that varies with the state laws. Usually the payee must call at the state unemployment insurance office in person to arrange for the collection of his check. He is expected to take any job that the state finds for him, providing that the wages paid by the new employer equal the wages paid on his last job.

Uniform Commercial Code. The compilation of laws governing the handling of commercial transactions. This code has been adopted by the various state legislatures.

The code had its inception with the National Conference of Commissioners on Uniform State Laws. The commission is made up of Commissioners appointed by the governors of the states. This national body has as its purpose (1) the promotion of *uniformity* in state laws on all subjects where uniformity is deemed desirable and practicable; (2) to draft model acts on (a) subjects suitable for interstate compacts, and (b) subjects in which uniformity will make more effective the exercise of state powers and promote interstate co-operation; and (3) to promote uniformity of judicial decisions throughout the United States.

See also UNIFORM LAWS.

Uniform Laws. Conflicting state statutes have led to the adoption, in many fields of business and commercial interest, of similar laws by the various states. The laws are known as *uniform laws.* Some of the more important uniform laws are the Uniform Negotiable Instruments Act, the Uniform Partnership Act, the Uniform Stock Transfer Act, and the Uniform Warehouse Receipt Act.

In all states the uniform laws have been supplemented by the UNIFORM COMMERCIAL CODE.

Union Label. A mark that a union puts on articles that have been manufactured by union help. The union wants to assure to customers that wholesome conditions and fair terms of employment are maintained in the establishment from which the goods come. The union, of course, wants customers to buy union made merchandise and employers to hire only union men.

United States Code. A compilation of all general and permanent laws of the United States, as of January 6,

1959, arranged under general subject headings with a detailed index. Annual supplements are published.

United States Code Annotated is a publication arranged in parallel fashion to United States Code. It gives Federal and state decisions pertaining to each law in the code. Revised volumes are issued periodically. See SLIP LAWS and STATUTES AT LARGE.

United States Code Annotated. See UNITED STATES CODE.

Upper Case. Pertaining to capital letters of the alphabet, as opposed to small (lower case) letters. To uppercase a letter is to change if from a small letter to a capital.

Usury. Contracting for or receiving something in excess of the amount of interest allowed by law for the loan or forbearance of money, as in the sale of goods on credit or under the installment plan. In the majority of states, a lender who charges a usurious rate of interest loses his rights to collect any interest, although a few states permit him to collect the legal rate. In some states, both principal and interest are forfeited. Service charges, investigation fees, and commissions charged by an agent are not usually considered interest and may be added to the legal rate without usury. In some states the parties to a contract may agree upon a rate of interest higher than the legal rate but within a statutory limit; in a few states, they may agree on any rate. In some states loans to corporations, but not to individuals, may be made at more than the legal rate. Certain types of loans, such as small personal loans, are not covered by the usury law but are subject to special laws.

V

Vagrancy. The conduct of an idle person in wandering from place to place with no visible lawful means of support. The idler subsists on charity and does not work though able to do so. The mere possession of funds will not prevent a person's being a vagrant, however. Professional gamblers and those who live by AIDING AND ABETTING prostitutes have been held as vagrants.

Valued Policy. An insurance agreement where the value of the article insured is settled by agreement between the parties and inserted in the policy. See OPEN POLICY.

Vendee. One who enters into a CONTRACT OF SALE and agrees to purchase the REAL PROPERTY of another (VENDOR). Every contract of sale must have a vendee ("purchaser" or "buyer"). If two or more vendees desire to take TITLE as joint tenants, the contract of sale must describe them as such tenants. The buyer may be an individual or a CORPORATION. If he is an individual, he must be an adult of sound mind. If the vendee is a corporation, the purchase must have been duly authorized by the corporation's board of directors. A seller who enters into a contract of sale with a corporation as vendee should make certain that the CORPORATION is actually in existence and that it has power under its charter to purchase the real property. A trustee or an executor seldom has power to purchase real estate.

Vendee's Lien. The LIEN of a purchaser (VENDEE) on land as security for repayment of any monies paid in the event the seller (VENDOR) refuses or is unable to convey good TITLE. In order that the vendee's lien may be effective as against innocent purchasers from the seller, the vendee must file suit to enforce his lien.

The CONTRACT OF SALE may specifically provide that all sums paid on account of the CONTRACT and the reasonable expenses of title examination shall be a lien on the property in favor of the purchaser if the seller cannot complete his contract, but that such lien shall not continue after DEFAULT by the purchaser under the contract.

Vendor. One who enters into a CONTRACT OF SALE and agrees to sell his REAL PROPERTY to another (VENDEE). Every contract of sale must have a vendor or "seller." The vendor may be an individual, a PARTNERSHIP, a CORPORATION, or a representative. The individual may be either an adult or a minor, or he may enter into the contract in a representative capacity. If the vendor is a minor or an incompetent, the contract of sale should indicate that fact and give the name of his guardian, together with the date of the court order under which he was appointed. If the vendee is a representative, such as an agent or an executor, the contract should set forth the source of his authority.

Vendor's Lien. (Real estate.) The LIEN which a VENDOR (seller) has on the land sold, to secure payment of any part of the purchase price by the VENDEE (purchaser) remaining unpaid after delivery of the DEED. The lien is subject to FORECLOSURE like a MORTGAGE, and a deficiency JUDGMENT may be obtained by the seller against the purchaser. (The vendor's lien exists whether or not the CONTRACT OF SALE provides for it.) Such a lien is, however, of little value unless specifically provided for in the deed, for an innocent purchaser from the first vendee acquires TITLE free of the vendor's lien.

Where the vendor reserves in his deed to the vendee a lien on the land to secure payment of the balance of the purchase price, the lien has priority over (1) prior judgments against the buyer, and (2) any subsequent lien or ENCUMBRANCE on the REAL PROPERTY. The buyer is not personally liable for his debt unless he has signed a note or other instrument making him personally liable. One who purchases from the buyer is not personally liable to the holder of the vendor's lien unless he assumes and agrees to pay the debt under his deed. If the debt is assigned, the assignee may foreclose the lien.

A vendor's lien is used in lieu of a MORTGAGE in Louisiana and some other states, just as a WARRANTY DEED is used in Georgia and similar states.

Venue. The county and state where the facts of a case are alleged to have occurred, and in which the trial is held. If it can be shown that justice requires trial in another county, the case is removed by *change of venue.* The venue of a case in Federal court may be changed to another state.

Venue is also used to refer to the clause in a sworn statement showing the state and county or other political subdivision where the instrument was executed.

The venue always appears in legal instruments such as an AFFIDAVIT or COMPLAINT; or in a part of a legal instrument, such as an ACKNOWLEDGMENT or VERIFICATION and in court papers such as a FORECLOSURE action, or NOTICE OF MOTION. The venue does not have to do with the power of the court, but with its right to proceed in a given case by reason of the residence of the parties, the place of performance of the contract or the place of happening of the incident.

How the secretary types the venue. Type the statement of the venue in solid caps, bracket it, and follow with *ss.,* the abbreviation for *scilicet* (sc, though correct, is not used in legal papers). The abbreviation may be caps or small letters. Like all abbreviations, it is followed by a period. Technically, a colon should also follow because scilicet means "to wit," but few law offices observe this technicality.

Verbal. Relates to either written or spoken words. *Verbal* is used carelessly in place of *oral* with reference to spoken words.

435

Verification. A sworn statement by a qualified person that the allegations contained in a PLEADING are true. The statutes require that many pleadings and supporting papers be verified, and some law firms follow the practice of verifying all pleadings whether the statute requires it or not. Some of the papers commonly verified are complaints, answers, petitions and bills of particulars.

If the complaint is verified, the answer *must* be verified. The verification always recites the VENUE and always has a jurat, or "sworn to" clause. One of the duties of a NOTARY PUBLIC is to administer the oath to a person verifying a pleading. The proper procedure is for the notary to stand and raise his right hand and ask the verifier to do the same. Then the notary administers the oath in the following, or similar words: "Do you solemnly swear that the con-

```
COMMONWEALTH OF VIRGINIA)
                         : SS.
COUNTY OF HENRICO        )


        AUSTIN L. NELSON, being duly sworn, deposes and
says: That he is the treasurer of Southwestern Pine, Inc.,
the plaintiff in the above entitled action; that he has read
the foregoing complaint and knows the contents thereof; that
the same is true of his own knowledge; except as to matters
therein stated to be alleged upon information and belief,
and as to those matters he believes it to be true.



                                      _____


Given under my hand and seal this
    day of September, 19—.


        _____
        Notary Public
My commission expires
```

Verification: **Figure 1.** Verification of complaint by officer of domestic corporation.

tents of the foregoing instrument subscribed by you are the truth, the whole truth, and nothing but the truth, so help you God?" The verifier should answer "Yes" or "I do." Figure 1, page 436, is an illustration of a verification of complaint by an officer of a domestic corporation.

Versus. (vs., v.) Against.

Visa. (See PASSPORT).

Vital Statistics. For birth and death records, write:

Superintendent of Documents
U. S. Printing Office
Washington, D.C. 20402

Ask for "Where to Write for Birth and Death Records." For Divorce Records, write as above. Ask for "Where to Write for Divorce Records." For Marriage Records, write as above. Ask for "Where to Write for Marriage Records." See GOVERNMENT PUBLICATIONS

Void; Voidable. That which is void is of no legal force or effect; that which is voidable may be rendered void. For example, a gambling or wagering contract is void (see CONTRACT, 3); whereas an infant's contracts are merely voidable at his election (see CONTRACT, 2).

Voting Trust. A method devised for concentrating the control of a company in the hands of a few people. A voting trust is usually organized and operated under a *voting trust agreement*. This is a contract between the stockholders and those who manage the corporation, called the voting trustees. The stockholders transfer their stock to the trustees, giving them the right to vote the stock during the life of the agreement. The trustees in turn, issue certificates of beneficial interest, called *voting trust certificates,* to the stockholders, who are entitled to the dividends. All stockholders may become parties to the agreement, which is generally subject to statutory regulation. The trust is usually for a definite period of time. When it is terminated, the certificate-holders are notified to exchange their trust certificates of stock.

Voyage Charter. See CHARTER-PARTY.

W

Waiver. The surrender, either expressed or implied, of a right to which one is entitled by law. Thus, a stockholder might sign a waiver of notice of meeting, or he might impliedly waive that notice by participation in the meeting. The essence of the waiver is conduct that indicates an intention not to enforce certain rights or certain provisions of an agreement. A widow may waive her right to share in the estate of her husband; a buyer may waive delivery on a certain date by accepting the goods at a subsequent date. For *waiver of citation* in a probate proceedings, See PROBATE OF A WILL.

Warrant. A directive from a competent authority in pursuance of law, directing the doing of an act, and affording him protection from damage if he does it. See SEARCH AND SEIZURE.

Warranty. Affirmation of a material fact or promise by the seller, which acts as an inducement for the buyer to make a purchase. A warranty may be express (a direct statement made by the seller), or implied (one that is indicated by the nature of the contract). Warranties relate to many things: fitness of the goods sold for a special purpose; merchantability of the goods; title to real or personal property; and quiet enjoyment of premises. All representations made by an applicant for insurance, whether material or not, are deemed warranties. The term *guaranty* is loosely used in the sense of warranty. The common guaranty of a product is, strictly, a warranty and not a guaranty. (See GUARANTY.) Any warranty made by a seller which proves to be false gives the buyer a right of legal action.

Warranty Deed. 1. Upon a sale of REAL PROPERTY, a DEED under which the GRANTOR covenants that he will forever warrant TITLE to real property conveyed. A full covenant or *general* warranty deed may enumerate all the COVENANTS OF TITLE. In many states it is necessary to set forth all the covenants of title in full in the warranty deed; the usual covenants are implied if the deed contains certain words of conveyance, such as *grant, bargain, and sell,* or *convey and warrant,* or if a phrase such as the following is included after the description: *and grantor warrants the title to the same,* or *with warranty,* or *with warranty covenants.*

A warranty deed does not correct a bad TITLE; nor does it cure defects in former deeds. It merely gives the GRANTEE the right to sue the grantor for breach of warranty if anyone later makes a claim against the property.

2. Upon a loan, an instrument used to secure payment of the debt. In some states, particularly Georgia, a warranty deed to secure a debt is used in lieu of a

MORTGAGE. In the event of the death of the mortgagor (borrower), the mortgage, as a claim against his estate, is junior to expenses of administration, to a year's support for the widow and children, and to certain other claims. In all states, a warranty deed that is in fact given to secure a debt is treated as a mortgage. Such an instrument is sometimes used in states where a mortgage does not provide adequate security under the law. A warranty deed to secure a debt usually contains the same provisions as a mortgage.

Watered Stock. Stock issued as fully-paid, for which the CORPORATION has received assets worth palpably less than the par or stated value of the stock. Watered stock is created, generally, by an over-valuation of the property given the corporation as consideration for stock.

The term "watered stock" gets its name from the old practice of letting cattle fill themselves up with water just before they were to be weighed in and sold at market. The water would bring up the weight and the buyer would be paying an unfair price for "watered stock." See also CAPITAL STOCK.

We. The editorial *we* instead of *I* in a letter written on behalf of a company should be avoided. Use *I* when referring to the writer individually and *we* when referring to the company. *I* and *we* may be used in the same letter.

I [the writer] will look after this order. You can be sure *we* [the company] will ship it tomorrow.

Weekly Call. See CALENDAR CALL.

Wharf. See WHARFAGE.

Wharfage. Wharfage is the money paid for tying a vessel to a wharf, or landing goods upon, or loading them from, a wharf. A wharf is the structure alongside navigable waters to which vessels can be moored and, when desired, loaded or unloaded.

Wherefore Clause. The final paragraph of a COMPLAINT in which formal demand for a judgment against the defendant is made. The *wherefore clause* may demand judgment for a specified sum of money, or in EQUITY actions "pray" for or seek other relief to which the plaintiff believes he is entitled. Thus, the wherefore clause may also be called the *prayer*. See COMPLAINT; PARTIES TO AN ACTION.

White-collar Worker. An employee identified by the fact that he wears conventional attire while working. Some groups of workers that would fall under this classification are schoolteachers, salespeople, and office workers.

White Slave. A term used in the United States statutes to indicate a female with reference to whom an offense is committed under the so-called Mann White Slave Traffic Act of June 25, 1910 (18 U.S.C.A. Sec. 2421-2424), prohibiting the transportation in interstate and foreign commerce of women and girls for immoral purposes.

Widow. *Printing.* A short last line of a paragraph carried over from the previous page or column to the top of a page or column. The text should be adjusted to avoid a widow.

Will. An instrument that is an effective expression of its maker's intention as to what shall be done with property under his control at the time of his death. Usually it must be in writing and executed in strict conformity with the applicable statutory requirements. A will takes effect only at the maker's death. As long as the maker lives he may revoke the will, or make any changes in its terms that he may wish.

A *holographic will* is one written entirely in the handwriting of the maker, even though there is no ATTESTATION by any witness. Before a holographic will is admitted to probate, the handwriting of the maker must be proved. A Holographic Will is not legal in some states.

A *nuncupative will* is one that is made orally. Oral wills are allowed in most states under certain limited conditions.

Typing a will. Figures 1 and 2 (pages 441, 442) illustrate the first and last pages of a will. The typing of a will offers a greater challenge to the typist than possibly any other typing that she does. Many wills are short, but many of them are very long and involved, ranging from 10 to 50 or more pages, all of which are dictated. The lawyer chooses his words very carefully and the dictation, therefore, is not rapid. The transcription should cause no difficulty; the challenge lies in the typing of the final copy. There should be no erasures in names or amounts, and no discernible erasures in other parts. PROBATE OF A WILL has been refused when material provisions have been erased, because the courts could not tell whether an alteration was made before or after execution. The typing should begin and end at the same point on every page, except the last, and yet there must be continuity from page to page, which means that no page should end with the close of a paragraph or sentence. The purpose of the continuity

is to avoid the omission, or the possible insertion, of a page. Some lawyers go so far as to require that the last word on each page be hyphenated. The placement of the signature with reference to the testimonium and ATTESTATION clauses is of prime importance in a will.

Frequently the lawyer will tell the secretary to copy a certain paragraph from another will, or from a skeleton form. She should be on the lookout for differences between the will she is typing and the form she is following, such as a change from singular to plural, or from *his* to *her,* and the like.

Signature page and preceding page of a will. The placement of the signature often presents a problem. Good practice makes the solution obligatory in some respects, permissible in others.

It is obligatory that at least one line of the testimonium clause be on the same page as part of the will (Figure 3, page 443). In other words, a new page cannot begin with the testimonium clause, because this arrangement would increase the possibility of the loss of a page, or permit the insertion of a page without detection.

It is obligatory that at least one line of the attestation clause be on the page with the signature (Figure 4, page 443). The purpose of this requirement is to tie in the witnesses' signatures with that of the testator.

The most desirable setup of the signature page is to have at least three lines of text on the page with the testimonium clause, the signature, and the attestation clause and witnesses' signatures (see Figure 2).

It is permissible, though not desirable, to have the signature and attestation clause on a page containing only one line of the testimonium clause.

THE LAST WILL AND TESTAMENT OF

THOMAS I. DEAN

I, THOMAS I. DEAN of Centerville, Center County,
State of Florida, being of sound mind and disposing.memory,
do make, publish and declare this to be my Last Will and
Testament, and hereby revoke any and all former wills and
codicils by me made.

ARTICLE I.

I hereby direct my executors hereinafter named,
to pay all my just debts and funeral expenses as soon after
my demise as can be lawfully done.

ARTICLE II.

I give and devise my farm located just outside and
to the West of Centerville, to my son Richard and his heirs
and assigns forever.

ARTICLE III.

I give and bequeath to my daughter Anne fifty (50)
shares of common stock of United States Steel, Inc.

ARTICLE IV.

I give and bequeath the following sums of money to
the following persons, to-wit:

(a) The sum of Seven Hundred Fifty Dollars ($750.)
to Robert Jones of Allentown, Georgia.

(b) The sum of One Thousand Dollars ($1,000.) to
Edna Jones of Ellisville, Florida.

ARTICLE V.

I give and bequeath to the Merchants' Loan and
Trust Company, a corporation, organized under the laws of

Will: **Figure 1.** First page of Will.

requesting him to appropriate it or so much of it as he shall think proper for presents to servants in our employ at the time of my death.

     IN WITNESS WHEREOF, I have signed my name at the foot and end of this my Last Will and Testament and affixed my seal this   day of May, 19—.

_____ [L.S.]

    The foregoing instrument, consisting of ten pages, including this page, each page being typewritten only on one side, was at the date thereof by the said THOMAS I. DEAN signed, sealed, published and declared to be his Last Will and Testament in the presence of us, who, at his request, in his presence and in the presence of each other, have subscribed our names as attesting witnesses thereto.

_____ residing at _____

_____ residing at _____

_____ residing at _____

Will: **Figure 2.** Last page.

How to gauge and test the page length. Unless a will is very short and simple, a draft, triple spaced, is always typed.

1. Count the lines, exclusive of the testimonium clause, signature line, attestation clause, and witnesses' signatures.

2. Assume the draft is 15 pages, 25 lines to the page (drafts are triple-spaced), or a total of 375 lines.

3. Plan on a top margin of five double spaces and an inch margin at the bottom, on 13-inch paper; this will leave room for 32 lines of typing.

4. Divide the total number of lines by the lines per page. You will have 11 typewritten pages with 23 lines left over for the 12th page. A triple space between the text and a three-line testimonium clause, plus three spaces for the signature line places the signature line at the bottom of the page without room for any of the attestation clause. But it is obligatory that at least one line of the attestation clause be on

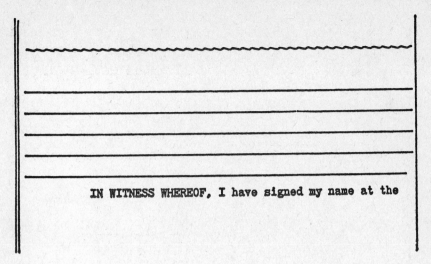

Will: Figure 3. One line of testimonium clause on page with part of text of Will.

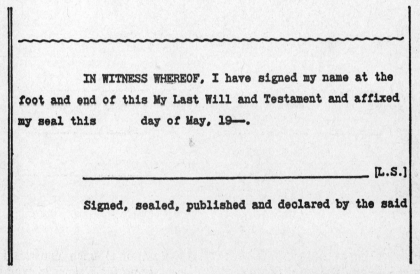

Will: Figure 4. One line of attestation clause on page with signature.

the page with the signature. So, you must try another plan.

Plan on a top margin of six double spaces, instead of five, and type 31 lines to the page. This will give 12 typewritten pages with three lines remaining for the 13th page. You then have ample room for the testimonium clause, the signature, the attestation clause, and the witnesses' signatures (see Figure 2).

Of course, in counting the lines in the draft, you must allow for interlineations and deletions that were made on the draft. If a paragraph is changed considerably, so that you cannot tell how many lines it contains, retype it before counting the lines of your draft. You must also take into consideration triple spaces between articles or items, if you plan to use them. In the illustration in Figure 1, there is a triple space between the title and the introductory paragraph; also, each article is separated from the preceding one by a triple space, making a total of six extra spaces, which is equivalent to 3 double spaces, on that page. Although the page length is 32 lines, that page actually has only 28 lines of typing. The extra spaces throughout the will must be added to the total number of lines.

Witnessing a will. The procedure of witnessing a will is rather formal. The practice in most states is for the testator to "publish" the will in the presence of the witnesses by declaring that the document is his will. He also asks the witnesses to witness the signing of it. The testator not only signs the will but initials the left margin of the other pages. Each witness signs in the presence of the testator and of each other, and no one leaves the room while the will is being signed, witnessed, and sealed. Notice from Figure 2 that space for the address of the witness is provided. The address is important because the witness will be called upon to prove the will after the testator's death in states where this is required.

Certifying copies of will. It is customary in many law offices for the secretary to certify the copies of a will. This certification is not for the purpose of the formal affidavit required when the will is probated but is for authentication of the carbon copies made when the will was typed. Type the form of certification on the copies and, after the copies have been conformed to the original, sign the certification. The following is a form of certification to be used when the typist conforms the copies.

I certify that this carbon copy is one that I typed simultaneously with the original will and that after the execution of the original, I conformed this copy to the original by adding the initials, date, signatures, and the addresses of the witnesses.

. . . .

If someone other than the typist of the will conforms it, the form of certification to be signed by the typist should be changed to read:

I certify that this carbon copy is one that I typed simultaneously with the original will and that after the execution of the original, this copy was conformed to the original by the addition of the initials, date, signatures, and the addresses of the witnesses.

. . . .

Some law firms use the following form of certification:

We, the undersigned, hereby certify that we have compared the foregoing copy with the original will or . . . . dated . . . . and find it to be a true and accurate copy thereof.

. . . .
. . . .

This last form of certification requires the reading of the will by three persons, or more if more than two copies are made. One person reads the original will aloud and signs the top line of the certification on each of the copies. Each person who follows a copy signs the second line of the certification on the copy that she has followed.

Capitalization and punctuation. The secretary will notice from Figure 1 that the testator's name is written in solid caps, whereas all other names are underscored. (preferably with red ink). The words *last will and testament* are written with initial caps in the will and in the attestation clause. In the phrases *make, publish and declare* and *give, devise and bequeath,* no comma precedes the conjunction *and.* Many lawyers prefer that *executor* and *trustee* be capitalized. The secretary will notice from Figure 2 that the words *in witness whereof* are written in solid caps and are followed by a comma. These arrangements are arbitrary but are followed extensively in law offices that give considerable attention to these details.

"Do's and don't's" in preparing a will. Unless otherwise instructed the secretary should follow these directions when preparing a will.

1. Type first in draft form unless the will is only a few pages in length.

2. In the final typing, make an original and two copies, the original and one copy for the testator and the other copy for your files. (If a bank or other institution is named executor, ask if an extra copy is to be made for it.)

3. Use the best LEGAL CAP available or specially printed white heavy stock with LAST WILL AND TESTAMENT printed at the top, and white heavy stock backs and matching envelopes.

4. Place the responsibility line at the top of the office copy *only.*

5. Double space, except the attestation clause.

6. Type the same number of lines on each page.

7. Number each page no more than double space below the last line, except the last page, which should be numbered one-half inch from the bottom of the page.

8. Don't forget to precede and follow the page number with a hyphen. Type the hyphen preceding the number at 42 on the typewriter scale, if a pica type machine is used or page 1 of 10, etc.

9. Type space between the text of the will and the testimonium clause.

10. Start the signature line at point 30 on the typewriter scale, if a pica, and continue the line to 67, writing the first bracket in [L.S.]or [SEAL] at point 68. These two scale points are important: the first to accommodate a long signature, and the second to permit a neat application of the seal.

11. If wax seal is used, omit the typed seal. Have wax and ribbon available.

12. Single space the attestation clause. Start it at the regular left margin, indenting the first line five spaces. Set the right margin stop at 55 on the typewriter scale. (If necessary to conserve space at the end of the will, type the attestation clause all the way over to the right ruled margin of the paper.)

13. Start the first witness line three spaces below the attestation clause, at the left margin, and underscore for 25 spaces; then type "residing at" and underscore for another 25 spaces.

14. Triple space between the witness lines.

15. Collate.

16. Check and double check spelling of names.

17. Endorse the back as shown in Figure 5, on page 446, using a back engraved with firm's name. Back the original and first carbon.

18. Have someone compare with her any descriptions of real estate devised by the will.

19. Bind firmly and securely. After the will is signed and it is witnessed:

20. Conform copies to original.

21. Certify the copies.

22. If her office is to retain the original of the will for safekeeping, give

the testator a receipt, signed in the firm's name by one of the lawyers or herself, reading as follows: "The will

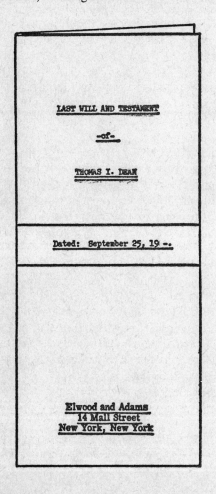

LAST WILL AND TESTAMENT

-of-

THOMAS I. DEAN

Dated: September 25, 19-.

Elwood and Adams
14 Mall Street
New York, New York

Will: Figure 5. Endorsed back of Will.

of ....., dated ....., is in our possession for safekeeping."

23. Enclose the original in an envelope, marked "Last Will and Testament of ...., dated ....."

24. If an institution is named executor, forward conformed copy with covering letter.

25. If a copy of a former will by the testator is in your file, note on it that a later will, of a certain date, has been executed.

Codicil. A CODICIL is written and executed with the same formality as the will. It is not attached to the will, but should be placed in a separate envelope on which it typed, "Codicil to Last Will and Testament of ...., dated ...." A testator may make more than one codicil.

Suggestion for red-inking a will. The usual method of red-inking a will is as follows:

Draw *double* red lines:
  Under the name of the testator in the introductory paragraph and on the cover
  Under each Article number
  Under "IN WITNESS WHEREOF"

Draw *single* red lines:
  Under each name appearing in the will
  Under "Executor" and "Trustee"
  Under everything appearing on the cover, including the engraved name of the law firm but excepting the name of the testator which has double lines under it.

Will Contest. A proceeding *sui generis,* a suit *in rem,* having for its purpose determination of question whether there is or is not a will.

Withholding. Deductions from INCOME as it is earned. The purpose of withholding money from a salary or wage is to cover the recipient's INCOME TAX and other tax liability as required by Federal, state, or local laws. The amounts withheld approximate the recipient's tax liability on wages earned.

Withholding for Federal income tax. If an employer-employee relationship exists, the responsibility of withholding for Federal income taxes rests with the employer. Every employer who is not exempted by statute must withhold from wages regardless of the number of employees or how long each is employed. "Wages" constitutes cash, whether termed vacation pay, bonus, commission, or the like, and other forms of payment such as stocks or other property.

The amount of tax withheld is computed by Government withholding tables. The amount is based on the wages earned and the number of exemptions claimed by an employee.

Without Recourse. A phrase used in an ENDORSEMENT which relieves the endorser from assuming liability in the event the maker fails to do something mentioned in the order.

Witness. To subscribe one's name to a deed, will, or other document, for the purpose of attesting its authenticity, and proving its execution, if required, by bearing witness thereto.

Witness Clause. See ATTESTATION.

Words and Phrases. A legal dictionary in 73 volumes and supplemented annually that attempts to give every definition appearing in court decisions. See LEGAL DICTIONARIES.

Workmen's Compensation. The name commonly used to designate the method and means created by statutes for giving protection and security to the workman and his dependents against injury and death occurring in the course of employment. Workmen's compensation laws generally impose an absolute liability (or liability without fault) on the employer. He must compensate his employees for injuries sustained in their employment even though he takes every precaution to prevent injury and the employee is, himself, negligent. See NEGLIGENCE.

Writ. An order issued by a court, or judge, in the name of the state, for the purpose of compelling the defendant to do something mentioned in the order. For specific writs, see MANDAMUS; CERTIORARI; HABEAS CORPUS; QUO WARRANTO; PROHIBITION; WRIT OF ERROR.

Writ of Error. A mandatory precept, under seal, issued out of a court of competent jurisdiction. It is directed to the judges of a court of record in which final judgment has been given. The writ commands that the record be examined in order that some alleged error in the proceedings may be corrected. In some cases, the writ commands the judges to whom it is issued to examine the record; in other cases, it commands them to send the record to another court of appellate jurisdiction.

Writ of Execution. See JUDGMENT CREDITOR.

Wrongful Death Action. A statutory provision that allows the EXECUTOR of the decedent, for the benefit of the next of kin, to sue one who wrongfully caused the decedent's death. If it was not for this law, a man who injures someone could be sued if the victim lives but would escape suit if the man dies. In order for the executor to bring a wrongful death action, however, the decedent must have had an enforceable cause of action at the time of his death. In other words, there could be no suit by an executor if the decedent could not sue were he alive. For example, if the decedent's CONTRIBUTORY NEGLIGENCE is a cause of his own injury and death, his executor will not be able to sue. As another example, the executor is barred from suing if the decedent had allowed the STATUTE OF LIMITATIONS to run before he died from his injury.

Y

Yearly Retainer. The fee that a lawyer and his client agree upon when the client engages the lawyer on an annual basis. The yearly retainer usually covers certain services, such as professional advice, the drawing up of ordinary business documents, contracts, deeds, mortgages and the like. When a client is on a yearly retainer, the secretary should know whether a specific matter is covered by the retainer or is to be charged for separately.

Year's Allowance. The amount set by the Court or the appraisers in some states for the support of the surviving spouse and/or minor children for one year after decedent's death.

Yellow-dog Contract. An agreement made by workers, as a condition of employment, not to belong to a union during the period of their employment and not to engage in certain activities, such as collective bargaining or striking. The yellow-dog contract was used effectively by management to keep out unions and preserve the absolute right to employ and discharge workers at will. Legislation has now prohibited the use of anti-union contracts.

York-Antwerp Rules. A set of regulations drafted in 1890 to bring about uniformity in the calculation of GENERAL AVERAGE LOSS claims in the major maritime nations. While these rules, revised in 1924 and 1950, have never been enacted into law, parties are free to incorporate them into marine insurance policies or other maritime contracts. Today, the York-Antwerp Rules are widely referred to and incorporated into bills of lading (see BILLS OF LADING) throughout the world.

Z

"Z" Ruling. See PRINTED LAW BLANKS.

Zoning. A regulation, enforced under the police power of municipalities and states and applied to the use of both lands and buildings, whereby land use is restricted to specific purposes and building construction is controlled as to type, intensity, and volume. Most of the larger cities in the United States now have regulatory zoning laws, which exercise powerful influences upon land values.